TRADITIONAL BALLADS OF VIRGINIA

TRADITIONAL BALLADS OF VIRGINIA

COLLECTED UNDER THE AUSPICES OF
THE VIRGINIA FOLK-LORE SOCIETY

EDITED BY

ARTHUR KYLE DAVIS, Jr.

UNIVERSITY OF VIRGINIA

THE UNIVERSITY PRESS OF VIRGINIA
CHARLOTTESVILLE

REPRINTED BY ARRANGEMENT WITH
THE HARVARD UNIVERSITY PRESS AND A. K. DAVIS, JR.
FIRST PUBLISHED BY THE UNIVERSITY PRESS OF VIRGINIA 1969
STANDARD BOOK NUMBER: 8139-0269-X
LIBRARY OF CONGRESS CATALOG CARD NUMBER: 78-79458
PRINTED IN THE UNITED STATES OF AMERICA

To the Memory of

C. ALPHONSO SMITH

THROUGH WHOM THE VIRGINIA BALLAD COLLECTION CAME INTO BEING

And to the Many

BALLAD WORKERS AND BALLAD LOVERS OF VIRGINIA

WHOSE NAMES HE WOULD HAVE HERE JOINED WITH HIS OWN

THIS BOOK IS INSCRIBED BY ITS EDITOR

PREFACE

THE editor of this volume did not know the bliss of being a ballad collector in the young days of the Virginia Folk-Lore Society. In the fascinating emprise of hunting out the singers of ballads and recording the words and music of the otherwise all too perishable songs that fell from their lips, he bore no part. Perhaps if he had, he might feel as did Miss Dorothy Scarborough, that "personally, I have had so much fun collecting . . . songs that I should regard any future deprivation or calamity as merely a matter of evening up. It is not fair for one being to have all the fun and enjoyment in life." By the same token, the present editor, who knew not the joys of collecting but only the grim business of editing, looks forward to a giddy time in years to come.

Toward the end of 1923, Professor Alphonso Smith's failing health made it apparent to him that he would be unable to undertake the editing of the Virginia ballad collection which had been brought together under his leadership by the Virginia Folk-Lore Society. No other member of the Society seems to have been both qualified and willing to take up the work. Moreover, as the ballad movement had been a state-wide movement centering at the state university, Dr. Smith was especially anxious that the collection should be edited by some one connected with the University of Virginia. Accordingly, he consulted with Dean J. C. Metcalf, Chairman of the Department of English at the University of Virginia, and the nomination fell to one who, though he knew himself no ballad authority, was flattered by the invitation and did not pause to investigate properly the burden he was accepting. Would he edit the fifty Virginia ballads? Only fifty ballads? Certainly, and have them ready in a few months' time! What were fifty ballads to him, fresh from the rigors of a dissertation? Little did he think that the editing of these so-called fifty ballads would dwarf anything he had previously done. He did not foresee (and, indeed, those two kindly yet canny souls who approached him must hardly have foreseen, certainly did not overemphasize) the magnitude of the task: the long period of preparation for work in a highly specialized field; the fifty ballads expanding into six hundred and fifty versions, variants, and fragments of fifty-one different ballads, with one hundred and forty-eight melodies; the tediousness of recapturing the data of collection for each of these six hundred and fifty items; the often illegible and unsatisfactory state of the material, requiring much minute editorial attention and textual criticism; the bulky files of correspondence extending over a dozen years from hundreds of ballad correspondents all over the state; the tedious and microscopic process of comparing all the versions and variants of a single ballad with each other and with all the other printed texts of the same ballad from Child through the latest American ballad publication; the ticklish business of selecting and rejecting texts; the interminable proof-reading; the finding of qualified and efficient assistance in the musical line; the writing of elaborate head-notes and an introduction; the seeing of the book through the press. He who goes through this book carefully, reading through all fifty-one head-notes, will gain a fair idea of the extent and the exacting character of the work; but he should also examine the state of the original material.

The death of Dr. Smith on June 13, 1924, removed the very person to whom the editor would most naturally look for enthusiastic moral support and for authoritative technical help. So, practically from the first, the editor found himself solely responsible for the preparation, editing, and publication of the richest collection of genuine ancient ballads so far brought together in America. He has, of course, been interested in other things meanwhile; but he has no apology that some four years have elapsed from the time when he received the material to the book's going to press. Only those who are ignorant of what ballad editing means will be critical of this lapse of time.

How the task has been accomplished, others must say, and doubtless will say to his mortification. But before the coming of the ordeal by reviewer, the editor who knows his own epicurean leanings all too well may be pardoned a moment, not of self-gratulation, but rather of astonished contemplation of his stoic achievement.

Fortunately, the task called for no particular editorial brilliance; only for sustained labor of reasonable intelligence, and a certain scholarly conscience. These, the editor would like to believe, he was able to bring to his task, and as time went on he developed a genuine interest in his subject which showed itself in the preparation of several papers dealing with ballad problems and read before the Popular Literature group of the Modern Language Association of America. It is to be hoped that this genuine interest may now and then show through the routine labor of the pages to follow. Not only does any subject on which we have bestowed honest work take on life for us, but ballads, it seems, exercise a peculiar fascination whereby even the indifferent worker becomes a dedicated spirit. There is a well-known type of romance in which at first acquaintance the man is indifferent to the woman, even cordially dislikes her, but finally comes to realize he cannot live without her. The editor's ballad romance has been like that.

But fortunately, again, the worth of this volume depends not upon the skill of its editor but upon the well-nigh indestructible value of its material. As no editor could greatly enhance the wealth of this material, so none but the most bungling could greatly detract from its richness. The book stands or falls by the quality of its ballad content, and it was the value of the material that led the Harvard University Press to accept the volume for publication sight unseen and before the editor himself was more than half acquainted with his material. If the editing has added some little to the value of the material, it is well; if not, the book is still a worth-while addition to the growing library of American balladry.

At any rate, the editor is happy to be able to discharge a trust (perhaps too hastily assumed) confided to him by the late C. Alphonso Smith, Dean J. C. Metcalf, and the Virginia Folk-Lore Society. Since ballads are but concentrated life-histories of men and women, the editor might slightly emend Robert Browning and say to them,— and with a profound sense of relief and great satisfaction he does now say, — "Here they are, your fifty men and women!"

It is a pleasure here to acknowledge certain indebtednesses. The first must go to Professor George Lyman Kittredge, of Harvard University. Though this book was not, as have been so many ballad and folk-song publications, the offspring of his inspiration, he has throughout taken in it an interest by no means stepfatherly. Dean John Calvin Metcalf, of the Department of Graduate Studies, University of Virginia, has lent valuable encouragement at critical moments. Mrs. C. Alphonso Smith, of Charlottesville, Virginia, has cheerfully turned over certain useful papers of her husband, and has been an ever faithful friend of the book. Mr. John Stone, of the Virginia Folk-Lore Society, has always been ready to give what help he could. Miss Margaret Snowden Broomall, of New York City, and Miss Betty Booker, of Charlottesville, Virginia, have given cordially that expert musical assistance without which this volume would have been bereft of all its song. Miss Emily S. Calcott, M.S., Graduate Student of English in the University of Virginia, gave valuable bibliographical help. Miss Alfreda M. Peel and Miss Caroline Melbard, of Salem, Virginia, are the donors of most of the photographs used in illustration of the ballad country. Especial thanks are due to Professor James M. Grainger, of the State Teachers College, Farmville, Virginia, for a careful and suggestive reading of the galley proofs. The Houghton Mifflin Company has generously granted permission to quote certain copyrighted material from Child's introductions in his *English and Scottish Popular Ballads*. G. P. Putnam's Sons have similarly allowed the use of material previously printed in Campbell and Sharp's *English Folk-Songs from the Southern Appalachians*. Since this ballad work unexpectedly overran its time and diverted the editor somewhat from another project, he acknowledges an obligation to a Sterling Research Fellowship in the Graduate School of Yale University for leisure to complete this study. The Research Committee of the University of Virginia, the officers of the Harvard College Library and of the Harvard University Press, each in their proper sphere, have contributed materially toward the fulfilment of this task. To each and all of the above, the editor tenders his very genuine thanks and appreciation. And in all conscience he must add gratefully the members of his own family in Petersburg, Virginia, who bore with him through several summers of intensive ballad work.

ARTHUR KYLE DAVIS, JR.

UNIVERSITY OF VIRGINIA
October, 1929

CONTENTS

I. BALLADS

II. BALLAD MUSIC

LIST OF ILLUSTRATIONS

LIST OF REFERENCES

ABBREVIATIONS

Barry: Phillips Barry, *Ancient British Ballads*, etc. (A privately printed list.)

Belden: H. M. Belden, *A Partial List of Song-Ballads and Other Popular Poetry Known in Missouri.* Second Edition (1910).

Brown: F. C. Brown, *Ballad-Literature in North Carolina.* Reprinted from *Proceedings and Addresses of the Fifteenth Annual Session of the Literary and Historical Association of North Carolina*, December 1–2, 1914.

Bulletin: *The Virginia Folk-Lore Society Bulletin.* (Nos. 1–12, 1913–1924.)

Campbell and Sharp: Olive Dame Campbell and Cecil J. Sharp, *English Folk-Songs from the Southern Appalachians.* New York, 1917.

Child: Francis James Child, *The English and Scottish Popular Ballads.* Boston, 1883 ff.

Colcord: Joanna C. Colcord, *Roll and Go, Songs of American Sailormen.* Indianapolis, 1924.

Combs: Josiah H. Combs, *Folk-Songs du Midi des États-Unis.* Paris, 1925.

Cox: John Harrington Cox, *Folk-Songs of the South.* Cambridge, 1925.

Finger: Charles J. Finger, *Frontier Ballads.* New York, 1927.

Gray: Roland Palmer Gray, *Songs and Ballads of the Maine Lumberjacks with Other Songs from Maine.* Cambridge, 1925.

Heart Songs: *Heart Songs, Dear to the American People and by them Contributed in the Search for Treasured Songs Initiated by the National Magazine.* Boston, 1909.

Hudson: Arthur Palmer Hudson, *Specimens of Mississippi Folk-Lore.* 1928.

Jones: Bertrand L. Jones, *Folk-Lore in Michigan.* Reprinted from *Kalamazoo Normal Record*, May, 1914. Western State Normal School, Kalamazoo, Michigan.

Journal: *The Journal of American Folk-Lore.*

McGill: Josephine McGill, *Folk-Songs of the Kentucky Mountains.* New York, 1917.

Mackenzie: W. Roy Mackenzie, *The Quest of the Ballad.* Princeton, 1919.

Mackenzie, *Ballads*: W. Roy Mackenzie, *Ballads and Sea Songs from Nova Scotia.* Cambridge, 1928.

Pound, *Syllabus*: Louise Pound, *Folk-Song of Nebraska and the Central West, A Syllabus.* Nebraska Academy of Sciences, *Publications*, Vol. IX, No. 3.

Pound, *Ballads*: Louise Pound, *American Ballads and Songs.* New York, 1922.

Sandburg: Carl Sandburg, *The American Songbag.* New York, 1927.

Sargent and Kittredge: Helen Child Sargent and George Lyman Kittredge, *English and Scottish Popular Ballads, Student's Cambridge Edition* (one volume). Cambridge, 1904.

Scarborough: Dorothy Scarborough, *On the Trail of Negro Folk-Songs.* Cambridge, 1925.

Sharp, *Songs*, I: Cecil J. Sharp, *American-English Folk-Songs Collected in the Southern Appalachians. First Series.* New York, 1918.

Sharp, *Songs*, II: Cecil J. Sharp, *Folk-Songs of English Origin Collected in the Appalachian Mountains. Second Series.* London.

Shearin: Hubert G. Shearin, *British Ballads in the Cumberland Mountains.* Reprinted from the *Sewanee Review*, July, 1911. Sewanee, Tennessee.

Shearin and Combs: Hubert G. Shearin and Josiah H. Combs, *A Syllabus of Kentucky Folk-Songs* (Transylvania Studies in English, II)., Lexington, Kentucy, 1911.

Shoemaker: Henry W. Shoemaker, *North Pennsylvania Minstrelsy.* Second Edition. Altoona, Pennsylvania, 1923.

C. A. Smith: C. Alphonso Smith, *Ballads Surviving in the United States.* Reprinted from the *Musical Quarterly*, January, 1916. New York.

Reed Smith: *The Traditional Ballad and Its South Carolina Survivals. Bulletin of the University of South Carolina*, No. 162, May 1, 1925. Columbia, South Carolina.

Reed Smith, *Ballads*: *South Carolina Ballads.* Cambridge, 1928.

Wyman and Brockway: Loraine Wyman and Howard Brockway, *Lonesome Tunes, Folk-Songs from the Kentucky Mountains.* New York, 1916.

Wyman and Brockway, *Songs*: Loraine Wyman and Howard Brockway, *Twenty Kentucky Mountain Songs.* Boston, 1920.

TRADITIONAL BALLADS
OF VIRGINIA

INTRODUCTION

I. PRELIMINARY MATTERS

WHAT IS A BALLAD?

WITH so many satisfactory definitions of the ballad ready to one's hand, it would be platitudinous, or even impertinent, to present a definition of one's own. Like other English words, and perhaps more noticeably than most others, the term *ballad* may be used either loosely or strictly, in its broadest or in a more specialized sense. Professor Kittredge's oft-quoted dictum runs that

a ballad is a song that tells a story, or — to take the other point of view — a story told in song. More formally, it may be defined as a short narrative poem, adapted for singing, simple in plot and metrical structure, divided into stanzas, and characterized by complete impersonality so far as the author or singer is concerned.[1]

And Professor Gummere — to avoid his more familiar but controversial definitions in terms of origin — has said that

the ballad is a conglomerate of choral, dramatic, lyric, and epic elements which are due now to some suggestive refrain, now to improvisation, now to memory, now to individual invention, and are forced into a more or less poetic unity by the pressure of tradition in long stretches of time.[2]

Both, it is clear, are appropriating the word to a use somewhat more exact than the sense in which it is ordinarily employed, somewhat different from its accepted sense among musical composers, and somewhat more restricted and specialized than a dictionary maker would insist upon. They are defining the type which is sometimes called "the ballad proper," "the early ballad" or "the popular or folk ballad." But there is ample precedent for referring to this form simply as "the ballad," without modification. And this is the type of ballad with which this volume is concerned.[3]

[1] *English and Scottish Popular Ballads* (Cambridge ed.), Introduction, p. xi.

[2] *The Popular Ballad* (Boston, 1907), p. 321.

[3] The so-called "broadside ballad" is simply a ballad, traditional or other, usually other, printed on a single sheet, often with appropriate ornamentation. This is the "ballad in print o' life" which Autolycus sells and which Mopsa loves. (See *The Winter's Tale*, IV, iv.) Such ballads were widely known and sold in the late sixteenth and early seventeenth centuries especially. The traditional ballads so printed were usually vulgarized and debased.

The term *folk-song* in its broadest and most obvious sense includes both the ballad and other traditional songs of the people. But in a more specialized sense it is used in opposition to the term *ballad* and applied only to those traditional songs which lack the ballad quality.

> The distinction between the ballad and the song [writes the late Cecil J. Sharp] is more or less arbitrary and is not easy to define with precision. Broadly speaking, however, the ballad is a narrative song, romantic in character and, above all, impersonal, that is to say, the singer is merely the narrator of events with which he personally has no connection and for which he has no responsibility. The song, on the other hand, is a far more emotional and passionate utterance and is usually the record of a personal experience — very frequently of an amatory nature.[1]

The ballads of this volume, then, are folk-songs in the broader sense, not in the narrower one.

Recently a British poet and critic, Mr. Robert Graves,[2] has listed the distinguishing features of the ballad, as follows:

1. The ballad-proper has no known author.
2. There is never an authoritative text of such a ballad.
3. It is incomplete without music, music of a repetitive kind that excites and sustains.
4. Though it may treat of Kings and Queens and notable figures in history, it is local, not cultural.
5. It is oral, not literary.
6. It is not highly advanced technically.
7. It does not moralize or preach or express any partisan bias.
8. It "begins in the last act" of the drama and moves to the final climax without stage directions.

So far without controversy. But Mr. Graves is on disputed ground when he adds "this ninth which includes the other eight":

9. The ballad-proper is best understood not primarily as a narrative poem or as a song, but as a song and chorus evolved by the group-mind of a community, a group-mind which is more than the sum of the individual minds that compose it, more than the conviction of the strongest or most active clique.

This theory of the "communal composition" of ballads, which has long been held by a most distinguished company of scholars and critics of the ballad, has of late years been severely attacked, and perhaps somewhat damaged, by believers in "individual authorship," who protest that the making of a

[1] *English Folk-Songs from the Southern Appalachians*, Introduction, p. xii.

[2] See *The English Ballad* (London, 1927), Introduction, p. 9.

ballad is not so vastly different from the making of an ordinary poem. The "communal theory" had its origin in Germany more than a century ago. Herder has been regarded as its prophet, and as its leading teachers Jacob and Wilhelm Grimm (especially the former), Steinthal, Grundtvig, ten Brink, Gaston Paris, Andrew Lang, and other great modern philologists, possibly Francis James Child. But the position of Professor Child on the subject is not altogether certain; his article on "Ballad Poetry" in *Johnson's Universal Cyclopaedia* has been quoted approvingly by both sides; yet it is clear that those scholars who were most impregnated with his thought on this problem — Francis B. Gummere, George Lyman Kittredge, William Allan Neilson — have in one form or another defended the "communal" or "popular" idea, though in a form much modified from the more extreme pronouncements of Jacob Grimm. Professor Gummere, because he gave to this problem the fullness of his thought [1] and defended his position with great learning and with much controversial deftness, has for some years been looked to as the leading exponent of this modified "communal" idea. "I do not for a moment maintain," he says, "that individual impulses did not assert themselves in earliest song; without them there can be no poetry at all; but what I urge is the great predominance of homogeneous and choral elements and the subordination of individual impulses." [2] He conceived his position as a middle ground between Grimm and the individualists. He sought to explain the "epic objectivity" of ballads as "by no means the simple matter of miraculous popular conception that Jacob Grimm thought it to be, by no means the artistic triumph that traditional criticism assumes." [3] He was as ready as were his opponents to discard "the immaculate conception of poetry, the people that make an epic and the song that sings itself." [4] But this moderation did not save him from bearing the brunt of the individualists'

[1] See the copiously documented Introduction to *Old English Ballads*, Boston, 1894; "The Ballad and Communal Poetry," in the Child Memorial Volume of *Studies and Notes in Philology and Literature*, Boston, 1896; *The Beginnings of Poetry*, New York and London, 1901; the three brilliant papers replying to his critics under the title "Primitive Poetry and the Ballad," in *Modern Philology*, I, 193-202, 217-234, and 373-390, Chicago, 1903-04; and especially *The Popular Ballad*, Boston and New York, 1907. There can be little doubt that Professor Gummere clarified, even modified, his ideas as later volumes or articles appeared.

[2] "Primitive Poetry and the Ballad," I, *Modern Philology*, I, 200.

[3] "Primitive Poetry and the Ballad," II, *Ibid.*, p. 219.

[4] "Primitive Poetry and the Ballad," III, *Ibid.*, p. 390.

attack, which came chiefly from Professors Scherer and Alois Brandl in Germany, Messrs. T. F. Henderson and Gregory Smith in Great Britain, and Miss Louise Pound in America.[1] No wonder he felt that "the middle way in theories of the beginnings of poetry, of the origin of ballads, may be a way of pleasantness, but it is not a path of peace." [2]

Of these, Miss Pound [3] has proved herself the most conspicuous and unrelenting antagonist of what she calls the "communal prepossession." She is now the outstanding representative of the individualist position. Her contention in a recent article is that

> such a "communal mind" or "mob mind" or "gesammtgeist," as you may choose to call it, has no actuality which science or sense can observe. If history and indeed ethnology betray clearly one fact it is that there is no such "mental homogeneity" among men. As a critical hypothesis the whole communal prepossession has led mainly into misconception and misvaluation; its service (for service of a sort it is) has been to arouse an interest and an industry in its support which have only succeeded in demonstrating its futility. In other words, it is honorably shelved by its own inability to stand the test of substantial evidence.[4]

But Miss Pound's contention is more far-reaching. As presented in *Poetic Origins and the Ballad*, the most adequate discussion of the "anti-communal" position, it is that

> the following assumptions which have long dominated our thought upon the subject of poetic origins and the ballads should be given up, or at least should be seriously qualified; namely, belief in the "communal" authorship and ownership of primitive poetry; disbelief in the primitive artist; reference to the ballad as the earliest and most universal poetic form; belief in the origin of narrative songs in the dance, especially definition of the English and Scottish traditional ballad type as of dance origin; belief in the emergence of traditional ballads from the illiterate, that is, belief in the communal creation

---

[1] These, of course, follow a long line of distinguished British believers in the "minstrelsy theory" of ballad origins, including Bishop Percy, Sir Walter Scott, Professor W. A. Courthope, and more recently the late Professor Sir Walter Raleigh, and Sir Arthur Quiller-Couch. In opposition to these the names of Andrew Lang and Cecil J. Sharp spring to mind.

[2] "Primitive Poetry and the Ballad," I, *Modern Philology*, I p. 193.

[3] Miss Pound's numerous papers contributed to the *Publications of the Modern Language Association of America*, to *Modern Philology*, to *The Mid-West Quarterly*, and to *Modern Language Notes*, she has reprinted, with modifications and additions, as *Poetic Origins and the Ballad*, New York, 1921; see also her chapter on "Oral Literature" in *The Cambridge History of American Literature*, Vol. IV, chap. XXVII (New York, 1917–21); her valuable Introduction to *American Ballads and Songs*, New York, 1922; and especially "The Term: 'Communal'," *P. M. L. A.*, XXXIX (1924), 440–454. Add "A Recent Theory of Ballad-Making," *P. M. L. A.* XLIV (1929), 622–630.

[4] "The Term: 'Communal'," *P. M. L. A.*, XXXIX (1924), 444.

rather than *re*-creation of ballads; belief in the special powers of folk-improvisation; and belief that the making of traditional ballads is a "closed account." [1]

In the judgment of scholarship not all these positions have been gained; on the other hand, certain of the points would hardly be questioned by modern scholars of the first rank. Miss Pound's discussion has made for clarification and for the elimination of views uncritically accepted on the authority of tradition or because of their own fascination. She has certainly helped to clear away mistakes and extravagances of the older doctrine which offered themselves for popular misconception.

Her attack, whether one agrees with her or not, is an able, serious, and scholarly one, quite unlike the derisive laughter of certain light-hearted critics who have not always fully understood the theory they were attacking, a theory which rather lends itself to the derision of the unsympathetic. In a recent lecture before the Royal Society of Literature, a distinguished English poet [2] expresses herself as follows:

> With regard to the making of ballads, a theory respecting them has been propounded by a learned American, Professor Gummere.[3] It is called the communal theory, and affirms that the People — that is, a crowd of people all together — composed them. This reminds me of the programme of a lecture by Mr. Bernard Shaw which I once saw. The subject of the lecture was "Government by the People for the People," and it must have been delivered when Mr. Shaw was in an anti-democratic frame of mind. I remember among the headings given in the programme, "*Sculpture by the People for the People; Dentistry by the People for the People*," and finally "*Government is an Art.*" Poetry is still more an art; and works of art have never, so far as we can trace them, been produced by crowds, but by individuals. Indeed anyone who has ever produced a work of art, on however small a scale, must feel the improbability of their being produced otherwise. . . . This spinning-song example hardly convinces me that a thrillingly dramatic ballad such as "Binnorie," a masterpiece of pity and terror such as "Clerk Saunders," a grim "tabloid" tragedy such as "The Twa Corbies," or a well-knit and delightful tale such as that of "Allen-a-Dale's Wedding," were cast together like a cairn of stones by a contributory crowd. It is more probable that they sprung like an Elizabethan play, lyric, or any other bit of fine literature, whole and alive, from the brain of a man of genius.[4]

These latter remarks show clearly that Mrs. Woods, like many another literary visitor to the field of the ballad, has not rightly

[1] Preface, p. vii.

[2] Mrs. Margaret L. Woods, in "Ballads," a paper read January 20, 1926, and published in *Essays by Divers Hands* (ed. by G. K. Chesterton, London, 1926), VI, 25–42.

[3] Mrs. Woods does not mention that the theory was originally proposed by the Grimms, if not by the earlier hints of Herder or by A. W. Schlegel, who later recanted.

[4] Pages 32–33.

understood the theory of Professor Gummere and of those who think with him. They have stated quite explicitly that they do not hold that the *extant* traditional ballads were communally composed. In the very earliest of his books on the ballad, Professor Gummere writes, "All of the English and Scottish ballads, by the very conditions of their preservation, lie this side of the purely communal stage." [1] "Nobody will hold," writes Professor Kittredge, "that 'Robin Hood and the Monk' or 'King Estmere' is the direct result of communal composition. It is unlikely that even the simplest of our extant ballads were made in this fashion." [2] Yet otherwise reputable critics and scholars continue to make this glaring and fundamental error in attributing to the "neo-communal" theorists a belief which probably Jacob Grimm himself would hardly have held.

If there is one lesson to be learned from an examination of the history of the controversy, it is that allegiance is not lightly to be given to either side without a somewhat thorough examination and understanding of the bases — sociological, anthropological, ethnological — of the problem. The difficulty is that hitherto each side has been able to present and to interpret favorably to its contention the evidence of primitive societies. Perhaps the ultimate solution of the problem — if, indeed, the "fascinating mystery" is ever to be resolved — must await the amassing and the disinterested interpretation of further evidence bearing more directly upon the ballad problem, if such evidence is at all procurable. But this much one may say at the present juncture: The individualists seem to have made good their contention for the exclusion of the term "communal" from definitions of the ballad on the ground that it is not a necessary or indubitable fact of the ballad's origin; they have also cast doubt upon several notions previously accepted about the origin of poetry and the ballad's connection with it; but, though they may have diminished the emphasis to be put upon it, they have not yet reasoned out of existence the influence of the group in determining the ballad form or idea, or the possibility of such a carefully qualified act of so-called "communal composition" as that described by Professor Kittredge. Further than this the would-be impartial summer-up, who knows the unwisdom of premature entry into this great field of

[1] *Old English Ballads*, Introduction, p. lxvii.

[2] *English and Scottish Popular Ballads* (Cambridge ed.), Introduction, p. xix. Cf. p. xviii, ll. 9–10, and p. xxvii, ll. 3–6.

historico-literary controversy, can only record that the world of scholarship — whose opinion alone is of weight in the matter — is not yet agreed how the ballad originated or what is its relation to earlier poetry.

Miss Pound, like Professor Gummere, has shown some disposition to conciliate.

> I wish to make clear in advance [she wrote in an article published in 1917] that I have no desire to deny the general social inspiration of song. In a broad sense, all art is a social phenomenon — the romanticists to the contrary. Song is mainly a social thing at the present time, and it was yet more prevailingly social among our remote ancestors.[1]

One feels that if a polemic past could be forgotten and the academic allurement of a battle of words could be resisted, the best minds on either side would not be far apart on essential points. The difference at the present time is, more largely than has been admitted by either side, one of emphasis.[2]

And finally, it may be well to recall that we are here interested not primarily in the far-distant origins of primitive poetry, but in the origin of the English and Scottish ballads, the bulk of which, in the form in which we know them, date from the fifteenth and early sixteenth centuries and even later. These represent "a second growth of the genuine popular song . . . some of it springing, doubtless, out of shoots from the old stock which had lived through this long interval, some of it a fresh product of the age." The words are those of Professor Child.[3] The distinctive quality of these surviving ballads, especially their impersonality, the absence of any obvious traces of individual authorship, is to be explained by the fact of oral tradition or transmission, by which they are mainly preserved, rather than by any theory as to their ultimate origin or connection with primitive poetry.

THE BALLAD IN AMERICA

In the latter days of the last century, with the publication of the later volumes of Professor Child's collection of the *English and Scottish Popular Ballads*, public attention was directed to

[1] "The Beginnings of Poetry," *P. M. L. A.*, XXXII (1917), 209.

[2] The Introduction to a collection of this sort is hardly the place to present controversial matter. The editor therefore refrains from elaborating his own personal views. He hopes, however, that the above clarifying summary may point the way to a possible solution of the problem.

[3] See his article on "Ballad Poetry," in *Johnson's Universal Cyclopaedia.*

the fact that many of these old ballads were still known and sung in different parts of America, and the interest of scholars and ballad lovers was aroused in collecting and preserving these antiques before they should vanish from tradition. The latter part of this Introduction, "A History of the Ballad Movement in Virginia," gives a fairly complete account of the ballad quest in Virginia, with a mention of some of the pioneer workers in the field of American balladry. Good summary accounts of the progress of ballad work in America will be found in Miss Pound's Introduction to her anthology of *American Ballads and Songs*, and still more recently, in Professor Reed Smith's account of "The Traditional Ballad To-day," in his *South Carolina Ballads*. Every volume named in the List of References given in the front of this book contributes something toward the full picture of the ballad in America. Of the earlier articles, Professor H. M. Belden's "Balladry in America" [1] is one of the best and the best-known. For a brief introduction to the subject, written at the peak of popular interest in the ballad quest, no better article could be recommended than C. Alphonso Smith's "Ballads Surviving in the United States," [2] which, as the one notable piece of ballad criticism from the leader of the Virginia ballad movement, would be a fitting introduction to this book.

II. THE VIRGINIA VOLUME

CONTENTS

THIS volume presents what seems an adequate selection from the ballad archives of the Virginia Folk-Lore Society.[3] The material consists entirely of versions, variants, and fragments, with their melodies, of the genuine English and Scottish popular ballads surviving in oral tradition in Virginia. Of the three hundred and five ballads recognized by Professor Child and included in his great five-volume work,[4] fifty-one have been found in Virginia. These, with their numerous texts and tunes, are the matter of this volume.

[1] See *Journal*, Vol. XXV.

[2] See *Musical Quarterly*, Vol. II, No. 1 (January, 1916), pp. 109–129.

[3] Appendix A gives a supplementary list of Virginia ballad material not used in this book, with the data of collection for each item.

[4] *The English and Scottish Popular Ballads*, Boston, 1883–98.

SPECIALIZATION[1]

The Virginia volume is somewhat more specialized than other recent American ballad and folk-song publications, partly because it can afford to be. It is rich enough in these genuine antiques to devote a whole volume to the older type of traditional ballad. Other publications have invariably accorded this type the position of honor, but generally because of its scarcity they have also included later broadside ballads and songs of more recent American adaptation or origin. Some collectors, like Mr. John A. Lomax, have been genuinely more interested in these later songs. But the Virginia Folk-Lore Society set itself as its first task the collection of all the old English and Scottish survivals in the state. Its success was phenomenal, far surpassing that of any other state or local organization. Later volumes may perhaps be devoted to later types of ballad and folk-song, many of which streamed in to the archivist unbidden. The editor is not inclined to draw too hard and fast a distinction between the Child ballads and all other ballads. But the first publication of the Virginia ballad material must be limited exclusively to genuine old-world ballad survivals, both because such was the obvious intention of the founder and workers of the Virginia Folk-Lore Society and because, indeed, one stout volume can hold no more.

MANY VARIANTS

Where several variants are available, a ballad may not be adequately represented by a single variant, for "a ballad is not one text, but many texts." Multiplicity of variants is a constituent element of its very nature, and as such must be accepted by ballad readers. One text, or one melody, is only part of a ballad, and no single version may be regarded as the standard or authoritative one. "All versions that have been collected from folk-singers have equal authority, though one may be very noble and another very base," says Professor Gerould. "The ballad does not exist, it is fair to say, except in its variants. Some are good, some are bad, but all of them con-

[1] This and the other sub-sections that follow may seem not only explanation to the reader, but a sort of G.B.S. "First Aid to Critics," of course without the Shavian cleverness. For the present editor's more extended consideration of some of the general problems of ballad publication and a discussion of recent American practice in their solution, see his article, "Some Problems of Ballad Publication," *Musical Quarterly*, Vol. XIV, No. 2 (April, 1928), pp. 283–296.

stitute — in a very real sense — the ballad." And again, "If the ballad be considered not as a single text, which has suffered various alterations good and bad, but as a group of versions, collected and uncollected, which have circulated in oral tradition, it becomes clear that any ultimate or original text is not only undiscoverable but comparatively unimportant." [1]

For the multiplicity of variants there must be no apology, for it constitutes the chief value not only of this volume but of the whole American ballad quest. Recent American ballad collectors have unearthed no hitherto lost ballad of tradition, but new versions are almost as important as new ballads, and through their efforts some ninety-five [2] ballad-cycles have been rendered more complete — by the Virginia collectors, fifty-one. Since the time of Professor Child a stream of new material from the purest traditional sources has been pouring in to enrich and refresh the ballad heritage of the English-speaking peoples — a stream which but for the efforts of recent American collectors might have been cut off forever with this generation; for ballad-singing is in a phase of lingering disappearance. The Virginia contribution, then, though it includes several ballads not found elsewhere in America, consists largely in its wealth of added variants, which may not be further reduced without loss.

SCHOLARLY AND POPULAR INTEREST

While this volume contains much that may be of general interest, its most obvious appeal is to the ballad lover and the ballad scholar. American balladry has thus far lived upon the Child tradition of scientific scholarship. This is, of course, no indication that it will never follow the example of such British collectors as Bishop Percy, Sir Walter Scott, William Allingham, and Sir Arthur Quiller-Couch in presenting to the public volumes less academic and scientific and more tasty to the popular palate—but without the liberties taken by some of these eminent editors. Miss Pound's anthology of *American Ballads and Songs* is already a step in this direction, and many recent folk-song publications like Miss Scarborough's *On the Trail of Negro Folk-Songs*, Professor Mackenzie's *The Quest of the Ballad*, and Professor Rickaby's *Ballads and Songs of the Shanty-Boy* show distinct concessions to popular interest. But, particularly as

[1] See "The Making of Ballads," *Modern Philology*, XXI (1923), 15-28.

[2] See Reed Smith, *South Carolina Ballads*, p. 171. The totals there given are: New England, 25; the South, 69; the United States, 92; Canada, 15; America, 95. This makes clear the comparative importance of Virginia's 51.

far as the English and Scottish ballads are concerned, it will be well to wait until all the source volumes have appeared and until all the material is available before compiling the more readable volumes which will appeal mainly to popular favor. It would be a pity to have the break in the scholarly tradition of American balladry come too soon, whatever the clamor of popular reviewers and whatever the present indifference of the public.

FOR THE GENERAL READER

If the scholar's interest may be taken for granted, it is also to be hoped that herein may be found something to intrigue that lordly abstraction, the general reader. The fifty-one head-notes to individual ballads have been designed to provide him with an adequate introduction to each ballad, and at the same time to satisfy the demands of his exacting antithesis, the ballad scholar. The notes to each variant make the attempt, without stooping to triviality, to preserve some of the human factors of ballad collecting, and the historical section of this Introduction sketches some of the leading personalities among the collectors and singers. After all, though many variants are provided, it is not necessary that the general reader gorge himself upon them. He may sample here and there, as in any other book of verse. The music assembled at the back of the book provides him with a hundred and forty-eight actually singable songs. Some of the melodies are irresistible.

CONCERNING ARTISTIC QUALITY

Whether this concentration on English and Scottish ballad survivals alienate the general reader or not, there is no doubt that its effect upon the quality of the poetry is a happy one. As poetry or as dramatic narrative the later broadside ballads and modern American songs cannot compare with the older traditional ballads. One has but to examine a book of modern ballads like the recently published *Minstrelsy of Maine* to be convinced of the truth of Sir Arthur Quiller-Couch's judgment that

> the ballad has been dead, or as good as dead, for two hundred years. It would seem to have discovered, almost at the start, a very precise Platonic pattern of what its best should be; and having exhausted itself in reproducing that, it declined (through a crab-apple stage of broadsides) into sterility. Therefore [he continues in introducing the *Oxford Book of Ballads*[1]] this anthology cannot be brought down to the present day, and therefore the first half of it contains far finer poetry than the second.

[1] Preface, p. vii.

The exclusion of later ephemeral material from this volume, then, is an exclusion in favor of a high aesthetic standard. As Professor Mackenzie remarks in introducing the heterogeneous balladry of his native Nova Scotia,

> I have no inclination, and no warrant, to become boastful about the achievements of my fellow-countrymen in the matter of ballad composition. The art of ballad-making, indeed, has never risen to any great heights in any part of this western continent, and if we have cause for gratulation in our dealings with folk-song, as I believe we have, this is due mainly to the affectionate persistence of our singers in cherishing the ballads which they and their forefathers brought to these shores from the British Isles.[1]

CONCERNING PATRIOTISM

The superiority of artistic quality is part of the answer, but by no means the whole answer, to the "patriotic" question, Why so much effort to collect ballads of European origin rather than native American ballads? As Miss Pound says, "American folk-song as a whole has been imported from the Old World." [2] The nearest approach to an American body of folk-lore is the folk-lore of European origin transplanted and adapted in America — unless, forsooth, we should prefer to regard as representatively American the tribal and ceremonial songs of the Red Indian, which are American in no sense except the geographical, or the folk-songs of the Negro, which, beautiful as they often are, are obviously the heritage of the "Homo Africanus" transplanted in America, not the possession of our white majority. Try as we may, we cannot if we would — and there are those who would not if they could — controvert the historical fact that the American stock is European in origin. Hence it follows that the English and Scottish popular ballads (which are English or Scottish in language but Western European in culture, since their counterparts are to be found in most European literatures) are as American as any thing of tradition can be. By long adoption, by adaptation, sometimes by almost complete re-creation, we have made them as truly American as anything old that is not Red Indian. Professor Smith once made an enthusiastic remark to a journalist who was interviewing him, that "the search for the ballad is now the most interesting phase of *American* literature." The italicized adjective is significant here, though we may question the superlative. The patriotic preference for one hundred per cent

[1] *Ballads and Sea Songs from Nova Scotia* (Cambridge, 1928), Introduction, p. xxiii.
[2] See *American Ballads and Songs*, Introduction, p. xxvi.

American ballads rather than ballads of European origin now existing in America, is based on ignorance of the nature of folk-song, perhaps also on ignorance of the true meaning of Americanism, as well as upon an indifference to artistic standards.

THE STATE BOUNDARY

The ballads in this volume were actually sung, or recited, within the boundaries of Virginia. But the Virginia achievement in ballad collecting is no mere matter for state pride, though any state not too absorbed in the idea of modern progress might well be proud of so rich a heritage of old ballads. It is a matter of much wider interest — Southern Appalachian, American, English-speaking — and of importance to the literary and musical worlds. The state is, of course, not a ballad unit at all. Ballads, like coal deposits, are to be found chiefly in the mountain section of each state, and the Southern Appalachian mountain region, running through a part of Virginia, West Virginia, Kentucky, Tennessee, North Carolina, and a little of South Carolina, Georgia, and Alabama, is a district far more homogeneous and far more significant in balladry than any state division. The doctrine of state sovereignty, whatever its political standing to-day, has no reference to the ballad. This Virginia volume, then, may be viewed as a contribution, in ballads the richest single contribution, toward the larger Southern Appalachian collection, which in turn will contribute toward the complete American collection.

But this rather artificial line of demarcation, the state line, is hardly to be regretted. It gained for the collecting movement the impetus of state pride and the *esprit de corps* of a political division of long standing. It resulted in the tapping of certain ballad localities which under any other than a state plan of collection would almost certainly have remained untapped. It also suggested and made possible an interesting experiment as to the state-wide distribution of the ballad in Virginia. The experiment proved that ballads or fragments of ballads were to be found in every one of the one hundred counties of Virginia — in the Tidewater and Piedmont as well as the Mountain and Valley sections of the state.[1] The yield from the non-mountainous counties was comparatively small, but it was worth harvesting, and under any other than a state organization like

[1] A fuller account of this investigation will be found in Part III of this Introduction, "A History of the Ballad Movement in Virginia."

the Virginia Folk-Lore Society this yield would doubtless have been lost and some interesting data about the territorial distribution of ballads would be lacking. The state boundary, then, admittedly artificial as applied to the ballad, has many compensations and, even if not final, has been justified by its results.

THE MUSIC AND ITS TREATMENT

One of the most difficult problems of the volume was presented by the music.[1] The original notations varied all the way from the impeccable copy of Mr. Cecil J. Sharp to the musical monstrosities of less gifted contributors. The chief problem has been how to present the air in a technically correct form musically without doing violence to the original copy. Editing, at this point, had to proceed with caution. It would not do to say, "I believe this is what the recorder had in mind," and to alter an unusual melodic sequence, bar division, or time count to a more conventional form. Not standardization, but the preservation of what the singer actually sang, was desired. But could not a more expert musical editor enable a somewhat clumsy musical interpreter to come at what the singer actually sang and to set down accurately what the recorder intended to record? Possibly, but it is ticklish business for an editor who knows neither singer nor recorder nor tune, or even if he knows all three, to decide which aberrations are those of the transcriber, which of the singer. And the latter must be preserved at all cost, just as an obvious verbal intrusion (if one may speak of an "intrusion" here) must be preserved in the text, whether or not it makes sense, because it is preserved by the folk. Every one of the hundred and forty-eight airs of this volume comes from a traditional source, is, or recently was, actually sung in Virginia. Not one, so far as is known, can be traced to a printed source. In the matter of editing, then, obvious musical errors have been eliminated; in a few instances, after consultation, the musical editors have made minor alterations which, in their considered opinion, bring the text nearer to what the singer must actually have sung; but in all cases the original music has been left as undisturbed as possible. The music here given is not what the editor thinks an effective rendition of the song, not what he thinks the singer ought to have sung, but, purged

[1] The first problem under this head was the finding of competent musical assistance, which was ably provided by Miss Booker and Miss Broomall. See Preface.

of obvious error, what was recorded by the original hearer as what the singer actually sang.

Whether what was recorded was what was actually sung depends, of course, upon the trustworthiness of those who did the recording. The ballad collectors in Virginia varied a good deal in their musical ability. Some, like Mr. Cecil J. Sharp, were expert enough to take down the tune, as they took down the words, from the lips of the singer. Some, like Mr. John Stone, have good musical ears and memories and some little knowledge of musical technique, but not enough to enable them to record an air acceptably without the help of a musical instrument and some hard study. Some, like Miss Alfreda M. Peel, know and sing the songs, but have to rely entirely upon musical friends for the recording of the airs. And many collectors who have neither good ears nor a knowledge of music are totally incapacitated as collectors of tunes, can be looked to for the words only. This is why so many texts must appear without tunes. This last class of collector has generally known its limitations; where it has ventured beyond its depth, there has been trouble for the musical editor. The music of the first class is evidently the most trustworthy, but there is no reason to suspect the products of the second or third classes, especially when they bear the mark of the conscientious ballad lovers numbered among the Virginia collectors.

The fitting of the words to the tune has also given some trouble. Very seldom did the collector unite the two before he sent them in. The music sent in was usually a bare sequence of notes at the foot of the page, or on an additional sheet. (Notable exceptions to this rule are all of Mr. Sharp's music, much of Miss Peel's, some of Mr. Stone's, Miss Davis's, and Miss Fauntleroy's.) For some time the editor thought of leaving the words and music independent of one another; but the interweaving of the two makes the song so much more singable (and the ballad being essentially a combination of words and music), the final decision was to unite the two even where the distribution of the words over the tune was problematic. The usual procedure has been to scan both words and tune and to fit the accents of the one to the accents of the other. This, of course, is what the ballad singers themselves frequently if not generally do, unconsciously and often imperfectly. But different singers, or even the same singer at different times, will distribute the words differently. And some folk-singers have "the habit of dwelling arbitrarily upon certain notes of the melody, generally the weaker accents." [1] Hence the distribution of the words over the tune is in only a few cases to be accepted as final; rather as a possible way, and the most natural way, for the song to be sung. The words of the first stanza have been set to the tune, even when the presence of certain extra notes has indicated that the collector or singer had in mind another stanza in setting down the music. Such extra notes have generally been put in parentheses, or else tied, to indicate that they may be needed in another stanza. And conversely, extra notes are sometimes needed for the words of the first stanza. The extra note has generally been inserted as a tied note, but at times the arrangement of the words under the music is deemed sufficient to show how many words are spoken on the same note. The ballad singer does not hesitate occasionally to cast timing to the winds and indulge in a long recitative on a single note. In a few instances where the words have been written under the music by the contributor and the verbal accents have not coincided with the musical accents, the original has been left unchanged. A few cases where the interwoven words have not quite agreed with the separately written text have not been altered as errors of copying, but left as interesting variants.

It is evident that the method of singing these ballads is important, and in itself presents difficulties of musical notation. The strange sing-song sometimes unappreciatively referred to as the "mountain whine" is apt to display a lack of accuracy in pitch and accent. Individual singers often permit themselves certain embellishments on single notes. For instance, at a long pause or at the ending there is sometimes a slur to a short note on the third above, and the habit of dwelling arbitrarily on a weaker accent has already been referred to. Such peculiarities make recording difficult even for the musical expert, but they add greatly to the effectiveness of the ballad singer's performance.

> The wonderful charm [says Mr. Sharp], fascinating and wellnigh magical, which the folk-singer produces upon those who are fortunate enough to hear him is to be attributed very largely to his method of singing, and this, it should be understood, is quite as traditional as the song itself. The genuine folk-singer is never conscious of his audience — indeed, as often as not, he has none — and he never, therefore, strives after effect, nor endeavours in this or

---

[1] Cecil J. Sharp, *English Folk-Songs from the Southern Appalachians*, Introduction, p. x.

in any other way to attract the attention, much less the admiration of his hearers. So far as I have been able to comprehend his mental attitude, I gather that, when singing a ballad, for instance, he is merely relating a story in a peculiarly effective way which he has learned from his elders, his conscious attention being wholly concentrated upon what he is singing and not upon the effect which he himself is producing.[1]

A musical accompaniment is, of course, no part of a ballad or folk-song, and therefore none appears in this volume. There is no objection to such an accompaniment, provided it is understood that the musician has added something which does not strictly belong to the ballad. It is an embellishment, designed to make the song available in convenient form to a larger public, in the musical home, or on the concert stage. Accompaniments to these ballads are very simple, would consist usually of but three chords, built on the first, fourth, and fifth notes of the scale in which the tune is written. If one is neither a natural ballad singer nor interested in reproducing the conditions of folk-song, the accompaniment, which may easily be supplied, will be found to add something to his rendition of these ballads.

The editor makes no apology for the profusion of musical variants printed in this volume. On the contrary, he regrets that a few whole ballads and of course many variants, must stand without music because the music was not sent in. As to the importance of musical rendition to the ballad, a few ballad authorities may be briefly cited. The late Cecil J. Sharp declares that

it is greatly to be deplored that the literature of the ballad has, in the past, attracted so much more attention than the music. Properly speaking, the two elements should never be dissociated; the music and the text are one and indivisible, and to sever the one from the other is to remove the gem from its setting.[2]

The late C. Alphonso Smith concludes his article on "Ballads Surviving in the United States" with these words: "The truth is that the ballad heritage of the English-speaking race has been studied as poetry but not as song. Yet it is as song that the ballad was born and it is as song that it survives." [3] And Miss Louise Pound declares that

the salvage of melodies is desirable, for folk-music, like folk-literature, has its interest and its distinctive ways. Generally the melody and the words are so associated in the minds of the singers that the one cannot be recalled without

---

[1] *English Folk-Songs from the Southern Appalachians*, Introduction, p. x.
[2] *Ibid.*, p. xii.
[3] *Musical Quarterly*, Vol. II, No. 1, p. 129.

the other. The song is the life of the words the two are not to be separated. . . . In America, at least, pieces do not seem to be continued in tradition through recital or chanting. They persist because they are sung. It is the music, however it fluctuates, which keeps them alive.[1]

In this volume enough musical variants are presented to enable the ballad authority to study the music and its fluctuations. The editor confesses to a certain amount of regret that the music could not be printed in the body of the book, each tune at the head of the variant to which it belongs. But there are arguments, other than that of expense, against such an arrangement. The plan of segregation finally adopted at least clearly indicates for musical and for non-musical readers their respective bailiwicks. The interweaving of the words of the first stanza with the music makes this a book of easily singable songs.[2]

Concerning the music which he himself had collected in Virginia (much of which appears in this volume), Mr. Sharp says, "I have found the tunes in Virginia extraordinarily beautiful; I think of greater musical value than those I have taken down elsewhere in America." [3] In view of the quality of this music, Mr. Sharp might perhaps be as willing to prefix to this volume as to his own his statement:

It is my sober belief that if a young composer were to master the contents of this book, study and assimilate each tune with its variants, he would acquire just the kind of education that he needs, and one far better suited to his requirements than he would obtain from the ordinary Conservatoire or College of Music.[4]

This, be it understood, was the deliberate conclusion of the English-speaking world's leading authority on folk-music.

HEAD-NOTES, FOOT-NOTES, TEXT

The general head-notes to each of the fifty-one ballads aim to give an adequate introduction to the whole ballad and to its Virginia representatives taken collectively, with a bibliography of the ballad's American texts already printed or otherwise reported. Head-notes to individual variants preserve the data of collection for each variant and any available facts of its pro-

[1] *American Ballads and Songs*, Introduction, pp. xxvi-xxvii.

[2] See the sub-section on "The Problem of Music Publication" in the present editor's article, "Some Problems of Ballad Publication," *Musical Quarterly*, Vol. XIV, No. 2, p. 283.

[3] In a letter to Professor Smith, September 1, 1918.

[4] *English Folk-Songs from the Southern Appalachians*, Introduction p. xx.

venience. The data recorded in these minor head-notes, wherever possible, are:

1. The title of the variant as given by the collector or contributor — generally a local title but often an identification.
2. The name of the collector or contributor (with place of residence where that of the singer is not given).
3. The name of the singer or reciter, with place of residence.
4. The Virginia county to which the item is to be credited (usually but not always the county of the singer's present residence).
5. The date, usually that of receipt by the archivist, but in a few cases where obtainable, the date of collection.
6. The statement whether or not the item is accompanied by music, the words "With music" indicating the variants that have tunes.
7. Any facts about the previous history of the song or its singer, with any interesting or significant remarks of the collector. These are presented usually in the form of an excerpt from the letter with which the variant was sent in — the editor's only source of information.

Where not all these data are obtainable, the nearest approximation to them is given.[1]

The foot-notes perform the usual service of their kind. They supply variant readings, interpret or comment upon difficult words or passages, and now and then offer comparisons with other texts. They are neither formidable in number nor massive with learning. The idea has been to reduce them as far as possible.

No editorial liberties have been taken with the text. In every case, it is given as it was sent in, presumably as it was sung, essentially without emendation. Punctuation has, of course, been supplied where it was lacking or inaccurate; bad or unusual spelling, where it had no connection with the original pronunciation or rendition, has been corrected; stanza divisions have been provided, sometimes conjecturally, in order to present the words in a standard and readable form. But the essential folk quality of these ballads has not been tampered with. No attempt has been made to "improve upon" oral tradition, after the manner of Bishop Percy, Sir Walter Scott, and others. The endeavor has been to present it as accurately as possible.

These tedious preliminaries now being over, the reader may be allowed to hear how the Virginia ballad collection was brought together with the more human stories of the collectors.

[1] Appendix A, at the back of the book, records these data plus the number of stanzas for the remainder of the Virginia ballad collection; that is, for the ballad material excluded, for one reason or another, from this book.

III. A HISTORY OF THE BALLAD MOVEMENT IN VIRGINIA

The ballad, of course, had enjoyed a long and honorable life, both in Virginia and elsewhere in America, long before it was so nearly lost or forgotten that its presence in our midst had to be rediscovered by scholars toward the end of the nineteenth century. So quietly and unobtrusively as to be scarcely perceptible to historians, the ballad had played a distinguished part in the social history of the country. Unfortunately, the story of ballad-singing in America before the twentieth century has to be based more largely upon inference than upon documentary proofs, but the inference seems valid enough.

Some of the ballads in this volume were known and sung in England, Scotland, and Ireland before Columbus discovered America; others sprang up and gained popularity in the centuries following, when America was being colonized. It is quite natural, therefore, that some of these ballads should have been brought over to America with the earlier settlers, to whom printed books would have been an encumbrance but whose memories were charged with the oral traditions of their race. These traditions were well preserved in the isolation of their adopted land. Later immigrants no doubt added variety; and a comparatively primitive and homogeneous society, especially as the population pushed out toward the mountain fastnesses, gave the conditions necessary for the preservation of the ballad heritage intact or with such adaptation as might be expected of oral tradition in a new country.

As to the ballad past of Virginia, it would perhaps not be giving too free a rein to the imagination to suggest that some of the ballads of this volume may actually have landed at Jamestown in 1607; that many others were added as succeeding boatloads, whether of Cavaliers or of indentured servants, arrived; that they were known and sung by the families both of great planters and of petty yeomen; that they fell gracefully from the lips of Colonial dames, and were no less movingly sung by the poorest nurse-maids; that Negro slaves learned them from master or mistress or even from "po' white trash," and preserved them with great fidelity or with characteristic variations; that they were not unknown around the camp-fires of Revolutionary soldiers; that later immigrations, especially that of Scotch-Irish settlers into the Valley of Virginia, greatly enriched the ballad tradition; that rural social gatherings in the early nineteenth century were often given over to ballad-singing; that even as late as the Civil War, some soldiers at the front and matrons at home both knew the solace of these old songs; but that with the growth of population and the progress of industry and education in the nineteenth century, ballad-singing betook itself more and more to the mountain communities and the more out-of-the-way places suited to the unmolested survival of antiques — where for a time they linger still. Virginia, the seat of the first permanent English settlement in America, still dominantly English in stock, with a strong Scotch and Scotch-Irish infusion, with a large rural population given to sociability but until recently none too well provided with transportation facilities, traversed by two picturesque mountain ranges inviting habitation but not communication with the outside world; Virginia, whose traditions were not too far scattered by migration into the interior or adulterated by admixture with alien types or throttled by urbanization, presents an especially fair field for the ballad collector.

Now that the interest of scholars has been redirected to the ballad, it will probably not be long before substantial evidence as to the past of the ballad in America is accumulated. One such bit of evidence as to Virginia, for instance, is to be found in Senator William Cabell Bruce's *Life of John Randolph of Roanoke* (1922), where Randolph, writing to a niece, February 20, 1822, asks if she knows a certain ballad that used to be sung to him as a child by a mulatto servant girl. "I pr'y thee get me that ballad," he says. "I can give you the tune." It is a fact in no wise due to this letter that in the mountains of Virginia the well-known ballad of "Lord Randal" is sometimes sung as "Johnnie Randolph!" But one feels that Randolph's interest in ballads as attested by the letter gives a certain poetic justice to the ballad's tribute to him. Perhaps this letter would entitle Randolph to mention as an early Virginian ballad collector.

But American interest in balladry was not really awakened until Professor Francis James Child, of Harvard, had begun the publication of his great collection which appeared in ten parts between 1882 and 1898 and which was to contain "every obtainable version of every extant English or Scottish ballad." In collecting and editing these ballads, Professor Child looked chiefly to England and Scotland, and to printed or manuscript sources rather than to oral tradition, for his texts — though he did not entirely ignore the traditional source. It is probable that he did not suspect the richness of certain sections of his own country in the traditional ballad that he went so far to seek. As the successive parts of his great work appeared, American survivals of the old ballad began to flow in to him and were soon included either in the body of the work or in the "Additions and Corrections" appended to succeeding parts of the work.

As far as Virginia is concerned, the credit of being the pioneer collector and publisher of ballads surviving within her borders must go to Mr. W. H. Babcock, lawyer and author, of Washington, D.C. In the *Folk-Lore Journal* (London) for January–March, 1889, he published his finds under the curious title of "The London Ballads." Not until one has read the article's first sentence — "They come from that prosperous but out-of-the-way county of Virginia, in the corner between the Potomac and the Blue Ridge" — does one discover that "London" is a misprint or a misspelling for "Loudoun," the Virginia county described. Mr. Babcock continues:

> Plain people of the conservative overseer and small-tenant class have transmitted them from mother to daughter, through the years and lives that have passed since the first settlement, as in England before it. Of course they do not think of writing them down, and know nothing of the books in which the relics of balladry are treasured.

In his account of how the ballads were obtained, Mr. Babcock foreshadows the methods of later collectors.

> One evening as we approached our home near Washington [he writes], a ballad, then heard for the first time, came chanted to us out of the open windows. The new house girl, white, and from up the river, was singing the smaller children to sleep. When the song of many words ended, another was taken up, and after it another. Plainly the services of the collector were called for, and most members of the family enlisted, as opportunity offered. Unfortunately the pace of the music kept ahead of the reporters; and when she undertook to recite the line deliberately, something was sure to be omitted or confused. Memory depended in part on the swing and excitement of her habitual mode of utterance. But a fair approach to completeness, in some cases, was made by repetition and comparison; and the results in full were read to the young woman's mother, who made some notable additions, and declared the ballads to be substantially correct. She could not explain anything which is not obvious, nor, indeed, tell us anything of them but what I have said in the beginning.

With this introduction, Mr. Babcock prints six songs, three of them genuine old ballads. These are: "Wilson," a version of

"Lady Isabel and the Elf Knight"; "The Brown Girl," a version of "Lord Thomas and Fair Annet"; and "Come Along, Come Along, My Pretty Lass," a version of "The Lass of Roch Royal." In speaking of "Lady Isabel and the Elf Knight," Mr. Babcock says, "That cycle, so carefully studied and preserved by Professor Child, cannot afford to leave this stray member wandering unrecorded over Virginia foot hills." Professor Child was evidently of the same opinion, for in the "Additions and Corrections" published with Part VI later in 1889, all three of these Virginia survivals are printed, of course with proper acknowledgment to Mr. Babcock and to the *Folk-Lore Journal.* For the fourth and final ballad included from Virginia, "Lamkin," Professor Child is indebted not to Mr. Babcock but to the singing of the "negroes of Dumfries, Prince William County," who have the ballad "orally transmitted from the original Scottish settlers of that region," as reported by a Mrs. Dulany.

Evidently, with this paltry total of four reported from Virginia, Professor Child made no serious attempt to recapture the American survivals of the old ballads, though he used what came to him. For the whole country, he reported only thirty versions of eighteen ballads found in the Atlantic states from Maine to South Carolina. But at least he pointed the way to a field from which succeeding collectors have reaped a rich harvest of ballad material. And richest of all has been the harvest in Virginia.

On April 17, 1913, in Richmond, Virginia, at a meeting of those interested in the collection and preservation of ballads and other folk-lore, the Virginia Folk-Lore Society was founded and its constitution adopted. Its purpose, as stated in the constitution, was "to discover, collect, publish and thus preserve the folk-lore of Virginia and of the states recruited by immigration from Virginia." As a matter of fact, the formation of similar organizations in neighboring states caused the Society to limit its operations to Virginia; and it was decided to postpone the collection of other varieties of folk-lore while the Society devoted its first attention exclusively to the ballad. Thus the immediate object of the Society was stated as "to collect and thus to preserve the words and music of the English and Scottish ballads that drifted across with our first settlers and that have been transmitted from century to century by oral tradition." Its first purpose, then, was to run down all the Virginia versions of the Child ballads.

So for a round dozen years the workers of the Society have been scouring the mountains, raking the Piedmont, and even combing the Tidewater sections of the state for old ballads, which they have copied down hot from the lips of the singers and sent off to gladden the heart and plump the files of the archivist.

How well the task has been accomplished may be judged from this volume, the first publication of the Virginia material which is, I believe, the largest and richest collection of authentic ballads so far brought together in any single state or in any one ballad locality in America. Fifty-one of the original ballads have been rescued, and of these fifty-one some six hundred and fifty versions or variants or fragments. Tunes have been recovered for all except seven of these fifty-one ballads — for some, various tunes. And what is more, as an indication of the widespread distribution of ballads in the state, ballads or fragments of ballads have been found in every one of the one hundred counties of Virginia — a record not approached in any other state.

Difficult as it may be in a brief Introduction to give an idea of the activities of many people over a period of a dozen years, it should be interesting, now that the ballad phase of the Society's work has come to a close, to glance back and see just how this rich collection was brought together, and, more particularly, to hear from the collectors themselves some account of their adventures, experiences, and impressions in running down ballads all over the state.

The movement was fortunate, in the first place, in having at its head a man of extraordinary vision, energy, and magnetism. C. Alphonso Smith, at that time Edgar Allan Poe Professor of English in the University of Virginia, founded the Virginia Folk-Lore Society on his own initiative, and as its first president and later as its permanent archivist, he somehow managed to kindle and to keep alive among its many workers an enthusiasm almost equal to his own.

That the idea of searching for American survivals of the old ballads was not original with Professor Smith, has already been shown. Not only had the way been pointed by Professor Child, but there had also sprung up in the decade following his death

C. ALPHONSO SMITH
(1864–1924)

Edgar Allan Poe Professor of English, University of Virginia, 1909–17; Head of Department of English, United States Naval Academy, 1917–24.

Founder of the Virginia Folk-Lore Society

a group of interested collectors in several localities. At the time when the Virginia Folk-Lore Society was founded, the work of recovering ballads in America had already been ably carried forward by such leaders as Professor W. W. Newell, who may be regarded as the pioneer in the American field; Professor George Lyman Kittredge, and Mr. Phillips Barry, of Massachusetts; Messrs. Hubert G. Shearin and Josiah H. Combs, of Kentucky; Mr. H. M. Belden, of Missouri; Miss Louise Pound, of Nebraska; Mr. John A. Lomax, of Texas; Mr. F. C. Brown, of North Carolina; and especially by the *Journal of American Folk-Lore*, under the editorship of Professor Franz Boas, of Columbia University. Many distinguished names have since been added to this roster of American ballad workers. But the success of the ballad quest in Virginia was due, first of all, to the energy and scholarly interest of C. Alphonso Smith.

How Professor Smith came to interest himself in ballads, he has himself described.

> I first became interested in ballad research [he once said] when I found that Professor Child, in his authoritative *English and Scottish Popular Ballads*, reported that only four remained in North Carolina. I had already learned that many times that number could be found in the state. This started me to work. However, when in 1908 I was notified of my appointment as Roosevelt Exchange Professor to Berlin, all my ballad work stopped. When I came back in 1911 and went to the University of Virginia, I found that many times the four assigned by Child to that state, too, were in existence there. So I took up the search for the elusive ballad.

A particularly valuable version of "Barbara Allen" brought in by a student of the University of Virginia and published with elaborate commentary in the *University of Virginia Magazine* for April, 1913, may have given the final push to his intentions. Once the Virginia Folk-Lore Society was organized, its founder was insatiable. Something of the infectious enthusiasm of the man may be caught from his words quoted in a press interview.

> It is perfectly fascinating work [he said]. The search for the ballad is now the most interesting phase of American literature. It is a revelation of tremendous historical importance to anyone who realizes how closely our present is built on our past, or how intimate are the ties of tradition which still link us to the lands across the waters. Many of these old songs that scholars have been searching for are being sung at their very doors, but they did not dream of it.

Is there any wonder that, under such leadership, the Virginia ballad quest flourished?

One of the first decisions reached by the Virginia Folk-Lore Society was that a systematic search for the ballads surviving in Virginia should be conducted through the teachers in the public schools of the state, on the ground that these constituted an intelligent class spread into all the far corners of the state and that to them an appeal might legitimately be made in the name of education. Accordingly, at the instigation of Professor Smith, the Department of Public Instruction in Virginia issued a circular giving all necessary information about the collecting of ballads and asking the help of teachers, pupils, and school patrons "in the great movement to collect and save to the state and nation these old songs still surviving in the commonwealth." The importance of collecting at once these American survivals was stressed:

> If our American versions are not collected quickly [says the bulletin], they can never be collected at all. It is now or never. Many influences are tending to obliterate them. Catchy, but empty songs not worthy of comparison with them, the decadence of communal singing, the growing diversity of interests, the appeal to what is divisive and separative in our national life, the presence of the artificial and self-conscious in modern writing, are depriving our homes and schoolrooms of a kind of literature which, for community of feeling, for vigor of narrative, for vividness of portraiture, and for utter simplicity of style and content is not surpassed in the whole history of English or American song.

A similar appeal by Professor Smith addressed to the teachers of the nation had been issued just before this Virginia circular by the Bureau of Education in Washington, with a Preface by the Honorable P. P. Claxton, United States Commissioner of Education. Indeed, Professor Smith was commissioned by the Bureau of Education to institute a nation-wide search for versions of these old ballads that "helped to mould the character of men and women who made up the larger part of the Colonial population of this country." Mr. Claxton, in his Preface, speaks of the part played by the ballad in our national culture, and adds, somewhat poetically,

> Before the march of the public school, the public library, urban civilization, and modern industrial and commercial life, they have vanished like the fresh, cool mists of the morning before the heat of the sun, but they still have their value, and we should not permit them to be lost out of our national life. The Nation will be the poorer if we do.

Copies of this pamphlet were sent to thirty thousand teachers in all parts of the country. Thus was the work of the Virginia

Folk-Lore Society linked up with the nation-wide quest of the ballad.

In addition to these manifestos, much newspaper publicity was given to the work of ballad hunting, so that contributors might do their work intelligently. The *Virginia Journal of Education*, sent to all public school teachers, was generous in its space, as were various other publications. The Society itself published an annual bulletin.

The response to these several appeals was immediate and gratifying. Before the end of the year 1913, in the April of which the Virginia Folk-Lore Society was organized, twenty of the old ballads had been recaptured and safely stored in the archives of the Society — with several variants of each. Each succeeding year brought new ballad finds, so that, as far as the ballad is concerned, the results seem to justify the statement found in the first bulletin of the Society, that "no state of the Union offers so rich a field for the student of folk-lore as Virginia."

But the story of ballad collecting in Virginia is of especial interest not only because of the richness of its results, but also because of the widespread, democratic character of the movement, and because Virginia was the first to undertake to collect ballads through the teachers in the public schools. English teachers and other educators, chiefly of college rank, formed an interested nucleus of informed ballad lovers for the charter membership of the Virginia Folk-Lore Society. It was early decided to hold the annual meeting of the Society at the time and place designated by the Virginia State Educational Association, then known as the State Teachers Association, for its annual meeting, in the attempt to interest the teachers in the work of the Society and in ballad hunting. As to the results of this policy, it will be well to quote Professor Smith, who was especially anxious to give credit to the teachers. "That Virginia has found and rescued more of these old-world treasures than any other single state," he wrote, "is due more to the interest and perseverance and intelligence of the teachers than to any or to all other causes."

One of the most effective ways of catching the interest of prospective teachers was found to be the formation of ballad clubs at the state normal schools or teachers' colleges. These schools offered a particularly promising field because their students came from all parts of the state and soon went out again as teachers in intimate touch with the people in every county. The most flourishing of these clubs was that organized at the Farmville Normal School, now State Teachers College, in late April, 1913, under the tutelage of Professor James M. Grainger, of the English Department there, an ardent lover of ballads. This club soon numbered about fifty members, representing both faculty and students, and interesting ballad programs were rendered at its bi-weekly meetings. Of the work of the club in actually running down ballads, Professor Grainger himself has spoken.

> The collecting of ballads has been carried on [he says] largely by means of systematic canvasses of the entire school community. At certain intervals, on a day set apart for the purpose, a member of the faculty explains the nature of the canvass at the morning assembly, discusses the ballad briefly, and quotes one or two. During that day every member of the Club interviews personally, in regard to their knowledge of ballads, all the students assigned to her by the committee. These "ballad hunts" have given the members valuable first-hand experience and training in collecting and have unearthed several new variants of old ballads . . . and a mass of other folk material which is exceedingly interesting.

Much of this material was published in the students' monthly magazine, *The Focus*, from which all printed ballad material was clipped and sent, usually along with the original manuscript, to Professor Smith. However, the greatest value of this and similar clubs was felt when their members went out as teachers in remote parts of the state and, retaining their interest in balladry, sent in their finds to the Folk-Lore Society.

But as in all human activities the bulk of the labor devolves upon a few enthusiastic individuals, so the quest for ballads in Virginia, comparatively general as it was, was carried forward primarily by a few zealous workers. Though scores, if not hundreds, of people made valuable contributions to the archives of the Society, the bulk of its collecting was done by four, or perhaps six, devoted workers. The four are Miss Martha M. Davis, of Harrisonburg, Va.; Miss Juliet Fauntleroy, of Altavista, Va.; Miss Alfreda M. Peel, of Salem, Va.; and Mr. John Stone, of Mt. Fair, Va. It is interesting to note that all of these were teachers in the public schools of the state, and that all of them hail from the mountain section of the state. The other two who must be mentioned are Professor James M. Grainger, whose yeomen service at Farmville, already described, entitles him to rank in this select company; and the eminent English ballad authority, Mr. Cecil J. Sharp, whose collecting in Virginia was done with the coöperation of Professor Smith, and who very courteously presented to the Virginia Folk-Lore Society not only typed copies of the texts, but also his original musical notations, of the ballads he found in Virginia. All of these collectors have given the Society in letters to the archivist or in narratives specially written some account of their experiences in ballad collecting. Indeed, the thousand or more letters and reports written to Professor Smith as President and Archivist, accompanying and often explaining or discussing their precious ballad freight, constitute a mass of material of even greater interest, and of scarcely less value than the ballads themselves. Professor Grainger has already spoken, and the other five collectors may be called upon to tell of their own ballad adventures.

First, a characteristic letter from that indefatigable walker, singer, collector, and "character," Mr. John Stone, who later, after the resignation of Professor Smith, became President of the Virginia Folk-Lore Society. Under date of November 15, 1915, he writes to the archivist:

> I enjoy the excitement of running down the ballad, but I hate the details. Could I write as fast as I can talk, I could tell you some interesting experiences. In Culpeper one day, I walked fourteen miles, raised four blisters on my feet and walked lame for a month. The next day, in spite of blisters, I walked seven more, but finished with versions of "Lord Lovel," "Barbara Allen," more news of "The Hangman" and the trail of "Robin Hood." At the present time, I am waiting for the return to this county of an old gentleman over seventy-five who has been and is a great singer of old songs. From him I hope to get good news.

It was this letter that led Professor Smith to remark to the Society at its next meeting, "If we ever select a flag or standard for our Society, I propose for its heraldic device a hurrying heel or a fleeting foot glorified with four large blisters and underneath it these inspiriting words: 'In hoc signo vinces.'" Of Mr. Stone we shall hear more later on.

Miss Martha M. Davis, then a teacher in the Harrisonburg High School, may be called the pioneer contributor of the Society. During 1913 her efforts were so successful that her own county of Rockingham furnished exactly half of the ballads collected by the Society during the first year of its life. Her valuable correspondence with Professor Smith began almost as soon as the Society was organized. On May 3, 1913, she writes to him: "The University, your own prestige, and the inspiration of your presence can give character and solidity to this movement not always accorded to popular movements. It will not be difficult for you to win the sympathy and coöperation of the entire state."

Miss Davis's interest in folk-lore was not limited to ballads. Her letter of May 26, 1913, begins:

> Thank you for all the pleasant things you say about my contributions to the Society in the way of ballads. I have kept other folk-lore in abeyance, as it seemed best to you to report first the English and Scottish ballads, if possible. I am collecting, however, on witchcraft and superstitions, primitive customs and social games, Indian legends, negro improvisations, old ballads. . . . Any English and Scottish ballads that may turn up during the summer I shall be glad to report at once.

Again, in a letter of January 3, 1914:

> You will be glad to see the enclosed ballads, I feel sure, "The House Carpenter," "Our Goodman," and the fragment of "Jock o' Hazelgreen." The mountain woman who gave me these ballads is a domestic in the family of some friends I have just been visiting for a day or two. We called her into the living room and found her mind a storehouse of English and Scottish lore. Her great grandfather fought in the Revolutionary War, and her own story reads like a novel. She also gave me several stanzas of "The Lass of Roch Royal," "Lord Randal," "The Hangman's Tree" — quite a full version — besides some stanzas of interesting things I hope to report to you later in less fragmentary state. She learned many of these ballads from her mother and another woman, a weaver, whom she was helping at the loom in her young days.

Again, on August 6, 1913, she writes enclosing several ballads:

> The memory of the immortal ladies, "The King's Daughter," "Barbara Allen," and "Lady Marget" is still fresh in western Rockingham, as you will see from the records enclosed. . . . This version of "Barbara Allen" may be superfluous, but it seems worth while as a piece of genuine oral tradition. The Mrs. Adam Gowl who dictated "Barbara" and "The King's Daughter" belongs to the good plain people, small farmers, millers, weavers, and the like, whose folks have lived time out of mind among the foot-hills of the mountains in western Rockingham Co. In her youth she was a domestic and can barely read and write. Mrs. William Keister, who dictated "Lady Marget," lives in the same neighborhood. All these things are still sung, "Barbara" to the English air, not the Scottish.

The letter continues with enthusiasm:

> Thus far I have had only pleasure in collecting. There is nothing like an old song, it seems, to stir up memory, unless it be the perfume of a flower, and so these songs of the simple folk for me have not only their own story to tell,

but a chapter from the life of the narrator and a page from the human heart. So much for "old wives' tales." How many ballads do we need to put Virginia at the head?

Miss Davis is a ballad critic of much astuteness. In sending a version of "Lamkin," September 5, 1915, she remarks: "This version of 93 is suggestive of 'K' in Kittredge. I wonder if it could be a fragment of something older, or if it is merely another instance of what an English ballad becomes in the hands of the negro." She continues: "I am reasonably sure that this county as yet has yielded only a tithe of her lore. There are several neighborhoods under suspicion, but it will take a fortunate combination of circumstances to reach them." Two months later she sends another report:

> Some weeks ago I had the opportunity to hear the mountain woman sing again — the same who has given me quite a number of interesting ballads. This woman belongs to a clan that has lived in the hollow of the mountain near Swift Run Gap (Spottswood's) since pre-Revolutionary times, and there is not the slightest doubt that her ballads are genuine oral tradition.

Miss Davis's ballad conscience is apparent in this letter of March 2, 1916:

> I am also glad to see that the version — a variant — of "The Seven Brothers" reported from Rockingham Co. has been found elsewhere. I was a little afraid my mountain woman had made up a jargon of her own. I have also found it again in Harrisonburg from an old woman who learned it many years ago in Rappahannock County.

The ballad talk continues:

> "Lady Gay" (79) comes from an illiterate woman I see sometimes in our mission Sunday School. Like the old granny from Rappahannock, she "has always known it." A few days after I had received the words of (79), a man from the neighborhood of the mission was cleaning the sidewalk. I found he knew "Lady Gay," so I asked him to come into the mission and sing it. He has a rich baritone, and he sang it well. It was like an echo from a past age. I wrote the air down at once in the same key in which he sang it. These old airs in a minor key are often so sad.

Her letter of May 9, 1916, shows that she is contemplating an article on her ballad experiences, but her conclusion is, "I am within too close range to write freely for print about many interesting things in connection with collecting."

But here we must leave Miss Davis and her interesting correspondence, and turn to her friendly rival in a neighboring county, Miss Juliet Fauntleroy, of Altavista, Virginia.

Like most of those who bore the brunt of the collecting in Virginia, Miss Fauntleroy first had her attention called to ballad hunting by one of the many speeches which Professor Smith made in the interest of the Folk-Lore Society. Her first letter, dated March 9, 1914, begins:

> It was with great interest that I heard you speak at the Educational Convention in Lynchburg last fall on the preservation of our old ballads. . . . My attention having been called to ballad hunting, I have tried to discover any still handed down in my own immediate neighborhood — and with better results than I ever anticipated. Those that I have collected I am sending you now. All of them I wrote down from the singing of the people who gave them to me, and who all said they had never seen them in print or in writing in their lives. On each ballad I have written the name of the person who gave it to me, and the date of collection.

She then adds some brief information about several of the ballad singers:

> Mr. and Mrs. Dan Maxie were originally from Franklin County, and only moved to Altavista two months ago. They are good plain people, of very little education. Mr. Maxie said he learned his songs chiefly from an aunt who had such a sweet voice that the neighbors often used to come in just to hear her sing. He said they all used to sing a great deal at their "sociables" and parties, and that he was a great singer himself. Mrs. Maxie had learned her songs from her mother and older sisters — she was one of twelve children. . . . Mrs. John Maxie, née Lily Stone, has always lived here, and has little education. She knows fragments of several ballads learned from her mother and her friends. . . . Mr. Alonzo Hogan and his sister learned their songs by singing with their mother when they all sat together in the evenings; and Mrs. Hogan had them from an old aunt who raised her. . . . All of these songs (except one) I collected in the homes of the people who sang them.

If Miss Davis had dominated the returns for 1913, Miss Fauntleroy was the outstanding contributor of 1914. Professor Smith was shrewd enough to stimulate a friendly rivalry between the good ladies of Rockingham and Campbell counties — a rivalry that was very profitable for the Folk-Lore Society. The competitive spirit appears here and there in Miss Fauntleroy's letters. On May 24, 1914, she writes: "If after all my efforts Rockingham is still ahead of old Campbell, I shall be quite disappointed!" And on June 13, 1914, she adds a postscript to a long letter, as follows: "I feel hopeless of catching up with Rockingham! I might send in other versions of 'The Brown Girl' or 'The House Carpenter,' but nothing else is in sight." Not until September, 1915, did she finally overtake her rival, and on the eighteenth of that month she wrote to Professor Smith:

Of course Campbell County's primacy in the ballad line is most gratifying, but I feel assured that when some of our other counties, and particularly our mountain counties, really wake up, they will make as good a showing, or a better one. And probably there are other ballads in Campbell if I can only find them. But my researches are necessarily restricted for the most part to my own immediate neighborhood. And I have never been able to find any of the rarer ballads, such as "Robin Hood," "The Gypsy Lad," "The Hunting of the Cheviot," etc.

Perhaps the most interesting excerpt from Miss Fauntleroy's correspondence is her testimony about the religious antagonism to the ballads.

In making enquiries in regard to ballads [she writes], I have in several cases encountered a strong Puritanical feeling against them. One lady told me she had "prayed to the Lord to take them fool songs out of her mind," and now she never thought of them. She said if she were to allow her children to sing her such songs they would soon be playing on the banjo, and playing *dance* music! Her tone implied that there could be no greater depth of sin! A man informed me brusquely, as if I had reflected on his personal character in asking about ballads, that in the last seven years he had not lost seven days from his work, and those on account of his wife's illness. He said he was never in a magistrate's court in his life, either as accused or as witness; no, indeed, *he* knew no ballads! So you see some people regard our ballad singing friends as quite beyond the pale. Is n't it fortunate that everybody is n't of this mind?[1]

Miss Fauntleroy was particularly interested in the musical side of the ballads, and was continually plying Professor Smith with questions and with suggestions as to the ballad airs she was sending in. On June 30, 1914, she writes:

I am surprised to know that so few ballad tunes have been published. But probably in England and Scotland, as here, many of the melodies are so simple and monotonous that no one has considered them worth collecting. So that our tunes may be traditional after all. I do hope you will publish all the airs

---

[1] For this Puritanical attitude toward ballads, compare W. Roy Mackenzie's Introduction to *Ballads and Sea Songs from Nova Scotia*, p. xvi:

"But to the Scotchmen of Nova Scotia there came a time when all customs were to be subjected to the most rigorous standards that could be derived from or ascribed to the tenets of Holy Writ,— a time when all things which, so scrutinized, could not be adjudged as lovely and of good report must be consigned to the merely ungodly, where, it might secretly be hoped, they would remain as a visible sign of unregeneracy in the world."

For an early Puritan example of the same attitude, see the diary of Cotton Mather, entry for September 27, 1713: "I am informed that the minds and manners of many people about the Countrey are much corrupted by foolish Songs and Ballads, which the Hawkers and Peddlers carry into all parts of the Countrey. By way of antidote, I would procure poetical Composures full of Piety, and such as may have a Tendency to advance Truth and Goodness, to be published, and scattered into all Corners of the Land." It would seem that the worthy man's zealous propaganda reached as far as Virginia, as that Puritanism he represented reached much further through American civilization, Cavalier or other, at a later stage.

you can find. Ballads can never live without music. Can you not induce other collectors to write down the music also, or to get some musical friend to do it for them? Some trained musician might correct for you any conspicuous errors in notation in the scores sent in. Mine need correction, I know, as to the value of the rests, etc.

And on August 1, 1914, her musical conscience again asserts itself:

Since sending you the ballad airs [she writes], I have had an opportunity of correcting my notation of those Mrs. Christian sang, by hearing her sing them again. The notation I am now sending is correct, she says. So won't you destroy or return to me the first copies I sent of these four airs? The other airs I sent I had already verified. I think, however, that I failed to write the signature to Mrs. Jesse Maxie's tune for "Barbara Allen." It should be in the key of F (one flat). The tune sung by Mr. Hall and Miss Callie Hogan to "Barbara Allen" is the one generally known to "My Pretty Little Pink."

Strangely enough, the people who sing ballads know them not as ballads but simply as "old songs." Collectors uniformly report no response to their ballad inquiries until they have asked for "old songs." Indeed, to the mountain singer the word "ballad" or "song ballad" means something rather different from our present usage of the word. In the same letter, Miss Fauntleroy adds an interesting note showing the survival of this antique meaning:

The people who know ballads, when I ask about any particular one, often tell me they have n't the ballad of that, but maybe they can remember it for me. Ballad with them seems to mean a manuscript or printed copy. One old lady brought forth with pride a box of "ballads" she had. They proved to be old songs she had copied off years ago, before she was married.

This meaning of ballad or "ballet" is, of course, familiar to the student of the history of the ballad.

Miss Fauntleroy is somewhat disturbed by the liberties which certain ballad singers seemed to take with both words and music of their songs. She admits, however, that not all singers are so careless. In her letter of September 11, 1915, she writes:

Some ballad singers, probably most ballad singers, like Mrs. Jesse Maxie, would regard the slightest deviation in words or tune as hardly short of a crime, while others, of less exact memories or less strict ideals, sometimes sing unimportant words or lines differently, and even vary the melodies, which is even more confusing.

Some of the variations which trouble Miss Fauntleroy are the following: in "Barbara Allen," the change from "choir" to "Ohio"; in "The Wife of Usher's Well," "To hear my must resign" instead of "To him I must resign" — the latter of which clearly makes much better sense. Of course, ballad singers often use words which they do not understand and which convey little or no meaning to others, as when the "castle-gate" of "Lord Lovel" is mutilated into "cassy-gate." But a more usual custom is for the singer to substitute a familiar for an unfamiliar word, as "speed" for the rather highfalutin' "steed," or "Aiken" for "eke in." Most singers have a perhaps unconscious tendency to rationalize words or expressions which they do not understand, as when "Come a link, come a long summer's day" is rationalized to "Come the length of a long summer's day" in "Lady Isabel and the Elf-Knight," and in "The Cruel Mother" the refrain "All along and lonely" is altered to "All alone and lonely." At any rate, such changes are necessary to the ballad as oral tradition, and Miss Fauntleroy is exceedingly punctilious in recording them.

Another intensely interesting part of Miss Fauntleroy's correspondence is that in which she names the ballad singers of her community with a brief description of each. For the most part, they are people of little education — farmers' wives, carpenters, seamstresses, and so on. But now and then a new type of singer appears, such as one whom she describes as "a man of good family and some education, but a poor inefficient creature, who lived as an object of charity in this neighborhood for many years, and was finally sent to the poor house. I remember he used to make rhymes by the hour to the tune of 'Vive l'Amour.'" But perhaps her complete list, with brief identifications, of the "Ballad Singers of Campbell County, Virginia, 1914–1915" is a record worth preserving. It runs as follows:

Miss Callie Hogan	Seamstress.
Mr. Alonzo Hogan	Carpenter, brother of Miss Callie.
Mr. Jesse Maxie	Employed at tobacco warehouse.
Mrs. Jesse Maxie	His wife; has several children.
Mrs. John Maxie	Works out as a cleaner. Her husband is a rough carpenter.
Mrs. Essie Yowell	Keeps a boarding house for cotton mill employes.
Mrs. Lit Arthur	Wife of a farmer; has three children.
Mrs. Bob Stone	Wife of a farm foreman.
Mr. J. B. Crawford	Foreman in road building.
Mrs. J. B. Crawford	His wife; has eight children.
Mrs. James Sprouse	Her husband is 40 years her senior — used to be a section foreman on R.R.
Mrs. Lloyd Poe	Her husband works at the cedar chest factory; has three children.

Mrs. Virgie Kesee	Wife of a farmer; has many children; cannot read or write.
Mr. Ed. Stinnet	A wood chopper and ditcher; cannot read or write; has many children.
Mrs. John W. Wildman	Wife of a farmer.
Mr. Morgan Hall	A tenant farmer.
Mrs. Fanny Stone	Mother of Mrs. John Maxie; old and feeble.
Jesse Burgess	Fourteen years old; in the first grade; belongs to a cotton mill family.
Mr. Walker	An excellent carpenter.
Mrs. Quarles	Wife of a farmer.
Mrs. Kegley	Her son works at the cotton mill.
Miss Mary Colbird	Works at the cotton mill.
Miss Hooney Wright	Works at the cotton mill. (N.C.)
Miss Maggie Wright	Works at the cotton mill. (N.C.)
Charles Henry Payne	An old colored man; cannot read or write.
Pamela Payne	A colored woman; works in the field.
Willie Walker	Wife of Isaiah Walker, a colored farm hand; has many children.
Mr. H. W. Adams	A large landowner and farmer.
Mrs. H. W. Adams	His wife; has six children.
Miss Charlotte Rodé	Stenographer at a bank.
Miss Jennie Nelson	A teacher, related to Thos. Nelson Page.
Miss Ethel Hancock	A teacher, from Franklin Co., Va.
Mrs. James Dearing	Widow of General Dearing, from Prince George Co. originally; musical talent.
Mrs. Frank P. Christian	Wife of Judge Christian; has a fine ear for music; daughter of Mrs. Dearing.

Again, Miss Fauntleroy seems to suspect ballads which come from educated folk.

I have been wondering [she writes, November 1, 1915] whether the version of "Lord Lovel" I sent you was strictly the product of oral tradition. Mrs. Christian, who gave it to me, first learned it from Mrs. Thomas Walker, herself an educated woman, the wife of a well-known physician. Both Mrs. Christian and Mrs. Walker were great readers and may have been influenced by printed copies even though they first learned the ballad orally, and never had the printed music for it. So if it seems to you suspiciously like the printed copies we will not print it.

There is need of no further laboring of the point to prove that the Virginia collection was brought together, in the main, by workers of superior intelligence, conscience, and ballad sympathy. As Misses Davis and Fauntleroy dominated the earlier collecting of the Society, so Miss Peel and Mr. Stone were the outstanding contributors during its later years. As a dividing line may be mentioned the visit to Virginia during 1916 (and again in 1918) of the great English balladist, the late

Cecil J. Sharp, then President of the British Folk-Lore Society. Mr. Sharp tarried for some days in Albemarle County and there collected a number of ballads, copies of which, together with their tunes, he very generously handed to Professor Smith as a gift to the Virginia Folk-Lore Society. Thus the Society's archives received the first of several rich donations from an eminent contributor.

The relation of Mr. Sharp to the Virginia ballad quest will best be exhibited by a selection from his interesting correspondence with Professor Smith. These letters also give a good deal of the inside history behind Mr. Sharp's own publications, especially his *English Folk-Songs from the Southern Appalachians* and *American-English Folk-Songs*, the material for which he himself noted down with the help of his secretary, Miss Maud Karpeles, during their jaunts through the Southern mountains.

The first letter, dated September 10, 1916, from Asheville, N. C., is a masterpiece of diplomacy, broaching a rather delicate matter.

You may remember [he says to Professor Smith] that when I had the pleasure of meeting you at Cincinnati University last June I told you it was my intention to do some ballad collecting in these mountains during the months of August and September. You will, I am sure, be interested to know that I have been able to carry out my intention, with the result that in the last six weeks I have taken down about 250 songs and ballads with their tunes. The wealth of these districts in the matter of traditional song is to me simply amazing. I enclose a list of the ballads noted by Child, which I have found, to many of which I have collected several tunes.[1] This week I am going to pay a flying visit to a district in Georgia, where I have reason to believe I can get hold of some good singers. My present plan is to spend the following fortnight — which will bring my holiday to a conclusion — in the middle of Kentucky. But in looking through the list, which you and others have published, of the "Child" ballads which have been discovered in America I find that the majority of those which I have not yet myself come across, have been found in Virginia. Mrs. John Campbell, with whom I am collaborating in this matter and who, together with her husband, has so far been directing my movements, tells me that she believes that these Virginian ballads have probably been discovered by your students, and at your instigation. I have an idea, though it may be a wrong one, that in the majority of cases it is the text only and not the tune that has been noted. If I am right, it seems to me very important that the investigation, initiated by your students, should be followed up by some one, like myself, who can take down the tunes; for I am sure you will agree with me that the tune is every whit as essential a part of the ballad

[1] The enclosed list of ballads already found by Mr. Sharp in America consists of Child, Nos. 3, 4, 7, 12, 13, 20, 53, 54, 62, 68, 73, 74, 75, 79, 81, 84, 85, 95, 99, 200, 209, 243, 248, 272, 274, 277, 295, 299 — twenty-eight in all.

as the text. So it has occurred to me that it might be more profitable for me to spend my last fortnight in your neighborhood rather than in Kentucky. But I should not wish to do this without your approval or unless I felt assured of your coöperation. It is to ascertain this that I am now writing to you, feeling quite sure that you will be frank with me and tell me just what you would like me to do. Apart altogether from the question of collection, it would be a great pleasure to me to visit Charlottesville, show you the tunes and ballads that I have already taken down and discuss them with you. So that I have a double reason for wishing to spend my last fortnight in Virginia. . . . If you will be kind enough carefully to consider the suggestion made above and give me your frank opinion upon it I shall be deeply grateful to you.

Professor Smith's reply must have extended a hearty welcome, for Mr. Sharp's letter of September 17, 1916, reads:

Your very cordial letter reached me yesterday at Hot Springs, where I have just concluded a week's work — and a very successful one too. I added 70 tunes to my collection, including fine versions of "The Two Sisters", "The Cruel Brother," "The Two Brothers," "Lamkin," and "The Golden Trinity," ballads which I had not previously come across out here in America. Tomorrow I am going to take you at your word and make a start to Charlottesville, breaking the journey at Black Mountain where I shall prospect for a day or two. I will let you know directly I reach Charlottesville.

Mr. Sharp and Miss Karpeles spent about ten days in Charlottesville, with Professor Smith as their official host and "liaison officer." He accompanied them on their visits to local ballad singers, and was much interested to note how the two collaborated in the taking down of songs. The Smith home, one of the pavilions upon the University Lawn, extended its hospitality, and on September 27 Mr. Sharp spoke informally at a smoker of the Colonnade Club, the faculty club of the University of Virginia. The next letter, dated October 3, 1916, is from Chicago, whither Mr. Sharp had gone to do some teaching. "I am sending you," it begins, "the music of the Child ballads I collected during my recent visit to your town. I have not troubled to copy the songs I took down because I know your interest is chiefly in ballads, but chiefly for lack of time." Then, after more personal bits about his teaching and about the war, he concludes, "I am looking forward with eagerness to my next visit to Charlottesville and to the plunder which I shall no doubt then make. We both enjoyed our ten days tremendously, very largely owing to the kindness which we received from you and Mrs. Smith."

Incessant travel is the penalty of the serious ballad collector, and the Briton who collects in America must add the ocean passage to his inland mileage. Back at his home in Hampstead,

London, Mr. Sharp was soon hard at work preparing for the press his garner of songs from the Southern ballad region. That Professor Smith had some part in furthering the publication of *English Folk-Songs from the Southern Appalachians* is shown by Mr. Sharp's letter of January 24, 1917, which also reveals plans for more collecting in America.

I have been intending for some time [runs the letter] to write to you and thank you for answering Mr. Putnam's enquiries in a way which induced him to undertake the publication of the songs I recently collected in the mountains. It was evident that what you and also Dr. Gummere said induced Putnam's to accept my book. I am glad to say that I am sending to New York this week the last of the MSS. Miss Karpeles and I have had to work very hard at it to get it done in these few weeks and it is a great relief to us to have got to the end of our task. I am sure that there are many people in America, besides yourself, who will be glad to have the material which we collected in a convenient form. I hope it will not be long before I begin further investigations, and it is quite possible that I may get to work again in April or May. I am sure there is a great deal to be had in your neighborhood, but then there is Kentucky also, which I must not neglect.

His sailing plans are given, with the remark that he expects to be in New York "once again by about the 20th of next month."

The news of Professor Smith's appointment as Head of the English Department of the U. S. Naval Academy at Annapolis was not altogether good news to his English ballad friend, who writes from Champaign, Illinois, March 22, 1917:

Hearty congratulations on your new appointment which, I presume, offers wider opportunities than the position you are vacating. I am sorry, of course, because my collecting in Virginia will now have to be done without your cooperation. However, you have given me a good start for which I cannot be too thankful. It is kind of you to offer to write to Miss Davis about me and I shall be very glad if you will do so fairly soon, as it is quite probable that I may be going to Virginia in the course of the next three or four weeks. My plans are not yet settled, but in any case I shall be going South to collect more songs some time in April, so it will be as well to make preparation betimes. I leave here at the end of the present week for Pittsburgh, etc.

The Miss Davis to whom he was referred is, of course, Miss Martha M. Davis, of Harrisonburg, whose correspondence has already been examined. Mr. Sharp's disappointment at Professor Smith's leaving the state was mild as compared with that of the Virginia ballad workers. But the archivist agreed to continue his duties from Annapolis, and did so faithfully, returning each year for the annual meeting of the Virginia Folk-Lore Society, of which his report was always the feature.

But Mr. Sharp's later correspondence is far more interesting and significant. It appears that he did not arrive in Virginia until late April, 1918. From somewhere in Virginia, May 8, 1918, he writes to Professor Smith:

I have been collecting for 3 weeks in your state. The first week I got absolutely nothing trying out the upper part of the Shenandoah Valley only to find it hopelessly and irretrievably Dutch. However, in the last fortnight walking around Afton (Nelson Co.) and Buena Vista I have done much better. So far I have got 15 Child ballads as per enclosed lists.[1] The 2 "Earl Brand" tunes and texts are quite good ones, especially the tunes, while one of the "Two Crows" is quite a fine one. I expect all that I have yet found in Virginia you have already collected, although I am not quite sure about "Earl Brand." If you would like me to send you copies I will try and find time to do so. Tomorrow I go to the Tye River and Rockfish valleys for a week, after which I return to Washington for 4 or 5 days as I am giving a lecture there. . . . The other day I had been climbing up a mountain outside Crozet after a singer — who proved a very good one — and was returning when a young man in his shirt sleeves driving a motor car offered us a lift, which needless to say we accepted with alacrity. I told him what we had been doing and he at once commended the work with great enthusiasm and spoke of it with some knowledge, saying that he had graduated at Virginia University and had been in your class and attended your lectures on Ballads! His name was O'Neill and he is the son of a well known orchardist near Crozet. I am sure this will interest you as it did me profoundly — an experience which, alas, I should not be likely to meet with in England!

Mr. Sharp's letter of September 1, 1918, written from North Carolina, is a most valuable summary of the ballad situation in Virginia as seen by a world-famous authority on folk-song.

I have been working in Virginia since I spent that very pleasant day with you in April last [he writes], with the exception of a few weeks in June and July when I had to return to New York to direct my Summer School. I started down the Shenandoah Valley, but did not hit the trail till I struck Afton. Since then I have explored more or less thoroughly the mountain districts in Nelson, Bedford, Franklin and Patrick Counties, and, on the other side of the Ridge, the section around Buena Vista. Altogether, counting those that I noted in Albemarle Co. in 1916, I have taken down something over 400 tunes in Virginia. Experience has shown me that the songs are to be found in large numbers on the south-eastern slopes of the Blue Ridge, but that very few are to be gathered on the other side. I found plenty of old houses and favorable conditions on the north-western slopes, but the residents were for the most part new-comers, not old settlers, the original settlers having apparently trekked further west in search, presumably, of more fertile land, or

[1] The list reads as follows: "Barbara Ellen (4), Brown Girl (2), Two Brothers, Lord Thomas (2), Two Sisters (2), Little Musgrave, Fair Margaret (2), Earl Brand (2), Gipsy Laddie (2), Wife of Usher's Well, Young Hunting, Daemon Lover, Lord Randal (2), The Two Crows (2)." Total, 25 variants of *14* ballads.

maybe attracted by the lure of the coal-mines. This may or may not be the reason, but I think I may say that I have established the fact that from the point of view of the folk-song the south-eastern slopes of the Blue Ridge are far more fertile than the north-western.

I have also found that although the songs are to be gathered with comparative ease in Virginia, they are only to be found in the memories of the older inhabitants. In other words, the conditions in Virginia are similar to those which obtain in England; the tradition is steadily approaching extinction owing to the establishment of schools and the contaminating influence of what is usually called modern progress. In North Carolina every one sings and the folk-song tradition is still vital. In Kentucky the tradition was, I imagine, in full blast up to a few years ago, and still is in some of the most remote districts, but is now being rapidly killed in its prime by industrialism. In Kentucky it is a case of sudden death; in Virginia, of euthanasia. Bearing this in mind, the fact that although the Virginians remember their tunes with great fidelity, their texts are generally speaking very corrupt, becomes intelligible. To a similar reason, too, we must ascribe the fact that the Virginian singers use the 7-note scale more frequently than the 5-note, as in England. That is to say, they have advanced to a later stage of evolution than have the singers in Kentucky and North Carolina.

Again, for some reason, which I am unable to give, I have found ballad-singing in Virginia less prevalent than in the other states, the singers evidently being more attracted by the songs. This may be because they are more interested in the tunes than the words and, of course, in the ballad the text is the dominant factor.

To sum up, I may say that I have found the tunes in Virginia extraordinarily beautiful; I think of greater musical value than those that I have taken down anywhere else in America. On the other hand, the texts that I have recovered in Virginia are not very good, certainly not so valuable as those that I have noted in the other states.

The ballad findings of the Virginia Folk-Lore Society would suggest that Mr. Sharp's conclusions are based on too limited a survey of the state, a very large part of which he left untouched. Professor Smith hints at this in his reply, when he says, "I am not sure but that when you try the counties north of Albemarle you will find not only more ballads but more singers of them." But granting that Mr. Sharp happened upon some unfavorable ballad territory and that the picture of the ballad in Virginia is not so dark as he paints it, yet the files of the Virginia Folk-Lore Society with their large number of fragmentary or garbled texts give ample warrant for the remark that the Virginia texts in general leave something to be desired — and this in spite of a large number of first-class texts. Whatever derogation there may be in this is offset by the tunes — "extraordinarily beautiful; I think of greater musical value than those that I have taken down anywhere else in America."

After this very informing if slightly controversial summary, the letter continues:

I enclose a list of the Child ballads that I have discovered in Virginia with the number of variants, i.e., tunes, that I have taken down in each case. I believe that very nearly all of these have already been discovered by other collectors in Virginia, but I think there are two or three that have not previously been noted, e.g., "The Suffolk Miracle," "The Death of Queen Jane," "Edward," "Earl Brand," and "Geordie."

I left Patrick Co. on Friday last and am now in Winston-Salem, but I leave for Marion, N.C., tomorrow and shall probably spend the next six or eight weeks in this state. Some time or other, however, I mean to return to Virginia and try out the counties north of Albemarle, which I missed when I came down the Shenandoah Valley. . . . Miss Karpeles will be very pleased to send you copies of the texts of those ballads in the list which have not hitherto been found in Virginia, if you would care to have them. If we had time, we would send you copies of all of them.

The accompanying list, Mr. Sharp's final list for Virginia, with the number of tunes, consists of "Lady Isabel and the Elf-Knight" (6), "Earl Brand" (4), "The Two Sisters" (4), "Lord Randal" (7), "Edward" (4), "Sir Lionel" (1), "The Cruel Mother" (3), "The Three Ravens" (3), "The Two Brothers" (3), "Young Beichan" (1), "Young Hunting" (4), "Lord Thomas and Fair Ellinor" (17), "Fair Margaret and Sweet William" (10), "Lord Lovel" (3), "The Wife of Usher's Well" (4), "Barbara Allen" (3),[1] "The Maid Freed from the Gallows" (7), "Sir Hugh" (1), "The Gypsy Laddie" (4), "Geordie" (2), "The Daemon Lover" (9), "The Suffolk Miracle" (3), "The Wife Wrapt in Wether's Skin" (1), "The Farmer's Curst Wife" (1), "The Golden Vanity" (1), "The Brown Girl" (3), "Jack of the Hazelgreen" (2), "The Mermaid" (1), and "The Death of Queen Jane" (1) — a total of 113 tunes to 29 ballads. All of these ballads except "The Death of Queen Jane," "Geordie," and "The Suffolk Miracle" were represented in the Virginia files, and Mr. Sharp soon sent these three. Mr. Sharp and Miss Karpeles are represented in this volume by many variants of twenty-three different ballads — their entire contribution to the Virginia archives.

The final letter, written from the Grove Park Inn, Asheville, N.C., October 14, 1918 (note the date), is full of the war news but fuller still of ballad talk. "We have just left the mountains and are now resting here for a week to recuperate. We leave for New York on Saturday next," runs the more personal part of

[1] "This is widely known, but I only took down a few versions."— C. J. S.

the letter. "We had a very good time in N.C. and I got a lot of very interesting stuff, chiefly in Yancey Co., where I made Burnsville my centre."

There follows a sort of valedictory to his American collecting, with a valuable summary of his material.

> And now [he says] I suppose I have finished all the work I shall ever do in the Appalachians, for before next season comes around I shall pretty certainly have left for England. Work of this sort is never, of course, really finished — there are always other variants to be found — but I feel that I have recorded the bulk of the songs and ballads that are now being sung in these mountain districts. Altogether I have spent 52 weeks actually searching for songs and have noted 1620 tunes: 17 weeks in Kentucky (525 tunes); 15 weeks in N. C. (565 tunes); 15 weeks in Virginia (415 tunes); and 4 weeks in Tennessee (115 tunes); one abortive week in West Virginia.
>
> I am itching to publish more of the results of my work, but until the war is over I must possess my soul in patience. Putnam's are very ready to continue the series, but of course they cannot undertake an expensive publication of this sort just at present. There are many other places in America besides the Appalachians which I should like to investigate and which assuredly should be searched, but I do not see how I shall be able to spare the time even if I had the money and the strength! However, one never knows what the future may hold in store.

That neither of the two correspondents should live to see the publication of the Virginia ballad volume, in which both were so deeply interested, is but part of the tragedy of the taking off of two such men.

The narrative of Miss Alfreda M. Peel is full of local color. It is a series of four sketches of the ballad trail, each representing a season of the year. The first is spring.

> One day early in the spring of 1911 [she writes], I was riding over a mountain road in southwest Virginia. I did not know then about the ballad quest nor had I ever heard a ballad sung. It was May Day, and the little spring winds were shaking down the Judas bloom and rippling the snowy dogwood below us in many a deep ravine. Where the forest ends and the orchards begin stood a little log cabin and in the doorway a woman was sitting:
>
> "'T wuz in thuh lovely month of May
> When all the buds wuz swellin',
> Sweet William on his death bed lay
> Fer the love o' Barbara Allen."
>
> She sang loudly and in a melancholy minor. When she saw the wagon she stopped suddenly and looked with the silent interest that lonely people have for a chance passer-by.
>
> "She's a powerful singer," said our driver solemnly.
>
> "What is it she's singing? I never heard a song like that before."

"Hit's song ballets, awful lonesome tunes. She learned 'em from her mammy who was right smart of a hand to sing 'em too. They allus make me feel kinder lonesome an' sad. I'd a heap rather hear a dance tune," said the wagoner.

Two days later, sitting in the doorway of that cabin, I heard her sing two ancient ballads in her melancholy nasal minor. She seemed to be quite glad to let me write them down. And thus began my ballad quest.

Miss Peel's method of collecting was more adventurous, less sedentary, than that employed in Rockingham and Campbell Counties.

The best method I have found to hunt ballads [she says] is to board at a farm house in some lonely mountainous county and on horseback and on foot visit every person within the neighborhood who "makes music" on any instrument or sings songs of any description. By carefully explaining your mission, and with much tact, you will soon receive much kindness and coöperation.

A good illustration of this tact and its results is the summer adventure of Miss Peel and her friend, Miss Caroline Melbard, of Salem, Virginia. The narrative is vivid, and well charged with almost photographic description:

"Hit's eight miles to the lumber camp, an' you better be mighty keerful o' rattlesnakes," said the saw-mill hand, looking in astonishment at the strange town women who, mounted on two rough farm horses, had lost their way on the wilderness road. . . . And eight miles back. Heavens! And on these horses!

The day was hot — midsummer. It was a blessing that the road wound through dense woods where rhododendron and laurel overhung the path and the spruce pine grew darkly over the rocky brown streams. Where the trees parted a little we could see the green mountain spurs over which hung thunder heads, seeming motionless in the heat, and from which issued a low growl of warning.

Again we plunged into a rocky stream, and our horses struggled up a steep road scraped by logging teams to the little shanties that clung to the edge of a rocky gorge. An old woman with a pet owl on her shoulder stood in the doorway of one of the shanties. She was the saw-mill cook whom we knew for a "singing woman."

"May we wait here till the storm is over?" we asked, as the thunder rolled over our heads ominously.

"Come right in. Me an' Bill'll git yer saddles off."

Inside the shanty were long oil-cloth covered tables piled with soiled dishes. We told her of our quest and asked her to sing for us.

"I declare, I ain't got no time, fer I got to git my dishes washed."

My friend volunteered to wash them, so after many excuses the old woman finally consented.

"We better set in the porch. I killed a right big rattler in the room yestiddy. It was lyin' in the bunk, so it makes me kinder nervous to set in thar."

So, accompanied by the owl which made strange noises, we sat in the porch while the rain dripped from the eaves and the storm rolled away among the mountains. Ballad after ballad she sang in her cracked and quavering voice, but still they were all familiar.

"Do you know one about the devil?" I asked hopefully.

"I kin sing one about 'The Devil an' the Nine Questions':

"'Ef you don't answer me questions nine,
  Sing ninety-nine and ninety,
I'll take you off to hell alive,
  And you're the weaver's bonny.'"

This was the ancient ballad of "Riddles Wisely Expounded," recorded here for the first time in the New World in this remote corner of the Southern Appalachians.

Autumn, too, has its appropriate vignette.

A muddy road in late November stretching away from the three-room school at the cross-roads is also a ballad trail. It leads to a little house beside the creek where Mabel, the pupil who has asked me home to supper, lives. It is a great occasion for us both.

"Git a lamp and play fer yer teacher, Mabel," says the mother, after the usual formalities. "Mabel is a powerful hand ter sing 'song ballets' when she takes a notion."

An organ decorated with Christmas tree trimmings stands in the corner. Mabel opens a box full of folded scraps of paper on which songs are scribbled. The organ begins to wheeze and groan, and Mabel sings:

"Ge-e-orge Collins rode out one cold winter ní-ight,
Ge-e-orgie Col-lins rode home so fi-ine . . . "

"Please let me see your song collection," I ask eagerly.

"You can't read none of 'em, they're wrote so bad."

They certainly are a badly spelt, poorly written jumble, and among a mixture of hymns and sentimental songs I find two ballad treasures, "The Seven King's Daughters," and "George Collins."

Many times since have I examined similar collections of songs such as these, and hardly ever have I failed to find either a fragment or a full ballad among them.

Winter rounds out the ballad hunter's calendar.

Blep-blep goes the woodchopper's axe. He has walked a long way from his cabin in the hollow along a road swept by an icy wind. The sky is gray and the hoary mountains look bleak and sharply ridged. Inside the kitchen of the farm-house it is warm and cosy.

"Get the poor old fellow to come in and warm. He must be nearly frozen out there," says the farmer's wife kindly.

He comes tottering across the yard and into the kitchen. He is a very old man, tall and thin, with a ruddy face and sparse chin-whiskers. No one gives him credit for knowing much. He warms his knotted hands before the fire and wipes his rheumy eyes on a bandanna handkerchief. Somehow you wonder if in his dim memory there may not be some ancient fragment of song.

"Wall," he says, after your careful questioning, "I heered one one time from my grandmammy." He brightened visibly. "Hit certainly wuz a fine ballet. Hit showed what punishment comes ter sinful people. Wicked folks got what was coming to them in them days." He shook his head mournfully over the present day ideas of justice.

"Won't you try and sing it?"

"I ain't got no voice and I can't think of none of it now. Looks like sence I had that spell last winter I'm so fergitful."

At last, after much persuasion, and with great embarrassment, he began to repeat a ballad of the shameful love of "Lady Barnard and Little Musgrave" and the swift retribution which followed in its wake. Many of the lines were imperfect and its phrases changed to common diction but the substance was unchanged, and the version, an excellent one, was thus rescued from oblivion.

In spite of these illustrations, Miss Peel makes it clear that the ballad singers are not confined to any one class.

All sorts of people have sung me ballads [she writes]. An old lady whose home was once one of the famous houses on the James River sang me the fragment of a ballad her grandmother had sung to her. Another whose ancestors fought with the Stuarts repeated the three verses of "Mary Hamilton," which I believe are all that have been found in this country. A grave-digger, a bootlegger, a night watchman, a scrubwoman in an insane asylum, and an old woman whose chief duty seemed to be "to set up with the dead" have all contributed their quota of song.

No wonder, with such varied and fascinating experiences, that Miss Peel was able to write vividly of them!

With America's entry into the Great War, the Society's activities suffered a decided slump, naturally enough; but after the armistice the work began anew. Even the Great War caused only one lapse in the publication of the annual bulletin in which the Society was accustomed to report its finds and its doings. The report for 1918 and 1919 was issued as one bulletin.

The interruption of the War past, Professor Smith was especially anxious to determine how widely distributed the ballad might be in the state. That certain mountain counties were the richest field for the collector, had been well established, but Professor Smith had an earnest conviction that the silent counties were not really ballad vacua, and he wished to test this conviction and to enrich the Virginia ballad collection from regions hitherto untapped. Accordingly, an arrangement was made whereby Mr. John Stone, one of the most successful and reliable workers of the Society, should make a series of tours in quest of ballads into the counties from which hitherto no ballads had come. The expense money for these trips was provided by a timely and generous appropriation from the Colonial Dames of America in the State of Virginia, whom Professor Smith had interested in the ballad as Colonial literature and Colonial folklore.

Mr. Stone gives an account of his ballad jaunts in his own inimitable style. His introduction to ballad hunting was due to Professor Smith, as the beginning of his narrative shows:

> Sitting in the gallery of Cabell Hall on a summer morning some ten years ago [written in 1924] during the session of the University of Virginia Summer School, I heard Dr. C. Alphonso Smith talk on ballads and the work of the Virginia Folk-Lore Society in collecting and saving those English and Scottish ballads still surviving in Virginia by oral tradition. Right then I decided that I had found some use for my fondness for singing old songs. I became a ballad hunter.

And a very successful hunter he was for years before he was called upon to undertake a special task for the Society.

Mr. Stone's first long trip was in the summer of 1921, to the south and east of Richmond. On the eve of his departure, a letter of instruction from Professor Smith ended with a note of solemnity:

> This is a big work, Stone, and my best wishes and sincerest benedictions will be with you in it during every day and night of your quest. It's an experiment made possible by the patriotism and generosity of the Colonial Dames of Virginia but an experiment which I am confident your devotion and enthusiasm will vindicate.

Undertaken in this spirit, the quest brought in a rich harvest of ballads from all the non-reporting counties of the state, so that Virginia achieved the record of "a ballad from every one of its one hundred counties." Mr. Stone gives the attendant circumstances:

> The report of the archivist at the meeting in 1920 showed that sixty counties were on the reported list, but that from the other forty counties no report of any kind had come, although many of them were in promising territory. The Colonial Dames of Virginia came to the rescue by giving us $500.00 with which to carry the search into the non-reporting counties. The missing ones were scattered from the mountains to the Atlantic and from the Potomac to Carolina, so that to make the money last there was need of the maximum of energy together with the minimum of expense. My interest in the work having led me rather far afield at times, I was sent out to round up the forty counties. During the summer of 1921 I was out twice — a month each time — and again for a month in the summer of 1922. I went not only into the forty counties but also into a number of others, and brought back about 175 ballads, including fragments and duplicate versions.
>
> My adventures were many and varied. At one time or another, I was mistaken for a revenue officer, an aviator, a globe trotter, and an eminent novelist.

More than once night found me far from shelter, so that my bed was in some convenient field, fence corner, or deserted road. To strangers who wanted to know what pay I received, I replied that I got something to eat and a place to sleep, provided I did n't sleep too often or eat too much. During the whole time I met only two people who were not interested in what I was doing. One thought I was a revenue officer in disguise, and met me at the gate with the salutation, "Go on away. I don't want nothing you got." When I said that I was not trying to sell anything but that I was looking for old songs, the answer was prompt — "I don't know any old songs and I would n't sing 'em for you if I did. I don't encourage tramps. You ought to be at work." The other did n't believe in such frivolous pastimes. One of the pleasant features of the hunt was the meeting with all kinds and conditions of people. One day I would be talking to people of culture and refinement and a day or two later I would be up in the hills among those some of whom were little better than outlaws — all of them interested and doing what they could to help.

At the end of his first trip, into southeastern Virginia, Mr. Stone listed four things that impressed him: (1) the number of people who had never heard of ballads; (2) the number of people who, having once sung ballads, had forgotten them and could recall only fragments; (3) the number of people who are interested in the subject but who do not know how to find ballads or do not hunt for them; and (4) the realization that what is going to be done ought to be done quickly.

Mr. Stone's second trip led him into the far southwest corner of the state —"that land of blue grass, parallel mountain ranges, and beautiful narrow valleys. It is a land of ballads. I stayed nearly thirty days and brought back ninety-four ballads, including duplicate versions and fragments. . . . The people whom I met belonged to all classes from the best to the worst."

No ballad hunter could fail to be impressed with the scenic beauties of this region. "While we were going from Chilhowie to Konnarock the driver stopped the car at the top of the Iron Mountains in order that I might get a view of the Holston Valley from that point. My vocabulary is inadequate to do justice to that view." But this ballad hunter was no mere aesthete, and very soon he settled to his task.

Having passed over the top of the mountain, we dropped down into a region different in every way, not only in topography but also in people and pursuits. Hoping to find an old man who I had been told could sing songs, I started up the side of White Top, the highest mountain in Virginia. I found the man [Mr. George Hart], and sitting there on the mountain-side on a green bank under a large tree, I wrote from his singing and dictation seventeen ballads ranging in length from twenty-eight stanzas to a fragment of one stanza. For nearly six hours I did not get off the ground. The old man's dinner bucket was at his elbow, but he did not lift the lid. He told me he had gotten up from the

GLIMPSES ALONG THE BALLAD TRAILS
IN VIRGINIA

supper table to sing and had stopped singing to wash his face for breakfast. The next day a gentleman told me the statement was true because he was there at the time. The singer could neither read nor write. Four times on my trip into that part of Virginia, people told me that when they were young they had sung all night.

Alternate thrills and disappointments were the lot of the ballad hunter:

Sometimes I found ballads when I had no previous knowledge of the singer, and at other times I made long trips on foot to see some special singer and found nothing. On one occasion I walked ten miles up into the hills on a hot September day to see an old man who I thought would be a wonder. I was weak and sick from the effects of a severe cold, so that only high hopes of a big ballad find could have induced me to make the trip. When I finally found the old man about sundown, he added nothing whatever to my list. . . . At another time when I was wandering rather aimlessly about a small town where I happened to be for the day, I found an excellent version of a ballad that I was especially anxious to add to my list ["Fair Annie"]. It was after supper when I called. The lady who sang the song [Mrs. Martha Elizabeth Lethcoe] said that she had forgotten it. I asked her to try and recall the words. We sat facing each other in a chair swing. Slowly, with the far-away look of the ballad singer and with long intervals of thought between, she either sang or recited stanza after stanza. The sun went down and the darkness came on; a neighbor with his milk bucket came and stood by the swing; but the song went on. Finally, when it was so dark that I could not see a line of what I was writing, she finished the last stanza — twelve in all. If I had followed my schedule and had gone back to Glade Springs that afternoon, I should have missed that ballad.

One of the pleasant incidents of the trip was a call upon the old lady who had sung for Mr. Cecil J. Sharp when he was hunting ballads in Virginia. Mr. Stone writes:

I had stopped at a small way station, only to find that my trail led exactly nowhere. Having heard that the old lady lived not far away, I decided to call on her. She lived in a log house in a small cove not far away. Seeing no one as I approached, I went around to the back of the house. An old lady in the sixties, her large pleasant face topped by gray hair, upon which perched a small straw hat, was sitting on a small porch at the kitchen door. She was peeling potatoes and singing "The Old Time Religion is Good Enough for Me." "Don't stop," I said, "That's just why I have come — to hear you sing." She sang several songs for me and showed much interest in what I was doing. . . . We both agreed that the simple life was the one to live, even though there might be snakes and such other little inconveniences to contend with. That call upon one who seemed to embody so many of the finer traits of the ballad singer was a fitting close to the active work of the trip.

Mr. Stone's last trip was more trying. In the summer of 1922, thirteen counties still remained to be heard from, one group of counties along the York River, another at the northern extremity of the Shenandoah Valley. So Mr. Stone set out on another thirty-day trip — a trip that was "a succession of bus rides, rides on mail cars, long hikes, nights in the open, more bus rides, more hikes, more nights in the open, till finally every one of the one hundred counties of Virginia was on the reporting list, and the job was done."

Still, ballads turned up with refreshing unexpectedness, to relieve the tedium of travel:

> I stumbled over ballads till it was almost uncanny. I passed a little country store three times without stopping. Having stopped at the same store to make a small purchase as I was leaving the community, I asked about ballads and as a result found five. Another day I declined a cordial invitation to spend the night and pushed on into strange territory. Shortly before sundown, a gentleman gave me a lift in his car. He had to go some distance from the road to see a friend. While he talked business on one side of the car, I sat on the running board on the other side and wrote an excellent version, the only ballad I found in that county. If I had accepted the invitation or had missed the ride, I should not have found that ballad. On a former trip I was lost and walked for an hour in a circle. Later I decided to go on instead of stopping for supper at a hotel. Nearly five miles farther on a storm overtook me in front of a gentleman's home where there had been a birthday party that day. I stopped, and instead of having an all-night supperless hike, I feasted right royally, had a delightful visit among congenial people, rode around the next day with the gentleman's son and as a result carried home nine ballads and fragments instead of one. If I had not walked in a circle, or if I had stopped for supper, or if there had been no storm, I should have missed those ballads.

Whether or not Mr. Stone owes much to chance, it is clear that the Virginia ballad collection owes much to the tall pedestrian who with stout stick, stout legs, and stouter heart — not to mention his little satchel and old rag hat — carried the ballad hunt into places hitherto silent or inaccessible. From a calm study window, now that the dust of those breathless ballad-hiking days has cleared away, one is inclined to regret the emphasis that was put upon the "ballad from every county" objective at this point. A careful reading of the reports of these trips, telling of their breakneck pace from county to county, and a careful examination of the material that resulted from these trips, so much of it one- and two-stanza fragments, show conclusively enough that the county record was achieved at the sacrifice of a more substantial harvest of ballad material. Some may think the record, with its data about the distribution of ballads in the state, worth the sacrifice. But in the long view this appears doubtful. For surely the finding of good ballad texts and tunes is more important than any local record or county representation in the ballad totals. At any rate, there is nothing in this suggestion to detract from the glory of Mr. Stone's almost heroic work. His trips would have been abundantly worth while if one Mr. George Hart, of Konnarock, Va., had been their only discovery. With their full gleaning of texts, tunes, and record, this series of trips remains perhaps the most impressive incident of the Virginia ballad quest.

Mr. Stone's successful tours were capped in 1924 by Mr. B. C. Moomaw's finding of the fiftieth ballad in Virginia, an excellent version of "Dives and Lazarus" (Child, No. 56). This was in reality the fifty-first ballad, since the fiftieth had lain dormant and unreported in the files of the archivist for some time, to be rediscovered by the present editor in 1927.[1] At any rate, with this so-called fiftieth ballad the Society attained the objective it had arbitrarily set for itself as the mark to be reached before it should undertake to publish its material, and with this its ballad labors reached their climax.

As the later years of the Virginia Folk-Lore Society dragged on, adding but little to the weight of its ballad treasure, it became increasingly apparent that Professor Smith was not to undertake the editing of the Virginia collection. His absence from Virginia, and his feeling that the editor should be identified with the University of Virginia, under whose aegis he had launched the movement and made it a state-wide popular movement; perhaps the sheer labor and infinite detail of the task for a man of his years and breadth of interest; his ill health; these and doubtless other factors told against his undertaking the burden of publication. As early as November 8, 1917, he had written to Mr. Stone, then President of the Virginia Folk-Lore Society, "The time has come when we must think about putting our ballad finds into book form. With my new work and being absent from Virginia I see now that it will be impossible for me to do this work myself." And he discusses the plan of inviting a certain professor at the University of Virginia (not the present editor, who was then in academic swaddling-clothes) to undertake the task. Mr. Stone's reply is one of violent disapproval. "I don't like your plan," he says laconically, and after some argument and not a little talk of "associations," he concludes:

> If you have n't time now to put on the finishing touches,[2] why not wait until you have? If we have waited this long to go to press we can wait longer,

[1] For an explanation of this, see the head-note to "The Death of Queen Jane" (Child, No. 170), No. 35 of this volume.

[2] The editor may be pardoned for finding this expression a trifle naïve.

if we get a better product by doing so. I may be an oddity; but these old songs are my personal friends, and I'd hate for such valued acquaintances to be introduced to strangers by one who maybe does n't appreciate their full worth.

On the back of this letter Professor Smith has endorsed, "Wrote Nov. 16 saying plan will not be presented — we'll go on as before."

Six years later, with the collection more than doubled in size, the question of an editor could no longer be postponed. Professor Smith's failing health, moreover, made imperative the finding of his successor. The Society itself could supply no one both qualified and ready to carry on the work. Again Professor Smith looked to the University of Virginia and consulted with Dean J. C. Metcalf, Chairman of the Schools of English Language and Literature, who ten years before had acted as chairman of the first meeting of the Virginia Folk-Lore Society and had kept up his interest in the ballad work. As a result, the nomination fell to the present editor, and was accepted. At the ensuing meeting of the Virginia Folk-Lore Society, December 1, 1923, the appointment was announced and confirmed, and the new editor was elected archivist. After a brief introduction of the editor, Professor Smith declared, "I shall turn over all of our ballads to him and he will select, reject, and edit as he thinks best." Early in 1924 the transfer was made by express — a large wooden box full of letter files crammed with twelve years' accumulations of ballads and correspondence.

Whatever qualms the new editor may have felt were allayed by reassuring letters from the late archivist.

You are to have full responsibility and full independence in your editorial work [wrote Professor Smith, December 18, 1923]. It is to be your work and I want you to feel that the full credit of it will be yours. I shall give any advice I can and will serve you in every way possible. I shall appreciate of course your mentioning the fact that I founded the Virginia Folk-Lore Society on my own initiative and have given it the very best efforts of my life during the last ten years. There have been many times when pressure was brought to bear to side-track my main aim and to make the Society merely an agency for the loose record of all sorts of popular stuff. But I have kept our prow pointed steadily to the collection of these old world songs in which I knew Virginia was rich and in which she now occupies a position far ahead of any other state in the Union.[1]

---

[1] This personal letter obviously not intended for publication has been presented not only for its historical importance, but because the editor considers it an essentially modest statement from an essentially modest man.

The letter also explains why the Virginia collection was limited to the older ballad survivals. In 1923, Professor Smith was of the opinion that the Virginia Folk-Lore Society, having accomplished its purpose in the collecting of these ballads, should terminate its existence. But at its annual meeting, the Society decided to maintain its organization and to enlarge the scope of its activities by collecting not only ballads but also other old songs and miscellaneous folk-lore, such as witch tales, ghost stories, superstitions, legends, proverbs, charms, tokens, the origins of place names, folk games, and quaint customs of all sorts. But this new phase of the Society's activity has been held largely in abeyance pending the appearance of the ballad volume.

Then came swift catastrophe to Virginia balladry in the death on June 13, 1924, of its able leader and influential friend, C. Alphonso Smith, long recognized as the leading ballad scholar of the South. The annual meeting of the Virginia Folk-Lore Society in November, 1924, was largely one of commemoration. Speaking on this occasion, Dean J. C. Metcalf, of the University of Virginia, appraised Professor Smith's contribution to folk-lore in the following terms:

> With Child and Kittredge and Gummere should be coupled the name of Alphonso Smith as an authority on balladry. He stimulated investigation in native regions which their researches had barely touched. They were looking backward in their assembling and appraisal, while Smith was looking about him and hearkening to the living voices in Southern hill and valley and quiet countryside, the voices of our contemporary ancestors in old Virginia. He of course depended upon the sure foundation laid by these New England scholars, but he showed the instinct and the practice of the true explorer, the original investigator, sensing the game and directing the chase. I think it is safe to say that wherever in the Southern states, whether in the highlands or the lowlands, the hunt for ballads and their preservation may now be in progress, his influence is felt as a stimulating incentive to what is essentially a patriotic as well as a poetic task. And even beyond the bounds of his own South, the movement for preserving folk-poetry, so ably and effectively led by him, owes much to Alphonso Smith's intelligent initiative and energy. . . . As for . . . the lingering ballad, it will be associated with his name as its finest interpreter to this generation when the history of Southern folk-lore shall be adequately recorded.

The death of Professor Smith was more than a personal sorrow to his friends and fellow workers in Virginia balladry, for he was equipped as no one else could be to advise and assist in the editing and publication of the material that he had gathered with the assistance of the Virginia Folk-Lore Society. Lacking his help, the editor has had a heavy responsibility and a solitary and difficult, though not uninteresting, task.

The story of the Virginia ballad movement from the end of 1924 to the present time is told in the preparation of this volume. Another volume or more to be devoted to later folk-songs and to other types of folk-lore from Virginia may appear in the course of time.

I. BALLADS

BALLADS

I

RIDDLES WISELY EXPOUNDED

(CHILD, No. 1)

ONLY one variant of this rare ballad has been recovered in Virginia, but both text and tune are excellent. Except in the similarity of the questions and answers, the Virginia text is not specially close to any one of the Child versions. As a colloquy between the devil and the maiden, it is certainly closer to Child C and D than to A and B; and as it lacks the first seven stanzas about the widow and the daughters found in C, perhaps it is closest to D. Still, it is like Child A and B in that the questions are asked and answered two at a time, not all together. Nor will it escape the reader that the devil's "nine" questions are really eight.

American texts of this ballad are almost unknown. See *Bulletin*, No. 10, p. 5; *Jones*, p. 300 (fragment); *Journal*, XII, 129 (Cooke, fragment, Louisiana). For Miss Peel's picturesque account of her finding of this ballad, see Introduction, pp. 46–47.

The ballad seems to be known locally as "The Devil's Nine Questions," "The Nine Questions," or "The Devil and the Nine Questions." The Virginia text is the only complete, or nearly complete, version recovered in America.

"The Devil's Nine Questions." Sent in by Miss Alfreda M. Peel. Sung by Mrs. Rill Martin. Giles County. September 11, 1922. With music.

1 "If you don't answer me questions nine,
Sing ninety-nine and ninety,
I'll take you off to hell alive,
And you are the weaver's bonny.[1]

2 "What is whiter than milk?
Sing ninety-nine and ninety;
What is softer than silk?
Say you're the weaver's bonny."

3 "Snow is whiter than milk,
Sing ninety-nine and ninety;
Down is softer than silk,
And I'm the weaver's bonny."

4 "What is louder than a horn?
Sing ninety-nine and ninety;
What is sharper than a thorn?
Sing I am the weaver's bonny."

[1] Variant line: "An -a you the weaver's bonny." See music.

5 "Thunder's louder than a horn,
Sing ninety-nine and ninety;
Death is sharper than a thorn,
Sing I'm the weaver's bonny."

6 "What is higher than a tree?
Sing ninety-nine and ninety;
What is deeper than the sea?
Sing I'm the weaver's bonny."

7 "Heaven's higher than a tree,
Sing ninety-nine and ninety;
And hell is deeper than the sea,
Sing I'm the weaver's bonny."

8 "What is innocenter than a lamb?
Sing ninety-nine and ninety;
What is worse than woman kind?
Say I'm the weaver's bonny."

9 "A babe is innocenter than a lamb,
Sing ninety-nine and ninety;
She devil's worse than woman kind,
Sing I'm the weaver's bonny."

10 "You have answered me questions nine,
Sing ninety-nine and ninety;
You are God's, you're not my own,
And you're the weaver's bonny."

2

THE FAUSE KNIGHT UPON THE ROAD

(CHILD, No. 3)

THE idea underlying this ballad, as Child has pointed out, is that the devil can carry off the youngster if he can nonplus him. In the Virginia version, as elsewhere, the boy more than holds his own in the repartee, and presumably goes on to school unmolested, though we have not the positive assurance to that effect given in Pound, *Ballads*, No. 20: "And he pitched him in the well and went on to school."

Only one variant of this ballad has been found in Virginia. It bears close resemblance to Child A, B, and C, though the third stanza does not appear in any one of them. American texts are scarce. See Barry, No. 26; *Bulletin*, No. 7, p. 4; Campbell and Sharp, No. 1 (two versions, Tennessee, North Carolina; cf. Sharp, *Songs*, I, No. 4); *Journal*, XXIV, 344 (Barry, Maine, fragment); and XXX, 286 (Kittredge, Virginia); Pound, *Ballads*, No. 20 (Missouri, from Virginia). It might be noted that of these American texts three emanate from Virginia either immediately or ultimately. For additional references, see *Journal*, XXX, 286.

"The False Knight on the Road." Collected by Miss Martha M. Davis. Sung by Mrs. Sarah Finchum,[1] of Elkton, Va. Rockingham County. November 23, 1918. With music.

1 "Where are you going?" said the false, false knight,
Said the false so rude.[2]
"I am going to school," said the child;
And still it stood.

2 "What have you got there?" said the false, false knight,
Said the false so rude.
"I have good books in my hand," said the child;
And still it stood.

3 "Are you a child of God?" said the false, false knight,
Said the false so rude.
"I say my prayers at night," said the child;
And still it stood.

4 "I wish you were in the well," said the false, false knight,
Said the false so rude.
"And you as deep in hell," said the child;
And still it stood.

[1] "The mountain woman who has contributed so many ballads" (Miss Davis).
[2] Variant: "false *or* rude." Cf. Child B: "And false, false was his *rede*."

3

LADY ISABEL AND THE ELF-KNIGHT

(Child, No. 4)

This ballad is one of the few most frequently found in Virginia, where it is variously known as "Pretty Polly," "The Seven King's Daughters," "The King's Daughter," "The Pretty Gold Leaf," "The Salt Water Sea," "Miss Mary's Parrot," and under several other titles. Its polyonymity is almost equal to its ubiquity — twenty-eight variants under sixteen different titles. In Virginia it does not, however, when compared with "Barbara Allen," "The House Carpenter," and several others, quite live up to its general reputation of having obtained the widest circulation of all ballads.

Child's remarkable introduction to this ballad discusses at some length its extraordinary currency in the southern as well as the northern nations of Europe. Space is also given to a consideration of the hypothesis that the ballad is a wild shoot from the story of Judith and Holofernes, with Holofernes the original of the Elf-Knight. Child concludes: "It is a supposition attended with less difficulty that an independent European tradition existed of a half-human, half-demonic being, who possessed an irresistible power of decoying away young maids, and was wont to kill them after he got them into his hands, but who at last found one who was more than his match, and lost his own life through her craft and courage. A modification of this story is afforded by the large class of Bluebeard tales."

All the Virginia texts correspond much more closely with the Child series C–G (and Sargent and Kittredge H) than to A and B.

Warning might perhaps be given of the confusion of Pollies in most of the Virginia texts. The girl and the parrot have the same name and are not always immediately distinguishable.

For American findings of this ballad see Barry, No. 4; Belden, No. 1 (fragment); Brown, p. 9 (North Carolina); *Bulletin*, Nos. 2–4, 6–12; Campbell and Sharp, No. 2 (Massachusetts, North Carolina, Kentucky, Georgia); Child, III, 496 (Virginia, from *The Folk-Lore Journal*, VII, 28); Cox, No. 1 and p. 521 (fragment and melody); Hudson, No. 1 (Mississippi); Jones, p. 301 (fragment); *Journal*, XVIII, 132 (Barry, Massachusetts, text and melody); XIX, 232 (Belden, Missouri); XXII, 65 (Beatty, Wisconsin), 76 (Barry, New Jersey, melody only), 374 (Barry, Massachusetts, text and melody, Missouri), 344 (Barry, Massachusetts); XXVII, 90 (Gardner, Michigan); XXVIII, 148 (Perrow, North Carolina); XXXV, 338 (Tolman and Eddy, Ohio); Mackenzie, *Ballads*, No. 1, and p. 391 (melody); Sandburg, p. 60 (R. W. Gordon Collection); Scarborough, p. 43 (Texas, text and melody); Shearin, p. 3; Shearin and Combs, p. 7; Reed Smith, No. 1; Reed Smith, *Ballads*, No. 1; Wyman and Brockway, p. 82. For additional references, see Cox, p. 3; *Journal*, XXIX, 156; XXX, 286; XXXV, 338.

A

"The King's Daughter; or Pretty Polly." Collected by Miss Martha M. Davis. Sung by Mrs. Adam Gowl. Rockingham County, July 31, 1913.

1 He followed her up, he followed her down,
He followed her into the room,
She had n't the heart one word to say,
Nor the tongue to tell him nay, nay, nay,
Nor the tongue to tell him nay.

2 "Go gather up your father's gold,
Likewise your mother's fee,
And two of your father's best horses,
Wherein there stood thirty and three, three, three,
Wherein there stood thirty and three."

3 He mounted upon his bonny black,
And she on the bible [1] bay,
And they rode along the broad water side,
One lonesome long summer day, day, day,
One lonesome long summer day.

4 "Get you down, get you down, my pretty Polly,
And chat here awhile with me,
For six king's daughters I've drowned here,
And the seventh you shall be, be, be,
And the seventh you shall be.

5 "Pull off, pull off that costly robe,
And lay it on yon lea,[2]
For it is far too costly a robe,
To rot in the salt water sea, sea, sea,
To rot in the salt water sea."

6 "Turn your body around about,
Your face unto the sea,
For I think you are a false-hearted wretch,
A naked woman to see, see, see,
A naked woman to see."

7 He turned his body around about,
His face toward the sea.
She picked him up in her arms so strong,
And tossed him into the sea, sea, sea,
And tossed him into the sea.

[1] Probably for *piebald*. Cox suggests *dapple*.

[2] Variant: *on yonder sand*.

8 "Some help! some help! my pretty Polly,
Some help! some help!" cried he,
"And if I ever recover again
I surely will marry thee, thee, thee,
I surely will marry thee."

9 "Lie there, lie there, you hard-hearted wretch,
Lie there instead of me,
For six king's daughters you've drowned there,
And the seventh you shall be, be, be,[1]
And the seventh you shall be."

10 She mounted upon the bonny black,
And led the bible bay,
And when she arrived at her father's house,
It was just two hours till day, day, day,
It was just two hours till day.

11 She placed the money in the drawer,
The horses where they stood,
And when she got to her own bed room,
It was just one hour till day, day, day,
It was just one hour till day.

12 Up spake her kind and good little parrot,
In its cage where it did stay,
"Where have you been, my pretty Polly,
This lonesome, long summer day, day, day,
This lonesome, long summer day?"

13 "Hush up, hush up, my pretty Polly,[2]
And tell no tales on me,
Your cage shall be made of a pure piece of gold,
And the door of ivory, -ry, -ry,
And the door of ivory."

14 Then up spake the kind and good old man,
From the bed wherein he lay,
"What makes you speak, my pretty Polly,[2]
So long before, 'tis day, day, day,
So long before 'tis day?"

15 "There were two cats at my cage door,
Offering violence unto me,
And I have called to pretty Polly,
To drive those cats away, -way, -way,
To drive those cats away."

[1] Variant line: "And the seventh *drowned* you shall be, be, be."
[2] "Polly" here refers to the parrot.

B

"Pretty Polly." Sent in by Miss D. Roxie Martin and Mr. J. M. McManaway, of Charlottesville. Sung by Hill Jackson (Colored),[1] of Brown's Cove, Va. Albemarle County. June 1, 1917. With music (sent by Mr. John Stone, November 3, 1920).

1 "He followed me up, he followed me down,
He followed me all the way;
I had not the heart to say one word,
Nor heart to say him nay, nay, nay,
Nor heart to say him nay."

2 "You get all of your father's gold,
Likewise your mother's fee,
And two of your father's best horses
Which are of thirty and three,
And come along with me."

3 She jumped upon the bonny, bonny, brown,
And he the piebald bay,
And rode along by the broad water side
That lonely lazy summer day, day, day,
That long summer day.

4 "Set you down, set you down, Pretty Polly,
And chat a while with me;
For here I've drownded six king's daughters,
And you were the seventh to be, to be,
And you were the seventh to be."

5 "No, Jimmy, my pretty Jimmy,
That's not what you promised me;
You promised to take me to the marriage land,
And there to marry me, me, me,
And there to marry me."

6 "Pull off, pull off those costly robes,
And hang them on yonder tree;
They are too costly and fine
To swim in the salt water sea, sea, sea,
To swim in the salt water sea."

7 "Turn your face about
Into the leaves of the tree."
She picked him up in her arms so strong
And plunged home[2] into the sea, sea, sea,
And plunged home into the sea.

[1] The collectors also record that "an old negro woman sang Pretty Polly years ago, she tells it now." The tune is Hill Jackson's.

[2] A strange substitute for the expected *him*.

8 "Lie there, lie there, you false-hearted wretch,
Lie there, instead of me;
Six king's daughters you've drownded there,
And I the seventh was to be, be, be,
And I the seventh was to be."

9 "Oh no, Polly, oh no, Polly,
All I want is help from thee,
And if I get to shore again,
I'm sure to marry thee, thee, thee,
I'm sure to marry thee."

10 She jumped upon the bonny, bonny, brown,
And he the piebald bay,[1]
And arrived at her father's house
Three hours before 't was day, day, day,
Three hours before 't was day.

11 She put the gold into its place,
And the horses where its would be,[2]
And arrived into her chamber fair,
Two hours before 't was day, day, day,
Two hours before 't was day.

12 Then up rised that pretty parrot
. . . .
"Oh, what are you doing up
So long before 't was day, day, day,
So long before 't was day?"

13 "Set you down, get you down, Pretty Polly,
Don't tell no tales on me;
Your cage shall be made of hand-beaten gold,
The door out of ivory, -ry, -ry,
The door out of ivory."

14 Then up rose that good old man,
Then up rose that good old man.
"What are you doing up
So long before 'tis day, day, day.
So long before 'tis day?"

[1] This line is evidently repeated gratuitously from stanza 3, the singer momentarily forgetting that the gentleman is in distress in the sea, if not already drowned. "And led the piebald bay" is the usual line here.

[2] Here is a neat puzzle for those who enjoy tinkering with oral tradition. The manuscript is unmistakable here.

15 "There are three cats at my cage door,
Trying to do violence to me,
And I'm just call (-ing) Miss Polly
To drive those cats away, -way, -way,
To drive those cats away."

C

"The Salt Water Sea." Collected by Mr. Ben C. Moomaw, Jr. Sung by Mr. Sam Pritt, of Barber, Va. Alleghany County. November 28, 1924.

1 He followed her up and he followed her down,
He followed her into the room;
She had no power to flee from his arms,
Nor the tongue to answer him nay, nay, nay,
Nor the tongue to answer him nay.

2 "Oh, gather up your father's gold,
Likewise your mother's too;
And tell me of two of the very, very best,
Where in stalls stand sixty-three."

3 She gathered up her father's gold,
Likewise her mother's too,
And told him of two of the very, very best,
Where in stalls stood sixty-three.

4 She mounted on her milk-white steed,
And he on his iron gray;
She rode along the long, long road
Till she came to the salt water sea.

5 "Mount off, mount off, Pretty Polly," he said,
"And chat awhile with me.
Six king's daughters I've drownded here,
And you the seventh shall be."

6 "Pull off your clothes, Pretty Polly," he said,
"Pull off your clothes," said he,
"Because they are too rich and fine
To rot in the salt water sea."

7 "Oh, turn your face to yonder hill,
And gaze on yonder tree;
For it's no proper sight for a man to behold
To gaze on a maiden like me."

8 He turned his face to yonder hill,
And gazed on yonder tree;
She picked him up as he were a babe,
And cast him in the salt water sea.

9 "Some help, some help, Pretty Polly," he cried,
"Some help, some help," cried he.
"If ever I recover from this place," he said,
"I'll surely marry thee."

10 "No help, no help," Pretty Polly, she cried,
"No help, no help from me.
Your clothes are not too rich and fine
To rot in the salt water sea."

11 She mounted on her milk-white steed
And she led the iron gray;
She rode along the long, long road
Till she came to her father's dwelling.

(*Some stanza about a bird, not fully remembered.*)

12 "I wish I had a little willow bow,
And a string to fit my arrow;
I'd shoot a dart right through your heart,
And your notes you'd sing no more."

D

"The King's Daughter" or "Come a Link, Come a Long." Collected by Miss Juliet Fauntleroy. Sung by Mr. Ed. Stinnet, of Lynch Station, Va. Campbell County. April 11, 1924. With music.

1 "You followed me up, you followed me down,
You followed me day by day,
You neither had the tongue for to tell me yea,
Nor the heart for to turn me away."

2 "I followed you up, I followed you down,
I followed you day by day,
I neither had the tongue for to tell you yea,
Nor the heart to turn you away."

3 She got up on the little pony [1] brown,
He got up on the gray,
They rode till they came to the blue, salt sea,
Come a link, come a long summer day.

[1] Probably for *bonny*.

4 "Get down, get down, my pretty fair Miss,
And fold your silk veil on my knee,
For it's cost your father too much money
To rot in the blue salt sea."

5 He turned his head around and about
Till he faced to the leaves of the tree,
[She took him hastily up in her arms] [1]
And she splunged [2] him into the blue, salt sea.

6 "Oh, hand me down your white lily hand,
Oh, hand it down to me,
[Oh, hand me down your white lily hand,]
And married we shall be."

7 "No, sir, for you have drownded
Nine of the king's daughters [fair]
[Bear you them company].
You lie there in the place of me."

8 She got on the little pony brown,
And she led the iron gray,
She rode till she came to her father's gate,
Just three hours till day.

9 "Wake up, wake up, dear parents,
And tell no tales on me.
All the crimes that I have done
Hangs on a green willow tree."

10 She got on the little pony brown,
And she started off at full speed.
The golden rings flew off her fingers,
And her nose begin to bleed.

11 "And I wish to the Lord I had never been born,
Or had died when I was young,
I'd never been here to shed a tear,
Nor to listen to your lying tongue." [3]

[1] The bracketed words appear to be those about which the collector is uncertain or which she has supplied.

[2] Either expressive for *plunged* or the remains of "she has plunged."

[3] The final stanza and part of the one before have been contaminated from a later folk-song.

E

"Seven King's Daughters." Collected by Miss Alfreda M. Peel, of Salem, Va. Roanoke County. September 11, 1922.

1 He followed her up, he followed her down,
He followed her into her room,
Saying, "Gather up your own father's gold
And go along with me, me, me,
And go along with me."

2 She gathered up her own father's gold
And two of his finest horses,
And rode till they came to the salt water sea,
All on a long summer day, day, day,
All on a long summer day.

3 It's "Get you down a while," said he,
"And talk a while with me;
For six king's daughters have I drowned,
And the seventh one you shall be, be, be,
And the seventh one you shall be."

4 She looked around the blooming trees
And took him in her arms,
And tossed him in the sea, sea, sea.
And tossed him in the sea.

5 It's "Reach me here your hand," said he,
"And up to my promise I shall be.
I promised that I would marry you
And a fair lady you should be, be, be.
And a fair lady you should be."

6 "Swim on, swim on, my false true love,
Swim on, swim on," said she.
"Your clothing is not a bit too fine
To rot in the salt, salt sea, sea, sea,
To rot in the salt, salt sea."

7 She mounted on her milk-white horse,
And led her iron grey,
And rode till she came to her father's door
Two hours before the day, day, day,
Two hours before the day.

8 She put her horses where they stood,
And money in the same place,
And into her bed-chamber she did go,
With the rest all fast asleep, sleep, sleep,
With the rest all fast asleep.

9 It's "Where have you been, my pretty princess,
That you have come before day?
I'm sure you have drowned your own true love,
And the same you would do to me, me, me,
And the same you would do to me."

10 It's "Hold your tongue, my pretty parrot,
Don't tell those tales on me,
And your cage shall be made of the purest gold
And hang on a willow tree, tree, tree,
And hang on a willow tree."

F

"Seven King's Daughters." Collected by Miss Alfreda M. Peel. Sung by Miss Odell Roop, of Vinton, Va. Roanoke County. September 11, 1922. With music.

1 There was a man out in the land,
He courted a maiden fair;
He promised to take her to northern lands,
There the marriage should be.

2 "Go get some of your father's gold,
Some of your mother's fee;
Get two of the horses that stand in the stalls,
That stand by forty and three.

3 "Dismount, dismount your milky steed
And deliver it unto me;
For six king's daughters have I drowned,
And the seventh one you shall be.

4 "Pull off, pull off your silky robe
And deliver it unto me;
For I think it is too costly
To roll in the deep blue sea."

5 "If I must pull off my silky robe,
Please turn your back on me;
For I think it's not nice, you know,
A naked maiden to see."

6 He turned his back all unto her;
She wept most bitterly;
She grabbed him round his thin small waist
And tumbled him into the sea.

7 He waved on high, he waved on low,
He waved till he came to her (side?):
"Take hold of my hand, my pretty Pauline,
And you shall be my bride."

G

"Song Ballad of Pretty Polly." Sent by Mrs. Olin F. Wiley, of Richmond, Va. Wise County. December 1, 1916.

1 "Rise up, rise up, Pretty Polly, rise up,
Rise up, rise up," says he,
"And I'll take thee to some North Scotland
And there I'll marry thee.

2 "Go get some of your father's gold,
Likewise some of your mother's theme; [1]
I got a horse out of yonder stable
And there stands thirty three."

3 She mounted on her snowy white horse,
And him the dapple gray;
Straightway they made for some salt water sea
Three hours before it was day.

4 "Get off, get off, Pretty Polly," says he,
"Get off, get off," says he,
"For six king's daughters have I drownded here,
And those never shall be."

5 "Get out those sickles and cut those nettles
That stand so near the brim,
For fear they tangle in her long yellow hair
And sting her snowy white skin."

6 He got out of those sickles and *he* cut those nettles
That staid [*sic*] so near the brim,
For fear they would get tangled in her long yellow hair
And sting her snowy white skin.[2]

7 "Pull off, pull off, those fine silk clothes,
Pull off, pull off," says he,
"For they are too fine and costly too
For to rot in the bottom of the sea."

[1] Variation of the usual *fee*.

[2] Stanzas 5 and 6 link this version definitely with Child F. It is the only Virginia version that has the sickle and nettle incident. Compare Campbell and Sharp, No. 2, D.

8 "Turn your back on the leaves of the trees
And your face toward the sea,
Till I pull off my fine silk clothes,
So myself you may not see."

9 He turned his back on the leaves of the trees
And his face toward the sea,
And Pretty Polly with a trembling heart
Threw False William in the sea.

10 "O help me, O help, Pretty Polly," says he,
"Reach down your hand to me,
And I'll take thee to North Scotland
And there I'll marry thee."

11 "Lay there, lay there, False William," says she,
"Lay there, lay there," cried she;
"For six King's daughters have you drownded here,
You with those seven shall be."

12 She mounted on her snowy white horse
And led the dapple gray,
And away she rode to her old father land
An hour before it was day.

H

"Miss Mary's Parrot." Sent in by Miss Juliet Fauntleroy. Sung by Mrs. James Sprouse (*née* Pribble), of Lawyers, Va. Campbell County. March 20, 1915.

1 "Go bring me a portion of your father's gold
And some of your mother's fee,
And bring your father's choice horse
That stands on sixty-three."

2 So she brought him a portion of her father's gold
And some of her mother's fee,
And she brought him her father's choice horse
That stands on sixty-three.

3 So he mounted upon the milk-white steed,
And she on the iron gray;
And they arrived at the salt sea side,
'T was the length of a long summer day.

4 "I will light you down, Miss Mary dear,"
Was the words he said to me.
"I have drownded six of the King's daughters here,
And the seventh one you shall be.

8 "Lie there, lie there, you hard-hearted whelp,
Lie there in the place of me.
You drowned six of the king's daughters here;
Go keep them company."

9 "Lend me your hand, my pretty Polly Anne,
Lend me your hand," said he,
"And all of those tales that I've ever told you,
I'll double them thirty times three."

10 "Lie there, lie there, you false young man,
Lie there in the place of me.
For it's a scandal and a shame for a man like you
To drown a lady like me."

11 She mounted on the milk-white steed,
And her hand on an iron gray,
And she rode home to her father's hall
Three long hours before it was day.

12 "O where have you been, my pretty Polly Anne,
O where have you been?" says he.
"Hush up, hush up, my pretty parrot,
And tell no tales on me,
And I'll build you a castle out of yellow gold bead,
And I'll swing it to the willow tree."

J

"Pretty Gold Lee." Collected by Miss May Blankenship, of the Farmville Ballad Club. Sung by her cousin, of Naruna, Va. Campbell County. May, 1914. Printed in *The Focus* for May, 1914, p. 212.

1 "Go bring me some of your father's gold,
And some of your mother's fee,
And two of the prettiest nags in the stall,
Wherein stands thirty and three, three, three,
Wherein stands thirty and three."

2 He mounted upon his milk-white horse,
And she the dapple gray,
And they safely arrived at the salt sea side,
And 't was three hours till day, day, day,
And 't was three hours till day.

3 "Light off, light off with the dapple gray,
And deliver it unto me;
For six king's daughters have I drowned here,
And now the seventh shall be thee, thee, thee,
And now the seventh shall be thee."

4 He turned his back and looked around,
The green leaves for to see;
She picked him up in her arms so strong,
And threw him in the sand salt sea, sea, sea,
And threw him in the sand salt sea.

5 "Reach forth, reach forth your lily-white hand,
And help me from the sea,
And I'll take you away to some foreign land,
And there I'll marry thee, thee, thee,
And there I'll marry thee."

6 "Lie there, lie there, you false-hearted man,
Lie there instead of me,
For six pretty ladies you drowned here,
And the seventh shall now drown thee, thee, thee,
And the seventh shall now drown thee."

7 She mounted upon the milk-white horse,
Leading the dapple gray.
She safely arrived at her father's house,
And 't was two hours till day, day, day,
And 't was two hours till day.

8 And there bespoke the pretty parrot,
Where in his cage he stay,
"Where have you been, my Pretty Gold Lee?"
And 't was one hour till day, day, day,
And 't was one hour till day.

9 "Oh hush, oh hush, my pretty parrot,
And don't tell tales on me.
Your cage shall be made of yellow gold,
And the doors of ivory, -ry, -ry,
And the doors of ivory."

10 And then bespoke the king so high,
Where in his chamber he lay,
"Oh, what is the matter with my pretty parrot
So long before 't is day, day, day,
So long betore 't is day."

11 "The cat is coming to my cage
To carry me away,
And I am calling my Pretty Gold Lee,
To drive the cat away, -way, -way,
Go drive the cat away."

8 "Lie there, lie there, false-hearted young man,
Lie there instead of me;
Six pretty fair maids you have drowned here,
And the seventh one drowneth thee."

9 "Help me out, help me out, my pretty fair maid,
Help me out, help me out," cried he.
"I'll take you back to your father's home,
And there I'll marry thee."

10 "Lie there, lie there, false-hearted young man,
Lie there, lie there," cried she,
"Six pretty fair maids you have drowned here,
And the seventh one drowneth thee."

11 She mounted on her milk-white steed,
Whilst leading the iron gray,
She rode away to her father's house,
'T was just one hour from day.

M

"King's Seven Daughters." Sent in by Mrs. N. E. Clement, of Chatham, Va. Pittsylvania County. July 25, 1917.

1 "Go take part of your father's,
Likewise of your mother's fee,
And take two horses from your father's barn,
Where stand thirty and three."

2 She took part of her father's gold
Likewise her mother's fee,
And took two horses out of the barn,
Where there were thirty and three.

3 She mounted the bonny, bonny brown,
While he the dapple grey,
And rode until they came to the sea, salt sea,
And 't was just three hours to day.

4 "Take off, take off those costly gems,
And hang on yonder tree;
For six of the King's daughters I have drowned,
And the seventh you shall be.

5 "Take off, take off your white silk gown,
Hang it on yonder tree;
For 't is too rich and too costly
To rot in yonder sea."

6 "You turn your body round about,
With your back to yonder tree,
For ain't it a pity for a rebel like you
A naked woman to see."

7 He turned his body round about
With his back to the leaves of the tree;
She tripped him into the sea, salt sea,
And she tripped him into the sea.

8 "Lie there, lie there, you false-hearted man,
Lie there instead of me;
For you promised to take me to fair Scotland,
And there to marry me."

9 She mounted the bonny, bonny brown,
And led the dappled grey,
And rode till she came to her own father's home;
'Twas just an hour till day.

10 "O hush, O hush, my pretty little bird,
Don't patter so long before day;
For your cage shall be made of beaten, beaten gold
And the doors of ivory."

N

"The Six King's Daughters" or "The Seventh King's Daughter" or "Pretty Polly." Collected by Miss Mary E. Peck, of the Farmville Ballad Club. Sung by her father (when she was a child). Prince Edward County. May, 1914. Printed in *The Focus* for May, 1914, p. 214.

1 "Go gather up your mother's gold,
Likewise your father's fee,
For I have drowned six king's daughters,
And you the seventh shall be, shall be,
And you the seventh shall be."

2 He mounted on his iron gray,
And she the dappled bay,
And off they rode to the broad seaside,
Three hours before 't was day, day, day,
Three hours before 't was day.

3 "Go turn your back to the salt-water sea,
Your face to the limbs of the tree."
She picked him up so manfully
And plunged him into the sea, sea, sea,
And plunged him into the sea.

There is a struggle, the maid frees herself and throws the knight into the pool, then sings:

5 "Lie there, lie there, you false young man,
. . . .
For six king's daughters you've drownded here
But the seventh one's drownded you, -u, -u,
But the seventh one's drownded you."

Q

"The Seven King's Daughters." Collected by Miss Juliet Fauntleroy. Sung by Mrs. Dan Maxie (*née* Holland), of Altavista, Va. Franklin County. March 23, 1914. With music. Miss Fauntleroy writes: "This is evidently only the ending, but it is all that Mrs. Maxie can remember. She used to hear her mother sing it when she was a child."

She picked him up so shyly,
She hauled him in the sea.
"Lie there, lie there, you false-eyed vilyun
Instead of me.
Six of the king's daughters you've drownded,
And the seventh one *you* shall be."

R

"The False Hearted Knight." Collected by Miss Alfreda M. Peel. Sung by Mrs. Harrington, of Roanoke, Va. Roanoke County. December 17, 1916. With music.

Miss Peel's letter of this date supplies an introduction to the following fragment: "The singer had forgotten the first, but told me that the ballad was about a maiden being lured to a lonely spot. When she had reached there, a false knight, her supposed lover, demanded that she strip and give him her jewels." She replies thus:

1 "Now turn your back to me
And your face to the leaves on the tree;
Such a wicked man as thou 'rt is n't fit
A naked woman to see."

2 And turning his back to her
And his face to the leaves on the tree,
She picked him up in her own strong arms
And threw him in the sea.

3 "Lie there, lie there, false-hearted knight,
Lie there instead of me;
Three king's daughters you have drowned,
But I the fourth shan't be."

4 And mounting on her own bay horse
And leading the dapple gray,
She then arrived at her father's house
One hour and a half before day.

5 Her father hearing her come in
Got up, and thus did say:
"Who enters here, who enters here,
When 't is so near to day?"

6 The pretty parrot began to talk
And laugh so fitfully:
"The cat was before my little cage door
And about to have eaten me."

7 The girl came up and thus did say
To the pretty parrot blithe and gay:
"O mistress Polly, you keep still
And tell no tales on me;
Your cage shall be made of beaten gold,
And hang on a willow tree."

S

"Lady Isabel and the Elf-Knight." Collected by Miss Alfreda M. Peel. Sung by Lucile Noel, of Vinton, Va. Roanoke County. November 30, 1923. With music.

"Go get me of my father's gold,
And some of my mother's feed;
Get two of the horses that stand in the stall,
That stand by forty and three."

10 He rode, he rode, ...
He rode with his lady so dear.
Until he came to his own mother's stile,
Who he did love so dear.

11 "Mother, oh mother, make my bed,
And make it soft and wide,
That I may lie down and rest for awhile
With my lady by my side."

12 Lord William he died about midnight,
Lady Margret just before day;
The old woman died for the grief of her son,
So there was seven [1] lives lost.

B

"The Seven Brothers, or The Seven Sleepers." Collected by Miss Martha M. Davis. Sung by Mrs. Rosie Morris, of Elkton, Va. Rockingham County. August 30, 1922. With music.

1 "Get ye up, get ye up, ye seven sleepers,
Put on your armor so bright;
For it never shall be said that a daughter of mine
Could stay with Sweet William all night."

* * * * * *

2 He mounted her on the milk-white steed,
And himself on the dapple grey;
He drew his pistol all down by his side,
And away they went riding away.

3 "Get ye down, get ye down, Lady Margot," he cried,
"And hold my steed for a while;
Until I fight your seven brothers bold
And your father you love so well."

4 She held, she held, she better had held,
And never delayed any time;
Until she saw her seven brothers fall
And her father she loved so well.

5 "Stop your hand, stop your hand, Sweet William," she cried,
"Stop your hand, stop your hand for a while;
It's a many a sweetheart I could have had
But a father I'll never have again."

[1] Bad arithmetic. The number should be *eleven*, as in other variants.

6 "You can choose for to go, or to stay alone."
. . . .
"I'll go, I'll go, Sweet William, you know
You've left me without any guide."

7 He mounted her on the milk-white steed,
And himself on the dapple grey;
He drew his pistol down by his side,
And away he went bleeding away.

8 They rode, they rode, and better they rode,
And never delayed any time;
Until they came to his mother's stile,
And a mother she was to him.

9 "O mother, O mother, go make my bed,
And make it both soft and wide,
And lay my lady down by my side
So I may rest for a while."

10 Sweet William he died before midnight,
Lady Margot died before day.
The mother died for loss of her son,
And eleven lives were lost for one.

C

"The Seven Brothers." Sent in by Miss Martha M. Davis. Collected by Mrs. Herbert Cover, of Elkton, Va. Rockingham County. November 22, 1913.

1 "Arise, arise, ye seven brothers,
Put on your armor so brave;
For I never intend for a daughter of mine
To stay with Sweet William[1] a day."

2 He jumped upon his milk-white steed,
She on her viper[2] bay.
He buckled his sword down by his side,
And away they went singing away.

3 They rode, they rode, at length they rode,
He with his love so dear;
Until he met her seven brothers bold
And her father she loved so dear.

[1] Also sung as "Lord William." [2] Sometimes *dapple*.

APPENDIX

"I'll Tell You of a Soldier." Collected by Miss Martha M. Davis. Sung by a mountain woman. Rockingham County. April 1, 1915. For references see Cox, p. 375. See also introductory head-note to this ballad, Virginia, No. 4.

1 I can tell you of a soldier who late returned from war,
Who courted a lady with honor and great store.
Her fortune was so great it scarcely could be told,
And yet she loved the soldier because he was so bold.

2 "Now," says the lady, "I'd freely be your wife
But for my cruel father, I fear him for my life."
He drew his sword and pistol and swung them by his side,
And swore that he'd get married, let what would betide.

3 They went to the parson and returned home again,
They met her cruel father and seven armed men.
"O now," said the lady, "I fear we shall be slain."
"Fear nothing in the world," said the soldier again.

4 "Now," said the soldier, "there's no time to prattle,
I am but a small man not fitten for a battle."
He drew his sword and pistol which caused them to rattle,
And the lady held the horse while the soldier fought the battle.

5 The first one he came to he ran it through the man;
The next one he came to he ran it through again.
"O, run," said the rest, "I find it all in vain;
Fight a gallant soldier I never will again."

6 Up spoke the old father, "Please spare my life.
You may have my daughter, five thousand pounds in hand."
"Fight on," said the lady, "The portion is too small."
"O hold your hand, brave soldier, and you may have it all."

7 "Run," said the rest, "we all shall be slain;
For fighting of a soldier we know we are to blame."

8 They mounted the horses and home they did ride,
And a fine wedding supper at home they did provide.

5

THE TWA SISTERS

(Child, No. 10)

One might expect to find this ballad rather abundantly in Virginia, as Child reports it as one of the very few old ballads which are not extinct as tradition in the British Isles. The thirteen Virginia items are known variously as "The Two Sisters," "The Old Man of the North Countree," "Sister Kate," "The Miller and the Mayor's Daughter," "I'll Be True to My Love," "The Three Sisters," and by other like titles.

All the Virginia variants, except the final fragment (K), belong with Child R and Y, and perhaps with the kindred fragments S and U between, as is shown by the refrain and the details of the story. The final fragment (K) is a different version: it has a refrain similar to Child G and J, but the drowned girl is a king's daughter, as in Child A. All of the Virginia texts are without that striking but rather gruesome detail found in more complete and uncorrupted forms of the ballad — the use of some part of the body of the drowned girl to furnish a musical instrument which then makes known the murderer. The ballads that follow do not tell how the miller's guilt was discovered, but they state satisfyingly that he was hung at his mill gate. No punishment is mentioned for the elder sister. The miller is always the villain, never the innocent rescuer of the body as in Child A and B, etc.

For American texts, see Barry, No. 3; Belden, No. 2 (fragment); *Bulletin*, Nos. 2–8, 12; Campbell and Sharp, No. 4 (North Carolina, Virginia; cf. Sharp, *Songs*, II, No. 4); Child, I, 137 (New York); II, 508 (New York); Cox, No. 3, p. 521 (fragment and melody); Gray, p. 75; Hudson, No. 3 (Mississippi); *Journal*, xviii, 130 (Barry, Rhode Island, text and melody, Maine); xix, 233 (Belden, Kentucky, Missouri, fragment, reprinted from James Ashby's Missouri ballad-book); xxx, 286 (Kittredge, Missouri, Nebraska); Pound, *Syllabus*, p. 11 (fragment); Pound, *Ballads*, No. 4; Shearin, p. 4; Shearin and Combs, p. 7 (fragment). For additional references, see *Journal*, xxx, 286 and Cox, p. 20. It will be noted that Campbell and Sharp give three texts and three melodies from Virginia.

A

"The Old Lord of the North Country" or "The Three Sisters." Collected by Mr. John Stone. Sung by Mr. A. S. Furcron. Fauquier County. November 10, 1919. With music.

1 There lived an old lord in the North Countree,
Bow down.
There lived an old lord in the North Countree,
Bow down you bittern to me.
There lived an old lord in the North Countree
And he had daughters, one, two, three.
If this be true, true love, my love, my love, be true to me.

7 "No, I'll not reach you my hand nor my glove,
For you shan't have my own true love."

8 She bowed her head and she swam away;
She swam into the miller's bay.

9 The miller he took his old grab-hook,
And fished the girl out of the brook.

10 Said, "Miller, I'll give you these ten gold chains
To bring me to my home again."

11 The ten gold chains the miller took
And pushed the girl back in the brook.

12 They hanged the miller on yonder gate
For the murder of the sister Kate.

C

"The Two Sisters." Collected by Miss Juliet Fauntleroy. Sung by Mrs. J. B. Crawford. Albemarle County. May 26, 1915.

1 There was an old man in the North Countrie,
Bow down, bow down.
There was an old man in the North Countrie,
And he had daughters, one, two, three.
Love will be true, true to my love,
Love will be true to you.

2 There was a young man came courting there,
And he did choose the youngest fair.

3 He gave to the youngest a gay gold ring,
And to the oldest not a single thing.

4 He gave to the youngest a beaver hat,
And the oldest she thought hard of that.

5 "Sister, O sister, let's walk the sea shore,
To see the ships come sailing o'er."

6 They were walking along on yonder sea-brim
When the oldest shoved the youngest in.

7 "O sister, O sister, hand me your hand,
And you may have my house and land.

8 "O sister, O sister, hand me your glove,
And you may have my own true love."

9 "I'll neither hand you hand nor glove,
For all I want is your true love."

10 So down she sank and away she swam
Until she reached the old mill dam.

11 The miller threw out his old grab-hook
And pulled the fair maiden out of the brook.

12 "O miller, O miller, here's three gold rings,
If you'll take me to my father's again."

13 He up with her fingers and off with her rings
And threw her back in the brook again.

14 The miller was hung at his mill gate
For drowning of my sister Kate.

D

"The Two Sisters" or "Sister Kate" or "The Miller and the Mayor's Daughter." Collected by Miss Juliet Fauntleroy. Sung by Mrs. L. L. Arthur and Mrs. Bob Stone (*née* Taylor) of Altavista, Va. Campbell County. March 14, 1914. With music.

1 There was a Lord Mayor in our town,
Bow down.
There was a Lord Mayor in our town,
Bow it's been to me.[1]
There was a Lord Mayor in our town,
And he had daughters, one, two, three.
Love will be true, true to my love,
Love will be true to you.

2 There was a young man went courting there,
And he did choose the youngest fair.

3 "O sister, O sister, let's we walk out
And view the ships all sailing about."

4 The oldest pushed the youngest in,
And down she sank and away she swam.

5 "O sister, O sister, Oh, loan me your hand
And you may have my house and land.

6 "Sister, O sister, Oh, loan me your glove,
And you may have my own true love."

[1] Cf. Cox variants, "Bow and bend to me" and "The bough has been to me," pp. 21–22.

9 The miller got her golden ring,
The miller pushed her back again.

10 The miller was hung at his mill gate
For drownding my poor sister Kate.

G

"The Two Sisters." Collected by Mr. Cecil J. Sharp and Miss Karpeles. Sung by Miss Louisa Chisholm, at Woodridge, Va. Albemarle County. September 23, 1916. With music. Printed by Campbell and Sharp, p. 18.

1 There lived an old lord by the northern sea,
Bow down,
There lived an old lord by the northern sea,
The boughs they bend to me,
There lived an old lord by the northern sea,
And he had daughters one, two, three,
That will be true, true to my love,
Love and my love will be true to me.

2 A young man came a-courting there,
He took choice of the youngest there.

3 He gave this girl a beaver hat,
The oldest she thought much of that.

4 "O sister, O sister, let's walk out
To see the ships a-sailing about."

5 As they walked down the salty brim,
The oldest pushed the youngest in.

6 "O sister, O sister, lend me your hand,
And I will give you my house and land."

7 "I'll neither lend you my hand or glove,
But I will have your own true love."

8 Down she sank and away she swam,
And into the miller's mill (or fish) pond she ran.

9 The miller come out with his fish hook
And fished the fair maid out of the brook.

10 And it's off of her finger took five gold rings,
And into the brook he pushed her again.

11 The miller was hung at his mill gate,
For drowning of my sister Kate.

H

"The Lady of the North Country." Collected by Miss Roxie Martin and Mr. J. M. McManaway. Albemarle County. June 1, 1917. "A school girl wrote this as her father sang it to her" (Miss Martin and Mr. McManaway). If so, the original manuscript is an interesting commentary upon school-girl literacy.

1 There lived an old lady in the Northern Country,
Bow down,
There lived an old lady in the Northern Country,
The bow has been to me.
There lived an old lady in the Northern Country,
She had daughters one, two, three.
True to my love, my love be true to thee.

2 There came a young man a-courting there,
Bow down,
There came a young man a-courting there,
The bow has been to me.
There came a young man a-courting there,
He made a choice of the youngest there.
True to my love, my love be true to thee.

3 He made her a present of a beaver's hat,
Bow down,
He made her a present of a beaver's hat,
The bow has been to me.
He made her a present of a beaver's hat,
The oldest thought a heap of that.
True to my love, my love be true to thee.

4 "O sister, O sister, just walk out,"
Bow down,
"O sister, O sister, just walk out,"
The bow has been to me.
"O sister, O sister, just walk out,
See those vessels a-sailing about."
True to my love, my love be true to thee.

5 The oldest one pushed the youngest in,
Bow down,
The oldest one pushed the youngest in,
The bow has been to me.
The oldest one pushed the youngest in,
She did struggle, she did swim.
True to my love, my love be true to thee.

K

No title given. Collected by Miss Martha M. Davis. From the singing of her grandmother. Rockingham County. January 8, 1914. Miss Davis writes: "My grandmother sang this ballad in broad Scotch, but this is all we can recover."

1 The miller's daughter went out one day,
Hey ho, my honey, O,
To get some water to make her bread,
And the swan swam so bonny, O.

* * * * * *

2 The miller went and stopped his dam,
Hey ho, my honey, O,
And placed the king's daughter on dry land,
And the swan swam so bonny, O.

6

LORD RANDAL

(CHILD, No. 12)

THE famous old story-bearing dialogue between a mother and her son who is poisoned masquerades in Virginia as "John Willow, My Son," "Johnnie Randolph, My Son," "Johnny Rillus" (or "Rilla" or "Rolus" or "Riller" or "Reynolds"), "Ransel, My Son," "McDonald," "John Elzie," "Billy Randall, or A Rope and a Gallows," and "Where Have You Been to, My Dear Son?," seldom as "Lord Randal."

In "Johnnie Randolph, My Son," the fame of a distinguished Virginian, John Randolph of Roanoke, has penetrated into ballad tradition. Cox finds the same title in West Virginia. One is glad to find in Bruce's *Life* evidence that Randolph was himself a ballad fancier and that therefore he may be considered worthy of the ballad's tribute to him. Writing to a niece, February 20, 1822, Randolph says: "Do you know a ballad that used to be sung to me when I was a child by a mulatto servant girl of my cousin Patsy Banister, called Patience, about a rich suitor offering 'his lands so broad' and his golden store to a girl of spirit whose reply was somehow thus?

What care I for your golden treasures?
What care I for your house and land?
What care I for your costly pleasures?
So as I get but a handsome man.

I pry' thee get me that ballad. I can give you the tune."

The fame of still another John may be linked with this ballad. Scott's preface to this ballad in his *Minstrelsy of the Scottish Border* quotes a manuscript chronicle of England which recounts the death of King John of England in a manner not unlike the ballad account of Lord Randal's death.

Most of the Virginia variants belong with Child A or B, but some show relations with other versions, notably D. Most of the texts here given prefer the "hell and fire" ending of A to the "rope and gallows" idea of B (one substitutes "a keg of powder to blow her sky-high"), but all except two follow B in eliminating the death of the dogs, which elsewhere serves as an indication that the master, too, is poisoned. A general verbal similarity with Child D is to be noted.

Two very interesting survivals among the archives have been excluded as not strictly Virginian. One, "as sung by boys from the East Side of New York City," has the son "Henry" (cf. Child C) answer that he has been "down at grandma's" (cf. Child I, K, R), and finally leave the rope, etc., not to his sweetheart, but to his *brother*. The other, which comes from Oklahoma and is known as "Durango," indicates the grandmother as the poisoner (cf. Child I). They appear as Appendices A and B.

For American texts, see Barry, No. 10; Brown, p. 9 (North Carolina); *Bulletin*, Nos. 2–5, 7–11; Campbell and Sharp, No. 6 (North Carolina, Georgia); Child, I, 163 (Massachusetts), 499; Cox, No. 4; Hudson, No. 4 (Mississippi); *Journal*, XIII, 115 (Newell, Ohio, New York, New Brunswick,

Scotch variant obtained in America); xvi, 258 (Barry, Rhode Island, Massachusetts, five texts and four melodies); xviii, 195 (Barry, Rhode Island, Maine, text and melody, Massachusetts, nine texts and seven melodies, Connecticut, text and melody, Vermont), 303 (Barry, Vermont, text and melody); xxii, 77 (Barry, Pennsylvania, melody only), 376 (Barry, Maine, text and melody); xxiv, 345 (Barry, Maine); xxix, 157 (Tolman, fragment); xxx, 289 (Kittredge, Indiana, fragment, New York, fragments, Missouri, fragment and melody); xxxv, 339 (Tolman and Eddy, Illinois, fragment and melody); xxxix, 81 (Whiting, Maine); McGill, p. 19; Pound, *Syllabus*, p. 9 (fragment); Pound, *Ballads*, No. 1; Shearin, p. 4; Shearin and Combs, p. 7; Shoemaker, p. 139; C. A. Smith, p. 19 (New York, fragment, Oklahoma, and Great Britain, melodies only); Reed Smith, No. 2; Reed Smith, *Ballads*, No. 2; *Focus*, December, 1913, February and March, 1914; and *The Crimson Rambler* (Tonkawa, Oklahoma), Vol. 8, No. 4. For additional references see *Journal*, xxix, 157; xxx, 289.

A

"John Willow, My Son." Collected by Miss Juliet Fauntleroy. Sung by Mrs. James B. Crawford, of Altavista, Va. Campbell County. September 9, 1915. With music.

1 "Oh, where have you been, John Willow, my son,
Oh, where have you been, my dear little one?"
"I've been to my sweetheart's. Mother, make my bed soon;
There's a pain in my heart, and I want to lie down."

2 "What did you have for your supper, John Willow, my son,
What did you have for your supper, my dear little one?"
"Eels fried in batter. Mother, make my bed soon;
There's a pain in my heart, and I want to lie down."

3 "What did you do with your leavings, John Willow, my son,
What did you do with your leavings, my dear little one?"
"I gave them to my dogs. Mother, make my bed soon;
There's a pain in my heart, and I want to lie down."

4 "Where are your dogs, John Willow, my son,
Where are your dogs, my dear little one?"
"They lay down and died. Mother, make my bed soon;
There's a pain in my heart, and I want to lie down."

5 "I'm afraid you are poisoned, John Willow, my son,
I'm afraid you are poisoned, my dear little one."
"Oh yes, I am poisoned. Mother, make my bed soon;
There's a pain in my heart, and I want to lie down."

6 "What do you will to your father, John Willow, my son,
What do you will to your father, my dear little one?"
"My house and my land. Mother, make my bed soon;
There's a pain in my heart, and I want to lie down."

7 "What do you will to your mother, John Willow, my son,
What do you will to your mother, my dear little one?"
"I wish you a home in heaven. Mother, make my bed soon;
There's a pain in my heart, and I want to lie down."

8 "What do you will to your sister, John Willow, my son,
What do you will to your sister, my dear little one?"
"My horse, saddle, and bridle. Mother, make my bed soon;
There's a pain in my heart, and I want to lie down."

9 "What do you will to your sweetheart, John Willow, my son,
What do you will to your sweetheart, my dear little one?
"Hell-fire and brimstone, to scorch her so brown;
She's the cause of this pain, and I want to lie down."

B

"Johnny Rillus." Collected by Mr. John Stone. Sung by Mrs. Emily Via, of Stage Junction, Va. Fluvanna County. November 3, 1920. With music.

1 "Where have you been, Johnny Rillus, my son,
Where have you been, my dearest little one?"
"I've been out a-courting, mother, make my bed soon;
I've a pain in my heart and I want to lie down."

2 "Have you been to your supper, Johnny Rillus, my son,
Have you been to your supper, my dearest little one?"
"Yes, been to my supper, mother, make my bed soon;
I've a pain in my heart and I want to lie down."

3 "What did you have for your supper, Johnny Rillus, my son,
What did you have for your supper, my dearest little one?"
"Fresh eel and butter, mother, make my bed soon;
I've a pain in my heart and I want to lie down."

4 "What color were your eels, Johnny Rillus, my son,
What color were your eels, my dearest little one?"
"White and black spotted, mother, make my bed soon;
I've a pain in my heart and I want to lie down."

5 "You are dying, Johnny Rillus, my dearest little son,
You are dying, Johnny Rillus, my dearest little one."
"Yes, dying, mother; mother, make my bed soon;
I've a pain in my heart and I want to lie down."

6 "What will you leave to your sister, Johnny Rillus, my son,
What will you leave to your sister, my dearest little one?"
"A fine horse and saddle, mother, make my bed soon;
I've a pain in my heart and I want to lie down."

7 "What will you leave to your mother, Johnny Rillus, my son,
What will you leave to your mother, my dearest little one?"
"Sweet fields in heaven, mother, make my bed soon;
I've a pain in my heart and I want to lie down."

8 "What will you leave to your sweetheart, Johnny Rillus, my son,
What will you leave to your sweetheart, my dearest little one?"
"Brimstone and fire, mother, make my bed soon;
I've a pain in my heart and I want to lie down."

9 "Where do you want to be buried, Johnny Rillus, my son,
Where do you want to be buried, my dearest little one?"
"Down in the green meadow where the grass grows so tall,
Where my sweetheart can see me, for she was the cause of it all."

C

"McDonald." Sent in by Miss Alfreda Peel. Sung by Mrs. W. W. McClurg, of Salem, Va. Roanoke County. November 10, 1918.

1 "Whar have you been, McDonald, McDonald,
Whar have you been, McDonald, my son?"
"I've been out hunting, mother; make my bed soon,
I'm a weary, weary wanderer in a pain to lie down."

2 "Where are your grey hounds, McDonald, McDonald,
Where are your grey hounds, McDonald, my son?"
"They're still out a-sunning; mother, make my bed soon,
I'm a weary, weary wanderer in a pain to lie down."

3 "What did you have for dinner, McDonald, McDonald,
Whar did you get your dinner, McDonald, my son?"
"I dined with my sweetheart; mother, make my bed soon,
I'm a weary, weary wanderer in a pain to lie down."

4 "What had you for dinner, McDonald, McDonald,
What had you for dinner, McDonald, my son?"
"We had white fish and poison; mother, make my bed soon,
I'm a weary, weary wanderer in a pain to lie down."

5 "What will you will your father, McDonald, McDonald,
What will you will your father, McDonald, my son?"
"I will will him my gold staff; mother, make my bed soon,
I'm a weary, weary wanderer in a pain to lie down."

6 "What will you will your mother, McDonald, McDonald,
What will you will your mother, McDonald, my son?"
"I will her my gold watch; mother, make my bed soon,
I'm a weary, weary wanderer in a pain to lie down."

7 "What will you will your sister, McDonald, McDonald,
What will you will your sister, McDonald, my son?"
"I will her my jewelry; mother, make my bed soon,
I am a weary, weary wanderer in a pain to lie down."

8 "What will you will your sweetheart, McDonald, McDonald,
What will you will your sweetheart, McDonald, my son?"
"I will her a keg of powder to blow her sky high,
For I'm a weary, weary wanderer in a pain to lie down."

D

"Ransel, My Son." Collected by Mr. John Stone. Sung by Mr. George Hart, of Konnarock, Va. Washington County. November 8, 1921.

1 "O where have you been, O Ransel, my son?
O where have you been, my sweet and pretty one?"
"O mother, I've been courting; mother, make my bed soon,
I'm sick to the heart and in pain to lie down."

2 "What did you eat for your supper, O Ransel, my son?
What did you eat for your supper, my sweet and pretty one?"
"A cup of cold pizen, mother, make my bed soon,
I'm sick to the heart and in pain to lie down."

3 "What will you will to your old father, O Ransel, my son?
What will you will to your old father, my sweet and pretty one?"
"A dead son to bury, mother, make my bed soon,
I'm sick to the heart and in pain to lie down."

4 "What will you will to your old mother, O Ransel, my son?
What will you will to your old mother, my sweet and pretty one?"
"A sick son for to nurse, mother, make my bed soon,
I'm sick to the heart and in pain to lie down."

5 "What will you will to your oldest brother, O Ransel, my son?
What will you will to your oldest brother, my sweet and pretty one?"
"My hounds and my bugle, mother, make my bed soon,
I'm sick to the heart and in pain to lie down."

6 "What will you will to your youngest brother, O Ransel, my son?
What will you will to your youngest brother, my sweet and pretty one?"
"My horse, whip, and saddle, mother, make my bed soon,
I'm sick to the heart and in pain to lie down."

7 "What will you will to your oldest sister, O Ransel, my son?
What will you will to your oldest sister, my sweet and pretty one?"
"My chest and my money, mother, make my bed soon,
I'm sick to the heart and in pain to lie down."

8 "What will you will to your youngest sister, O Ransel, my son?
What will you will to your youngest sister, my sweet and pretty one?"
"My land and my buildings, mother, make my bed soon,
I'm sick at the heart and in pain to lie down."

9 "What will you will to your old sweetheart, O Ransel, my son?
What will you will to your old sweetheart, my sweet and pretty one?"
"The rope and the gallows, mother, make my bed soon,
I'm sick at the heart and in pain to lie down."

E

"Where Have You Been to, My Dear Son?" Sent in by Professor J. M. Grainger. Reported by Miss Evelyn Purcell, of Schuyler, Va. Sung by her mother. Albemarle County. November 20, 1913. Printed in *The Focus* for December, 1913, p. 397.

1 "Where have you been to, my dear son?
Where have you been to, my dear son?"
"Courting, mother, courting, mother; make my bed smooth,
For I'm sick at my heart, and fain would lie down."

2 "What did you have for your supper, my son?
What did you have for your supper, my son?"
"Eel's broth, mother, eel's broth, mother; make my bed smooth,
For I'm sick at my heart, and fain would lie down."

3 "What sort of eel's broth was it, my son?
What sort of eel's broth was it, my son?"
"Black back, mother, speckled breast, mother; make my bed smooth,
For I'm sick at my heart and fain would lie down."

4 "What will you leave to your father, my son?
What will you leave to your father, my son?"
"House and plantation, mother; make my bed smooth,
For I'm sick at the heart and fain would lie down."

5 "What will you leave to your mother, my son?
What will you leave to your mother, my son?"
"Carriage and horses, mother; make my bed smooth,
For I'm sick at my heart, and fain would lie down."

6 "What will you leave to your sister, my son?
What will you leave to your sister, my son?"
"Hook, crook, and a bagnet, mother; make my bed smooth,
For I'm sick at my heart, and fain would lie down."

7 "What will you leave to your brother, my son?
What will you leave to your brother, my son?"
"Horse, saddle, and bridle, mother; make my bed smooth,
For I'm sick at my heart, and fain would lie down."

8 "What will you leave to your sweetheart, my son?
What will you leave to your sweetheart, my son?"
"Brimstone and fire for to burn her heart brown,
For she was the cause of my lying down."

F

"Jonny Rilla." Collected by Mr. John Stone. Sung by Mrs. Ella Wood, of Doylesville, Va. Albemarle County. November 10, 1919. With music.

1 "Where have you been, Jonny Rilla, my son,
Where have you been, my dear little one?"

2 "Courting my sweetheart. Mother, make my bed soon;
I have a pain at my heart and I want to lie down."

3 "Have you been to your supper, Jonny Rilla, my son,
Have you been to your supper, my dear little one?"

4 "I have been to my supper. Mother, make my bed soon;
I have a pain at my heart and I want to lie down."

5 "What did you have for your supper, Jonny Rilla, my son,
What did you have for your supper, my dear little one?"

6 "Fresh eel and butter. Mother, make my bed soon;
I have a pain at my heart and I want to lie down."

7 "What color were the eels, Jonny Rilla, my son,
What color were the eels, my dear little one?"

8 "Black and yellow spotted. Mother, make my bed soon;
I have a pain at my heart and I want to lie down."

9 "They were rattlesnakes, Jonny Rilla, my son,
They were rattlesnakes, my dear little one.[1]

10 "You are going to die, Jonny Rilla, my son,
You are going to die, my dear little one.

11 "What will you will to your sister, Jonny Rilla, my son,
What will you will to your sister, my dear little one?"

12 "Fine horse and saddle. Mother, make my bed soon;
I have a pain at my heart and I want to lie down."

[1] Here the dialogue ceases while the mother speaks three consecutive stanzas.

13 "What will you will to your mother, Jonny Rilla, my son,
What will you will to your mother, my dear little one?"

14 "A sweet home in Heaven. Mother, make my bed soon;
I have a pain at my heart and I want to lie down."

15 "What will you will to your sweetheart, Jonny Rilla, my son,
What will you will to your sweetheart, my dear little one?"

16 "Brimstone and hell-fire to scorch her right brown,
She caused this pain at my heart and I want to lie down."

G

Name unknown. Collected by Dr. Hugh Mercer Blain, Baton Rouge, Louisiana. Sung by his grandmother, Mrs. Susan Isham Blain, in Va. (County unmentioned.) February 24, 1914.

1 "Where have you been to, my dear son?
Where have you been to, my dear son?"
"Courting, mother. Courting, mother. Make my bed warm,
For I'm sick at my heart and fain would lie down."

2 "What did you eat for your supper, my son?
What did you eat for your supper, my son?"
"Eel broth, mother. Eel broth, mother. Make my bed warm,
For I'm sick at my heart and fain would lie down."

3 "What sort of eel broth was it, my son?
What sort of eel broth was it, my son?"
"Black-back, mother. Speckled belly, mother. Make my bed warm,
For I'm sick at my heart and fain would lie down."

4 "What will you leave for your father, my son?
What will you leave for your father, my son?"
"House and plantation, mother. Make my bed warm,
For I'm sick at my heart and fain would lie down."

5 "What will you leave for your mother, my son?
What will you leave for your mother, my son?"
"Carriage and horses, mother. Make my bed warm,
For I'm sick at my heart and fain would lie down."

6 "What will you leave for your brother, my son?
What will you leave for your brother, my son?"
"Horse, saddle, and bridle, mother. Make my bed warm,
For I'm sick at my heart and fain would lie down."

7 "What will you leave for your sweetheart, my son?
What will you leave for your sweetheart, my son?"
"Brimstone and fire, mother. Make my bed warm,
For she was the cause of my lying down."

H

"Johnnie Randolph, My Son." Sent in by Miss Martha M. Davis. Sung by Mr. Edgar J. Steele. Rockingham County. January 20, 1914. "This ballad was taught me by a domestic whose home was in the mountains of West Rockingham" (Edgar J. Steele). "Edgar J. Steele is one of our high school boys. The woman from whom he learned 'Johnnie Randolph' about twelve years ago could scarcely read and write" (Miss Davis, January 20, 1914).

1 "What did you have for your supper, Johnnie Randolph, my son?"
"Eel fried in butter; mother, make my bed soon,
I have a pain on my heart and I want to lie down."

2 "What did you will to your mother, Johnnie Randolph, my son?"
"My love and my kindness; mother, make my bed soon,
I have a pain on my heart and I want to lie down."

3 "What did you will to your father, Johnnie Randolph, my son?"
"My horse, saddle, and bridle; mother, make my bed soon,
I have a pain on my heart and I want to lie down."

4 "What did you will to your brother, Johnnie Randolph, my son?"
"My boots and my clothes; mother, make my bed soon,
I have a pain on my heart and I want to lie down."

5 "What did you will to your sister, Johnnie Randolph, my son?"
"A sweet stay in heaven; mother, make my bed soon,
I have a pain on my heart and I want to lie down."

6 "What did you will to your true love, Johnnie Randolph, my son?"
"Hell-fire and brimstone; mother, make my bed soon,
I have a pain on my heart and I want to lie down."

I

"Billy Randall, or A Rope and A Gallows." Sent in by Professor J. M. Grainger. Collected by Miss Kathleen Hale, of the Farmville Ballad Club. Sung by Mrs. E. W. Hale. Giles County. March 16, 1914. Printed in *The Focus* for March, 1914, p. 100.

1 "Where've you been, Billy Randall,
Billy Randall, my son?
Where've you been, Billy Randall,
My own dearest one?"
"A-courting, a-courting, mother, make my bed down,
For I'm sick to the heart and fain to lie down."

2 "What's the matter, Billy Randall,
Billy Randall, my son?
What's the matter, Billy Randall,
My own dearest one?"
"A potion of poison, mother, make my bed down,
For I'm sick to the heart and fain to lie down."

3 "What's your will for your father,
Billy Randall, my son?
What's your will for your father,
My own dearest one?"
"My land and my houses, mother, make my bed down,
For I'm sick to the heart and fain to lie down."

4 "What's your will for your mother,
Billy Randall, my son?
What's your will for your mother,
My own dearest one?"
"My cattle and horses, mother, make my bed down,
For I'm sick to the heart and fain to lie down."

5 "What's your will for your brother,
Billy Randall, my son?
What's your will for your brother,
My own dearest one?"
"My clothes and my silver, mother, make my bed down,
For I'm sick to the heart and fain to lie down."

6 "What's your will for your sister,
Billy Randall, my son?
What's your will for your sister,
My own dearest one?"
"My books and my treasures, mother, make my bed down,
For I'm sick to the heart and fain to lie down."

7 "What's your will for your sweetheart,
Billy Randall, my son?
What's your will for your sweetheart,
My own dearest one?"
"A rope and a gallows to stretch her neck long!
For she's the occasion for my lying down."

J

"Johnny Reynolds." Collected by Mr. John Stone. Sung by Mrs. M. C. Hurt, of Wytheville, Va. Wythe County. November 8, 1921.

1 "Where have you been,
Johnny Reynolds, Johnny Reynolds, my son?"
"A-hunting for the best, the best that can be found;
Mother, make my bed soon,
I've a pain in my heart and I long to lie down."

2 "What did you have for your supper,
Johnny Reynolds, Johnny Reynolds, my son?"
"Sweetbread and white coffee (*or* fried snakes);
Mother, make my bed soon,
I've a pain in my heart and I long to lie down."

3 "What will you leave to your father,
Johnny Reynolds, Johnny Reynolds, my son?"
"My home and farm to live on;
Mother, make my bed soon,
I've a pain in my heart and I long to lie down."

4 "What will you leave to your mother,
Johnny Reynolds, Johnny Reynolds, my son?"
"Gold and silver to live on;
Mother, make my bed soon,
I've a pain in my heart and I long to lie down."

5 "What will you leave to your sister,
Johnny Reynolds, Johnny Reynolds, my son?"
"Six horses and a coach for her to ride in;
Mother, make my bed soon,
I've a pain in my heart and I long to lie down."

6 "What will you leave to your brother,
Johnny Reynolds, Johnny Reynolds, my son?"
"My dog and gun to hunt with;
Mother, make my bed soon,
I've a pain in my heart and I long to lie down."

7 "What will you leave to your wife,
Johnny Reynolds, Johnny Reynolds, my son?"
"Brimstone and hell-fire to burn her bones brown;
Mother, make my bed soon,
I've a pain in my heart and I long to lie down."

K

"Lord Randall." Collected by Miss Corita Seoane, of Merrifield, Va. Sung by an old Negress. Fairfax County. January 10, 1915.

1 "Where have you been wandering,
Tom Randall, my son?"
"I've been to see my sweetheart."

Chorus

"Mother, make my bed soft;
For I'm sick at my heart,
And I'll freely lie down."

2 "What did you have for your supper,
Tom Randall, my son?"
"Fried eels' heads and butter."

3 "What will you leave your sister
Tom Randall, my son?"
. . . .

4 "What will you leave your sweetheart,
Tom Randall, my son?"
"Hell-fire and brimstone to roast her bones in."

5 "What will you leave her brother,
Tom Randall, my son?"
"The highest gallows that he can swing from." [1]

L

"Lord Randal, My Son." Collected by Miss Juliet Fauntleroy. Sung by Miss Bab Lynch, and her sister Mrs. Creasy, near Altavista, Va. Campbell County. August 29, 1916. "I never heard before that Lord Randal's sweetheart gave him *rattlesnake* and eel broth. That was a dose! And Mrs. Creasy says that although Lord Randal knew his sweetheart had poisoned him, he forgave her and still loved her" (Miss Fauntleroy's letter of September 15, 1916). The bequest of the fine horse and buggy, thus interpreted, indicates a considerable alteration in the story. Its powerful close has been toned down to a more sentimental ending.

1 "Where have you been, Lord Randal, my son?
Where have you been, my dearest little one?"
"I've been to my sweetheart's, mother, make my bed soon,
For I'm sick at my heart, and I want to lie down."

[1] This gives a new turn to the story, indicating the sweetheart's brother as the poisoner, or as the accomplice of the sweetheart herself in the deed. The double curse (stanzas 4 and 5) is unusual.

SOME BALLAD SINGERS OF THE VIRGINIA MOUNTAINS — I

2 "What have you been eating, Lord Randal, my son?
What have you been eating, my dearest little one?"
"Eating rattle and eel broth, mother, make my bed soon,
For I'm sick at my heart, and I want to lie down."

3 "What do you will to your mother, Lord Randal, my son,
What do you will to your mother, my dearest little one?"
"My fine house and home, mother, make my bed soon,
For I'm sick at my heart, and I want to lie down."

4 "What do you will to your sisters, Lord Randal, my son,
What do you will to your sisters, my dearest little one?"
"All of my gold and my silver, mother, make my bed soon,
For I'm sick at my heart, and I want to lie down."

5 "What do you will to your brothers, Lord Randal, my son,
What do you will to your brothers, my dearest little one?"
"All of my fine clothing, mother, make my bed soon,
For I'm sick at my heart, and I want to lie down."

6 "What do you will to your sweetheart, Lord Randal, my son,
What do you will to your sweetheart, my dearest little one?"
"My fine horse and my buggy, mother, make my bed soon,
For I'm sick at my heart, and I'm mighty near gone."

M

"John Elzie." Collected by Miss Martha M. Davis. Sung by Mrs. Rosie Morris, of Elkton, Va. Rockingham County. August 30, 1922.

1 "Where were you last night, John Elzie, my son?
Where were you last night, my dear little one?"
"I was to see my true love;
Mother, make my bed soon,
I've a pain at my heart, and I want to lie down."

2 "Have you been to your supper, John Elzie, my son?
Have you been to your supper, my dear little one?"
"Yes, I've been to my supper," etc.

3 "What had you for supper?"
"Fresh eels fried in butter."

4 "What d' you will to your father?"
"House, stock, and fine building."

5 "What d' you will to your brother?"
"Horse, bridle, and saddle."

6 "What d' you will to your sister?"
"A sweet tree in heaven."

7 "What d' you will to your true love?"
"Hell-fire and brimstone to scorch her so brown."

8 "Where do you want to be buried?"
"Down in the meadow where the grass grows so green."

N

"Lord Randal." Contributed by Miss Alfreda M. Peel, of Salem, Va. Bland County. November 30, 1923. With music.

1 "What will you will to your father, Lord Randal, my son?
What will you will to your father, my dearest sweet one?"
"My horse and my buggy. Mother, make my bed soon,
For I'm sick to the heart, and would freely lie down."

APPENDICES

A

"Lord Randal." Contributed by Miss Adelia Dodge, of the Farmville Ballad Club. Sung by boys from the East Side of New York City. February, 1914.

1 "Where have you been all day, Henry, my son?
Where have you been all day, my loving one?"
"Down at grandma's, down at grandma's!
Make my bed, I've a pain in my head,
And I want to lie down and die."

2 "What did you eat at grandma's, Henry, my son?
What did you eat at grandma's, my loving one?"
"Milk and poison, milk and poison!
Make my bed, I've a pain in my head,
And I want to lie down and die."

3 "What did you leave to your father, Henry, my son?
What did you leave to your father, my loving one?
"Gold and silver, gold and silver!
Make my bed, I've a pain in my head,
And I want to lie down and die."

4 "What did you leave to your mother, Henry, my son?
What did you leave to your mother, my loving one?"
"Silks and satins, silks and satins!
Make my bed, I've a pain in my head,
And I want to lie down and die."

5 "What did you leave to the baby, my son?
What did you leave to the baby, my loving one?"
"A kiss from heaven, a kiss from heaven!
Make my bed, I've a pain in my head,
And I want to lie down and die."

6 "What did you leave to your brother, Henry, my son?
What did you leave to your brother, my loving one?"
"A rope to hang him, a rope to hang him!
Make my bed, I've a pain in my head,
And I want to lie down and die."

B

"Durango." Sent in by Miss Martha M. Davis. From "The Crimson Rambler," Tonkawa, Oklahoma. Sung by the mother of E. A. Rippey. January 14, 1914. "This old ballad was sung to the writer by his mother, while he was a small child. . . . It is clear that some stanzas of the poem have been lost, and the story is rather vague. A child has just returned from a visit to its grandmother who has poisoned it in order to secure an inheritance. As to how this inheritance is to become hers is left to the imagination" (E. A. Rippey, January 14, 1914).

1 "What had you for supper, Durango, my son?
What had you for supper, my darling one?"
"An eel fried in batter; mother, make my bed soon,
For I'm faint and I'm weary, and I want to lie down."

2 "What will you leave mother, Durango, my son?
What will you leave mother, my darling one?"
"A coach and fine horses; mother, make my bed soon,
For I'm faint and I'm weary, and I want to lie down."

3 "What will you leave sister, Durango, my son?
What will you leave sister, my darling one?"
"A box of fine jewels; mother, make my bed soon,
For I'm faint and I'm weary, and I'm almost gone."

4 "What will you leave grandmother, Durango, my son?
What will you leave grandmother, my darling one?"
"A rope for to hang her; mother, make my bed soon,
For I'm faint and I'm weary, and I'm gone, gone, gone!"

7

EDWARD

(CHILD, NO. 13)

THIS ballad, like the preceding, is a colloquy between mother and son. The son has killed some one, usually a father or brother, and the mother by persistent questioning extracts the truth from him. The final stanza in Child usually implicates the mother. All the Virginia texts, however, are strikingly filial: the mother is never cursed or implicated in the murder, nor is the father ever the victim. The tragedy is always fratricidal, with the "little brother" as victim. They are more closely related to Child A than to B, in form, in language, and in the identity of the victim, but the absence of the mother-cursing stanza and her implication in the guilt distinguishes them sharply from all the Child versions. Whether this change is the result of American filial sentimentality or of an unconscious rationalization of a somewhat unnatural conversation, there is some loss of dramatic force at the close. For a man to say that he will be back

When the sun and moon set on yonder hill,
And that will never be

is an inadequate substitute for the compressed meaning when he tells his "ain mither deir" what he will leave her:

The curse of hell frae me sall ye beir,
Sic counceils ye gave to me O.

In Virginia the ballad is usually known by its repeated first line, as "What Is That on the End of Your Sword?" "What Is That on Your Sword So Red?" and "How Come That Red Blood on Your Coat?"

American texts are few. See *Bulletin*, Nos. 2–4, 6, 9, 10; Campbell and Sharp, No. 7 (North Carolina); Hudson, No. 5 (and *Journal*, XXXIX, 93; Mississippi); Pound, *Ballads*, No. 9; Sharp, *Songs*, I, No. 1 (Tennessee); Shearin, p. 4; Shearin and Combs, p. 7; Perrow reported the ballad from Kentucky in a letter to Kittredge (1914).

A

"How Come That Red Blood on Your Coat?" Collected by Mr. John Stone. Sung by Mrs. M. C. Hurt, of Wytheville, Va. Wythe County. November 8, 1921.

1 "How come that red blood on your coat?
Pray, Son John, tell it to me."
"It is the blood of my fine horse
That ran away with me."

2 "How come that red blood on your coat?
Pray, Son John, tell it to me."
"It is the blood of my fine gilligohound [1]
That trailed the track for me."

[1] Cf. *gay gilleon* or *gergilleon* in other versions. Cf. also *greyhound* of Child A.

3 "How come that red blood on your coat?
Pray, Son John, tell it to me."
"It is the blood of my poor little brother
That rode along with me."

4 "What did you and your little brother fall out about?
Pray, Son John, tell it to me."
"We fell out about a chestnut bush
Which you might call a tree."

5 "What will you do when your father comes home?
Pray, Son John, tell it to me."
"I'll set my feet in yonders boat
And sail across the sea."

6 "What will you do with your pretty little wife?
Pray, Son John, tell it to me."
"I'll set her down by my side
And sail across the sea."

7 "What will you do with your sweet little baby?
Pray, Son John, tell it to me."
"I'll set him down betwixt my knees
And sail across the sea."

8 What will you do to get rid of the law?
Pray, Son John, tell it to me."
"I'll set my feet in yonders boat
And sail across the sea."

9 "When will you be back?
Pray, Son John, tell it to me."
"When the sun and the moon set on yonders hill,
And that will never be."

B

"What Is That on the End of Your Sword?" Sent in by Professor James M. Grainger. Collected by Miss Evelyn Purcell, of the Farmville Ballad Club. From the singing of her mother. Albemarle County. November 20, 1913. Printed in *The Focus* for December, 1913, p. 398. The version of Mrs. Susan Isham Blain has been excluded because it is practically identical with this except that it lacks one stanza (5 or 6) and its last stanza begins: "When the red sun sets on yonder hill."

1 "What is that on the end of your sword,
My dear son, tell to me?
What is that on the end of your sword,
My dear son, tell to me?"

"'T is the very blood of an English crane
My father sent to me.
'T is the very blood of an English crane
My father sent to me."

2 "Crane's blood is not so red,
My dear son, tell to me.
Crane's blood is not so red,
My dear son, tell to me."
"'T is the very blood of my dear little brother,
And I wish it had never been.
'T is the very blood of my dear little brother,
And I wish it had never been."

3 "What will your father say to you,
My dear son, tell to me?
What will your father say to you,
My dear son, tell to me?"
"I will put my foot in the bottom of the boat
And sail away to sea.
I will put my foot in the bottom of the boat
And sail away to sea."

4 "What will you do with your pretty little wife,
My dear son, tell to me?
What will you do with your pretty little wife,
My dear son, tell to me?"
"She shall put her foot in the bottom of the boat
And sail away with me.
She shall put her foot in the bottom of the boat
And sail away with me."

5 "What will you do with your dear little boy,
My dear son, tell to me?
What will you do with your dear little boy,
My dear son, tell to me?"
"I will leave him with his grandparents
To make him think of me.
I will leave him with his grandparents
To make him think of me."

6 "What will you do with your sweet little girl,
My dear son, tell to me?
What will you do with your sweet little girl,
My dear son, tell to me?"
"I will leave her to her grandmother
To make her think of me.
I will leave her to her grandmother
To make her think of me."

7 "When do you expect to return again,
My dear son, tell to me?
When do you expect to return again,
My dear son, tell to me?"
"When the sun and the moon set on yonder hill,
And that will never be.
When the sun and the moon set on yonder hill,
And that will never be."

C

"What Is That on the End of Your Sword?" Collected by Miss Martha M. Davis. Sung by Mrs. Archibald Cummins, of Berryville, Va. Clark County. April 23, 1913. With music. "Mrs. Cummins was formerly of Lynchburg (Campbell County), Va. The ballad has been traditional in her family for several generations as a nursery song" (Miss Davis, April 23, 1913).

1 "What is that on the end of your sword,
My dear son, tell to me?"
"'T is the blood of an English crow
And I wish it had never been."

2 "Crow's blood was ne'er so red as that,
My dear son, tell to me."
"'T is the blood of my dear little brother,
And I wish it had never been."

3 "How did it happen,
My dear son, tell to me?"
"'T was digging round the hollow tree,
And I wish it had never been."

4 "What will you do with your dear little son,
My dear son, tell to me?"
"I will leave him with his grandpapa
To make him think of me."

5 "What will you do with your dear little daughter,
My dear son, tell to me?"
"I will leave her with her grandmama
To make her think of me."

6 "What will you do with your dear little wife,
My dear son, tell to me?"
"She will put her foot on yonder boat
And sail away with me."

7 "When will you come back,
My dear son, tell to me?"
"When the sun and moon set on yonder hill
And that will never be."

D

"Edward." Collected by Mr. John Stone. From Mrs. Travers D. Moncure, of Aylett, Va. King William County. September 13, 1917. With music. "Mrs. Moncure learned the song from her mother, who learned it from *her* mother. She has never heard it sung out of her family. She is a direct descendant of Col. William Byrd, of Westover. I imagine that the song has come down directly from old Colonial days" (Mr. Stone).

1 "What is that on your sword so red?
   Dear son, pray tell unto me."
"'T is the blood of a gay gilleon.[1]
   Dear mother, pity me.
'T is the blood of a gay gilleon.
   Dear mother, pity me."

2 "No gilleon's blood was e'er so red.
   Dear son, pray tell unto me."
"'T is the blood of my dear brother.
   O mother, pity me.
'T is the blood of my dear brother.
   O mother, pity me."

3 "What will you do when your father comes home?
   Dear son, tell unto me."
"I'll get aboard of yonder ship
   And sail away to sea.
I'll get aboard of yonder ship
   And sail away to sea."

4 "When will you return, my son?
   Dear son, pray tell unto me."
"When the sun and the moon set on yonder hill,
   And that will never be.
When the sun and the moon set on yonder hill,
   And that will never be."

E

No local title. Collected by Mr. John Stone. Recited by Miss Thelma Stevens, of Igo, Va. King George County. September 11, 1922.

1 "Willie, my son, what have you done,
   With blood all over your clothes?"
He mumbled out with all his might,
   "Been bleeding out of my nose."

[1] "Neither of us knew what a 'gay gilleon' was; so we spelt it as two words. It may be 'gergilleon'" (Mr. Stone).

8

SIR LIONEL

(CHILD, No. 18)

A COMPARISON with the Child texts will show how vastly this ballad has been altered by its American tradition. Child summarizes the composite story of the ballad about as follows:

"A knight finds a lady sitting in (or under) a tree, who tells him that a wild boar has slain (or worried) her lord and killed (or wounded) thirty of his men. The knight kills the boar, and seems to have received bad wounds in the process. The boar belonged to a giant, or to a wild woman. The knight is required to forfeit his hawks and leash and the little finger of his right hand (or his horse, his hound, and his lady). He refuses to submit to such disgrace, though in no condition to resist; the giant allows him time to heal his wounds, and he is to leave his lady as security for his return. At the end of the time the knight comes back sound and well, and kills the giant as he has killed the boar. C and D say nothing of the knight having been wounded. The wild woman, to revenge her "pretty spotted pig," flies fiercely at him, and he cleaves her in two. The last quarter of the Percy copy [which is lost] would, no doubt, reveal what became of the lady who was sitting in the tree, as to which traditional copies give no light."

The Virginia ballad is not so pretentious as this, but it is vigorous and amusing. It limits itself generally to introducing the hunter and telling of his successful encounter with the ferocious wild boar, but one version introduces the lady and has her agree to marry the hunter. The Virginia ballad is much more jovial than its Child fellows. To turn from "Sir Lionel" to "Old Bangum" is to turn from Arthurian romance to semi-burlesqued melodrama in homespun. The Virginia ballad is also known as "Old Bang'em," "Bangum and the Boar," "Bingham," etc. Ferocious as the ballad is, it is often used as a lullaby or nursery song. Note the "cuddle down" of the refrain in Virginia B and D.

For American texts, see Belden, No. 3 (fragment); *Bulletin*, Nos. 3–5, 9; Campbell and Sharp, No. 8 (North Carolina, Virginia); *Journal*, XIX, 235 (Belden, Missouri, fragment); XXV, 175 (Belden, Missouri); XXX, 291 (Kittredge, Missouri, British version); McGill, p. 79; Scarborough, p. 51 (Virginia, text and melody); J. R. Moore, *Modern Language Review*, XI, 396 (two stanzas from Missouri). Note two Virginia texts and two melodies previously printed. For additional references see *Journal*, XXX, 291.

A

"Bangum and the Boar." Collected by Miss Juliet Fauntleroy. Sung by Mr. H. W. Adams, near Altavista, Va. Campbell County. May 24, 1914. With music. With the title compare "Bangrum" and "Bangry Rewey" of Campbell and Sharp versions, p. 28.

1 Old Bangum came riding across the glen,
Dillum, down, dillum.
Old Bangum came riding across the glen,
Kimmy-ko.

Old Bangum came riding across the glen,
He was the bravest of all brave men.
Dillum down, kimmy-ko, kwam.

2 A pretty fair maid came riding astride,
Dillum, down, dillum.
A pretty fair maid came riding astride,
Kimmy-ko.
A pretty fair maid came riding astride,
Old Bangum rode up by her side.
Dillum down, kimmy-ko, kwam.

3 "Oh, pretty fair maid, will you marry me?"
Dillum, down, dillum.
"Oh, pretty fair maid, will you marry me?"
Kimmy-ko.
"Oh, pretty fair maid, will you marry me?"
"Oh, yes, kind sir, I do agree."
Dillum down, kimmy-ko, kwam.

4 "There is a wild hog in this wood,"
Dillum, down, dillum.
"There is a wild hog in this wood,"
Kimmy-ko.
"There is a wild hog in this wood
That'll eat your flesh and drink your blood."
Dillum down, kimmy-ko, kwam.

5 The wild hog came in such a rash,
Dillum, down, dillum.
The wild hog came in such a rash,
Kimmy-ko.
The wild hog came in such a rash
He tore his way through oak and ash.
Dillum down, kimmy-ko, kwam.

6 Old Bangum drew his trusty knife,
Dillum, down, dillum.
Old Bangum drew his trusty knife,
Kimmy-ko.
Old Bangum drew his trusty knife
And deprived the wild boar of his life.
Dillum down, kimmy-ko, kwam.

7 Old Bangum rode to the wild boar's den,
Dillum, down, dillum.
Old Bangum rode to the wild boar's den,
Kimmy-ko.
Old Bangum rode to the wild boar's den
And spied the bones of a thousand men.
Dillum down, kimmy-ko, kwam.

B

"Old Bang'em." Reported by Professor James M. Grainger. Contributed by Miss Evelyn Purcell, of the Farmville Ballad Club. As handed down from her great grandfather, who lived at least 150 years ago. Albemarle County. November 20, 1913. With music. Printed in *The Focus* for February, 1914, p. 48. Note the similarity of the first stanza with the first stanza of the familiar nursery song "A Frog He Would A-wooing Go" (Campbell and Sharp, No. 119; Cox, No. 162).

1 Old Bang'em would a-hunting ride,
Dillem, down, dillem.
Old Bang'em would a-hunting ride,
Dillem down.
Old Bang'em would a-hunting ride,
Sword and pistol by his side.
Cubby, ki, cuddle down,
Killi, quo, quam.

2 "There is a wild boar in this wood,"
Dillem, down, dillem.
"There is a wild boar in this wood,"
Dillem down.
"There is a wild boar in this wood
Will eat your meat and suck your blood."
Cubby, ki, cuddle down,
Killi, quo, quam.

3 "Oh, how shall I this wild boar see?"
Dillem, down, dillem.
"Oh, how shall I this wild boar see?"
Dillem down.
"Oh, how shall I this wild boar see?"
"Blow a blast and he'll come to thee."
Cubby, ki, cuddle down,
Killi, quo, quam.

4 Old Bang'em blew both loud and shrill,
The wild boar heard on Temple Hill.
Cubby, ki, cuddle down,
Killi, quo, quam.

5 The wild boar came with such a rush
He tore down hickory, oak and ash.
Cubby, ki, cuddle down,
Killi, quo, quam.

6 Old Bang'em drew his wooden knife
And swore that he would take his life.
Cubby, ki, cuddle down,
Killi, quo, quam.

7 "Old Bang'em, did you win or lose?"
He swore that he had won the shoes.
Cubby, ki, cuddle down,
Killi, quo, quam.

C

"Old Bangum." Collected by Miss Ellen Dana Conway. Spottsylvania County. November 1, 1915.

1 Old Bangum would a-hunting ride,
Sword and pistol at his side.
Dellum-down dellum.
Old Bangum would a-hunting ride,
Sword and pistol at his side.
Dellum-down, kimmy-quo-quan.

2 There lived a wild boar in the wood,
He'd eat your flesh and drink your blood.
Dellum-down dellum.
There lived a wild boar in the wood,
He'd eat your flesh and drink your blood.
Dellum-down, kimmy-quo-quan.

3 Old Bangum passed the wild boar's den,
He spied the bones of a thousand men.
Dellum-down dellum.
Old Bangum passed the wild boar's den,
He spied the bones of a thousand men.
Dellum-down, kimmy-quo-quan.

4 The wild boar came in such a wrath
He made his way from south to north.
Dellum-down dellum.
The wild boar came in such a wrath
He made his way from south to north.
Dellum-down, kimmy-quo-quan.

5 Old Bangum drew his wooden [1] knife
To deprive him of his life.
Dellum-down dellum.
Old Bangum drew his wooden knife
To deprive him of his life.
Dellum-down, kimmy-quo-quan.

[1] "I have heard it suggested that the hero's knife was properly 'woodsman's' and not 'wooden' but put it down as it is sung" (Miss Conway).

6 They fought nine hours of the day
And then the wild boar ran away.
Dellum-down dellum
They fought nine hours of the day
And then the wild boar ran away.
Dellum-down, kimmy-quo-quan.

D

"Old Bangum." Contributed by Dr. Hugh Mercer Blain and Miss Mary Randolph Blain, of Baton Rouge, La. Sung by his grandmother, Mrs. Susan Isham Blain, of Virginia, about 75 years ago. (No county given.) February 24, 1914.

1 Old Bangum would a-hunting ride,
Dillum down dillum,
Old Bangum would a-hunting ride,
Dillum down,
Old Bangum would a-hunting ride
With sword and pistol by his side.
Cubby rye, cuddle down, rilly quor quam.

2 "There is a wild boar in this wood,"
Dillum down dillum,
"There is a wild boar in this wood,"
Dillum down,
"There is a wild boar in this wood
Will eat your flesh and drink your blood."
Cubby rye, cuddle down, rilly quor quam.

3 "Oh, how shall I this wild boar see?"
Dillum down dillum,
"Oh, how shall I this wild boar see?"
Dillum down,
"Oh, how shall I this wild boar see?"
"Blow a blast and he'll come to thee."
Cubby rye, cuddle down, rilly quor quam.

4 Old Bangum blew both loud and shrill,
Dillum down dillum,
Old Bangum blew both loud and shrill,
Dillum down,
Old Bangum blew both loud and shrill,
The wild boar heard on Temple Hill.
Cubby rye, cuddle down, killy quor quam.

5 The wild boar came with such a rush,
Dillum down dillum,
The wild boar came with such a rush,
Dillum down,
The wild boar came with such a rush,
He tore down hickory, oak, and brush.
Cubby rye, cuddle down, rilly quor quam.

6 "Old Bangum, did you win or lose?"
Dillum down dillum,
"Old Bangum, did you win or lose?"
Dillum down,
"Old Bangum, did you win or lose?"
He swore by blank [1] he had won the shoes.[2]
Cubby rye, cuddle down, rilly quor quam.

E

"Bingham." Contributed by Miss Maria P. Duval, of Staunton, Va. Sung by her mother. Augusta County. March 10, 1914.

1 There was a wild boar lived in the wood,
Dillum, dune, dillum.
There was a wild boar lived in the wood,
He'd eat your flesh and drink your blood,
Dillum, dune,
Killum, kune,
Dillum, dune, dillum.

2 Bingham vowed that he would ride,
Dillum, dune, dillum,
Bingham vowed that he would ride,
Sword and pistol by his side,
Dillum, dune,
Killum, kune,
Dillum, dune, dillum.

3 He fought three hours by the day,
Dillum, dune, dillum.
He fought three hours by the day,
And then the boar he ran away,
Kum-a-ka,
Killum, kune,
Kum-a-ka, kune.

[1] Puritan influence discernible. [2] Metonymy for *spurs?*

F

"Ole Bangum." Contributed by Mrs. Landon Randolph Dashiell and Miss Dorothy Scarborough. Sung by Mrs. Dashiell and in her family for many years. Fauquier County. April 11, 1921. With music. "From years of memory and iteration" (Mrs. Dashiell).

1 "Ole Bangum, will you hunt an' ride?"
Dillum down dillum.
"Ole Bangum, will you hunt an' ride?"
Dillum down.
"Old Bangum, will you hunt an' ride,
Sword an' pistol by your side?"
Cubbi Ki, cuddle dum,
Killi quo quam.

2 There is a wil' bo' in these woods,
Dillum down dillum.
There is a wil' bo' in these woods,
Dillum down.
There is a wil' bo' in these woods,
Eats men's bones an' drinks their blood,
Cubbi ki, cuddle dum,
Killi quo quam.

3 Ole Bangum drew his wooden knife,
Dillum down dillum.
Ole Bangum drew his wooden knife,
Dillum down.
Ole Bangum drew his wooden knife,
An' swore by Jove he'd take his life,
Cubbi ki, cuddle dum,
Killi quo quam.

4 Ole Bangum went to the wil' bo's den,
Dillum down dillum.
Ole Bangum went to the wil' bo's den,
Dillum down.
Ole Bangum went to the wil' bo's den,
An' found the bones of a thousand men,
Cubbi ki, cuddle dum,
Killi quo quam.

5 They fought fo' hours in that day,
Dillum down dillum.
They fought fo' hours in that day,
Dillum down.

They fought fo' hours in that day,
The wil' bo' fled an' flunk away,
Cubbi ki, cuddle dum,
Killi quo quam.

6 "Ole Bangum, did you win or lose?"
Dillum down dillum.
"Ole Bangum, did you win or lose?"
Dillum down.
"Ole Bangum, did you win or lose?"
He swore by Jove he'd won the shoes,
Cubbi ki, cuddle dum,
Killi quo quam.

G

"Sir Lionel." Collected by Mr. Cecil J. Sharp and Miss Karpeles. Sung by Mrs. Betty Smith and Mr. N. B. Chisholm, at Woodridge, Va. Albemarle County. September 28, 1916. With music. Printed by Campbell and Sharp, p. 28.

1 There is a wild boar in these woods,
Dellum down, dellum down,
There is a wild boar in these woods,
He'll eat your meat and suck your blood,
Dellum down, dellum down.

2 Bangum [1] drew his wooden knife
And swore he'd take the wild boar's life.

3 The wild boar came in such a flash
He broke his way through oak and ash.

[1] See Campbell and Sharp, p. 28. *Bangrum* there would seem to be a misprint. It does not appear on the typed carbon sent to Dr. Smith.

9

THE CRUEL MOTHER

(CHILD, No. 20)

THE story of the full ballad is briefly recounted by Child, as follows: "A young woman, who passes for a leal maiden, gives birth to two babes, puts them to death with a penknife, and buries them, or, ties them hand and feet and buries them alive. She afterward sees two pretty boys, and exclaims that if they were hers she would treat them most tenderly. They make answer that when they were hers they were differently treated, rehearse what she had done, and inform or threaten her that hell shall be her portion." The Virginia variants, several of which are mere fragments, omit all antecedent action about the identity of the young man and details of the birth and of the crime. They consist entirely of the dialogue between the cruel mother and the two babes whom she subsequently meets, in which the antecedent action is sufficiently indicated. This absence of preliminary narrative, plus a similarity of refrain, connects the Virginia texts with the Child series K, L, M, N. "The Cruel Mother" seems to be the usual title of the ballad, but it is also known in Virginia as "The Three Little Babes" and "Greenwood Side."

For American texts, see *Bulletin*, Nos. 3–5; Campbell and Sharp, No. 9 (North Carolina, Georgia, Tennessee, Virginia; cf. Sharp, *Songs*, II, No. 1); Cox, No. 5 and p. 522 (3 texts, melody); Jones, p. 301 (fragment); *Journal*, xxv, 183 (Mackenzie, Nova Scotia); McGill, p. 83; Mackenzie, p. 104; Mackenzie, *Ballads*, No. 3, and p. 391 (fragment and melody); Shearin, p. 4; Shearin and Combs, p. 7. For additional references see Cox, p. 29; *Journal*, xxx, 293.

A

"The Cruel Mother." Collected by Miss Juliet Fauntleroy. Sung by Mrs. James B. Crawford, of Altavista, Va. Campbell County. September 11, 1915. With music.

1 As I was going to my father's house,
All along and lonely,
I saw two babies playing with a ball,
Down on the green river sidey.

2 "Oh babes, Oh babes, if you were mine,"
All along and lonely,
"I'd dress you up in scarlet fine,"
Down on the green river sidey.

3 "Oh mother, Oh mother, when we were thine,"
All along and lonely,
"You would not dress us in scarlet fine,"
Down on the green river sidey.

4 "You stuck a pen-knife to our tender little heart,"
All along and lonely,
"And buried us down in brush in the dark,"
Down on the green river sidey.

(*One stanza forgotten here about the mother's grief, Mrs. Crawford says.*)

5 "Oh babes, Oh babes, if you could tell,"
All along and lonely,
"How long on earth have I to dwell?"
Down on the green river sidey.

6 "Seven long years on earth to dwell,"
All along and lonely,
"The balance of your time you'll spend in hell,"
Down on the green river sidey.

B

"The Cruel Mother." Collected by Miss Juliet Fauntleroy. Sung by Mrs. Virgie Keesee (*née* Mayhew). Pittsylvania County. May 26, 1915. With music. "Mrs. Keesee is sixty-three years old and cannot read or write. She says she learned this ballad from her uncle, Henry Dalton, who learned it while on a visit to Tennessee" (Miss Fauntleroy).

1 One day I was setting in my father's hall,
I saw three babes a-playing ball.
All day long and I love you all,
Down by the greenwood side-y, Oh!

2 "Oh, little babes, if you was mine,
I'd dress you up in scarlet fine."
All day long and I love you all,
Down by the greenwood side-y, Oh!

3 "Oh, dear mother, when we was thine
You neither put on our coarse nor fine."
All day long and I love you all,
Down by the greenwood side-y, Oh!

4 "Oh, little babes, if you could tell,
How long on earth have (am) I to dwell?"
All day long and I love you all,
Down by the greenwood side-y, Oh!

5 "Seven long years on earth to dwell,
The balance of your time you'll spend in hell."
All day long and I love you all,
Down by the greenwood side-y, Oh!

C

"The Cruel Mother." Collected by Miss Martha M. Davis, of Harrisonburg, Va. Sung by a mountain woman. Rockingham County. May 9, 1916. With music. "Words and air collected from a woman who learned them from her grandmother, an illiterate old body who died many years ago" (Miss Davis).

1 As Lily was walking out on the strand,
O, lily of the lowlands! [1]
Out come two babes a-playing in the sand,
Down by the greenwood side.

2 "O, little babes, if you were mine,"
O, lily of the lowlands!
"I'd dress you up in silks so fine,"
Down by the greenwood side.

3 "O mother, O mother, when we were thine,"
O, lily of the lowlands!
"You neither gave us coarse nor fine,"
Down by the greenwood side.

4 "You buried us here beneath the ground,"
O, lily of the lowlands!
"You buried us without a sheet or a gown,"
Down by the greenwood side.

D

"Cruel Mother" or "Three Little Babes" or "Greenwood Side." Collected by Miss Corita G. Seoane, of Merrifield, Va. Fairfax County. January 10, 1914.

1 "O Lord, babes, if you were mine
I would dress you up in silk so fine."

2 "False-heart mother, when thee [2] were thine,
You neither dressed us coarse nor fine.

3 "You took a knife both keen and sharp
And pierced it through our little heart.

4 "You dug a grave both wide and deep
And wrapped us in a winding sheet,

5 And buried us a way down in the greenwood side."

[1] The refrain seems to be a significant part of the story.
[2] *Thee* should evidently be *we*, but the manuscript is unmistakable.

Said one old crow unto his mate,
"What for our dinner shall we eat?"
And they all flapped their wings and cried:
  Caw, Caw, caw,
  Billy Magee Magaw.

3 "In yonder field there lies a horse,"
  Billy Magee Magaw,
"In yonder field there lies a horse,"
  Billy Magee Magaw,
"In yonder field there lies a horse,
And we will dine upon his corse."
And they all flapped their wings and cried:
  Caw, caw, caw,
  Billy Magee Magaw.

4 "We'll perch ourselves on his backbone,"
  Billy Magee Magaw,
"We'll perch ourselves on his backbone,"
  Billy Magee Magaw,
"We'll perch ourselves on his backbone,
And pluck his eyes out one by one."
And they all flapped their wings and cried:
  Caw, caw, caw,
  Billy Magee Magaw.

B

"Two Crows." Contributed by Miss Martha M. Davis, of Harrisonburg, Va. Sung generally in her vicinity. Rockingham County. October 5, 1915. "This is quite generally known, and is sung to the air of 'Bonny Doon'" (Miss Davis). The last stanza (cf. D, E) reminds one of the famous sea song "Poor Old Horse," popular in both England and America. For a text and references see Gray, p. 104.

1 There were two crows sat on a tree,
And they were black as they could be.

2 The one crow said unto his mate,
"What shall we do for food to eat?"

3 "There is an old horse on yonders plain
By evil nature lately slain.

4 "We'll pounce upon his old breastbone [1]
And pick his eyes out one by one."

5 "Old horse, old horse, you've carried many passengers,
But soon you'll be ground up and blown into snassengers."

[1] Sometimes *backbone*.

C

"The Three Ravens." Collected by Mr. John Stone. Sung by Mr. W. T. Davis, of Goochland C. H., Va. Goochland County. June 29, 1921. Mr. Stone writes that Mr. Davis got it fifty years ago from a music teacher named Morrison.

1 There were three crows upon a tree
And they were black as crows could be. Skubaugh.[1]

Chorus

They all flew down upon a limb.
They flapped their wings and cried,
Caw, caw, caw. Skubaugh, skubaugh.

2 Said one black crow unto his son,
"Before I'd die, I'd always run." Skubaugh.

3 Said one black crow unto his sister,
"Does mustard always draw a blister?" Skubaugh.

4 Said one black crow unto his aunt,
"Sometimes it can, sometimes it can't." Skubaugh.

5 Said one black crow unto his brother-in-law,
"Please give me a tobacco chaw." Skubaugh.

6 "There is a horse on yonders plain
That very lately has been slain." Skubaugh.

7 "We'll sit upon his old backbone
And pick his eyes out one by one." Skubaugh.

D

"The Three Ravens." Collected by Mr. John Stone. Recited by Mr. R. B. Rouzie, of Tappahannock, Va. Essex County. September 11, 1922.

1 There were three crows sat upon a tree
And they were as black as crows could be.

2 One said unto his mate,
"What shall we do for food to ate?"

3 "There lies a horse on yonders plain
Whose body for three days we have slain.

[1] The Virginia mountain form of *usquebaugh*. "Distilled spirit made by the Celtic people of the British Islands, originally from barley. In this sense the term is still used in Scotland for malt whiskey" (The Century Dictionary and Cyclopedia).

1 Three old crows sat on a tree,
Just as black as crows could be,
Poor old crow . . .

2 The old he-crow says to his mate,
"What shall we do for meat to eat?"
Poor old crow . . .

J

"The Three Crows." Collected by Mrs. J. B. Ferneyhough, of Richmond, Va. Sung by Miss Elizabeth Grubb. Norfolk County. October 15, 1919. With music.

1 There were three crows sat on a tree,
And they were black as crows could be.

2 Said one old crow unto his mate,
"What shall we do for bread to ate?"

3 "There lies a horse in yonder shed
That has been now some three weeks dead.

4 "We'll perch upon his bare backbone
And pick his eyes out one by one."

K

"Three Crows." Contributed by Mrs. J. B. Ferneyhough, of Richmond, Va. Norfolk County. December 2, 1919. With music (differing slightly from J).

1 There were three crows sat on a tree
And they were black as crows could be.

2 Said one old crow unto his mate
"What shall we do for grub to ate?"

3 "There lies a horse in yonder shed
Who has been now some three weeks dead.

4 "We'll perch upon his bare backbone
And pick his eyes out one by one."

L

"The Three Crows." Collected by Mr. John Stone. Sung by an Englishman near Scottsville, Va. Albemarle County. November 10, 1919. Mr. Stone writes: "Nearly twenty years ago I heard an Englishman named Marshall sing this song in the lower part of Albemarle County. I think he came from York or Hull. He lined it off two lines at a time and then sang the words to the tune of 'Bonny Doon.' Two years ago I was telling Dr. J. C. Blair, of

Scottsville, Albemarle County, about it, and he told me that he had heard it sung in the same way to practically the same tune when he was a boy years ago. He did not know Mr. Marshall. Burns wrote 'Bonny Doon' late in the eighteenth century and sang it to the tune of an old Caledonian war-song. Did 'The Three Crows' get its tune from the war-song, or the war-song get its tune from 'The Three Crows,' or did some latter-day wag fit the words to the tune of 'Bonny Doon'? The crow song evidently came from 'The Three Ravens.'"

1 There were three crows sat on a tree,
As black as any crows could be. (All sing.)

2 One of these crows said to his mate,
"What shall we do for food to eat?" (All sing.)

3 "There lies a horse in yonder lane
That has been only three days slain. (All sing.)

4 "We'll sit upon his bare backbone
And pick his eyes out one by one." (All sing.)

M

"The Three Crows." Collected by Mr. John Stone. Recited by a lady in Stafford County. September 11, 1922.

1 There were three crows sat on a tree,
Quack, quack, quack,
As black crows as black could be,
Quack, quack, quack.

2 One black crow said to its mate,
Quack, quack, quack,
"Old horse would make good bait,"
Quack, quack, quack.

N

"The Three Crows." Collected by Mr. John Stone. Sung by Mrs. Wyndham Robertson, of Plasterco, Va. Washington County. November 8, 1921.

1 There were three crows sat on a tree,
Skubaugh.
There were three crows sat on a tree.
They all flew down upon a limb,
They flapped their wings and cried,
Caw, caw, caw,
Skubaugh, skubaugh.

11

THE TWA BROTHERS

(Child, No. 49)

This is one of the very few ballads of which American texts were known to Child, included in the body of his work, and actually commented upon in his head-note. "It is interesting," he says, "to find the ballad still in the mouths of children in American cities,— in the mouths of the poorest, whose heritage these old things are. The American versions, though greatly damaged, preserve the names John and William, which all the other copies have." And in a foot-note he quotes W. W. Newell, who obtained the American version, to this effect: "I have heard it sung at a picnic, by a whole carful of little girls. The melody is pretty. These children were of the poorest class."

The Virginia singers seem to have found no distinctive title for "The Two Brothers." The bulk of the Virginia versions differ from the bulk of the Child versions in that only two of the Virginia texts out of a total of eleven leave even the possibility that the fratricide was accidental. Of the other nine, some leave the stabbing as an outburst of passion, some indicate that the two brothers were in love with the same girl and that jealousy was therefore the motive. This essential point, and others, connect the bulk of the Virginia texts with Child B. The other two may be related to A in this respect, otherwise, especially verbally, to B.

In all of the Virginia texts the age of the "little boys" is incompatible with the rest of the story, the love-affair in particular. Several variants, like Child B and C, conclude the ballad with stanzas taken from "Sweet William's Ghost" (Child, No. 77), but none follows Child D, E, F, G, in supplementing the story with more or less of the ballad of "Edward" (Child, No. 13). As Child C differs in several essential points (accidental killing, the mother's parting anger with the younger son, etc.), we are led back to Child A and B, especially B, for our closest relationship.

The brothers, when not simply older and younger, are John and William, as in Child. The girl, when not merely true-love or little sweetie, is Susie, not Margaret as in Child B.

For American texts, see Barry, No. 33; *Bulletin*, Nos. 3–5, 7, 9, 10; Campbell and Sharp, No. 11 (North Carolina, Virginia); Child, I, 443 (Massachusetts, New York); Cox, No. 7; Hudson, No. 7 (Mississippi); *Journal*, XXVI, 361 (Pound, Nebraska); XXVIII, 300 (Barry, Massachusetts, text and melody); XXIX, 158 (Tolman, Indiana); XXX, 294 (Kittredge, Kentucky, Missouri, both fragments); McGill, p. 55; Pound, *Syllabus*, p. 10 (fragment); Pound, *Ballads*, No. 18; Sharp, *Songs*, I, No. 2 (Kentucky); Shearin, p. 4; Shearin and Combs, p. 7. For additional references see Cox, p. 33; *Journal*, XXIX, 158; XXX, 292.

A

"The Two Brothers." Collected by Mr. John Stone. Sung by Miss Etta Shifflett, of Blackwell's Hollow, Va. Albemarle County. November 10, 1919. With music. "I got this song and its tune from Etta Shifflett, the little daughter of Raz Shifflett, of Blackwell's Hollow. She and her brothers can sing it" (Mr. Stone).

1 There were two brothers in one school.
One evening coming home
The oldest said to the youngest one,
"Let's have a wrestle and fall."

2 The oldest threw the youngest one,
He threw him to the ground,
And out of his pocket he drew a pen knife
And gave him a deadly wound.

3 "Pull off, pull off your woolen shirt
And tear it from gore to gore
And wrap it around your bleeding wound,
And it will bleed no more."

4 So he pulled off his woolen shirt
And tore it from gore to gore,
He wrapped it around his bleeding wound
And it did bleed no more.

5 "Pick me all up upon your back
And carry me to yonder churchyard,
And dig my grave both wide and deep
And gently lay me down."

6 "What must I tell your loving father
When he calls for his son John?"
"Tell him I'm in some lonely green wood
Teaching young hounds to run."

7 "What must I tell your loving mother
When she calls for her son John?"
"Tell her I'm in some graded school,
A good scholar to never return."

8 "What must I tell your loving Susie
When she calls for her dear John?"
"Tell her I'm in my lonely grave,
My books to carry back home."

9 When loving Susie heard of this,
She took her horn and blew;
She charmed the birdies from the nest
And the fishes out of the sea.

4 "False brother, false brother, you have wounded me,
You have wounded me full sore.
There is not a man in this wide world
Can like my brother any more.

5 "Tear my shirt off my back,
And tear it from gore to gore,
And wrop it around those bleeding wounds,
That they may bleed no more."

6 He tore his shirt off of his back,
And tore it from gore to gore,
And wropped it around those bleeding wounds,
That they might bleed no more.

7 "If you see my father as you return home
And he inquires for his son John,
You can tell him I am gone to the king's high gate
To learn to sing and pray.

8 "If you see my mother as you return home
And she inquires for her son John,
You can tell her I am gone to the far-off land
To bring my new book home.

9 "If you see my true love as you return home
And she inquires for her love John,
You can tell her I am buried in the old churchyard,
And it is for her sake I'm gone.

10 "Bury my prayer-book at my head,
My Bible at my feet,
My little hymn-book by my side,
The sounder I might sleep."

11 He buried his prayer-book at his head,
The Bible at his feet,
His little hymn-book by his side,
The sounder he might sleep.

D

"The Two Brothers." Collected by Mr. Cecil J. Sharp and Miss Karpeles. Sung by Mr. Nuel Walton, at Mount Fair, Brown's Cove, Va. Albemarle County. September 28, 1916. With music. Printed by Campbell and Sharp, p. 35.

1 One evening, one evening,
Two brothers gone from school.
The oldest said to the youngest one:
"Let's take a wrastle fall."

2 The oldest threw the youngest down,
He threw him to the ground,
And from his pocket came a penknife
And give him a deathless wound.

3 "Pull off, pull off, your woolen shirt,
And tear it from gore to gore,
And wrap it around this deathless wound
And that will bleed no more."

4 He pulled off his woolen shirt
And tore it from gore to gore,
And wrapped it around this deathless wound
And it did bleed no more.

5 "It's take me up all on your back
And carry me to yonder churchyard,
And dig my grave both wide and deep
And gentle lie me down."

6 "What will you tell your father
When he calls for his son John?"
"You can tell him I'm in some low green woods
A-learning young hounds to run."

7 "What will you tell your mother
When she calls for her son John?"
"You can tell her I'm in some graded school,
Good scholar to never return."

8 "What will you tell your true love
When she calls for her dear John?"
"You can tell her I'm in some lonesome grave,
My books to carry home."

* * * * * *

9 "One sweet kiss from your clay, clay lips
Will bring my day short on."

E

"The Two Brothers." Collected by Miss Juliet Fauntleroy. Sung by Mr. Dan Maxie, of Altavista, Va. Franklin County. May 9, 1914. With music. "Mr. and Mrs. Dan Maxie were originally from Franklin County, and only moved to Altavista two months ago. They are good plain people, of very little education. Mr. Maxie said he learned his songs chiefly from an aunt who had such a sweet voice that the neighbors often used to come in just to hear her sing. He said they all used to sing a great deal at their 'sociables' and parties, and that he was a great singer himself" (Miss Fauntleroy).

G

"The Two Brothers." Collected by Miss Juliet Fauntleroy. Sung by Mrs. James Sprouse (*née* Pribble), of Lawyers, Va. Campbell County. May 29, 1915. "Mrs. Sprouse's explanation of this ballad is that both brothers were in love with the same girl, 'Little Sweetie'; therefore jealousy was the cause of the tragedy. This ballad was also sung for me by Miss Lilian Keesee, daughter of Mrs. Virgie Keesee. But I find less variation in the words and tune of this ballad than in most ballads. The tune has always been exactly the same" (Miss Fauntleroy).

1 Two brothers, dear brothers, walked out one day
To view the chestnut grove.
The youngest had a long, keen knife,
And stove it to the oldest one's heart.

2 "Oh brother, dear brother, take off thine shirt
And wrap my bleeding wound,
And bind them up so neat and strong
That they won't bleed any more.

3 "Oh brother, dear brother, go dig my grave,
Dig it wide and deep;
Place my Bible under my head,
My Testament under my feet,
My sword and pistol by my side,
Just like I was sound asleep.

4 "Oh brother, dear brother, when you go home,
My mother will ask for me;
You may tell her I've gone with some little play-mates
To bear their company home.

5 "Oh brother, dear brother, when you go home,
My father will ask for me;
You may tell him I've gone to London town
To view the chestnut grove.

6 "Oh brother, dear brother, when you go home,
Little Sweetie will ask for me;
You can tell her that I'm buried in the cold, clay ground,
Whose face she will no more see."

H

"The Two Brothers." Collected by Mr. Cecil J. Sharp and Miss Karpeles. Sung by Mrs. Rosie Smith (33), at Charlottesville, Va. Albemarle County. September 20, 1916. With music. Printed by Campbell and Sharp, p. 34.

1 Two brothers they have just returned,
Their pleasures are all sincere.
"I want to see my pretty Susie,
The girl I loved so dear."

2 "You're not the one that loved Susie,
And here I'll slip your blood."
He drew a knife both keen and sharp
And pierced it through his heart.

3 "What will you tell my father dear
When he calls for his son John?"
"I'll tell him you're in the western woods
A-learning your hounds to run."

4 "What will you tell my mother dear
When she calls for her son John?"
"I'll tell her you're in the Tennessee
A lesson there to learn."

5 "What will you tell my pretty Susie
When she calls for true love John?"
"I'll tell her you're in your silent grave,
Where never no more to return."

6 She took her Bible in her hand,
A-moaning (mourning?) she went on.
She moaned till she came to his silent grave,
In search of her true love John.

7 "What do you want, my pretty Susie?
What do you want with me?"
"I want a kiss from your clay cold lips,
'Tis all I ask of thee."

8 "If I were to kiss your rosy cheeks,
My breath it is so strong;
If I were to kiss your ruby lips,
You would not stay here long.

9 "So now go home, my pretty Susie,
And moan no more for me,
For you may moan to Eternity,
My face no more you'll see."

12

YOUNG BEICHAN

(CHILD, No. 53)

IN VIRGINIA the ballad is known as "Lord Bateman," "The Turkish Lady," or as "Lord Bateman and the Turkish Lady." This would indicate, what is indeed the case, that the Virginia variants are closely related to Child L, "The Loving Ballad of Lord Bateman." The story is well known. Lord Bateman, an Englishman of high degree, is discontented and must needs take a sea voyage. He is captured by the Turks and imprisoned. A lady, daughter of his Turkish captor, sees him in prison and is enamored of him. The attraction is mutual, and after they have vowed that for seven long years neither would wed another, she sets him free and he returns home. At the end of this period, having heard nothing of her lover, she sets out to find him. Lord Bateman has just brought home his bride, but when his Turkish love appears he bids the bride's mother take back her daughter, who is none the worse for him, and forthwith he marries the Turkish lady. The Virginia variants, in the main, follow Child L fairly closely, but often they show traces not found in the Child version, such as the hole bored in the captive's shoulder (see other Child versions), the lady's statement that she wants not his gold and silver but only his body, and the naming of India rather than England as the home of the noble lord. There are also certain fairly persistent exclusions, such as the stanza about the tree in the prison (Child L 3) and that about the harbor and the ship of fame (Child L 9). But the likenesses are quite sufficient to prove a common source.

Child says that "'Young Beichan' is a favorite ballad, and most deservedly. There are beautiful repetitions of the story in the ballads of other nations, and it has secondary affinities with the extensive cycle of 'Hind Horn,' the parts of the principal actors in the one being inverted in the other." The story of the ballad, he also points out, agrees in general outline, and also in some details, with a well-known legend about Gilbert Beket, father of St. Thomas, which legend he recounts at length. But his conclusion is, "That our ballad has been *affected* by the legend of Gilbert Beket is altogether likely. . . . But the ballad, for all that, is not derived from the legend."

For American texts, see Barry, No. 12; Brown, p. 9 (North Carolina); *Bulletin*, Nos. 2, 3, 5–9, 12; Campbell and Sharp, No. 12 (North Carolina, Kentucky); Cox, No. 8; Hudson, No. 8 (Mississippi); *Journal*, XVIII, 209 (Barry, Massachusetts); XX, 251 (Kittredge, Kentucky); XXII, 64 (Beatty, Kentucky), 78 (Barry, Pennsylvania, melody only); XXIII, 451 (Barry, Pennsylvania, melody; *The Forget-me-not Songster*, text); XXVI, 353 (Pound, Nebraska, fragment); XXVIII, 149 (Perrow, North Carolina); XXX, 294 (Kittredge, Indiana, West Virginia, North Carolina, all fragments); Mackenzie, p. 115; Mackenzie, *Ballads*, No. 5 and p. 392 (melody); Pound, *Syllabus*, p. 9 (fragment); Pound, *Ballads*, No. 14; Shearin, p. 4 (fragment); Shearin and Combs, p. 7; Reed Smith, No. 3 (text and melody); Reed Smith, *Ballads*, No. 3; Wyman and Brockway, p. 58. For additional references, see *Journal*, XXX, 294.

A

"Lord Bateman." Reported by Miss Edith M. Payne. Collected by Miss Grace Ward. Sung by her grandmother, Mrs. L. G. Davis, as sung by her mother about sixty years ago. Princess Anne County. January 20, 1914.

1 In England lived a noble lord,
His riches were beyond compare,
He was the darling of his parents,
To their estate the only heir.

2 He had gold and he had silver,
He had houses of high degree;
But still he never would be contented
Until a voyage he had been to sea.

3 He sailed east and he sailed west
Until he came to India's shore.
There he was taken and put in prison
Where he could see and hear no more.

4 The jailer had an only daughter,
A gay young lady of airs was she.
As she was walking by the door
She chanced Lord Bateman for to see.

5 She stole the keys of her father's prison,
She said Lord Bateman she would (set) free.
She went unto the prison door
And opened it without delay.

6 "What will you give to the fair lady
If she from bondage set you free?"

7 "I have gold and I have silver,
I have houses of high degree.
I'll give them all to the fair lady
If she from bondage set me free."

8 "It's not your gold nor yet your silver,
It's not your houses of high degree;
All that I crave to make me happy
And all I want is your body.

9 "Let's make a bargain and make it strong,
For seven long years this bargain shall stand.
That you will wed no other woman,
And I will wed no other man."

10 She sailed east, she sailed west,
Till she sailed to Lord Bateman's home,
"Who's there? who's there?" cried the proud young porter,
"Who's there that raps so loud and strong and won't come in?"

11 . . . .
"Is Lord Bateman himself within?"
"Oh yes, oh yes," cried the proud young porter,
"He has just taken his young bride in."

12 "Go tell him of the wine so strong,
Go tell him of the raging sea,
Go tell him of the Turkish lady
That out of prison set him free."

13 "Lord Bateman, there's a lady at your gate,
And she is of high degree.
She wears a ring on her forefinger
And on the other she wears three.

14 "She bade me remind you of the wine so strong,
She bade me tell of the raging sea,
She bade me tell of a Turkish lady
Who out of prison set you free."

15 Lord Bateman rose from his seat
And split his chair into pieces three.
"I'll lose my life for a Turkish lady,
Who out of prison set me free.

16 "Go take away this little bride,
Go take her straight away from me.
She came to me on a horse and saddle;
I'll send her home in a coach and three."

C

"The Turkish Lady, or Lord Bateman." Collected by Miss Corita G. Seoane. Sung by Mrs. Charles A. Wynkoop, of Fairfax, Va. Fairfax County. January 10, 1914.

1 In India lived a noble Lord,
His riches were beyond compare;
He had the fortune of his parents,
Of their estates their only heir.

2 He had gold and he had silver,
He had houses of high degree,
But still he never could be contented
Until a voyage he'd been to sea.

3 He sailed east and he sailed west
Until he came to the Turkish shore,
There he was taken and put in prison
Where he could neither see nor hear.

4 For several months he lay
Lamenting in iron chains;
He happened to see a brisk young lady,
Who set him free from his iron chains.

5 The jailer had an only daughter,
A brisk young lady gay was she;
As she was walking cross the floor,
She chanced Lord Bateman for to see.

6 She stold the keys of her father's prison,
And said Lord Bateman she'd set free.
She went to the prison door
And opened it without delay,

7 Saying, "Have you gold and have you silver?
Have you houses of high degree?
What will you give to this fair lady
If she from bondage should set you free?"

8 "Yes, I've gold and I have silver,
I have houses of high degree.
I'll give it all to this fair lady
If she from bondage shall set me free."

9 "Then let us make a bargain,
For seven long years it shall stand;
You'll not wed no other woman
And I'll not wed another man."

10 When seven years had come and gone,
When seven years were at an end,
Packing all her richest clothing
Said, "Now I'll go and see my friend."

11 She sailed east and she sailed west.
Till she came to England's shore,
She could not be contented
Until Lord Bateman she did inquire,
Lord Bateman's palace and every corner of the street
Of every person she chanced to meet.

12 When she came to Lord Bateman's palace,
She knocked so loud upon the door,
There was no one so ready as the brisk young porter
As to rise and let the fair one in.

10 "She bids you mind of the wine so strong,
She bids you mind of the roaring sea,
She bids you mind of the Turkish Lady
That out of bondage set you free."

11 Lord Bateman rose on hearing this,
His table he did smash in three.
"I owe my life to this Turkish Lady
Who out of bondage set me free.

12 "Go take my bride to her father's hall,
Oh, she is none the worse by me;
Oh, she came here on horse and saddle,
But take her back in coaches fine."

E

"Lord Bateman." Collected by Miss Roxie Martin and Mr. J. M. McManaway. Sung by a Negro woman. Albemarle County. August 4, 1916. "A 'religious' Negro woman sings 'Lord Bateman,' but she says 'The Lord will forgive me for it'" (Miss Martin). Religious antagonism to the ballads is not always removed by such sublime confidence of forgiveness. Moody and Sankey are among the ballad hunter's chief obstacles.

1 Lord Bateman was a noble lord,
A lord of high degree,
He shipped himself on board a ship
To some far country he'd go see.

2 They sailed him east, they sailed him west,
Until he came to a private [1] Turk;
There he was taken in prison
Until his life was almost gone.

3 In this prison there grew a tree,
It grew so stout and strong;
Lord Bateman was chained about the tree
Until his life was almost gone.

4 Now this Turk had a daughter,
The fairest creature his eyes could see;
She stole her father's prison keys
And said, "Lord Bateman I'll set free."

5 She took him to her father's hall,
Gave him drink and favor of wine,
Said, "Farewell, Lord Bateman,
I'll never see you again.

[1] For *pirate.*

6 "But seven long years I'll make a vow,
Seven years I'll keep it strong,
If you'll marry no other woman,
I'll marry no other man."

7 Seven years and fourteen days had past,
Since Lord Bateman went to sea.
She gathered all her gay clothing
And said, "Lord Bateman I'll go see."

8 She walked up to Lord Bateman's gate
And proudly rang the bell.
"Who's there, who's there?" cried the reporter,[1]
"Who's there?" as she appeared within.

9 "Is this Lord Bateman's castle
In which I'll question him?"
"Yes, he's just taken a new bride,
A new bride he's taken in."

10 "Go bid him send me a slice of cake
And a bottle of his very best wine;
Tell him, 'Never forget the fair girl
Who released him from close confine.'"

11 He went to Lord Bateman's room,
Told him there was a lady at the gate
With a ring on every finger
And on one there was three,
With enough gay clothing upon her
To buy the whole Northumberland.

12 Lord Bateman into a great rage flew,
Broke his sword in splinters three.
He said, "I'll give all my father's riches
Since Sophia has crossed the sea."

13 Out spoke the new bride's mother,
Who was never known to speak so free,
"Don't forget my only daughter,
If Sophia has crossed the sea."

14 "I've only made a bride of your daughter,
She's nothing more to me;
She came to me on horse and saddle,
She goes back on a coach and three."

[1] For *porter*.

15 They prepared for another marriage,
Both their hearts were full of glee.
He said, "I'll roam no more in foreign countries
Since Sophia has crossed the sea."

F

"Lord Bateman." Reported by Miss Martha M. Davis. Collected by Mrs. Herbert Cover, of Elkton, Va. From the recitation of a mountain woman. Rockingham County. November 22, 1913.

1 Lord Bateman sailed east, and he sailed west,
He sailed to the Turkey shore,
And there he was put in prison
And expected his freedom no more.

2 The jailor had as fine a daughter
As ever your two eyes did see.
She stole the keys of her father's treasure,
And said, "Lord Bateman I'll set free."

3 She took him to her father's closet,
And there they drank the wine so strong;
And at every health he tooken
He said, "Susan, I wish you were mine."

4 She took him to her father's cellar,
And there they both made bargains free (free bargain?)
That he was to marry no other woman
And she was to marry no other man.

* * * * * *

5 Susanna packed her gold and diamonds,
Likewise her treasures all.
She traveled until she crossed the sea
And came unto Lord Bateman's hall.

6 "Is this where Lord Bateman lives,
And is he at his home?"
"O yes, he's at his wedding table,
Just brought his new bride home."

7 "Tell him to send me a slice of cake,
Likewise a glass of wine,
And tell him not to forget the lady
That freed him from his prison strong."

8 "Lord Poter, here take back your daughter,
She's thought none the less of by me;
For I am going to marry Susanna
Who's lately come across the sea."

G

"Lord Bateman." Collected by Miss Martha M. Davis. From a mountain woman, of Elkton, Va. Rockingham County. January 20, 1914. "This is a supplement to the version of 'Lord Bateman' sent in November [Nov. 22, 1913]. The mountain woman of Elkton who contributed the version already submitted thought some of her friends 'knew more of Lord Bateman than she did.' Accordingly, she sent the enclosed version without explanation" (Miss Davis). It will be noted that this version takes up the story at the third stanza, evidently assuming the first two stanzas of the earlier version. And in addition to being more complete, it differs materially from the earlier version, even in the girl's name — *Sophia* in place of *Susan* or *Susanna.*

1 She took him to her father's palace
And gave to him the best of wine,
And every health that she drank to him
Was, "I wish, Lord Bateman, you were mine.

2 "For seven long years I'll make a vow,
And seven long years I'll keep it strong,
If you will wed no other woman,
I will wed no other man."

3 Then she took him to her father's harbor
And gave him a ship of fame.
"Farewell, farewell to you, Lord Bateman,
I fear I never shall see you again."

4 When seven long years were gone and past,
And fourteen days well known to me,
She packed up her gay gold and clothing
And said Lord Bateman she would see.

5 When she came to Lord Bateman's castle,
So boldly there she rang the bell.
"Who's there, who's there?" cried the young porter,
"Who's there, who's there, unto me tell."

6 "Oh, is this Lord Bateman's castle,
And is his lordship within?"
"Oh, yes, oh, yes," cried the proud young porter,
"He has just now taken his young bride in."

7 "Tell him to send me a slice of cake
And a bottle of the best of wine,
And not forget the fair young lady
That did release him when close confined."

8 Away, away went this proud young porter,
Away, away, away, went he;
Until he came unto Lord Bateman,
When on his bended knees fell he.

9 "What news, what news, my proud young porter?
What news, what news have you brought unto me?"
"Oh, there is the fairest of all young ladies
That ever my two eyes did see.

10 "She has got rings on every finger,
And on one of them she has got three,
And she has as much gold around her middle
As would buy Northumberland of thee.

11 "She tells you to send her a slice of cake,
And a bottle of the best of wine,
And not to forget the fair young lady
That released you when close confined."

12 Lord Bateman in a passion flew,
He broke his sword in splinters three.
"I'll give all my father's wealth and riches
Now if Sophia has crossed the sea."

13 Then up spoke his young bride's mother,
Who never was heard to speak so free,
"Don't you forget my only daughter,
Although Sophia has crossed the sea."

14 "I own I've made a bride of your daughter.
She's none the better or worse for me.
She came to me on a horse and saddle,
And she may go back in a carriage and three."

15 Then another marriage was prepared
With both their hearts so full of glee.
"I'll range no more to foreign countries
Since Sophia has crossed the sea."

H

"The Turkish Lady." Collected by Mr. John Stone. Sung by Mr. George Hart, of Konnarock, Va. Washington County. November 8, 1921.

1 "She bid you mind of the wine so strong,
She bid you mind of the roaring sea,
She bid you mind of the Turkish lady,
Who out of prison set you free."

2 "O take from me this fair young lady,
She is nothing more than a penny to me.
I'll give my life for the Turkish lady
Who out of prison set me free."

I

"The Turkish Lady." Collected by Miss Martha M. Davis. Sung by Mrs. M. Leake, of Harrisonburg, Va. Rockingham County. November 21, 1918. With music.

1 "I sailed east, I sailed west,
I sailed to the Turkey shore,
And there I was taken and put in prison
With hopes of freedom nevermore."

13

THE CHERRY-TREE CAROL

(CHILD, No. 54)

THE finding of the fragment C in Virginia in 1915 was the first evidence that "The Cherry-Tree Carol" still survived in America or had ever existed here in oral tradition. No other collector had reported it in 1915 (see *Bulletin*, No. 4, p. 6; also *Journal*, XXIX, 293 and 294, note).

The source of the carol story is to be found in the Pseudo-Matthew's gospel, chapter XX, which is thus briefly worded by Child: "On the third day of the flight into Egypt, Mary, feeling the heat to be oppressive, tells Joseph that she will rest for a while under the palmtree. Joseph helps her to light from her beast, and Mary, looking up from under the tree, and seeing it full of fruit, asks for some. Joseph somewhat testily expresses his surprise that she should think of such a thing, considering the height of the tree: he is much more concerned to get a supply of water. Then Jesus, sitting on his mother's lap, bids the palm to bow down and refresh his mother with its fruit. The palm instantly bends its top to Mary's feet." Most British versions of the carol alter this original story considerably: the tree is a cherry-tree, as of course it would be in England; Joseph's ill-humored reply is coupled with an insinuation of Mary's infidelity; the babe speaks, not from his mother's lap, but miraculously from her womb, to bring about the miracle which is a rebuke to Joseph; there are additional stanzas prolonging the story and sometimes known independently as "Joseph and the Angel."

In Virginia A, the only Virginia variant that is nearly complete, the first two stanzas are not to be found in any hitherto printed version. From the third stanza onward the ballad proceeds much as the British versions do through Child A 9, B 8, C 7, D 6, of course with differences of detail. The latter portion about the angel, found in all the British versions, is absent from the Virginia version. The other Virginia fragments, B and C, follow Child B and A, respectively, fairly closely. The melody is simple, but captivating.

An interesting letter from Miss Martha M. Davis, one of the staunchest Virginia collectors, concerns this ballad. Temporarily residing at Winthrop College, Rock Hill, S. C., she writes, as of February 21, 1921: "A few months ago several of the teachers here went to hear a Negro preacher one night, a picturesque exhorter of the old type. They came back with a marvelous story (to them) of Joseph and Mary Virgin pickin' cherries from a cherry tree, a part of the gospel story according to the preacher. Well, old ballads are often found in strange company." For other Negro utilizations of old ballad material, see Scarborough, Chapter II, and the head-note to No. 27 of this volume.

For American texts, see *Bulletin*, Nos. 4, 5; Campbell and Sharp, No. 13 (North Carolina); *Journal*, XXIX, 293 (McGill, Kentucky); McGill, p. 60; Pound, *Ballads*, No. 19; Scarborough, pp. 60–61; For additional references, see *Journal*, XXX, 297.

A

"Cherry Tree Carol." Reported by Miss Juliet Fauntleroy. Contributed by Miss Agnes O'Halloran, of Lynchburg, Va. Sung by her mother (*née* Margaret Shannahan), of County Clare, Ireland. Campbell County. January 22, 1916. Miss O'Halloran writes: "These ancient carols were learned seventy or seventy-five years ago in the south of Ireland, in sweet County Clare, where the silver Shannon flows. The neighbors brought their flax spinning wheels and cards and knitting, and whiled away the hours of labor by folk stories and old ballads and carols that took the peculiar coloring of the people's devotion to our Blessed Lady. Both of these carols are equally old and traditional." Mrs. O'Halloran was born in 1834, in the Parish of Cratloe, County Clare, but came to Virginia to live before the Civil War. The ballad is therefore Virginian by adoption, as well as by transmission to the daughter in Virginia.

1 "Lie down, Lady Mary,
And take a long sleep,
I am going to Jerusalem,
My sins for to weep."

2 Said Mary to Joseph,
So mild and so low,
"I'll go along with you, Joseph,
Wherever you go."

3 As Mary and Joseph
Were walking the green,
Said Mary to Joseph,
So mild and serene,
"Joseph, pull me a cherry,
I am surely with child."

4 Said Joseph to Mary,
So stubborn and unkind,
"Let the father of your baby
Pull cherries for you."

5 Well bespoke our blessed Saviour,
In his mother's womb,
"Cherries, bow down
Till my mother gather of you."

6 The highest of branches
Bowed down to the ground,
Mary gathered cherries
Till her apron overflowed.

B

"The Cherry-Tree Carol." Collected by Mr. John Stone. Sung by a Negro woman. Culpeper County. November 15, 1916. With music.

Joseph was an old man,
An old man was he;
And he married Mary,
The queen of Galilee.

C

"The Cherry-Tree Carol." Contributed by Miss Ellen Dana Conway. Sung by an old Negro nurse. Spottsylvania County. November 1, 1915. "I notice in the list you sent a ballad called 'The Cherry Tree Carol,' and I remember to have heard it sung when I was very young by just one person, my old Negro nurse, who has been dead for years. I can remember only the opening lines, which ran thus [as below]. This woman had been born a slave, and had originally belonged to the Graves family in Orange County. She may have heard it in that county, or in Spottsylvania, but unluckily there is no way of finding it out now. At least it proves that the ballad existed in Virginia within the last twenty-five years; and it may be yet lingering in either or both of the counties mentioned." (Extract from Miss Conway's letter of November 1, 1915.)

Joseph was an old man,
And an old man was he,
What time he married Mary
Way down in Galilee.

14

DIVES AND LAZARUS

(CHILD, No. 56)

THE text and melody here given are the only version of this ballad known to survive in America. No other collector has hitherto reported it from any state. This was the final ballad added to the Virginia collection. With it the Virginia Folk-Lore Society attained the objective it had arbitrarily set for itself at the time of its founding as the mark to be reached before it should publish its findings. The survival of more than fifty ballads in the state was felt to be exceedingly doubtful. The fiftieth ballad, however, was already in the archives, though it had not been counted. This was in reality the fifty-first.

The Virginia version differs entirely, except in the bald outline of the Biblical story, from the Child versions. The difference of language is just about complete. The Virginia text appears to be somewhat damaged in this respect. Its language here and there is certainly not the usual ballad language; note "condition," "damnation," "compassion," "communication," "persuaded." Rhyme has been almost completely lost, except in the first stanza. The moralistic close is also a bit stronger and more scriptural than in the Child texts. But it is a good vigorous ballad, with an impressive tune.

The only American reference would be to *Bulletin*, No. 12, p. 3, where the recovery of this item was first announced.

"Lazarus and Dives" or "The Rich Man Dives." Collected by Mr. Ben C. Moomaw, Jr. Sung by Mr. Sam Pritt, of Barber, Va. Alleghany County. November 28, 1924. With music.

1 There was a man in ancient times,
Dressed in purple and fine linen;
He ate, he drank, but scorned to pray,
Spent all of his days in sinning.

2 Poor Lazarus lying at his gate,
All helpless in his condition,
He asked the crumbs fell to the floor,
That fell from his rich table.

3 But not one thing would he bestow
To help him in his condition.
The dogs took pity and licked his sores,
More ready to relieve him.

4 At length it came the poor man died,
And angel bands surrounding,
Away to Abraham's bosom flies,
Where all his troubles ended.

5 At length it came the rich man died
In his horrible condition;
In hell he lifted up his eyes,
In hell in his damnation.

6 Seeing Lazarus lying afar off
All safe in Abraham's bosom,
"Father Abraham, have compassion on me,
Send Lazarus with cold water.
For I am tortured in these flames,
Oh, in an endless torture."

7 "Oh, don't you remember when on earth,
And at your gate a-lying,
He asked the crumbs fell to your floor,
That fell from your rich table?

8 "But not one thing would you bestow
To help him in his condition.
Besides there is an endless gulf
Cuts off all communication."

9 "Father Abraham, one more request
And I'll confine myself to torture;
Send Lazarus to earth my five brethren to warn,
They're going fast to ruin."

10 "There's Moses and the prophets too,
By them to be persuaded;
If one were risen from the dead
They would not be persuaded."

15

FAIR ANNIE

(Child, No. 62)

Only two other texts of this touching ballad have been reported in America, a fragment printed by Campbell and Sharp (No. 14, p. 45), found in North Carolina, and a complete version from West Virginia, printed by Combs, p. 129. The Virginia text is in a very good state of preservation, is, indeed, an excellent ballad. The story as given by Child but without all variations and references, is this:

Annie was stolen from home in her childhood by a knight from over sea, to whom she has borne seven sons, out of wedlock. Her consort bids her prepare to welcome a bride, with whom he shall get gowd and gear; with her he got none. But she must look like a maid, comb down her yellow locks, braid her hair. Annie meekly assents, for love (or for other reason). Annie receives the bride and her train and serves the tables, suppressing her tears and drinking water to keep her cheek from paling. She passes for servant or housekeeper. . . . When the married pair have gone to their bed-chamber, Annie, in a room near by, bewails her sad lot in song, to the harp or her virginals. The bride hears the lament, . . . goes to Fair Annie's chamber to see what gars her greet, inquires her parentage, and discovers that they are sisters. The bride, who had come with many well-loaded ships, gives all or most of them to her sister, and goes virgin home.

The Virginia text, while not particularly like any Child version in wording, perhaps shows its closest relationship to A, the "Lord Thomas and Fair Annie" first printed by Scott in his *Minstrelsy of the Scottish Border*, II, 102, 1802, as is shown particularly by the identity of the man's name, which both versions probably take over from "Lord Thomas and Fair Annet" (Child, No. 73). But the thirty-one stanzas of the Child text have been reduced to thirteen in the Virginia version, without the loss of a single essential detail. The Virginia and North Carolina texts are much more closely related verbally, and also in the bride's concluding suggestion of punishment for Lord Thomas, a detail not found in any Child text. The North Carolina variant suggests burning, the Virginia, hanging.

An especially interesting verbal similarity of the American texts, again not found in the Child versions, is the expression, "She looked *all under the sun*," which plainly means "looked all round," that is, to the four points of the compass. For other examples of the expression and a fuller discussion of it, see the article by C. Alphonso Smith in *Modern Language Notes*, 1922.

Comparison seems to show for the American texts a common source which is not shared by any Child version, with the possible exception of A. The lyric beauty of the ballad, on which Child has commented, is well sustained by the Virginia text and melody.

"Fair Annie." Collected by Mr. John Stone. Sung by Mrs. Martha Elizabeth Lethcoe, of Damascus, Va. Washington County. September 2, 1921. With music. "I called on Mrs. Lethcoe after supper. She said she knew a little of the ballad; but having gotten a start, she kept on. Darkness came on;

writing was difficult; but for fear of breaking her train of thought, I kept on. I wrote the last stanza without seeing it, taking a whole page of my notebook" (Mr. Stone).

1 "Comb back your hair, Fair Annie," he said,
"Comb it back into your crown,
For you shall look a fair maid's life
When I bring my bridal [1] home."

2 "How can I look a fair maid's life,
A maid all in her bloom,
When six fair sons I've had for you
And another yet to come?"

3 On the back door he hung a silk towel,
Hanging on a silver pin,
For Fair Annie to wipe her eyes
As she passed out and in.

4 Six months being gone and nine coming on,
Fair Annie thought the time long;
She took her spy glass in her hand
And up her bower she ran.

5 She looked east, she looked west,
She looked all under the sun,[2]
And she saw Lord Thomas
Bringing his bridal home.

6 "You are welcome, Lord Thomas," she said,
"You are welcomed home by me;
You and your men, your merry men
Are all as welcome as one."

7 She waited on them all day long
With strong brew ale and wine;
She taken herself of cold well water
To keep her spirits mild.

8 She waited on them all day long,
Fair Annie thought the time long;
She takened her flute in her hand
And up her bower she run.

9 She fluted east, she fluted west,
She fluted loud and shrill;
She wished her seven sons were seven grey hounds,
And her a wolf on the hill.

[1] For *bride*, probably substituted for metrical reasons. Compare *briden* of Campbell and Sharp text.

[2] See head-note to this ballad.

10 "Come down stairs, Fair Annie," she says,
"Come down stairs," says she.
"Tell me the name of your father dear
And I'll tell mine to thee."

11 "Prince Douglas [1] was my father's name,
Queen Chatten [2] was my mother,
King Henry was my brother dear,
Queen Mary was my sister."

12 "If Prince Douglas was your father dear,
Queen Chatten was your mother,
King Henry was your brother dear,
I'm sure I am your sister.

13 "I have seven ships sailing on the sea,
All loaded to the brim;
Six of them I'll give to you,
If you'll have Lord Thomas hung;
Six of them I'll give to you,
And one will carry me home."

[1] Cf. *Quince Dudley* of Campbell and Sharp text.
[2] Cf. *Queen Catherine* of Child B, and *Queen Chatry* of Campbell and Sharp text.

16

LADY MAISRY

(Child, No. 65)

The two bare fragments here given, found by a single collector in the same neighborhood in Virginia, are the shrunken remains of this ballad in America. No other collector has reported it on this continent.

The full story of the ballad is called for, to eke out these scattered crumbs. Child summarizes the moving story thus: "Lady Maisry rejects the suit of all the lords in the north country; she has given her love to an English lord. . . . It is discovered that Maisry goes with bairn. Her brother, or father, informed to this effect, requires her to renounce her English lord, but she refuses; her father offers her the choice of marrying an auld man or burning (in one version). In the other versions the family set about preparations for burning her without attempting any arrangement. Maisry, warned of her approaching fate, calls for a boy to carry word to England, and a light-footed and heartily devoted young messenger takes her errand. The English lord asks if his biggins are broken, his towers won, or is his lady lighter, and is told that his lady is to be burnt for him that very day. Horses are instantly saddled: a black, a brown, are foundered, a milk-white (a dapple-gray), fair fall the mare that foaled that foal! holds out. . . . Maisry, in the flames, hears her lover's horn, hears his bridle ring. 'Beet on!' she cries; 'I value you not one straw. Mend up the fire, brother; I see him coming that will soon mend it up to thee.' (In two versions), she cries out when her lover appears, that if her hands had been free she would have cast out his young son. He leaps into the fire for a last kiss; her body falls apart. He threatens an awful retaliation: he will burn father and mother, and the chief of all her kin (who, no doubt, had been concerned in this auto da fé). Vengeance glutted, he will throw himself into the flames." It is added that "the regular penalty for incontinence in an unmarried woman, if we are to trust the authority of romances, is burning."

In the Virginia fragment A, the heroine's name is Margerie, as in Child D, E, F, G, J, K, but the wording of the six lines corresponds very closely with Child B, the last two lines of stanza 5 and the whole of stanza 6. The resemblance to Child C, stanzas 1 and 2, is almost as close. The Virginia B stanza has only with some hesitation been assigned to this ballad at all, on the assurance of the collector that it came from the same neighborhood as A and was given to her as a part of the same song. It is quite similar to Child B 13, C 7, E 9, F 14, G 6, J 8, K 8, but a like stanza appears in several other ballads, notably in "Little Musgrave and Lady Barnard" (Child, No. 81). But there is no reason for refusing to accept Miss Peel's identification.

The two fragments taken together are a very pitiful remainder of a stalwart ballad, but they are at least evidence, and the only evidence so far presented, that this ballad survives in America.

See *Bulletin*, No. 11, p. 5, for the original announcement of this find.

SOME BALLAD SINGERS OF THE VIRGINIA MOUNTAINS — II

A

"Lady Maisry." Collected by Miss Alfreda M. Peel. Sung by Miss Isobel Nicewander, of Bland, Va. Bland County. September 3, 1923.

1 . . . .
. . . .
"How now, how now, little Margerie,
You'll soon become a whore."

2 She said, "I am no whore,
And never will be; [1]
I'm with child by an English lord,
And hope he will marry me."

B

"Lady Maisry." Collected by Miss Alfreda M. Peel. Sung by Mrs. Rosa Tickle, of Bland, Va. Bland County. September 3, 1923.

When he got to the river
He smote his breast and swum,
And when he got to dry land
He took to his heels and run.

[1] Variant line: "And never wanted to be."

17

YOUNG HUNTING

(CHILD, NO. 68)

THE hero, who is usually Lord Henry, returning from the hunt, is courteously invited in for the night by his mistress, who is usually Lady Margaret. Lord Henry refuses the invitation rather brusquely, saying that another lady whom he loves more than he loves her is awaiting him. As he leans over to kiss her good-bye, Lady Margaret wounds him sorely with a little pen-knife. In the conversation that ensues, he indicates that he really loves Lady Margaret. He dies, and Lady Margaret, sometimes with the help of her maids whom she offers to reward for silence, throws his body into a deep well. Her parrot speaks accusingly to her, and she tries to cajole the bird with promises, then threatens it, but to no avail. The wily parrot is not to be deterred, and presumably betrays her guilt.

Here the Virginia texts end, as does Child F. They do not go ahead, like Child A and other fuller versions of the ballad, to the coming of the king's duckers, their finding of the body by candle light after a hint from the bird, the lady's protestations of innocence and her attempt to throw the guilt on one of her maids, the trial by fire, which leaves the maid unscathed but consumes the guilty lady.

The names and title of Virginia A, "Lord Barnet and Fair Eleonder," seem to be borrowed partly from "Little Musgrave and Lady Barnard (Barnett)" (Child No. 81) and partly from "Lord Thomas and Fair Ellinor" (Child, No. 73). "Proud Lady Margaret," "Lord Henry," sometimes "Love Henry," and "Sir Henry and Lady Margaret," are the titles more properly its own.

A point of special interest in these Virginia variants is their obvious contamination with stanzas from "Lady Isabel and the Elf-Knight" (Child, No. 4). Note the stanzas about the bird in all texts, and also stanza 8 of Virginia E. E has also many interesting verbal expressions.

A, B, C, D are all excellent ballads, well preserved. The four tunes are also good, especially the strangely wild hunting tune of B.

For American texts, see Barry, No. 18; *Bulletin*, Nos. 5–7, 10; Campbell and Sharp, No. 15 (North Carolina, Georgia, Virginia); Cox, No. 9; Hudson, No. 9 (Mississippi); *Journal*, XVIII, 295 (Barry, Vermont, melody only); XX, 252 (Kittredge, Kentucky); XXX, 297 (Kittredge, Kentucky, text and melody, Missouri, Indiana); Reed Smith, No. 4 (text and melody); Reed Smith, *Ballads*, No. 4; Sandburg, p. 64 (North Carolina); Sharp, *Songs*, I, No. 3 (Kentucky); Shearin, p. 3; Shearin and Combs, p. 8. For additional references, see Cox, p. 42; *Journal*, XXX, 297.

A

"Lord Barnet and Fair Eleonder." Collected by Mrs. Henry Semones, of Roanoke, Va. Smyth County. December 2, 1917.

1 Lord Barnet he went out a-hunting,
A-hunting he did ride,
With his hunting horn around his neck
And his broadsword by his side.

2 He rode till he came to fair Eleonder's hall,
He tinkled at the ring;
There was none so ready as fair Eleonder
To rise and let him in.

3 "Come light, come light, Lord Barnet," she said,
"And tarry with me all night;
And you shall have both candle and coal
And fire a-burning bright."

4 "I cannot light nor I will not light,
And I cannot light at all;
For there is a ten times fairer lady than you
Sitting in Lord Barnet's hall."

5 He stooped over out of his saddle,
Thinking to kiss her so sweet;
But she having a little pen-knife
She ran him very deep.

6 "What have you done, fair Eleonder?" he said,
"What have you done to me?
You have killed your own sweet
Who loved you so dear."

7 "Come live, come live, Lord Barnet," she said,
"Come live just one hour,
And all the doctors in the town
They shall be at your bower."

8 "I cannot live and I will not live,
And I cannot live at all,
For don't you see my own heart's blood
Down on the ground doth fall?"

9 She called up her maidens all
Three hours before it was day.
"Lord Barnet he lies here in my bower;
I want to get him away."

10 Some took him by his lily-white hands,
Some took him by his feet,
And they threw him into yon deep well
Which was fifty fathoms deep.

11 "Lie there, lie there, Lord Barnet," she said,
"I hope you may not swim;
That ten times fairer lady than me,
I'm afraid she might you win."

12 Then up jumped a pretty little bird
And sit upon a briar,
"Go home, go home, false lady," it said,
"And pay your maids their hire."

13 "Come here, come here, my pretty little bird,
And sit upon my hand,
And you shall have a cage of the beaten gold
And hung under yon ivory (willow) tree."

14 "I cannot come and I will not come,
And I can't come off of this briar;
For I know very well you would kill me
As you have done the worthy squire."

B

"Sir Henry and Lady Margaret." Collected by Miss Alfreda M. Peel. Sung by Mrs. Witt, of Salem, Va. Roanoke County. February 9, 1919. With music.

1 Late last Friday night,
When Margaret was going to bed
She heard the sound of a bugle horn,
Which made her heart full glad.

2 She thought it was Sir Henry
Returning from his wild hunting,
With a sword and pistol by his side,
And a bugle horn 'round his neck.

3 "Get down, get down, Sir Henry,
And stay all night with me;
I'll give to you my silver and gold
To spend at your command."

4 "I won't get down, I won't get down,
Nor stay all night with thee;
There is a bonny lass in a merry green land
That's longing for my return."

5 Bending over his precious beast,
He gave her kisses three;
And holding a knife in her right hand
She pierced him to his heart.

(*Here two stanzas have been forgotten.*)

6 Some took him by his feet and hands,
Some by his long yellow hair,
And throwed him in the wild waters
Which run both wide and deep.

7 "Lay there, lay there, Sir Henry,
Till the flesh rots off your bones.
And the bonny lass in the merry green land
Shall long for your return."

8 Then sitting over her head
Her parrot sang in a tree,
"How could you murder your own true love,
When you then I did see?"

9 "Come down, come down, my pretty parrot,
And sit in my right hand.
I'll give to you a cage of gold
To hang in a willow tree."

10 "I won't come down, I won't come down,
Nor sit in your right hand;
For if you would murder your own true love,
The sooner you'd murder me."

11 "I wish I had my bow to bend,
My arrow and my string;
I would pierce you to your heart so deep
That you would no more sing."

12 "I wish you had your bow to bend,
Your arrow and your string;
I would fly from tree to tree,
You'd always hear me sing."

C

"Proud Lady Margaret." Collected by Miss Roxie Martin and Mr. J. M. McManaway. Sung by a woman of Blackwell's Hollow, Va. Albemarle County. June 1, 1917.

1 As Lady Margaret was going to bed
She heard a musical horn,
It made her heart feel glad and sad
To think it was her brother John
Returning from his ring.
But who should it be but her true love Hannaree
Coming in from his wild hunting.[1]

2 "Oh light! oh light, love Hannaree,
And stay all night with me
And you shall have the cheers of a cheery cold girl,
The best I can give thee."

3 "Oh, I will not light, I shall not light
And stay all night with thee.
For there is a girl in the merry green lea
I love far better than thee."

4 As he stooped over her soft pillow
To give her a kiss so sweet,
With a pen-knife in her right hand
She wounded him awful deep.

5 "Woe be! woe be! Lady Margaret," he cried,
"Woe be, woe be to thee!
For don't you see my own heart's blood
Come trickling down my knee?"

6 She called unto a maid of hers,
"Keep a secret, keep a secret for me,
And all of these fine robes on my body
Shall always belong to thee."

7 One took him by his long yellow hair,
And the other by his feet;
They threw him into a well of water
Which was so cold and deep.

8 "Lie there, lie there, love Hannaree,
Till the flesh rots off your bones,
And that pretty girl in the merry green lea
Will think long of your coming home."

[1] For the irregularity of stanza 1, compare the Sharp variant following, Virginia D.

9 Up spoke, up spoke a pretty little parrot
A-sitting on a willow tree:
"There never was a girl in narry green lea
He loved half as well as thee."

10 "Come down, come down, my pretty parrot,
And sit upon my knee,
And your cage shall be made of pure, pure gold,
Instead of a willow tree."

11 "I won't come, nor shan't come
And sit upon your knee;
For you have murdered your true love Hannaree,
And sooner you'd kill me."

12 "If I had my arrow in my hand,
My bow on tuneful string,
I'd shoot a dart within your heart
So you could no longer sing."

13 "If you had your arrow in your hand,
Your bow on tuneful string,
I'd take flight and fly, fly away,
And tune my voice to sing."

D

"Young Hunting." Collected by Mr. Cecil J. Sharp and Miss Karpeles. Sung by Mrs. Orilla Keeton, at Mount Fair, Brown's Cove, Va. Albemarle County. September 28, 1916. With music. Printed by Campbell and Sharp, p. 50.

1 As Lady Margret was a-going to bed
She heard a sound of a musical horn,
Which made her heart feel glad and sad
To think that it was her brother John, brother John,
Coming in from his wild hunt.
But who should it be but her true love Henery
Returning from his king.

2 "O light, O light, love Henery,
And stay all night with me,
And you shall have the cheers (*or* chairs) of the cheer (*or* cheery) gold (*or* cold) girl,
The best I can give you."

3 "I will not light and I shall not light
To stay all night with thee,
For there's a pretty girl in Merry Green Lee
I love far better than thee."

4 He bended over her soft pillow
And gave her a kiss so sweet,
But with a pen-knife in her right hand
She wounded him in full deep.

5 "Woe be, woe be, Lady Margret," he cried,
"Woe be, woe be to thee;
For don't you see my own heart's blood
Come twinkling down my knee?"

6 She called unto a maid of hers;
"Keep a secret, keep a secret on me.
All these fine robes on my body
Shall always be to thee."

7 One taken him by his long yellow hair
And the other one by his feet,
And they threw him into the well waters
Which was so cool and deep.

8 "Lie there, lie there, love Henery,
Till the flesh rots off your bones,
And that pretty girl in Merry Green Lee
Thinks long of your coming home."

9 Up spoke, up spoke a pretty little parrot
Exceeding [1] on a willow tree:
"There never was a girl in Merry Green Lee
He loved so well as thee."

10 "Come down, come down, my pretty little parrot,
And sit upon my knee,
And you shall have a cage of a pure, pure gold
Instead of the willow tree."

11 "I won't come down, nor I shan't come down
To sit upon your knee;
For you have murdered your true love Henery,
More sooner you would kill me."

12 "If I had my arrow in my hand,
My bow and tuneful string,
I'd shoot a dart that would win your heart,
So you could no longer sing."

13 "If you had your arrow in your hand,
Your bow and tuneful string,
I'd take a flight and fly, fly away
And tune my voice to sing."

[1] For *a-sitting?*

ℰ

"Lord Henry." Collected by Miss Alfreda M. Peel, of Salem, Va. Giles County. April 23, 1922. With music. This fragment contains many interesting expressions such as "wild match woods," "wounded Lord Henry for lee," "ride under the sun," "fairly dame," which justify its inclusion here. The final stanza comes directly from "Lady Isabel and the Elf-Knight" (Child, No. 4).

1 "Come in, come in, Lord Henry," said she,
"And stay this night with me."
"I won't come in, nor I won't sit down,
I have not a moment's time."

2 "Away, away to the wild match woods,
Is where you stayed last night."

3 He reached down over to kiss her white cheek.
. . . .
She had a pen-knife in her hand.
She wounded Lord Henry for lee.

4 "You'll neither ride east, you'll neither ride west,
You'll neither ride under the sun.
There's never a doctor that has lungs,
Can cure what I have done."

5 She picked him up by his coal-black hair,
And also by his feet;
She pitched him into a deep draw-well,
Sixteen fathoms deep.

6 "Lie there, lie there, Lord Henry," said she,
"And let your blood run cold;
You've rode your last to the wild match woods
To see that fairly dame."

7 She hung her love on a green willow
Three hours before it was day.

8 "Turn your back, turn your back, turn your back," says she,
"You might as well be there as me.
Your clothes are not a bit too fine
To rot in the salt, salt sea."

F

"Young Hunting." Collected by Mr. John Stone. Sung by Mrs. Brice Walton, at Mount Fair, Va. Albemarle County. November 10, 1919. With music. Compare the Sharp text and melody (Virginia D) from the same place.

As Lady Margaret was going to bed,
She heard the sound of a musical horn,
Which made her heart feel glad and sad
To think that it was her Brother John, Brother John,
Coming in from his wild hunt.
But who should it be but her true love Henery,
Returning from his king?

18

LORD THOMAS AND FAIR ANNET

(CHILD, No. 73)

THE three lovely ballads that follow (Nos. 18, 19, and 20) are so closely akin and so frequently blended with one another that it will be well to mention their distinguishing marks in advance. All are concerned with the tragedy that follows in the wake of the betrayal or too long deferring of true love. In 18 and 19 the man loves one woman but marries another, for her money or following the advice of friends or family. In 18 the true love comes to the wedding and outshines the bride, who kills her through jealousy and is herself killed by the lover, who then kills himself. In 19 the bridegroom in his marriage bed dreams that his true love appears to him. He dresses and rides to her home, to find her dead of a broken heart. He dies of grief and remorse. Both deaths are natural, as also in 20. But in 20 the triangle disappears; the lover is not unfaithful, only laggard, and he returns to find his lady dead of love too long deferred, then himself dies of grief. All three, then, are lovers' tragedies. In 18 there is a triangle with three violent deaths; in 19 there is a triangle, with the two lovers' deaths, neither violent; in 20 the triangle disappears, and the two lovers die without violence, of love-longing and of sorrow. By this analysis the pure forms may be distinguished from the blended texts.

With these three ballads, also, the familiar "rose-and-brier" ending is most frequently associated. Child speaks of this in his introduction to "The Douglas Tragedy." As he says, "The beautiful fancy of plants springing from the graves of star-crossed lovers, and signifying by the intertwining of stems or leaves, or in other analogous ways, that an earthly passion has not been extinguished by death, presents itself, as is well known, very frequently in popular poetry. Though the graves be made far apart, even on opposite sides of the church, or one to the north and one to the south outside the church, or one without kirk wall and one in the choir, however separated, the vines or trees seek one another out, and mingle their branches or their foliage:

> 'Even from the tomb the voice of Nature cries,
> Even in our ashes live their wonted fires!'"

In the Virginia texts, this fanciful idea is seldom found in 18 (see B), but regularly in 19 and 20. And the appendage appears again a little later in the Virginia texts of "Barbara Allen" (No. 24), which as another love tragedy is also akin to this group.

No. 18 is known in Virginia as "Lord Thomas and Fair Ellinor," "Lord Thomas," "The Brown Girl," "Lord Thomas and the Brown Girl," "The Three Lovers," "Fair Ellen," "Lord Thomas and Fair Ellen," and by other like titles. The simple name Eleanor goes through many changes of spelling and pronunciation, from Ellinor to Ellender. The thirty-seven texts and seven tunes of this ballad collected in Virginia indicate its great, and deserved popularity. Most of the texts are complete or nearly so, and in an excellent state of preservation. But they all seem to be more closely related to the Child D group than to any other version. They follow the English rather than the Scottish form of the ballad.

Several of the Virginia variants begin with a description of Lord Thomas and Fair Eleanor. But in most of the variants, as Cox says of the West Virginia texts, "the story begins by the hero's asking his mother to solve the riddle as to whether he shall marry Fair Eleanor or bring the brown girl home. Since the brown girl has house and lot (land) and Fair Eleanor has none, she advises him to marry the brown girl. Thereupon he dresses himself up in state, takes his merry men with him, rides to Fair Eleanor's hall, and invites her to his wedding on the morrow. She says that it is very bad news to her for she expected to be his bride. Later she asks her mother to solve the riddle as to whether she shall go to Lord Thomas's wedding or stay at home. Her mother advises her to stay at home since she will have few friends at the wedding and many enemies, but she is determined to go. Thereupon she arrays herself in her finery, takes her merry maids with her, and rides to Lord Thomas's hall. In answer to her knocking, Lord Thomas himself lets her in, leads her into the hall, and chooses for her the highest seat. Fair Eleanor twits him with having married such a brown wife, whereupon the brown girl stabs her with a pen-knife between the short ribs and the long. Lord Thomas asks her why she looks so pale and she suggests that he must be blind not to observe her heart's blood trickling down to her knee. With a little hand-sword Lord Thomas cuts off the head of the brown girl, kicks it against the wall, and then slays himself with the same sword. Before he dies, he requests that Fair Eleanor be buried in his arms and the brown girl at his feet." This summary by Cox may stand for the typical Virginia text as well.

American texts of this ballad are very numerous, showing its great popularity in the New World. See Barry, No. 2; Belden, No. 4 (fragment); Brown, p. 9 (North Carolina); *Bulletin*, Nos. 2, 3, 5–10; Campbell and Sharp, No. 16 (North Carolina, Georgia, Tennessee, Massachusetts, Virginia); Child, III, 509 (Virginia from *The Folk Lore Journal*, VII, 33, 1889); Cox, No. 10; Hudson, No. 10 (and *Journal*, XXXIX, 94; Mississippi); *Journal*, XVIII, 128 (Barry, Vermont, text and melody, Massachusetts, fragment), 295 (Barry, Vermont, melody only); XIX, 235 (Belden, Missouri, Arkansas); XX, 254 (Kittredge, Kentucky); XXVII, 71 (Barry, melody only); XXVIII, 152 (Perrow, North Carolina); XXIX, 159 (Tolman, Pennsylvania, fragment); McGill, p. 28; Mackenzie, p. 97; Mackenzie, *Ballads*, No. 6 and p. 392 (text and melody); Pound, *Syllabus*, p. 11 (fragment); Pound, *Ballads*, No. 12; Sandburg, p. 157 (North Carolina); Shearin, p. 3; Shearin and Combs, p. 8; Shoemaker, p. 155; Reed Smith, No. 5 (texts and melodies); Reed Smith, *Ballads*, No. 5; Wyman and Brockway, *Songs*, p. 14 (Kentucky). For additional references, see Cox, p. 45; *Journal*, XXIX, 159.

A

"Lord Thomas and Fair Elenor." Collected by Messrs. Carpenter and Stone. Sung by Mrs. J. A. Mitchell, Miss Mary Mitchell and Mrs. H. Hoffman. Madison County. November 3, 1920. With music.

1 Lord Thomas he was a bold young man,
  A keeper of our king's deer;
Fair Elenor was a fair lady,
  Lord Thomas he loved her dear.

2 He went unto his mother dear,
"Mother dear, mother dear," says he,
"Must I marry the brown-skin girl
Or bring Fair Elenor home?"

3 "The brown-skin girl has house and land,
Fair Ellen she has none;
Therefore I charge you with my blessing
To bring the brown girl home."

4 He dressed himself in attire of red,
His man he trimmed in green;
And every village as he passed by
He was taken to be some king.

5 He rode up to Fair Ellen's door,
He knocked and so loudly it did ring;
There was none more ready than Fair Ellen herself
To rise and let him in.

6 "What news, what news have you brought unto me?
What news, what news?" says she.
"I've come to ask you to my wedding today."
"O that's sad news to me."

7 She went unto her old mother dear.
"Mother dear, mother dear," says she,
"O shall I go to Lord Thomas' wedding
Or stay at home with thee?"

8 "There'll be ten of your friends and ten of your foes,
And that you plainly see;
Therefore I charge you with my blessing
To tarry at home with me."

9 She dressed herself in scarlet red,
Her maid she dressed in green;
In every village that she passed by
She was taken to be some queen.

10 She rode up to Lord Thomas' door
And knocked, and so loudly it did ring;
There was none so ready as Lord Thomas himself
To rise and let her in.

11 He took her by her fair lily hand
And led her through the hall.
He seated her in a gold leaf chair
Among the quality all.

12 "Is this your beautiful bride, Lord Thomas?
I'm sure she is quite brown.
You could have married a fair-skin girl
As ever the sun shone on."

13 The brown-skin girl had a knife in her hand,
It was so keen and sharp;
Between the short ribs and the lungs
She pierced Fair Ellen's heart.

14 Lord Thomas he had a sword in his hand,
It was so rusty and dull;
He cut the head of his own bride off
And kicked it against the wall.

15 He put the handle next to the floor,
The point next to his heart.
Were there ever three lovers that met so soon,
So soon as these to part?

16 "O mother, mother, go dig my grave,
Dig it both wide and deep;
Bury Fair Ellen at my right side
And the brown-skin girl at my feet."

B

"Lord Thomas and Fair Eleanor." Reported by Miss Juliet Fauntleroy. Contributed by Miss Mary Finch. Sung by Miss Jennie Nelson, of Rustburg, Va. Campbell County. May 24, 1924. With music.

1 Lord Thomas he was a bold forester,
A keeper of the King's deer;
Lady Eleanor was a fair ladye,
She loved Lord Thomas dear.

2 "'T is time you were wed," his mother she said,
"'T is time you were wed," said she.
"So, son, I charge you upon my blessing
To bring home a bride to me."

3 "Then riddle this riddle, my mother," he said,
"And riddle it well," said he.
"Full long have I loved the fair Eleanor,
And the brown girl she loves me."

4 "The brown girl she has houses and lands,
Fair Eleanor she has none;
So, son, I charge you upon my blessing
To bring me the brown girl home."

5 Lord Thomas he rode to fair Eleanor's door,
With his merrie men all in green;
And who so ready as fair Eleanor
To let Lord Thomas in?

6 "What news, what news, Lord Thomas?" she cried,
"What news do you bring to me?"
"I've come to bid you to my wedding,
And that is sad news for thee."

7 "Sad news, sad news, Lord Thomas," she cried,
"They fill my heart with gloom;
For I thought myself to have been the bride,
And you to have been the bridegroom."

8 Lady Eleanor mounted her milk-white steed,
With her merrie men all in green;
And every borough that she rode through
They took her to be some queen.

9 "Is this your bride, Lord Thomas?" she cried,
"Methinks she looks wondrous brown;
You might have married the fairest woman
That ever trod English ground."

10 "Nay, blame her not, fair Ellen," he cried,
"Nay, blame her not to me;
For better I love thy little finger
Than the brown girl's whole body."

11 The brown girl took her little pen-knife,
Which was both long and sharp,
And 'twixt the short ribs and the long
She pierced fair Eleanor's heart.

12 "Now how is this, fair Ellen?" he cried,
"Methinks you look wondrous wan;
You used to be the fairest woman
That ever the sun shone on."

13 "Oh, what is this, Lord Thomas?" she cried,
"And can you not very well see,
That this is now my own heart's blood
Comes trickling down to my knee?"

14 Lord Thomas he wore a sword by his side,
It leaped from his side with a bound.
It touched the brown girl on the throat;
Her head rolled on the ground.

15 The hilt against a tree he placed;
The point against his heart.
Did ever true lovers so sadly meet,
So sadly soon to part?

16 They laid them both in the old churchyard,
They buried them in the church choir;
And out of her bosom there grew a white rose,
And out of hisn a brier.

17 They grew to the top of the old church tower,
And when they could grow no higher
They twined themselves in a true lovers' knot
For (all) true lovers to admire.

C

"Lord Thomas and Fair Ellender." Collected by Mr. John Stone. Sung by Mr. George Hart, of Konnarock, Va. Washington County. November 8, 1921.

1 Lord Thomas, Lord Thomas, he was a stockkeeper,
A keeper of our king's deer.
Fair Ellender, she was a fair damsel,
Lord Thomas he loved her well.
Fair Ellender, she was a fair damsel,
Lord Thomas he loved her well.

2 "O mother, O mother, come riddle us both,
Come riddle us both as one,
And tell me whether to marry Fair Ellen
Or bring the Brown Girl home."

3 "The bonnie Brown Girl has house and land,
Fair Ellender she has none;
And it's my advice to you, my son,
The Brown Girl bring home."

4 He called out his waiting men,
He called them by one, two, and three,
Saying, "Go and saddle my stage white horses.
Fair Ellender I'll go see."

5 He dressed himself in silk so fine,
His waiting men in green;
And every city that he rode through,
They took him to be some king.

6 He rode till he came to Fair Ellender's hall,
And knocked so loud at the ring;
And none was so ready as Fair Ellender herself
To rise and let him come in.

7 "What news, what news, Lord Thomas?" she says,
"What news have you brought unto me?"
"I've come to invite you to my wedding.
Tomorrow's the day it's to be."

8 "Bad news, bad news, Lord Thomas," she says,
"Bad news you have brought unto me.
I was hoping to be the bride myself
And you the bridegroom be."

9 "O mother, O mother, come riddle us all,
Come riddle us all as one,
And tell me whether to go to the wedding
Or tarry at home today."

10 "Fair Ellender, you've a heap of friends
Besides all other foes,
And it's my advice to you, my daughter,
At home to tarry today."

11 She called out her waiting maids,
She called them by one, two, and three,
Saying, "Go and saddle my stage white horses.
Lord Thomas's wedding I'll see."

12 She dressed herself in silk so fine,
Her waiting maids in green;
And every city that she rode through,
They took her to be some queen.

13 She rode till she came to Lord Thomas's hall,
And danced upon the ring;
And none was so kind as Lord Thomas himself
To rise and bring her in.

14 He took her by the little white hand
And led her through the hall,
He set her down at the head of the table
Amongst the quality all.

15 "Is this your bride, Lord Thomas?" she says.
"She looks most wonderful brown;
When you might have gotten as fair a gay lady
As ever the sun shined on."

16 The bonnie Brown Girl, she had a pen-knife,
It were both keen and sharp;
Between the long ribs and the short
She pierced Fair Ellender's heart.

17 "Lord Thomas, Lord Thomas, what makes you look so pale?"
"To think I see my own heart's blood
A-streaming to the ground,
To think I see my own heart's blood
A-twinkling down my knees."

18 He took the Brown Girl by the hand,
He led her through the hall,
And with a sword he cut off her head
And kicked it against the wall.

19 He put the handle against the wall,
The point unto his heart,
Saying, "Here's the end of three true loves.
Lord, send our souls to rest.

20 "Go dig my grave both wide and deep."
Saying, "Lay Fair Ellender in my arms
And the Brown Girl at my feet."

21 They buried the Brown Girl in his arms,
Fair Ellender at his feet;
They laid the Brown Girl in his arms
And let her go to sleep.

D

"Fair Ellen." Collected by Miss Alfreda M. Peel. Sung by Sis Sears, of Salem, Va. Roanoke County. November 5, 1916. With music.

1 "Oh mother, dear mother, come riddle to me,
Come riddle to me the sport:
Shall I marry fair Ellen-der
Er bring the brown girl home?"

2 "The brown girl she has house and lands,
Fair Ellen she has none;
So I would advise as your own dear mother
To bring the brown girl home."

3 He rode and he rode till he came to the hall,
And jingled around the ring,
There was none so ready as fair Ellen herself,
To rise and let him in.

4 "Good news, good news, good news, you bring,
Good news," fair Ellen said she.
"I've come to invite you to my wedding;
Is that good news to thee?"

5 "Sad news, sad news, you bring to me,
Sad news," fair Ellen said she,
"I thought that I was to be your bride
And you the bridegroom to be."

6 "So now, old mother, come riddle to me,
Come riddle the sport this once:
Must I go to Lord Thomas's wedding
Or tarry at home?" said she.

7 . . . .
. . . .
"I'll venture my life, I venture my death,
At Lord Thomas's wedding I'll be."

8 She dressed up her milk-white steed,
Her waist was made of green;
And every city that she passed through,
She was taken to be some queen.

9 She rode and she rode till she came to the hall,
She jungled around the ring;
There was none so ready as Lord Thomas himself
To rise and let her in.

10 He taken her by her lily-white hand
And led her through the hall,
And set her down at the head of the table,
Amongst those ladies all.

11 "Lord Thomas, Lord Thomas, is this your bride?
She is wonderful brown,
When you might have had as fair a ladye
As ever the sun shined on."

12 The brown girl she had a little pen-knife,
Which was both keen and sharp;
She thrust it in fair Ellen's breast,
It entered near her heart.

13 "Oh, what's the matter, my own true love,
Oh, what's the matter with thee?"
"Oh, don't you see my own heart's blood
Go trickling down from me?"

14 He taken the brown girl by the hand,
And led her through the hall,
And drew a big sword, and cut off her head,
And stove it against the wall.

15 "Oh mother, dear mother, go dig my grave,
Go dig it both wide and deep;
Place fair Ellen in my arms
And the brown girl at my feet."

16 He put the sword against the wall,
The point against his breast.
"Oh, here is the death of three true lovers;
God, send them home for rest."

E

"The Brown Girl." Collected by Miss Juliet Fauntleroy. Sung by Mrs. Essie Wallace Yowell, of Altavista, Va. Campbell County. June 13, 1914.

1 "Come father, come mother, come riddle us both,
Come riddle us both as one,
And tell me whether to marry fair Ellender
Or bring the brown girl home, home,
Or bring the brown girl home."

2 "The brown girl has a house and home,
Fair Ellender she has none,
Therefore I would advise you as my best son
To bring the brown girl home, home,
To bring the brown girl home."

3 He rode, he rode, till he came to the hall,
He rattled the bell and it rang;
None was more ready than fair Ellender herself
To arise and let him in, in,
To arise and let him in.

4 "What news, what news, Lord Thomas," she cried,
"What news do you bring to me?"
"I've come to invite you to my wedding day;
And is that good news to thee, thee,
And is that good news to thee?"

5 "Sad news, sad news, Lord Thomas," she cried,
"Sad news you bring to me.
I thought that I was to be the bride
And you the bridegroom for me, me,
And you the bridegroom for me."

6 "Come mother, come mother, come tell me your mind,
Come tell me a story or two.
And tell me whether to attend the wedding
Or tarry at home with you, you,
Or tarry at home with you."

7 "Ten thousand of your friends will be there,
Ten thousand of your foes,
Therefore I advise you as my best daughter
To tarry at home with me, me,
To tarry at home with me."

8 She dressed herself in robes of white,
Her wait-maids were dressed in green;
And every town that she rode through,
They taken her to be some queen, queen,
They taken her to be some queen.

9 She rode, she rode, till she came to the hall,
She rattled the bell and it rang;
None was more ready than Lord Thomas himself
To arise and let her in, in,
To arise and let her in.

10 He took her by her lily-white hand
And led her across the hall,
And seated her at the head of the table
Among those ladies all, all,
Among those ladies all.

11 "Is this your bride, Lord Thomas?" she cried,
"She is most wonderful brown;
You once could have married as fair-skinned a girl
As ever the sun shined on, on,
As ever the sun shined on."

12 "Fair Ellender, fair Ellender, fair Ellender," he cried,
"What makes you look so pale?"
"Oh, can't you see my own heart's blood
Comes trickling down by me, me,
Comes trickling down by me?"

13 The brown girl had a sharp pen-knife,
It being both sharp and keen,
She pierced it in fair Ellender's side,
Which entered into her heart, heart,
Which entered into her heart.

14 Lord Thomas he had a very bright sword
Which hung up in the hall;
He took it down and cut her head off,
And kicked it against the wall, wall,
And kicked it against the wall.

15 "Here goes the life of three true lovers.
Lord, take them home to rest."

F

"The Three Lovers." Reported by Professor W. A. Montgomery. Contributed by Mrs. Olin Fisk Wiley, of Richmond, Va. Wise County. June, 1915.

1 Lord Thomas was a nice young gentleman,
He rode a many a town;
He courted a girl they called fair Eleanor
And one called Sally Brown.

2 "Father and mother, I'll ask you both as one,
Whether I must marry fair Elender[1]
Or bring the Brown girl home?"

3 "Foes they may be many, Lord Thomas.
The Brown girl she has house and land,
And Fair Elender she has none;
You take the warning by such a kind friend
And bring the Brown girl home."

4 He went up to fair Elender's gate
And loudly he tingled and called;
There was none so ready to let him in
But fair Elender herself.

5 "What have you brought me, Lord Thomas?" said she,
"I've come to invite you to my wedding,
Tomorrow it shall be."

6 "Father and mother, I'll ask you both as one,
Whether I must go to Lord Thomas' wedding
Or whether I must stay at home?"

7 "Foes they may be many, fair Elender,
And friends they may be few;
If you'll take warning of such a kind friend,
You'll stay with your mother at home."

8 "I care nothing for friends or foes,
But Lord Thomas's wedding I'll go."

9 She dressed herself in silk so fine,
Her waist was diamond green;
And every town that she rode through,
They took her to be some queen.

[1] The contributor draws attention to the change of name here.

10 She rode up to Lord Thomas's Hall
And tingled in the ring;
But there was none so ready as Lord Thomas himself
Rising to let her in.

11 He took her by the lily-white hand,
And led her through the Hall,
And sat her down at the head of the table,
Among the ladies all.

12 She said, "Is this your bride, Lord Thomas?
I think she is dreadful brown;
You once could have married as fair a girl
As ever the sun shined on."

13 The Brown girl had a long pen-knife,
The point both keen and sharp;
She put it against fair Elender's breast
And stove it to her heart.

14 Lord Thomas took the Brown girl by the hand,
And led her through the hall,
And took a sword, cut off her head,
And kicked it against the wall.

15 He put the handle against the floor,
The point against his breast;
"This is the end of three true loves;
Lord, send our souls to rest.

16 "Go bury fair Elender in my arms,
The Brown girl at my feet,
And in both hands a glass of wine,
Happy that we all may sleep."

G

"Lord Thomas and Fair Ellender." Collected by Mr. John Stone. Sung by Misses Fannie and Hattie Via. Fluvanna County. November 3, 1920. "They learned it from Mrs. Orilla Keyton, of Mountfair, Albemarle County. Mrs. Keyton sang four songs for Prof. Sharp, two of which were ballads; but none of the three sung by the Via children were in the list sung to Prof. Sharp" (Mr. Stone).

1 Lord Thomas, Lord Thomas was a nice young man,
A captain all of the hall;
He asked the relief of his kind old mother,
"O mother, which must I take, Fair Ellen or the brown-skin girl?"

2 "The brown-skin girl has house and land,
Fair Ellen she has none;
And if I've got to invite you with all my heart,
Go bring the brown girl home."

3 Lord Thomas he called for a horse and saddle,
A bridle and saddle to ride.
"I'm going to invite Fair Ellen all to my wedding,
All to my wedding day."

4 He rode and he rode till he came to the hall,
And jingled was loud at the ring;
And who was so ready as Fair Ellen herself
To rise and welcome him in?

5 "Sad news, sad news, I've come to tell,
Sad news I've come to tell;
I've come to invite you all to my wedding,
All to my wedding day."

6 Fair Ellen she called for a horse and saddle,
A bridle and saddle to ride.
"I'm going all to Lord Thomas's wedding,
All to his wedding day."

7 Fair Ellen she dressed herself in white,
And trimmed herself in green;
And every town that she passed by,
They taken her to be some queen.

8 She rode and she rode till she came to the hall,
And jingled was loud at the ring;
And who was so ready as Lord Thomas himself
To rise and welcome her in?

9 He taken her by her lily-white hand
And led her through the hall,
He set her down at the head of the table
Among those ladies all.

10 "Lord Thomas, Lord Thomas, is this your bride?
I think she is wonderfully brown,
When you once could have married a fair-skin girl
As ever the sun shone on."

11 The brown-skin girl had a little pen-knife,
It being both long and keen;
And between the long rib and the short one
She cut Fair Ellen's heart.

12 "Lord Thomas, Lord Thomas, Lord Thomas," cried she,
"Lord Thomas," cried she,
"Don't you see my own heart's blood
Come trickling down my knee?"

13 Lord Thomas he had a sword in his house,
It being both long and keen;
He clipped all off his own bride's head
And kicked it ag'in the wall.

14 He put the sword all to the floor,
Its point all to his breast.
"Did you ever see three true lovers meet
As quick as we have parted?"

H

"Lord Thomas." Reported by Miss Mary Washington Ball. Contributed by Miss Arline Eubank, of Richmond, Va. Sung by her grandmother. Henrico County. May 20, 1914.

1 Lord Thomas, he went to his mother one day
And kneeled low at her knee.
"Oh riddle my riddle to me, mother,
And riddle it unto me,
Whether will I bring the Brown Girl
Or bring Fair Ellen to thee?"

2 "The Brown Girl has houses and lands," she said,
"And Fair Ellen, she has none.
So for my blessing, Lord Thomas," she said,
"Bring me the Brown Girl or none."

3 Lord Thomas went unto Fair Ellen
And kneeled low at her knee.
"What news, what news, Lord Thomas?" she said,
"What news have you brought to me?"
"I have come to bid you to my wedding."
"Oh, very bad news for me."

4 Fair Ellen went unto her mother
And kneeled low at her knee,
Saying, "Whether will I go to Lord Thomas's wedding,
Or tarry at home with thee?"

5 "There'll be some of your friends there," she said,
"But far more of your foe.
So for my blessing, Fair Ellen," she said,
"To Lord Thomas's wedding don't go."

6 "There'll be some of my friends there," she said,
But far more of my foe.
So let weel or woe betide," she said,
"To Lord Thomas's wedding I'll go."

7 She dressed her six maids all in red;
She dressed her self in green;
And every village that she came to,
They took her to be some queen.

8 And when she came to Lord Thomas's gates
She tinkled low at the ring.
The very first person to let her in
It was Lord Thomas himself.

9 He took her by the right hand
And led her twice round the hall;
Then set her in their very best chair,
Which amazed the bride most of all.

10 "Is this the bride, Lord Thomas?" she said,
"She looks so wonderful brown.
And you might have had the fairest lady
That ever the sun shone on."

11 "Hold your tongue, Fair Ellen," he said,
"Hold your tongue, let me be.
I'd rather have your little finger," he said,
"Than the Brown Girl's whole body."

12 "Where got you the water, Fair Ellen," she said,
"That washed your face so fair?"
"'T was in my father's garden," she said,
"And under a sycamore tree;
Where if you were to look till your eyes go blind,
Never a drop would you see."

13 The Brown Girl had a little knife,
It was both sharp and keen.
She stuck it in Fair Ellen's breast —
Such a wedding never was seen.

14 "Oh, what is the matter, Fair Ellen," he said,
"You look so white and pale?
You used to be the fairest lady
That ever the sun shone on."

15 "Oh, are you blind, Lord Thomas," she said,
"Or can't you very well see?
For I feel my heart's warm blood," she said,
"Come trickling down to my knee."

16 Lord Thomas had a little sword,
It was both sharp and keen.
He chopped off the Brown Girl's head —
Such a wedding never was seen.

17 He placed his foot 'gainst Fair Ellen's chair,
And his head against the wall;
And he cut his throat with his little sword,
And at Fair Ellen's feet did fall.

I

"Lord Thomas and Fair Ellender." Collected by Mr. John Stone. Sung by Mr. Jeff Doss, of Damascus, Va., who learned it from his brother. Washington County. November 8, 1921.

1 "O mother, dear mother, come riddle my riddle,
And riddle my riddle as one,
Whether I shall marry Fair Ellender
Or the Brown Girl bring home."

2 "The Brown Girl she has house and land,
Fair Ellender she has none;
I charge you now by my experience
The bonny Brown Girl bring home."

3 He rode till he came to Fair Ellender's hall,
He knocked till he tingled the ring;
There was none so ready as Fair Ellender herself
To rise and let him in.

4 "O what's the news? O what's the news?
O what's the news?" cried she.
"I come to axe you to my wedding,
Sad news, sad news," says he.

5 "O mother, O mother, come riddle my riddle,
Come riddle my riddle in one,
Whether I must go to Lord Thomas's wedding
Or wither and tarry at home."

6 "One might be your friend, dear girl,
Five hundred might be your foe.
I charge you now by my experience
You'd better tarry at home."

7 She dressed herself in solid green,
The prettiest I ever seen;
And every city that she passed through,
They took her to be some queen.

8 She rode till she came to Lord Thomas's hall,
She knocked till she tingled the ring;
There was none so ready as Lord Thomas hisself
To rise and let her in.

9 He took her by the lily-white hand,
He led her into the hall;
He set her down at the head of the table
Amongst the gentlemens all.

10 "Is this your bride, Lord Thomas?" she cried.
"She looks most wonderful brown.
You might have had as fair a one
As ever the sun shined on."

11 The bonny Brown Girl had a knife in her hand,
The point grew thin and sharp;
Between the long ribs and the short,
She entered Fair Ellender's heart.

12 "O what's the matter? O what's the matter?
O what's the matter?" cries he.
"It's don't you see my own heart's blood
Come twinkling down from me?"

13 He took the bonny Brown Girl by the hand,
He led her into the hall,
And with his sword he chopped off her head
And slammed it against the wall.

14 He put the butt against the wall,
The point against his breast.
"Here ends the life of three lovers, dear lovers.
Lord, take our souls to rest."

15 "O mother, dear mother, you are the cause of this,
You are the cause of all these deaths.
Bury Fair Ellender in my arms,
The bonny Brown Girl at my feet."

J

"Lord Thomas and Fair Ellen." Contributed by Misses Ethel and Hallie Rodes. Found in Bryant, Va. Nelson County. March 26, 1917.

1 "The brown girl she has house and land,
Fair Ellen she has none;
I therefore charge you with all my blessing,
Go bring the brown girl home."

2 He rode to fair Ellen's hall,
He rattled, the bell did ring;
No one was so ready as fair Ellen herself
To arise and let him in.

3 "What news, Lord Thomas," she says to me,
"What news, what news, have you brought?"
"I come to invite you to my wedding.
Oh, isn't that bad for thee."

4 "Mother, spend your opinion
And tell your stories true;
Must I to Lord Thomas's wedding go
Or stay at home with you?"

5 "You have a great many friends,
Likewise as many foes;
I therefore charge you with all my blessing
Lord Thomas's wedding not go."

6 "I have a great many friends,
Likewise as many foes;
Betide my life, betide my death,
Lord Thomas's wedding I'll go."

7 She dressed herself in robes of white,
Her maids all dressed in green;
And every town she passed through,
They thought she was some queen.

8 She rode to Lord Thomas's hall,
She rattled, the bell did ring;
No one was so ready as Lord Thomas himself
To arise and let her in.

9 He took her by her lily-white hand
And led her through the hall,
Where there were four and twenty gay ladies,
And she the flower of all.

10 "Is this your bride, Lord Thomas," says she,
"That looks so wonderfully brown?
You might have married as fair a young lady
As ever the sun shone on."

11 "Depise her not," Lord Thomas he says,
"Despise her not to me;
For I do love your little finger
Better than her whole body."

12 The brown girl had a little pen-knife,
Both very keen and sharp;
Between the lungs and her short ribs
She pierced fair Ellen's heart.

13 "What makes you faint?" Lord Thomas he says,
"What makes you faint so soon?
You once did wear as rich a color
As ever a rose in June."

14 "Oh, are you blind, Lord Thomas," she says,
"Or can't you plainly see?
The beautiful color that was once in my cheek
Goes twinkling down my knee."

15 He had his sword all by his side;
He walked across the hall,
And cut off his own bride's head
And threw it against the wall.

16 He placed his sword all on the floor,
The point all towards his heart.
Was ever the like ever known,
Three lovers so soon to part?

17 "Oh, mother, dig my grave,
Dig it both wide and deep,
And place fair Ellen by my side,
The brown girl at my feet."

K

"The Brown Girl." Collected by Miss Lauretta M. Yost. Sung by Miss Maude Boyd. Floyd County. March 11, 1916.

1 "O mother, O mother, come riddle my sport,
Come riddle it all as one,
Whether I shall marry Fair Ellender,
Or bring the Brown Girl home."

2 "The Brown Girl, she has house and land,
Fair Ellender she has none;
Therefore I advise you as a blessing,
To bring the Brown Girl home."

3 "Go saddle up my milk-white horse,
Go saddle him up in speed,
For I am going to invite Fair (Ellender)
To my wed-wed-wedding."

4 He rode and he rode till he came to the Hall,
He jingled at the ring;
There was none so ready as Fair Ellender
To rise and let him in.

5 "What news, what news, Lord Thomas," she cried,
"What news you bring to me?"
"I have come to invite you to my wedding;
Ain't that good news to thee?"

6 "Bad news, bad news, Lord Thomas," she cries,
"Bad news you bring to me,
For I once thought I was to be your bride,
And you the bridesgroom to be."

7 "O mother, O mother, come riddle my sport,
Come riddle it all as one,
Whether I shall go to Lord Thomas' wedding,
Or tarry with you at home?"

8 She dressed herself in scarlet red,
Her beauty dressed in green;
And ever' city that she rode through,
She was taken for to be some queen.

9 She rode and she rode till she came to the Hall,
She jingles at the ring;
There was none so ready as Lord Thomas,
Himself to rise and let her in.

10 He took her by her lily-white hand,
He led her through the hall;
He sat her down at the head of the table,
Among them ladies all.

11 "Is this your wife, Lord Thomas?" she cries,
"A wonderful brown is she,
When you once could have married as fair young lady
As ever the sun shined on."

12 The Brown Girl she has a little pen-knife,
The blade both keen and sharp,
She pitched it in Fair Ellender's side,
Which entered near her heart.

13 "What's the matter, what's the matter, my old true love?
Oh, what's the matter with thee?"
"Oh, don't you see my own heart's blood
Come twinkling down by me?"

14 He took the Brown Girl by the hand,
He led her through the hall,
He drew her so he cut her head off,
He threw it against the wall.

15 "O mother, O mother, go dig my grave,
Go dig it both wide and deep,
And bury Fair Ellender in my arms,
The Brown Girl at my feet."

16 He put his sword against the wall,
The point against his breast.
Sing here the death of three true lovers;
God send them home to rest.

L

"The Brown Girl'' or "Lord Thomas and Fair Ellender." Collected by Miss Juliet Fauntleroy. Sung by Mrs. Dan Maxie (*nêe* Holland), of Altavista, Va. Franklin County. March 9, 1914. With music.

1 The brown girl had both house and lands,
Fair Ellender she had none.
"I would advise you, as a blessing,
To bring the brown girl home."

2 "Oh mother, oh mother, come riddle these sports,
Come riddle them all as one;
I'm going to invite fair Ellender
Unto my wedding tonight."

3 He rode and he rode till he came to the walls,
With jingles all and rings.
There was none so ready as fair Ellender herself
To rise and let him in.

4 "What news, what news, Lord Thomas," she cried,
"What news do you bring to me?"
"I've come to invite you to my wedding,
Unto my wedding tonight."

5 "Bad news, bad news, Lord Thomas," she cried,
"Bad news, bad news, indeed.
You promised that I was to be your bride,
And you the bridegroom be."

6 "Oh mother, oh mother, come riddle these sports,
Come riddle them all as one;
Whether I shall go to Lord Thomas's wedding
Or dwell with thee at home."

7 She dressed herself in scarlet red,
Her wait-men she in green,
And every town that she rode through,
They taken her to be some queen.

8 She rode and she rode till she came to the walls,
With jingles all and rings.
There was none so ready as Lord Thomas himself
For to rise and let her in.

9 He taken her by her lily-white hand
And led her across the hall;
He seated her down in a golden chair
Among the ladies all.

10 "And is that your bride, Lord Thomas?" she cried,
"She is the most dismal brown,
When you could have married as fair a young lady
As ever the sun shone on."

11 The brown girl she had a sharp-pointed knife,
It was both sharp and wide;
She stuck it in fair Ellender's side,
And it returned to her heart.

12 He taken the brown girl by the hand
And led her across the hall;
He took a sharp sword and cut her head off
And staved it against the wall.

13 "Oh mother, oh mother, go dig my grave,
Go dig it both wide and deep,
And bury fair Ellender in my arms,
And the brown girl at my feet."

14 "What is the matter, Lord Thomas?" she cried,
"What is the matter with you?"
"Oh, don't you see my own heart's blood
A-floating down by me?"

15 Here lies the death of three true loves.
God send them home to rest.

M

"Lord Thomas." Collected by Miss Nancy Johnston. Contributed by Miss Ruth Stone, of Martinsville, Va. Henry County. April 15, 1914.

1 "Mother, come riddle this vote,
Come riddle it as one:
Whether I shall marry Fair Ellen,
Or bring the brown girl home."

2 "The brown girl, she has house and land,
Fair Ellen she has none;
Therefore I advise you at my blessing
To bring the brown girl home."

3 "Go saddle my milk-white beast,
Saddle him with speed;
I am going to invite Fair Ellen
To my wedding."

4 He rode till he came to town
And dingled around the ring;
But none so ready as Fair Ellen herself
To rise and let him in.

5 "What news do you bring to me?"
"Good news, good news I bring.
I come to invite you to my wedding.
Is that good news to you?"

6 "Bad news, bad news you bring to me,
Bad news you bring.
I thought that I were to be your bride,
And you the bridegroom to be."

7 She dressed herself in scarlet red,
Her waist was braided green;
And each town that she passed through,
They took her to be some queen.

8 She rode and rode till she came to the hall,
And dingled around the ring;
But none so ready as Lord Thomas
To rise and let her in.

9 He took her by her lily-white hand
And led her across the hall,
And set her down at the head of the table
Among the ladies all.

10 "Lord Thomas, is this your bride
That looks so pale and brown,
When you could have married as fair a young girl
As ever the sun shined on?"

11 The brown girl having a little pen-knife,
It being both keen and sharp,
She pierced it in Fair Ellen's side,
And it entered to the heart.

12 "What's the matter?
What's the matter with thee?"
"O don't you see my own heart's blood
Come tingling down to me?"

13 He took the brown girl by her hand
And led her across the hall,
And drew a bright sword, and cut her head off,
And stowed [1] it against the wall.

14 He put the sword against the wall,
The point towards his breast,
Saying, "Here is the death of three true loves;
God send us all home to rest."

15 "Mother, dig my grave,
Dig it both deep and wide;
Bury the brown girl at my feet,
Fair Ellen by my side."

N

"Lord Thomas and Fair Ellen." Collected by Mr. John Stone. Sung by Mrs. Ellen Mullens, at Saltville, Va. Smyth County. November 8, 1921.

1 Lord Thomas rode unto the gate,
He knocked so loud at the ring,
And none so ready as Fair Ellen
To rise and let him in.

2 "What is the matter, Lord Thomas?" says she,
"What is the matter with thee?"
"I've come to ask you to my wedding,
Most sorrowful news to thee."

3 "God forbid it had a been so soon.
I wanted to be the bride myself,
And you the bride sweet groom."

[1] Probably for *stoved* or *stove*.

4 When her old mother came to know,
"To Lord Thomas's wedding you shall not go."
"If my death-coffin stood at the door,
To Lord Thomas's wedding I would go."

5 Fair Ellen dressed up
All in her green,
And every town she marched round,
They took her to be some queen.

6 She rode up unto the gate,
And knocked so loud at the ring,
And none so ready as Lord Thomas
To rise and let her in.

7 He took her by her lily-white hand
And led her through the merry maids all;
He set her down in a golden chair
Among those ladies all.

8 "Is this your bride, Lord Thomas?" said she.
"She looks most wonderful brown;
When you might have had as fair a lady
As ever the sun shined on."

9 The brown girl had a pen-knife in her hand,
One of those keen and sharp;
Between the long ribs and the short
She pierced Fair Ellen's heart.

10 "What is the matter?" Lord Thomas says he,
"What is the matter with thee?
You used to have pretty rosy cheeks,
But now they are all fading away."

11 "What makes you talk so foolish to me?
I think I feel my own heart's blood
Come twinkling over my knee."

12 Lord Thomas had a sword in his right hand;
He cut off the brown girl's head.
He stove the sword against the ground,
The point went to his own heart.

13 "Bury the brown girl at my feet,
Fair Ellen at my right side;
If I had lived to have seen that day,
Fair Ellen would have been my bride."

O

"Lord Thomas." Contributed by Professor James M. Grainger. From the Farmville Ballad Club. Patrick County. May, 1913. Printed in *The Focus* for May, 1913.

1 "O mother, O mother, come riddle this riddle,
Come riddle it all as one;
Whether I shall marry Fairelenda
Or bring the Brown girl home."

2 "The Brown girl she has house and land,
Fairelenda she has none;
Therefore I advise as your best friend
To bring the Brown girl home."

3 "Go saddle me up my milk-white steed,
Go saddle him up in haste;
For I'm going to invite Fairelenda
To my wedding feast."

4 He rode and he rode till he came to the hall;
He tingled on the ring;
There was none so ready as Fairelenda
To rise and let him in.

5 "What news, what news, Lord Thomas," she cried,
"What news you bring to me?"
"I come to invite you to my wedding.
Isn't that good news to thee?"

6 "Bad news, bad news, Lord Thomas," she cried,
"Bad news you bring to me.
I thought I was to be your bride
And you the bridegroom be."

7 "O mother, O mother, come riddle this riddle,
Come riddle it all as one:
Whether I shall go to Lord Thomas's wedding
Or stay with thee at home."

8 She dressed herself in scarlet red,
Her waiting-maid in green,
And every town that she passed through,
They took her to be some queen.

9 She rode and she rode till she came to the hall;
She tingled on the ring;
There was none so ready as Lord Thomas
To rise and let her in.

10 He took her by her lily-white hand
And led her across the hall;
He sat her down at the head of the table
Amongst the ladies all.

11 "Is this your bride, Lord Thomas?" she cried,
"She is most wondrous brown;
You once could have married as fair a young girl
As ever the sun shone on."

12 The Brown girl she had a little pen-knife,
The point being both keen and sharp.
She stabbed it into Fairelenda's side
And plunged it to her heart.

13 "What's the matter, what's the matter, Fairelenda?" he cried,
"What's the matter, what's the matter with thee?"
"O don't you see my own heart blood
Come trickling down by me?"

14 He took the Brown girl by her hand;
He led her across the hall;
He drew a bright sword and cut her head off
And stove it against the wall.

15 "O mother, O mother, go dig my grave,
Go dig it both deep and wide;
And bury Fairelenda in my arms
And the Brown girl at my side."

P

"Lord Thomas and Fair Ellinor." Reported by Miss Martha M. Davis. Collected by Mrs. Herbert Cover, of Elkton, Va. Sung by a mountain woman. Rockingham County. November 22, 1913.

1 Lord Thomas, a brave young soldier,
Was captain of his own hall;
Fair Ellinor, fair beautiful damsel,
He loved her better than all.

2 "Mother, O mother, come tell me true,
Come tell to me which one;
Must I marry the brown-skinned girl
And leave fair Ellinor alone?"

3 "The brown-skinned girl has house and lands,
Fair Ellinor she has none;
If I must charge you with all my heart,
Go bring the brown girl home."

* * * * * *

4 "Is this your bride?" Fair Ellinor said,
"I'm sure she's wonderful brown,
When you could have married as fair a lady
As ever the sun shone on."

5 "O hush your tongue, Fair Ellinor," said he,
"Don't say one word to me;
I would not give your finger's end
For all her whole body."

6 The brown-skinned girl had a little pen-knife,
It was both keen (long?) and sharp;
Between Fair Ellinor's long ribs and short,
She pierced her to the heart.

7 Lord Thomas had a sword down by his side
It was both keen and sharp.[1]
He clipped his own bride's head off
And kicked it against the wall.

8 He placed the handle against the wall,
The point against his breast.
Did you ever see true lovers meet
And part as quick as this?

Q

"The Brown Girl." Collected by Miss Corita G. Seoane, of Merrifield, Va. Fairfax County. January 10, 1914.

1 Said he, "Dig my grave wide and long,
And dig it wide and deep,
And bury fair Ellender at my side
And the Brown girl at my feet.

2 "At my head and feet a marble stone,
On my breast a turtle dove,
So every one can see and know
And know I died for love."

[1] Variant line: "As he walked about the hall."

R

"Lord Thomas and Fair Ellinor." Collected by Mr. Cecil J. Sharp and Miss Karpeles. Sung by Mrs. Kate Campbell, at Woodridge, Va. Albemarle County. September 28, 1916. With music. Music and one stanza printed by Campbell and Sharp, p. 60.

1 "O mother, O mother, O mother," says he,
"Pray tell your willing mind,
Whether I must marry fair Ellington,
Or bring the brown girl home."

2 "The brown girl she has house and land,
Fair Ellington she has none.
If I must charge you with all my heart,
Go bring the brown girl home."

3 He rode up to fair Ellington's house,
And loudly at the ring.
And none was so ready as Ellington
As to rise and welcome him in.

4 "Good news, good news, good news, good news,
Good news I bring to thee.
I've come to invite you unto my wedding,
Unto my wedding day."

S

"Fair Ellender." Collected by Miss Martha M. Davis, of Harrisonburg, Va. Rockingham County. May 9, 1916. Music only.

19

FAIR MARGARET AND SWEET WILLIAM

(CHILD, No. 74)

FOR a general introduction to Nos. 18, 19, and 20, see the head-note to No. 18.

The twenty-nine items collected for this ballad indicate that it is fairly widespread in the state, though it is somewhat less popular than either of its immediate neighbors, which boast thirty-seven items each. The ballad is known not only as "Fair Margaret and Sweet William," but also as "Lady Marget," "Lydia Marget," "Sweet William," "Sweet William's Bride," "Sweet William and Lady Margaret." As in the case of Eleanor in the preceding ballad, the name Margaret is variously spelled and pronounced. Eight melodies have been recovered.

The normal Virginia text shows no very exact similarity to any one of the Child versions, A, B, or C, though it has some likenesses to each. It is like A in that the dream is William's and in the "such dreams" stanza, which is common to both. It is like B verbally, in the conversation that takes place between William and Margaret's ghost, and in the direct rose-and-briar ending, without aftermath. It is like C in that no hint is given that the bride is brown. This touch, characteristic of "Lord Thomas and Fair Annet," has slipped into Child A and B but does not appear in any Virginia text. All told, a general likeness to Child B is most apparent, but the Virginia text would surely have to be printed as a version separate from the Child versions.

The story of the Virginia text is this: Sweet William arises one morning and dresses himself in blue. He denies that there is anything of moment between Lady Margaret and himself, and says that on the following day Lady Margaret will see his bride. Lady Margaret stands at her window as he and his bride pass by; she throws down her ivory comb in her emotion, and is never more seen there. That night Lady Margaret's ghost appears at the foot of Sweet William's bridal bed and inquires how he likes his bride. He replies that best of all he likes the lady that stands at his bed's feet. He wakes, hints to his wife of his ominous dream, and gets her permission to go and see Lady Margaret. Her brother lets him in and informs him that Lady Margaret is in her coffin. After taking farewell kisses of her, he dies of sorrow. The two lovers are buried nearby, and sympathetic plants grow from their graves and entwine to symbolize their love transcending death.

For American texts, see Belden, No. 5 (fragment); Brown, p. 9 (North Carolina); *Bulletin*, Nos. 2–6, 8–10; Campbell and Sharp, No. 17 (Tennessee, Kentucky, North Carolina, Virginia); Child, V, 293 (Massachusetts); Cox, No. 11 and p. 522 (seven texts, two melodies); Hudson, No. 11 (Mississippi); *Journal*, XIX, 281 (Belden, Missouri); XXIII, 381 (Combs, Kentucky); XXVIII, 154 (Perrow, North Carolina); XXX, 303 (Kittredge, Missouri); XXXI, 74 (Waugh, Ontario, text and melody); XXXV, 340 (Tolman and Eddy, Ohio, text and melody); McGill, p. 71; Mackenzie, p. 124; Mackenzie, *Ballads*, No. 7; Pound, *Ballads*, No. 16; Shearin, p. 3; Shearin and Combs, p. 8; C. A. Smith (Virginia, two melodies only); Wyman and Brockway, p. 94. For additional references, see Cox, p. 65; *Journal*, XXIX, 160; XXX, 302.

A

"Sweet William." Collected by Miss Roxie Martin and Mr. J. M. McManaway. Sung by a school girl. Albemarle County. June 1, 1917. "A schoolgirl sings 'Sweet William and Lady Margaret' as she heard the people in the mountains sing it" (Miss Martin and Mr. McManaway).

1 Sweet William rose one early May morning
And dressed himself in blue:
"And it's come to tell of the long, long love
Between Lady Margaret and you."

2 "I know nothing of Lady Margaret,
Lady Margaret knows nothing of me;
But before tomorrow night
Lady Margaret my bride shall see."

3 Lady Margaret was sitting in her dining-room door
Combing back her long yellow hair,
But who did she spy but Sweet William and his bride
In the churchyard as they passed by?

4 And down she threw her ivory comb,
And back she threw her hair,
And down she fell from her dining-room door.
She was never more seen there.

5 The day's spent, the night is coming on,
Most of the men are asleep;
And who did he spy but Lady Margaret's ghost
A-standing at his bed's feet?

6 "It's how do you like your bed?
How do you like your sheet?
And how do you like your new wedded wife
Who is is now in your arms asleep?"

7 "And I do like my bed," says he,
"And better do I like my sheet;
But best of all is the pale-faced ghost
Who stands at my bed's feet."

8 The night's been spent, the day's coming on,
Most of the men are awake.
Sweet William says, "I'm troubled in my head
With a dream I dreamed last night.

9 "Such dreams! such dreams! they can't be good.
Such dreams, they may come true.
I dreamed my hall was full of white swine
And my loved bride was flown in tears."

10 He called and he called to his merry men,
He called them one by one,
And he got release from his new wedded wife
Lady Margaret to go to see.

11 He rode and he rode till he came to the door;
Loud did he knock and call.
And who was more ready than Lady Margaret's brother
To come down and let him in?

12 "Where is Lady Margaret?" says he,
"Is she in her kitchen? Is she in her hall?
Or is she in her highmost chamber
Among her merry maids all?"

13 "She's neither in her kitchen hall,
She's neither in her kitchen hall;
She's in that coffin, made of white lead,
With her pale face to the wall."

14 "Fold down, fold down, that lily-white sheet
That's made of hollens [1] so fine,
And let me kiss the clay cold lips
That oftentimes kissed mine."

15 And it's once he kissed her lily-white breast,
And twice he kissed her chin,
And it's three times he kissed her cold clay lips;
Then perished her heart within.

16 Lady Margaret died like today,
Sweet William died like tomorrow.
Lady Margaret was buried 'neath one willow tree,
Sweet William was buried 'neath the other.

17 Out of Lady Margaret's grave grew a red rose,
And out of Sweet William's grew a brier.
They grew and they grew to the church steeple top
Until they could grow no higher,
And there they entwined in a true lover's knot
For all true loves to admire.

[1] For *Holland* (linen).

B

"Lydia Marget." Sent in by Miss Martha M. Davis. Contributed by Mr. Wilmer P. Dove. Sung by his mother, at Dovesville, Va. Rockingham County. January 20, 1914. "After my little talk to the Rockingham Teachers' Association on the subject of ballads last November, Mr. Dove, who is one of the teachers of the county, told me his mother knew 'Lady Marget.' I suppose this is his mother's version" (Miss Davis).

1 Sweet William he rose one May morning
And dressed himself in blue.
"Come tell unto me that long, long love
That's betwixt Lydia Marget and you."

2 "I know nothing of Lydia Marget,
Lydia Marget knows nothing of me;
But tomorrow morn by eight o'clock
Lydia Marget my bride shall be.

3 Lydia Marget was sitting at her by-window,[1]
Combing back her golden hair;
And who did she spy but Willie and his bride
At the churchyard as they passed by.

4 Down she threw her ivory comb,
And back she threw her hair,
And down she fell from her by-window,
Never to see there any more.

5 The day passed and the night came on
When most men were asleep;
And who did appear but Lydia Marget's ghost
A-standing at Willie's bed feet?

6 "Oh, how do you like your bed?" said she,
"And how do you like your sheep? [2]
And how do you like that new married lady
That is lying in your arms asleep?"

7 "Very well, very well, do I like my bed,
And better do I like my sheep;
But the best of all is that young lady
That is standing at my bed foot."

8 The night being gone, and the day came on,
When most men were at work;
Sweet William said he was troubled in his mind
Of a dream that he dreamed last night.

[1] The manuscript has *bi window*. *By-window* does no violence to the original sound, and adds the sense of *side-window*. Only a trace of *bower-window* is left.

[2] Nonsense, of course. The singer has sacrificed sense for a more perfect rhyme than the merely assonantal *sheet*.

9 "Such a dream, such a dream, it can't be true,
Such a dream, it can't be true;
I dreamed my room was full of white swine
And my bride's bed a-flowing in tears."

10 He ask a leave of his many maids all,
By one, by two, by three;
He ask a leave of his new married lady,
Lydia Marget he might go to see.

11 He came and he knocked so loud,
He called till he almost screamed;
And who was so early but Lydia Marget's brother
To arise and let him in.

12 "Oh, is she in the kitchen?" says he,
"Or is she in the hall?
Or is she in her highest chamber
Among her many maids all?"

13 "She's neither in the kitchen," says he,
"Nor is she in the hall;
She's lying under her cold coffin lid
With her pale face turned to the wall."

14 "Tears down, tears down those silk white robes,
Tears down those reannents [1] so fine,
And let me kiss those clay-cold lips
That ofttimes have kissed mine.

15 "It was once I kissed her rosy cheeks,
It was twice I kissed her chin,
Three times I kissed her ruby lips,
But never will again."

16 Sweet William he died on eventide,
Lydia Marget she died on the morn;
Lydia Marget she died of pure, pure love,
And Sweet William he died from sorrow.

17 Ever in the churchyard green
Together they were laid,
And out of her grave grew a red rose,
And out of his a briar.
They wrapped themselves in a true lover's knot,
The red rose 'round the briar.

[1] *Raiments* is probably the word, but the manuscript spelling is unmistakable, and it is more than a misspelling. The manuscript *r* does bear some resemblance to an *s* which might suggest *cerements*.

C

"Lady Margret and Sweet William." Collected by Miss Juliet Fauntleroy. Sung by Mr. Dan Maxie, of Altavista, Va. Franklin County. March 3, 1914.

1 Sweet William he arose on a merry May morn,
He dressed himself in blue.
He sang the long, long love that lies
Betwixt Lady Margret and you.

2 "I know no harm of Lady Lady Margret,
And I hope she has none of me;
But tomorrow morning at eight o'clock,
My bride Lady Margret shall see."

3 She was sitting at her bower window,
Combing back her hair,
When she saw Sweet William in his bridegroom suit,
She knew him as he drew near.

4 She dashed down her ivory comb,
And with silk tied up her hair;
That fair maid went out of that room,
And was never no more seen there.

5 The day being gone, and the night had come,
And they were all asleep.
Lady Margret appeared unto Sweet William,
Standing at his bed feet.

6 "Oh, how do you like your bed?" she said,
"Or how do you like your sheet?
How do you like the gay lady,
That lies in your arms and sleeps?"

7 "Very well do I like my bed," he said,
"Much better do I like my sheet;
But the best of them all is the gay lady
That stands (*or* A-standing) at my bed feet."

8 The night being gone, the day being come
When they were all awake,
Sweet William laid down his merry men all,
By one, (by) two, (and) by three.

9 He goes unto her uncle's house,
And knocked on the ring;
There was none so ready as her eldest brother
To arise and let him in.

10 "Oh, is she in her kitchen?" he says,
"Or is she in her hall?
Or is she in her sitting room,
Among her merry men (merry maids?) all?"

11 "She is neither in her kitchen," he said,
"Nor neither in her hall,
But she is in her parlor room,
Laid out against the wall."

12 "Take the sheets off of Lady Margret,
Made out of the silk so fine,
And let me kiss her clay-cold lips
That oft-times kissed mine."

13 And first he kissed her clay-cold lips,
And then her ruby chin,
And then he kissed her clay-cold lips;
That pierced to his heart within.

14 "Take the sheets off Lady Margret's corpse,
Made out of the silk so fine.
Today they laid over Lady Margret's corpe,
Tomorrow they'll lay over mine."

15 Lady Margret died like unto today,
Sweet William like tomorrow;
Lady Margret died for pure true love,
Sweet William died for sorrow.

16 Lady Margret was buried under a high church tree (*or* chest tree),
Sweet William under a pear;
From Lady Margret's breast grew a red rose,
From Sweet William's grew a green brier.

17 The brier and the rose, they grew so high,
They grew to the chest tree top;
There they linked and joined together,
And tied in a true lover's knot.

D

"Sweet William." Reported by Professor James M Grainger. Contributed by Miss Mary Clay Hiner. Sung by her aunt, Mrs. Bucher. Augusta County. December 19, 1914. Mrs. Bucher learned it from her grandmother, a native of Wales.

1 It was early one morning Sweet William arose,
He dressed himself in blue.
"Now tell unto me that long, long love
That lies between Lady Margaret and you."

2 "Oh, I know nothing of Lady Margaret,
And Lady Margaret knows nothing of me.
But tomorrow morning before 't is eight o'clock,
Lady Margaret my bride shall see."

3 Lady Margaret was standing in her bowing door,
A-combing back her hair,
When who should she see but Sweet William and his bride
A-going to the infair.[1]

4 Down she dashed her ivory comb,
And back she threw her hair,
And down she fell in her bowing door;
Never more was she seen there.

5 But they rode on till they came there.
This couple went to bed;
And about midnight when they two awoke,
A ghost stood at their feet,

6 Saying, "How, kind Sir, do you like your bed,
And how do you like your sheet,
And how do you like that gay lady
That lies in your arms and sleeps?"

7 "Oh, very well do I like my bed,
Much better I like my sheet;
But the best of all is that lady
That stands at my bed's feet."

8 It was early next morning Sweet William arose,
He arose to tell his dream.
He dreamed that his courts were all filled with wine,
And his garments stained with blood.

9 Sweet William asked his gay lady
If Lady Margaret he might go and see;
"Oh, yes," said she, "These twenty-four hours
Lady Margaret you may go and see."

10 He mounted on his milk-white steed,
So gaily he rode away;
Gold rings bursted off his fingers,
And his nose began to bleed.

[1] This word, also and preferably spelled *infare*, from Anglo-Saxon *infaer*, is still in use in the mountain districts for the reception of the bride into the home of the groom, following the wedding at the bride's home. Sweet William was already married; hence Lady Margaret's tragic behavior when she saw him "a-going to the infair."

11 But he rode on till he came there;
So loudly he rattled the ring.
But no one was so ready to rise and let him in
As her own servant brother.

12 "Is Lady Margaret in her bowing door?
Or is she in the hall?
Or is she in her very fine room
Among her merry maids all?"

13 "Lady Margaret is not in her bowing door,
Nor is she in her hall;
But she is in her own coffin cold,
A corpse against the wall."

14 "Unfold those winding sheets," said he,
"Unfold from head to feet,
That I may kiss those cold, cold cheeks
That look so cold and sweet."

15 First he kissed her cold, cold cheeks
And then he kissed her chin
And then he kissed her cold ruby lips
That filled his heart within.

16 Lady Margaret was buried in the churchyard,
Sweet William by her side;
And out of her grave grew a red rose
And out of his a briar.

17 They grew as high as the church top,
Till they could grow no higher;
And then they grew into a true lover's knot,
And the rose wound round the briar.

E

"Sweet William and Lady Margaret." Collected by Mr. John Stone. Sung by Mr. T. C. Clark, of Whitehall, Va. Albemarle County. November 3, 1920. With music. "Mr. Clark is seventy-seven years old. He learned this ballad when a boy of fifteen from James Ripitoe, a boy of about the same age and son of Capt. Ripitoe, at that time sheriff of Albemarle. Mr. Clark was unable to recite the words, but could sing them. He said he had not sung them more than a few times in the last twenty years" (Mr. Stone).

1 Sweet William arose one May, May morning
And dressed himself in blue.
"Come tell unto me this long, long love
Between Lady Margaret and you."

2 "I know nothing of Lady Margaret,
And the least she knows of me;
Before tomorrow morning at ten o'clock
Lady Margaret my bride shall be."

3 Lady Margaret was standing at her dormer window
Combing her long yellow hair.
Who did she spy but Sweet William and his bride
In the churchyard as they passed by?

4 'T was down she threw her ivory comb,
And back she threw her hair,
And from her dormer window she fell,
And was no more seen there.

5 The night being spent and the day coming on
And most of the men were awake,
Sweet William he said he had troubles in his head,
The dreams that he dreamt last night.

6 "Such dreams, such dreams, they must be true,
Such dreams they must be so;
I dreamed my hall was full of white swine
And my love bed floating in tears."

7 He called his maid from the bed,[1]
By one, by two, by three;
And he asked leave of his new wedded bride,
Lady Margaret he might go see.

8 He rode till he came to Lady Margaret's hall,
He knocked and he loudly called;
And who was so ready as Lady Margaret's brother
To rise and let him in.

9 "Is Lady Margaret in the kitchen?" he said,
"Or is she in the hall?
Or is she in the upper chamber
With her merry maids all?"

10 "She is neither in the kitchen," he said,
"Nor neither in the hall;
She is in her coffin made of lead
With her pale face turned to the wall."

11 "Fold down, fold down those lily-white sheets
Which makes the olive so fine,[2]
That I may kiss her pale, cold lips,
As ofttimes she kissed mine."

[1] Variant line: "He called unto his merry men all."
[2] Variant line for, "Made of the holland so fine."

12 It's "Once I kissed her lily-white breast,
Twice I kissed her chin,
Three times I kissed her pale, cold lips,
Which breaks my heart within."

13 Lady Margaret died on Whitsun Monday,
Sweet William died tomorrow;
Lady Margaret died for pure, pure love,
Sweet William died for sorrow.

14 Lady Margaret was buried under one willow tree,
Sweet William was buried under another;
Out of Lady Margaret's grave grew a red rosy bush,
And out of Sweet William's a briar.

15 They grew till they grew to the church steeple top,
Till they could grow no higher,
And the leaves spread about and the branches they did meet
And they tied a true lover's knot.

F

"Lady Marget." Collected by Miss Martha M. Davis. Sung by Mrs. William Keister. Rockingham County. July 31, 1913. With music.

1 Lady Marget stood by her high dawning[1] window,
Combing her long yellow hair,
When whom should she spy, but Sweet William and his bride
As the church door they drew nigh?

2 Lady Marget threw down her ivory comb,
Forced back her long yellow hair.
She left her high dawning window,
And never more was seen there.

* * * * * *

3 "Oh, how do you like your bed?" she said,
"And how do you like your sheet?
And how do you like your newly made bride
That lies in your arms asleep?"

4 "Very well do I like my bed," he said,
"Very well do I like my sheet;
But the dearest of all is the dear little maid
That's standing at my bed's feet."

5 He rode all day and he rode all night,
Till he came to Lady Marget's hall.
. . . .
. . . .

[1] Possibly for *dormer*.

6 "Oh, is she in her kitchen room,
Or is she in her hall?
Or is she in her chamber
With her merry maidens all?"

7 "She's neither in her kitchen room,
Nor is she in her hall,
But under her cold coffin lid,
Her face turned to the wall." [1]

8 "Fall down, fall down, ye milk-white sheets,
White fallies [2] are so fine,
That I may kiss the clay-cold lips
That ofttimes have kissed mine."

9 Three times he kissed her on each cheek,
Three times he kissed her chin,
Three times he kissed the clay-cold lips
That bound his heart within.

10 Lady Marget died on Whitsuntide Monday,
Sweet William died on the morrow;
Lady Marget died for pure, pure love,
Sweet William died for sorrow.

11 They buried her in the old churchyard,
They buried him in the tower;
Out of her breast grew a red rose bush,
And out of his a green briar.

12 They wound and they wound to the top of the church,
And they could not well go higher;
And there they tied in a true lover's knot,
Which many did admire.

G

"Fair Margaret and Sweet William." Collected by Miss Nancy Pearson. Sung by Mr. Armistead, of Cobbs Creek, Va. Mathews County. September 14, 1915. With music. According to the original manuscript, the last two lines of some stanzas are repeated, but irregularly. The music does not indicate this repetition, but it can easily be made at the singer's pleasure. Tbe changes from "Margaret" to "Margret" are preserved.

---

[1] Variant lines for 7 c and d, marked "original" by Miss Davis:

"But yonder lies under her cold coffin lid
With her pale face turned to the wall."

[2] Evidently for *farlies;* that is, novelties.

1 Young William he rose early in the morning,
Dressed himself in blue.
"Come tell with me the long courtship
Between Lady Margaret and you."

2 "I know nothing of Lady Margaret
And she knows nothing of me;
But before to-morrow ten, ten o'clock,
Lady Margret, my bride you'll see."

3 Lady Margret was standing at the high way window
Combing back her hair,
And who did she spy but William and his bride
To the church as they passed by?

4 Lady Margaret threw down her comb and brush,
And also threw back her hair,
And away she ran from the high way window,
And no more came there.

5 "I had a dream the other night,
I'm sure it was no good;
I dreamed that my hall was full of white swan,
And my bride's bed was floating in blood.

6 "I dreamed I saw Lady Margret's ghost
Standing at my bed feet
Say, 'How do you like your covering,
And how do you like your sheet?
And how do you like that new lady bride
That lies in your arms asleep?'"

7 "I like my coverin' very well,
And I also like my sheets;
But I love, I love that pretty fair bride
That lies at my bed feet."

8 Young William he rose and called for his horse,
He rode to her father's gate;
Saying, "Is she in the kitchen?
Or is she in the hall?
Or is she in some upper chamber
Among those fair ladies all?"

9 "She's neither in the kitchen,
She's neither in the hall;
Cold, O cold, cold clay corpse
Lies up on yonders wall."

10 "Pull down them linen sheets
That look so neat and fine,
And let me kiss them cold clay lips
Which ofttimes have kissed mine."

11 Lady Margret was buried in the new churchyard,
Young William was buried in the choir;
Out of her bosom there sprang a red rose,
And out of William's a briar.

12 They grew and they grew to the church steeple top,
Until they could grow no higher;
They tied themselves in a true lovers' knot
For all true love to admire.

H

"Lady Margaret." Collected by Miss Juliet Fauntleroy. Sung by Miss Bab Lynch, near Altavista, Va. Campbell County. August 24, 1916. The irregular repetition of the last two lines of a stanza is to be noted in the original manuscript.

1 Sweet William he rose in the morning of May,
And he dressed up himself in blue:
"Oh, come and tell me the long, long love,
Between Lady Margaret and you."

2 "Though I know no harm of Lady Margaret,
Though she knows no harm of me,
But tomorrow morning about eight o'clock,
Lady Margaret my bride shall see."

3 Lady Margaret was sitting by her violet door,
Combing of her pretty yellow hair;
The first that she spied was Sweet William and his bride,
To the churchyard they drew nigh.

4 Oh, the morning's come and gone,
And the evening shades have appeared,
Sweet William he said, "From the strutters in my head,
From the dream that I dreamt last night.

5 "The dream that I dreamt last night
Was an awful dream, I'm sure;
I dreamt that my hall was full of idle swine,
And true lovers swimming in blood."

6 He called his waiting maids,
He called them all by one, by two, by three;
He called his Lady out of Galilee,
Lady Margaret to go and see.

7 He ran and he ran till he got just there,
. . . .
And there was no one there but her own brother
To rise and let him in.

8 "Is she in her room,
Or is she in the hall?"
"No, she is in her own coffin,
Which sets by the side of the wall."

9 "Unfold, unfold them lily-white sheets,
Unfold them down so fine,
That I should kiss her red, rosy cheeks
Just as often as she has kissed mine."

10 It's first he kissed her cheeks,
And the next he kissed was her chin,
The next he kissed was her cold, cold lips,
Which had no breath within.

11 Lady Margaret she died for love,
And Sweet William he died for sorrow.
It sprung a red rose from Lady Margaret's breast
And from Sweet William's a brier.
At length they tied in a true lover's knot,
For all true lovers to admire.

I

"Fair Margaret and Sweet William." Collected by Mr. Cecil J. Sharp and Miss Karpeles. Sung by Mr. N. B. Chisholm, at Woodridge, Va. Albemarle County. September 23, 1916. With music. Printed by Campbell and Sharp, p. 69.

When the night was spent and the day coming in
And the most of them was awake,
Sweet William arose with trouble in his mind
Of the dream that had been last night.

J

"Fair Margaret and Sweet William." Collected by Mr. Cecil J. Sharp and Miss Karpeles. Sung by Mrs. Orilla Keeton, at Mt. Fair, Brown's Cove, Va. Albemarle County. September 26, 1916. With music. Music and one stanza printed by Campbell and Sharp, p. 69.

1 O down she threw her ivory comb,
And back she tossed her hair,
And down she fell from that high, high window
And never was more seen there, seen there,
And never was more seen there.

2 "O I knew nothing of Lady Margret,
And she knew nothing of me.
Tomorrow morning at eight o'clock
Lady Margret my bride shall be, shall be,
Lady Margret my bride shall be."

K

"Sweet William and Lady Margaret." Collected by Mr. John Stone. Sung by Mrs. C. A. Dickson. Highland County. November 3, 1920. With music. "She learned it from an old nurse, Nanny Dever, who used to rock her asleep with it" (Mr. Stone).

1 Lady Margaret was standing in her drawing-room door,
Combing back her long yellow hair;
And who did she spy but Sweet William and his bride,
Going to the church to be tied.

2 Down she threw her iron comb,
And back she threw her long yellow hair,
And down she knelt in her drawing-room door,
Never to arise any more.

3 "Oh! how do you like your new made bed?
And how do you like your sheet?
And how do you like your new wedded lady
That lies in your arms asleep?"

4 "Very well do I like my new made bed,
Very well do I like my sheet,
Still better do I like my new wedded lady
That lies in my arms asleep."

L

"Fair Margaret and Sweet William." Collected by Miss Corita G. Seoane, of Merrifield, Va. Fairfax County. January 19, 1914. This is evidently a mixture of "Barbara Allen" and "Fair Margaret and Sweet William." The first stanza is taken from "Barbara Allen."

1 As I was going across the fields,
I heard those bells a-tolling.
"Lie down, lie down thy corpse," she said,
"And let me look upon him."

2 Fair Margaret died of true, true love,
Sweet William died for sorrow;
Fair Margaret was buried at the east of the church,
Sweet William close by her.

3 There sprang a rose from Fair Margaret's grave
And from Sweet William's a briar.
They grew till they got to the top of the church,
Till it could not grow no higher,
And there they tied in a true love's knot,
A red red rose and a briar.

M

"Lady Margret." Collected by Miss Juliet Fauntleroy. Sung by Mr. Alonzo Hogan and Miss Callie Hogan, of Lynch Station, Va. Campbell County. February, 1914. With music.

1 Lady Margret was sitting in her bower window,
Combing out her long yellow hair;
Who should she spy but Sweet William and his bride
As they were riding near.

2 Lady Margret fell from her bower window,
Combing out her long yellow hair.
. . . .
. . . .

3 "Such a dream, such a dream, as I dreamed last night,
Such a dream, it may come true.
I dreamed my bed was full of whitened twine,
And my bride bed was filled with the tears."

4 "Hold down, hold down, your lily-white cheeks,
Hold down, hold down, so fine;
Let me get as many kisses from your cold clear lips
As ever you kissed from mine."

5 Lady Margret died today at twelve o'clock,
Sweet William died like tomorrow.
Lady Margret was buried under a tall willow tree,
Sweet William was buried under another.

N

"Sweet William's Bride." Contributed by Misses Ethel and Hallie Rodes, of Bryant, Va. Nelson County. March 26, 1917.

1 Sweet William's bride rose one merry morning
And dressed herself in blue.
"Pray tell to me the long, long love
Betwixt Lady Margaret and you."

2 "I know nothing of Lady Margaret
Nor neither does she of me;
But before tomorrow eight o'clock
Lady Margaret my bride shall be." [1]

3 As Lady Margaret was sitting in her low window,
Combing her yellow gold hair,
She saw Sweet William and his bonnie bride
Come riding close by there.

4 Down fell her ivory white comb,
Back flew her yellow gold hair,
And she fell back with a dying groan;
Never more was she seen there.

5 Sweet William came to the low window,
Saying, "Where is Lady Margaret to-day?
I want to see her one more time
Before I go away."

6 "She is neither in her bed chamber,
Nor is she in the hall,
But she is in her lead coffin
That sits against the wall."

7 "Oh, hold me back the lid,
And fold me back the sheet,
And let me kiss those clay-cold lips,
Where once so soft and sweet."

8 First he kissed her snowy white hands,
And then he kissed her chin,
And then he kissed those clay-cold lips,
Where there was no breath in.

9 Lady Margaret died like it might be today,
Sweet William died like tomorrow;
Lady Margaret died from pure true love,
Sweet William died from sorrow.

10 Lady Margaret was buried in the green churchyard,
Sweet William was buried there by her;
From Lady Margaret's breast there grew a red rose
And from Sweet William's a briar.

11 They grew and they grew to the top of the church
Until they could grow no higher;
And there they met in a true lovers' knot,
For all young people to admire.

[1] A slip in sense from the usual *see*.

O

"Lady Margaret and Sweet William." Collected by Mr. John Stone. Recited by Mrs. Mary Jett Armstrong, of Falmouth, Va. Stafford County. September 11, 1922.

1 Lady Margaret was buried at a choir church,
Sweet William at Ohio;[1]
There sprang a red rose out of Lady Margaret's grave,
And out of Sweet William's a briar.

2 They grew and grew to the church steeple top,
Till they could grow no higher;
They twined and twined in a true lover's knot
For all true lovers to admire.

P

"Lady Margaret and Sweet William." Collected by Mr. John Stone. Sung by Mr. Raz Shifflett, of Blackwell's Hollow, Va. Albemarle County. November 2, 1920. Music only.

---

[1] An interesting intrusion of American geography into an old ballad. *Ohio* is substituted for the *choir* of other variants because *choir* has already been used in the line above and because burial "in the choir" is not familiar to the American folk.

20

LORD LOVEL

(CHILD, No. 75)

FOR a general introduction to Nos. 18, 19, and 20, see the head-note to No. 18.

The wide popularity of "Lord Lovel" in America has frequently been mentioned, as in the head-notes of Cox and Reed Smith. The thirty-seven items of the Virginia collection can be more succinctly represented here because they all belong to a single version, and because several variants are almost identical. They all agree in the general outlines of the story, differ only in minor details and in phraseology. There are, however, some remarkably interesting minor variations. The thoughts that came into Lord Lovel's mind, for instance, are sometimes "languishing," but also "lingering," "laughing," "angry," "anguish," "strange," "languid," and "languish"; and the church whose bells are tolling is sometimes "St. Pancras," but also "St. Patrick's," "St. Pauthry's," "St. Varney's," "St. Vincent's," "St. Mary's," and "St. Rebecca." The lovers preserve their names with some constancy. Lady Nancybell (variously spelled) is only once Lady Annie, later Lady Annie the belle, which is quite close to the Ouncebell of Child A; and Lord Lovel slips only once, and quite naturally, into Lord Lover.

The Virginia texts are all closely related, in phraseology and in story, to Child H. The story is familiar. Lord Lovel tends his horse at his castle gate, when up comes Lady Nancybell to bid her lover good speed. In answer to her inquiries, he tells her that he is going strange countries for to see, and for what length of time he will be gone. In one text, A, she says that his intended stay is too long, and that she will be dead when he returns. Lord Lovel goes, but before his intended stay is up he languishes for Lady Nancybell and returns. In London he is greeted by funeral bells and is told the name of the dead, Lady Nancybell. He has the grave opened and the shroud turned back that he may kiss the dead, and himself dies of grief. They are buried near one another, and the rose and brier, springing from their graves, entwine their branches as a sign of love transcending death.

Miss Mary Johnston, the novelist, in a letter to Dr. Smith, of the Virginia Folk-Lore Society, tells of hearing a mountain woman sing the first two lines of "Lord Lovel" thus:

Lord Lovel stood at his *cassy*-gate,
A-combing his milk-white *speed*.

"It is probable," Dr. Smith explains, "that 'steed,' meaning nothing to the hearer, found itself easily replaced by the equally meaningless 'speed,' while 'cassy,' which often appears as 'casten' related itself vaguely in the singer's mind with the 'cast' of 'cast-iron.'" But the substitution of "cassy" for "castle" does not need such elaborate explanation. The ways of popular etymology are strange.

The four melodies, all much alike, are rather lilting, even tripping, with their double or triple repetition of the last word of the fourth line, followed by the repetition of the line. They are quite out of harmony with the deep tragedy of the ballad story. To sing the tune is to mitigate the tragedy, perhaps even to run the risk of burlesquing it.

Parodies of "Lord Lovel" may be partially attributed to the tune, but also to the nature of the story. As Child says, "'Lord Lovel' is peculiarly such a ballad as Orsino likes and praises: it is silly sooth, like the old age. Therefore a gross taste has taken pleasure in parodying it. . . . But there are people in the world who are amused even with a burlesque of Othello." A Civil War parody about Abe Lincoln, from oral tradition in Virginia, forms a perhaps excusable appendix to the ballad. Cox refers to various parodies in his headnote, p. 78.

For American texts, see Barry, No. 14; Belden, No. 6 (fragment); Brown, p. 9 (North Carolina); *Bulletin*, Nos. 2–10; Campbell and Sharp, No. 18 (North Carolina); Child, v, 294 (Massachusetts); Cox, No. 12; Jones, p. 301; *Journal*, xviii, 291 (Barry, Massachusetts, Connecticut, fragment and melody, Rhode Island, fragment, melody reprinted from Mus. 401, 2, Harvard University Library); xix, 283 (Belden, Missouri, version reprinted from James Ashby's ballad-book); xxiv, 337 (Barry, melody only from Hudson MS. No. 336); xxxi, 352 (Pound, Nebraska, fragment); xxxv, 343 (Tolman and Eddy, Ohio, fragment and melody); Pound, *Syllabus*, p. 9 (fragment); Pound, *Ballads*, No. 2; Sandburg, p. 70 (South Carolina); Scarborough, p. 55 (North Carolina, text and melody); Shearin, p. 3; Shearin and Combs, p. 8; Shoemaker, p. 140; Reed Smith, No. 6; Reed Smith, *Ballads*, No. 6. Parody satirizing a Confederate officer, Belden, No. 128. Confederate parody substituting Lincoln for Lovel, *Bulletin*, No. 6, p. 6. For additional references, see Cox, p. 78; *Journal*, xxix, 160; xxxv, 343.

A

"Lord Lovel." Collected by Miss Roxie Martin and Mr. J. M. McManaway. Sung by a white woman of Blackwell's Hollow, Va. Albemarle County. June 1, 1917. In another copy of this ballad from the same source, Lord Lovel becomes Lord Lover after the first stanza. The fourth stanza of this variant is not found in Child H or in any other Virginia text.

1 Lord Lovel he stood at his castle gate
Combing his milk-white steed,
When up came Lady Nancy Bell
Wishing her lover good speed, good speed,
Wishing her lover good speed.

2 "Where are you going, Lord Lovel?" she said.
"Where are you going?" said she.
"I'm going, my Lady Nancy Bell,
Strange countries for to see."

3 "When will you be back, Lord Lovel?" she said,
"When will you be back?" said she.
"In a year or two or three, at least,
I'll return to fair Nancy."

4 "Too long, too long, Lord Lovel," she said,
"Too long, too long," said she.
"In a year or two or three, at least,
The grass will grow o'er me."

5 He hadn't been gone quite a year and a day
Strange countries for to see,
When laughing thoughts came into his mind,
Lady Nancy Bell he would go and see.

6 So he rode and he rode on his milk-white steed,
Until he came to London town,
And there he heard Saint Pancreas' bells
And the people all mourning around.

7 "Oh, what is the matter?" Lord Lovel he said,
"Oh, what is the matter?" said he.
"A lord's lady dead," the woman replied,
"And some call her Lady Nancy."

8 So he ordered the grave to be opened wide
And the shroud to be turned down,
And then he kissed her clay-cold lips,
Until the tears came trickling down.[1]

9 Lady Nancy she died as it might be today,
Lord Lovel he died tomorrow.
Lady Nancy she died out of pure, pure grief,
Lord Lovel he died out of sorrow.

10 Lady Nancy was laid in Saint Pancreas' church,
Lord Lovel was laid in the choir;
And out of her bosom there grew a red rose,
And out of her lover's a brier.[2]

11 It grew and it grew to the church steeple top,
Until it could grow no higher,
And there it entwined in a true lovers' knot,
For all true loves to admire.[3]

[1] Variant line: "Until the tears came *tinkle* down."
[2] Variant line: "And out of her *lover* a brier."
[3] Variant line: "For all true *lovers* to admire."

B

"Lord Lovel." Collected by Miss Alfreda M. Peel. Sung by Mrs. John Roberts, of Roanoke, Va. Roanoke County. October 19, 1919. With music.

1 Lord Lovel stood at his castle gate
Combing his milk-white steed;
Lady Nancybell came riding by,
Wishing her lover good speed, speed, speed,
Wishing her lover good speed.

2 "Oh, where are you going, Lord Lovel?" she cried,
"Oh, where are you going?" cried she.
"I am going away, Lady Nancybell,
Strange countries for to see, see, see,
Strange countries for to see."

3 "When will you return, Lord Lovel?" she cried,
"When will you return?" cried she.
"In a year or two or three or more,
I'll be back to my Lady Nancy, -cy, -cy,
I'll be back to my Lady Nancy."

4 He had not been gone but a year and a day
Strange countries for to see,
When a languishing thought came into his mind
Lady Nancybell to see, see, see,
Lady Nancybell to see.

5 So he rode and he rode on his milk-white steed,
Till he came to London Town,
And there he heard St. Vincent's bell
And the people all mourning around, -round, -round,
And the people all mourning around.

6 "Is there anyone dead?" Lord Lovel said,
"Is there anyone dead?" cried he.
"A lord's daughter's dead," the people all said.
And some said, "Lady Nancy, -cy, -cy,"
And some said, "Lady Nancy."

7 He ordered the coffin straightway to be opened,
And the shroud to be folded down;
And there he kissed her pale cold lips,
And the tears came trickling down, down, down,
And the tears came trickling down.

8 Lady Nancy died it might be today,
Lord Lovel died tomorrow;
Lady Nancybell died of pure, pure love,
Lord Lovel died of sorrow, -orrow, -orrow,
Lord Lovel died of sorrow.

9 They buried them in the new churchyard,
Lady Nancy, Lord Lovel beside her.
And on her breast there grew a red rose
And on his breast a green briar, -riar, -riar,
And on his breast a green briar.

10 They grew and they grew to the new church tower,
Till they could grow no higher,
And there they entwined a true lover's knot
For all true loves to admire, -rire, -rire,
For all true loves to admire.

C

"Lord Lovel." Contributed by Miss Alice Maude Ewell, of Haymarket, Va. Through Col. E. Berkeley. Prince William County. February 2, 1914.

1 Lord Lovel stood at his castle gate,
Combing his milk-white steed,
When by came Lady Nancibel
To wish her fond lover good speed, good speed,
To wish her fond lover good speed.

2 "Now, where are you going, Lord Lovel?" she said,
"And where are you going?" said she.
"I'm going, my Lady Nancibel,
Strange countries for to see, to see,
Strange countries for to see."

3 "How long will you stay, Lord Lovel?" she said,
"How long will you stay?" said she.
"A year and a half or two years at most,
And then I'll return to thee, to thee,
And then I'll return to thee."

4 He had n't been gone a year and a day
Strange countries for to see,
When languishing thoughts came into his head
To return to his Lady Nancie, Nancie,
To return to his Lady Nancie.

HOMES OF BALLAD SINGERS IN THE
MOUNTAINS OF VIRGINIA

5 He rode and he rode as fast as he could,
Until he reached London Town,
And then he saw a funeral
With people all mourning around, around,
With people all mourning around.

6 "Now, who is dead?" Lord Lovel he said,
"And who is dead?" said he.
"Our Lord's only daughter," the people replied,
"And some call her Lady Nancie, Nancie,
And some call her Lady Nancie."

7 He ordered the grave to be opened straightway,
And her face-cloth pullèd down,
And he pressed a kiss on her clay-cold lips,
While the tears came trickling down, a-down,
The tears came trickling down.

8 Lady Nancie died it might be today,
Lord Lovel he died tomorrow;
Lady Nancie died of pure, true love,
Lord Lovel he died of sorrow, of sorrow,
Lord Lovel he died of sorrow.

9 Lady Nancie was buried in St. Mary's Church,
Lord Lovel was buried in the Choir,
And out of her bosom there grew a red rose,
And out of Lord Lovel's a brier, a brier,
And out of Lord Lovel's a brier.

10 They grew and they grew till they reached the church top
And they could grow no higher;
So they twined all into a true-love's knot
For all true-loves to admire, admire,
For all true-loves to admire.

D

"Lord Lovel." Reported by Miss Mary Washington Ball. Contributed by Miss Arline Eubank, of Richmond, Va. Sung by her grandmother. Henrico County. May 20, 1914.

1 Lord Lovel stood at his castle gate
A-combing his milk white steed,
When along came his Lady Nancy Belle
A-wishing her lover God speed, -speed, -speed,
A-wishing her lover God speed.

2 "Oh, where are you going, Lord Lovel?" she said,
"Oh, where are you going?" said she.
"I am going, my Lady Nancy Belle,
A foreign land for to see, see, see,
A foreign land for to see."

3 "And when will you be back, Lord Lovel?" she said,
"And when will you be back?" said she.
"In a year or two or three at most,
I'll return to my Lady Nancy, -cy, -cy,
I'll return to my Lady Nancy."

4 Lord Lovel had been gone but a year and a day
Strange countries for to see
When languishing thoughts came into his head
His Nancy Belle he would see, see, see,
His Nancy Belle he would see.

5 He rode and he rode on his milk-white steed
Till he came to London Town;
There he heard St. Varney's bells
And all the people murmuring 'round, 'round, 'round,
And all the people murmuring 'round.

6 "Oh, is any one dead?" Lord Lovel he said,
"Oh, is any one dead?" said he.
"A Lord's daughter is dead," was an old woman said,
"And some call her Lady Nancy, -cy, -cy,
And some call her Lady Nancy."

7 He ordered the grave stone to be taken up,
And the coffin lid to be opened,
And there he kissed her clay-cold lips
Till the tears came trinkling down, down, down,
Till the tears came trinkling down.

8 Lady Nancy died as it were today,
Lord Lovel died tomorrow.
Lady Nancy died for true, true love,
Lord Lovel died for sorrow, -orrow, -orrow,
Lord Lovel died for sorrow.

9 They buried one in the old church yard,
They buried the other in the choir;
And out of her bosom there grew a red rose
And out of Lord Lovel's a briar, -iar, -iar,
And out of Lord Lovel's a briar.

10 And they grew till they reached the church-steeple top,
And then they could grow no higher;
And there they tied in a true lover's knot
Which all true lovers admire, -ire, -ire,
Which all true lovers admire.

E

"Lord Lovel." Collected by Miss Juliet Fauntleroy. Sung by Mrs. Frank P. Christian, of Lynchburg, Va. Campbell County. May 24, 1914. With music.

1 Lord Lovel he stood at his castle gate,
Combing his milk-white steed,
When up came Lady Nancy Belle,
To wish her lover good speed, speed, speed,
To wish her lover good speed.

2 "Oh, where are you going, Lord Lovel?" she said,
"Oh, where are you going?" said she.
"I'm going, my Lady Nancy Belle,
Strange countries for to see, see, see,
Strange countries for to see."

3 "When will you be back, Lord Lovel?" she said,
"When will you be back?" said she.
"In a year or two, or three at most,
I'll return to my Lady Nancy, -cy, -cy,
I'll return to my Lady Nancy."

4 He had not been gone a year and a day,
Strange countries for to see,
When languishing thoughts came into his head,
Lady Nancy Belle he would see, see, see,
Lady Nancy Belle he would see.

5 So he rode and he rode and he rode and he rode,
Till he came to London Town,
And there he heard St. Patrick's bells,
And the people all mourning around, -round, -round,
And the people all mourning around.

6 "Who's dead, who's dead?" Lord Lovel he said,
"Who's dead, who's dead?" said he.
"A Lord's lady is dead," the people replied,
"And some call her Lady Nancy, -cy, -cy,
And some call her Lady Nancy."

7 So he ordered the grave to be opened wide,
And the coffin to be undone,
And there he kissed her clay-cold lips
Till the tears came trickling a-down, down, down,
Till the tears came trickling a-down.

8 Lady Nancy she died as it might be today,
Lord Lovel he died as tomorrow;
Lady Nancy she died out of pure, pure grief,
Lord Lovel he died out of sorrow, -orrow, -orrow,
Lord Lovel he died out of sorrow.

9 Lady Nancy was buried in the church yard,
Lord Lovel he lay in the choir;
And out of her bosom there grew a red rose,
And out of her lover's a brier, -rier, -rier,
And out of her lover's a brier.

10 They grew and they grew to the church-steeple top,
And there they could grow no higher,
So there they entwined in a true lover's knot,
That all true lovers admire, -rire, -rire,
That all true lovers admire.

F

"Lord Lovel." Collected by Mr. John Stone. Sung by Mrs. Wyndham Robertson, of Plasterco, Va., who learned it from her father. Washington County. November 8, 1921.

1 Lord Lovel he stood at his castle gate
Combing his milk-white steed.
Lady Nancy Bell stood on him to wait,
A-wishing her lover good speed, speed, speed,
A-wishing her lover good speed.

2 "O where are you going, Lord Lovel?" she said,
"O where are you going?" said she.
"I'm going away, my Lady Nancy,
Strange countries for to see, see, see,
Strange countries for to see."

3 "When will you return, Lord Lovel?" she said,
"When will you return?" said she.
"In a year or two more, at least three or four,
I'll return to my Lady Nancy, -cy, -cy,
I'll return to my Lady Nancy."

4 He had not been gone but a year and one day
Strange countries for to see,
When a languishing thought came over his heart
Concerning his Lady Nancy, -cy, -cy,
Concerning his Lady Nancy.

5 He rode all that day and all the next night,
Till he reached great London Town;
And there he heard the bells all ringing,
And the people all mourning around, around,
And the people all mourning around.

6 "Is anyone dead?" Lord Lovel he said,
"Is anyone dead?" said he.
"The squire's daughter is dead," the people all said,[1]
"Some call her the Lady Nancy, -cy, -cy,
Some call her the Lady Nancy."

7 He rode right straight to the churchyard gate
Somewhere out of the town;
He kissed and kissed the pale cold lips,
Till the tears came trickling down, down, down,
Till the tears came trickling down.

8 Lady Nancy Bell died as it were today,
Lord Lovel he died tomorrow;
Lady Nancy Bell of pure, pure love,
Lord Lovel he died of sorrow, sorrow, sorrow,
Lord Lovel he died of sorrow.

9 . . . .
. . . .
And out of her grave grew a red, red rose,
And out of his grew a briar, -iar, -iar,
And out of his grew a briar.

10 They grew and they grew to the old church spire,
And there they could grow no higher;
They linked and twined in a true lover's knot
For all true lovers to admire, -ire, -ire,
For all true lovers to admire.

[1] An occasional tendency toward internal rhyme is to be noted in this variant. Cf. 3 c and 6 c. Note also G 5 a, H 6 c, I 6 c, K 6 c, etc.

G

"Lord Lovel." Reported by Miss Ellie Hammock, of the Farmville Ballad Club. Received from Miss Ocieneal Hammock. Sung by Mrs. Dickson. Nottoway County. May, 1914. Printed in *The Focus* for May, 1914, p. 215.

1 "Where are you going, Lord Lovel," she said,
"Where are you going?" said she.
"I'm going to leave old England,
Strange countries for to see, see, see,
Strange countries for to see."

2 "When will you be back, Lord Lovel," she said,
"When will you be back?" said she.
"In a year and a half or two or three,
Then, love, I'll return to thee, thee, thee,
Then, love, I'll return to thee."

3 Lord Lovel had not been gone more than a year,
Strange countries for to see,
When an angry thought came in his mind,
Lady Annie he must go and see, see, see,
Lady Annie he must go and see.

4 He rode and he rode on his milk-white steed,
Till he came to London Town,
And there he heard St. Rebecca Church bells,
And the people all gathered around, 'round, 'round,
And the people all gathered around.

5 "Who is dead, who is dead?" Lord Lovel said,
"Who is dead, who's dead?" said he.
"The king's daughter, Lady Annie the Bell,[1]
Some call her Lady Nancy, Nancy, Nancy,
Some call her Lady Nancy."

6 He ordered the grave to be opened wide,
The shroud to be drawn down,
And there he kissed her clay-cold lips,
Till the tears came trinkling down, down, down,
Till the tears came trinkling down.

7 Lady Annie, she died as it might be today,
Lord Lovel he died on tomorrow;
And one of them died of pure true love,
And the other one died of sorrow, sorrow, sorrow,
And the other one died of sorrow.

[1] Close to the Lady *Ouncebell* of Child A. Note the shifting of the lady's name in this variant.

8 Lady Annie was buried in St. Rebecca's Church yard,
Lord Lovel was buried in the choir,
And out of her grave grew a pretty red rose,
And out of her lover's a briar, briar, briar,
And out of her lover's a briar.

9 They grew and they grew to the church steeple top,
And could not grow any higher,
And they twinkled and twined in a true lover's knot,
For all young lovers to admire, admire, admire.
For all young lovers to admire.

H

"Lord Lovel. Contributed by Dr. John W. Wayland. Written down from memory in 1849 by his mother (*née* Anna M. Kagey), of Mt. Jackson, Va. Shenandoah County. December 28, 1914.

1 Lord Lovel he stood at his castle gate
Combing his milk-white hair;[1]
Up came Lady Nancy Belle
To wish her lover good speed.

2 "Where are you going, Lord Lovel?" she said,
"Where are you going?" said she.
"I am going, my Lady Nancy,
Strange countries for to see."

3 "When will you be back, Lord Lovel?" she said,
"When will you be back?" said she.
"In a year or two or three at the most
I'll return to my fair Lady Nancy Belle."

4 He had not been gone but a year and a day
Strange countries for to see,
When anguish thoughts came into his head
That Lady Nancy he would go see.

5 He rode and he rode on his milk-white horse
Till he came to London town,
And there he heard St. Pauthry's bell
And the people all mourning around.

6 "What is the matter?" Lord Lovel he said,
"What is the matter?" [said he].
"The Lord's lady that died," the woman replied,
"Some calls her Lady Nancy."

[1] Evidently Lord Lovel's milk-white steed has got itself mixed up with Lady Nancy Belle's hair, which usually figures in a later stanza.

7 He ordered the grave to be opened wide
And her shroud to be turned down;
And there he kissed her clay-cold lips
Till tears were trickling down.

8 Lady Nancy died pure, pure grief,
Lord Lovel he died out of sorrow;
Lady Nancy died as it might be today,
Lord Lovel he died tomorrow.

9 Lady Nancy was laid
In St. Pauthry's church choir, choir;
And out of her bosom there grew a red rose,
And out of her lover a brier.

10 It as high as the church steeple top,
And it twined all 'round in a true lover's knot
For all true lovers to admire, -rire,
For all true lovers to admire.

I

"Lord Lovel." Contributed by Mr. Wilson E. Somers. Sung near Bloxom, Va. Accomac County. March 30, 1918.

1 Lord Lovel he stood at his castle gate
A-combing his milk-white steed,
When up came Lady Nancy Belle
To wish her lover good speed, speed, speed,
To wish her lover good speed.[1]

2 "O, where are you going, Lord Lovel?" she cried,
"O, where are you going?" cried she.
"I am going, my Lady Nancy Belle,
Strange countries for to see, see, see,
Strange countries for to see.

3 "When will you be back, Lord Lovel?" she cried.
"When will you be back?" cried she.
"In a year or two or three at the most,
I'll return to my Lady Nancy, -cy, -cy,
I'll return to my Lady Nancy."

4 He had not been gone but a year and a day
Strange countries for to see,
When languishing thoughts came into his mind;
Lady Nancy Belle he would go see, see, see,
Lady Nancy Belle he would go see.

[1] "Instead of 'to wish' in these lines 'for to wish' seems also to have been in use" (Mr. Somers).

5 He rode and he rode on his milk-white steed
Till he came to London Town,
And there he beheld what turned his blood cold,
Was the people all mourning around, 'round, 'round,
Was the people all mourning around.

6 "O, what is the matter?" Lord Lovel he cried,
"O, what is the matter?" cried he.
"A lady is dead," a woman said,
"And some called her Lady Nancy, -cy, -cy,
And some called her Lady Nancy."

7 He ordered her grave to be opened wide,
The shroud to be turned down,
And there he kissed her clay-cold lips,
Till the tears came trickeling down, down, down,
Till the tears came trickeling down.

8 Lady Nancy Belle died as it may be today,
Lord Lovel he died tomorrow,
Lady Nancy Belle died out of pure, pure grief,
Lord Lovel he died of sorrow, 'orrow, 'orrow,
Lord Lovel he died of sorrow.

9 Lady Nancy was laid in St. Patrick's churchyard,
Lord Lovel was laid in his choir,
And out of her bosom there grew a red rose,
And out of her lover's a brier, -ier, -ier,
And out of her lover's a brier.

10 They grew and they grew to the church steeple top
Until they could grow no higher,
And there they entwined in a true lover's knot,
For all true lovers to admire, -ire, -ire,
For all true lovers to admire.

J

"Lord Lovel." Collected by Mr. John Stone. Sung by Miss Susie Stringfellow, of Elkwood, Va. Culpeper County. November 15, 1915.

1 Lord Lovel stood at his castle gate
Combing his milk-white steed.
And by came Lady Nancy Bell
Wishing her lover good speed, speed, speed,
Wishing her lover good speed.

2 "Oh, where are you going, Lord Lovel?" she said,
"Oh, where are you going?" said she.
"I'm going abroad, Lady Nancy Bell,
Strange countries for to see, see, see,
Strange countries for to see."

3 "When will you be back, Lord Lovel?" she said,
"When will you be back?" said she.
"In a year or two or three at most
I'll return to my Lady Nancy, -cy, -cy,
I'll return to my Lady Nancy."

4 He had n't been gone but a year and a day,
A year and a day had he,
When a languishing thought came into his mind
Lady Nancy for to see, see, see,
Lady Nancy for to see.

5 He rode and he rode till he reached London town,
He rode and he rode, did he;
And there he heard St. Varney's Church bells
And the people all mourning around, -round, -round,
And the people all mourning around.

6 "Is any one dead?" Lord Lovel he said,
"Is any one dead?" said he.
"A lady is dead," the people said,
"They called her the Lady Nancy, -cy, -cy,
They called her the Lady Nancy."

7 He caused the grave to be opened wide
And the shroud to be folded down;
And there he kissed her clay-cold lips,
Till the tears came trickling down, down, down,
Till the tears came trickling down.

8 Lady Nancy was laid in the old churchyard,
Lord Lovel was laid close by her;
And out of her bosom there grew a red rose,
And out of his backbone a briar, -iar, -iar,
And out of his backbone a briar.

9 They grew and grew till they reached the church top
And they could n't grow any higher;
And there they twined in a true lover's knot
For all true lovers to admire, -ire, -ire
For all true lovers to admire.

10 Lady Nancy died as it might be today,
Lord Lovel died tomorrow.
Lady Nancy died of pure, pure grief,
Lord Lovel died of sorrow, -orrow, -orrow,
Lord Lovel died of sorrow.

K

"Lord Lovel and Lady Nancy Bell." Contributed by Miss Lucy T. Latané, of Baltimore, Maryland. Sung by her mother's "mammy" in Virginia. Louisa County. November 18, 1913. "The version of Lord Lovel that has always been repeated and sung in our family. My mother and aunt learned it from their 'mammy' in Louisa County [Va.] in the forties" (Miss Latané).

1 Lord Lovel he stood at his castle gate
A-patting his milk-white steed,
When down came the Lady Nancy Bell
A-wishing her lover good speed, speed, speed,
A-wishing her lover good speed.

2 "O where are you going, Lord Lovel?" she said.
"O where are you going?" said she.
"I'm going, my dear Lady Nancy Bell,
Strange countries far to see, see, see,
Strange countries far to see."

3 "When will you be back, Lord Lovel?" she said,
"When will you be back?" said she.
"A year or two or three at the most.
Strange countries I must go see, see, see,
Strange countries I must go see."

4 But he had not been gone a year at the most
Strange countries far to see,
When languishing thoughts came into his heart.
His Nancy Bell he must go see, see, see,
His Nancy Bell he must go see.

5 So he rode and he rode on his milk-white steed
Till he came to London town,
And there he hear St. Pancras bell
And the people all hurrying 'round, 'round, 'round.
And the people all hurrying 'round.

6 "O what is the matter, good people?" he said,
"O what is the matter?" said he.
"A lord's lady is dead," a poor woman said,
"And they called her the Lady Nancy, cy, -cy,
And they called her the Lady Nancy."

7 He ordered the grave to be opened wide
And the shroud to be laid aside,
And there in all . . . [1]
Lady Nancy Bell he espied, -spied, -spied,
Lady Nancy Bell he espied.

8 Lady Nancy she died as it might be today,
Lord Lovel he died tomorrow,
And out of her breast grew a lily-white rose
And out of her lover's a brier, -rier, -rier,
And out of her lover's a brier.

9 And they grew and they grew till they reached the church tower,
And when they could climb no higher,
They twined together in a true-lover's knot
For all true-lovers to admire, -rire, -rire,
For all true-lovers to admire.

L

"Lord Lovel." Collected by Mr. John Stone. Sung by Mr. Thomas H. Bailey, of Marksville, Va. Page County. November 10, 1919. With music. "Mr. Bailey got this song years ago from a man named Oliver Cave, who lived on the top of the Blue Ridge mountains. The tune is almost identical with that of 'The Bonny Blue Flag.' I have an idea that 'The Bonny Blue Flag' got its tune from 'Lord Lovel'" (Mr. Stone). But Mr. Fred P. Myers, who sends the same text from the same singer states that it was "sung by Mr. Bailey from memory of one hearing from Miss Lee Koonz, of Marksville, Page County, Va., 1868. Heard first at an 'apple-butter boiling.'" Perhaps Mr. Bailey's memory was at fault.

1 Lord Lovel who stands at the castle gate
A-combing his milk-white steed,
In up comes Miss Nancy my dear,
A-wishing her lover could stay, stay, stay,
A-wishing her lover could stay.

2 "Where are you going, Lord Lovel?" said she,
"Where are you going?" said she.
"Away, away to strange countries to see, see, see,
Away to strange countries to see." [2]

[1] Variant line from same family: "And there, oh there, in the cold, cold ground."

[2] A conjectural standardization of this stanza would substitute for its last two lines these three:

"Away, away to strange countries,
Away to strange countries to see, see, see,
Away to strange countries to see."

3 "When will you be back, Lord Lovel?" said she,
"When will you be back?" said she.
"One year or two or three at the most
I'll return to my Lady Nancy, -cy, -cy,
I'll return to my Lady Nancy."

4 He having been gone but a very short time,
Not more than a month and one day,
Languish thoughts came into his mind,[1]
His lady he would go see, see, see,
His lady he would go see.

5 He saddled his pony and he did ride,
He rode till he came to the town;
And there he heard the large church bell,
The people was mourning all 'round, 'round, 'round,
The people was mourning all 'round.

6 "What is to matter?" Lord Lovel says he,
"What is to matter?" says he.
The ladies replied, "The Governor's daughter is dead.
Some called her the lady Nancy, -cy, -cy,
Some called her the lady Nancy."

7 He ordered her coffin to be opened wide
And the shroud to be fold down.
And there he kissed her clay-cold lips
Till the tears came trickling down, down, down,
Till the tears came trickling down.

M

"Lord Lovel." Collected by Mr. John Stone. Recited by Mrs. H. G. Saunders, of Shirley, Va. Charles City County. June 29, 1921. "She heard it sung at an entertainment when she was a little girl" (Mr. Stone).

It twistled and twistled till it could n't twistle no higher;
And there it formed a true lover's knot,
For all true lovers to admire, -ire, -ire,
For all true lovers to admire.

[1] Variant line: "*Before languid* thoughts came into his mind."

N

"Lord Lovel." Collected by Mr. John Stone and Miss Sarah Doughty. Sung by Mr. John Doughty, of Cape Charles, Va. Northampton County. November 8, 1921. The second stanza gives an unusual ending to the ballad.

1 Lord Lovel was buried in St. Patrick's Hall,
Lady Nancy Bell was buried in the choir;
And out of her breast there grew a red rose
For all true lovers to admire.

2 It grew so high and it grew so tall,
'T was a wonder to all the town;
And the rose and the brier would still have been there,
If the sexton had not cut it down.

O

"Lord Lovel." Collected by Mr. John Stone. Sung by Mrs. Mary E. Bell, of Shirley, Va. Charles City County. September 13, 1917. With music.

Lord Lovel stood at his castle gate,
Combing his milk-white steed,
When up stepped Lady Nancy Bell,
A-wishing her lover good speed, speed, speed,
A-wishing her lover good speed.

APPENDIX

Parody of "Lord Lovel." Collected by Mr. John Stone. Received from Mrs. T. C. Cummins, of Rumford, Va. King William County. June, 1917. "She heard it soon after the War between the States. I think it was an army song. Evidently the ballad itself was sung in those days. . . . As fragments of the ballad itself, Mrs. Weathers gave me the expression 'sorrow-orrow-orrow' and Mrs. Mary E. Bell, of Shirley, Va., gave me the expression 'it thristled and thristled and thristled and grew' in place of 'it grew and grew to the church steeple top'" (Mr. Stone).

1 Abe Lincoln stood at the White House gate
Combing his milk-white steed,
When along came Lady Lizzie Tod,
Wishing her lover good speed, speed, speed,
Wishing her lover good speed.

2 "Where are you going, Abe Lincoln?" she said.
"Where are you going?" said she.
"I'm going, my dearest Lizzie Tod,
O'er Richmond for to see, see, see,
O'er Richmond for to see."

3 "When will you be back, Abe Lincoln?" she said.
"When will you be back?" said she.
"In sixty or ninety days at the most,
I'll return to my Lady Lizzie, -zie, -zie,
I'll return to my Lady Lizzie."

4 He had n't been gone more than one or two days
O'er Richmond for to see,
When back to the White House gate he came,
All tattered and torn was he, he, he,
All tattered and torn was he.

5 "How do you flourish, Abe Lincoln?" she said.
"How do you flourish?" said she.
"The rebels have killed my old Scotch horse
And I have skedaddled, -dee, -dee, -dee, -dee,
And I have skedaddled, -dee, -dee."

6 Abe Lincoln rode his Burnside horse
Which started at the rebels' fire.
He threw the baboon heels over head,
And there he stuck tight in the mire, -ire, -ire,
And there he stuck tight in the mire.

21

THE LASS OF ROCH ROYAL

(Child, No. 76)

No complete or nearly complete text of this ballad has been recovered in Virginia. Only two stanzas definitely belonging to the ballad have been found, the "shoe my foot" stanzas. These appear often alone, often in combination with other songs. The stanzas correspond roughly to Child A 18–21, Child B 1–4, Child D 1–4, Child E 1–4, Child F 1–2, Child H 1–2, Child J 1–2. But the closest correspondence is, perhaps naturally, to be found with the last two stanzas of the seven-stanza ballad printed in Child III, 511–512, from *The Folk-Lore Journal* VII, 31, "as sung in Virginia"; with the succeeding two-stanza fragment obtained in the "Carolina mountains" (Child III, 512); and with West Virginia B (Cox, p. 87).

The story of "The Lass of Roch Royal," not to be gleaned from the Virginia fragments, is a most touching and tragic one. The Lass of Roch Royal, in great distress and far gone in pregnancy, goes in quest of her lover, Love Gregory, or Love Gregor. When she comes to his castle, his mother, who is evidently hostile to her, answers for the son and asks for the love tokens that have passed between the two. These the girl gives, only to be told that Love Gregory is not at home but away upon the sea. It is here that, according to Child A, she inquires who will take care of her and who will be her bairn's father till Love Gregory comes home, and the mother answers that she will do all the other things but none can be the bairn's father till Love Gregory comes home (the "shoe my foot" stanzas). But the girl departs to continue her quest. Soon Love Gregory, who has been at home asleep, awakes and tells his mother of his dream that the Lass of Roch Royal was knocking at the door. The mother tells him that the dream is true, and that the girl has just left. After speaking his mind to his mother for her failure to wake him, he mounts his swiftest horse in pursuit of the lass, but he finds only her dead body (sometimes with that of his young son), over which he bitterly laments before he joins her in death. In most versions, the "shoe my foot" stanzas come at the beginning of the ballad, before the lass sets out from home, where the reply that father, mother, brother, etc. will support her but there is none to be her bairn's father till Love Gregory returns, comes more properly.

The two "shoe my foot" stanzas often occur by themselves, as a separate song, and often in combination with other songs. The variants A-U are pure texts, fragmentary of course; the appendices A-I, are texts in combination.

Of the pure fragments standing alone, the Virginia title is usually a repetition of the first line, or "Love Gregor." Compare West Virginia B, which is known as "My Lady's Slipper." The twenty-one texts A-U, which are modifications of the two identical stanzas, are an interesting study in ballad variation. Of these twenty-one items, no two are identical, and often the variation is significant. In some texts there are two speakers, in some only one, who answers his or her own questions; where there are two speakers, sometimes the man speaks first and the girl answers, sometimes the girl is the questioner and the man answers. Several times the two stanzas are expanded into six by repetition; see A and footnote, and Appendix A. The girl's reply to the crucial question who will kiss her ruby lips, is as variable as woman herself; and even the land to which he or she is going is a place of infinite variety.

The "shoe my foot" stanzas may be thought of as the hydrogen ion of balladry because of their readiness of combination, illustrated by Appendices A-I. In Virginia the stanzas seem to be so frequently combined with certain stanzas, particularly the "Adieu" chorus, of "There is a Tavern in the Town," that there was a temptation to admit texts of this sort to the full status of variants rather than print them as appendices. But caution ruled, and they appear as Appendices A and B. The tavern song, which is a familiar college song in this country, is better known in English folk-song as "There is an Alehouse in Yonder Town," and in longer broadside form as "A Brisk Young Sailor."

This combination with the chorus (or more) of the tavern song is widely current in Virginia. And there are other exhibits (Appendices C-I) to show how readily the "shoe my foot" stanzas become part of any song about the parting of friends, a lovers' farewell, or any sort of lover's lament. They are found regularly or often in "The True Lover's Farewell," "Cold Winter's Night," "The Rejected Lover," "John Hardy," "Careless Love," "The False Young Man," "Kitty Kline," and the like. Appendices C-I give some interesting examples of the combination of the stanzas in songs known in Virginia as "Bright Day," "The Irish Girl," "Turtle Dove," "Cold Winter's Night," "Negro Dancing Song," as well as "The Lass of Roch Royal" and "Who Will Shoe My Pretty Little Feet?" Virginia 40, Appendices A and B, may also be regarded as appendices of this ballad, and the title of B, "A-Roving," may be listed here.

The "Lass of Roch Royal" stanzas are frequently found in Virginia in association with "The House Carpenter" (Child, No. 243). See Virginia 40, R, S, Appendix A and Appendix B. Compare "The New-Slain Knight" (Child, No. 263). Particular attention should be called to Virginia 40, Appendix A, because its chorus supplies the only other "Lass of Roch Royal" stanza found in Virginia, the stanza spoken by the lass when she is about to set forth from home in quest of Love Gregory, and by Love Gregory when he goes in pursuit of her:

> "Saddle me the milk-white horse,
>   Saddle me the brown,
> Saddle me the swiftest horse
>   That ever laid foot on ground."

To be quite accurate, then, "The Lass of Roch Royal" in Virginia boasts the "shoe my foot" stanzas plus this one, which seems to turn up quite by chance in another song.

For other American texts, see Belden, No. 91 (fragment); Brown, p. 9 (North Carolina); *Bulletin*, Nos. 2–10; Child, II, 224 (Michigan); III, 511 (Virginia, from *The Folk-Lore Journal*, VII, 31; "the Carolina Mountains"); Combs, p. 134 (West Virginia); Cox, No. 13; *Journal*, XXII, 240 (Bascom, North Carolina, fragment); Sandburg, p. 98 (Indiana, R. W. Gordon Collection); Shearin, p. 4; Shearin and Combs, p. 8. For additional references, see *Journal*, XXX, 305.

A

"Lass of Roch Royal." Collected by Mr. John Stone. Sung by Mrs. Terry. King William County. November 15, 1916. With music. This variant is an interesting prolongation of the usual two stanzas. The singer has tripled the length of the song without introducing new words. "I have found fragments of 'Roch Royal' in various counties of the state; namely, Nelson, Alexandria, Amherst, Augusta, Henrico, Montgomery, Middlesex, Culpeper, New Kent, and Campbell. Some have 'No one will kiss my ruby-red lips,' while others have, 'You will kiss my ruby-red lips, when you return from a foreign land.' Some have 'rosy-red lips'" (Mr. Stone). Similar texts, in which each line is expanded into a stanza, were later reported by Mr. Stone from Arlington and Lee counties.

1 "Who will shoe your pretty little feet,
Who will shoe your pretty little feet,
Who will shoe your pretty little feet,
When I'm in a foreign land?"

2 "My father will shoe my pretty little feet,
My father will shoe my pretty little feet,
My father will shoe my pretty little feet,
When you're in a foreign land."

3 "Who will glove your lily-white hand,
Who will glove your lily-white hand,
Who will glove your lily-white hand,
When I'm in a foreign land?"

4 "My brother will glove my lily-white hand,
My brother will glove my lily-white hand,
My brother will glove my lily-white hand,
When you're in a foreign land."

5 "Who will kiss your ruby red lips,
Who will kiss your ruby red lips,
Who will kiss your ruby red lips,
When I'm in a foreign land?"

6 "My mother will kiss my ruby red lips,
My mother will kiss my ruby red lips,
My mother will kiss my ruby red lips,
When you're in a foreign land."

B

"Love Gregor." Collected by Mr. John Stone. Recited by Mr. J. A. Cooper, of Williamsburg, Va. James City County. July 13, 1921. Mr. Cooper "first heard it in Rowan County, North Carolina, about forty years ago" (Mr. Stone).

1 "Who will shoe your pretty little foot, foot, foot?
Who will glove your lily-white hand, hand, hand?
Who will kiss your ruby lips
When I am in that far distant land?

2 "Your father will shoe your pretty little foot, foot, foot;
Your mother will glove your lily-white hand, hand, hand;
Your kind friends will kiss your ruby lips
When I am in that far distant land."

C

No title given. Contributed by Miss Addie Mason, of Roanoke, Va. Franklin County. July 28, 1916.

1 "Who will shoe my pretty little feet?
Who will glove my hands?
Who will kiss my red rosy cheeks,
When I'm in a foreign land?

2 "Papa will shoe my pretty little feet;
Mama will glove my hand;
Johnny will kiss my red rosy cheeks,
When I'm in a foreign land."

D

"Who Will Shoe My Pretty Little Feet?" Collected by Mrs. W. H. Taliaferro. Sung by Mrs. M. E. McDaele, of Buffalo Junction, Va. Mecklenburg County. March 15, 1915.

1 "Who will shoe my pretty little feet?
My father'll shoe my pretty little feet,
My mother will glove my pretty little hand,
When I am in a foreign land.

2 "Who will kiss my pretty little lips
When I return again?
My sweetheart will kiss my pretty little lips
When I am at home again."

E

"Love Gregory." Collected by Mr. John Stone. Sung by Mr. C. F. Carpenter of Bolar, Va. Highland County. November 3, 1920.

1 "Who will shoe my bony, bony feet?
And who will glove my hand?
And who will kiss my ruby red lips,
When you are in some foreign land?

2 "My father will shoe my bony, bony feet;
My mother will glove my hand;
No one will kiss my ruby red lips,
When you are in some foreign land."

F

"Lass of Roch Royal." Collected by Mr. John Stone. Sung by Miss Bertha Mayo, of Wilmington, Va. Fluvanna County. November 3, 1920. "She learned it from her father and brother, who were both absent when I called; consequently, I missed hearing them sing. They are natives of Fluvanna" (Mr. Stone).

1 "Who will shoe my pretty little foot?
Who will glove my hand?
Who will kiss my red rosy cheeks,
When you are in the promised land?

2 "My papa will shoe my pretty little feet;
My mamma will glove my hand;
My sister will kiss my red rosy cheeks,
When you are in the promised land."

G

"Love Gregor." Collected by Mr. John Stone. Sung by Mrs. Mollie Binns, of Claremont, Va. Surry County. July 13, 1921.

1 "O who will shoe my pretty, pretty foot?
O who will glove my lily-white hand?
And who will kiss my pretty, pretty lips,
While you are gone to the foreign land?

2 "My father will shoe my pretty, pretty foot;
My mother will glove my hand;
And you shall kiss my pretty, pretty lips,
When you are in from the foreign land."

H

"Love Gregor." Collected by Mr. John Stone. Recited by Mrs. Martha C. Throckmorton, of Bluemont, Va. Loudoun County. September 23, 1922. "Mrs. Throckmorton used to play it as a ring game when she was a child" (Mr. Stone).

1 "O, who will shoe my pretty little foot
And hold my lily-white hand?
And who will kiss my sweet little lips
When I go to distant lands?"

2 "O, I will shoe your pretty little foot,
And I will hold your lily-white hand,
And I will kiss your sweet little lips
When you go to distant lands."

I

"Love Gregor." Collected by Mr. John Stone. Recited by Mrs. Margaret A. Pound, of Oakgrove, Va. Westmoreland County. September 11, 1922.

1 "Who will shoe my pretty little foot?
Who will glove my hand?
Who will kiss my ruby lips,
When you are in some foreign land?

2 "My father will shoe my pretty little foot;
My mother will glove my hand;
No one will kiss my pretty little lips
When you are in some foreign land."

J

"Love Gregor." Collected by Mr. John Stone. Sung by Mr. J. W. Wyatt, of Dante, Va. Russell County. November 8, 1921.

1 "Who will shoe your pretty little foot?
Who will glove your hand?
Who will kiss your rosy cheeks,
When I am in a foreign land?"

2 "My father will shoe my pretty little foot;
My mother will glove my hand;
And you will kiss my rosy cheeks,
When you return from a foreign land."

K

"Love Gregor." Collected by Mr. John Stone. Sung by Mrs. Sidney Smith, of Yorktown, Va. York County. July 13, 1921. "She heard her mother sing it when she was a child" (Mr. Stone).

1 "O who will shoe my pretty little foot?
And who will glove my lily-white hand?
And who will kiss my rosy lips,
When I am far from land?

2 "My father will shoe my pretty little foot;
My mother will glove my lily-white hand;
And my sweetheart will kiss my rosy lips,
When I am far from land."

L

"Love Gregor." Collected by Mr. John Stone. Sung by Mr. and Mrs. Claude Rhame, of Cape Charles, Va. Northampton County. July 13, 1921. "Mr. Rhame heard his mother sing it when he was a boy in South Carolina. Mrs. Rhame heard her mother sing it here in Virginia when she was a child" (Mr. Stone).

1 "O, who will shoe my pretty little foot?
O, who will glove my lily-white hand?
O, who will kiss my ruby lips
When you are in a { far off (*Mrs. R.*) / foreign (*Mr. R.*) } land.

2 "My father will shoe my pretty little foot;
My mother will glove my hand;
My { beau / lover } will kiss my ruby lips,
When you are in a { far off / foreign } land."

M

"The Lass of Roch Royal." Contributed by Miss Katherine Middleton, of Rich Creek, Va. Sung by her mother in Rockbridge County. July, 1914.

1 "Oh, who will shoe my pretty little foot?
And who will hold my lily-white hand?
And who will kiss my ruby lips,
When you are in some distant land?

2 "My father, he will shoe my pretty little foot;
My sister hold my lily-white hand;
But none may kiss my ruby lips
When you are in some distant land."

N

"Love Gregor." Collected by Mr. John Stone. Sung by Mr. Sam Kirby, of Bland Court House, Va. Bland County. November 8, 1921. "He [Mr. Kirby] heard Mr. Jim Thompson, Thompson's Valley, Tazewell County, Virginia, sing it about twelve years ago" (Mr. Stone).

1 "Who's a-going to shoe my pretty little feet?
Who's a-going to glove my hand?
Who's a-going to kiss my red ruby lips,
When I'm in a western land?

2 "My papa's going to shoe my pretty little feet;
My mamma's going to glove my hand;
My brother's going to kiss my red ruby lips,
When I'm in a western land."

O

"Love Gregor." Reported by Prof. James M. Grainger. Collected by Miss Mae Cox, of the Farmville Ballad Club. Albemarle County. February, 1914. Printed in *The Focus* for February, 1914.

1 "Oh, who will shoe your foot, my dear?
And who will glove your hand?
And who will kiss your red rosy lips,
When I am gone to the far-off land?"

2 "My papa will shoe my foot, my dear;
My brother will glove my hand;
My mamma will kiss my red rosy lips,
When you have gone to the far-off land."

P

"Love Gregor." Collected by Mr. John Stone. Sung by Miss Rena Louise Trice, of Walkerton, Va. King and Queen County. September 11, 1922.

1 "Who will shoe my pretty little foot?
Who will glove my lily-white hand?
Who will kiss my ruby lips,
In all this distant land?

2 "My pa will shoe my pretty little foot;
My ma will love my lily-white hand;
My beau will kiss my ruby lips,
In all this distant land."

Q

"Love Gregor." Collected by Mr. John Stone. Sung by Dr. S. E. Richardson, of Urbana, Va. Middlesex County. September 11, 1922.

1 "Who will shoe that pretty little foot?
Who will glove that lily-white hand?
Who will kiss those ruby lips,
When I am in a foreign land?"

2 "Pa will shoe that pretty little foot;
Ma will glove that lily-white hand;
Kind friends will kiss those ruby lips,
When I am in a foreign land."

R

"The Lass of Roch Royal." Collected by Miss Lemma Garrett, of the Farmville Ballad Club. Sung by a Negro in Charlotte County. March, 1913. Printed in *The Focus* for March, 1913.

1 "I, who gwine to shoe my foot?
I, who gwine to glove my hand?
I, who gwine to kiss my red ruby lips?
For I'm gwine to a far distant land.

2 "Daddy gwine to shoe my foot,
Mammy gwine to glove my hand,
My true love will kiss my red ruby lips,
For I'm gwine to a far distant land."

S

"The Lass of Roch Royal." Collected by Miss Ellen B. Bouldin. Sung by Mr. John L. Bouldin, of Houston, Va. Halifax County. February 12, 1914. "These my brother, John L. Bouldin, heard a Negro sing in Charlotte County, Virginia, and has often sung them for us" (Miss Bouldin).

1 "Who gwine to shoe my feet?
Who gwine to glove my hand?
Who gwine to kiss my red rosy cheek?
For I am goin' to a far distant land.

2 "My father gwine to shoe my feet;
My mother gwine to glove my hand;
My true love gwine to kiss my red rosy cheek,
For I am goin' to a far distant land."

T

"Love Gregor." Collected by Mr. John Stone. Recited by Mr. and Mrs. B. F. Pollard, of Claremont, Va. Surry County. July 13, 1921.

1 "Who will shoe your pretty little feet?
  Who will glove your hand?
Who will kiss your ruby lips,
  When I am gone?"

2 "My father will shoe my pretty little feet;
  My mother will glove my hand;
My brother will kiss my ruby lips,
  When you are gone."

U

"Love Gregory." Collected by Mr. John Stone. Sung by Mrs. C. A. Dickson. Highland County. November 3, 1920. With music.

"My father loves my lily-white hands;
  My sister loves my face so fair;
But none shall kiss my ruby lips,
  When you are in some distant land."

APPENDICES

A

"Lass of Roch Royal." Collected by Mr. John Stone. Sung by Mrs. Nathaniel Stone, of Culpeper, Va. Culpeper County. November 15, 1916. With music.

1 "Adieu, kind friend, adieu, adieu,
I cannot linger long with you;
I'll bid farewell to all my fears
  While I am in a foreign land.
I'll bid farewell to all my fears
  While I am in a foreign land.[1]

2 "Must I go bond and you go free?
Must I go bond and you go free?
O, must I act the foolie's part
  And die for a man that would break my heart?
O, must I act the foolie's part
  And die for a man that would break my heart?

[1] In other variants of the same combination song, this "Adieu" stanza appears after the "shoe my foot" stanzas or — and more generally — as a chorus.

3 "O, who will shoe those pretty little feet?
O, who will glove those lily-white hands?
O, who will kiss those ruby lips,
While I am in a foreign land?
O, who will kiss those ruby lips
While I am in a foreign land?"

4 "My father will shoe my pretty little feet;
My brother will glove my lily-white hands;
My mother'll kiss my ruby lips,
When you are in a foreign land.
My mother'll kiss my ruby lips
When you are in a foreign land."

B

No title given. Collected by Miss Alice Crawley. Sung by Mrs. Drake, of Courtland, Va. Southampton County. January 10, 1917.

1 "Who will kiss my ruby lips?
Who will kiss my ruby lips?
Who will kiss my ruby lips,
When you are far away?"

2 "Kind friends will kiss your ruby lips,
When I am far away;
Kind friends will kiss your ruby lips,
When I am far away;
Kind friends will kiss your ruby lips,
When I am far away."

3 "Who will glove my lily-white hand?
Who will glove my lily-white hand?
Who will glove my lily-white hand,
When you are far away?"

4 "Your mother will glove your lily-white hand,
When I am far away;
Your mother will glove your lily-white hand,
When I am far away;
Your mother will glove your lily-white hand,
When I am far away."

5 "Who will shoe my pretty little feet?
Who will shoe my pretty little feet?
Who will shoe my pretty little feet,
When you are far away?"

6 "Your father will shoe your pretty little feet,
When I am far away;
Your father will shoe your pretty little feet,
When I am far away;
Your father will shoe your pretty white feet,
When I am far away."

7 "I'll hang my heart on the willow tree,
And go for the fellow that goes for me;
I'll hang my heart on the willow tree,
And go for the fellow that goes for me;
I'll hang my heart on the willow tree,
And go for the fellow that goes for me."

C

"Bright Day." Collected by Miss Juliet Fauntleroy. Sung by Mrs. John Maxie (*née* Lily Stone), near Altavista, Va. Campbell County. February 28, 1914.

1 "I wish I was in my own room,
A-sitting on a bed of down;
I never would give to you my hand
To sail to a foreign land."

2 "Hush, oh hush, my dearest,
I hate to hear you cry,
The best of friends do part,
And why not you and I?

3 "Oh, don't you see yonder lonesome dove,
Flying from pine to pine,
Mourning for its own true love,
Just like I have mourned for mine.

4 "Oh, I wish to the Lord I'd never been born,
Or had died when I was young;
I'd never been here to shed a tear
For no girl under the sun.

5 "Oh, who will shoe your pretty little foot?
And who will glove your hand?
And who will kiss your rosy red lips
When I'm in some foreign land?"

6 "My father will shoe my feet, my love;
My mother will glove my hand;
And you may kiss my rosy red lips
If you ever return again."

7 "Supposing I go so far away,
Be taken sick and die;
Who will hear me when I cry (pray),
And who will see me when I die?"

8 "Oh, if you go so far away,
Be taken sick and die,
Your father will hear you when you cry (pray),
Your mother will see you when you die."

9 "And if ever I prove false to the one I love,
Bright day will surely turn to night,
My own true love,
Bright day will turn to night.[1]

10 "Oh, I wish to the Lord I had never been born,
Or had died when I was young;
I'd never been here to shed a tear
For no girl under the sun.

11 "That for me the cradle had never been rocked,
Nor to me my mother sung,
Then would I not have been here
To part from you, my dear.[1]

12 "Oh, if ever I prove false
To you, my own true love,
Bright day will turn to night,
And the raging sea shall burn;
If I false prove to the one I love,
The elements shall mourn.[1]

13 "Oh, if I had never been born,
Or had died when I was young,
I'd never been here to shed a tear
For nary girl under the sun."

D

"Who Will Shoe My Pretty Little Feet?" Collected by Mrs. Olin F. Wiley, of Richmond, Va. Found in Wise County. December 1, 1916.

1 As I walked out last winter's night,
A-drinking of sweet wine,
Conversing with that pretty little girl
Who stold this heart of mine,

[1] The line divisions of stanzas 9, 11, and 12 are doubtful.

2 Her cheeks were like some pink or rose
Just bloomed in the month of June,
Her voice was like some new instrument
Just been put in tune.

3 "Five thousand miles, my own true love,
Through Scotland, France, and Spain,
And if you were to take sick and die,
And you so far from home.

4 "No one to ease you of your pain,
To hear your pitiful cry.
I wish to God I'd never been born,
Or died when I was young.

5 "I never would bathe my cheeks in tears,
About no old man's son.
The rocks shall melt just by the sun,
The raging sea shall burn.

6 "Oh, who will shoe your feet, my love?
Or who will glove your hand?
Or who will kiss those ruby lips,
When you are in a foreign land?"

7 "My father will shoe my feet, my love;
My mother will glove my hand;
And you may kiss my ruby lips
When you return again."

E

"Negro Dancing Song." Collected by Miss Juliet Fauntleroy. Sung by Irene Douglas and Willie Walker, two Colored servants, of Lynch Station, Va. Campbell County. March, 1914.

1 "Who's going to shoe your pretty little feet?
Who's going to curl your hair?"
"Papa's going to shoe my pretty little feet,
Mama's going to curl my hair."

2 "I wish I had a bosom friend
To tell my secrets to.
This old sinful heart of mine
Has told every thing I do.

3 "If I had a needle and thread,
The finest I could sew,
I'd sew my baby to my side,
Carry him every where I go.

4 "I've told you once, I've told you twice,
I've told you a thousand times,
If you don't like the way I do,
You move on down the line.

5 "I told that girl when I left town,
Don't she grieve and cry;
If I live and don't get killed
I'd see her by and by.

6 "Where you been, my darling,
Where you been so long?"
"I've been around the whole round world,
And don't you want to go?"

7 "Where'd you get your brand new shoes,
Your dress you wear so fine?"
"Got my shoes from a railroad man,
My dress from a golden mine."

F

"The Irish Girl." Collected by Mr. John Stone. Sung by the Misses Rosalie and Ruby Broadus, of Alexandria, Va. Arlington (formerly Alexandria) County. November 10, 1919. "This is one of several songs I have found having the 'shoe my foot' lines. They include England, Ireland, and France in their geography" (Mr. Stone).

1 One evening I took a walking out,
Down by the salt sea side;
I cast my eyes all around me
And a loving little girl I spied.

2 How costly were the jewelry
This Irish girl did wear;
So red and rosy were her cheeks,
And coal black was her hair.

3 The tears came rolling down her cheeks
And she began to cry:
"My true love is in Ireland,
And truly forsaken am I."

4 "My true love gone, my joy gone,
My pleasure went with him;
He hated to leave his darling,
But he knew we had to part."

5 "Here is whiskey, boys, here brandy, boys,
We will drink before we go;
We will cross the British old ocean,
Let the tides run high or low."

6 "I wish I was in Old Ireland,
A-sitting in my chair,
With pen and ink in my hand,
A-writing to my dear."

7 "O who's going to shoe your pretty little feet?
Who's going to glove your hands?
Who is going to kiss your red ruby lips,
When I am in a foreign land?"

8 "My papa will shoe my pretty little feet;
My mamma will glove my hands;
And you will kiss my red ruby lips
When you return from a foreign land."

G

"Cold Winter's Night." Collected by Miss Juliet Fauntleroy. Sung by Mrs. Maxie (*née* Holland), of Altavista, Va. Franklin County. April 7, 1914. With music.

1 I was roving out one cold winter night,
A-drinking of sweet wine,
And a-loving of that pretty little girl
That stole this heart of mine, mine, mine,
That stole this heart of mine.

2 Her cheeks were like some pinky rose
That blooms in the month of June;
Her tongue was like some musical banjo
Just newly put in tune.

3 Oh, don't you see that black-eyed boy,
A-sitting on his knee?
Parting me and my true love,
Shall be the death of me.

4 I wish I had listened at the singing birds
That sing among the trees,
When I was a-listening at your flattering tongue,
When you were a-flattering me.

5 "Who will shoe your pretty little foot?
Who will glove your hand?
Who will kiss your red rosy lips
When I'm in a fair run (foreign) land."

6 "My father will shoe my pretty little foot;
My mother will glove my hand;
No one shall kiss my red rosy lips
When you are in a fair run (foreign) land."

7 Suppose you go the Lord knows where,
Suppose you go away,
Suppose you go the Lord knows where
And leave me here for to stray.

8 Suppose you go so far away
That you get sick and die,
Who'll be there to hear you moan,
And hear you groan and cry?

9 Don't you see that lonesome dove,
That flies from vine to vine,
Lamenting for his own true love
As I lament for mine?

H

"Lass of Rock Royal." Collected by Miss Alfreda M. Peel. Sung by Mrs. Crop, of Salem, Va. Roanoke County. June, 1921.

1 As I was walking out one day,
A-drinking of sweet wine,
I had to part with a pretty little maid
Who stole this heart of mine.

2 "Oh hush, oh hush, my dearest dear,
I hate to hear you cry;
The best of friends have to part
And why not you and I?

3 "The darkest time I ever saw
Has surely turned to light;
If ever I prove false to you,
Bright day will turn to night.

4 "If you were carried far away
And taken sick to die,
Oh, who will mourn my own true love?
Oh, who will hear you cry?"

5 "If I am carried far away
And taken sick to die,
My mamma she will hear me mourn,
My papa hear me cry."

6 "Oh, who will shoe my pretty little foot?
    And who will glove my hand?
And who will kiss my ruby lips,
    When you're in a far distant land?"

7 "My papa he will shoe my foot;
    And mamma will glove my hand;
And you will kiss my sweet ruby lips
    When you come from the western land."

I

"Turtle Dove." Collected by the Misses Ethel and Hallie Rodes, of Bryant, Va. Nelson County. March 26, 1917.

1 "Oh! don't you see that turtle dove
    Sitting on yonder pine?
She is mourning the loss of her true love,
    And why not me for mine?

2 "It's hard to love and not be loved,
    It's hard to please your mind.
You've broken the heart of a many poor girl,
    But you never shall break mine."

3 "Oh! who will shoe your pretty little foot?
    And who will glove your hand?
And who will kiss your sweet little lips,
    While I'm in the foreign land?"

4 "My father will shoe my pretty little foot;
    My mother will glove my hand;
Somebody will kiss my sweet little lips,
    While you're in the foreign land."

5 "Oh, fare ye well, Oh, fare ye well,
    Oh, fare ye well for a while;
I'm going away to return again
    If I go ten thousand miles."

22

THE WIFE OF USHER'S WELL

(CHILD, No. 79)

THE Child title is unknown in Virginia, where the ballad is called "The Lady Gay," "The Three Little Babes," "The Beautiful Bride," or (once) "Lady Gains." The Virginia variants all belong to the same version, which is neither Child A, B, nor C. The religious cast of the Virginia version seems to relate it to Child C, but in other respects it is nearer to Child A. It is practically identical with the American text printed in Child, V, 294, except that the mother's prayer for the return of the children is not usual in the Virginia texts; indeed, appears only once. The motive for the children's return — to forbid the mother's obstinate grief — is found in most of the Virginia variants, as in other American texts, but not in Child A. In practically all Virginia texts the ghosts disappear for two reasons: the crowing of the cock and the summons of the Saviour. In this respect they are like West Virginia B. The Virginia texts do not add much except minor variations to the texts already published from America.

The story of the composite Virginia text runs as follows: — A lady gay sends her three children to school in the north country, where, after a time, they die. (The mother grieves for her children and prays for their return.) About Christmas time they appear to her. She prepares a feast for them, but they refuse to eat, because the Saviour forbids. She spreads a bed with rich covering for them, but they bid her take it off, as it represents mere worldly pride. With the approach of dawn and by appointment with their Saviour, they depart, warning the mother that her tears but wet their winding sheet. The Virginia and other American texts are more sternly puritanical and have less human warmth than Child A. Another interesting feature of the Virginia texts concerns the sex of the babies. In old-country texts the children are always sons. In Virginia the sex is normally unspecified; they are simply "children" or "babes." But occasionally they actually become girls. See F 6, line 2, and G 5, line 4. Perhaps the same change of sex is indicated by the "normal school" variant of C 1, line 3.

For American texts, see Belden, No. 77; Brown, p. 9 (North Carolina); *Bulletin*, Nos. 3–5, 9; Campbell and Sharp, No. 19 (North Carolina, Tennessee); Child, V, 294 (North Carolina); Cox, No. 14; Hudson, No. 12 (and *Journal*, XXXIX, 96; Mississippi); *Journal*, XIII, 119 (Newell, North Carolina); XXIII, 429 (Belden, Missouri); XXX, 305 (Kittredge; California, Nebraska, Kentucky, Tennessee); XXXII, 503 (Richardson, West Virginia); McGill, p. 5; Pound, *Syllabus*, p. 10 (fragment); Pound, *Ballads*, No. 7; Shearin and Combs, p. 9. For additional references, see *Journal*, XXX, 305.

A

"The Lady Gay." Collected by Mr. John Stone. Sung by Mr. George Hart, of Konnarock, Va. Washington County. November 8, 1921.

1 Nancy bride and children three,
  And children she had three;
She sent them away to a northern countrie
  To learn some grammaree.

2 They had n't been gone but about three year,
  Till their mother was a-standing in the door,
And who should she see but her three little babes
  Come hastening home once more.

3 She sot them a table both wide and long,
  And on it sot bread and wine,
Saying, "Come and eat, my three little babes,
  Come eat and drink of mine."

4 "O mother, O mother, I can't eat your bread,
  Nor neither can I drink of your wine;
For yonder stands our Saviour dear,
  To him we must resign."

5 She spread them a bed in a backward room,
  And on it spread a white sheet,
And on the top of that spread a golden spread,
  To make her babes lie sweet.

6 "Take it off, take it off," say the oldest one,
  "For it's nothing but the pride of life;
And yonder stands our Saviour dear
  To bear our souls away."

7 "Rise up, rise up," says the next oldest one,
  "For the chickens is a-crowing for day,
And yonder stands our Saviour dear
  To bear our souls away."

8 "Put a marble stone around our head,
  And cold clay around our feet,
For the tears that you shed over us last night
  Has wet our winding sheet."

B

"The Lady Gay." Collected by Mr. John Stone. Recited by Mrs. Jennie Allison, of Saltville, Va. Smyth County. November 8, 1921. "She learned it from her cousin, Mrs. Mandy Rogers" (Mr. Stone).

1 There was a lady, a lady gay,
  And children she had three;
She sent them away to the north country
  To learn their grammaree.

2 They had n't been gone but a very short time,
  A month, six weeks, or so,
Till their sweet death came hasting along
  And swept those babes away.

* * * * * *

3 She on the table spread a table cover,
  And on it set bread and wine:
"Come eat and drink, my three little babes,
  Come eat and drink of mine."

4 "No, mother, we do not want your bread,
  Neither do we want your wine;
For yonder stands our Saviour dear,
  And to him we'll resign."

5 She went into a low back room,
  And on the bed spread a sheet,
And over this sheet spread a golden cover,
  For those three babes to sleep.

6 "Wake up, wake up," said the oldest one,
  "The chickens will soon crow for day,
And yonder stands our Saviour dear;
  We must go without delay."

7 "Wake up, wake up," said the next oldest one,
  "The chickens has done crowed for day;
And to the Saviour we must go
  Without further delay."

8 "Place a marble stone at our head, dear mother,
  For cold clay lies at our feet;
And to our Saviour we must go,
  For his love is complete."

C

"The Lady Gay." Collected by Miss Juliet Fauntleroy. Sung by Miss Maggie Wright, of Altavista, Va. Campbell County. September 18, 1915.

1 There lived a lady, lady gay,
  And children she had three.
She sent them off to a {northern / normal} school,
  To learn their grammaree.

2 They had n't been gone but a very short time,
  Scarcely three months and a day,
Until cold death came over the land
  And stole those babes away.

3 "There lives a King in Heaven," she cried,
  "Who used to wear a crown.
Pray send me back my babes tonight
  Or in the morning soon."

4 . . . .
  . . . .
She saw three babes come hastening along
  To greet their mother home.

5 She spread her table wide and long,
  Put on it bread and wine.
"Come eat, come drink, my sweet little babes,
  Come eat, come drink of mine."

6 "No, mother, we don't want your bread,
  Nor either want your wine,
For yonder stands our Saviour dear,
  To him we are resigned."

7 She fixed her bed in a narrow back room,
  Put on it white, white sheets,
And on the top a golden spread,
  That they might better sleep.

8 "Take it off, take it off," the oldest cried,
  "For the chickens now do crow,
And yonder stands our Saviour dear,
  To him we now must go."

D

"Lady Gains." Collected by Miss Martha M. Davis. Rockingham County. March 2, 1916.

1 Lady Gains had children three;
She sent them off into the North
To learn their grammaree.

2 They had n't been gone but a very short time,
No longer than a month and a day,
Until cold death came passing by
And stole those babes away.

3 She set a table wide and long,
Put on it cake and wine.
"Come eat, come drink, my three little babes,
For you are surely mine."

4 "I want none of your bread, mother,
I want none of your wine;
For yonder stands my own Saviour,
So we are not wholly thine."

5 She made a bed in her fine parlor,
Put on it sheets so fine,
And on the top a golden spread
That they might slumber on.

6 "Wake up, wake up," said the oldest one,
"The chickens crow for day;
And yonder stands my own Saviour,
And I must haste away."

7 "Wake up, wake up," said the second one,
"The chickens crow for day;
And yonder stands my own Saviour,
And I must haste away."

8 "Wake up, wake up," said the youngest one
"The chickens crow for day;
And yonder stands my own Saviour,
And we must haste away."

E

"The Lady Gay." Collected by Mr. John Stone. Sung by Mr. Jeff Doss, of Damascus, Va., who learned it from his mother. Washington County. November 8, 1921.

1 There was a lady and a lady fair,
And children she had three;
She sent them away to some low countree
To learn them their grammaree.

2 They had n't been gone but a very short while,
Scarcely three months and a day,
Till sickness spread over the whole town
And swept those babes away.

3 It being nigh about Christmas time,
When the nights grew long and cold,
Here come all three of her sweet little babes
Down through their mother's room.

4 She fixed them a table of her own,
Put cake and wine on it.
"Go eat and drink, my three little babes,
Go eat and drink of mine."

5 "We'll neither want your cake
Nor drink your wine,
For early in the morning at the close of day
We'll join our Saviour here."

6 She fixed them a bed in the most back room,
Clean sheets she spread on it,
And on the top spread a golden cloth,
To make those ventures sleep.

7 "Take it off, take it off," says the oldest one.
"Take it off again, I say;
For pride has been the cause of your three little babes
Now lying in cold clay.

8 "Cold clay, cold clay, lies at our feet,
Green grass grows at our head;
And for the tears you have shed for us
Would have wept[1] those winding sheets."

[1] For *wet*. And there are other confusions.

F

"The Beautiful Bride" or "The Lady Gay." Collected by Mr. John Stone. Given by Mrs. Teressa Farris, of Saltville, Va. Smyth County. November 8, 1921.

1 There was a bride, a beautiful bride,
And three little babes had she;
She sent them away to some northern country
To learn their grammaree.

2 It being close to Christmas time,
The nights being long and cold,
Till in came running those three little babes
Into their mother's home.

3 She took them into her dining room
And over the table spread fine,
And over the table spread bread and wine,
"Go eat and drink of mine."

4 "We can't eat any of your bread, dear mother,
Or either drink any of your wine;
For it has n't been long since prayers be gone
And there stands the Saviour."

5 She took them to her backward room
And over the bed spread fine,
And over the bed spread a golden spread
Where those three little babes were lying.

6 "Take it off, take it off," says the oldest one,
"Take it off, take it off," says she,[1]
"For we can't stay here in this wide wicked world,
When there's a better one for me."

7 "Cold clods, cold clods down by my side,
Cold clods at my feet,
For the tears my dear mother has shed for me
Would wet a winding sheet."

[1] At least one child is a girl. See general head-note to this ballad.

G

"The Three Little Babes." Collected by Miss Juliet Fauntleroy. Sung by Miss Mary Colbird, of Altavista, Va. Pulaski County. September 13, 1915.

1 There was a lady, and a lady for to be,
And children she had three.
She sent them off to some foreign land,
Their grammaree for to learn.

2 And Christmas times were drawing near,
And the nights were dark and cold,
Those three little babes came chattering down the steps.
"Come home to your mama."

3 She spreaded on her table cloth,
And covered it with bread and wine,
Saying, "Sit you down, my three little babes,
And eat and drink of mine."

4 "I cannot eat your bread, mother,
Nor neither drink your wine,
For yonder stands my Saviour so dear
To hear my must resign." [1]

5 She fixed a bed all in her backest room,
And covered it with a white sheet,
The toppest sheet was a golden sheet,
Saying, "Sleep, three damsels,[2] sleep."

6 "Wake up, wake up," said the oldest one,
"Wake up, it's almost day;
How can you sleep in this dark, lonesome world
While there's a brighter one beyond?"

7 "The cold clay lies over my head, mother,
And the green grass grows on my feet,
And every tear that rolls down your cheeks,
It seems so dear to me."

[1] The line might be corrupted from, "To Him I must resign."
[2] The children are evidently all girls. See general head-note to this ballad.

H

"The Lady Gay." Collected by Mr. John Stone. Sung by Mr. J. W. Fields, of Coeburn, Va. Wise County. November 8, 1921.

1 There was a lady, a lady gay,
And babies she had three;
She sent them off to the north country
To learn their grammaree.

2 They had n't been there two weeks or more,
I'm sure it was not three,
Till the news came hastening, hastening home,
Those babes she might not see.

3 They had n't been gone three weeks or more,
I'm sure it was not four,
Till the news came hastening, hastening home,
Those babes, they was no more.

4 She made a table long and wide,
On it she put bread and wine:
"Come eat and drink, my three little babes,
Come eat and drink of mine."

5 "I will not eat your bread, dear mother,
Neither drink your wine;
For yonder stands our Saviour dear,
To him we must resign."

6 She made a bed both long and wide,
And over this spread a sheet,
And over this a golden spread,
That they might better sleep.

7 "Wake up, wake up," said the oldest one,
"Wake up, for it is almost day,
For yonder stands our Saviour dear,
And him we must obey."

I

"The Three Little Babes." Collected by Miss Juliet Fauntleroy. Sung by Mrs. Seely Ann Kegley, of Altavista, Va. Grayson County. September 13, 1915. "Mrs. Kegley, originally from Grayson County, Virginia, said she used to hear her mother sing this ballad long ago, but she could not remember the first verses, except the line, 'About three months to a day'" (Miss Fauntleroy).

1 As Christmas time was drawing nigh
(And the nights were dark and cold),
Those three little babes came running home
Into their mother's hall.

2 She fixed her table both neat and fine,
And on it put both bread and wine,
Saying, "Sit you down, my three little babes,
And eat and drink of mine."

3 "Pray take it away," said the oldest one,
"I cannot eat your bread nor either drink your wine,
For yonder stands our Saviour dear,
Unto whom we must resign."

4 She fixed her bed in the backward room,
And on it she put a white sheet,
And over the top a golden spread,
"And here is where you'd better sleep."

5 "Rise you up, rise you up," said the oldest one,
"The chickens are crowing for day.
For woe unto ye in this wide, wicked world
Since pride has been in view.

6 "Place marble stones at our head, mother dear,
Cold clay around our feet,
For the tears that were shed for you last night
Have wet our winding sheet."

J

"The Three Little Babes." Collected by Miss Juliet Fauntleroy. Sung by Mrs. James Sprouse, of Lawyers, Va. Campbell County. March 20, 1915. With music. "Mrs. Sprouse said there were other verses to this, but she could not recall them" (Miss Fauntleroy).

1 There was a lady, lady gay,
Who had babies one, two, three;
She sent those babes to the north countrie
To learn their grammaree.

2 They hadn't been there but a month and a day
Before swift death came on,
Before swift death came on
And taken those babes away.

3 "There is a King who lives in Heaven
Who used to wear a crown;
Pray send me back those three little babes
Tonight or in the morning soon."

4 "Come in, come in, my three little babes,
And eat this bread and wine."
"O mother, I cannot eat your bread,
I cannot drink your wine."

K

"The Lady Gay." Collected by Dr. C. Alphonso Smith. Sung by Mr. J. C. Mays, of Goshen, Va. Augusta County. December 17, 1914. "I met him on the train — a good banjoist — and secured this and ballads 73 and 243. He learned them in Amherst County from his mother" (Dr. Smith).

1 Once there was a lady gay,
And children she had three;
She sent them away to the North Countree
For to learn their grammaree.

2 They had not been there very long,
Scarcely six months and a day,
Before cold death came hasting along
And stole those babes away.

3 She fixed a table down in the front room
And on it spread bread and wine:
"Come eat, come drink, my sweet itta [1] babes,
Come eat and drink of mine."

4 "Neither do we want your bread, mother,
Neither do we want your wine,
For yonder stands our sweet Saviour
Whose heart has our design."

5 The mother hung her head and wept,
And says, "I'll do my best;
I'll give those babies to the Lord,
And I will trust the rest."

L

"Lady Gay." Collected by Miss Martha M. Davis. Rockingham County. March 2, 1916. With music.

There was a lady fair and gay,
And children she had three;
She sent them far into the north
To learn their grammairie.

[1] The usual baby talk for *little*.

23

LITTLE MUSGRAVE AND LADY BARNARD

(CHILD, No. 81)

THE seven variants found in Virginia have the titles, "Lord Arnold's Wife," "Lord Daniel's Wife," "Lord Vanner's Wife," "Lord Darnold," "Little Matthew Groves," and "Little Mosie Grove and Lord Burnett's Wife." A general concurrence with Child A is to be noted, but the divergences are many. In the Virginia texts, the lady is more definitely the aggressor; the stanza in which Little Matthew recognizes her as Lord Barnett's wife by her rings (found in Child D, E, F, H, J, K, and L, but not in A) is included, while the stanzas in which the two lovers profess their past affection are excluded; except in Virginia A, no regret is expressed by Lord Barnett for either of his killings; except in Virginia B where the lady is shot, she dies by stroke of sword, not by the barbarity of Child A; Lord Barnett's instructions for the lovers' burial are omitted; repetition is frequent in the Virginia texts.

The story told by the Virginia texts is this: On a certain holiday Little Matthew (Mathy, Marthy, Mosie) Grove (Groves) goes to church and there sees Lord Barnett's (Burnett's, Daniel's, Arnold's, Darnold's) wife, who makes advances and invites him to lie with her that night. He at first refuses, as he sees by her ring that she is Lord Barnett's wife, but is reassured when she informs him that her husband is away. A little foot-page hears the assignation, and runs off to inform Lord Barnett, who returns and surprises the lovers in bed. He generously offers his best sword to Little Matthew and kills him in fair fight. In A, he regrets his rash act. When he finds that his lady loves little Matthew more than she loves him (B, D, and E), he kills her also.

For American texts, see Brown, p. 9 (North Carolina); *Bulletin*, Nos. 3, 6, 7, 9, 11; Campbell and Sharp, No. 20 (North Carolina, Tennessee, Kentucky); Cox, No. 15; *Journal*, XXIII, 371 (Mackenzie, Nova Scotia); XXV, 182 (Mackenzie, Nova Scotia); XXX, 309 (Kittredge, Kentucky, three texts and two melodies, Missouri, text and melody); Mackenzie, pp. 14, 88 (fragment); Mackenzie, *Ballads*, No. 8; Pound, *Ballads*, No. 15; Shearin, p. 3; Shearin and Combs, p. 8; Reed Smith, No. 7; Reed Smith, *Ballads*, No. 7; Wyman and Brockway, *Songs*, pp. 22, 62. For additional references, see *Journal*, XXX, 309.

A

"Little Mosie Grove and Lord Burnett's Wife." Collected by Miss Alfreda M. Peel. Sung by an old man of Salem, Va. Roanoke County. July 31, 1918.

1 One holiday, one holiday,
  The highest day in the year,
Little Mosie Grove went to the church,
  God's holy word to hear.

2 Some came dressed in satin fine,
Some came dressed in blue,
But the finest of all was Lord Burnett's wife,
The finest of the whole crew.

3 She stepped up to Mosie Grove
Whom she was standing by,
And asked him to go home with her,
With her all night to lie.

4 He saw by her middle finger ring
That she was Lord Burnett's wife;
He dare not go home with her
Lest he should lose his life.

5 A little foot-page was standing by
And heard what they did say.
He said Lord Burnett should hear of this
Before the break of day.

6 He had three long miles to run
And one he had to swim.

7 And when he came to Lord Burnett's door,
He jingled at the ring;
There was none so ready as Lord Burnett himself
To rise and let him in.

8 "What news? what news?" Lord Burnett said,
"What news you bring to me?"
"Little Mosie Grove is at your old hôme,
In bed with your fair lady."

9 He told him, if that be true
About his fair lady,
"I have not but one daughter
And you shall married be.

10 "If it was a lie you tell unto me
About my fair lady,
A new gallows shall be built so high
And you shall hangèd be."

11 "If this be a lie I tell unto thee,
What good would it be unto me?
A new gallows you need not build,
But hang me on a tree."

12 He would not let a horn be blown
    Nor yet a drum be beat.
. . . .
    . . . .

13 One of his merry men
    Who loved his daughter dear,
Put his horn unto his lips
    And blew it loud and clear.

14 Little Mosie Grove in his bed
    Said, "Hark, what do I hear?
I think I hear Lord Burnett's horn
    Come sounding loud and clear."

15 She said, "Lie still, lie still, little Mosie Grove,
    Lie still, keep my back from the cold;
It is my father's shepherd boys
    Driving the sheep from the fold."

16 He went to the house
    Where in bed they lie on,
And bid him rise from out the bed
    And put his garments on;
For it should not be said when he was dead
    That he killed a naked man.

17 But he could not rise
    For fear of his life;
For Lord Burnett had two great broadswords
    And he not so much as a knife.

18 He rose up and took one sword
    And wounded Lord Burnett sore;
But the very next blow Lord Burnett gave,
    Little Mosie lay dead on the floor.

19 "Curses be to my merry men all
    Which here around do stand;
You let me kill the prettiest man
    That ever was in the land."

20 He went into the other room
    Where his fair lady lay;
And seized [her] by her little white hand
    And cut her head away.

B

"Little Matthew Groves." Collected by Mr. John Stone. Sung by Mr. George Hart, of Konnarock, Va. Washington County. November 8, 1921. The irregular repetitions of the original manuscript are preserved. Stanzas 7 to 10 of this variant seem to be a crossing of this ballad with "Lady Maisry." Compare Child, No. 65, A, 21 and 23, and B, 13 and 16. Compare also Virginia, No. 16, B.

1 Tum-a-high-lo, boys, tum-a-high-lo, boys,
On the very first day of the year
Little Matthew Groves to preaching go
The gospel for to hear, hear,
The gospel for to hear.

2 The first came down were Lady Gay,
The next come down were a boy,
The next come down were Lord Daniel's wife,
The prince amongst them all.

3 As he passed by, as she passed by,
She cast her eye upon him,
Saying, "Come go home with me, Little Matthew Groves,
On purpose for to lie, lie,
On purpose for to lie."

4 "How dear I am to go home with you,
How dear I am for my life;
For I know by the ring that you wear on your finger
That you are Lord Daniel's wife."

5 "It's what if I am Lord Daniel's wife?
Lord Daniel's not at home;
He's gone away to the knee breast key,[1]
And no one for to see, see,
And no one for to see."

6 The little foot-page were a-standing by,
And he heard what they did say;
He fell to his breast and he buckled up his shoes
And he took to his heels and he ran, ran,
And he took to his heels and he ran.

7 He ran till he came to the broad waterside,
And he bowed to his breast and he swum,
And he bowed to his breast and he swum, swum,
And he bowed to his breast and he swum.

[1] Probably for *Nebraska*, another American geographical intrusion.

8 He swum till he came to the broad dry land,
And he buckled up his shoes and he run,
And he buckled up his shoes and he run, run,
And he buckled up his shoes and he run.

9 He run till he come to the king's high gate,
And he blowed both loud and keen,
And he blowed both loud and keen, keen,
And he blowed both loud and keen.

10 "It's my log cabin's burning down
Or my retires one?"[1]
"It's your log cabin's not burning down
Nor your retires none;
Little Matthew Groves is at your house
And in the bed with your wife, wife,
And in the bed with your wife."

11 "If this be a lie, my little foot-page,
That you do tell to me,
It's out of a rope a gallows prepared
And hanged you shall be,
And hanged you shall be, be,
And hanged you shall be.

12 "If this be the truth, my little foot-page,
That you've to tell to me,
I've only one daughter dear to my heart,
Your wedded wife shall be, be,
Your wedded wife shall be."

13 "If this be a lie," says the little foot-page,
"That I've to tell to thee,
You need not have a gallows prepared;
You can hang me to a tree,
You can hang me to a tree, tree,
You can hang me to a tree."

14 He ordered him up a army of men,
He rode both keen and swift,
He ordered not a word to be said,
Nor never a horn should blow, blow,
Nor never a horn should blow.

[1] Evidently for *towers won.* See head-note to this variant, and cf. especially Child, No. 65, B 16:

"Is my building broke into?
Or is my towers won?"

15 Little Matthew he had a very good friend,
A very good friend indeed;
He put his bugle to his mouth
And he blowed both loud and keen, keen,
And he blowed both loud and keen.

16 "I must get up and get away from here,
Lord Daniel 's coming home;
For I hear Lord Daniel 's bugle horn,
It blowed both loud and keen, keen,
It blowed both loud and keen."

17 "Lie down, lie down, Little Matthew Groves,
And keep the cold from me;
It's nothing but my daddy's dogs
A-driving sheep from food, food,[1]
A-driving sheep from food."

18 From that they fell to hugging and kissing,
From that they fell to sleep;
When they waked up there stood Lord Daniel
Right at the foot of the bed, bed,
Right at the foot of the bed.

19 "It's how do you like my new coverlids?
It's how do you like my sheets?"
"Very well do I like your new coverlids;
Very well do I like your sheets;
Much better do I like your gay lady bride
Who lies in my arms and sleeps, sleeps,
Who lies in my arms and sleeps."

20 "Get up, get up, Little Matthew Groves,
And putteth on your clothes;
For it never shall be said when I am dead
That I slew a naked man, man,
That I slew a naked man."

21 "I must get up and putteth on my clothes;
It's fighteth for my life;
You have two swords all by your side
And me not so much as a knife, knife,
And me not so much as a knife."

22 "I have two swords all by my side,
And you not so much as a knife;
I'll give to you the best of them,
And I will keep the worst, worst,
And I will keep the worst.

[1] For *fold* , by an easy phonetic transition.

23 "And you may have the very first lick,
    And I will take the next,
And I will take the next, next,
    And I will take the next."

24 The very first lick Little Matthew struck,
    He wounded deep and sore;
The very first lick Lord Daniel struck,
    Little Matthew didn't fight any more, more,
    Little Matthew didn't fight any more.

25 He took his bride upon his knee,
    He dandled her up and down.
"It's which of those do you like the best,
    Little Matthew Groves or me, me,
    Little Matthew Groves or me?"

26 "Very well I like your red rose cheeks,
    Very well I like your chin;
Much better do I like Little Matthew Groves
    Than Lord Daniel and all of his kin, kin,
    Than Lord Daniel and all of his kin."

27 He drew a revolver from his side,
    He shot her as she sot,
Saying, "Here's the end of two true loves
    No quicker than they could part."

C

"Lord Darnold." Collected by Mrs. Olin F. Wiley, of Richmond, Va. Wise County. December 1, 1916.

1 Today it was the holy day,
    The first day in the year
To church little Mathey Groves
    Did go to hear the holy word.

2 The first came was dressed in white,
    The second she in green,
The third came in Lord Darnold's wife,
    The fairest of the three.

3 She cast her eyes all round and round,
    She cast her eyes on me:
"You got a go home with me tonight,
    A bed feller to be."

4 "Oh no, oh no," said Mathey Groves,
"I cannot for my life.
I can tell by the ring that is on your fingers
You are Lord Darnold's wife."

5 "Well, if I am Lord Darnold's wife,
As you possess me,
Lord Darnold's gone to the big white house
King Johnny for to see."

6 The little foot-page was standing by,
He took to his heels and run,
He run till he came to the water's side,
He bowed his breast and swam.

7 When he got out on the other side,
He took to his heels and run,
He run till he came to the big white house;
He rattled the bells and rung, rung.

8 "What news have you for me to-night,
What news have you for me?"
"Little Mathey Groves is at your house
Gone home with your gaily deal.[1]

9 He placed his men all round and round,
He placed his men all fow;[2]
Not nary word then should be spoken,
Or easy[3] horn should blow.

10 His brother came with a bugle horn,
He blowed it loud and shrill,
And at the tuning of every tune,
"I wish I was a . . . ."

11 Little Mathey felt one sweet kiss,
And dramp a dream so sweet,
And when little Mathey Groves awoke,
Lord Darnold was standing at his feet.

12 The very first lick Little Mathey struck,
He wound Lord Darnold deep;
The very first lick Lord Darnold struck,
Little Mathey fell dead at his feet.

[1] For *gay lady*. [2] For *four*. [3] Usually *any*.

D

"Little Matthew Groves." Collected by Mr. John Stone. Sung by Mrs. M. C. Hurt, of Wytheville, Va. Wythe County. November 8, 1921.

1 Little Matthew Groves went to church
The very first day in the week
Those holy words for to hear, for to hear,
Those holy words for to hear.

2 The very first one that came down
Was dressed all in white;
The very next one that came down
Was Lord Donald's wife.

3 The little foot-page he took to his heels
And he ran and he ran till he came to Olinglunt;[1]
And there he knocked so loud till it rang, rang,
There he knocked so loud till it rang.

4 "Little Matthew Groves went home with your wife
And there with her for to lie, lie,
And there with her for to lie, lie,
And there with her for to lie."

5 "If this be the truth, which I suppose it to be,
I have a daughter in Olinglunt[1]
And a wedded man you shall be, be,
And a wedded man you shall be.

6 "If this be a lie, which I suppose it to be,
I have a rope in Olinglunt,[1]
And a hanged man you shall be, be,
And a hanged man you shall be."

7 "Little Matthew Groves, rise and fight for your life."
"'T is hard to rise and fight for my life
When you have two bright swords in hand,
And me not so much as a knife, knife,
And me not so much as a knife."

8 "O yes, I have two bright swords in my hand,
And you can take the very best
And I will take the worst, worst,
And I will take the worst."

[1] *Old England?*

9 Little Matthew Groves struck the very first lick
And wounded him full sore;
Lord Donald struck the very next,
Little Matthew struck no more, more,
Little Matthew struck no more.

10 He took his wife by her lily-white hand
And set her on his knee:
"Which do you love the best
Little Matthew Groves or me, me,
Little Matthew Groves or me?"

11 "It's very well I love your red ruby lips,
It's very well I love your skin;
Much better do I love little Matthew Groves
Than you and all your kin."

12 He took her by her lily-white hand
And placed her on the plane;
He took in hand his new bright sword
And split her head to the brain.

E

"Lord Arnold's Wife." Collected by Miss Juliet Fauntleroy. Sung by Charles Henry Payne (Colored), near Altavista, Va. Campbell County. June 6, 1914. Miss Fauntleroy writes: "I copied this down myself from the singing of the old Colored man, with the repetitions, etc., just as he gave them, and it is as nearly accurate as I can make it. This is the same old man from whom John Adams got the copy I sent you before. . . . From something the old man said I think he meant *George's* in the second verse, and not *gorgeous;* alluding probably to one of the former King Georges of England."

1 Lord Arnold's wife she went to church
The first day in the year;
She cast her eyes all round the room
To see who would go with her home,
To see who would go with her home.

2 Little Marthy Grove was standing aside,
She said, "Come and go with me home;
Lord Arnold is gone to the King's white house,
George's (gorgeous?) white horses to see,
George's (gorgeous?) white horses to see."

3 A little foot-page was standing aside,
He took to his heels and he ran;
He ran and he ran to the water side,
He vented his breath and he swam,
He vented his breath and he swam.

4 He swam and he swam to the other side,
He took to his heels and he ran.
He ran, he ran to Lord Arnold's house:
"What news, what news do you bring,
What news, what news do you bring?"

5 "Bad news, bad news, I bring to you,
Bad news, bad news I bring to you."
"If 't is the truth you are telling me,
As probably it may be,
As probably it may be.

6 "But if it is a lie you are telling me,
Your neck it shall be hung,
To the tallest tree is on the roadside
Your neck it shall be hung,
Your neck it shall be hung."

7 "Oh hush, oh hush, little Marthy Grove,
I think I heard Lord Arnold's horn,
I think I heard Lord Arnold's horn,
It rings so loud and clear,
It rings so loud and clear.

8 "Oh hark, oh hark, little Marthy Grove,
You keep my back so warm."
"It's nothing but my father's horn,
Blowing sheeps under the globe (glebe?),
Blowing sheeps under the globe." [1]

9 "Rise you up, little Marthy Grove,
And put you on some clothes;
I won't have it said in the old country
I murdered a naked man,
I murdered a naked man.

10 "You may take the two bright swords
And I will take the dull;
You may make the very first lick,
And I will make the next,
And I will make the next."

11 The very first lick little Marthy made,
He ruined Lord Arnold's song.
The very first lick Lord Arnold made,
Little Marthy did n't fight no more,
Little Marthy did n't fight no more.

[1] Probably a phonetic substitute for *fold*. Cf. A 15, B 17, etc.

12 "The better I like your pillows and dines (downs?),
The better I like your silk sheet,
The better I like your pretty fair maid,
That lies in my arms asleep,
That lies in my arms asleep."

13 "The better I like your pillows and dines (downs),
The better I like your silk sheet,
The better I like your pretty fair maid,
I like little Marthy the best,
I like little Marthy the best."

14 He raised his sword up above his head
And he cut her all up into twain;
He raised his sword up above his head
And he cut her all up into twain,
And he cut her all up into twain.

F

"Lord Daniel's Wife" or "Lord Vanner's Wife." Collected by Miss Alfreda M. Peel. Sung by Mrs. Nancy Kitts, of Bland, Va. Bland County. September 3, 1923. With music.

1 Down came a lady,
Down came two,
Down came Lord Daniel's wife,
And she was dressed in blue.

2 She spied Little Mathy
By the light,
"I must invite you
To lie with me tonight."

3 "I cannot, I will not,
By my life;
By the ring on your finger,
You are Lord Daniel's wife."

4 "If I'm Lord Daniel's wife,
Lord Daniel ain't at home;
He's gone away to the little bonnie brown cabin
Old Mackie for to see."

5 The little page was standing by,
He took to his heels and run.

6 And when he came to the river,
He smote his breast and swum;
And when he got to dry land,
He took to his heels and run.

7 "If it's a lie,
As I suppose may be,
Build me a gallows,
And hanged you shall be."

8 "If it be a lie,
As you suppose may be,
You need not build a gallows,
But hang me on a tree."

* * * * * *

9 He put a horn to his mouth,
And blew it loud and clear.

10 "Lie still and keep me
From the cold;
It is my father's horn,
Blowing his sheep to the fold."

11 They locked and they linked
And at last they fell asleep;
The first time Little Mathy woke,
Lord Daniel was at his feet.

12 "How do you like your bed, sir?
How do you like my sheet?
How do you like my gala dame
That lies in your arms asleep?"

13 "Very much I like your bed, sir;
Very much I like your sheet;
But best I like your gala dame
That lies in my arms asleep."

14 "Rise up, rise up, Little Mathew,
And put you on some clothes;
It never shall be said of me
That a naked man I slew."

15 He took Mrs. Daniel by the hand,
And led her through the hall;
He drew his sword, cut off her head,
And threw it against the wall.

24

BONNY BARBARA ALLAN

(CHILD, No. 84)

OF the Virginia ballads, "Barbara Allen" is *facile princeps* in the number of items collected, both of texts and of music. Her ninety-two Virginia progeny are something of a record achievement, certainly for a lady who, according to the ballad, scorned her lover. One is thankful she did not encourage him! Many of these ninety-two items are, of course, mere repetition and fragmentation; but when all refuse is set aside, a surprising number of healthy and differing texts remain, of which some thirty-six are here presented. Many of the excluded texts were discarded only after an editorial pang, and have perhaps an equal claim to appear. An even dozen melodies, many of them quite similar but never identical, uphold the ballad's prestige in the musical line.

The ballad is known in Virginia as "Barbara Allen" or "Barbara Ellen" — with variant spellings — once as "Barbara Allen's Cruelty." In marked contrast to the fidelity with which Barbara's name is preserved are the many titles of her lover. In the texts that follow he appears as Sweet William (9 times), Sweet Willie (4 times), Young Jimmy (3 times), Young Jimmy Grove (2 times); once each he is William, Willie, William Ryley, Sweet Jimmy, Young Jimmy Groves, Sweet Jimmy Grove, Young Jimmy Grame, Sir James Graham, Sir James the Graham (and Sweet Jimmy), Sir James of the Grave, Young Jamie Grove, John Green, and Johnny; and once (not counting the "music only" fragments) he is unnamed.

Both the Child A and B versions are represented in the Virginia texts, with many variations, additions, and combinations of the two. To record, with references, all the variations and affiliations of the Virginia texts would require a statistician, not an editor. But certain interesting features may be here pointed out, and some slight guidance offered through the texts that follow.

In the first place, the familiar "rose-and-brier" ending (see head-note to Virginia 18, above), which does not appear in any Child version of the ballad, appears more or less regularly in Virginia texts. Whether or not this was originally supplied from "Fair Margaret and Sweet William," as is suggested also by the hero's name in many variants and by a general similarity of theme in the two ballads, the ending has become an integral part of the most popular Virginia version of "Barbara Allen." Excluding fragments, there are only some half dozen Virginia texts without this ending (see L–O). These conclude usually with Barbara's farewell exhortation to "the virgins all" to "shun the fault she fell in." Cf. Cox, A 16, p. 98.

Still more interesting and important is the fact that the young man's defence of himself against Barbara's accusation of his slighting her appears with some regularity in the Virginia texts (see A–I, L, and P). No such defence is found in any Child version. Moreover, in Virginia A and B, two stanzas of accusation from Barbara are replied to in turn by the man. In A he distinguishes clearly between his love for her and his interest in "the ladies all." In B he defends himself against the first accusation and pleads guilty to the second. Dr. Smith's article on "Ballads Surviving in the United States" (*Musical*

Quarterly, II, 109–129) has some interesting comments on these additional stanzas. Having just quoted Child A in full, he remarks: "The printed versions vary but little from the incidents as here narrated. But the story as a story has always seemed to me to be flawed by the silence of Sir John under the accusation brought against him. The reader infers, of course, that Barbara's charge in stanza five is unjust but, in view of the tragic dénouement, artistic balance demands some sort of exculpatory answer from Sir John. At any rate, I felt a sense of profound relief when a version came in from Buchanan County, Virginia, with four additional stanzas. The singer had never seen a printed copy of the song but had always heard it and sung it with these stanzas in place of stanza five. [Here he quotes Virginia A 7–10.] It is possible of course that this better constructed version may be as old as any version known to us." And he proceed to establish this fact.

Virginia texts C–I, L, and P all have one stanza of accusation, one of defence. J has one stanza of accusation and another, also by Barbara, elaborating its consequences, with no defence offered by the man. In K the man acknowledges the slight, as in B 8. In several other texts the accusation is made without reply from the man, the usual Child A form. The *two* stanzas of accusation and *two* of self-defence are extremely rare. An excellent text of this sort from northern Louisiana, sent by Professor Pierce Butler, of the H. Sophie Newcomb Memorial College, New Orleans, found its way into the Virginia collection, and the four significant stanzas may be here given for comparison with Virginia A and B:

"Oh, do you remember last Saturday night
When you sat in the alehouse drinking?
You drank to the health of a pretty fair maid,
Nor thought of Barbara Allen."

"Oh, yes, I remember last Saturday night
When I sat in the alehouse drinking.
I drank to the health of a pretty fair maid,
But I thought of Barbara Allen."

"And do you remember that night at the ball,
With the lights about us gleaming?
You danced with many a pretty fair maid,
And you slighted Barbara Allen."

"Oh, yes, I remember that night at the ball,
With the lights about us gleaming.
I danced with many a pretty fair maid,
But I dreamed of Barbara Allen."

And more properly belonging here are the three analogous stanzas of a Virginia text sent by Mr. Henry A. Wise from the Eastern Shore of Virginia. The full text, though recorded, is not to be found among the Virginia archives, but Reed Smith's head-note gives these stanzas in which the lover replies so differently:

"O Jimmie, don't you remember the time
When you walked into the tavern,
And passed the health of the ladies all around,
And slighted Barbara Allen?"

"You go look under the head of my bed,
And there you'll find a basin;
And in that basin, one drop of my blood
To remember Barbara Allen.

"You go look under the foot of my bed,
And there you'll find a napkin;
And in that napkin a gay gold ring
For the love of Barbara Allen."

In P and Q the young man in his farewell breathes an ominous curse for Barbara, and in P Barbara returns the curse in her dying farewell. Usually the man dies with a mere farewell to Barbara or with kind expressions for her; sometimes he even heaps gifts upon her. And Barbara is elsewhere uniformly repentant at the close.

In R–T the young man offers presents to Barbara (seven ships in R) or leaves her money (five thousand pounds in S) or does both (a gold watch and ten thousand pounds and fifty in T). In U Barbara rides away in a fine carriage, possibly a present from her lover. The victim's generosity stands out in contrast to Barbara's cruelty and adds to the poignancy of the tragedy. These texts, S and T especially, may be thought of as showing some connection with the ballad in Buchan's MS., mentioned by Child, in which "the dying lover leaves his watch and gold ring, his Bible and pen-knife, a mill and thirty ploughs, nine meal-mills and the freights of nine ships, all to tocher Barbara Allan."

V, like A, mentions that Barbara is chosen from three maids or three ladies with whom she dwells — a detail not found in Child.

In W Barbara blames her cruelty on her mother (as quite explicitly in J 9), and the mother also joins the lovers in death, as she does also in X and Y, but without being otherwise implicated in the tragedy. In many versions, after the mother has been called on to make the daughter's bed, the father is called on to dig the daughter's grave — a quite natural division of labor.

Of the miscellaneous later variants, Z has a line contaminated from "Pretty Peggy O." In AA the messenger is a nephew of the sick man; in BB a little boy is hired, and Barbara resides in Strawberry Town (cf. Cox D). CC–JJ are fragments or music only.

C is an especially interesting Negro version of the ballad. Miss Scarborough, who "had wondered if the Negroes had failed to appreciate and appropriate this most familiar and beloved of all ballads," was especially pleased when Dr. Smith sent her this text. Another Negro text has an occasional "Lord, hand me down" refrain and the ending

"Lord, Lord, hand me down.
That the last of Bober Allen."

A frequent shift of the angle of narration is to be noted in many Virginia texts. Child B changes from first to third person after the first stanza, but the shifting is hardly carried to the protean extreme of Virginia D and other Virginia texts which more or less follow Child B. See the footnote to Virginia D.

Five of the twelve melodies in the book were printed by Dr. Smith in his *Musical Quarterly* article, along with two British melodies, and from the comparison he draws important conclusions about the relationship of British and American ballad airs. He says: "Among the following musical arrangements of *Barbara Allen*, one from Scotland, one from England, and five recently transcribed from the lips of the singers in Virginia, no one of whom understood music, the differences are so great that it would hardly be safe to select any two and say that they are related by direct derivation, though four are current in the same county: [Here are printed seven notations of the ballad: A, from "Select Melodies of Scotland"; B, from "The Minstrelsy of England"; C, from Rockingham County, Va. (Virginia HH); and D, E, F, and G, from Campbell County, Va. (Virginia AA, II, H, and U, respectively)].

"Even if a similar strain be heard in A, C, and F, and if E be found to suggest G, the relationship would seem to be collateral rather than lineal. Priority, in other words, can hardly be affirmed of any of these melodies until more data be thrown upon the scales. When Pepys in 1666 lauded the 'little Scotch song of *Barbary Allen*' and when Goldsmith a century later declared that 'the music of the finest singer is dissonance to what I felt when our old dairy-maid sung me into tears with *Johnny Armstrong's Last Goodnight* or *The Cruelty of Barbara Allen*,' both may have been praising, so far as we know, a melody unrecorded in books and heard today, if heard at all, only in some shadowed lane or mountain cove or lonely farm-house of the United States. Who can say?"

For other American texts and melodies, see Barry, No. 22; Belden, No. 7; *Bulletin*, Nos. 2–10; Campbell and Sharp, No. 21 (Georgia, North Carolina, Tennessee, Kentucky, Virginia); Cox, No. 16, and p. 523 (nine texts and two melodies); *Heart Songs*, p. 247; Hudson, No. 13 (and *Journal*, XXXIX, 97; Mississippi); Jones, p. 301 (fragment); *Journal*, VI, 132 (Edmands, North Carolina); XIX, 286 (Belden, Missouri, Indiana); XX, 256 (Kittredge, Kentucky); XXII, 63 (Beatty, Kentucky); XXVI, 352 (Pound, Nebraska, fragment); XXVIII, 144 (Perrow, Mississippi); XXIX, 160 (Tolman, Virginia), 198 (Rawn and Peabody, Georgia, fragment); XXXV, 343 (Tolman and Eddy, Ohio, fragment and melody, Kentucky, fragment and melody); XXXIX, 211 (M. E. Henry, North Carolina); McGill, p. 40; Mackenzie, p. 100; Mackenzie, *Ballads*, No. 9, and p. 393; Pound, *Syllabus*, p. 9 (fragment); Pound, *Ballads*, No. 3; Sandburg, p. 57; Scarborough, p. 59 (Virginia, sent by C. A. Smith); Shearin, p. 3 (fragment); Shearin and Combs, p. 8; Shoemaker, p. 122; C. A. Smith, p. 12 (British version), p. 13 (Virginia, fragment), p. 20 (Great Britain, Virginia, seven melodies only); Reed Smith, No. 8; Reed Smith, *Ballads*, No. 8; Wyman and Brockway, p. 1. For additional references, see Cox, p. 96; *Journal*, XXIX, 160; XXX, 317; XXXV, 343.

A

"Barbara Ellen." Contributed by Mr. W. E. Gilbert. Found in Southwest Virginia. Buchanan County. March 31, 1913 (found in fall, 1912). For a full analysis and critique of this version see the article entitled "A Discovery in Ballad Literature" by Stewart A. Steger and Loyal C. Morrow, in *The University of Virginia Magazine*, April, 1913, pp. 329–335. See also the head-note to this ballad, Virginia 24, above.

1 So early in the month of May,
When the green buds they were swelling,
This young man on his death-bed lay,
For the love of Barbara Ellen.

2 Three maids, three maids, three maids they be,
The maids that live in the dwelling,
And the only one that he called his own,
And that was Barbara Ellen.

3 He called his servant to his bed,
And lowly he said to him,
"Go bring the one that I love best,
And that is Barbara Ellen."

4 Slowly, slowly he got up,
And went to the dwelling,
Saying, "I'm sent for the one that he loved best,
And that is Barbara Ellen."

5 Slowly, slowly she got up,
And slowly she went to him.
The very first word when she got there:
"Young man, I'm afraid you're dying."

6 He whirled his face upon the wall,
His back toward the people:
"Adieu! adieu! to my friends all
And a woe to Barbara Ellen."

7 "Do you remember the other day
When we were at the tavern drinking,
You drank a health to the ladies all
And you slighted Barbara Ellen."

8 "Yes, I remember the other day
When we were at the tavern drinking;
I drank a health to the ladies all
And three to Barbara Ellen."

9 "Do you remember the other night,
When we were at the ball room dancing?
You gave your hand to the ladies all
And slighted Barbara Ellen."

10 "Yes, I remember the other night
When we were at the ball room dancing;
I gave my hand to the ladies all
And my heart to Barbara Ellen."

11 "Cursed, cursed be my life,
And cursed be my nature;
I might have saved this young man's life
If I had done my duty.

12 "As I walked down the streets the other day
I heard the death-bells ringing,
And every sound just seemed to say:
'Hard hearted Barbara Ellen.'

13 "I looked east, and I looked west,
And I saw the pale corpse coming:
'Lie down, lie down, you cold pale corpse,
Till I can smile upon you.'"

14 William died on Saturday night,
And Barbara on next Monday;
And her mother died for the love of them
All on the eve of Monday.

15 William was buried in one church yard,
And Barbara in another.
Out of her grave sprang a rose,
And out of his a briar.

16 They grew so high and they grew so tall
They could not grow any higher;
They grew till they tied in a true love knot,
The rose around the briar.

B

"Barbara Ellen." Collected by Miss Nancy Pearson, of Christiansburg, Va. Montgomery County. October 9, 1916.

1 'T was in the early month of May,
The June buds they were swellin',
Young Jimmy lay on his death-bed
For the sake of Barbara Ellen.

2 He sent a servant to the town
Where this young maid was a-dwellin',
Saying, "Come, oh come, to my master's house,
If your name be Barbara Ellen."

3 La, lo, la, lo, oh! she got up,
La, lo, la, lo, she came near him,
And the words she said when she got there were,
"Young man, I think you're dyin'."

4 "Come pity me, my pretty fair maid,
For I'm on my death-bed dyin'.
How much better I might have been
If it had n't been for Barbara Ellen."

5 Says she, "Do you remember in younder's town
Those ladies you were treating?
You drank your health to the ladies all round
And you slighted Barbara Ellen."

6 Says he, "I remember in younder town
Those ladies I was (were) treating.
I drank a health to the ladies all round
And three to Barbara Ellen."

7 Says she, "You remember in the ball room
Those ladies you were greeting?
You gave your hand to the ladies all round
And slighted Barbara Ellen."

8 Says he, "I remember in the ball room
Those ladies I were greeting.
I gave my hand to the ladies all round
And slighted Barbara Ellen."

9 He turned his pale face to the wall
And his back to all good people.
"No better, no better I never will be
If I can't get Barbara Ellen."

10 She got right up and walked out the door,
Hard-hearteder than ever.
"No better, no better you never will be,
For you can't get Barbara Ellen."

11 She had n't gone no more than three miles,
The death-bell she heard ringing,
And every strike it seemed to say,
"Hard-hearted Barbara Ellen."

SCENES FROM THE BALLAD REGION
OF VIRGINIA

12 She turned her body round and round,
And spied the corpse a-coming.
"Oh, lay him down upon the grass
That I may gaze upon him."

13 She looked upon him with scornful eye,
Her cheeks were red like smiling,
And all his friends around him cried,
"Hard-hearted Barbara Ellen."

14 "Oh! mither go and make my bed,
Go make it soft and narrow;
Young Jimmy died for me today,
And I shall die for him tomorrow.

15 "Oh! father you go dig my grave,
Go dig it long and narrow;
Young Jimmy died for pure, pure love
And I shall die for sorrow."

16 They buried him in the green church yard
And they buried her on the morrow,
And off his grave sprung forth a red rose
And off hers sprung a green briar.

17 They grew up to the old church wall
Till they could grow no taller;
They looped themselves in a true lover's knot,
The rose around the brier.

C

"Bob-ree Allin." Contributed to "Songs We Used to Sing," August 18, 1912. As sung by the Virginia darkies. December, 1913. See Scarborough, p. 59, and compare Reed Smith, No. 8, E, a very similar version. And see head-note, above.

1 In London town, whar I was raised,
Dar war a youth a-dwellin',
He fell in love wid a putty fair maid,
Her name 't war Bob-ree Allin.

2 He co'ted her for seben long years;
She said she would not marry;
Poor Willie went home and war takin' sick,
And ve'y likely died.

3 He den sen' out his waitin' boy
Wid a note for Bob-ree Allin.
So close, ah, she read, so slow, ah, she walk:
"Go tell him I'm a-comin'."

4 She den step up into his room,
And stood an' looked upon him.
He stretched to her his pale white hands:
"Oh, won't you tell me howdy?"

5 "Have you forgot de udder day,
When we war in de pawlor,
You drank your health to de gals around,
And slighted Bob-ree Allin?"

6 "Oh, no; oh, no, my dear young miss;
I think you is mistaking;
Ef I drank my healt' to de gals aroun',
'T war love for Bob-ree Allin.

7 "An' now I'm sick and ve'y sick,
An' on my deathbed lyin',
One kiss or two fum you, my dear,
Would take away dis dyin'."

8 "Dat kiss or two you will not git,
Not ef your heart was breakin',
I cannot keep you from death,
So farewell," said Bob-ree Allin.

9 He tu'n his pale face to de wall,
An' den began er-cryin';
An' every tear he shed appeared,
"Hard-a-hearted Bob-ree Allin."

10 She walked across de fiel's nex' day
An' heerd de birds a-singin',
An' every note dey seemed to say:
"Hard-hearted Bob-ree Allin."

11 She war walkin' 'cross de fiel' nex' day,
An' spied his pale corpse comin'.
"Oh, lay him down upon de groun',
An' let me look upon him."

12 As she war walkin' down de street
She heerd de death bells ringin',
An' every tone dey seemed to say:
"Hard-a-hearted Bob-ree Allin."

13 "Oh, fader, fader, dig-a my grave,
An' dig it long an' narrow;
My true love he have died today,
An' I must die tomorrow.

14 "Oh, mudder, mudder, make-a my s'roud,
An' make it long and narrow;
Sweet Willie died of love for me,
An' I must die tomorrow."

15 Sweet Willie war buried in de new church-yard,
An' Bob-ree Allin beside him.
Outen his grave sprang a putty red rose,
An' Bob-ree Allin's a briar.

16 Dey grew as high as de steeple top,
An' could n't grow no higher,
An' den dey tied a true-love knot,
De sweet rose roun' de briar.

D

"Barbara Allen." Collected by Mr. John Stone. Sung by Mrs. Lizzie Alley and Mrs. Pearl Wilson, of Dante, Va. Russell County. November 8, 1921. Note how frequently and irrationally the angle of narration shifts in this variant. The young man begins the story in the first person (stanzas 1–3); the fourth stanza begins in the third person, but slips back to the first person in the third line; dialogue follows to the end of stanza 7; here the first person is resumed, but with Barbara as narrator (stanzas 8–10); then back to the third person again (stanzas 11–14).

1 Way down South where I came from,
That's where I got my learning,
I fell in love with a pretty little girl,
Her name was Barbara Allen.

2 I courted her for seven long years,
Till she said she would not marry,
And I went home and was taken sick
And very likely of dying.

3 As I lay there on the dying-bed,
I wrote my love a letter.
She moved so slow, she walked so slow:
"Tell him I am a-coming."

4 She walked up to his bedside lay,
He turned his back upon her;
The only words I heard her say,
"Young man, I think you're dying."

5 "Yes, I'm sick, I'm very sick,
Lovesick here I'm lying;
A kiss or two from Barbara's lips
Would surely save me from dying."

6 "O do you remember the other night
When we was down town drinking,
You drank your health to the ladies all around
And slighted Barbara Allen?"

7 "No, O no, you surely are mistaken;
I drank my health to the ladies all around,
But my love was for Barbara Allen."

8 As I went through yonders woods,
I heard some birds a-singing;
It seemed to me as they would say,
"Hard-hearted Barbara Allen."

9 As I went through the town,
I heard some church bells ringing;
It seemed to me as they would say,
"Go back, go back, Barbara Allen."

10 As I got about a mile from town,
I saw some corpse a-coming.
"Set him down, set that young man down
And let me gaze upon him."

11 The more she gazed the more she mourned,
Till she bursted out to crying:
"Sweet Willie died for me today,
And I'll die for him tomorrow.

12 "Mother, O mother, go make my shroud,
Go make it long and narrow;
Sweet Willie died for pure, pure love,
And I'll die for him for sorrow."

13 They buried him in the old church-yard,
And her next to the choir;
From Willie's breast sprang a red, red rose,
And from hers a briar.

14 They grew and grew to the old church-top,
Till they could n't grow any higher;
They wrapped and tied in a true lover's knot,
And the rose wrapped round the briar.

E

"Barbara Allen." Collected by Miss Juliet Fauntleroy. Sung by Miss Mary Colbird, of Altavista, Va. Pulaski County. September 15, 1915.

1 "Oh, way down south where I came from,
There's where I got my learning;
I fell in love with a pretty little girl,
Her name was Barbara Allen.

2 "I courted her for seven long years,
And she told me she could not marry."
Sweet Willie went home and was taken sick,
And very like of dying.

3 As he lay all on his bed side
He wrote his love a letter.
"Oh, I am sick and very sick,
No hopes of getting any better."

4 So slow she fixed, so slow she came,
So slow she drew unto him.
When she got there she says,
"Young man, I think you are a-dying."

5 She says, "Young man," she says, "Young man,
I think you are a-dying."
He handed her out his lily-white hand,
All for to tell her howdy.

6 "Oh no, oh no, don't you remember,
In yonders town a-drinking,
You filled full glasses all around,
But you slighted Barbara Allen?"

7 "Oh yes, oh yes, I remember,
In yonders town a-drinking,
I'll drink my health with my living friends,
And my love to Barbara Allen."

8 He turned his pale face towards the wall,
As death came creeping upon him.
"Adieu, adieu, I'll bid to you,
Adieu, adieu, forever."

9 As she returned from the church one day,
She heard some bells a-ringing;
They rung so near, they rung so clear,
"Hard-hearted Barbara Allen."

10 She looked to the east, she looked to the west,
She saw some corpse a-bringing —
"Pray set you down this cold corpse clay
And let me look upon it."

11 The more she looked, the more she fell,
She bursted out a-crying,
"Pray take away this cold corpse clay,
I think I am a-dying."

12 "Oh mother, oh mother, go fix my bed,
And fix it soft and narrow;
Sweet William died for me today,
I'll die for him tomorrow."

13 They buried one in the old church yard,
And the other on top of Ohio.[1]
And out of William's breast sprung a red rose,
And out of Barbara's a brier.

14 They grew till they grew to the old church top,
And they could not grow any higher,
And there they tied in a true lover's knot,
And they could not grow any higher.

F

"Barbara Allen." Collected by Mr. John Stone. Sung by Mr. George Hart, of Konnarock, Va. Washington County. November 8, 1921.

1 All in the merry month of May,
When green buds they were swelling,
Sweet William lay on his death-bed low
For the love of Barbara Allen.

2 He sent his servant to the town
Where Barbara she were dwelling,
Saying, "Come, come to my bedside
If your name be Barbara Allen."

3 So slowly she put on her clothes,
And so slowly she come nigh him;
And all that she said when she got there:
"Young man, I think you're dying."

4 "O yes, O yes, I'm low indeed,
And death is in me dwelling;
But never better will I be
Till I get Barbara Allen."

[1] For *the choir*.

5 "O don't you remember in the town,
The town where you were drinking,
You drank a health to those young ladies round
And you slighted Barbara Allen?"

6 "O yes, I remember in the town,
The town where I were drinking;
I drunk a health to those young ladies round
And I treated Barbara Allen."

7 "If you be a-lying on your death-bed,
What need of a tale be telling?
I cannot keep you from your death.
Farewell," says Barbara Allen.

8 He turned his pale face to the wall,
His back upon the dwelling,
And all of his friends cried out, "For shame!
Hard-hearted Barbara Allen."

9 She had n't got more than a mile from the town
Till she heard some death-bell a-ringing,
And every knock it seemed for to say,
"Hard-hearted Barbara Allen."

10 She had n't got more than another mile
Till she spied the corpse a-coming.
"Lie down, lie down that cold pale corpse
And let me gaze upon him."

11 The longer she gazed, the louder she cried,
And all of his friends a-telling,
"The loss of your Sweet William dear
Was the loving of Barbara Allen."

12 Sweet William he died like it might be today,
And Barbara died tomorrow;
Sweet William he died out of pure love
And Barbara died for sorrow.

13 Sweet William was buried in the new church-yard,
And Barbara in another;
And out of his grave there grew a red rose,
And Barbara's grew a briar.

14 The briar and the rose they grew together
Till they could not grow any higher;
They wrapped and they tied in a true lover's knot
For all true lovers to admire.

G

"Barbara Allen." Collected by Miss Juliet Fauntleroy. Sung by Mrs. Seely Ann Kegley, of Altavista, Va. Grayson County. September 21, 1915. With music.

1 It was in the fall season of the year,
When yellow leaves were falling,
Sweet William he was taken sick
By the love of Barbara Allen.

2 He sent his servant to the town,
The town where she was dwelling,
"My master's sick and very sick,
For the love of Barbara Allen."

3 Slowly, slowly she rose up,
And slowly she went to him.
She drew the curtains from his bed,
"Young man, I think you're dying.

4 "You're low, you're low, you're low indeed,
And death is in you dwelling;
And the better never will you be
By the getting of Barbara Allen.

5 "Do you remember in yonders town,
In the town where you were all drinking,
You drank a health to all around
And slighted Barbara Allen?"

6 "Yes, I remember in yonders town,
In the town where we were drinking,
I drank a health to all around,
And my love to Barbara Allen."

7 He turned his pale face to the wall,
She turned her back upon him.
"Adieu, adieu, to all around,
Adieu to Barbara Allen."

8 As she was a-walking along the street,
She heard the death-bell ringing.
She thought she heard her own heart say,
"Come here, Barbara Allen."

9 She looked to the east, she looked to the west,
She spied the corpse a-coming.
"Lie down, lie down, your master called,
And let me look upon him.

10 The more she looked, the more she grieved,
She bursted out a-crying.
"I might have saved this young man's life
By using my endeavor.

11 "Go mother, go mother, go make my bed,
And make it soft and narrow;
For my true love has died today,
And I shall die tomorrow."

12 They taken them both to the new church yard,
And there where they were buried,
And out of his grave grew a white rose,
And out of hers a brier.

13 They met and tied in a true love's knot
Till they could not grow any higher;
They met and tied in a true love's knot,
The rose around the brier.

H

"Barbara Allen." Collected by Miss Juliet Fauntleroy. Sung by Mrs. John Maxie, *née* Lily Stone, of Altavista, Va. Campbell County. June 29, 1914. With music.

1 'T was in the merry month of June,
Sweet flowers they were bloomin';
Sweet William lay on his death-bed
For love of Barbara Allen.

2 He sent his servant to the town,
The town where she was dwellin',
Saying, "Master's sick and very sick,
All for the love of Barbara Allen."

3 And slowly, slowly she rose up,
And got her bonnet and started;
And all she said when she got there,
"Young man, I think you're dyin'."

4 He turned his pale face to the wall,
And bursted out a-cryin',
Saying, "Yes, I'm sick and very sick,
All for the love of Barbara Allen."

5 "You drank your health in the greatest of wealth,
You drank to the ladies all round you;
You drank your health in the greatest of wealth,
And slighted me, Barbara Allen."

6 "I drank my health in the greatest of wealth,
And I drank yours, Barbara Allen."
She turned her pale face towards the sky
And bursted out a-cryin'.

7 She mounted to her stage on high,
And through the town went sailin';
And every door as she passed by,
"Hard-hearted Barbara Allen!"

8 She looked to the east, she looked to the west,
She spied the pale corpse comin';
"Father, oh father, go dig my grave,
And dig it long and narrow.

9 "And on my breast place a mournful dove
To prove to the world I died in love;
Sweet William died for me today,
I'll die for him tomorrow."

10 Sweet William died on Easter Friday,
And Barbara died on Saturday;
They both were driven to the new church yard
And buried there together.

11 From his breast there sprung a red rose,
And from hers grew a brier;
They grew and they grew to the new church top,
And then they could grow no higher.

12 There they tied in a true lover's knot,
They lived and died together;
There they tied in a true lover's knot,
They lived and died together.

I

"Barbara Ellen." Collected by Miss Alfreda M. Peel. Sung by Texas Gladden, near Salem, Va. Roanoke County. May 27, 1917. With music.

1 "Way down yonder in London town,
That's where I got my learning,
I fell in love with a nice young girl,
Her name was Barbara Ellen.

2 "I courted her for seven long years,
She said she would not marry."
Sweet Willie went home and taken down sick,
And sent for Barbara Ellen.

3 She dressed so slow for she hated to go,
"Go tell him I am coming."
As she went walking through the room,
She heard some birds a-singing.

4 She walked up to Sweet Willie's bedside:
"Young man, I think you're dying."
He turned his face to the cold, cold wall
And busted out a-crying.

5 "Do you remember the other day,
We were down at the tavern a-drinking,
You drank your health to the ladies all around,
And slighted Barbara Ellen?"

6 "Oh no, oh no, oh no," said he,
"I think you are mistaken;
I drank my health to the ladies all around,
My love to Barbara Ellen."

7 She went walking to the road,
She heard some birds a-singing,
And every one it seemed to say,
"Hard-hearted Barbara Ellen."

8 She looked to the East and then to the West,
She spied a corpse a-coming.
"Oh, bring him here and lay him down,
That I might look upon him."

9 The more she looked the more she wept,
She busted out to crying.
"I might have saved this young man's life
And kept him from hard dying.

10 "Oh mother, make my bed
And make it long and narrow;
Sweet Willie died for the love of me,
And I shall die for sorrow."

11 They buried Sweet Willie in the new church yard
And Barbara in attire [1];
In Willie's grave sprang a bright red rose
And on Barbara Ellen's a green brier.

12 They grew as tall as the new church top,
They could not grow any higher;
They wrapped and tied a true bow-knot,
And the rose ran down the brier.

[1] Variant for *in the choir.*

J

"Barbara Allen." Sent in by Professor J. M. Grainger. Collected by Miss Kathleen Hale, of the Farmville Ballad Club. Sung by Mrs. E. W. Hale, of Pembroke, Va. Giles County. March 16, 1914.

1 'T was in the early month of May,
When green buds were a-swelling,
Sweet Jimmie Grove on his death-bed lay,
For the love of Barbara Allen.

2 He sent his servant to the town,
In which that she was dwelling;
"Say, my master's sick and sent for you,
If your name be Barbara Allen."

3 Then slowly, slowly got she up
And swiftly she went to him;
She softly walked the chamber round —
"Young man, I think you are dying."

4 "Oh yes, I'm sick, I'm very sick,
And death is in my dwelling;
Oh yes, I'm sick, and very sick
For the love of Barbara Allen."

5 "Do you not recall in yonder town,
While we were all a-drinking,
You treated all the ladies round
And slighted Barbara Allen?

6 "And though you are sick, and very sick,
Though death be in your dwelling,
Because of the slight you gave to me,
You'll never get Barbara Allen."

7 He turned his white face to the wall
And his back to Barbara Allen;
"Adieu, adieu to all my friends!
Be kind to Barbara Allen."

8 She had n't gone more than a mile from the place
Till she heard his death-bell ringing;
Nor had she gone more than five miles from the place,
Till she saw his corpse a-coming.

9 "Oh, lay him in the cold, cold clay
And let me look upon him!
O mother dear, you caused all this;
You would not let me have him.

10 "And father, father, dig my grave,
And dig it deep and narrow.
Sweet Jimmie dies for me today,
I'll die for him tomorrow."

11 Sweet Jimmie was buried in the South Church yard,
And Barbara in the other.
A rose bush sprang from one of their breasts,
A briar from the other.

12 They grew, they grew, till they reach the church-top;
They grew till they could n't grow higher;
They grew and tied a true love-knot,
The rose wrapped round the briar.

K

"Barbara Allan." Collected by Mr. John Stone. Recited by Mrs. Rhoda O'Bryhin, of Falmouth, Va. Stafford County. September 11, 1922.

1 'T was in the merry month of May,
And green buds they were swelling,
Young Jimmy he was taken sick
And sent for Barbara Allan.

2 "O was it for my gold you sent,
Or was it for my silver?
Or was it for my pure, pure love
That you sent thereafter?"

3 "It was n't for your gold I sent,
It was n't for your silver;
It was only for your pure, pure love
That I sent thereafter,
And one kiss from your sweet lips
Will keep me now from dying."

4 "O don't you remember in your home town,
In the town where you were dwelling,
You bought your wine and strewed it round
And slighted Barbara Allan?"

5 "O yes, I remember in yonders town,
In the town where we were dwelling;
I bought my wine and strewed it round
And slighted Barbara Allan."

6 Slowly, slowly she rose up,
And slowly she went from him.
She had not gone more than a mile or two
Before she heard the death-bell tolling,
And every toll it seemed to say,
"Hard-hearted Barbara Allan."

7 "O mother, mother, make my bed,
O make it long and narrow;
Young Jimmy died for me today;
I'll die for him tomorrow."

8 From Jimmy's grave there sprung a leaf,
From Barbara's sprung a briar;
They grew and tied in a true love's knot
For all true loves to admire.

L

"Barbara Ellen." Contributed by Mrs. Olin F. Wiley, of Richmond, Va. Wise County. December 1, 1916.

1 It was one morning, one morning in May,
The little flowers were blooming,
Sweet William on his death-bed lay
For the love of Barbara Ellen.

2 "Go send a servant to the town,
To Barbara Ellen's dwellin',
'Rise up, rise up, and go to my store
If your name be Barbara Ellen.'"

3 Slowly, slowly, she got up,
And slowly she went unto him,
And all she said when she got there,
"Young man, I think you are dying."

4 "O, I am sick and very sick;
I am lone, sick and a-dying,
I am no better nor never can be,
For I can't get you, Barbara Ellen."

5 "O, yes, you're sick and very sick,
You are lone, sick and a-dying,
You're no better nor never will be,
For you can't get Barbara Ellen.

6 "Do you remember the other day
When we were in the bar room,
You gave a drink to the ladies all around,
And slighted Barbara Ellen?"

7 "O, yes, I remember the other day,
When we were in the bar room;
I gave a drink to the ladies all around,
But — my love to you, Barbara Ellen."

8 He turned his pale face to the wall,
He turned his (back?) upon her,
And then he cried until he died,
For the love of Barbara Ellen.

9 As she went walking down the street,
She heard the death bells tolling,
. . . .
. . . .

10 She look east and she look west,
She saw the corpse a-coming,
She cried, "Lay, O lay him down,
And let me look upon him.

11 "O mamma, O mamma, go make my bed,
Go make it smooth and narrow;
Sweet William has died for pure true love,
And I must die for sorrow.

12 "O papa, O papa, go dig my grave,
Go dig it deep and narrow;
Sweet William has died for me today,
And I must die for him tomorrow."

13 Now those two, those two are dead;
Their parents grieve, but no relief.
Their funerals will be preached tomorrow.

M

"Barbara Allan." Collected by Miss Roxie Martin and Mr. J. M. McManaway. Sung by Miss Hazel L. Garrison, of Brown's Cove, Va. Albemarle County. June 1, 1917.

1 In Scarlet town where I was born,
There was a fair maid dwellin',
Made very youth cry well away!
Her name was Barbara Allan.

2 All in the merry month of May,
When green buds were swellin',
Young Jimmy Grove on his death-bed lay,
For the love of Barbara Allan.

3 "And death is printed on his face,
And o'er his heart is stealin';
Then haste away to comfort him,
O lovely Barb'ra Allan."

4 So slowly, slowly she came up,
And slowly she came nigh him.
And all she said when there she came,
"Young man, I think you're dyin'."

5 He turn his face unto her straight,
With deadly sorrow sighing:
"Oh pretty maid, come pity me,
I'm on my death-bed lying."

6 "If on your death-bed you do lie,
What needs the tales you are telling?
I can't keep you from your death.
Farewell," says Barbara Allan.

7 He turn his face unto the wall,
And death was with him dealin',
"Adieu, adieu, my friends all,
Adieu to Barbara Allan."

8 As she was walking o'er the fields,
She heard the bells a-knellin',
And every stroke did seem to say,
"Unworthy Barbara Allan."

9 She turn her body round about
And spied the corpse a-comin'.
"Lay down, lay down the corpse," she said,
"That I may look upon him."

10 With scornful eyes she looked down,
Her cheeks with laughter swellin',
Whilst all her friends cried, "Well away,
Unworthy Barb'ra Allan."

11 When he was dead and in his grave,
Her heart 't was struck with sorrow.
"O mother, mother, make my bed,
For I shall die tomorrow.

12 "Hard-hearted creature him to slight
Who loved me so dearly.
Oh, that I'd been more kind to him,
When he was alive and near me!"

13 She on her death-bed as she lay
Begged to be buried by him
And sore repented of the day
That she did ever deny him.

14 "Farewell," she said, "ye virgins all,
And shun the fault I fell in;
Henceforth take warning by the fall
Of cruel Barb'ra Allan."

N

"Barbara Allen." Collected by Miss Nancy Pearson, of Christiansburg, Va. Pulaski County. October 9, 1916.

1 In the town where I was born
There was a fair maid dwelling,
Made every youth to weal or woe,
Her name was Barbara Allen.

2 It was in the merry month of May,
The green buds they were swelling;
Young Jimmy Grame on his death-bed lay,
For the love of Barbara Allen.

3 He sent his man unto her then,
Unto the tavern where she was dwelling.
"You must go to my master dear,
If your name be Barbara Allen."

4 Slowly, slowly she fixed up,
And slowly she came near him,
And the words she said when there she came,
"Young man, I think you're dying."

5 He turned his face upon her straight
With deathly sorrow sighing,
"Come, pretty maid, come pity me,
For I am on my death-bed lying."

6 "If on your death-bed you do lie,
What need the tale you're telling?
I can not keep you from your grave.
Farewell," said Barbara Allen.

7 He turned his face upon the wall,
A deathly pang he fell in.
"Adieu, adieu, my dear friends all,
Adieu to Barbara Allen."

8 As she was crossing o'er the fields,
She heard the bell a-knelling,
And every stroke did seem to say,
"Hard-hearted Barbara Allen."

9 She turned her body round about,
She spied the corpse a-coming,
"Lay down, lay down the corpse," she cried,
"That I may look upon him."

10 With scornful eyes she looked down,
Her cheeks with laughter swelling,
While all her friends cried out, "Amen.[1]
Unearthly Barbara Allen."

11 When on her death-bed she did lay,
She begged to be buried by him,
And sore repented of the day
That ever she did deny him.

O

"Barbara Allen." Sent in by Miss Edith B. Payne. Collected by Miss Grace Ward. Sung by Mrs. L. G. Davis, of Kempsville, Va. Princess Anne County. January 20, 1914.

1 It fell about St. Martamus[2] day
When the green leaves were falling,
Sir James Graham of the west countrie
Fell in love with Barbara Allen.

2 "What is thy name, my bonnie maid?
And where hast thou thy dwelling?"
She answered him most modestly,
"My name is Barbara Allen."

3 "Oh, see ye not yon seven ships
So gaily as they are sailing?
I'll make you mistress of them all,
My bonnie Barbara Allen."

4 But it fell out upon a day
At the wine as they were drinking,
He made the glass go around and around
And slighted Barbara Allen.

[1] For *amain*, doubtless.
[2] For *Martinmas*. St. Martin's day is November 11.

5 Oh, she has taken it so ill!
She'll no longer look upon him,
And for all the letters he could send
Still say she'll never marry him.

6 "Oh, if I had a man, a man!
A man within my dwelling,
I'd write a letter with my blood
And send to Barbara Allen."

7 His man is off with all his speed
To the place where she is dwelling.
"Here is a letter from my master dear,
And give ye to Barbara Allen."

8 All slowly, slowly she rose up,
And slowly she went to him,
And softly drew the curtain by:
"Young man, I think you are dying."

9 "Oh, I'm sick, I'm very sick,
"It's all for you I'm pining.
One kiss or two from your sweet lips
Will save me from the dying."

10 All slowly, slowly she rose up
And slowly, slowly left him,
And sighing said she could not stay,
Since death of life had 'reft him.

11 As she was walking down the street,
She saw the corp' a-coming.
And all around cried loud and long,
"Unworthy Barbara Allen."

12 "Oh mother, mother, make my bed!
Make it hard and narrow.
My true love died for me today,
I'll die for him tomorrow."

P

"Barbara Allen." Collected by Mr. John Stone. Sung by Mrs. M. C. Hurt, of Wytheville, Va. Wythe County. November 8, 1921. The young man's name in stanza 9 is evidently supplied from one of the three ballads about William Reilly: "William Reilly's Courtship," "Reilly's Trial," and "Reilly's Answer, Releasement, and Marriage with Coleen Bawn." See Cox, No. 101.

1 He sent his servant to the country
Where she was dwelling.
"My master's sick and very sick
And on his death-bed lying."

2 "Your master's sick and very sick
And on a death-bed lying;
No better will he ever be;
He'll never get Barbara Allen."

3 How slow she reads, how slow she moves:
"Go tell him I am coming."
O slowly slow she raised the curtain,
"Young man, I think you're dying."

4 O yes, I'm sick and very sick,
And on a death-bed lying.
One kiss or two from your sweet lips
Would save me from a-dying."

5 "Do you remember the other night,
When you were in your tavern,
You drank the health with the girls all around
And slighted Barbara Allen?"

6 "O yes, O yes, I remember well
When I was in my tavern;
I drank to health with the girls all around,
Within my heart was Barbara Allen."

7 He turned his pale face to the wall
And bursted out a-crying:
"Adieu, adieu to all friends on earth,
And woe to Barbara Allen."

8 As she was riding through the town,
She spied those corpse a-coming.
"O put him down, O put him down,
So I may look upon him."

9 She looked upon him with a scornful eye
And bursted out crying:
"Adieu, adieu to all friends on earth,
And a woe to William Ryley."

Q

"Barbary Ellen." Collected by Miss Eunice Harris and Mrs. J. S. Harris. Sung by Mrs. Goodwin, of Prospect, Va. Prince Edward County. March 23, 1914. Printed in *The Focus*, April, 1914.

1 In the early month of May,
When the green buds were swelling,
Sweet William lay on his death-bed
For the love of Barbary Ellen.

2 He called unto his serving man
To go and get his gelding;
Make no delay till he got there,
And bring him Barbary Ellen.

3 He started off at top of speed
And reached her father's dwelling:
"Sweet William sent me here for you,
If your name be Barbary Ellen."

4 Then very slowly she rose up
And remarked that she was going,
But all she said when she got there was,
"Young man, I think you are dying."

5 He turned his face toward the wall,
Yes, turned his back upon her.
"Adieu," he said, "to kind friends and all,
And woe to Barbary Ellen."

6 "Don't you remember last country day,
While at your table drinking,
You drank a health to the ladies all,
And slighted Barbary Ellen?"

7 As she was returning home,
She heard the death-bell ringing,
And oft she stopped and listened while
The mourners still kept coming.

8 "It was today that Sweet William died,
And I will die tomorrow."
Out of his grave there grew a red rose
And out of Barbary's a briar.

9 They grew as high as a steeple top,
And could grow no higher,
When the two linked in a true love knot.
The rose wrapped round the briar.

R

"Barbara Allen." Collected by Mr. John Stone. Sung by Mrs. Leona Dever, of Mustoe, Va. Highland County. September 9, 1920. "She learned it from her mother, Mrs. Acy Doyle, who learned it from her father, an Irishman who came to this country from Ireland either in 1798 or 1800. . . . Mrs. Doyle learned the song nearly seventy years ago" (Mr. Stone).

1 'T was in and about the Martinmas Day,
When the green leaves were a-falling,
Sir James the Graham in the western country
Fell in love with Barbara Allen.

2 She was a fair and comely maid,
A maid near to his dwelling,
Which made him admire the beauty,
The beauty of Barbara Allen.

3 They fell out upon a day,
A day which they were drinking;
He made the health go round about
And slighted Barbara Allen.

4 She has taken so allow
She looks no more upon him;
And all the letters he could send,
She still swore she never would have him.

5 "Oh! seven ships have I at sea,
Bonny as they are sailing;
I'll make you mistress of them all,
My bonny Barbara Allen."

6 "Oh! mind you not, young man,
When you were in the tavern,
You made the healths go round about
And slighted Barbara Allen?"

7 He turned his back then to the wall,
His eyes then to the ocean;
And all the words that he did say,
"Farewell to Barbara Allen.

8 "If I had a man,
A man within my dwelling,
Would write a letter with my blood
And carry it to Barbara Allen."

9 The man is off with all his speed
To the place where she was dwelling.
"Here is a letter from my master dear.
Can you be Barbara Allen?"

10 Holy, holy rose she up,
And loudly, loudly laughed she;
Before she read the letter through,
The tears did fall and blind her.[1]

11 She slightly threw the curtains by
And viewed the corpse all in the coffin.
. . . .
. . . .

12 "O mother, mother, make my bed
And make it soft and narrow;
Since Jimmy died for me today,
I'll die for him tomorrow."

13 She had not gone a mile out of town
Till she heard the death-bell tolling
And every knell the death-bell made,
"Woe, woe to Barbara Allen."

14 Barbara Allen was buried in the churchyard,
Sweet Jimmy was laid in the choir;
Out of her grave grew a red rose
And out of his a briar.

15 They grew to the churchyard steeple top,
Till they could grow no higher,
They entwined in a true lover's knot,
Till the red rose hung in the briar.

S

"Barbara Ellen." Contributed by the Misses Ethel and Hallie Rodes, of Bryant, Va. Nelson County. March 26, 1917.

1 It was in the merry month of May,
When the green leaves were a-shining,
Young Jimmy Groves on his death-bed lay,
For the sake of Barbara Ellen.

[1] Stanza 10, evidently an interloper here, belongs not to "Barbara Allen" but to "Sir Patrick Spens" (Child, No. 58) or to "Lord Derwentwater" (Child, No. 208) or to "Geordie" (Child, No. 209). Compare Mackenzie, *Ballads*, No. 9, A, stanza 10. It is interesting to find in Virginia this corroboration of a corruption reported in far-off Nova Scotia. An excluded Virginia text has a similar stanza.

2 He sent his servant man to her house,
 To the house that she lived dwelling,
Saying, "You must unto my master go,
 If your name be Barbara Ellen."

3 Slowly, slowly she got up,
 Slowly went to him,
And when she got to his bedside
 She says, "Young man, you're dying.

4 "I see death printed all in your face,
 And I can't save you from dying."

5 He turned his face unto the wall,
 And streams of sorrow came flowing,
While he counted five thousand pounds
 For the sake of Barbara Ellen.

6 He turned his face unto the wall,
 And streams of sorrow came flowing,
Saying, "I bid adieu to one and all,
 And adieu to Barbara Ellen."

7 And as she walked up and down the street
 She heard some bells a-ringing,
And as they rung they seem to say,
 "Hard-hearted Barbara Ellen."

8 As she walked up and down the street,
 She met his corpse a-coming,
"Come, sit him down and let me look,
 And take the last look at him."

9 The more she looked the more she laughed
 Until she got farther from him,
And her friends and parents cried out, "Shame,
 Hard-hearted Barbara Ellen."

T

"Barbara Ellen." Collected by Mr. John Stone. Sung by Mr. N. H. McKay, of Tunstall, Va. New Kent County. September 11, 1922. Mr. McKay "learned it from his mother when he was a boy on Cape Breton Island. When he gave me the song he was on his way to work, but stopped long enough to write the words for me" (Mr. Stone).

1 In Ireland I was bred and born,
 In Dublin I was dwelling,
I fell in love with a pretty fair maid,
 Her name was Barbara Ellen.

2 I courted her for weeks and months,
Thinking to gain her favor;
But I took sick on my death-bed
And sent for her come and see me.

3 She came into my father's house,
Saying she, "Young man, you are dying."
"Dying, my dear, that never shall be;
One kiss from you shall save me.

4 "Look up, look up at my bed's head,
A gold watch you'll see hanging;
It has been mine, but it shall be thine,
Hard-hearted Barbara Ellen.

5 "Look down, look down at my bedside,
A basin you'll see sitting
With just a drop of my heart's blood;
It was shed for Barbara Ellen.[1]

6 "Bring down, bring down ten thousand pounds,
Ten thousand pounds and fifty,
And give it to this pretty maid
That came so far to see me."

7 They both were buried in the same churchyard,
They both were buried together,
And out of her grave there grew a rose
(And?) out of his a briar.

U

"Barbara Allen." Collected by Miss Juliet Fauntleroy. Sung by Mr. Hall, near Altavista, Va. Campbell County. May 28, 1914. With music.

1 It was one lovely month of May,
Sweet flowers they were blooming;
Sweet Willie is now on his death-bed,
In love with Miss Barbara Allen,
In love with Miss Barbara Allen.

2 He sent his servant to the town
To search in every tavern,
"My master is sick and sends for you,
If your name is Miss Barbara Allen."

[1] With stanzas 4 and 5 of this variant, compare the Wise fragment from the Eastern Shore of Virginia, quoted in the general head-note to this ballad.

3 Slowly, slowly she arose,
And slowly she went to him;
And all she said when she got there,
"Sweet Willie, I think you're dying."

4 "Yes, I am now so very sick,
I think that death is on me;
I can not live another day
Without you, Miss Barbara Allen."

5 She jumped into her fine carriage
And through the town she traveled;
And every tavern she passed by,
"There goes Miss Barbara Allen."

6 She has not driven but a mile from town,
She heard the death-bells ringing;
And all that they did seem to say,
"Hard-hearted Barbara Allen."

7 She looked to the east, she looked to the west,
She saw the corpse a-coming.
"Stop, oh stop, and open the corpse,
And let me look upon him.

8 "Oh mother, oh mother, dig my grave,
Dig it deep and narrow;
Sweet Willie died for me today,
And I will die for him tomorrow.

9 "Sweet Willie died for pure true love,
And I will die for sorrow."
Both were buried in the old church yard,
And both were buried together.

10 From one grave there sprang a rose,
The other was a brier.
They grew, they grew to the steeple top,
And there they could grow no higher.

11 And there they tied in a true lover's knot,
And lived and died together.
And there they tied in a true lover's knot,
And lived and died together.

V

"Barbara Allen." Collected by Miss Juliet Fauntleroy. Sung by Mrs. Berry Barbour (*née* Bowles), of Sycamore, Va. Pittsylvania County. April, 1916.

1 "In Quelick town where I was born
There was three ladies dwelling;
There was but one I called my own,
Her name was Barbara Allen."

2 He sent his servants to the town,
To the tavern she was dwelling,
Saying, "My master is sick and sent for you,
If your name be Barbara Allen."

3 "Go back, go back, go back again,
And tell him I am coming;
For the better of me he never will be,
If his own heart were breaking."

4 Slowly, slowly she rose up,
And slowly she went to him,
And all she said when she got there,
"Young man, I think you're dying."

5 He turned his face over to the wall,
His back to Barbara Allen.
"Adieu, adieu, to my friends all,
Be kind to Barbara Allen."

6 As she returned from church next day,
She met the corpse a-coming,
"Fold down, fold down the corpse of clay
And let me look upon him.

7 "Mother, mother, make my bed,
Make it soft and narrow;
John Green died for me today,
I will die tomorrow.

8 "Mother, mother, dig my grave,
Dig it deep and narrow;
John Green he died for pure true love
And I will die for sorrow."

9 John Green was buried in one church yard,
Barbara Allen was buried in the other;
Out of John Green's sprung a red rose,
Out of Barbara Allen's a green brier.

10 They grew and grew to the high church top,
Until they could not grow any higher,
And then retreated back again,
And the rose wrapped round the brier.

W

"Barbry Allen." Collected by Mrs. W. H. Taliaferro, University, Va. Sung by Mrs. M. E. McDade, of Buffalo Junction, Va. Mecklenburg County. March 15, 1915. The varied spellings of Barbara — "Barberey," "Barbrey," "Barbry" — are preserved because they may indicate differences of pronunciation at different points of the song.

1 'T was in the merry month of May,
When flowers were just a-blooming,
"A young man sick and sent for you,
If your name is Barberey Allen."

2 So slowly, slowly she got up,
And slowly went unto him,
And all she said when she got there:
"Young man, I think you are dying."

3 "Oh yes, I am sick and very sick,
I know my heart is sinking;
I'll never live to get well again
If I don't get Barbrey Allen."

4 "Oh now, remember when you were well,
You rode around my dwelling,
And drank your health to the ladies all
And slighted Barbrey Allen."

5 He turned his pale face to the wall,
She turned her back upon him.
"Adieu, adieu to the ladies all,"
Returned to Barbry Allen.

6 She went five miles below the town,
She heard the bells a-ringing;
The more they rang it seemed to say,
"Hard-hearted Barbry Allen."

7 She looked to the east, she looked to the west,
She saw the corpse a-coming.
"I pray you all to let him down,
And let me gaze upon him."

8 The more she looked the more she grieved,
She bursted out a-crying:
"I might have saved that young man's life,
But, mother, you indulged me.[1]

9 "Oh, take me up and carry me home,
Make my bed both soft and narrow;
This young man died for me today,
And I'll die for him tomorrow."

10 The young man died on Saturday,
And Barbry died on Sunday,
The old lady died for the love of the two,
She died on Easter Monday.

11 The young man was buried in the high church yard,
And Barbry was buried beside him;
Out of his grave sprung a red rose rose,
And out of Barbry's a brier.

12 The rose grew and grew to the high church top
And could not grow any higher;
There it met and tied in a true lover's knot
For all true lovers to admire.

X

"Barbara Allan." Collected by S. Bruce Jones, of Baywood, Va. Grayson County. April 1, 1914.

1 Away down yonder in London town
Is where I got my learning,
A-courting of a pretty little miss,
And her name was Barbara Allan.

2 I courted her for a very long while,
She said she would not marry.
Sweet William he was taken sick
And sent for Barbara Allan.

3 She turned her face toward the wall,
"Go tell him I am coming."
She turned around and walked so slow
To where William was lying.

4 "Sweet William, you are sick,
And very sick indeed,
. . . .
I am afraid you are dying."

[1] A significant addition. Cf. stanza 10, and see head-note to Virginia, No. 24.

5 "Oh yes, I am sick and very sick,
And sick and like of dying;
No better will I ever be
Until I get Barbara Allan."

6 "Oh yes, you are low, you are low indeed,
And death is in you dwelling;
No better will you ever be
By getting Barbara Allan."

7 She walked on through the distant town,
She heard some church bells ringing,
And every one did seem to say,
"Hard-hearted Barbara Allan."

8 She walked on through the meadows green,
She heard the spring birds singing,
And every one did seem to say,
"Sweet William now is dying."

9 She looked to the east, she looked to the west,
She saw the corpse a-coming.
"Oh, lay him down, my pale pale face,
And let me look upon him."

10 She drew the cover from over his face
And bursted out a-crying.
"Oh, take away my true sweetheart;
Oh mother, I am dying."

11 "Dear father, dear father, go dig my grave,
And dig it deep and narrow.
(My true love died for me today
I will die for him tomorrow.)"

12 Sweet William died on Saturday night,
And Barbara Allan died on Sunday,
The mother died for the love of both [1]
And was buried on Easter Monday.

13 They buried Sweet William in the old churchyard
And Barbara Allan beside him,
And out of his grave grew a lily-white rose
And out of hers a briar.

14 They grew and they grew to the top of the church,
And could not grow any higher;
There they lapped and they tied in a true love knot,
The white rose and the briar.

[1] Cf. the variant preceding.

Y

"Barbara Allen." Collected by Mr. John Stone. Sung by Mr. Ed. Davis, of Shipman, Va. Nelson County. November 15, 1915. With music. "Mr. Frank Wilson, of Shipman, Va., learned the same tune from his great-aunt years ago in Rockbridge County. She was a very old lady and brought it from Ireland" (Mr. Stone).

1 'T was early in the month of May,
The rosebuds they were swelling,
Sweet Jimmy on his death-bed lay
For the love of Barbara Allen.
Sweet Jimmy on his death-bed lay
For the love of Barbara Allen.

2 He called his servant to his side:
"Go to the town she's dwelling;
Say, 'My master's sick and sent for you,
For you, Miss Barbara Allen.'"

3 So slowly, slowly she did ride,
And slowly she went to him,
And all she said when she got there
Was, "Young man, I think you're dying."

4 "Oh yes, oh yes, I'm very sick,
The pain of death's upon me;
I know I'll never see another well day
Unless I get you, Barbara Allen."

5 He turned his pale face to the wall,
She turned her back upon him.
"Adieu, adieu, to all my friends,
Be kind to Barbara Allen."

6 As she was riding through the town
She heard the bells a-tolling,
And every sound seemed to say,
"Hard-hearted Barbara Allen."

7 She looked to the east and looked to the west,
She saw the corpse a-coming,
"Driver, drive over to my side
That I may gaze upon him."

8 The more she looked the more she sighed,
And finally burst out crying.
"Mother, father, take me home,
For, mother, I am dying."

9 Sweet Jimmie died on Saturday night,
Barbara Allen died on Sunday,
The mother died the love of them both,
And was buried on Easter Monday.

10 They both were carried to the same graveyard
And they were buried together,
And on one grave sprung a red rose
And on the other a briar.

11 They grew and grew to the church steeple top,
They could not grow any higher;
They linked and twined in a true lover's knot
For all true lovers to admire.

Z

"Barbara Allen." Contributed by Miss Elizabeth Painter, of the Farmville Ballad Club. Pulaski County. September 1915. Printed in *The Focus*, for September, 1915, pp. 282–283. Note the shift from "Allen" to "Ellen."

1 "Way down, way down, in Gordon town,
(That's where I got my learning),
I fell in love with a lady like a dove,[1]
Her name was Barbara Allen.

2 "I courted her for seven long years,
She said she would not marry."
Poor Willie went home,
Was taken sick and the very like of dying.

3 He sent his servant down to town
To the place where she was dwelling,
"My master sent me here today
For the sake of you, Miss Ellen."

4 Very slowly she put on her wraps,
Very slowly she went toward him,
And all she said when she got there,
"Young man, I think you are dying."

5 "I'm low, I'm low, I'm low, I know,
And death on me is dwelling;
No better will I ever be
Till I get you, Miss Ellen."

[1] The line is taken from "Pretty Peggy O." See Campbell and Sharp, No. 95.

6 "You're low, you're low, you're low, I know,
And death on you is dwelling,
No better will you ever be
By getting Barbara Allen."

7 He turned his pale face to the wall,
He turned his back upon her,
"Adieu! adieu! to all my friends,
Adieu to you, Miss Ellen."

8 She had n't been gone but an hour and a half
Till she heard the death-bell ringing;
She thought she heard her own heart say:
"Hard-hearted Barbara Ellen!"

9 She turned around and started back;
She spied the corpse a-coming:
"Oh, lay him down! Oh, lay him down!
Oh, let me gaze upon him!"

10 The more she looked the more she wept
Until she fell to crying,
"Oh take him on! Oh take him on!
My heart has done denied him!

11 "Oh mother, Oh mother, go dig my grave,
Go dig it long and narrow;
Poor Willie has died for pure, sweet love,
And I must die for sorrow.

12 "When I die you must bury me in the old church yard,
Bury me beside of Willie."
A briar has sprung from Willie's side,
And a rose from that of Barbara.

13 They grew and grew to the church yard
Till they could grow no higher,
They linked and tied, they withered and they died,
They linked and tied in a true love knot.

AA

"Barbara Allen." Collected by Miss Juliet Fauntleroy. Sung by Mrs. H. W. Adams, of Altavista, Va. Campbell County. June 21, 1914. With music.

1 'T was all in the merry, merry month of May,
When green buds they were swelling,
Young Jamie Grove on his death-bed lay,
For the love of Barbara Allen.

2 "My uncle's sick and very sick,
And death is dwelling near him;
No better, no better will he ever be
Till he gets you, Barbara Allen."

3 Slowly, slowly she got up,
And slowly she went to him,
And what she said when she got there,
"Young man, I think you're dying."

4 "Oh yes, I'm sick and very sick,
And death is hovering near me;
No better, no better will I ever be
Till I get you, Barbara Allen."

5 "No better, no better will you ever be,
For you'll not get Barbara Allen.
Remember the time that you passed the merry wine,
But you slighted Barbara Allen."

6 She had not gone more than a mile from town
Till she saw the cold corpse coming.
"Stop, oh stop, and open the corpse,
And let me gaze upon him."

7 The harder she gazed, the harder she wept
She said, "I'll die of sorrow.

8 "Oh mother, oh mother, go dig my grave,
And dig it long and narrow;
My true love died for me today,
I'll die for him tomorrow."

9 A red, red rose grew on his breast,
And from hers there grew a brier;
They grew and they grew to the church steeple door,
And then they went no higher.

10 They doubled and they twisted in a true lover's knot,
Never to part any more;
They doubled and they twisted in a true lover's knot,
Never to part any more.

BB

"Barbara Allen." Contributed by Mrs. Virginia Michie, of Charlottesville, Va. Loudoun County. May 17, 1913. The ballad was taken down by Emily Hewson Michie from Mrs. Virginia Michie's dictation. Mrs. Michie heard the song in Loudoun County, Va., in the '40's and had never seen it in print.

1 'T was late-*lie*, late-*lie* in the fall,
'T was when the leaves were dying,
That Johnny from the back countree
Fell in love with Barbara Allen.

2 And oh, he hired a little boy
To run for him an errand,
To run for him to Strawberry town
To fetch him Barbara Allen.

3 Slow-*lie*, slow-*lie* she came down
To where her love was dying;
Every word she said to him was,
"Young man, I think you're dying.

4 "For death is written on your brow,
The color's fading from you;
I cannot save you from the grave,
So fare you well, dear Johnny."

5 The more she looked the more she laughed
The farther she went from him;
And all her friends cried out, "For shame!"
Hard-hearted Barbara Allen.

* * * * * *

6 "Mother, mother, make my bed,
Make it both long and narrow;
For Johnny died for me today,
And I'll die for him tomorrow."

(*The two following verses are sometimes sung with "Barbara Allen" and sometimes with "Lord Lovell."*)

7 They buried him all in the church yard,
They buried her beside him;
Out of his grave a red rose grew
And out of hers a brier.

8 The red rose grew and the brier grew
Till they could grow no higher,
And there they tied a true lovers' knot
For all true lovers to admire.

CC

"Barbara Allen." Collected by Mr. John Stone. Sung by Mrs. Ellen Mulleins, of Saltville, Va. Smyth County. November 8, 1921.

1 "Don't you remember in yonders town
You were buying cakes and candy,
You gave treat to the ladies all around
And slighted Barbara Allen?"

2 "I remember in yonders town
I was buying cakes and candy;
I gave treat to the ladies all around,
And treated Barbara Allen."

3 "Mother, mother, make my bed,
And make it long and narrow;
Sweet William died for pure good love,
And I will die for sorrow."

DD

"Barbara Allen." Collected by Mr. John Stone. Sung by Mrs. C. A. Dickson, of Trimble, Va. Highland County. November 3, 1920. With music. "Mrs. Dickson did not remember the rest of the song. She heard an old lady, Mrs. Millway, sing it many years ago" (Mr. Stone).

1 It was early in the month of May,
When the buds they were a swelling,
Young Johnny lay on his death-bed
For the love of Barbara Allen.
Young Johnny lay on his death-bed
For the love of Barbara Allen.

2 He turned his pale face to the wall,
When death came creeping o'er him.
"Adieu, adieu, to all my friends,
Adieu to Barbara Allen."

EE

"Bonny Barbara Allen." Collected by Miss Corita G. Seoane. Sung by Mrs. C. W. Wynkoop, of Merrifield, Va. Fairfax County. February 11, 1914.

1 It was in the merry month of May,
And the green leaves they were swelling,
Sir James of the grave and the West country
Fell in love with Barbara Allen.

2 She was a fair and comely maid,
A maid near to his dwelling,
Which made him to admire the more
The beauty of Barbara Allen.

FF

"Barbara Allen." Collected by Miss Alfreda M. Peel. Sung by Sis Sears, of Salem, Va. Roanoke County. November 30, 1923. With music.

'T was in the lovely month of May,
When the green buds was swelling,
Sweet William on his death-bed lay
For the love of Barbara Allen.

GG

"Barbara Allen." Collected by Mr. John Stone. Heard in many places in Virginia. September 15, 1915. With music.

'T was in the merry month of May,
When the green buds were swelling.
Sweet William on his death-bed lay
For the love of Barb'ra Allen.

HH

"Barbara Allen." Collected by Miss Martha M. Davis, of Harrisonburg, Va. Sung by old people in Rockingham County. December 14, 1914. "These old people," Miss Davis writes, "know it only by oral transmission." Music only.

II

"Barbara Allen." Collected by Miss Martha M. Davis. Sung by Mrs. N. W. Hough, of Lynchburg, Va. Campbell County. December 12, 1914. Music only.

JJ

"Barbara Allen." Collected by Mr. Cecil J. Sharp. Sung by Mr. N. B. Chisholm, of Woodridge, Va. Albemarle County. September 28, 1916. Music only. Printed by Campbell and Sharp, p. 98.

25

LADY ALICE

(CHILD, No. 85)

THE eighteen items belonging to this ballad in the Virginia collection may be quite adequately represented by the eight here given, since the most widespread version of the song represented by C, D, E, F, and G shows an unusually constant and standard text, and there is no need of reprinting the identity or near-identity. The eighteen variants belong to two quite distinct versions, both of which differ widely from any Child version. One version, represented by A and B and known as "John Collins" or "Johnny Collins," has been found in only one county of the state, Highland. The other version, represented by all the other variants and known as "George Collins," "Giles Collins," "George Collin," or "George Collie," is quite widely known and sung. Some exceptionally fine melodies are the four which belong to the more popular version (see C, D, and E). The editor can personally testify to the special effectiveness of the second melody to D as it is sung in the Blue Ridge mountains. The air is poignant and dirge-like, conforming to the mournful quality of the story, not mitigating it as the lilting air of this ballad's counterpart, "Lord Lovel," mitigates the tragedy of that ballad. Reed Smith reports the ballad from a young man who "frequently heard it sung in the Dismal Swamp region of Virginia." It would be appropriate to that region! The other air given with B clearly belongs to a different version. The appendix shows that this ballad, like "Lord Lovel," is easily parodied.

For American texts, see Brown, p. 9 (North Carolina); *Bulletin*, Nos. 2–10; Campbell and Sharp, No. 22 (North Carolina, Tennessee); Child, II, 279 (Pennsylvania); Cox, No. 17; Hudson, No. 14 (and *Journal*, XXXIX, 102; Mississippi); *Journal*, XXVIII, 151 (Perrow, North Carolina); XXXII, 500 (Richardson, West Virginia, text and melody); Reed Smith, No. 9; Reed Smith, *Ballads*, No. 9. For additional references, see Cox, p. 110; *Journal*, XXX, 317.

A

"John Collins." Collected by Mr. John Stone. Sung by Miss Shaffir. Highland County. November 3, 1920.

1 Johnny Collins rode out to the fields one day,
When the flowers were all in full bloom;
It what did he spy but his own true love
A-washing a white marble tomb.

2 She screamed, she cried,
She threw up her lily-white hand,
"Come here, come here, young Collins, my dear,
For fear that your life is at hand."

3 He swam and he swam
Till he came to his own father's door,
"O father, dear father, get up, I pray,
And let me in once more.

4 "And if I die this very night,
Which I think in my heart that I will,
Go bury me at the foot of the white marble tomb
At the foot of Fair Ellen's green hill."

5 Fair Ellen was sitting in her door one morn,
All dressed in her silk so fine;
It what did she spy but a coffin a-coming,
As far as her eyes could adorn.

6 "Whose coffin, whose coffin,
Whose coffin so neat and so fine?"
"It's young Johnny Collins' coffin a-coming,
An old true lover of mine."

7 She ordered the coffin to be opened
When it landed on Dublin shore,
That she may kiss his cold clay lips
Which ofttimes had kissed them before.

8 She ordered a shroud to be brought to her
That she may trim it so fine.
"Today it waves over Collins' grave,
And tomorrow it shall wave over mine.

9 "O send the news up, O send the news down,
O send the news all around,
That six fair maidens all died last night,
All died for young Collins' sake."

B

"Johnny Collins." Collected by Mr. John Stone. Sung by Mrs. Julie Simmons. Highland County. November 3, 1920. With music.

1 Johnny Collins rode out to the fields one day,
When the flowers were all in full bloom;
Who did he spy but his own fair Ellen
A-washing a white marble stone.

2 She screamed, she cried,
She raised her hand,
Saying, "Come here, young Collins, my dear,
For fear your life at an end."

3 "Whose coffin, whose coffin, whose coffin," she cried,
"Whose coffin so neat and fine?"
"It's young Johnny Collins' coffin a-coming,
An old true lover of mine."

4 She ordered her shroud to be brought to her,
That she might trim it so fine:
"Today it waves over Collins' grave,
And tomorrow it shall wave over mine."

5 She ordered the coffin to be opened,
And the shroud to be folded down,
And she kissed his clay-cold lips,
Till the tears came twinkling down.

C

"George Collins." Collected by Miss Juliet Fauntleroy. Sung by Mrs. Lit Arthur (*née* Taylor), of Altavista, Va. Campbell County. March 14, 1914. With music. Miss Fauntleroy describes this as "the version most frequently met with in this neighborhood" (Campbell County). Note that it differs from most of the other variants in reversing the order of stanzas 4 and 5, and in having an additional stanza (7) which appears in only one other variant. Miss Alma Wilkinson reports the ballad as sung almost identically by school children in Carroll County, except that "Miss Mary" has become "Lady May."

1 George Collins rode home one cold winter night,
George Collins rode home so fine,
George Collins rode home one cold winter night,
Was taken sick and died.

2 See Miss Mary in yonders hall,
Sewing her silk so fine;
When she heard that George had died,
She laid her silk aside.

3 She followed him up, she followed him down,
She followed him to his grave.
She fell upon her bending knees,
She wept, she mourned, she prayed.

4 "Set down the coffin, screw off the lid,
Turn back the linen so fine;
I want to kiss his cold, pale cheeks,
For I know he will never kiss mine."

5 "Daughter, dear daughter, what makes you weep so?
There's more young men than George."
"Oh mother, dear mother, George won my heart,
And now he's dead and gone.

6 "Don't you see that lonesome little dove,
Sitting on yonders pine,
Mourning for its own true love,
Why can't I mourn for mine?

7 "The happiest hours I ever spent
Were by George Collins' side.
The saddest news I ever heard
Was when George Collins died."

D

"George Collins." Collected by Miss Alfreda M. Peel. Sung by Mrs. Lester, of Roanoke, Va. Roanoke County. May 27, 1917. With music (two tunes).

1 George Collins rode home one cold winter night,
George Collins rode home so fine,
George Collins rode home one cold winter night,
He was taken sick and died.

2 Oh, see Miss Mae in yonder hall,
Sewing her silks so fine;
But when she heard poor George was sick,
She laid her silks aside.

3 She followed him up, she followed him down,
She followed him to his grave;
She fell upon her bended knees,
She wept, she prayed, she mourned.

4 "Oh daughter, oh daughter, why do you weep so?
There are more young men than George."
"Oh mother, oh mother, he won my heart,
And now he's dead and gone.

5 "Set down the casket, unscrew the lid,
Lay back the linen so fine;
For I want to kiss his dear sweet lips,
I am sure he will never kiss mine.

6 "See that dove in yonder grove,
Flying from pine to pine,
Mourning for his own true love,
As I mourn for mine."

E

"George Collins." Collected by Miss Juliet Fauntleroy. Sung by Mrs. Dan Maxie (*née* Holland), of Altavista, Va. Franklin County. March 2, 1914. With music.

1 George Collins drove home one cold winter night,
George Collins drove home so fine,
George Collins drove home one cold winter night,
And was taken sick and died.

2 Sweet little Nellie in yonder hall,
Sewing her silk so fine;
But when she heard that George was dead,
She laid her silk aside.

3 She followed him up, she followed him around,
She followed him to his grave,
And there she fell on her bended knees,
She wept, she mourned, she prayed.

4 "Oh daughter, Oh daughter, what makes you weep so?
There's more young boys than George."
"Oh mother, Oh mother, he has my heart,
And now he's dead and gone.

5 "Set down the coffin, unscrew the lid,
Lay back the linen so fine,
And let me kiss his clay-cold lips,
For I'm sure he will never kiss mine.

6 "Don't you see that lonely little dove
A-sitting on yonder pine?
He's mourning for his own true love,
And why not I for mine?"

F

"George Collins." Reported by Professor James M. Grainger. Contributed by Miss Ella Lester, of the Farmville Ballad Club. Patrick County. April, 1913. Miss Lester writes: "The ballad came from Patrick County. I first heard it in the public school when all the girls sang it for pure love of singing. None of us had any idea where it originated." Printed in *The Focus*, April, 1913.

1 George Collins rode home one cold winter night,
George Collins rode home so fine;
George Collins rode home one cold winter night,
And was takened sick and died.

2 His maid was sitting in yonders room,
A-sewing on her silks so fine,
And when she heard George Collins was dead,
She laid her silks aside.

3 She followed him up, she followed him down,
She followed him to his grave;
And down upon her bended knees,
She wept, she mourned, she prayed.

4 "Set down the coffin, take off the lid,
Lay back the linen so fine;
For I want to kiss his cold, white lips,
For I'm sure they'll never kiss mine."

5 "O daughter, dear daughter, what makes you weep so?
There are more young men than George."
"O mother, dear mother, he has won my heart;
And now he is dead and gone.

6 "O don't you see that turtle dove
A-sitting on yonders pine?
He's mourning for his own true love,
Just like I mourn for mine."

G

"Giles Collins." Reported by Miss Corita G. Seoane, of Merrifield, Va. Contributed by Miss Edith Thompson. Fairfax County. February 11, 1914.

1 Giles Collins drove home on a cold winter night,
Giles Collins drove home so fine;
Giles Collins drove home on a cold winter night,
And taken sick an died.

2 I saw a maid in yonder home,
A-sewing her silk so fine;
But when she heard poor Giles was dead,
She laid her silk aside.

3 She followed him up, she followed him down,
She followed him to his grave,
And knelt upon her bended knees,
She mourned, she wept, she prayed.

4 "Dear daughter, dear daughter, what makes you weep so?
There are more young men than Giles."
"Dear mother, dear mother, he won my heart;
But now he is dead and gone.

5 "Set up the casket, open the lid,
Throw back his linen so fine.
And let me kiss poor Giles's lips,
For I know he will never kiss mine.

6 "I see a dove in yonder field,
Flying from pine to pine,
Is mourning for its lost true love.
Why can't I mourn for mine?"

APPENDIX

The "Giles Scroggins" which follows is evidently a burlesque of "Giles Collins," though this fact seems not to have been mentioned in previous publications of the familiar song. For the following bibliographical note on "Giles Scroggins," the editor is indebted to Professor Kittredge: "This was a favorite shop song in the first half of the 19th century. The music was adapted by Wm. Reeve (born 1757, died 1815) from an old air. The words have also been ascribed to him,— also (but erroneously, I think) to Dibdin. For words and music see *Davidson's Universal Melodist*, II (London, 1848), 406; Baring-Gould, *English Minstrelsie*, I (1895), 26. Baring-Gould gives some information on p. XXVIII,— including the remark that Reeve 'published his version in 1830.' [But Reeve died in 1815! See *Gentleman's Mag.*, Vol. 85 (1815, NO. 1), p. 648, for an obituary notice.] The song was a favorite in this country and is included in early American songbooks: *e.g.*, *The New England Pocket Songster*, Woodstock, Vt.; *The Singers Own Book*, Woodstock, Vt., 1838; *The Songster's Companion*, Brattleborough, Vt., 1815. See also Ford, *Massachusetts Broadsides*, No. 3126; Ford, *The Isaiah Thomas Collection*, No. 95."

"Giles Scroggins." Reported by Professor J. M. Grainger. Contributed by Miss Evelyn Purcell, of the Farmville Ballad Club. Albemarle County. December 21, 1913.

1 Giles Scroggins courted Molly Brown,
Fol lol de riddle rol de ray,
The fairest girl in all the town,
Fol de rol de riddle rol de ray.
"If you love me as I love you,
No knife can cut our love in two."
Says she, "I love Giles Scroggins too."
Fol de rol de riddle rol de ray.

2 But scissors cut as well as knives,
Fol lol de riddle rol de ray,
And quite uncertain 's all our lives,
Fol de rol de riddle rol de ray;

For just as they were going to wed,
Fate's scissors cut poor Giles's thread,
And so they were not marrièd.
Fol de rol de riddle rol de ray.

3 Poor Molly laid her down to weep,
Fol lol de riddle rol de ray,
And cried herself quite fast asleep,
Fol de rol de riddle rol de ray,
When standing there by her bed-post,
A figure tall her sight engrossed,
Said he, "I am Giles Scroggins's ghost."
Fol de rol de riddle rol de ray.

4 "Oh, Molly, you must come with me."
Fol lol de riddle rol de ray.
. . . .
Fol de rol de riddle rol de ray.
. . . .
"I won't", she said and screamed a scream,
And when she awoke she found 't was a dream.
Fol de rol de riddle rol de ray.[1]

[1] The first three stanzas are practically identical with the standard version of the song, but the fourth stanza is a compressed and fragmentary representative of the usual fourth and fifth stanzas, which (minus refrain) run thus:

4 The Ghost it said all solemnly,
"Oh Molly, you must go with *I*,
All to the grave your love to cool."
Says she, "I am not dead, you fool."
Says the Ghost, says he, "Fie, that's no rule."

5 The Ghost he seized her all so grim,
And for to go along with him,
"Come, come," said he, "e're morning beam."
"I won't," she cried, and gave a scream,
Then she woke and found she dreamed a dream.

These stanzas come from Harold Scott's *English Song Book*, New York, 1926, p. 67. "Giles Scroggins" is there described as "a clown song; undoubtedly in Grimaldi's repertory."

26

LAMKIN

(CHILD, No. 93)

THE first evidence that this ballad survived in America came from Virginia. Child's Additions and Corrections (III, 515) report that "the negroes of Dumfries, Prince William County, Virginia, have this ballad, orally transmitted from the original Scottish settlers of that region, with the stanza . . .

> Mr. Lammikin, Mr. Lammikin,
> oh, spare me my life,
> And I'll give you my daughter Betsy,
> and she shall be your wife."

It is to be noted that all the Virginia variants, except, of course, the fragment D, have the stanza which makes this unnatural offer (A 14, B 7, C 5). Of the twenty-six versions printed by Child, this stanza is found in only three (F 19, T 15, X 16), but the resemblance is not otherwise close to any one of these three, or indeed to any Child version. The Virginia texts seem to represent at least two separate versions (A and B) not found in Child.

The story, however, does not differ materially from that of the Child versions, thus summarized by Child: "A mason has built a castle for a nobleman, cannot get his pay, and therefore seeks revenge. The name given the builder is Lamkin [in Virginia, also Lampkin, Ward Lampkin, Beaulamkins, or Bow Lamkins]. . . . The Lord, having occasion to leave his family fears mischief from the man whom he has wronged, and enjoins his wife to keep the castle well fastened. Precautions are taken, but nevertheless his enemy effects an entrance through some aperture that has not been secured, or by connivance with a nurse. Most of the servants are away. To get at the lady, Lamkin, as we may call him, by advice of the nurse inflicts some hurt on the babe in the cradle, stabbing it or 'nipping' it, and the cries bring the mother down. The lady proffers large sums of gold to save her life, but Lamkin does not care for gold now. [She also offers her daughter. See above.] He gloats over his opportunity, and bids the nurse, or a maid-servant, or even one of the daughters of the house, to scour a silver basin to hold the lady's noble blood. The lord has a presentment of calamity at home, and, returning, finds his house red with the blood of his wife and child. Lamkin is hanged, or burned, or boiled in a pot full of lead. The nurse is burned, or hanged, or boiled in a cauldron." In Virginia texts, Lamkin is always hanged, the nurse always burned.

The tale has been localized in various parts of Scotland, as pointed out by Motherwell in his *Minstrelsy*, p. lxx, note 27, and p. 291. The name Lamkin Child explains as either (1) "a soubriquet applied in derision of the meekness with which the builder had submitted to his injury," or (2) "a simply ironical designation for the bloody mason, the terror of countless nurseries."

Four Virginia texts and one tune are here given. Of these, A and B are new and different versions, C is a badly mangled variant of A, and D is a fragment corresponding to Child D 13. The tune to B is conjecturally interpreted, but the original notation is also given.

For American texts, see Brown, p. 9 (North Carolina); *Bulletin*, Nos. 3, 9; Campbell and Sharp, No. 23 (North Carolina); Child, III, 515 (Virginia); V, 295 (North Carolina); Jones, p. 301 (fragment); *Journal*, XIII, 117 (Newell, New York); XXIX, 162 (Tolman, Ohio); XXXV, 344 (Tolman and Eddy, fragment and melody). For additional references, see *Journal*, XXIX, 162; XXX, 318.

A

"Beaulamkins" or "Bow Lamkins." Collected by Mr. John Stone. Sung by Mr. George Hart, of Konnarock, Va. Washington County. November 8, 1921.

1 Bow Lamkins was a fine mason
As ever laid stone;
He built him a frame house
Not far from Benone.

2 The landlord he bid her
Before he left home
To beware of Bow Lamkins
For he's come unbeknowns.

3 "What cares I for Bow Lamkins,
What cares I for him,
When my door is fast locked
And my windows barred in?"

4 Bow Lamkins he come
And he knocked on the ring,
And the false nurse she rose
And let him come in.

5 "O where is the landlord,
Or is he at home?"
"He is gone to fair England
To buy me a ring."

6 "O where is the lord's lady,
Or is she at home?"
"She is upstairs a-sleeping,"
Said the false nurse to him.

7 "O how will we get her down here?"
Said the false nurse to him,
"We will stick her little baby
Full of needles and pins."

8 Bow Lamkins he rocked,
And the false nurse she sung,
Till the tears and the red blood
From the cradle did run.

9 She come running downstairs,
Not a-thinking any harm;
And Bow Lamkins stood waiting
To catch her in his arms.

10 "O spare my life, Bow Lamkins,
O spare it one week;
Don't you hear my little baby
How mournful it weeps?"

11 "What cares I for your baby,
What cares I for it,
When I've got my heart's fortune
And it's all I do crave?"

12 "O spare my life, Bow Lamkins,
O spare it one day;
You may have as much gay gold
As your horse can tote away."

13 "What cares I for your gay gold,
What cares I for it,
When I can hardly keep my pen-knife
From your little white throat?"

14 "O spare my life, Bow Lamkins,
O spare it one hour;
You may have my daughter Betsy,
My own blooming flower."

15 "You may keep your daughter Betsy
To run through the blood
And to scour your silver basins
That catches your heart's blood."

16 "O stay, daughter Betsy,
Wherever you be,
Till you hear your old father
Come hard riding by."

17 "O father, dear father,
How can you blame me?
For Bow Lamkins and the false nurse
Has killed my mammy.
For Bow Lamkins and the false nurse
Has killed your lady."

18 Bow Lamkins he was hung
At the gallows so high;
And the false nurse she was burnt
At the stake standing by.

B

"Lampkin." Reported by Miss Martha M. Davis. Contributed by Mrs. Thomas Ware. Sung by an old Colored servant, Fanny Fletcher. Clark County. September 5, 1914. With music. "The old Negro servant who sang this song always gave an introduction, saying that 'Ward Lampkin had been in love with the Landlady, before her marriage to the Lord, and had always sworn to get his revenge. The Lord was going off on a trip and urged his wife to have some protection, to which the first stanza is her reply. Then the night after her husband went away, Ward Lampkin came and persuaded Fortunate, the nurse, that the baby was crying in the nursery, so that he would have a chance to get in while she was gone. Fortunate was afterwards punished with him, as she was accused of having helped him to murder her.' This old woman, Fanny Fletcher, was very proud of her high cheek-bones and hair, and never lost an opportunity to tell that her grandmother had been an Indian squaw" (Mrs. Ware).

1 "Why need I reward Lampkin?
Why need I reward him?
When my doors are fast bolted,
And windows pinned down?"

2 "Oh, Fortunate, Oh Fortunate!
Why do you sleep so sound?
Don't you hear that little baby,
How mournful it cries?"

3 "Landlady, landlady!
Why don't you come down,
For to see this fine gentleman
Just stepped into your room?"

4 "How can I come down,
When no candle is burning,
No fire gives light?"

5 "There's two silver candlesticks
A-setting in your room;
Why can't you come down
By the light of the one?"

6 Down stepped the landlady,
Not thinking of no harm;
Out stepped Ward Lampkin
And seized her by the arm.

7 "Mr. Lampkin, Mr. Lampkin,
Just spare me one hour,
And I'll gave you my daughter Betsy,
She's the flower of the flock."

(*Daughter Betsy was at school and had to be sent for.*)

8 "You can take your daughter Betsy,
And send her to the flood,
For to scour that silver basin,
To ketch your heart's blood."

9 "Mr. Lampkin, Mr. Lampkin,
Jest spare me one minute,
And I'll gave you as much money,
As you kin carry away."

10 "Ef you gave me as much money
As there's stars in the sky,
'T would not keep my bright sword
From your lily-white breast."

11 "Mr. Lampkin, Mr. Lampkin,
Jest spare me one secon',
And I'll gave you as many guineas
As you kin carry away."

12 "Ef you gave me as many guineas
As there's grains of sand on the sea,
'T would not keep my bright sword
From your lily-white breast."

13 Ward Lampkin was hung
On the gallows so high,
And old Fortunate was burned
In the fire close by.

C

"Beaulamkins" or "Bow Lamkins." Collected by Mr. John Stone. Recited by Mr. S. L. Riffey, of Park, Va. Grayson County. November 8, 1921. The stanza divisions are irregular and bad, but they are given just as they were sent in and presumably as recited. This is a fragmentary variant of A.

1 Bow Lamkins built a fine cation,[1]
Every load stone,
Pay he got none.
"Bow Lamkins has gone to Merry England
To buy me a ring."

[1] For *castle*, or a clipping short of (*fortifi-*)*cation*?

2 "Keep your windows bolted
And your door fast locked.
For Bow Lamkins will ketch you unbeknowns."

3 Bow Lamkins rose and knocked at the door,
False nurse she came stepping downstairs,
Thinking no harm;
There stood Bow Lamkins ready
For to catch her in his arms.

4 "Spare my life, Bow Lamkins,
Spare it one hour;
And I'll give you as much gold
As your horse can tote away."

5 "O spare my life, Bow Lamkins,
Just listen how mournful my baby do cry;
O spare my life, Bow Lamkins,
And I'll give you my daughter Betsy,
One blooming star.

6 "O spare my life, Bow Lamkins,
And just listen how mournful my baby do cry."
False nurse she said, "Stick her little baby
Full of needles and pins."

7 False nurse she rocked,
And she sung;
The tears and the red blood
From the cradle did run.

8 "O daughter Betsy, stay where you be,
And tell your dear father,
When he comes riding horse by,
Tell him Bow Lamkins has killed his lady."

9 Bow Lamkins was hung
At the gallows so high;
False nurse was burnt
At the stake a-standing by.

D

"Lamkin." Collected by Mr. John Stone. Recited by Mrs. Sarah Vest, of Deerfield, Va. Augusta County. July 31, 1922. "Mrs. Vest years ago could sing 'Bessie Bell and Mary Gray,' but she had forgotten it. Also she heard 'Johnny Scot' sung in Highland County, years ago. She heard her husband sing 'Lamkin'" (Mr. Stone).

"We have gave him breast milk,
We have gave him pap,
So come down, dearest madam,
And rock him in your lap."

27

THE MAID FREED FROM THE GALLOWS

(CHILD, No. 95)

THE first American text of this ballad to be printed came from Virginia (*via* North Carolina). Miss Backus, who transmitted it to Professor Child describes it as "an old English song, in the Yorkshire dialect, brought over to Virginia before the Revolution." Child includes it in V, 296, and Professor Kittredge has made it widely known by including it and discussing it in his Introduction to the one-volume edition of *English and Scottish Popular Ballads*, pp. xxv-xxvi. It is this version that, except for its Yorkshire dialect, most of the Virginia variants resemble. In language they most resemble Child B, though their quite universal use of the term "hangman" would link them to the Child fragment G, where alone does the term appear in Child. There is no trace among the Virginia variants of the strong ending of the Scottish version (Child I), in which the released prisoner turns upon her heartless relatives and flays them with curses. At least five Virginia texts (E, F, G, H, and I) are like the version of Child III, 516, in that the prisoner is a man, not a maid. Child suggests that "this may be a modern turn of the story, arising from the disposition to mitigate a tragic tale." And three Virginia texts (I, J, and K), like Child F, G, and H, give a suggestion of the offence for which the prisoner is in danger of hanging. But despite these other affiliations, the main resemblance is with the Child V, 296, version.

The thirty-one texts and five melodies collected in Virginia show the popularity of the ballad in the state, where it is generally known as "The Hangman's Tree," or "The Gallows Tree," or "Hangman," or "Freed from the Gallows," or "The Maid Saved," and by various Negro and other perversions of these titles, such as "The Hangerman's Tree," "Hangsman," and "Hangerman Tree," as well as by its Child title.

The ballad is a special favorite among the Negroes, who have all but appropriated it to their own uses. Not only do they sing it; they act it as well. Several records of its dramatization in Virginia are in the files of the Virginia Folk-Lore Society. Possibly the best account is found in a letter from Miss Mary I. Bell, formerly a teacher in the State Normal School of Harrisonburg, Va., dated May 27, 1913. The performance was at Scottsville, in Albemarle County, only some twenty miles from the University of Virginia:

> It was a long time ago — probably twenty-five years — at the Colored school-house, as a part of the closing exercises of the school. We young people always attended these exercises if possible, because we were sure of being highly entertained. This particular play I remember better than any other I ever saw there because we thought it so very funny, though plainly intended to be so very sad. They had on the stage a rather rude representation of the upper part of a scaffold. A rope the size of a man's wrist was thrown over the cross-beam, one end being tied around the neck of a most dejected-looking girl and the other end held in the hand of a middle-aged man of sternest aspect. She alone did any singing. The apparently endless

procession of relatives recited their parts very glibly until at last when her "true love" arrived he sang his part, and then the lovers ended the play with a joyous duet. I did not know then that it was a ballad.

The Negroes use the ballad as a game also. Mrs. Robert R. Morton, wife of the former executive of Hampton Institute, wrote to Dr. Smith, Dec. 2, 1915, saying, "When I was a child in Gloucester County, they used it as a game." And Mr. Stone reports of one of the tunes of the ballad (M), "The old time Negroes used it as the music to one of their games. Three instances of this kind were found in Nelson County." The words of some of the Negro versions, such as E and K, are highly entertaining. Dr. Smith attributes the popularity of this ballad among the Colored folk to "the adaptability of the theme and the easily remembered framework of the stanzas, qualities that mark the intersection of the ballad proper and the Negro camp-meeting song as types." For a fuller consideration of its use among the Negroes of the South, see Scarborough, Chap. II, pp. 34–43. Through the courtesy of Dr. Smith, Miss Scarborough presents a good deal of Virginia material in her discussion.

But white people as well as Negroes are known to have used the ballad as a play and as a game in Virginia. Mrs. James A. Otey writes from Montgomery County, February 21, 1916: "The apple tree still is here at Walnut Spring where the white children acted and sang this ballad as I have taken it down — about the year 1867, they think. It was given to me by two old scholars of the private school here. They never saw it in print." (See Virginia J.) Compare Child F, which is a children's game.

The wide currency of this ballad in Continental literature has been pointed out by Child, as has the fact that most of the English versions are defective and distorted in comparison with the European. Seldom is any explanation given of the danger in which the heroine (sometimes hero) finds herself (himself). In many versions in other languages, however, "a young woman has fallen into the hands of corsairs; father, mother, brother, sister, refuse to pay ransom, but her lover, in one case husband, stickles at no price which may be necessary to retrieve her," says Child. "Another tradition," says Miss Scarborough, "holds that the story is all allegory, the golden ball signifying a maiden's honor, which when lost can be restored to her only by her lover. That would explain the sentence of death; for, in old times, death by burning or hanging was the penalty for unchastity on the part of a maid or wife." Miss Scarborough gives also a more dialetic Negro interpretation, involving a lost golden ball and various magician's tricks. Of the three Virginia texts which attempt any explanation (I, J, and K), one has the sub-title "The Girl to Be Hanged for Stealing a Comb," the second also contains the inquiry whether the golden comb has been found, the third introduces the golden ball and the contributor attempts a fuller reconstruction of the story, as follows: "A man received a golden ball and promised never to part with it. Later he gave it to his sweetheart, but when questioned refused to tell what he did with it. He is to be hanged for this and is saved by his sweetheart who returns the golden ball."

As a guide to the variants following, A to D are normal but interesting Virginia texts; E to I reverse the sexes of the prisoner and rescuer; I to K give some explanation or inkling of the prisoner's offence; L to O are compressed but complete variants; P to V continue the series A to D, of normal Virginia texts with interesting variations. Nine variants have been excluded as adding little or nothing to the material included. They may be described as normal texts without significant variations from those included.

As appendices, for purposes of comparison, are given three texts which drifted in to the Virginia Folk-Lore Society from three other Southern states (Appendices A, B, and C). A is a quite different version, in which the victim is rescued by the mother; B has interesting verbal changes and a man as victim; C addresses the hangman as "Ropeman," and has other verbal changes. They are from North Carolina, Florida, and Mississippi, respectively.

For other American texts, see Barry, No. 25; Brown, p. 9 (North Carolina); *Bulletin*, Nos. 2–6; 8–10; Campbell and Sharp, No. 24 (Tennessee, North Carolina, Virginia); Child V, 296 (Virginia *via* North Carolina), 417 (North Carolina, melody only); Cox, No. 18; Hudson, No. 15 (and, *Journal*, XXXIX, 105; Mississippi); *Journal*, XIX, 22 (Hutchinson, Virginia, from *English and Scottish Popular Ballads:* Sargent and Kittredge, p. xxv); XXI, 56 (Kittredge, West Virginia); XXIV, 337 (Barry, melody only, reprinted from the Hudson MS. No. 355); XXVI, 175 (Kittredge, Massachusetts, fragment); XXX, 319 (Kittredge, New York, Missouri, text and melody, North Carolina); Pound, *Ballads*, No. 13; Sandburg, p. 72 (South Carolina); Scarborough, pp. 35 (Virginia), 39 (Florida, text and melody), 41 (Louisiana); C. A. Smith, pp. 6 (North Carolina), 10 (Virginia, fragments); Reed Smith, No. 10; Reed Smith, *Ballads*, No. 10; Wyman and Brockway, p. 44. For additional references, see Cox, p. 115; *Journal*, XXX, 318. For a recent consideration of this particular ballad, see Reed Smith, *Ballads*, Chapter VIII, "Five Hundred Years of 'The Maid Freed from the Gallows.'"

A

"The Hangman's Tree." Collected by Miss Martha M. Davis. Sung by a mountain woman of Elkton, Va. Rockingham County. January 3, 1914.

1 "O hangman, hangman, hold your rope,
O hold it for a while;
I think I see my father coming
Many and many a mile.

2 "O father, father, have you any gold,
The gold that will set me free?
Or have you come to see me hung
Beneath the willow tree?"

3 "O no, O no, I have no gold,
It 's gold that will set you free;
But I have come to see you hung
Beneath the willow tree."

4 "O hangman, hangman, hold your rope,
O hold it for a while;
I think I see my mother coming
Many and many a mile.

5 "Mother, O mother, have you any gold,
The gold that will set me free?
Or have you come to see me hung
Beneath the willow tree?"

6 "O no, O no, I have no gold,
It's gold that will set you free;
But I have come to see you hung
Beneath the willow tree."

7 "O hangman, hangman, hold your rope,
O hold it for a while;
I think I see my brother coming
Many and many a mile.

8 "O brother, brother, have you any gold,
The gold that will set me free?
Or have you come to see me hung
Beneath the willow tree?"

9 "O no, O no, I have no gold,
It 's gold that will set you free;
But I have come to see you hung
Beneath the willow tree."

10 "O hangman, hangman, hold your rope,
O hold it for a while;
I think I see my true love coming
Many and many a mile.

11 "O true love, true love, have you any gold,
The gold that will set me free?
Or have you come to see me hung
Beneath the willow tree?"

12 "O yes, O yes, I have some gold,
It's gold that will set you free;
For I have not come to see you hung
Beneath the willow tree."

B

"The Maid Freed from the Gallows." Collected by Mr. Cecil J. Sharp and Miss Karpeles. Sung by Mrs. Orilla Keeton, at Mount Fair, Brown's Cove, Va. Albemarle County. September 26, 1916. With music. Printed by Campbell and Sharp, p. 107.

1 "Hangman, hangman, spare my life,
Just spare my life a moment;
I think I hear my father coming,
A many, a many a mile.

2 "Father, father, have you gold,
The gold to set me free,
Or have you come to see me hung
Beneath the willow tree?

3 "Daughter, daughter, I have no gold,
Gold to set you free;
But I have come to see you hung
Beneath the willow tree."

In subsequent verses, mother, brother, sister, *etc., and finally* true love *are substituted for* father. *The last verse runs thus:*

15 "True love, true love, I have the gold,
Gold to set you free;
And I shan't come to see you hung
Beneath the willow tree."

C

"Hangman." Collected by Mrs. N. E. Clement. Sung by an old woman of Chatham, Va. Pittsylvania County. July 25, 1917.

1 "Hangman, hangman, hold your rope,
Wait a little while and see;
I think I see my mother dear,
A-sailing over the sea.

2 "O mother, have you brought me silver or gold,
Or money to pay my fee,
Or have you come to see me hanged
Upon the hangman's tree?"

3 "No, I've not brought you silver nor gold,
Nor money to pay your fee;
But I have come to see you hanged
Upon the hangman's tree."

4 "O hangman, hangman, stay your rope,
Wait a little while and see;
I think I see my father dear,
A-sailing over the sea.

5 "O father, have you brought me silver or gold,
Or money to pay my fee,
Or have you come to see me hanged
Upon the hangman's tree?"

6 "No, I've not brought you silver nor gold,
Nor money to pay your fee;
But I have come to see you hanged
Upon the hangman's tree."

7 "O hangman, hangman, stay your rope,
Wait a little while and see;
I think I see my sister dear,
A-sailing over the sea.

8 "O sister, have you brought me silver or gold,
Or money to pay my fee,
Or have you come to see me hanged
Upon the hangman's tree?"

9 "No, I've not brought you silver nor gold,
Nor money to pay your fee;
But I have come to see you hanged
Upon the hangman's tree."

10 "O hangman, hangman, stay your rope,
Wait a little while and see;
I think I see my brother dear,
A-sailing over the sea.

11 "O brother, have you brought me silver or gold,
Or money to pay my fee,
Or have you come to see me hanged,
Upon the hangman's tree?"

12 "No, I've not brought you silver nor gold,
Nor money to pay your fee;
But I have come to see you hanged,
Upon the hangman's tree."

13 "O hangman, hangman, stay your rope,
Wait a little while and see;
I think I see my sweetheart dear,
A-sailing over the sea.

14 "O love, have you brought me silver or gold,
Or money to pay my fee,
Or have you come to see me hanged,
Upon the hangman's tree?"

15 "Yes, I have brought you silver and gold,
And money to pay your fee,
And I have come to take you down,
And carry you home with me."

D

"The Gallows Tree." Collected by Miss Juliet Fauntleroy. Sung by Mrs. Essie Wallace Yowell, of Altavista, Va. Campbell County. April 17, 1914.

1 "Hangsman, hangsman, slacken your rope,
Oh, wait a few moments for me;
I think I hear my father coming,
A many long mile, a many long mile.

2 "Oh father, father, did you bring me any gold,
Did you come to pay my fee?
Or did you come to see me hung
On yonders gallows tree?"

3 "Oh no, oh no, I've brought you no gold,
I did n't come to pay your fee;
But I have come to see you hung
On yonders gallows tree."

4 "Hangsman, hangsman, slacken your rope,
Oh, wait a few moments for me;
I think I hear my mother coming,
A many long mile, a many long mile.

5 "Oh mother, mother, did you bring me any gold,
Did you come to pay my fee?
Or did you come to see me hung
On yonders gallows tree?"

6 "Oh no, oh no, I've brought you no gold,
I did n't come to pay your fee;
But I have come to see you hung
On yonders gallows tree."

7 "Hangsman, hangsman, slacken your rope,
Oh, wait a few moments for me;
I think I hear my brother coming,
A many long mile, a many long mile.

8 "Oh brother, brother, did you bring me any gold,
Did you come to pay my fee?
Or did you come to see me hung
On yonders gallows tree?"

9 "Oh no, oh no, I've brought you no gold,
I did n't come to pay your fee;
But I have come to see you hung
On yonders gallows tree."

10 "Hangsman, hangsman, slacken your rope,
Oh, wait a few moments for me;
I think I hear my sister coming,
A many long mile, a many long mile.

11 "Oh sister, sister, did you bring me any gold,
Did you come to pay my fee?
Or did you come to see me hung
On yonders gallows tree?"

12 "Oh no, oh no, I've brought you no gold,
I did n't come to pay your fee;
But I have come to see you hung
On yonders gallows tree."

13 "Hangsman, hangsman, slacken your rope,
Oh, wait a few moments for me;
I think I hear my love coming,
A many long mile, a many long mile.

14 "Oh love, oh love, did you bring me any gold,
Did you come to pay my fee?
Or did you come to see me hung
On yonders gallows tree?"

15 "Oh yes, oh yes, I've brought you gold,
I've come to pay your fee;
And by the help of God above
I'll take you home with me."

E

"The Hangerman's Tree" or "Freed from the Gallows." Collected by Miss Juliet Fauntleroy. Sung by Mrs. Maxie (*nêe* Holland), of Altavista, Va. Franklin County. March 23, 1914. With music. The prisoner in this variant is a man, as shown by stanzas 3, 6, and 13. Cf. F, G, H, I. It has been suggested that the change of sex in these variants may have some relation to the "Southern chivalry" which has made it difficult to convict a woman in the South.

1 "O hangerman, O hangerman, slack on your rope,
And wait a little while;
I think I see my father a-coming,
And he's traveled for many a long mile.

2 "O father, O father, have you brought me money,
And money to pay my fee;
Or have you come to see me hanged
Up on this hangerman's tree?"

3 "O no, my son, I've brought no money,
No money to pay your fee;
Yes, I have come to see you hanged
Up on this hangerman's tree."

4 "O hangerman, O hangerman, slack on your rope,
And wait a little while;
I think I see my mother a-coming,
And she's traveled for many a long mile.

5 "O mother, O mother, have you brought me money,
And money to pay my fee;
Or have you come to see me hanged
Up on this hangerman's tree?"

6 "O no, my son, I've brought no money,
No money to pay your fee;
Yes, I have come to see you hanged
Up on this hangerman's tree."

7 "O hangerman, O hangerman, slack on your rope,
And wait a little while;
I think I see my brother a-coming,
And he's traveled for many a long mile.

8 "O brother, O brother, have you brought me money,
And money to pay my fee;
Or have you come to see me hanged
Up on this hangerman's tree?"

9 "O no, my brother, I've brought no money,
No money to pay your fee;
Yes, I have come to see you hanged
Up on this hangerman's tree."

10 "O hangerman, O hangerman, slack on your rope,
And wait a little while;
I think I see my sister a-coming,
And she's traveled for many a long mile.

11 "O sister, O sister, have you brought me money,
And money to pay my fee;
Or have you come to see me hanged
Up on this hangerman's tree?"

12 "O no, my brother, I've brought no money,
No money to pay your fee;
Yes, I have come to see you hanged
Up on this hangerman's tree."

13 "O hangerman, O hangerman, slack on your rope,
And wait a little while;
I think I see my true love coming,
And she's traveled for many a long mile.

14 "O, my dear, have you brought me money,
And money to pay my fee;
Or have you come to see me hanged
Up on this hangerman's tree?"

15 "O yes, my love, I've brought you money,
And money to pay your fee;
I have not come to see you hanged,
Up on this hangerman's tree."

F

"The Maid Freed from the Gallows." Collected by Mr. Cecil J. Sharp and Miss Karpeles. Sung by Mr. N. B. Chisholm, at Woodridge, Va. Albemarle County. September 27, 1916. With music. Printed by Campbell and Sharp, p. 108.

1 "Hangman, hangman, hold your rope,
And hold it for a while;
I think I see my father coming
From a long many mile.

2 "Father, father, have you any gold,
Gold for to set me free,
Or have you come to see me hung
Beneath the gallows tree?"

3 "Son, O son, I have no gold,
Gold to set you free;
I've only come to see you hung
Beneath the gallows tree." [1]

The verses run thus until she has seen her mother, brother, sister, *etc., and finally her* sweetheart *arrives. The last verse is as follows:*

15 "Sweetheart, sweetheart, I have gold,
Gold to set you free;
And I have not come to see you hung
Beneath the gallows tree."

[1] How to reconcile this stanza with the title or with the words that follow, were a question above logic, but not, perhaps, above antiquarism. A vagary of the ballad singer has permitted the sex of the prisoner to change, and then to change back again. It seems a choice between these Zeus-like metamorphoses and the nodding of another Zeus — that is, Mr. Sharp. Such vagaries are not unknown to the ballad singer. But more probably the title is simply an identification, and the recorder simply nodded a moment when he wrote "*her* sweetheart."

G

"The Maid Freed from the Gallows." Collected by Mr. John Stone. Sung by Miss Mary Nash, of Onville, Va. Stafford County. September 11, 1922.

1 "Hangman, hangman, hold your rope,
Hold it for a while;
I think I see my father coming,
Coming many a mile.

2 "Father, father, have you gold,
If gold will set me free?
Or have you come to see me hung
Beneath the gallows tree?"

3 "No, my son, I have no gold,
If gold will set you free;
But I have come to see you hung
Beneath the gallows tree."

Repeat in groups of three stanzas for mother, brother, *and* sister. *Then continue:*

13 "Hangman, hangman, hold your rope,
Hold it for a while;
I think I see my true love coming,
Coming many a mile.

14 "True love, true love, have you any gold,
If gold will set me free?
Or have you come to see me hung
Beneath the gallows tree?"

15 "O yes, my lover, I have gold,
If gold will set you free;
And I've not come to see you hung
Beneath the gallows tree."

H

"The Gallows Tree." Collected by Miss Juliet Fauntleroy. Sung by Mrs. James Sprouse (*née* Pribble), of Lawyers, Va. Campbell County. September 4, 1915.

1 "Hangman, hangman, slacken your rope,
And a few more minutes for me;
I think I see my father a-coming,
He's coming from many a long mile.

2 "Oh father, Oh father, did you bring me any gold?
I'm obliged to pay my fee;
Or did you come to see me hang
Upon the gallows tree?"

3 "No sir, no sir, I brought you no gold,
Nor I won't pay your fee;
But I did come to see you hang
Upon the gallows tree."

Then in turn come mother, sister, *and* brother. *All make the same reply. Then comes the* true love, *who makes reply:*

15 "Yes sir, yes sir, I've brought you gold,
And I will pay your fee;
But I did not come to see you hung
Upon the gallows tree."

I

"Hangman's Tree." Contributed by Miss Nancy Pearson, of Christiansburg, Va. Pulaski County. October 9, 1916. "The story is this: The man received a golden ball and promised never to part with it. Later he gave it to his sweetheart, but when questioned refused to tell what he did with it. He is to be hanged for this and is saved by his sweetheart who returns the golden ball" (Miss Pearson).

1 "Oh mother, have you found my gold ball,
Or have you come to set me free?
Or have you come to see me hung
Upon this cursèd tree?"

2 "I have n't come to find your golden ball,
I have n't come to set you free;
But I have come to see you hung
Upon this cursèd tree."

J

"The Hangman's Tree" or "The Girl To Be Hanged for Stealing a Comb." Collected by Mrs. James A. Otey. Sung by two old women of Walnut Spring, Va. Montgomery County. February 21, 1916. Mrs. Otey writes, "The apple tree still is here at Walnut Spring where the white school children acted and sang this ballad as I have taken it down — about the year 1867, they think. It was given me by two old scholars of the private school here. They never saw it in print."

1 "Oh hangman, hangman, slack on the rope,
And gie me time to see
My father travelling night and day
To set his daughter free.

2 "Oh father, have you brought the comb
To set your daughter free?
Or have you travelled many a mile
This dreadful sight to see?"

3 "I have not brought the comb;
I can not set you free;
But I have travelled many a mile
To reach the hangman's tree."

Then in turn come mother, sister, *and* brother. *All make the same reply, until the* sweetheart *or* lover *comes. The final stanza runs:*

15 "I have bought a golden comb
To pay to set you free;
And I have come to take you home
Far from this cursèd tree."

K

"The Maid Freed from the Gallows." Contributed by Miss Henrietta G. R. Pendleton. Recited by a Colored girl in Gloucester County (who learned it from her grandmother). May 28, 1913. This is the only text in which the grandmother comes first. Probably the relatives appear in the order of seniority.

1 "O hangman, hold your holts, I pray!
O hold your holts awhile;
I think I see my grandmother
A-coming down the road.

2 "O have you found my golden comb? [1]
And have you come to set me free?
Or have you come to see me hanged
On the cruel hangman tree?"

3 "I have not found your golden comb,
Nor have I come to set you free,
But I have come to see you hanged
On the cruel hangman tree."

Then all the other members of the family until true love *comes.*

15 "Yes, I have found your golden comb,
And I have come to set you free.
I have not come to see you hanged
On the cruel hangman tree."

[1] A suggestion of the offence for which the girl is to be hanged.

JOHN STONE

Mt. Fair, Albemarle County, Va.

Ballad Hunter Extraordinary

L

"Hangerman Tree." Collected by Miss Alfreda M. Peel. Sung by Texas Gladden, of Salem, Va. Roanoke County. May 27, 1917.

1 "Hangerman, hangerman, hold your rope,
And hold it for a while;
I think I see my mother coming,
She's rode for many a mile.

2 "Have you come to see me hung,
Or come to pay my fee?"
"Yes, I have come to see you hung
Upon the gallows tree." [1]

3 "Hangerman, hangerman, hold your rope,
And hold it for a while;
I think I see my father coming,
A-riding through the air.[2]

4 "Have you come to see me hung
Or come to pay my fee?"
"Oh yes, I've come to see you hung
Upon the gallows tree."

5 "Hangerman, hangerman, hold your rope,
And hold it for a while;
I think I see my sweetheart coming,
He's rode for many a mile.

6 "Oh, have you come to see me hung,
Or come to pay my fee?"
"No, I've not come to see you hung,
And hung you'll never be."

M

"The Maid Saved." Collected by Mr. John Stone. Sung by Mr. Ed Davis, of Shipman, Va. Nelson County. September 15, 1915. With music. Mr. Stone writes: "Mr. Davis learned this ballad years ago from an old man who was fond of old songs. The music which I inclose is the tune I heard Mr. Davis sing. The old-time Negroes used it as the music to one of their games. Three instances of this kind were found in Nelson County. An old Colored woman told me that she heard it sung at a Negro entertainment last summer. In Cul-

[1] The usual two stanzas have been compressed into one. This elimination of one of the repeated stanzas, plus some curtailing of the procession of relatives, makes this a particularly handy complete version, without loss of essential elements.

[2] Perhaps this is a lapse of the recorder, a case of *contaminatio* with the well-known version printed in Professor Kittredge's *Introduction*, p. xxv (from Child). But that version "was brought over to Virginia before the Revolution." This "lapse" may be its lineal descendant.

peper County, Mrs. Nathaniel Stone remembered hearing the Negroes, years ago, sing and shout to the same song. In King William County, Miss Leah Arnold gave me the first verse, which Mr. Davis did not have in his version. When a child in Baltimore, Md., Miss Arnold sang it with her playmates to the tune of 'Good-bye, My Lover, Good-bye.' She learned the words from her mother, who learned them from her mother." This variant is especially interesting because it dispenses with the stanzas addressed to the hangman and lets the relatives appear without introduction.

["Hangman, hangman, hold your rope,
Hold it for awhile;
I think I see my father coming,
Riding many a mile.]

1 "Father, father, have you any gold,
Gold to set me free?
Or have you come to see me hung
Beneath the gallows tree?"

2 "O no, O no, I have no gold,
Gold to set you free;
But I have come to see you hung
Beneath the gallows tree."

3 "Mother, mother, have you any gold," etc.

4 "O no, O no, I have no gold," etc.

5 "Brother, brother, have you any gold," etc.

6 "O no, O no, I have no gold," etc.

7 "Sister, sister, have you any gold," etc.

8 "O no, O no, I have no gold," etc.

9 "Sweetheart, sweetheart, have you any gold," etc.

10 "O yes, O yes, I have (plenty of) gold,
Gold to set you free;
I have not come to see you hung
Beneath the hangman's (gallows) tree."

N

"Hangsman." Collected by Mr. John Stone. Sung by Mrs. J. D. Carpenter. Madison County. November 3, 1920. With music.

1 "Hangsman, hangsman, hold your rope,
And hold it for a while;
I think I see my father coming
Many and a many a mile.

2 "Father, father, have you any gold?
For gold will set me free;
Or have you come to see me hung
Beneath this hangsman's tree?"

3 "No, no, no, I have no gold,
For gold won't set you free;
Yes, I've come to see you hung
Beneath the hangsman's tree."

4 "Mother, mother, have you any gold," etc. [1]

5 "No, no, no, I have no gold," etc.

6 "Brother, brother, have you any gold," etc.

7 "No, no, no, I have no gold," etc.

8 "Sister, sister, have you any gold," etc.

9 "No, no, no, I have no gold," etc.

10 "True love, true love, have you any gold," etc.

11 "Yes, yes, yes, I have plenty of gold,
For gold will set you free;
I have not come to see you hung
Beneath the hangsman's tree."

O

"Hangman." Collected by Mr. John Stone. Sung by Mr. Joliffe, in Cape Charles, Va. Northampton County. July 13, 1921.

1 "Hangman, hangman, slack that rope,
Slack it for a while;
For I see my father come,
He's come for many a mile.

2 "Father, father, have you come
For to set me free?"
"No, I've come to see you hung
Under the old oak tree." [2]

Then come brother, sister, mother, *etc.*

[1] According to Mr. Stone's manuscript, the first stanza addressed to the "hangsman" is not repeated for the relatives who come after the father. But more probably he merely failed to indicate its repetition for the later relatives. The eleven stanzas would thus become fifteen.

[2] Again the compression of two stanzas into one, reducing the repeated group of stanzas to two instead of the usual three.

9 "Hangman, hangman, slack that rope,
Slack it for a while;
For I see my true love come,
She's come for many a mile.

10 "True love, true love, have you come
For to set me free?"
"Yes, I've come for to set you free
From under the old oak tree."

P

"The Maid Freed from the Gallows" or "The Hangman's Tree." Contributed by Miss Marrow Davis, of the Farmville Ballad Club. Sung by her cousin in Elizabeth City County. March, 1913. To Miss Davis belongs the distinction of being the first member of the Farmville Ballad Club to contribute a specimen of a real ballad still sung in Virginia.

1 "Hangman, hangman, hold the rope,
Hold it for a while;
I think I see my father
Coming many a mile.

2 "Father, father, did you bring me gold?
Or will you set me free?
Or have you come to see me hang
Upon the gallows tree?"

3 "I did not bring you gold,
I will not set you free,
But I have come to see you hang
Upon the gallows tree."

Repeat these three stanzas four times. At the first repetition substitute mother *for* father, sister *at the second, and* brother *at the third. At the fourth repetition substitute* sweetheart *for* father *in the first and second and let the last stanza read:*

15 "I have brought you gold,
I will set you free,
And I have come to cut the rope
And carry you home with me."

Q

"The Gallows Tree." Collected by Miss Juliet Fauntleroy. Sung by Mrs. John Maxie (*née* Lily Stone), near Altavista, Va. Campbell County. March 20, 1914.

1 "Oh hangsman, Oh hangsman, Oh hangsman, I say,
Oh, slacken your rope,
I think I see my father coming on,
Many far miles from here.

2 "Oh father, Oh father, Oh father, I say,
Some of your gold and some of your fee
Will keep me from hanging
On yonders gallows tree."

3 "None of my gold (now shall you have)
Nor (likewise) none of my fee,
But I have come to see you hang
On yonders gallows tree."

The verses run thus until the mother, *the* brother, *the* sister, *and the old* true love *have come. The* true love *says:*

15 "Here is my gold
And here is my fee;
I've come to keep you from hanging
On yonders gallows tree."

R

No title given. Collected by Miss Juliet Fauntleroy. Sung by Mrs. Creasy (*née* Lynch), near Altavista, Va. Campbell County. August 24, 1916.

1 "Hangman, hangman, slacken your rope,
And a few more moments for me;
I think I see my father coming,
He's coming for many a long mile.

2 "Father, Oh father, did you bring me gold,
Did you come to pay my fee?
Or did you come for to see me hung
By the high gallows tree?"

3 "Oh no, Oh no, I've brought you no gold,
I'm not a-goin' to pay your fee;
Yes, I have come to see you hung
On the high gallows tree."

Then come mother, brother, *and* sister, *who answer the inquiry in the same way. Last comes* darling, *who replies:*

15 "Oh yes, Oh yes, I've brought you gold,
And I'm going to pay your fee;
And if the Lord's in heaven above,
I'm goin' to take you home with me."

S

"The Hangman's Tree." Contributed by Miss Nancy E. Pearson, of Martinsville, Va. Giles County. November 10, 1917.

1 "Hangman, hangman, slack your rope,
O slack it for awhile,
Slack it till my mother comes,
She's gone a many a mile.

2 "Mother, O mother, have you brought me any gold,
To pay my fine likewise?
Or have you come to see me hung,
Hung down the gallows line?"

3 "No, O no, I have n't brought you any gold,
To pay your fine likewise;
But I have come to see you hung,
Hung down the gallows line."

(*Other friends and relatives come.*)

4 "True love, true love, have you brought me any gold,
To pay my fine likewise?
Or have you come to see me hung,
Hung down the gallows line?"

5 "Sweetheart, sweetheart, I have brought you gold,
To pay your fine likewise;
I have not come to see you hung,
Hung down the gallows line."

T

"Hangsman." Collected by Mr. John Stone. Sung by Mr. J. A. Wyatt, near Walkerton, Va. King William County. September 11, 1922.

1 "Hangsman, hangsman, slack your rope,
Slack it for a while;
I think I see my father coming,
Riding for many a mile.

2 "Father, did you bring me gold,
Or did you bring me free;
Or did you come to see me hung
Upon the gallows tree?"

3 "O no, I've not brought you gold,
And I've not brought you free;
But I have come to see you hung
Upon the gallows tree."

Repeat in groups of three stanzas for mother, brother, sister, *and* sweetheart. Sweetheart *speaks the last stanza:*

15 "O yes, I've brought you gold,
O yes, I've brought you free;
O yes, I've come to take you down
From the gallows tree."

U

"The Maid Freed from the Gallows." Collected by Mr. John Stone. Recited by Mrs. Margaret A. Pound, of Oakgrove, Va. Westmoreland County. September 11, 1922.

1 "Hangman, hangman, hold your rope,
Hold it for a while;
I think I see my father coming,
Coming a many a mile.

2 "Father, father, have you any gold?
Gold will set me free;
Or have you come to see me hanged
Beneath the gallows tree?"

3 "O no, O no, I have no gold,
For gold won't set you free;[1]
But I have come to see you hanged
Beneath the gallows tree."

Complete with four groups of three each. The others relate to mother, brother, sister, *and* true love. *Last stanza:*

15 "O yes, O yes, I have some gold,
If gold will set you free;
I have not come to see you hanged
Beneath the gallows tree."

[1] There seems to be a difference of opinion on a point of law here between the prisoner and the father. This line might possibly justify the father's inactivity, but for the two that follow. Even the true love seems uncertain about the efficacy of gold, but his concluding two lines are kinder and more reassuring. Of the reprieve there is little doubt.

V

No title given. Contributed by Miss Eva R. Tatum. Alleghany County. July 28, 1915.

1 "Oh hangman! oh hangman! slack your rope,
Oh, slack it for awhile,
Oh, slack it till my father comes,
He's come (gone) a many long mile.

2 "Oh father! Oh father! have you brought me any gold,
Wherewith to pay my fine?
Or have you come to see me hung,
Hung down the hangman's line?"

2 "Oh no, no, no, I've brought you no gold,
Wherewith to pay your fine;
For I have come to see you hung,
Hung down the hangman's line."

And so on with mother, brother, sister, uncle, auntie, cousin, *and* true love. *Last stanza:*

24 "Oh yes, yes, yes, I've brought you some gold,
Wherewith to pay your fine;
For I've not come to see you hung;
Put up the hangman's line."

APPENDICES

A

No title given. Collected by Professor Maurice G. Fulton, of Davidson, N. C. From a student of Davidson College, who obtained it from his aunt in North Carolina. December 8, 1915.

1 "Johnny Low, Johnny Low, my good Johnny Low,
Just pass your hands a while,
Methinks I see my good friend coming,
Riding so many miles.

2 "My friend, my friend, have you brought me any money,
Have you brought me any gold or silver,
To keep my body from the grave
And my neck from the gallows tree?"

3 "My friend, my friend, I've brought you no money,
I've brought you no gold nor silver;
I come this day to see you hung,
And hung, you shall be hung."

Then come in turn brother, sister, father, *and finally* mother, *whose reply is:*

15 "My son, my son, I've brought you money,
I've brought you gold and silver;
I don't come this day to see you hung,
And hung, you shall not be hung."

B

No title given. Contributed by Miss Margaret Munro, of Tampa, Florida. Sung by an old banjoist far back in the Florida woods. Hillsborough County. April 10, 1917.

1 "Hangman, hangman, spare the lines,
Spare them for a while;
Look away over yonder, see your father a-comin',
He has rode for many long miles.

2 "O father, O father, did you bring me any gold,
Any gold fer to pay my fine,
Or did you came fer to see me hanged, sir,
Hanged on the gallows line?"

3 "No, son, no, son, I bring you no gold,
No gold fer to pay your fine,
But I jes' came here fer to see you hanged, sir,
Hanged on the gallows line."

Then mother, *then* brother *appear and answer similarly; finally* true love *comes, and* she *replies:*

12 "Yes, love, yes, love, I brung you some gold,
Some gold fer to pay your fine,
But I never came here fer to see you hanged, sir,
Hanged on the gallows line."

C

"Ropeman's or Hangman's Ballad." Contributed by Professor F. M. Darnall, of Clarksville, Tennessee. Sung by an old woman in Harrison County, Mississippi. February 8, 1916.

1 "Ropeman, ropeman, slack your rope,
Slack your rope for awhile;
For I think I see my father dear
Coming from many a long mile.

2 "Father, O father, did you pay my fare,
Did you bring my gold along,
Or did you come here tonight to see me hang,
Hang on the gallows-tree?"

3 "Never paid your fare,
Never brought your gold along,
And I've come here tonight to see you hang,
Hang on the gallows-tree."

Similarly appear and similarly answer in turn mother, brother, sister. *Finally comes* true love, *whose reply is:*

15 "I paid your fare,
I brought your gold along,
And I've come here tonight to see you free,
Free from the gallows-tree."

28

THE BAILIFF'S DAUGHTER OF ISLINGTON

(CHILD, No. 105)

THE solitary text of this ballad found in Virginia is Virginian by fairly recent adoption. The contributor, Mrs. Levin Joynes, of Richmond, Virginia, writes, September 27, 1915: "'The Bailiff's Daughter of Islington' was sung to me in my childish days by a cousin, who lived in England, and I understood from her that it was an old English ballad. No doubt it was brought to Virginia by some of the early settlers. I have written it from memory, so no doubt it is very faulty." On the contrary, it is an excellent version, corresponding very closely with the Child text, the stanzas omitted or compressed being those which could best be spared or pared. Besides this text, Virginia tradition preserves a single stanza (B), with the tune.

The story is identical with that recorded by Child. "A fond youth and a coy maid, a bailiff's daughter, having been parted seven years, the maid disguises herself to go in quest of her lover, and meets him on her way. He asks her whether she knows the bailiff's daughter. The bailiff's daughter is dead long ago, she replies. Then he will go into a far country. The maid, assured of his faith, reveals herself, and is ready to be his bride."

The thirteen Child stanzas are represented by eight in the Virginia text, thus: Child 3, 4, and 5 are omitted, Child 8, 9, and 10 are compressed into Virginia 5 and 6, and Child 13 is dropped from the Virginia copy. In spite of minor variations, the two represent a single version.

During Professor Child's collecting days, Mr. F. H. Stoddard informed him that "'The Bailiff's Daughter' is still very much sung, and may be heard any day at a country cricket-match." It does not seem, however, to be current in oral tradition in Virginia. The present editor happens to be familiar with a lovely old air, but it comes from a juvenile song book he saw some years ago. The B melody is similar and is appropriate to this tender ballad with its happy ending.

For American texts, see *Bulletin*, No. 4, p. 7; Hudson, No. 16 (and *Journal*, XXXIX, 106; Mississippi); *Journal*, XXIX, 201 (Rawn and Peabody, Georgia. This survival, the author writes, is "similar" to the Child ballad); XXX, 321 (Kittredge, Missouri, Indiana, both fragments); Shearin, p. 4; Shearin and Combs, p. 8. For additional references, see *Journal*, XXX, 321.

A

"The Bailiff's Daughter of Islington." Contributed by Mrs. Levin Joynes, of Richmond, Va. Sung by her cousin. Henrico County. September 27, 1915.

1 There was a youth, and a well-beloved youth,
Who was the Squire's son.
He loved the bailiff's daughter dear,
Who lived in Islington.

2 But she was coy and never would
Her heart on him bestow,
So he was sent to London town,
Because he loved her so.

3 Full seven years had passed away.
She put on mean attire,
And straight to London she would go,
About him to enquire.

4 But as she passed along the road
Through weather hot and dry,
She rested on a grassy load
And her love came riding by.

5 "Oh, give me a penny, kind sir," she said,
"To help a maid forlorn."
"Before I give you a penny, sweet maid,
Pray tell me where you were born?"

6 "Oh, I was born in Islington."
"Then tell me if you know
The bailiff's daughter of that place?"
"She died, sir, long ago."

7 "If she be dead, then take my horse,
My saddle and bridle also,
And I'll away to some distant land,
Where no one shall me know."

8 "Oh, stay! oh, stay! thou goodly youth,
She standeth by thy side;
She is not dead but here alive
And ready to be thy bride."

B

"The Bailiff's Daughter of Islington." Contributed by Professor Willoughby Reade, of Alexandria, Va. From a childhood recollection. Arlington (formerly Alexandria) County. November 16, 1928. With music. Mr. Reade writes: "My father used to sing it to us children and I learned it from him when I was, perhaps, seven years old. It may have been a year or two later—one does not remember exact dates so far away!" Mr. Reade's father was an Englishman.

1 Oh, there was a youth, and a well-beloved youth,
And he was a Squire's son;
He loved the bailiff's daughter dear,
That lived at Islington.

29

JOHNIE COCK

(CHILD, NO. 114)

No other survival of this genuine old ballad has hitherto been found in America. This version of Mr. Stone and Mrs. Doyle is the only one discovered in Virginia. "On my way out of Highland County," writes Mr. Stone, November 3, 1920, "Mrs. Dever told me about the song which, from the foresters in it, I took to be 'The Douglas Tragedy' with its seven bold sons. I asked Mrs. Dever's little daughter to copy and send it to me, which she did. To my surprise I found it to be a new ballad."

The Virginia text is not quite complete, but it is in accord with the Child versions as to the primary points of the story. "A gallant young fellow, who pays no regard to the game-laws, goes out, despite his mother's entreaties, to ding the dun deer down. He kills a deer, and feasts himself and his dogs so freely on it that they all fall asleep. An old palmer, a silly auld, stane-auld carl, observes him, and carries word to seven foresters. They beset Johnie and wound him; he kills all but one, and leaves that one, badly hurt, to carry tidings of the rest. Johnie sends a bird to his mother to bid her fetch him away. . . . " The only significant additions of the Virginia version are that Johnny Cock blows a provocative blast upon his horn and rouses the seven foresters, who are then directed to him by the silly old man; that Johnny Cock says that no wolf would be guilty of so dastardly an attack as theirs; that he throws the wounded seventh forester across his saddle to carry the tidings home; that the bird is sent not to his mother but to fair Eleanor's window.

The Virginia text has no very close resemblance to any Child text, and it must therefore be set down as a separate version. Perhaps its relation is closest to either A or B, with about an equal number of points of likeness to each and with differences from either. Buck and Bouncer, the two names given to three bloodhounds, would seem to be corruptions of "busk" and "boun," meaning to make ready, prepare. Compare the second stanza of Child D,

> "Ye'll busk, ye'll busk my noble dogs,
> Ye'll busk and mak them boun."

and the opening line of the fragment, Child M, as sung by Carlyle's mother,

> "O busk ye, O busk ye, my three bluidy hounds."

"Come, Buck, come, Bouncer" would be a fairly natural modern interpretation of these two unfamiliar words. That the final stanza of this ballad is corrupted from "Lord Thomas and Fair Eleanor" is suggested with the more confidence since a variant of the last named ballad comes from the same family. Writes Mr. Stone, "Mrs. Dever's version of 'Lord Thomas and Fair Eleanor' can be traced back to an old Scotchman in Highland County years ago. Possibly 'Johnny Cock' came from the same source." In its present form the final stanza does not quite make sense, and the text, like Child B–G, must be adjudged incomplete.

In contrast to the broadside texts of some of the Robin Hood ballads that follow, "Johnny Cock" is an excellent specimen of the unspoiled traditional ballad.

The only reference to an American text would be to *Bulletin*, No. 8, p. 7, where this find was originally announced.

"Johnny Cock." Collected by Mr. John Stone and Miss Daisy Dever. Sung by Mrs. Acy Doyle. Highland County. November 3, 1920.

1 "Come, Buck,[1] come, Bouncer,[1] my three bloodhounds,
For tomorrow we must go
Away to the Broadway Low
To hunt the buck and doe."

2 Johnny's mother heard him say so
. . . .
"My blessings on you Johnny," she said,
"Take counsel and stay at home.

3 "There are the seven foresters
In the Broadway Low,
And for three drops of thy heart's blood
Would dare three sobs to hell."

4 Johnny heard his mother say so,
Made him wondrous keen;
He threw off his robes of red
And put on a light Lincoln green.

5 Johnny saddled his steed
And his three bloodhounds at his command,
And a sheaf of arrows at his side
As he rode along the strand.

6 Johnny shot and the dun deer left[2]
. . . .
Till he came to the waters wide;
There he laid himself down to sleep.

7 First he drew out his fine bugle horn
And blew a blast of pride,
Which awoke six of the seven foresters
That lay by the hawthorn side.

8 Up jumped the seventh forester
And said, "That is a blast well blown.
Are there a man among you all
Can blow such as him?"

[1] See head-note above.

[2] Possibly for *leapt*.

9 They rode over hills and vales
. . . .
Till they came to a silly old man,
By an ill death may he die.

10 "What news have you, old man, for me?
. . . .
Or else by the sword that hangs by my side,
By the point you shall die."

11 ". . . . .
No news have I for thee;
Only yonder lies the widow's fairest son
That ever my eyes could see."

12 They rode over hills
And mountains high
Till they came to the very spot
Where Johnny Cock did lie.

13 They bent three bows
And broad arrows did they let fly;
They wounded poor Johnny Cock
A little above the eye.

14 "Woe be to you, seven foresters,
That would do such a deed to I.
Is there a wolf in the Broadway Low
That would do such a deed to me?"

15 Johnny bent a bow
Bent of an ivory bone,
And shot among the seven foresters
And killed them all but one.

16 Besides he wounded the seventh forester
And broke his collar bone,
And threw him across his saddle
To carry the tidings home.

17 "Is there any pretty bird in the Broadway Low
That can whistle what I say,
That will go to fair Eleanor's [1] window
And take fair Johnny away?"

[1] See head-note.

30

ROBIN HOOD'S DEATH

(CHILD, No. 120)

NOT one of the three Robin Hood ballads of the Virginia collection has been found elsewhere in America, except in print. All three come from oral tradition in the Scotch-Irish family of Miss Martha M. Davis, of Harrisonburg, Rockingham County, Virginia, from her great-grandmother down. Miss Davis's letters accompanying the ballads contain interesting information. On April 8, 1913, she writes: "I enclose a variant of 'The Death of Robin Hood,' which has come down from our great-grandmother. When our grandmother was in her eighty-sixth year, in 1882, she dictated to my sister 'The Death of Robin Hood,' 'The Rescue of Will Stutly,' and 'Robin Hood and Arthur O'Bland.' 'Will Stutly' is complete, but 'Arthur O'Bland' lacks some lines. The air to 'The Death of Robin Hood,' as we know it, is quite simple and plaintive, in the peculiar minor of many of the old Gaelic airs." On April 26, 1913, she writes again. "The 'Will Stutly' seems to me a ballad with a fine flavor of the old days, but its place and value must be left to experts. They are all three, probably, 'The Death of Robin Hood,' 'Will Stutly,' and 'Arthur O'Bland,' broadsides from some collection; but what collection, and when? I have never seen the story of the last two in print. Will you tell me, please, whether they are in the Child collection? Our interest has been one chiefly of sentiment and association, with the hope that the missing lines would turn up in print some day. . . . Perhaps it is only proper to say that, apart from the present generation, so far as we know, these ballads do not belong to the oral traditions of Virginia. The ancestress from whom we have them lived in Cecil County, Md., in the last quarter of the eighteenth century, removed to a Scotch-Irish settlement in Pennsylvania in 1801, whence our forbears."

All three of these ballads, like their Child analogues, are in the seventeenth-century broadside style, and show clearly that some broadside is their source. They are, however, traditional in Virginia. They appear here, moreover, for the same reasons that gained them admission to Child's work: either that they have in them something of the old popular quality, or that they are believed to preserve the substance of a lost traditional ballad.

As to the character of Robin Hood, Child's introduction to "A Gest of Robyn Hood" (Child, No. 117) dispels some popular misconceptions. "Robin Hood is absolutely a creation of the ballad-muse," he says. "The earliest mention we have of him is as the subject of ballads. The only two early historians who speak of him as a ballad-hero, pretend to have no information about him except what they derive from ballads, and show that they have none other by the description they give of him; this description being in entire conformity with ballads in our possession, one of which is found in a MS. as old as the older of these two writers.

"Robin Hood is a yeoman, outlawed for reasons not given but easily surmised, 'courteous and free,' religious in sentiment, and above all reverent of the Virgin, for the love of whom he is respectful to all women. He lives by the king's deer (though he loves no man in the world so much as his king) and by levies on the superfluity of the higher orders, secular and spiritual, bishops and archbishops, abbots, bold barons, and knights, but harms no husbandman or yeoman, and is friendly to poor men generally, imparting to them of what he takes from the rich. Courtesy, good temper, liberality, and manliness are his chief marks; for courtesy and good temper he is a popular Gawain. Yeoman as he is, he has a kind of royal dignity, a princely grace, and a gentleman-like refinement of humor. This is the Robin Hood of the Gest especially; the late ballads debase this primary conception in various ways and degrees.

"This is what Robin Hood is, and it is equally important to observe what he is not. He is no sort of political character, in the Gest or any other ballad. This takes the ground from under the feet of those who seek to assign him a place in history."

The earliest known literary mention of Robin Hood is found in *Piers Plowman*, published about 1377, where the character Sloth confesses that he knows "rymes of Robyn Hood and Randolph, erle of Chestre" but is weak on his paternoster. In the century following, the references are very frequent, and it is not surprising that Michael Drayton in his *Polyolbion*, published 1613–1622, says of Robin Hood:

> In this our spacious isle I think there is not one
> But he hath heard some talk of him, and Little John.
> And to the end of time the tales shall ne'er be done
> Of Scarlock, George a Green, and Much the Miller's son.
> Of Tuck the merry Friar, which many a sermon made
> In praise of Robin Hood, his outlaws, and their trade.

Further evidence of Robin Hood's celebrity "is afforded by the connection of his name with a variety of natural objects and archaic remains over a wide extent of country." An imposing list of these is provided by Child.

In addition to the three ballads which follow, two other Robin Hood ballads have been reported from America, and one of them also comes ultimately, though not immediately, from Virginia. "Robin Hood and Little John," a ballad of twenty stanzas, recorded by E. L. Wilson, of Urbana, Illinois, and edited by H. S. V. Jones, appears in *Journal*, XXIII, 432. "This ballad," the editor records, "was sung in January, 1908, by William Shields McCulloch, of Normal, Illinois. Mr. McCulloch was born at Harper's Ferry, Virginia, December 10, 1816, and moved to Illinois in 1854. He learned this song from an old man whom he heard sing it about eighty years ago." But for the fact that it is not the policy of the present volume to repeat Virginia material from the *Journal*, a fourth Robin Hood ballad might properly appear in this volume of Virginia ballads. "Robin Hood and Guy of Gisborne" (Child, No. 118) is reported from North Carolina by Brown under the title of "Robin Hood and the Stranger."

The Virginia version of "The Death of Robin Hood" follows Child B more closely than Child A, but it shows more traces of the professional ballad writer, is less in the old popular ballad strain, than Child B. The story follows without significant deviation the story of this version as given by Child: "Robin Hood says to Little John that he can no longer shoot matches, his arrows will not flee; he must go to a cousin to be let blood. He goes, alone, to Kirkley nunnery, and is received with a show of cordiality. His cousin bloods him, locks him up in the room, and lets him bleed all the livelong day, and until the next day at noon. Robin bethinks himself of escaping through a casement, but is not strong enough. He sets his horn to his mouth and blows thrice, but so wearily that Little John, hearing, thinks his master must be nigh to death. John comes to Kirkley, breaks the locks, and makes his way to Robin's presence. He begs the boon of setting fire to Kirkley, but Robin has never hurt woman in all his life, and will not at his end. He asks for his bow to shoot his last shot, and where the arrow lights there his grave shall be. His grave is to be of gravel and green, long enough and broad enough, a sod under his head, another at his feet, and his bow by his side, that men may say, Here lies bold Robin Hood." The stanzas which tell of the excessive blood-letting (B 7 and 8 in Child) are lacking in the Virginia version. Except for the omitted stanzas and for certain differences near the beginning of the ballad, the two texts show a fairly close correspondence stanza for stanza, though hardly in language. The Virginia text lacks the final stanza of Child B.a., and has instead the first two lines of the epitaph found in Child B.b., wherein, following a later tradition, the attempt is made to identify Robin Hood as Robert, Earl of Huntingdon. The Virginia text, again like Child B.b., lacks the burden of Child B.a.

The only American reference would be to *Bulletin*, No. 2, p. 5, where this find was first announced.

"The Death of Robin Hood." Collected by Miss Martha M. Davis. Dictated by her grandmother, in 1882. Rockingham County. April 8, 1913. With music.

1 As Robin Hood and Little John
Walked by a bank of broom,
Said Robin in a mournful voice,
"I fear approaching doom.

2 "And since the day that we did meet,
Much mirth and joy we saw;
To many a poor man have we given
Since we became outlaw.

3 "But now, alas! these days are o'er,
For I am taken ill;
I must away to Kirkley Hall
To try physician's skill."

4 "Fare thee well," said Little John,
"O master dear, farewell;
And when I see your face once more,
Good news I hope you'll tell."

5 He is away to Kirkley Hall
As fast as he could hie,
But ere that he could reach that length
He was nigh like to die.

6 And when he came to Kirkley Hall,
He knocked and made great noise;
His cousin flew to let him in,
Full well she knew his voice.

7 "Will you sit down, dear cousin?" she said,
"And drink some wine with me?"
"I will neither eat nor drink
Until I blooded be."

. . . .

8 When he perceived their treachery,
Away he strove to fly
Out of the window, but could not,
It was so very high.

9 Then he picked up his bugle horn
That hung down by his knee;
He tried with all his might and main
If he could blow blasts three.

10 Then Little John heard his master's call
As he sat under a tree.
"I think," said he, "my master 's ill,
He blows so wearily."

11 Then he is away to Kirkley Hall,
Its doors broke open wide,
And when he came to Robin Hood
He knelt down by his side.

12 "What shall I do, dear master?" he said,
"That you avenged may be?
Shall I burn cursed Kirkley Hall
And all its nunnery?"

13 "O nay, O nay," said Robin Hood,
"I ne'er in all my life
Burned any kirk nor any nun,
Nor widow, child, nor wife.

14 "Nor shall it now be said of me
In this my dying hour
Upon the head of Christian folks
Destruction I did pour.

15 "Now bring me here my much-loved bow.
One arrow I'll let fly,
And wheresoe'er that arrow lights,
There let my body lie.

16 "Let green grass grow upon my grave,
By my side my bow so good,
At my head a stone that all may read,
'Here lies bold Robin Hood.'"

17 Underneath this little stone
Lies Robert, Earl of Huntingdon.

31

ROBIN HOOD AND THE TANNER

(CHILD, No. 126)

FOR a general introduction to the Robin Hood cycle, see the head-note to No. 30, preceding.

The story of the ballad as it appears in Child, is as follows: "Arthur a Bland, a Nottingham tanner, goes of a summer's morning into Sherwood forest to see the red deer. Robin Hood pretends to be a keeper and to see cause for staying the Tanner. The Tanner says that it will take more than one such to make him stand. They have a two hours' fight with staves, when Robin cries Hold! The Tanner henceforth shall be free of the forest, and if he will come and live with Robin Hood shall have both gold and fee. Arthur a Bland gives his hand never to part with Robin, and asks for Little John, whom he declares to be his kinsman. Robin Hood blows his horn. Little John comes at the call, and, learning what has been going on, would like to try a bout with the Tanner, but after a little explanation throws himself upon his kinsman's neck. The three take hands for a dance round the oak-tree."

The thirty-seven Child stanzas are represented by but twenty-four in the Virginia text. A significant variation in the Virginia text is that Arthur O'Bland is the forester who stays Robin Hood and provokes the fight. The first Virginia stanza is certainly a monstrosity from the popular ballad point of view; most of the rest of the ballad, like its Child analogue, has a good popular ring. All told, the two ballads are very similar. Among the corresponding stanzas are Child 7 and 8 to Virginia 5 and 6, Child 14 and 15 to Virginia 7 and 8, Child 18, 19–20, and 21 to Virginia 10, 9, and 11, Child 24 and 25 to Virginia 13 and 14, and Child 28 to 37 to Virginia 15 to 24.

The only American reference would be to *Bulletin*, No. 2, p. 6, where this find was first announced.

"Robin Hood and Arthur O'Bland." Collected by Miss Martha M. Davis. Dictated by her grandmother, in 1882. Rockingham County. April 8, 1913. With music.

1 When Phœbus had melted the shackles of ice
And likewise the mountains of snow,
Bold Robin Hood, that archer so good,
Went frolicking abroad with his bow.

2 He left his merry men all behind,
As through the green woods he passed.
There did he behold a forester bold
Who cried out, "Friend, whither so fast?"

3 "I'm going," said Robin, "to kill a fat buck
For me and my merry men all,
And likewise a doe before that I go,
Or else it will cost me a fall."

4 "You'd best have a care," the forester said,
"For these are His Majesty's deer.
Before that you shoot, that thing I'll dispute,
For I am head forester here."

5 ". . . . .
And you have such great command,
You must have more partakers in store
Before that you make me to stand."

6 "I have no more partakers in store,
Nor any at all do I need;
But if I get a knock on your bare scalp
. . . ."

7 "Let us measure our weapons," said bold Robin Hood,
"Before we begin the affray;
I would n't have mine any longer than thine
For that would be counted false play."

8 "I pass not for length," the stranger replied,
"For mine is of oak so free;
Six foot and a half will knock down a calf,
And I'm sure it will knock down thee."

9 About and about they lustily dealt
For almost two hours and more;
At every bang the woods they rang,
They plied their work so sore.

10 And Robin he raged like a wild boar
As soon as he saw his own blood.
Bland was in haste and laid on so fast,
As if he was cleaving of wood.

11 "Hold your hand," said jolly Robin,
"And let our quarrel fall.
Here we might thrash our bones to smash
And get no money at all."

12 "And what is your name?" said jolly Robin.
. . . .
. . . .
. . . .

13 . . . .
"In Nottingham long have I wrought;
And if you come there, I vow and declare,
I'll tan your hide for naught."

14 . . . .
"If you'll be so kind and free,
If you'll tan my hide for naught,
I'll do the same for thee."

. . . .

15 "Tell me, O tell me, where is Little John?
Of him fain would I hear,
For we are related by the mother's side,
And he is my kinsman near."

16 Then Robin he put his horn to his mouth
And blew both loud and shrill,
And quickly and soon appeared Little John
Tripping over the hill.

17 "What's the matter?" said Little John,
"O master, I pray thee me tell?
Why do you stand with your staff in your hand?
I fear that all is n't well."

18 "O man, I stand, and he makes me to stand,
The tanner who stands by my side;
He is a bold blade and master of his trade
And sorely he 's tanning my hide."

19 "He is to be commended," said Little John,
"If such a thing he can do;
If he is so stout we must have a bout,
And he shall tan my hide too."

20 "Hold your hand," said jolly Robin;
"As I do understand,
He's a yeoman good and of your own blood,
His name it is Arthur O'Bland."

21 Then Little John flung his staff away
As far as he could fling,
Then out of hand to Arthur O'Bland,
And about his neck he did cling.

22 For love and respect there was no neglect,
They neither were nice nor coy;
Each other did face with a comely grace,
And both did weep for joy.

23 Then Robin he took them both by the hand
And danced all around an oak tree,
And said, "Three merry men, and three merry men,
And three merry men are we.

24 "And ever hereafter, as long as we live,
We three shall be as one;
The woods they will ring and the old wives sing
Of Robin Hood, Arthur, and John."

32

ROBIN HOOD RESCUING WILL STUTLY

(CHILD, No. 141)

FOR a general introduction to the Robin Hood cycle, see the head-note to No. 30, preceding.

The story of the ballad as recounted by Child is as follows: "Robin Hood learns that Will Stutly has been captured and is to be hanged the next day. Robin and his men go to the rescue, and ask information of a palmer who is standing under the wall of the castle in which Stutly is confined; the palmer confirms the news. Stutly is brought out by the sheriff, of whom he asks to have a sword and die in fight, not on the tree. This refused, he asks only to have his hands loosed. The Sheriff again refuses; he shall die on the gallows. Little John comes out from behind a bush, cuts Stutly's bonds, and gives him a sword twitched by John from one of the sheriff's men. An arrow shot by Robin Hood puts the sheriff to flight, and his men follow. Stutly rejoices that he may go back to the woods."

The thirty-eight Child stanzas are represented by but twenty-one in the Virginia text. Except for stanzas omitted or combined in the Virginia version, the two texts are very close together. One significant deviation of the Virginia text, however, is that the eight stanzas of Will Stutly's address to the sheriff and the sheriff's reply are omitted, and in their place Little John when he appears asks the sheriff for permission to speak with Will and is curtly refused by the sheriff. The relations of the two may be more minutely indicated as follows: Child 1 and 2 are like Virginia 1 and 2; Child 3 is omitted in Virginia; Child 4 and 5 are like Virginia 3 and 4; Child 6 to 9 are omitted in Virginia; Child 10 to 15–16 are like Virginia 5 to 10; Virginia 11 does not appear in Child at this point but is like Child 6; Child 17 is like Virginia 12; Child 18 to 25 are omitted in Virginia; Child 26 to 28 correspond to Virginia 13 to 15 with the difference stated above; Child 29 to 32–33 are like Virginia 16 to 19; Child 34 is like Virginia 20; Child 35 and 36 are omitted in Virginia; Child 37–38 are combined into Virginia 21. The Child burden is omitted in Virginia.

Neither the Child nor the Virginia text has much of the popular quality or traditional style. Both are evidently ballads "made for print." The air, however, is much more in the traditional style.

The only American references would be to *Bulletin*, No. 2, p. 6, where this find was first announced, and to C. A. Smith, p. 4, where one stanza of it is used to illustrate word-substitution.

"The Rescue of Will Stutly." Collected by Miss Martha M. Davis. Dictated by her grandmother, in 1882. Rockingham County. April 8, 1913. With music. Miss Davis throughout has spelled the name *Stutely*, not *Stutly*. But the Child spelling has been adopted here, in the belief that no difference of pronunciation is indicated by Miss Davis's spelling, and to avoid needless confusion.

1 As Robin Hood in the green wood stood
Under a green wood tree,
Sad tidings came to him with speed,
Tidings for certainty.

2 That Stutly he surprised was,
In Aiken [1] prison lay.
Three varlets whom the king had hired
Did basely him betray.

3 When Robin Hood these news did hear,
He grievèd was full sore,
And likewise his brave bowmen bold,
Who all together swore

4 That Stutly he should rescued be,
Unto the woods again
Return with them to hunt the deer,
Or in his cause be slain.

5 "Will send one forth the news to hear
From yonder palmer there,
Whose cell is near the castle wall;
Some news he may declare."

6 Then stepped forth a brisk young man,
Of courage stout and bold,
And straight unto the palmer went,
Saying, "Ye palmer old,

7 "Tell me, if you can rightly tell,
When must Will Stutly die,
Who is of Robin Hood's brave men
That here in prison lie?"

8 "Alas, alas," the palmer said,
"That ever woe is me,
This day Will Stutly must be hung
Upon yon gallows tree.

9 "But did his noble master know,
He soon would succor send;
A few of his brave bowmen bold
Would save him from this end."

10 "That is true," the young man said,
"He soon would set him free;
So fare thee well, thou good old man,
With many thanks to thee."

11 Then Robin dressed himself in red,
His merry men all in green,
With swords and buckles and long bows
Most glorious to be seen.

[1] For *eke in*.

12 Not long from jail the young man went,
The gates were open wide,
When from the castle Stutly came,
Guarded on every side.

13 Not far from castle they had gone,
When appeared Little John,
And straight unto the sheriff went
And said to him, "Anon,

14 "Mr. Sheriff, with your leave,
I'll speak with him a while."
"No," said the sheriff, "you'll me seize;
Thou art an outlaw vile.

15 "I'll not consent," the sheriff said,
"But hangèd he shall be,
And so shall his vile master be
When in my custody."

16 Then in haste did Little John
Away cut Stutly's bands,
And from a man he twisted soon
The sword out of his hands.

17 Saying, "Will, take you this sword a while,
You can it better sway,
And now defend thy life from harm
For aid will come straight way."

18 And then they turned them back to back
And fought with valor good,
Until at length approachèd near
The valiant Robin Hood.

19 Then quick an arrow Robin sent
Which near the sheriff flew,
And quickly made him for to run,
And all his coward crew.

20 "O stay a while," said Will Stutly,
"And do not from us start;
O stay and hang up Robin Hood
Before you do depart.

21 "Thanks, O thanks, my master dear,
We'll in the green woods meet,
Where we will make our bow strings twang
Music for us most sweet."

33

SIR HUGH, OR THE JEW'S DAUGHTER

(CHILD, No. 155)

THIS familiar old ballad is founded upon what passed for an actual occurrence in England in the year 1255. Child summarizes the story told by a contemporary writer in the Annals of Waverley, in these words: "A boy in Lincoln, named Hugh, was crucified by the Jews in contempt of Christ, with various preliminary tortures. To conceal the act from Christians, the body, when taken from the cross, was thrown into a running stream; but the water would not endure the wrong done its maker, and immediately ejected it upon dry land. The body was then buried in the earth, but was found above ground the next day. The guilty parties were now very much frightened and quite at their wit's end; as a last resort they threw the corpse into a drinking-well. Thereupon the whole place was filled with so brilliant a light and so sweet an odor that it was clear to everybody that there must be something holy and prodigious in the well. The body was seen floating on the water, and, upon its being drawn up, the hands and feet were found to be pierced, the head had, as it were, a crown of bloody points, and there were various other wounds: from all which it was plain that this was the work of the abominable Jews. A blind woman, touching the bier on which the blessed martyr's corpse was carrying to the church, received her sight, and many other miracles followed. Eighteen Jews, convicted of the crime, and confessing it with their own mouth, were hanged." Additional circumstances are supplied by other contemporary or near-contemporary writers, and many other instances of child-murder or pretended child-murder by the Jews, with horrible Christian reprisals, are cited by Child, who concludes that they are "only a part of a persecution which, with all moderation, may be rubricated as the most disgraceful chapter in the history of the human race."

The English ballads founded upon the Hugh of Lincoln incident of course depart a good deal from the original occurrence, and doubtless, in the course of long tradition, from their original form. The story told by most of the Virginia texts is this: Some little boys are playing ball, and one tosses the ball into the Jew's garden, where no one dares to go. The Jew's daughter invites the boy in, but he refuses because he fears he may not come out again. She entices him in with a red apple or other attraction, leads him to a remote part of the house where none may hear him call, and there sticks him with a pin or stabs him with a carving-knife, after providing a basin in which to catch his heart's blood. (In D and E, the boy finds his own nurse within, picking a chicken; but she is deaf to his entreaties. Compare Child H and K.) The boy asks that a Bible be put at his head, a prayer-book at his feet, that his mother be told that he is asleep, his playmates that he is dead. In D and E, I and J, he is carried away and thrown into a deep well.

The sixteen Virginia texts, which clearly represent more than one version, show their closest relationship to the Child series G, H, I, J, K, but the likeness is by no means exact in any case. Stanza A 6 and the corresponding stanza in other Virginia texts are most like Child F 4 and N 6. In no Virginia text is the boy named (except in the title, which may be the work of the collector). The subsequent action of Child A–F, in which the mother sets out to seek her son, converses with him miraculously in the well, and finally has his body returned to her, with attendant miracles, is entirely lacking in the Virginia texts.

"The Jew's Daughter" is the most usual Virginia title, but "It Rained a Mist," "The Little School Boy," and "A Little Boy Threw His Ball So High" are also known. "Sir Hugh" and "Little Harry Hughes" are doubtless borrowed. Seven melodies are given, some related, some quite distinct.

For American texts, see Belden, No. 8 (fragment); *Bulletin*, Nos. 2–5, 7, 9, 11; Campbell and Sharp, No. 26 (North Carolina); Child, III, 248 (Pennsylvania, Maryland, New York from Newell's *Games and Songs of American Children*); Cox, No. 9; Hudson, No. 17 (and *Journal*, XXXIX, 108; Mississippi); Jones, p. 301; *Journal*, XV, 195 (reprinted from the *New York Tribune*, August 17, 1902; H. E. Krehbiel); XIX, 293 (Belden, Missouri, Kentucky); XXIX, 164 (Tolman, Indiana, Connecticut); XXXV, 344 (Tolman and Eddy, Ohio, text and melody); XXXIX, 212 (Rinker, Pennsylvania); Pound, *Ballads*, No. 5; Scarborough, p. 53 (Virginia, text and melody, Alabama from *The University of Virginia Magazine*, December, 1912); Shearin, p. 4; Shearin and Combs, p. 8; C. A. Smith, p. 15 (New York from Newell's *Games and Songs of American Children*, Virginia, three melodies only, Alabama, text and melody); Reed Smith, *Ballads*, No. 11. For additional references, see Cox, p. 120; *Journal*, XXIX, 164; XXX, 322; XXXV, 344.

A

"The Jew's Daughter." Collected by Miss Martha M. Davis, of Harrisonburg, Va. Rockingham County. April 26, 1913. With music.

1 It rained a mist, it rained a mist,
It rained all over the land.
Some little boys of our town
Went out to toss a ball, ball, ball,
Went out to toss a ball.

2 At first they tossed it up too high,
And then again too low,
Then over into a Jew's garden
Where no one dared to go, go, go,
Where no one dared to go.

3 Out came the Jew's daughter into the garden
All in her golden array,
"Come in, come in, my pretty little man
And you shall have your ball, ball, ball,
And you shall have your ball."

4 "I won't come in, I can't come in,
I have heard of you before;
Whoever goes in to your garden
Will never come out any more, more, more,
Will never come out any more."

5 At first she offered an apple so red,
And then again her ring,
And then she offered a cherry so ripe,
To entice this little boy in, in, in,
To entice this little boy in.

6 She took him by his lily-white hand,
And led him through the hall
Down into a cellar so dark and deep,
Where no one could hear him call, call, call,
Where no one could hear him call.

7 She bound him down on the floor of stone
. . . .
Where no one could hear him moan.

8 She bound him down on the floor so cold,
Where none could see his tears,
She called for a basin as bright as gold
To catch his heart's blood in, in, in,
To catch his heart's blood in.
. . . .

9 "O place my Bible at my head,
My prayer-book at my feet,
And if my mother asks for me,
O tell her that I am asleep, sleep, sleep,
O tell her that I am asleep.

10 "O place my prayer-book at my feet,
My Bible at my head,
And if my playmates ask for me,
O tell them that I am dead, dead, dead,
O tell them that I am dead."

B

"The Jew's Daughter." Collected by Miss Martha M. Davis, of Harrisonburg, Va. Sung by Mrs. Elmer Brunk. Rockingham County. November 6, 1913.

1 It rained, it snowed, in New Scotland,
It rained both wide and small,
And all the boys of our town
Went out to toss their ball.

2 At first they tossed their ball too high,
And then again too low,
And then into the Jew's garden,
Where no one dared to go.

3 The first came out was the Jew's daughter
All dressed in fairy green,
"Come in, come in, my lad," said she,
"You shall have your ball again."

4 "I won't come in, I shan't come in,
I've heard of you before;
Whoever goes in at the castle gate
Will never come out any more."

5 At first she showed him a mellow ripe apple,
And then a gay gold ring,
And then a cherry as red as blood
To entice this little boy in.

6 "I won't come in, I shan't come in,
I've heard of you before;
Whoever goes in at the castle gate
Will never come out any more."

7 She took him by the lily-white hand
And led him through the hall,
And then into a cellar below,
Where none could hear him call.

8 She tied him down, she chained him down,
She jug [1] him with a pin,
And then to scar [2] her basin bright
To catch his heart's blood in.

9 "Now lay my Bible at my head,
My prayer-book at my feet,
And if my playmates ask for me,
O tell them that I am asleep.

10 "Now lay my Bible at my feet,
My prayer-book at my head,
And if my mother asks for me,
O tell her that I am dead."

[1] Cf *jaggd* of Child F. [2] For *scour?*

C

"It Rained a Mist." Collected by Miss Alfreda M. Peel. Sung by Miss Marie Hatfield, of Vinton, Va. Roanoke County. April 24, 1923. With music. Miss Peel writes of Miss Hatfield: "This child is the great-niece of the famous 'Devil Anse,' the famous feud leader at Matewan, West Virginia."

1 It rained a mist, it rained a mist,
It rained all over the town;
And two little boys came home from school
To toss their balls around, around,
To toss their balls around.

2 At first they tossed their balls too high,
The second they tossed too low,
The third they tossed in the Jew's daughter's garden
Where no one was 'lowed to go, to go,
Where no one was 'lowed to go.

3 The Jew's lady came to the door,
All dressed in silk so fine,
"Come in, come in, my only son,
You may have your ball again, again,
You may have your ball again."

4 "I can't come in, and I won't come in.
I'll tell you the reason why:
I've heard of so many little boys coming in,
But never coming out alive, alive,
But never coming out alive."

5 At first she showed him a red rose apple,
And then a diamond ring;
And then she showed him a watch and chain
To toss the ball again, again,
To toss the ball again.

6 She took him by his little white arm,
And led him through the hall,
And took him in a little dark room,
Where no one could hear him call, him call,
Where no one could hear him call.

7 She pinned a napkin to his neck,
She pinned it with a pin;
And she took out her carving knife,
To carve his little heart in, oh in,
To carve his little heart in.

8 "Now place a Bible at my head,
A prayer-book at my feet,
And when my school-mates call for me,
Tell them I'm fast asleep, oh sleep,
Tell them I 'm fast asleep."

9 She placed a Bible at his head,
A prayer-book at his feet.
"And when my father calls for me,
You may tell him I am dead, am dead,
You may tell him I am dead."

D

"Sir Hugh, or The Jew's Daughter." Reported by Prof. James M. Grainger, of the Farmville Ballad Club. Contributed by Miss Evelyn Purcell, of Schuyler (Nelson County), Va. Albemarle County. November 20, 1913. The ballad can be traced back to Miss Purcell's great-grandfather's time. Printed in *The Focus* for December, 1913.

1 The little boy threw his ball so high,
The little boy threw it so low,
He threw it into a dusty garden
Among some flakes of snow.

2 "Come hither, come hither, my sweet little boy,
And you shall have your ball."
"I'll neither come hither, I'll neither come there,
Neither will I come for my ball."

3 She showed him an apple as yellow as gold,
She showed him a bright gold ring,
She showed him a cherry as red as blood,
And that enticed him in.

4 She enticed this little boy out of the hall,
She enticed him into the kitchen,
And there he met with his own dear nurse,
Picking of a chicken.

5 "Pray spare my life, my own dear nurse,
Pray spare my life or else never,
For if ever I live to be a man,
We'll spend our remains together."

6 "I'll neither spare your life, I'll neither spare your life,
For I minded you but when a babe;
I've been cleaning this basin the whole day long
To catch your heart's blood in."

7 She sat him down in a golden chair,
She fed him with sugar and sweet,
She laid him down on a dusty board
And stabbed him like a sheep.

8 "Pray put my Bible at my head,
My prayer-book at my feet,
And if any of my playmates should call for me,
Pray tell them I'm dead and asleep."

9 Some take hold of locks of hair,
And others the sole of his feet,
And drag him down in a deep dry well
Fifteen fathoms deep.

10 Some take hold of locks of hair,
And others the sole of his feet,
And drag him down in a deep dry well
Where weary travelers sleep.

E

"A Little Boy Threw His Ball So High." Contributed by Mrs. Landon Randolph Dashiell, of Richmond, Va. Sung by herself. Fauquier County. April 11, 1921. With music.

1 A little boy threw his ball so high,
He threw his ball so low;
He threw it into a dusky garden
Among the blades of snow.

2 "Come hither, come hither, my sweet little boy,
Come hither and get your ball."
"I'll neither come hither, I'll neither come there,
I'll not come get my ball."

3 She showed him an apple as yellow as gold,
She showed him a bright gold ring,
She showed him a cherry as red as blood,
And that enticed him in.

4 Enticed him into the drawing-room
And then into the kitchen,
And there he saw his own dear nurse,
A-pick-i-ing a chicken!

5 "I've been washing this basin this live-long day,
To catch your heart's blood in."
"Pray spare my life, pray spare my life,
Pray spare my life!" cried he.
"I'll not spare your life,
I'll not spare your life," cried she.

6 "Pray put my Bible at my feet,
My parer-book at my feet,
If any of my playmates should ask for me,
Oh, tell them I'm dead and asleep!"

7 She dragged him on his cooling board,
And stabbed him like a sheep.
She threw him into a dusky well
Where many have fallen asleep.

F

"It Rained a Mist." Collected by Miss Juliet Fauntleroy. Sung by Mr. Jesse Burgess, of Altavista, Va. Campbell County. April 30, 1915. With music. "This ballad," writes Miss Fauntleroy, "was sung to me by one of my pupils, Jesse Burgess, whose brother had heard it sung by a boy in Greensboro, North Carolina. Jesse Burgess is a boy of fourteen, but only in the first grade."

Miss Fauntleroy adds: "This same ballad was also sung to me by Mrs. Sinai Thomas (*née* Sales), from Wilkes County, North Carolina. But instead of 'Union yard' she sang it 'new-made yard'; instead of a 'charming gold ring,' she said 'diamond ring'; instead of 'little white hand,' 'lily-white hand'; instead of 'If ever I come to a joyous man,' she sang it, 'innocent man.' She sang the 6th stanza thus:

She pinned a napkin round his head,
She pinned it with a pin;
And with a knife she had in her hand,
She pierced his little heart in, etc.

"Edgar Thomas, a pupil of mine, and a son of Mrs. Sinai Thomas, said he had heard also the following lines:

She set him in a little arm chair,
She stuck him with a knife;
She called her servants to her side
To tell them what to do, to do,
To tell them what to do.

She laid him on a cooling board . . .

"This ballad was also sung for me by another pupil of mine, Lee Callaway, a little girl, who had learned it from her mother. She sang it pretty much as Jesse Burgess did."

1 It rained a mist, it rained a mist,
It rained all over the town,
When two little boys went out to play,
To toss their ball around, around,
To toss their ball around.

2 Then first they tossed the ball too high,
And then they tossed it too low;
They tossed it into the Union yard
Where no one was 'lowed to go, to go,
Where no one was 'lowed to go.

3 Here came young Miss, all dressed in silk,
All dressed in silk so fine;
"Come in, come in, my pretty little boys,
You shall have your ball again, again,
You shall have your ball again."

4 Then first she showed him a red rosy apple,
And then she showed him a peach,
And then she showed him a charming gold ring
Which charmed the little one in, one in,
Which charmed the little one in.

5 She took him by his little white hand,
She led him across the hall;
She took him into the dining room
Where none could hear him call, him call,
Where none could hear him call.

6 She pinned a napkin over his face,
She pinned it with a pin;
Then she took up a carving knife
And cut his little heart in, heart in,
And cut his little heart in.

7 "O spare my life, O spare my life,"
The little one he cried;
"If ever I come to a joyous man,
My joys will all be there, be there,
My joys will all be there."

8 "O place a prayer-book at my feet,
A Bible at my head,
And when my playmates call for me,
Pray tell them I am dead, am dead,
Pray tell them I am dead."

9 She placed the Bible at his head,
The prayer-book at his feet.
And when his playmates called for him,
She told them he was asleep, asleep,
She told them he was asleep.

G

"It Rained a Mist." Collected by Miss Juliet Fauntleroy. Sung by Miss Hooney Wright, from Surrey County, North Carolina, and Altavista, Va. Campbell County. September 18, 1915.

1 It rained a mist, it rained a mist,
It rained all over the town,
When two little boys went out to play,
To toss their ball around.

2 Then first they tossed the ball too high,
And then they tossed it too low;
They tossed it into the Jew lady's yard,
Where no one was 'lowed to go.

3 The Jew lady came to the door
And invited the little one in.
"Come in, come in, you bright little son,
You shall have your ball again."

4 "I can't come in, I won't come in,
Unless my playmate comes too.
I've often heard of boys going in
Who never were known to come out."

5 First she showed him a golden watch,
And then she showed him a chain;
And then she showed him a diamond ring
To entice the little one in.

6 She took him by his little white hand
And led him through the hall;
She took him to the dining room
Where no one could hear him call.

7 She pinned a napkin over his face,
She pinned it with a pin,
And then she took the carving knife
And carved his little heart in.

8 "Bury a prayer-book at my feet,
A Bible at my head,
And if my playmates call for me,
Just tell them I am dead."

H

"It Rained a Mist." Reported by Professor James M. Grainger, of the Farmville Ballad Club. Contributed by Miss Ruth Soyers, of Brim, North Carolina. Patrick County, Va. November 20, 1913. Printed in *The Focus* for December, 1913, pp. 396–397.

1 It rained a mist, it rained a mist,
It rained all over the ground,
When two little boys went out to play,
A-tossing their ball around, around,
A-tossing their ball around.

2 At first they tossed their ball too high,
And then they tossed it too low,
And then they tossed it in a general bound,
Where they were n't allowed to go, to go,
Where they were n't allowed to go.

3 On came a lady to the door,
All dressed in linen so fine;
"Come in, come in, you little one,
You shall have your ball again, again,
You shall have your ball again."

4 "I can't come in, I won't come in,
Unless my playmate comes too,
For I've often heard of little ones going in
And never coming out any more, any more,
And never coming out any more."

5 She first showed him a rose red apple
And led him across the hall;
She led him into the dining-room
Where no one could hear his call, his call,
Where no one could hear his call.

6 She pinned a napkin over his face,
She pinned it with a pin,
And then she took her little pen-knife
And carved his little heart in, heart in,
And carved his little heart in.

7 "Please spare my life, please spare my life,
Please spare my life," he cried.
"If ever I live to be a man,
My treasures shall be thine, be thine,
My treasures shall be thine.

8 "Please place the prayer-book at my feet,
The Bible at my head,
And when my playmate calls for me
You can tell him that I am dead, am dead,
You can tell him that I am dead."

I

"Sir Hugh, or Little Harry Hughes." Collected by Miss Juliet Fauntleroy. Sung by Miss Charlotte Rodé, near Rustburg, Va. Campbell County. March 1, 1914. With music. Miss Fauntleroy writes: "Miss Rodé heard this sung as a child by the poor white tenants and negroes on her father's farm near Rustburg. There were other verses, but she could not recall them when she sang these for me, when visiting my home."

1 A little school boy, he bounced his ball,
He bounced his ball so high,
He bounced his ball into the Queen's garden,
Where the lilies and roses lie.

2 "Come over, come over, you little school boy,
And you shall have your ball."
"I won't come over, I can't come over,
I won't come over at all."

3 She called up her servants one by one,
She called them three by three.
She said, "Oh, there's a little school boy,
I pray you bring him to me."

4 And some they took him by the hair of his head,
And others by his feet,
And they carried him and threw him into a well
That was ten thousand feet deep.

5 "Oh, put my Bible at my head,
My prayer-book at my feet,
And if my playmates ask for me,
Tell them I'm fast asleep."

J

"The Little School Boy." Collected by Miss Juliet Fauntleroy. Sung by Miss Charlotte Rodé and Mrs. Hattie Schäfer, near Altavista, Va. Campbell County. July 29, 1914.

1 A little school boy he bounced his ball,
He bounced his ball so high;
He bounced his ball into a lady's garden,
Where roses and lilies lie.

2 "Come over, come over, you little school boy,
And you shall have your ball."
"I won't come over, I can't come over,
Until my schooling is done."

3 She held up an orange as yellow as gold,
She held up a bright gold ring,
She held up an apple as red as blood,
And that enticed him in.

4 She took him and led him to a big arm chair,
She bled him like a sheep;
She laid him on a dusty board,
He lay like he was asleep.

5 She called up her servants one by one,
She called them two by two;
Said she, "Here lies a dead young man,
I pray you carry him too."

6 And some they took him by the hairs of his head,
And others by his feet;
They carried him and threw him into a well
That was ten thousand feet deep.

7 "Oh, lay my Bible under my head,
My prayer-book under my feet;
And when my playmates inquire for me,
Just tell them I'm fast asleep."

K

"The Jew's Daughter." Collected by Mr. John Stone. Sung by Mr. Ed. Davis and Mrs. Marion Browning, of Shipman, Va. Nelson County. November 15, 1916. With music.

1 It rained a mist, it rained a mist,
It rained all over the land,
It rained three days in the Jew's garden,
And no one could understand,-stand,-stand,
And no one could understand.

2 The boys went out to toss the ball,
To toss the ball, to toss the ball,
The boys went out to toss the ball
Upon the queen's highway,-way,-way,
Upon the queen's highway.

3 And first they tossed it up too high,
And then it went too low;
It went into the Jew's garden,
Where no one dared to go, go, go,
Where no one dared to go.

4 Out came the Jew's daughter, out came the Jew's daughter,
All dressed in finest of silk,
Saying, "You may come in, my pretty boy,
And you your ball shall win, win, win,
And you your ball shall win."

L

"Sir Hugh." Contributed by Mr. and Mrs. George D. McLaughlin of Benicia, California. Learned in Rockbridge County, Va. May 15, 1916. With music.

1 It rained a mist, it rained a mist,
It rained all over the town, town, town,
It rained all over the town.

2 And all the boys in our town
Went out to toss their balls, balls, balls,
Went out to toss their balls.

3 Some tossed too high, some tossed too low,
And one in the old Jew's garden did go,
In the old Jew's garden did go.

4 "Come in, my boy, come in, my boy,
Your ball you shall have again, 'gain, 'gain,
Your ball you shall have again."

5 And then she took his lily-white hand,
And led him in the hall, hall, hall,
And led him in the hall.

6 And then she called for the butcher knife
To stab his little heart in, in, in,
To stab his little heart in.

7 And then she called for the gold basin
To catch his heart's blood in, in, in,
To catch his heart's blood in.

M

"The Jew's Daughter." Collected by Mr. John Stone. Sung by Miss Gipson, of Charlottesville, Va. Albemarle County. November 10, 1919.

1 It rained a mist, it rained a mist,
It rained all over the land,
And every boy in our town
Went out to toss his ball, ball, ball,
Went out to toss his ball.

2 At first he tossed the ball too high,
And then again too low,
And then over a garden wall
Where no one dared to go, go, go,
Where no one dared to go.

3 Out came a Jewish maiden,
All clad in golden sheen,
Out came a Jewish maiden,
All clad in golden sheen, sheen, sheen,
All clad in golden sheen.

4 "Come in, my little man," she said,
"You shall have your ball again,
["Come in, my little man," she said]?
You shall have your ball again, 'gain, 'gain,
You shall have your ball again."

5 "I can't come in, I won't come in,"
In vain the little boy cried,
"For I have heard that he who goes,
That he who goes in there,
Will ne'er come out again, 'gain, 'gain,
Will ne'er come out again."

She offers him various gifts. He succumbs to a "red, red apple."

6 She took a great big carving knife,
And stabbed his little heart in;
She took a great big carving knife
And stabbed his little heart in, in, in,
And stabbed his little heart in.

7 "Pray lay the Bible at my head,
The prayer-book at my feet,
And if ever my playmates ask for me
Pray tell them that I am asleep, sleep, sleep,
Pray tell them that I am asleep.

8 "Pray lay the prayer-book at my feet,
The Bible at my head,
And when my parents ask for me,
Pray tell them that I am dead, dead, dead,
Pray tell them that I am dead."

34

THE HUNTING OF THE CHEVIOT

(CHILD, No. 162)

THIS ballad has received much commendation from eminent literary men. Sir Philip Sidney's oft-quoted words found in *An Apologie for Poetrie*, published in 1595, may apply as well to "The Battle of Otterburn," but in all probability referred to "The Hunting of the Cheviot" or "Chevy Chase." "I never heard the olde song of Percy and Duglas that I found not my heart mooved more than with a trumpet; and yet is it sung but by some blinde crouder, with no rougher voyce then rude stile: which, being so evill apparrelled in the dust and cobwebbes of that uncivill age, what would it worke trymmed in the gorgeous eloquence of Pindar!" Addison is authority for Ben Jonson's classic remark about "Chevy Chase," that "he had rather have been the author of it than of all his works." And Addison himself devotes two Spectator papers (Nos. 70 and 74, 1711) to a sympathetic critique of the ballad, which he declares to be "the favorite ballad of the common people of England." He quotes passages from the ballad and compares them to passages from Homer and Virgil, not altogether to the advantage of the latter. The service of Addison in turning public interest toward the ballad even in the early eighteenth century, is well known.

The fragment recovered from tradition in Virginia belongs to the same broadside version which was so greatly admired by Addison, Child B. The sixty-four stanzas of the Child text are represented by only twelve in the Virginia variant, but the contributor has summarized what he remembers of the story of the omitted parts. The Virginia stanzas 1–12 correspond, respectively, to Child 1, 3, 4 (lines 1 and 2) and 2 (lines 3 and 4), 2 (lines 1 and 2) and 4 (lines 3 and 4), 5, 9, 11, 12 (lines 1 and 2) plus ?, 17, 33, 35, 43. The story summarized by the Virginia contributor does not quite agree with the Child text as to the order and manner of the chieftains' deaths. According to Child B, Douglas, who has just bested Percy in fight, is struck and killed by an arrow from an English bow, much to Percy's sorrow, and Percy himself is thereafter killed by Sir Hugh Montgomery's spear. The last stanza (Virginia 12) applies in Child B to this spear-thrust, not to the English arrow. The last twenty-one stanzas of general fighting are entirely missing in the Virginia copy.

This ballad was not reported in the *Bulletin* of the Virginia Folk-Lore Society, though it has been in the Virginia archives since January 8, 1914. Beside it Dr. Smith had written "Not counted," evidently because the particular version sent in by Miss Davis came to her from an uncle who was then living in California. But as Miss Davis herself and other members of her family in Virginia were familiar with the ballad, which she describes as "traditional with us," it seems hardly fair to discriminate against it either as non-Virginian or as non-traditional. Of the uncle who copied the verses down from memory for her, Miss Davis writes, "This uncle has been living in California many years, but Chevy Chase is mine by ordinary generation, and I hope the Folk-Lore Society will acept it, at least until something better of its kind turns up." Her description of the ballad as "traditional with us" makes it almost impossible for the editor to exclude the ballad from the Virginia collection, as of course he might have done if other variants of strictly Virginia pedigree had presented themselves. The inclusion of this hitherto blacklisted ballad brings the Virginia total of Child ballads up to fifty-one. It is the present editor's belief that Dr. Smith would approve of this inclusion on the grounds stated above, now that no other version has come in. And aside from the quibble of whether or not the ballad is one hundred per cent Virginian, it would scarcely be published elsewhere, and balladry in general will surely be the richer by its inclusion here.

For American texts, see Barry, No. 16; Ford, *Massachusetts Broadsides*, Nos. 3011–3013 (cf. No. 833), and *The Isaiah Thomas Collection*, No. 41; *Journal*, XVIII, 294 (Barry, Massachusetts, melody only; two broadsides mentioned). For additional references, see *Journal*, XXX, 323.

"The Battle of Chevy Chase." Contributed by Miss Martha M. Davis, of Harrisonburg, Va. Traditional in her family, written down by her uncle in California. Rockingham County. January 8, 1914.

An uncle writes to Miss Davis: "Of the Robin Hood songs you know more than I know. I never wrote them down so they have faded from my memory, excepting three or four stanzas on Robin Hood's Death, but you no doubt have that. There was one song I often sang with Mother. It was called 'The Battle of Chevy Chase.' It must have happened away back in olden times before fire arms were in use when the weapons used were the cross bow and the sword and spear. It was all about the killing of some deer on Scottish ground. I know only a few verses, will write what I know of the song.

1 God prosper long our noble king,
Our lives and safeties all,
A woeful hunting once there did
In Chevy Chase befall.

2 Earl Percy of Northumberland
A vow to God did make
His pleasure in the Scottish woods
Two summer days to take,

3 The chiefest harts in Chevy Chase
To kill and bear away.
The child may rue that was unborn
The hunting of that day.

A forgotten verse which tells about the men who were his followers.

4 To chase the deer with hound and horn
Earl Percy took his way;
Like tidings to Earl Douglas came
In Scotland where he lay,

5 Who sent Earl Percy present word
He would prevent his sport;
The English Earl not fearing this
Did to the woods resort.

6 And long before the noon they had
A hundred fat bucks slain,
And having dined the drovers went
To rouse them up again.

7 Earl Percy to the quarry went
To view the nimble deer.
He says, "Earl Douglas promisèd
This day to meet me here.

8 "And if I thought he would not come,
No longer would I stay,
For we now have plenty killed
For us to bear away."

Just then Douglas and his clansmen come in view.

9 Earl Douglas on a milk-white steed,
Most like a baron bold,
Rode foremost of his company;
His armor shone like gold.

Another verse missing, hot words and a challenge from Douglas that they two fight it out, while the men looked on. They fought with swords. At last Douglas saw that Percy was weakening.

10 "Yield, yield, Earl Percy," Douglas said,
"For faith I will thee bring,
And thou shalt high renownèd be
By Jaḿes our Scottish King."

11 "Nay, nay, Earl Douglas," Percy said,
"Thy proffer I do scorn,
I would not yield to any Scot
That ever yet was born."

They fought on until Percy fell dead. Then an arrow from an English bow struck Douglas. The song says,

12 With such vehement force and might
It did his body gore,
The spear went through the other side
A good cloth yard or more.

Then the fighting became general—a hand to hand fight—neither side would yield until night came when there were only a few left. These deeds of valor of the men with their names were given in the song, but I cannot recall any more of the verse."

35

THE DEATH OF QUEEN JANE

(CHILD, NO. 170)

ONLY a fragment of "The Death of Queen Jane" has been recovered in Virginia, in interesting combination with the Virginia song of "The Brown Girl" (No. 50). In sending this ballad to Dr. Smith, Mr. Sharp wrote as follows, September 1, 1918: "You will be interested in the copy of 'The Death of Queen Jane,' which I herewith enclose, and which you will see is a delightful mixture, owing to the intrusion of 'The Brown Girl,' brought about, no doubt, by the doctor-and-bedside incident. Another singer in Bedford County (Va.) gave me a very corrupt version of 'The Brown Girl' and told me that the title of the song was 'King Henry.' This puzzled me at the time, but the mystery has now been solved. I should add that the tune to the text I am enclosing is a remarkably fine one, one of the best that I have found in Virginia or anywhere else." Unfortunately, in the excitement of the war news of the time, Mr. Sharp failed to send the tune, which therefore cannot be included here. Pending its receipt, Dr. Smith withheld his *Bulletin* announcement of this find. No mention of this ballad, therefore, appears in the Virginia *Bulletin*, nor can the present editor discover that any collector except Mr. Sharp has found it in America.

The full ballad of "The Death of Queen Jane" is a threnody of the wife of King Henry the Eighth, Jane Seymour, who, history records, died twelve days after the birth of Prince Edward on October 12, 1537. According to the ballad, Queen Jane is grievously ill, and begs for surgery to save her unborn child. King Henry is sent for, but he refuses to sacrifice the mother for the child. The operation, however, becomes necessary, the boy is delivered and christened amid rejoicing, but the mother dies and the funeral is held amid a general lamentation.

Of the ballad which follows, only three stanzas (1, 2, and 8) belong definitely to "The Death of Queen Jane," though the name of the woman — Sally, not Jane — is that found in American texts of "The Brown Girl." Stanza 3, where the song first becomes sidetracked from the former ballad to the latter, is reasonably common to both, though it belongs more definitely to "The Brown Girl." Stanzas 4, 5, 6, and 7 are also from "The Brown Girl." Except for the introduction of the royal suitor, King Henry, and the mourning stanza, the ballad here given does not differ materially from American versions of "The Brown Girl" in which the girl, Sally, is no longer brown and in which the sexes of the lovers are reversed. It is much like "Barbara Allen" with the ill lover changed from a man to a woman and the second death omitted. The title is an identification, not a local title.

"The Death of Queen Jane" (Combined with "The Brown Girl"). Collected by Mr. Cecil J. Sharp and Miss Karpeles. From Virginia (no county named). September 1 ,1918.

1 Poor Sally was sick,
Afflicted to her bed.
There's none knew what ailed her,
Or could relieve her from pain.

2 King Henry was sent for
On horseback and speed,
In the need of poor Sally,
In the time of her need.

3 "Am I the doctor
Was sent for to-day?"
"O yes, you're the doctor
Can kill or can cure,
And without your assistance
I am ruined, yes, I'm sure."

4 "I courted you with honor,
You slighted me with scorn.
I'll remind you of things, girl,
Of the time past and gone."

5 "Of the time past and gone,
Forget and forgive,
And 'low me two minutes
And let me still live."

6 "I'll allow you no minutes
Nor years to live,
But dance on your grave
Whilst you lie in cold clay."

7 It's off of her fingers
Pulled diamond rings twice three.
"Here, take those and wear them
While you're dancing on me."

8 O black was the mourning,
And yellow was the band,
And white was poor Sally,
Poor Sally of time.

36

MARY HAMILTON

(CHILD, No. 173)

THIS ballad has been reported from Virginia and West Virginia only. The two Virginia fragments seem to come from the same singer, but as they differ not only in the number and order of stanzas but also in certain minor points of wording, both are reproduced here. The four stanzas of A and the three of B come from the end of the ballad, where Mary Hamilton is making her last piteous remarks before her execution. Robert Burns, speaking of the wandering of the Scots in a letter to Mrs. Dunlop, January 25, 1790, gives the first known literary reference to the ballad, and quotes one of the stanzas of the Virginia fragment. He says, "I remember a stanza in an old Scottish ballad, which, notwithstanding its rude simplicity, speaks feelingly to the heart:

'Little did my mother think,
That day she cradled me,
What land I was to travel in,
Or what death I should die.'"

Child prints this as version R. The Virginia fragments are most like the four-stanza version, Child BB. But both lack its final stanza, which Child calls "clearly modern," and Virginia A has a fourth stanza (its third) which most resembles Child B 20.

Mary Hamilton is one of four Maries attendant upon Mary Stuart, at whose court the tragedy takes place. History records the names of the four Maries who went to France with Mary Stuart in 1548 and returned with her to Scotland in 1561 as Fleming, Livingston, Seton, and Beaton of Creich, but the ballad has altered the first two names to Hamilton and Carmichael. The usual story of the ballad is that one of these, Mary Hamilton, is with child, some versions hinting that the father is "the highest Stuart of all," or Darnley. The mother does away with the babe by wrapping it up and throwing it into the sea, but not before the queen has heard it cry and suspects the truth. The queen orders Mary to go with her to Edinburgh, where the trial takes place, and Mary is condemned to die. Before she goes to the gallows, she speaks to the assembly those touching stanzas of which the Virginia texts are a part.

Whether this ballad takes its rise in an incident which happened at the court of Mary, Queen of Scots, in 1563, in which a French woman attendant on the queen and the queen's apothecary were involved; or whether the source of the ballad is an instance of child-murder astonishingly like the ballad story which took place at the court of the Czar Peter the Great in 1718–19, involving a Mary Hamilton, attendant upon the Empress Catherine, and a Russian officer named Orlof; is a question which was long ago discussed at length by such authorities as Professor Child and Mr. Andrew Lang, and which continues to engage the attention of ballad investigators.

In sending the B text to Dr. Smith, Miss Peel writes, "The following is a fragment sung to me by my grandmother when I was little. The melody is lovely. Her family came from western England and she said her father sang her this ballad. . . . My grandmother's family all fought with the Stuarts, so this fragment is probably very old." The melody which is attached to A applies to B as well, and is indeed very lovely, even when sung with the Virginia "mountain whine" which Miss Peel can reproduce so perfectly.

See *Bulletin*, No. 10, p. 7, where this find was first announced; Combs, p. 141 (West Virginia).

A

"Mary Hamilton." Collected by Miss Alfreda M. Peel. Sung by Mrs. Marion Chandler, of Salem, Va. Roanoke County. May 14, 1922. With music.

1 "Little did my mother think,
When first she cradled me,
That I should die so far from home,
So far o'er the salt, salt sea.

2 "Last night there were four Maries,
Tonight there'll be but three;
There was Mary Seaton, Mary Beaton,
And Mary Carmichael and me.

3 "Last night I washed Queen Mary's feet
And carried her to her bed;
Today she'll give me my reward,
The gallows hard to tread.

4 "They'll tie a napkin 'round my eyes,
They'll ne'er let me see to die;
They'll ne'er let on to my father and mother
That I'm far away over the sea."

B

"Mary Hamilton." Collected by Miss Alfreda M. Peel. Sung by Mrs. Marion Chandler, of Salem, Va. Roanoke County. April 23, 1922. With music.

1 "Oh, little did my mother think
When first she cradled me,
That I should die so far from home,
Far over the salt, salt sea.

2 "They'll tie a napkin over my eyes,
They'll ne'er let me see to die;
They'll ne'er let on to my father and mother
That I'm far over the sea.

3 "Last night there were four Maries,
Tonight there'll be but three;
There was Mary Seaton, and Mary Beaton,
And Mary Carmichael and me."

37

THE GYPSY LADDIE

(CHILD, No. 200)

THE eight texts and three tunes of this ballad found in Virginia differ notably from one another, and all are included here. "The Gypsy Laddie" and "Gypsy Davy" are the usual titles.

The bald story of the ballad is recounted by Child for his A version as follows: "Gypsies sing so sweetly at our lord's gate as to entice his lady to come down; as soon as she shows herself, they cast the glamour on her. She gives herself over to the chief gypsy, Johny Faa by name, without reserve of any description. Her lord, upon returning and finding her gone, sets out to recover her, and captures and hangs fifteen gypsies." Of the historical prominence of Johnny Faa, Child cites numerous facts, among them that Johnnë Faw's right and title as lord and earl of Little Egypt were recognized by James V in 1540. But in the next year Egyptians were ordered to quit the realm within thirty days on pain of death. The gypsies were expelled from Scotland by act of Parliament in 1609. Soon after this date there are several records of the execution of Johnny, or Willie, Faa, and of other Egyptians. The execution of the notorious Johnny Faa seems to have made a considerable impression on the popular mind, as the ballad testifies. Later eighteenth century copies of the ballad seek to identify the lady as the wife of the Earl of Cassilis. But neither Johnny Faa nor the Earl of Cassilis is mentioned in any Virginia variant.

The Virginia variants pass very lightly over the first part of the story, the coming of the gypsies and the charming of the lady, and they also suppress the catastrophe of the hanging of the gypsies. The ballad ends with the lady's evidently final refusal to return with her husband. Only one text, Virginia B, has a spurious ending of two stanzas, in which the wife tires of the Gypsy, asks her husband to let her return, and is refused — a puritanical appendage in the interest of morals. The Virginia texts are most like the Child sequence H, I, J.

For American texts, see Barry, No. 9; Belden, No. 10 (fragment); Brown, p. 9 (North Carolina); *Bulletin*, Nos. 3, 5, 8, 9, 11; Campbell and Sharp, No. 27 (Tennessee, North Carolina, Virginia; cf. Sharp, *Songs*, II, No. 2); Child, IV, 72 (Massachusetts, New York, Maine); Cox, No. 21, and p. 524 (four texts, melody); Hudson, No. 18 (Mississippi); *Journal*, XVIII, 191 (Barry, Nova Scotia, text and melody, Massachusetts, four texts and two melodies, Rhode Island, fragment and melody); XIX, 294 (Belden, Missouri); XXII, 80 (Barry, Massachusetts, melody only); XXIV, 346 (Barry, Pennsylvania, Maine); XXV, 173 (Belden, Missouri, Ohio); XXVI, 353 (Pound, Nebraska, fragment); XXX, 323 (Kittredge, Massachusetts, text and melody); McGill, p. 15; Pound, Nebraska, fragment); XXX, 323 (Kittredge, Massachusetts, text and melody); McGill, p. 15; Pound, *Syllabus*, p. 10 (fragment). For additional references, see Cox, p. 130; *Journal*, XXX, 323.

A

"The Gypsy Laddie." Collected by Miss Alfreda M. Peel. Sung by Miss Myrtle Harmon, of Bland, Va. Bland County. August 28, 1923. With music.

1 Young Davie he came whistling by,
He whistled so loud and gaily,
He whistled till he made the green buds ring
And charmed the heart of a lady.

Chorus

Oh, rum, diddle dum, diddle dum, diddle dum,
Oh, rum, diddle dum, diddle do di,
Oh, rum, diddle dum, diddle doo, diddle dum,
Oh, rum, diddle dum, diddle do di.[1]

2 The lady she came stepping down stairs,
With her waiting maid behind her,
A glass of wine in her hand,
To drink a health to Davie.

3 The new Ingram lord came home that night,
Inquiring for his lady;
The waiting maid she vowed and said,
"She's gone with a Gypsy Laddie."

4 "Go saddle me my brightest bay,
My roan is not so speedy;
I'll ride all night and I'll ride all day
Till I overtake my lady."

5 He rode till he came to the broad waters
That run so deep and muddy,
And there the tears ran down his cheeks,
"And it's where will I find my lady?"

6 He overtook her at Gravel Hill,
Where the grass grows green and swarthy:
"Have you forsaken your house and home?
Have you forsaken your baby?
Have you forsaken your new Ingram lord
To go with Gypsy Davie?"

[1] The words of the manuscript chorus do not agree with those interwoven with the music. As the former cannot be sung to the tune without alteration, the words of the musical text have been adopted as more authoritative, at least more useful. The other jargon ran:

Rum a diddle dum, dum a diddle dum,
Rum diddle dum, diddle do di,
For a rum diddle dum, for a rum diddle dum
Diddle do di.

7 "Yes, I have forsaken my house and home,
Yes, I have forsaken my baby,
Yes, I have forsaken my new Ingram lord
To go with Gypsy Laddie."

8 "Last night you lay on a fine feather bed,
Your own true husband beside you;
Tonight you lie on the cold damp ground,
With Gypsy Davie beside you.

9 "Oh now pull off those high-heeled shoes,
That are made of Spanish leather,
And reach to me your little white hand,
And I'll bid farewell forever."

B

"Gypso Davy." Collected by Mr. John Stone. Sung by Mrs. Oscar Plummer and Miss Foxie Plummer, of Park, Va. Grayson County. November 8, 1921.

1 He come into his room one night,
A-quiring [1] for his lady;
The answer were made back to him,
"She's gone with the Gypso Davy."

2 "Go saddle, go saddle my little gray horse,
My black one ain't so speedy,
I'll ride all night, I'll ride all day
Till I overtake my lady."

3 He rode by the riverside
Where it was deep and muddy.
O who did he spy on yonder side?
Hard-hearted Gypso Davy.

4 "Come back, come back, my own true love,
Come back, come back, my lady;
I'll swear by the gold that hangs by my side
It's you shan't want for money."

5 "I won't come back, my own true love,
I won't come back, my baby,
For I would n't give a kiss from the gypsy's lips
For you and all your money."

6 "Would you forsake your house and land?
Would you forsake your baby?
Would you forsake those crowns of gold
And follow Gypso Davy?"

[1] *Inquiring. A-inquiring* easily becomes *a-quiring*.

7 "Yes, I'll forsake my house and land,
And I'll forsake my baby,
And I'll forsake those crowns of gold
And follow Gypso Davy."

8 "Pull off, pull off them high-top shoes,
They are made of Spanish leather;
And give to me your lily-white hand,
We'll bid farewell forever."

9 "I can't pull off my high-top shoes,
Though made of Spanish leather;
I'll give to you my lily-white hand,
We'll bid farewell forever."

10 "Last night you lay on your bed of rest
With your arms around your baby;
Tonight you can lay on the cold river banks
In the arms of the Gypso Davy."

11 He had n't been gone by about two weeks
Till she wrote him a letter:
"O come and get me, my old true love,
I'm tired of the Gypso Davy."

12 He wrote her back the very next day,
He wrote her back another:
He had him a sweet little babe,
She could stay with the Gypso Davy.[1]

C

"The Gypsy Laddie." Collected by Miss Martha M. Davis. Sung by a mountain woman. Greene County. March 9, 1914. Miss Davis notes: "Stanzas 8 and 2 (below) were given to me by a mountain woman in January. She thought she could find the rest of the ballad among her friends, and so she sent this version from a woman who learned it in Greene County."

2 "Saddle up, saddle up my milk-white steed,
Saddle up, saddle up in a hurry;
I'll ride my saddle to the base of the tree
Till I find the gypsy laddie."

1 "Are there any gypsies in the North?
Are there any in the country O?
They have taken from me my sweet little maid
Who has left her lands and money O.

[1] The last two stanzas are an interesting envoi to the ballad, though they completely change the effect of the story. This salutary warning to erring wives is evidently an addition of fairly recent date. It is without a parallel in the Child versions. Probably it is a Virginia contribution to the old ballad.

2 "Saddle up, saddle up my milk-white steed,
Saddle up, saddle up in a hurry O.
I'll ride all night until broad daylight
To overtake my lady O."

3 He rode to the east, he rode to the west
Until he came to sweet Bozey O,
And there he spied his sweet little maid
Along with the gypsy laddie O.

4 "Come back, come back, my sweet little maid,
Come back, come back, my honey O;
I'll lock you up in a chamber so high
That the gypsy can't come nigh O."

5 "I shan't come and I won't come back,
I shan't come back, my honey O;
I would n't give a kiss from the gypsy's lips
For all your land and money O."

6 "How can you forsake your house and land?
How can you forsake your money O?
How can you forsake your sweet little babe
To go with the gypsy laddie O?"

7 "O, I can forsake my house and lands,
O, I can forsake my money O,
O, I can forsake my sweet little babe
To go with the gypsy laddie O."

8 She was used to a feather bed
And servants all around her,
And now she has come to a bed of hay
With gypsies all around her.

D

"The Gypsy Laddie." Collected by Mr. John Stone. Sung by the Misses Fannie and Hattie Via, of Stage Junction, Va. Fluvanna County. November 3, 1920. With music. Mr. Stone notes that "they learned it from Mrs. Orilla Keeton in Albemarle County, when they lived in Albemarle County."

1 There are seven sweet gypsies in the North,
They are calling to sweet Baltimore,
They will sing a song that will charm your heart
And cause you to leave your husband.

2 It was eight o'clock the captain came,
He was calling for his honey O.
"O your honey and-er she is not here,
She is gone with the gypsies to Laddie O."

3 "Saddle up, saddle up my milk-white team,
Saddle up, saddle up in a hurry O;
I will ride all night till the broad daylight
Until I overtake my honey O."

4 He rode to the east, he rode to the west,
He rode on to sweet Baltimore.
When he got there he found his honey;
She had gone with the gypsies to Laddie O.

5 "Come back, come back, my pretty miss,
Come back, come back, my honey O;
It's how can you leave your three little babes
And go with the gypsies to Laddie O?"

6 "O yes, I can leave my three little babes,
O yes, I can leave my honey O;
For I'd rather have a kiss from the gypsy's lips
Than all of your land and money O."

7 She had n't been gone but a very short while
Until she spent all of her money O;
She spent the gold rings off of her fingers
And the breastpins off of her bosom.

8 It's once she was used to a feather bed
And servants to her parlor;
But now she is used to the old hay bed
And the gypsies all around her.

ℰ

"The Gypsy Laddie." Collected by Mr. John Stone. Sung by Mrs. Victoria Ryan, of Wytheville, Va. Wythe County. November 8, 1921. "She learned it when she was a little girl fifty years ago" (Mr. Stone).

1 There was Indians lived in the North
And they was bound for Barley O.
Sing a song of a-ru-sa-ma-lam [1]
And charm the heart of the laddie.

2 "Go saddle and bridle my milk-white horse,
Go saddle and bridle my pony, too;
I will ride both day and night
Till I overtake my honey."

[1] *Jerusalem* is recognizable.

3 The squire rode both east and west
Until he come to Barley;
And the Indians said: "She is not here;
She is gone with the gypsy laddie."

4 "Turn back, turn back, my dearest dear,
Turn back, turn back, my honey;
For I'll lock you up in a room so high
That the gypsies shan't come nigh you."

5 "I can't turn back, my dearest dear,
I can't turn back, my honey O;
For I'd rather have a kiss from the gypsy's lips
Than you and all your money." } *Repeat* [1]

6 "How can you leave your house and home?
How can you leave your husband, too?
It's how can you leave your sweet little babe
And go along with the gypsies?"

7 "I can leave my house and home,
I can leave my husband, too,
And I can leave my sweet little babe
And go along with the gypsies."

8 Then she sold all her fine things,
Likewise her velvet stockings, too,
Her gold rings off her fingers, too,
And her breastpin off of her bosom. } *Repeat* [1]

9 Saying, "Once I had a house and home
And servants to wait upon me, too;
But now I've come to a bed of straw
And the gypsies all around me.' } *Repeat* [1]

F

"Gypsen [2] Davy." Collected by Mr. John Stone. Sung by Mr. George Hart, of Konnarock, Va. Washington County. November 8, 1921.

1 The squire come home so late in the night,
Inquiring for his lady;
The servant gave him a quick reply:
"She's gone with the gypsen [2] Davy."

[1] The repetitions seem to be irregular. They are indicated for the fifth, eighth, and ninth stanzas only.

[2] This must have been very close to *Egyptian* in the original singing, but the manuscript wording is preserved.

Chorus

A radical gypsen, gypsen, gypsen,
A radical gypsen Davy.

2 "Go bridle and saddle my milk-white steed,
Go bridle and saddle him neatly,
I'll ride all night till broad daylight
Or overtake my lady."

3 He rode all night till broad daylight,
He rode to the head of Saluda;
There he spied his pretty little miss
On the knee of a gypsen Davy.

4 "It's how can you leave your house and land?
How can you leave your baby?
How can you leave your husband dear
And go with the gypsen Davy?"

5 "Very well I can leave my house and land,
Very well I can leave my baby,
For I'd rather have a kiss from the gypsen's lips
Than to have your land and money."

6 "Pull off, pull off them high-heeled shoes
Made out of Spanish leather,
And give to me your little white hand,
And I'll bid you farewell forever."

7 She soon run through with her gay bow dress,
Her velvet shoes and stockings;
The silver rings flew off of her fingers
And the gold plate off of her bosom.

8 "Once I had a house and land,
Feather beds and money,
But now I've come to the old straw pad,
And the gypsens all around me."

G

"The Gypsy Davy." Collected by Mr. John Stone. Sung by Mrs. Ellen Mulleins, of Saltville, Va. Smyth County. November 8, 1921.

1 "O saddle me up my big bay horse,
For the gray one is not so speedy;
I'll ride all day and I'll ride all night
Till I overtake my lady."

Chorus

Rum-a-doo-dle-dump-dum-do-di;
  Rum-a-doo-dle-dump-dum-do-da;
Rum-a-doo-dle-dump-tum-a-do-dol
  do-dol-do-dol-da-da.

2 "I rode till I got to the riverside;
  The water was low and muddy.
I looked away on the other side,
  And there I spied my lady."

3 "Last night I lay on a fine feather bed
  And the landlord he lay by me,
And tonight I lay on the cold ground
  And the Gypsy Davy beside me."

4 "Go hand me down those high-heeled boots,
  They are made of Spanish leather;
Give me your lily-white hand
  And I'll bid farewell forever."

H

"Gypsy Laddie." Collected by Mr. Cecil J. Sharp and Miss Karpeles. Sung by Mr. N. B. Chisholm, at Woodridge, Va. Albemarle County. September 27, 1916. With music. Music and second stanza only printed by Campbell and Sharp, p. 116.

1 "O Davy, I'm so glad to meet you,
  I've got something to tell you will fret you:
Way down there at the old barn door
  I saw your wife just a week ago."
    Ta de ra, etc.

2 Then he went unto the house,
  Enquiring for his baby.[1]
The answer that she made to him:
  "She's gone with the black boy Davy."
    Ta de ra, etc.

[1] *Lady* in Campbell and Sharp. But the manuscript is unmistakably *baby*.

38

BESSY BELL AND MARY GRAY

(CHILD, No. 201)

EXCEPT for the one West Virginia fragment, the four Virginia fragments are the only texts of this ballad recorded in America. The first stanza, generally found alone, seems to be fairly well known in the state. It accords very closely with the first stanza of the Child text. The second stanza of Virginia A does not appear in the Child version, seems, indeed, rather out of key with it. Its place, if any, in the four stanzas of the Child version would be between the second and third stanzas.

The two names celebrated by the ballad survive in Virginia not only in oral tradition but also as place names, applied to the two graceful little mountains which dominate the city of Staunton, in Augusta County. These names, however, may not have been taken directly from the ballad, but from two hills or mountains named from the ballad heroines in the County of Tyrone, Ireland. Waddell's *Annals of Augusta County*, pp. 362–364, recounts the story of the Scottish ballad, with a quotation from its first stanza, and records that "these names were carried from Scotland to Ireland, and applied to two mountains in County Tyrone, near the town of Omagh; and by our Scotch-Irish ancestors they were brought to the Valley of Virginia." See also Peyton's *History of Augusta County*, p. 106. A most interesting letter (of December 15, 1913) about this ballad and its local currency has been received from a distinguished Virginian who is a resident of Staunton, Mr. Armistead C. Gordon, who says: "The ballad of 'Bessie Bell and Mary Gray', as you know, contains the versified legend from which the two little mountains near Staunton take their names. The fact that these names mark the path of migration along which the Scotch settlers of the Valley of Virginia came on their way from Ayrshire to Ulster and thence to Virginia is more widely known than is the old ballad itself. These names were carried from Scotland to Ireland and applied to two mountains in County Tyrone, near the town of Omagh; and by the immigrants into the Valley from the North of Ireland in the first half of the eighteenth century they were brought to Augusta County. Other early settlers called another hill in Bath County, on the Cowpasture River, about a mile below Windy Cove Church, by the name of Betsie Bell or Bessie Bell, showing thereby how they cherished the associations of their former life in the old country. It would seem that the historical impression made by these names would have tended to preserve the ballad itself, but I have found no indication of its having done so. When I came to Augusta County to live, now nearly thirty-five years ago, I heard in a family where I frequently was a visitor, and among whose members were some elderly ladies, a variant of this ballad that I have never seen in print, and which does not appear either in Charles Kirkpatrick Sharpe's Ballads, nor in those in the smaller book of Dr. F. J. Child. This variant consists of a fifth verse, as follows:

Bessie kept the garden gate,
And Mary kept the pantry;
Bessie always had to wait,
While Mary lived in plenty.

This verse, however, I have no doubt, came to the old lady who recited it, not through tradition but out of a curious little volume of Scotch Ballads belonging to her husband, who was a Scotchman, and which unfortunately disappeared many years ago." [1]

Professor James M. Grainger also gives an interesting if less well-established tradition concerning the names: "You know also, I have no doubt, of the two mountains near Staunton which are known as Bessie Bell and Mary Gray. Tradition says that two girls by these names were lost on the mountains, and being caught by wolves, one was killed on Bessie Bell and the other on Mary Gray. This is very interesting to me as evidence of a familiarity with the ballad in that section. Several people have told me they had known the first stanza of the ballad all their lives, but had no idea it was a ballad." This tradition about the mountains takes no account of the ballad origin of the names, and is therefore hardly to be trusted.

The original Scottish tradition on which the ballad story is founded is to the effect that the two girls were intimate friends, Mary Gray's father being laird of Lednock and Bessie Bell's of Kinvaid; that while Bessie Bell was on a visit to Mary Gray, around 1645, the plague broke out and the two sought refuge from it by building themselves a bower near Lednock House, where for some time they lived; but before long the plague overwhelmed them, the infection being brought, it is said, by a young man who was in love with one or both of them and who was accustomed to bring them food; they were buried near the bower, in a spot which has since been marked and is frequently visited by pilgrims.

The Virginia fragments are reported in *Bulletin*, No. 5, p. 8 and No. 9, p. 7, and in C. A. Smith, p. 2. Add Cox, No. 22. For additional references see Cox, p. 134 and *Journal*, XXX, 325. Virginia B was the first text of this ballad to be found in America. No melody, Virginian or American, has been recorded.

A

"Bessie Bell and Mary Gray." Contributed by Miss G. B. Grinnan, of University, Va. Gloucester County. August 12, 1916.

1 Bessie (*or* Betsy) Bell and Mary Gray,
They were twa bonnie lassies;
They built a house upon the lea
And covered it with rushes.

[1] The rest of the letter is of more general interest, and may be relegated to a footnote: "I fancy that it is for the most part among the ignorant or illiterate, untouched by the influences of the printing press, that variants of the old ballads will be found to have come down by tradition in America. The people of this immediate section, as far as my observation goes, seem to have brought very little, if any, of the ballad tradition with them from the old country; but the historical and religious tradition is still strong among them; and since my first coming here I have heard, as a contemporary story, of a nurse hushing a crying child with the threat to 'Make Claverse catch it.' I am also told that the gentleman known in Scotland as 'the de'il' is sometimes mentioned in staunch Presbyterian households in the Valley of Virginia as 'the old Clavers'; but I do not vouch for this, for I am not sure that I have ever heard the spoken expression."

2 Bessie (*or* Betsy) kept the garden gate,
And Mary kept the pantry;
Bessie (Betsy) always came too late
While Mary lived in plenty.[1]

B

"Betsey Bell and Mary Gray." Collected by Professor James M. Grainger. Sung by Miss Jennie Tabb, of Farmville, Va. Amelia County. December 21, 1913.

O Betsey Bell and Mary Gray,
They were twa bonnie lasses;
They biggit a brig on yonder brae
And thichet it o'er with rashes.[2]

C

"Bessie Bell and Mary Gray." Collected by Mr. John Stone. Recited by Mr. Robert Fleming, of Norton, Va., who learned it years ago in Scotland. Wise County. November 8, 1921.

Bessie Bell and Mary Gray,
They were two bonnie lassies O;
They bigged a tower on yonder brae
And covered it over with rashes O.

D

"Bessie Bell and Mary Gray." Collected by Mr. John Stone. Recited by Mrs. G. P. Coleman, of Williamsburg, Va., who learned it from her grandfather when she was a child. James City County. November 8, 1921.

Bessie Bell and Mary Gray,
They were two bonnie lassies;
They built a cottage on the brae
And thatched it over with rashes.

[1] Compare the stanza in Mr. Gordon's letter, quoted in the head-note above.

[2] "Miss Jennie Tabb and her mother, formerly of Amelia County, now living in Farmville, both say they have always known a stanza running like this. . . . The 'Bessie' of the original has become 'Betsey' and the 'bower' has turned to a 'brig.' The latter change was evidently made after the first stanza became completely dissociated from the rest of the ballad, as a 'bridge' couldn't possibly function in the story or be thatched with rushes. Neither Miss Tabb nor her mother (who is just 60) had ever heard any more of the ballad. Former President John A. Cunningham, of this school, used to quote the stanza whenever he saw two pretty girls together, one of whom was named Bessie Bell. It seems that 'Betsey' is the form of the name used for one of the twin mountains near Staunton." Professor Grainger, letter of Dec. 21, 1913.

39

GEORDIE

(CHILD, No. 209)

THE four incomplete texts of this ballad found in Virginia all belong to a single version, and, like all the texts of "Geordie" so far recovered in this country, they show a closer relationship to the late seventeenth century broadside "The Life and Death of George of Oxford" than to the traditional forms of the story. But the Virginia version even more than the broadside itself, which Cox calls "a literary rifacimento of a traditional form of the song," shows distinctly the influence of the older traditional copies and exhibits stanzas which cannot possibly have come from the broadside. The ballad is either "Georgie" or "Geordie" in Virginia. One tune has been recorded, by Mr. Cecil J. Sharp in 1918, and not published by him.

The usual story of the traditional ballad is thus summarized by Child: "Geordie Gordon is in prison, on a charge endangering his life. He sends a message to his wife to come to Edinburgh. She rides thither with the utmost haste, and finds Geordie in extremity. She is told that his life may be redeemed by the payment of a large sum of money. She raises a contribution on the spot, pays the ransom, and rides off with her husband." In all the Child versions except F, Geordie is condemned either as a murderer or as a rebel. The only Virginia variant which mentions his offence agrees with Child F and with the "George of Oxford" broadside in saying that he has stolen some of the king's horses. In the Virginia version, moreover, the hero is not reprieved as in the traditional texts, but is actually hung, as in "George of Oxford" and in a still earlier seventeenth century broadside on the death of "George Stoole."

Let Virginia A stand for the Virginia version. Stanzas 1, 2, 4, and 5 correspond fairly closely to stanzas 1, 4, 7, and 15 of "George of Oxford," while stanzas 5 and 7 correspond fairly closely to stanzas 20 and 6 of "George Stoole." But when all possible identifications have been made, there is a goodly residuum (stanzas 3 and 4 especially) to be found in no black-letter piece, which must be identified with the traditional ballad of "Geordie." And if Mr. Stone's reporting is to be relied upon, Geordie and not Georgie is the name actually sung in two of the four Virginia fragments (C and D). Mr. Sharp's title is, of course, a mere identification.

For American texts, see Belden, No. 9 (fragment); *Bulletin*, Nos. 7, 9; Campbell and Sharp, No. 28 (North Carolina); Cox, No. 23; *Journal*, XX, 319 (Belden, Missouri); XXXII, 504 (Richardson, West Virginia); Pound, *Syllabus*, p. 11 (fragment); Shoemaker, p. 158. For additional references, see Cox, p. 135.

A

"Georgie." Collected by Mr. John Stone. Sung by Mr. George Hart, of Konnarock, Va. Washington County. September 2, 1921.

1 As I walked over London's bridge
So early in the morning,
I think I heard some poor Lemual say,
"Lord, spare me the life of Georgie."
I think I heard some fore lady say,
"Lord, spare me the life of Georgie."

2 "Go bridle and saddle my milk-white steed,
Go bridle and saddle him neatly;
I'll ride away to the yon castle fair
And plead for the life of Georgie."

3 She rode all day, she rode all night,
Till she came wet and weary,
A-combing back her long yellow locks,
A-pleading for the life of Georgie.

4 It's out of her pocket she drew a purse of gold,
The like I never saw any:
"Here, lawyers, come fee yourselves,
And spare me the life of Georgie."

5 It's up stepped George a-pleading for himself,
Saying, "I never killed anybody;
But I stole sixteen of the king's white steeds
And sold them in Goannie."[1]

6 The oldest lawyer was a-standing at the bar,
Saying, "George, I'm sorry for you,
That your own confession has condemned you to hang;
May the Lord have mercy on you.
That your own confession has condemned you to die;
May the Lord have mercy on you."

7 As George was walking up the streets,
He bid farewell to many;
He bid farewell to his own true love,
Which grieved him worse than any.

8 George was hung with a golden chain,
The like I never saw any;
'T was because that he come of a royal race
And courted a virtuous lady.

[1] Probably for *Guiana*.

MISS MARTHA M. DAVIS
HARRISONBURG, ROCKINGHAM COUNTY, VA.

MISS JULIET FAUNTLEROY
ALTAVISTA, CAMPBELL COUNTY, VA.

JAMES M. GRAINGER
FARMVILLE, PRINCE EDWARD COUNTY, VA.

MISS ALFREDA M. PEEL
SALEM, ROANOKE COUNTY, VA.

LEADING VIRGINIA BALLAD COLLECTORS

9 If I were on yonders hill
Where kisses I have many,
With my sword and pistols by my side,
I'd fight for the life of Georgie.

B

"Geordie." Collected by Mr. Cecil J. Sharp. Sung by Mrs. Laura Donald, at Dewey, Va. Bedford County. June 6, 1918. With music.

1 As I came over new London Bridge
One misty morning early,
I overheard a tender-hearted girl
A-pleading for the life of Georgie.

2 "Come saddle unto me my milk-white steed,
Come saddle unto me quite gaily,
That I might ride the livelong night
A-pleading for the life of Georgie."

3 Georgie was hung with a silken rope,
Such ropes they was not many,
But Georgie came of a noble race
And was loved by a virtuous lady.

C

"Geordie." Collected by Mr. John Stone. Smyth County. November 8, 1921. Mr. Stone writes: "I pieced this ballad together with the aid of four different people. While waiting for a train at Radford, I asked a stranger if he had ever heard the song. He gave me two stanzas and told me to see his father at Marion. I went to see his father, who was a very old man with failing memory. He told me when he was a young man he had sung all night, but now his memory was bad and he had forgotten the song. However, he told me to see his sister, Mrs. Ellen Mulleins, at Saltville. I did so. Mrs. Mulleins gave me some help, I think, and sent me to her daughter, who finished the song. I'm glad George was not a horse thief in this version. Some versions make him sell stolen horses in 'Old Virginny.'"

1 As I came riding across London Bridge
So early in the morning,
I thought I heard some poor Lemuel say,
"Lord spare me the life of Geordie."

2 "Go saddle and bridle my milk-white steed,
Go saddle and bridle him gay and neatly;
I'll ride away to the king's castles fair,
A-pleading for the life of Geordie."

3 She rode all day and she rode all night
Until she became tired and weary,
A-combing back her pretty yellow locks,
A-pleading for the life of Geordie.

4 Poor George walked up and down the street
And bid farewell to many;
He bid farewell to his own true love,
Which grieved him worse than any.

5 The oldest lawyer at the bar
Says, "George, I'm sorry for you,
That your own confession has condemned you to hang;
May the Lord have mercy on you."

6 Poor George was hung with a golden chain,
The like I never saw any,
Because he sprang from a royal race
And had courted a virtuous lady.

D

"Geordie." Collected by Mr. John Stone. Recited by Mr. W. G. Sawyer, at Radford, Va. Montgomery County. November 8, 1921. "This ballad was recited by Mr. Sawyer while we were both waiting for a train at Radford, Va. He learned it from his aunt years ago. Later I met his aunt, who added several stanzas. After that I met her daughter, who added more to it, and, finally, an old man in the mountains, who gave me a complete version" (Mr. Stone).

1 As I was riding across London Bridge
So early in the morning,
I thought I heard some poor Lemual say,
"O spare me the life of Geordie."

2 As I walked up and down the street,
I bid farewell to many;
I bid farewell to my own true love,
Which grieved me worse than any.

40

JAMES HARRIS (THE DÆMON LOVER)

(CHILD, No. 243)

NEXT to "Barbara Allen" in Virginia popularity stands "The House Carpenter," with fifty-two texts and seven melodies, of which twenty-nine texts and all seven melodies are here given. "The House Carpenter" is its almost invariable title, which yields only once to "The House Carpenter's Wife" (a slightly more appropriate title) and once to "On the Banks of the Sweet Laurie." "James Harris," which appears once, and "The Dæmon Lover," which appears three times at the head of manuscripts (and therefore in the table of contents), may be regarded merely as identifications, not as local titles. The lover has lost not only his name, but also, with the possible exception of four variants, all trace of his demoniac character.

The Virginia texts are most closely related to Child B, but with occasional stanzas and details that suggest other Child versions. But as all the Child versions are based upon A, with traditional modifications, the story of Child A may be profitably scanned as a preliminary step: "Jane Reynolds and James Harris, a seaman, had exchanged vows of marriage. The young man was pressed as a sailor, and after three years was reported as dead; the young woman married a ship-carpenter, and they lived together happily for four years, and had children. One night when the carpenter was absent from home, a spirit rapped at the window and announced himself as James Harris, come after an absence of seven years to claim the woman for his wife. She explained the state of things, but upon obtaining assurance that her long-lost lover had the means to support her — seven ships upon the sea — consented to go with him, for he was really *much* like unto a man. 'The woman-kind' was seen no more after that; the carpenter hanged himself."

The Virginia ballad cuts out all the antecedent action and the aftermath about the carpenter. It omits all names (except for the stolen "Fair Ellen" of Virginia F), and deprives the lover altogether of his ghostly character (with the possible exception of Virginia A, M, N, and Appendix A). The Virginia story, then, is a compressed and very human drama of illicit elopement and retribution. A seaman returns to find his old love married, it seems happily, to a house carpenter, by whom she has a child (or more). By his persuasiveness and by promises the old lover induces the wife to desert husband and babe and sail away with him. But soon she pines for the old ties, weeps for her sweet little babe, and (sometimes after she has had a vision of the torment in store for her) the ship springs a leak and sinks to the bottom of the sea. There is often a final stanza voicing her contrition, her curse upon deceiving men, or her warning to other women. In Virginia texts the carpenter does not reappear, as he does in Child B, to grieve and swoon at the news of the disaster and to curse such deluding mariners. Virginia A, M, N, and Appendix A are related to Child E and F; they contain the "hills of heaven and hell" stanzas, in which the so-called lover by interpreting the wife's vision assumes a more eerie and diabolical personality. But she never spies his cloven foot, as in Child E, F, and G, and even the vision stanzas are exceedingly rare in Virginia.

"The House Carpenter" is very often corrupted with other songs and ballads that fit in with its general motif. But it generally preserves its own identity; it does not, like "The Lass of Roch Royal" in Virginia, merely contribute certain stanzas to other songs. Of the texts that follow, A–Q are more or less pure and unalloyed variants, though the name "Fair Ellen" in F 9 and Q 4, and stanzas E 8, K 7, N 3, suggest "Lord Thomas and Fair Eleanor." But with R the combined texts begin. R–AA are marked by the intrusion of a stanza or more from some other source, but with the "House Carpenter" story still well preserved. Appendices A and B have been corrupted almost beyond recognition, but they still preserve two or three stanzas of the ballad. The "shoe my foot" stanzas of "The Lass of Roch Royal" appear in R 7 and 8, S 7 and 8, Appendix A 5 and 6, Appendix B 5 and 6; and the chorus of Appendix A is a stanza of "The Lass of Roch Royal" seldom found in Virginia. In variants T–AA stanzas are supplied from certain later songs which have something in common with "The House Carpenter," such as a lovers' greeting, a lovers' parting, a false lover, a remorseful lover, a betrayed lover's lament or warning, etc. Traces of "The False Young Man," "The True Lover's Farewell," "The Rejected Lover,' "The Wagoner's Lad," "Cold Winter's Night," "Careless Love," and perhaps other English folk-songs are to be found in the Virginia variants T–AA and in the appendices. "The False Young Man'' is the most frequent intruder. These variants in combination are a most interesting feature of the ballad in Virginia.

For other American texts, see Barry, No. 11; Belden, No. 11 (fragment); Brown, p. 9 (North Carolina); *Bulletin*, Nos. 2–12; Campbell and Sharp, No. 29 (North Carolina, Kentucky, Tennessee); Cox, No. 25 and p. 524 (five texts, melody); *The Focus*, April, 1914, p. 162 (fragment); Hudson, No. 19 (Mississippi); *Journal*, XIX, 295 (Belden, Missouri); XX, 257 (Kittredge, Kentucky); XXV, 274 (Barry, Pennsylvania, text and melody); XXXVI, 360 (Pound, Nebraska); XXX, 325 (Kittredge, two fragments and two melodies); XXXV, 347 (Tolman and Eddy, Ohio, fragment and three melodies); Pound, *Syllabus*, p. 10 (fragment); Pound, *Ballads*, No. 17; Sandburg, p. 66; Shearin, p. 3; Shearin and Combs, p. 8; C. A. Smith, p. 18 (Virginia, four melodies only); Reed Smith, No. 11; Reed Smith, *Ballads*, No. 12; Wyman and Brockway, *Songs*, p. 54 (Kentucky). For additional references, see Cox, p. 139; *Journal*, XXX, 325; XXXV, 347.

A

"The House Carpenter." Collected by Mr. Ben C. Moomaw, Jr. Sung by Mr. Sam Pritt, of Barber, Va. Alleghany County. November 28, 1924.

1 "Well met, well met, my own true love,
  Well met, well met," said he,
"I've just returned from the salt, salt sea,
  And it's all for the sake of thee.

2 "Oh, I could have married the King's daughter, dear,
  And she would have married me,
But I have refused the crowns of gold,
  And it's all for the sake of thee."

3 "If you could have married the King's daughter, dear,
I'm sure you are to blame;
For I am married to the house carpenter,
And he is a fine young man."

4 "If you'll forsake your house carpenter
And go along with me,
I'll take you to where the grass grows green
On the banks of the Sweet Willie."

5 "If I forsake my house carpenter
And go along with thee,
What have you got to maintain me upon
And keep me from slavery?"

6 "I've six ships sailing on the salt, salt sea,
Sailing for dry land,
And a hundred and twenty jolly young men
Shall be at your command."

7 Oh, she picked up her poor little babe
And kisses gave it three,
Saying, "Stay here with my house carpenter
And keep him companie."

8 She dressed herself in rich attire,
Most glorious to behold,
And as she tread upon her road
She shone like the glittering gold.

9 They had not sailed two weeks on sea,
I'm sure it was not three,
Till this fair maid began to weep,
And she wept most bitterly.

10 "Oh, do you weep for my gold?" he said,
"My houses, my land, or my store?
Or do you weep for your house carpenter
That you never shall see any more?"

11 "I do not weep for your gold," she said,
"Your houses, your land, nor your store;
But I do weep for my poor little babe
That I never shall see any more."

12 "Oh, what is that that shines so white,
That shines as white as snow?"
"Oh, those are the hills of Heaven itself,
Where we may never go."

13 "Oh, what is that that shines so black,
That shines as black as a crow?"
"Oh, that is the clouds of Hell itself,
Where you and I must go."

14 They had not sailed three weeks on sea,
I'm sure it was not four,
Till in the ship there sprung a leak,
And she sank to rise no more.

15 "Oh, cursed be a sailor's life
And an o'er-persuading man
That stole me from my house carpenter
And took away my life."

B

"The House Carpenter." Collected by Mr. John Stone. Sung by Mr. George Hart, of Konnarock, Va. Washington County. November 8, 1921.

1 "Well met, well met, my old true love,
Well met, well met," says he.
"I'm just returning from the sea, salt sea,
All for the sake of thee.

2 "I once could have married a king's daughter dear,
And she would have married me;
But I have refused her crowns of gold,
And it's all for the sake of thee."

3 "If you could have married a king's daughter dear,
I'm sure you are to blame;
For I am married to a house carpenter,
And I believe he is a fine young man."

4 "If you will forsake your house carpenter
And go along with me,
I'll take you to where the grass grows green
On the banks of the Sweet Willoree."

5 "If I was to forsake my house carpenter
And go along with thee,
What would you have to maintain me on
Or to keep me from slavery?"

6 "I have three ships all sailing on sea,
All sailing for dry land,
One hundred and ten brave bold young men;
You can have them at your command."

7 She picked up her sweet little babe
And kisses gave it three,
Saying, "You stay here, my sweet little babe,
And keep your pap company."

8 She went and she dressed in her richery,[1]
She went along her way,
She shined and she glittered and she boldly walked
The streets of Purity.

9 They had n't been on board but about two weeks,
And I am sure not three,
Till this young lady began for to weep,
And she wept most bitterly.

10 She cursed all the female kind,
She cursed the sailor's life.
"You've robbed me of my house carpenter
And deprived me of my life."

11 "Is it for my gold that you weep?
Or is it for my store?
Or is it for your house carpenter
Whose face you'll see no more?"

12 "It's neither for your gold I weep,
Nor neither is it for your store;
It's for that sweet little babe of mine
Whose face I'll see no more."

13 They had n't been on board but about three weeks,
And I am sure not four,
Till this young lady began for to weep,
And her weeping ceased no more.

14 They had n't been on board but about four weeks,
And I am sure not five,
Till the vessel sprung a leak and it sunk
And it sunk for to never rise.

[1] For *rich array*.

C

"The House Carpenter." Collected by Miss Alfreda M. Peel. Sung by Miss Rushia Richardson, of Vinton, Va., and by Sis Sears, of Salem, Va. Roanoke County. September 11, 1922. With music.

1 "Well met, well met, my own fair lady,
Well met, well met," cried she,
"I've just returned from my castle,
All for the sake of thee."

2 "Too late, too late, my own fair knight,
Too late, too late," cried she,
"I've just been wed to a house carpenter,
And I think he's a nice young man."

3 "If you will leave your house carpenter
And come along with me,
I'll take you where the grass grows green
On the banks of the salt, salt sea.

4 "If you will leave your house-carpenter
And come along with me,
I'll take you where the grass grows green
Beside my castles three.

5 "I have three ships on the salt, salt sea,
They are sailing for my lands;
One hundred and ten so jolly knights
You can have at your command."

6 She picked up her sweet little babe,
And kisses gave it three,
Crying, "Stay at home, my little babe,
And keep him company."

7 She was not on the sea three weeks,
I'm sure it was not three,
Before this lady began to weep
And wept most bitterly.

8 "Oh, is it for my gold you weep?
Or is it for my store?"
"I'm weeping for my sweet little babe
That I shall see no more.

9 "If I live till another fall
And God will give me grace,
I'll buy a bottle of Jenico wine
To wash your deceitful face.

10 "I wish to the Lord I had never been born
And died when I was young;
I never would wet my rosy cheeks
With no man's lying tongue."

11 She was not on the sea three weeks,
I'm sure it was not four,
Before the ship began to sink,
And sank to rise no more.

D

"The House Carpenter." Collected by Miss Juliet Fauntleroy. Sung by Mrs. Jesse Maxie, of Altavista, Va. Campbell County. February 19, 1914 and August 1, 1914. With music.

1 "I've come, I've come, my own true love,
I've come, I've come," said he.
"I've crossed the salty waters deep,
And it's all for the love of thee. } *Repeat* [1]

2 "I could have married a king's daughter fair,
She would have married me,
But 't was all for refuses of her silver and her gold,[2]
And all for the love of thee."

3 "If you could have married a king's daughter fair,
I'm sure you are to blame;
For I have married a house carpenter,
I'm sure he's a nice young man."

4 "If you will leave your house carpenter
And go along with me,
I'll carry you where the grass grows green,
On the banks of sweet Italy."

5 "If I should leave my house carpenter
And go along with thee,
What have you there to maintain me upon
And keep me from a slav'ry?"

6 "I have a hundred ships on sail,
All sailing for dry land,
Five hundred and ten brave, jolly sailor men [3]
Shall be at your command."

[1] "In singing this both Mrs. Maxie and Miss Callie Hogan repeat the last two lines. Mrs. Yowell repeats only the last line" (Miss Fauntleroy).

[2] Variant line: "But 't was all for the *refusal* of her *riches* and her gold."

[3] Variant line: "*One* hundred and ten, etc."

7 She called to her side her sweet little babe,
Her kisses was one, two, three,
Saying, "Stay at home, my sweet little babe,
And keep your papa company."

8 She had n't been on water two weeks,
I'm sure it was not three,
'Fore this fair lady she began to weep,
And she wept most bitterly.

9 "Are you weeping for your money, my love?
Are you weeping for your store?
Are you weeping for your house carpenter
That you left so far on shore?"

10 "No, I'm not weeping for my money, my love,
Nor neither for my store;
I'm weeping for my sweet little babe
That I never shall see any more."

11 She had n't been on water three weeks,
I'm sure it was not four,
'Fore this fair lady she began to weep,[1]
And sank for to rise no more.

12 Come all of you now, nice young girls,
Take warning now from me
And never leave your house carpenter
To go with a man on sea.

E

"On the Banks of the Sweet Laurie." Collected by Mr. Wilson E. Somers, of Disputanta, Va. Found in Accomac County. March 30, 1918.

1 "Well met, well met, my own true love,
Well met, well met," cried he.
"I have just returned from the sea, salt sea,
And 't was all for the sake of thee;
I have just returned from the sea, salt sea,
And 't was all for the sake of thee.

2 "I could have married a king's daughter,
So freely she'd marry me,
But I refused her golden fee,
And 'twas all for the sake of thee."

[1] Variant line: "*Before* this fair lady she *sprang a leap*." An interesting bit of "folk-etymology."

3 "If you could have married a king's daughter,
I think you are to blame;
For now I am married to a house carpenter,
And I think him a fine young man."

4 "If you forsake your house carpenter
And go along with me,
I will take you where the grass grows green,
On the banks of the Sweet Laurie."

5 "If I'll forsake my house carpenter
And go along with thee,
What have you there to maintain a wife upon,
And keep her from slavery?"

6 "Six ships, six ships are now at sea,
Seven more are on dry land,
One hundred and ten all bold sailor men,
Shall be at your command."

7 She took her pretty and her sweet little babe,
And gave it kisses three,
Saying, "Stay at home with your own papa,
And he will be kind to thee."

8 She dressed herself in the finest silk,
And her waitress all in green,
And every city that they came to pass,
They took her to be some queen.[1]

9 They had not sailed four weeks, four weeks,
Four weeks nor scarcely three,
When this lady fair, she began to weep,
And she wept most bitterly.

10 "Oh, why do you weep, my own true love?
Oh, why do you weep?" cried he.
"Oh, is it for your house or your house carpenter?
Or is it for your golden fee?"

11 "It's not for my house nor my house carpenter,
It's not for my golden fee,
But it is for my pretty and my sweet little babe
That I nevermore shall see."

12 They had not sailed five weeks, five weeks,
Five weeks nor scarcely four,
When this gallant ship, she began to sink,
And she sank to rise no more.

[1] The stanza is borrowed from "Lord Thomas and Fair Annet." See Virginia, No. 18, and cf. K 7, N 3, Y 7 and Z 5.

13 Oh, cursèd be these fair-faced men,
 And cursèd be their lives;
They are always robbing house carpenters
 And carrying away their wives.

F

"The House Carpenter." Collected by Mr. John Stone. Sung by Miss Lottie Shaffir, of Mustoe, Va., who got it from her mother, Mrs. L. A. Shaffir. Highland County. November 3, 1920.

1 "We've met, we've met," cried he,
 "I've just returned from the salt, salt sea,
And it was all for the sake of thee,
 And it was all for the sake of thee."

2 "I could have married the king's daughter fair
 And I know she would of (have?) married me,
But I refused all crowns of gold
 And 't was for the sake of thee."

3 "If you could of married the king's daughter fair,
 I am sure you are for the blame;
For I am married to a house carpenter
 And he is a fine young man."

4 "If you will forsake your house carpenter
 And go along with me,
I'll take you to where the grass grows green
 On the banks of Sweet Valley."

5 "If I forsake my house carpenter
 And go along with you,
What have you to maintain me upon
 And keep me from slavery?"

6 "I have seven ships all on the sea
 Sailing for dry land,
A hundred and ten bold jolly young men,
 And they shall be at your command."

7 She picked up her pretty little babe
 And kisses gave it three,
Saying, "Stay at home, my pretty little babe,
 And keep your father company."

8 She dressed herself in richrey,[1]
 Most beauty to behold;
And as she walked along the way
 She showed like glittering gold.

[1] For *rich array*.

9 She had not been on sea two weeks,
I am sure it was not three,
Until fair Ellen began for to weep,
And she wept most bitterly.

10 "It's what do you weep for? My gold?" he said,
"Or do you weep for my store?
Or do you weep for that house carpenter
That you never shall see any more?"

11 "I do not weep for your gold," she said,
"Nor do I weep for your store;
But I do weep for my pretty little babe
That I never shall see any more."

12 She had not been on sea three weeks,
I am sure it was not four,
Until her ship it sprang a leak,
And she sank to rise no more.

13 "It's woe be unto a wayfaring man,
And curses to a sailor,
For robbing me of my house carpenter
And taking away my life."

G

"The House Carpenter." Collected by Miss Martha M. Davis, of Harrisonburg, Va. Fairfax County. August 14, 1914. With music. "From the recitation of an old woman who goes out to nurse. She learned it from other children forty or fifty years ago when she was a child in Fairfax County, Va." (Miss Davis).

1 "Well met, well met, my own true love,
Well met, well met," says he;
"I've just returned from the salt, salt sea,
And it's all for love of thee.

2 "I could have married the king's daughter fair."
"You might as well," said she,
"For now I'm married to a house carpenter,
And a nice young man is he."

3 "If you will forsake your house carpenter
And go along with me,
I'll carry you away where the grass grows green
On the isle of sweet Willee."

4 "If I forsake my house carpenter
And go away with thee,
What have you to maintain me on
Or keep me from slavery?"

5 "I have ten ships on the sea sailing wide,
A-making on for land;
One hundred of my bold sailor men
Will be at your command."

6 She took her babe up in her arms
And kisses gave it three.
"Now stay at home, my sweet little babe,
For your father's company."

7 She dressed herself in her richest to wear,
And the weather being cold,
She walked, she walked the streets around,
She glittered like beaten gold.

8 She had n't been sailing more than two weeks,
I'm sure it was not three,
Before this damsel began for to weep,
And she wept most bitterly.

9 "What are you weeping for, silver or gold?
Are you weeping for my store?
Are you weeping for your house carpenter
You never shall see any more?"

10 "I neither weep for your silver nor gold,
Nor do I weep for your store;
I'm weeping for my sweet little babe
I never shall see any more."

11 She had n't been sailing more than three weeks,
I'm sure it was not four,
Before this ship had sprung a leak
And sunk to rise no more.

12 A curse, a curse to this young man
That sails the ocean wide;
He has robbed the poor house carpenter
And taken away his bride.

H

"The House Carpenter." Collected by Mr. John Stone. Sung by Mrs. J. A. Mitchell, Miss Mary Mitchell, and Mrs. Holland Hoffman, of Criglersville, Va. Madison County. November 3, 1920. With music. "They had a manuscript copy made about 1895 by Mrs. S. T. Rosser, of Criglersville, Va., who learned it from Mrs. Sally Yowell, long since dead" (Mr. Stone). But they all sang the song, and the words and music are those actually sung.

1 "Well met, well met, my old true love,
Well met, well met," says he,
"I have just returned from the salt-water sea,
And it's all for the sake of thee.

2 "I could have married a king's daughter dear,
How vain she would have married me;
I refused her gold and her silver too,
And it was all for the sake of you."

3 "If you could have married a king's daughter dear,
I'm sure you are to blame;
For I have married a house carpenter
And I think him a nice young man."

4 "Leave off, leave off your house carpenter,
And go along with me.
I will carry you where the grass grows green
On the banks of sweet relief." [1]

5 "What have you to keep me from slavery
Or any other disagree?"
"I have a hundred and ten of the nicest waiting-men,
And they shall all be at your command.

6 "There are seven ships all sailing on the sea,
All sailing for dry land,
And a hundred and ten of the nicest waiting-men,
And they shall all be at your command."

7 She picked up her sweet little babe
And gave it kisses three,
Saying, "Along, along with your pappy go,
And keep his company."

8 She was sailing on the ship about two weeks,
I'm sure it was not three,
Before the damsel began to weep,
And she wept most bitterly.

[1] One sang the line, "On the banks of the Sweet *Moree*."

9 "What are you a-weeping for? my gold?
Or are you for my store?
Or are you for that house carpenter
Whose face you will see no more?"

10 "I am neither a-weeping for your gold,
And neither for your store,
But a-weeping for my sweet little babe
Whose face I'll see no more."

11 She was sailing on the ship about three weeks,
I'm sure it was not four,
Before the vessel sprang a leak
And sank to rise no more.

12 "Cursed be, cursed be to a sailor's life
Or any other such a strife,
Who has robbed me off my house carpenter
And has taken away my life."

I

"The House Carpenter." Collected by Miss Martha M. Davis. Sung by a mountain woman at Elkton, Va. Rockingham County. January 20, 1914.

1 "Well met, well met, my own true love,
Well met, well met," said he.
"I've just returned from the salt, salt sea,
And it's all for the sake of thee.
I've just returned from the salt, salt sea,
And it's all for the sake of thee.

2 "I could have married a king's daughter
And she fain would have married me;
But I refused that crown of gold,
And it's all for the sake of thee.
But I refused that crown of gold,
And it's all for the sake of thee."

3 "If you could have married a king's daughter,
I'm sure you are to blame;
For I've married a house carpenter,
And I think he's a fine young man;
For I've married a house carpenter,
And I think he's a fine young man."

4 "If you will leave your house carpenter
And go along with me,
I'll take you where the grass grows green
On the banks of sweet Italy.
I'll take you where the grass grows green
On the banks of sweet Italy."

5 "If I should leave my house carpenter
And go along with thee,
What have you to support me upon
And to keep me from poverty?
What have you to support me upon
And to keep me from poverty?"

6 "I have three hundred armored men
And seven ships at sea,
And this is enough to support you upon
And to keep you from poverty.
And this is enough to support you upon
And to keep you from poverty.

7 "And I have many goods in store
And gems and gold for thee;
And this is enough to support you upon
And keep you from poverty.
And this is enough to support you upon
And keep you from poverty."

8 She picked up her sweet little babe,
Kisses gave it one, two, three:
"Stay at home, stay at home, my sweet little babe,
And keep your father company.
Stay at home, stay at home, my sweet little babe,
And keep your father company."

9 She had not been at sea two weeks,
I'm sure it had not been three,
Before she began to moan and weep,
And she wept most bitterly.
Before she began to moan and weep,
And she wept most bitterly.

10 "Oh, is it for my gold you weep,
Or is it for my store?
Or is it for your house carpenter
That you never shall see any more?
Or is it for your poor little babe
That you never shall see any more?"

11 "It is not for your gold I weep,
Neither is it for your store;
But it is for my house carpenter
That I never shall see any more;
But it is for my sweet little babe
That I never shall see any more."

12 She had not been at sea three weeks,
I'm sure it was not four,
Before the ship it sank in the deep,
And it sank to rise no more;
Before the ship it sank in the deep
And it sank to rise no more.

J

"The House Carpenter." Collected by Miss Nancy Pearson. Sung by Mr. Armistead, of Cobbs Creek, Va. Mathews County. November 15, 1915.

1 "I could 'a' married a king's daughter."
"I'm sure you're much to blame;
I have married a house carpenter,
And I'm sure he's a nice young man.
I have married a house carpenter,
And I'm sure he's a nice young man."

2 "If you forsake your house carpenter
And go along with me,
I'll take you where the grass grows green
On the banks of sweet O'lee.
I'll take you where the grass grows green
On the banks of sweet O'lee."

3 "If I forsake my house carpenter,
And go along with you,
What have you there to entertain me
And keep me from hard slavery?
What have you there to entertain me
And keep me from hard slavery?"

4 "I have hundreds of ships all out on sea
Or sailing for dry land,
With ten hundred and ten bold sailor men,
Which all shall be at your command;
With ten hundred and ten bold sailor men,
Which all shall be at your command."

5 She dressed herself in rich array,
As rich as she could afford,
And she walked the streets round and round,
And she shone like glittering gold;
And she walked the streets round and round,
And she shone like glittering gold.

6 Then she pressed her babe up to her lips
And give it a kiss or three,
Saying, "Stay at home, my darling little babe,
And keep your papa company";
Saying, "Stay at home, my darling little babe,
And keep your papa company."

7 She had not sailed more than two lengths at sea,
Not more than three, I'm sure,
Before this fair lady she began to weep,
And she weeps most bitterly;
Before this fair lady she began to weep,
And she weeps most bitterly.

8 "What are you weeping for? my gold?
Or either for my stores?
Or are you weeping for your house carpenter
That you never shall see any more?
Or are you weeping for your house carpenter
That you never shall see any more?"

9 "I'm not weeping for your gold,
Or neither for your stores,
But I'm weeping for my darling little babe
That I shall never see any more.
But I'm weeping for my darling little babe
That I shall never see any more."

10 They had not sailed more than three lengths at sea,
Not more than four, I'm sure,
Before the ship she springs a leak
And sinks to rise no more;
Before the ship she springs a leak
And sinks to rise no more.

11 "Now my poor husband is at home
Or wondering where I may be,
While my poor body is food for the fish
On the bottom of the deep blue sea;
While my poor body is food for the fish
On the bottom of the deep blue sea.

12 "Say here is a curse to all seafaring men,
Likewise to others' pure strife;
For they have robbed me of my house carpenter
And taken away my life;
For they have robbed me of my house carpenter
And taken away my life."

K

"The House Carpenter." Collected by Miss Juliet Fauntleroy. Sung by Miss Maggie Wright, of Altavista, Va. Campbell County. September 28, 1915.

1 "Well met, well met, my old true love,
Well met, well met," said he.
. . . .
. . . .

2 "I could have married a king's daughter fair,
She fain would have married me;
But I would not marry a king's daughter,
And it was all for the love of thee."

3 "If you could have married a king's daughter,
I'm sure you are to blame;
For I have married a house carpenter,
And I think he's a fine young man."

4 "If you will leave your house carpenter,
And go along with me,
I'll take you where the grass grows green
On the lakes of sweet Riley."

5 "If I forsake my house carpenter,
And go and live with you,
. . . .
. . . ."

6 She took her little babe up in her arms
And gave it kisses three,
Saying, "Stay at home, my sweet little babe,
And keep your papa's companie."

7 She went and dressed herself up in silk,
The finest ever was seen,
And as she marched along the street,
They took her to be some queen.

8 She had not been on water two weeks,
I'm sure it was not three,
Before this fair lady she began to weep,
And she wept most bitterly.

9 "Oh, are you weeping for my gold,
Or weeping for my store,
Or weeping for that house carpenter,
You never shall see no more?"

10 "I am not weeping for your gold,
Nor weeping for your store,
But weeping for my sweet little babe,
I never shall see no more.

11 "Cursed be the sailor man,
Cursed be his life;
He's robbed me of my sweet little babe,
He's robbed me of my life."

12 She has not been on water three weeks,
I'm sure it was not four,
Before the ship it sprang a leak
And sank to rise no more.

L

"The House Carpenter." Collected by Mr. John Stone. Contributed by Mr. H. E. Anderson, of Dante, Va. Sung by his mother in Grayson County. November 8, 1921.

1 "I've just returned, my old true love,
I've just returned to thee,
I've just returned from the saltsome sea,
And it's all for the sake of thee.

2 "I could have married a king's daughter,
I'm sure she would have married me,
But I refused the crowns of gold,
And it's all for the sake of thee."

3 "If you could have married a king's daughter,
And she would have married you,
I'm very sure she was the one,
For I have married a house carpenter,
And I think he's a nice young man."

4 "If you will refuse your house carpenter,
And go along with me,
I'll take you to where the grass grows green
On the banks of the Sweet Relea."

5 "If I refuse my house carpenter
And go along with you,
What have you got to maintain me on
To keep me from slavery?"

6 "I have sixteen boats all sailing on the sea,
Sixteen hundred and twenty jolly sailor boys
That you may have at your command
If you will go along with me."

7 She dressed herself in scarlet red,
And on it she put blue;
She glittered away in her golden purities
And walked them streets all through.

8 She picked up her sweet little babe
And kisses gave it three,
Saying, "You stay here, my sweet little babe,
And keep your pa company."

9 She had n't been on board not more than three weeks,
I'm sure it was not four,
Till she began to weep and to mourn,
The like I never saw before.

10 "What are you weeping for, my dear?
Are you weeping for your house carpenter?
Are you weeping for my store?
Are you weeping for your sweet little one
Whose face you shall see no more?"

11 "I'm not weeping for my house carpenter,
I'm not weeping for your store;
I'm weeping for my sweet little babe
Whose face I shall see no more."

M

"The Ship Carpender."[1] Collected by Mrs. Olin F. Wiley, of Richmond, Va. Found in Wise County. December 1, 1916.

1 "Well met, well met, my old true love,
. . . .
. . . . the salt sea,
And it is all for the sake of thee.

2 "I could have married a king's daughter,
And pailey[2] she would have me,
Although I refused that great rich crown,
All for the sake of thee."

[1] This ballad was copied from an old and hardly legible manuscript.
[2] Possibly *plainly* or *fainly* is the word.

3 "If you could get a king's daughter,
And painley [1] she would have ye,
You had better 'a' took her, my old true love,
Then 'a' waited so long for me.

4 "For I am married to a ship carpender,
And a ship carpender was he,
And by him I have a little son
Or, love, I would go to thee."

5 She picked up her baby all in her arms
And embraced it with kisses so sweet
And laid it down on a soft bed of down
And bid it go to sleep.

6 "What are you weeping for, my own true love?
Is it houses, land, or fee?
Or is it for some other man
You love far better than me?

7 "If you had ten thousand pounds
And would painley [1] give it to me,
You would never return to your dry land
Or again your baby you never shall see."

8 As she was sailing all by the sea side
And the water running bold
And silver sparkling to the top,
Just like the purest of gold,

9 "O what hills, what hills, my own true love,
That looks so white like snow?"
"It is the hills of heaven where
All true lovers go."

10 "What hills, what hills, my own true love,
That look so black and woe?"
"It is the hills of hell, my love,
Where you and I must go."

N

"The House Carpenter." Collected by Mrs. Olin F. Wiley, of Richmond, Va. Found in Wise County.[2] December 1, 1916.

1 "Oh! will you leave your house carpenter
And go along with me?
I'll take you where the grass grows green
On the banks of the deep blue sea."

[1] Possibly *plainly* or *fainly* is the word.
[2] "Found on the border of Virginia, close to Jenkins, Ky." (Mrs. Wiley).

2 And she picked up her three little babes,
And kisses gave them three.
"Stay here, stay here, my sweet little babes,
And keep your papa company."

3 She dressed herself in scarlet red,
Most glorious to the king;
And every city that she rode through,
She shined like glattering [1] gold.

4 She had n't been on the sea three weeks,
I'm sure not more than four,
When the ship sprung a leak and began to sink,
And sunk to rise no more.

5 "What are you weeping for?
Are you weeping for the house carpenter,
Or my silver and gold?"

6 "I'm neither weeping for the house carpenter,
Neither silver and gold;
I'm weeping for my three little babes,
I never shall see any more.

7 "What banks, what banks, behind I see?
They are white as any snow."
"The banks of Heaven," he cried unto her,
"Where the Christian people go."

8 "What banks, what banks, before me I see?
They are as black as any crow."
"They are the banks of Hell," he cried unto her,
"Where you and I must go."

9 This young lady began
To weep most bitterly,
Weeping for her sweet little babes,
She never shall see again.

O

"The Dæmon Lover." Collected by Mr. John Stone. Sung by Mrs. Mary Jett Armstrong, of Falmouth, Va. Stafford County. September 11, 1922.

1 "If you'll forsake your house carpenter
And go along with me,
I'll carry you where the grass grows green
On the banks of the sweet Willie."

[1] For *glittering*.

2 "I'll not forsake my house carpenter
To go along with thee;
I'll not forsake my sweet and pretty babe
For the banks of sweet Willie.

3 "What have you to support me on
The balance of my days
And keep me from starvation
And working like a slave?"

4 "I have three ships all on the sea,
The fourth one brought me to land,
With one hundred and ten bold jolly sailor men,
And all at your command."

5 "I'll not accept of your gold and silver,
I'll not accept of your house and land,
I'll not accept of your ships on the ocean,
If they are at my command."

6 She took her baby up
And gave it kisses three,
"Lie there, lie there, my sweet and pretty babe,
For your daddy's company."

7 "What are you weeping for, my dear?
Are you weeping for my store?
Or are you weeping for the house carpenter
You left on the other shore?"

8 "I am not weeping for the house carpenter,
I am not weeping for your store,
But I am weeping for my sweet pretty babe
I'll never see any more."

9 They had not been on sea three weeks,
I am sure it was not four,
Before the gallant ship sprang a leak
And sank to rise no more.

P

"The House Carpenter." Contributed by Mrs. Olin F. Wiley. Sung by Mr. Elisha McNew, III, of Wise, Va. Wise County. February 3, 1916.

1 "We have met, we have met, my old true love,
We have met, we have met," said he;
"I have lately crossed the old salt sea,
And it is all for the sake of thee.

2 "I have refused houses and lands,
And the rich King's daughter too,
Yet I have refused ten thousand pounds,
And it was all for the sake of you."

3 "You better have married the rich King's daughter,
Or have got you a house and land;
For now I am married to the house carpenter,
And I think he's a very fine man."

4 "Come, my love, and go with me,
I will take you where the grass grows green,
I will take you away to the Ivory."

5 She picked up her poor little babe,
And kisses she gave it three,
Saying, "Stay at home with the house carpenter,
And keep him company."

6 They had not been on sea but about two weeks,
I am sure it was not three,
When she fell across her lover's lap
And wept most bitterly.

7 "What are you weeping for, my love?
Are you weeping for a store?
Or are you weeping for the house carpenter,
Who you never shall see any more?"

8 "I am not weeping for the house carpenter,
Neither for any store,
I am weeping for my poor little babe,
Who I can never see any more."

9 They had not been over sea but about three weeks,
I am sure it was not four,
Till the ship it sank to the bottom of the lake,
And her voice was heard no more.

Q

"The House Carpenter." Collected by Mr. John Stone. Sung by Mr. C. F. Carpenter, of Bolar, Va, who learned it from his mother, when he was a boy. Highland County. November 3, 1920. With music.

1 "Well met, well met, my dearest dear,
Well met, well met," cried he.
"I've just returned from the salt, salt sea,
'T was all for the sake of thee,
'T was all for the sake of thee.

2 "If you'll forsake your house carpenter
And go along with me,
I'll take you to where the grass grows green
On the banks of Sweet Liberty."

3 So she picked up her pretty little babe
And gave it kisses three,
Saying, "Stay at home, my pretty little babe,
And keep your father company."

4 She had n't been on sea two weeks,
I'm sure it was n't three,
Before Fair Ellen began for to weep,
And she wept most bitterly.

5 "O do you weep for my gold?" he said,
"Or do you weep for my store?
Or do you weep for your house carpenter
That you never will see no more?"

6 "I do not weep for your gold," she said,
"Nor do I weep for your store;
But I do weep for my pretty little babe
That I never shall see no more."

7 She had not been on sea three weeks,
I'm sure it was not four,
Before the ship she sprung a leak,
And she sunk to rise no more.

8 "Woe be unto a wayfaring man,
Woe be unto a sailor's life,
For robbing me of my house carpenter
And taking away my life."

R

"The House Carpenter." Collected by Mr. John Stone. Sung by Mrs. Ellen Mulleins, of Saltville, Va., an old lady who learned it from her mother. Smyth County. November 8, 1921. The intruding stanzas here are 7 and 8. They are from "The Lass of Roch Royal."

1 "Well met, well met, my old true love,
Well met, well met," says she.
"I've just returned from the foreign land,
And it's all for the sake of thee.

2 "I could have married a king's daughter great,
And she would have married me,
But I refused her crown of gold;
It was all for the sake of thee."

3 "If you could have married a king's daughter great,
I'm sure you are to blame;
For I am married to a house carpenter,
And I think he is a nice young man."

4 "If you will leave your house carpenter
And go along with me,
I'll take you to where the grass grows green
On the banks of the deep blue sea."

5 "If I was to leave my house carpenter
And go along with thee,
What have you got to maintain me on
And keep me from slavery?"

6 "I have a hundred and ten young men
Stand ready at your command,
If you will come and go with me
And give me your lily-white hand."

7 "Who will shoe my pretty little foot?
Who will glove my hand?
Who will kiss my ruby lips,
When you are off in the foreign land?"

8 "My father will shoe your pretty little feet,
My mother will glove your hands,
And I will kiss your ruby lips,
When I return from the foreign land."

9 She picked up her pretty little babe
And kissed — she gave it three.[1]
"Stay here, stay here, my sweet little babe,
And keep your father company."

10 This lady had not been on the sea two weeks,
I'm sure it was not three,
Before this lady began to weep,
And she wept most bitterly.

11 "Is it for your land you weep?
Or is it for your store?
Or is it for that house carpenter
That you never shall see any more?"

12 "It is not for my land I weep,
Nor is it for my store,
But it is for my sweet little babe
That I never shall see any more."

[1] "And *kisses* she gave it three" is the normal line.

13 This lady had not been on sea three weeks,
I'm sure it was not four,
Before the ship it sprang a leak,
And she sank to rise no more.

S

"The House Carpenter." Collected by Miss Mabel C. Fuller. Sung by Mrs. Fuller, of Callands, Va. Pittsylvania County. August 9, 1916. The intruding stanzas here are 7 and 8, from "The Lass of Roch Royal." See the head-note to this ballad (Virginia, No. 40).

1 "Well met, well met, my old true love,
Well met, well met," cried he.
"I've just returned from a foreign land,
And it's all for the sake of thee.

2 "I once could 'a' married the king's daughter, dear,
I'm sure she'd 'a' married me,
But I refused her crown of gold,
And 't was all for the sake of thee."

3 "If you could 'a' married the king's daughter, dear,
I'm sure you are to blame;
For I have married a house carpenter
And I think him a nice young man."

4 "If you'll forsake your house carpenter
And go along with me,
I'll take you to where the grass grows green
On the banks of Sweet Willie."

5 "If I forsake my house carpenter
And go along with thee,
What have you got to support me on
And keep me from slavery?"

6 She called her babe up to her knee,
The kisses she gave it were three.
"Stay here, stay here, you darling little babe,
And keep your papa company.

7 "But who will shoe your pretty little feet,
And who will glove your hand,
And who will kiss your sweet little lips,
When I'm in a foreign land?"

8 "My papa will shoe my pretty little feet,
My papa will glove my hand,
No one shall kiss my sweet little lips,
When you're in a foreign land."

9 They had not been on board two weeks,
I'm sure that it was not three,
Before this lady began to weep,
And she wept most bitterly.

10 "Is it for my gold you're weeping?
Or is it for my store?
Or is it for your house carpenter?
His face you'll see no more."

11 "It is not for your gold I'm weeping,
Nor is it for your store;
It is all for the sake of the dear little babe
That I left alone on shore."

12 They had not been on board three months,
I'm sure that it was not four,
Before this vessel sprang a leak
And sank to rise no more.

T

"The House Carpenter." Collected by Miss Juliet Fauntleroy. Sung by Mrs. James Sprouse (*née* Pribble), of Lawyers, Va. Campbell County. September 4, 1915. Stanzas 1 and 2 are the intruders here. They belong to "The False Young Man." See Campbell and Sharp, No. 94. The similarity of these stanzas to the opening stanzas of "The House Carpenter" readily explains the intrusion.

1 "Come in, come in, my old true love,
And sit you down by me.
It's been over three quarters of a year
Since I spoke one word to you."

2 "I won't come in, I won't sit down,
I have n't a minute to stay.
I give you to understand you love another man,
And your heart is no more mine.

3 "I could have married a king's daughter dear,
She fain would have married me,
But I refused those crowns of gold,
'T was all for the sake of thee."

4 "If you could have married a king's daughter dear,
I'm sure you are to blame;
For I have married a house carpenter,
And he's a nice young man."

5 "Oh, won't you leave your house carpenter,
And go along with me?
I'll take you to where the grass grows green
On the banks of the sweet Willee."

6 "Yes, I will leave my house carpenter,
And go along with you,
If you'll take me to where the grass grows green
On the banks of the sweet Willee."

7 She went upstairs and dressed herself
As fine as fine could be.
She came down stairs and she kissed her little babe,
Said, "Stay and keep your papa's company."

8 She had n't been on sea two weeks,
I'm sure it was not three,
Before she began to weep and to mourn,
And she wept most bitterly.

9 "What are you weeping for, my dear?
Is it for my gold or store?
Or is it for the house carpenter
You never shall see no more?"

10 "'T is n't for your gold I weep,
Nor neither for the house carpenter.
It's all for the sake of the sweet little babe
That I never shall see no more."

11 She had n't been on water three weeks,
I'm sure it was not four,
Before the ship she sprang a leak,
And sank to rise no more.

U

"The House Carpenter." Collected by Mr. John Stone. Sung by the Misses Fannie and Hattie Via, who learned it from Mrs. Orilla Keeton, of Albemarle County. Fluvanna County. November 3, 1920. The intruding stanzas here are 10 and 11, evidently supplied from "The False Young Man." Compare Campbell and Sharp, No. 94.

1 "Well met, well met, my own true love,
Well met, well met," says he,
"I've lately returned from the salt water sea,
And it's all for the sake of thee.

2 "I once could have married the king's daughter dear,
And she would have married me,
But it's all the crowns of gold I refused,
And it was all for the sake of thee."

3 "If you could have married the king's daughter dear,
I'm sure you were to blame;
For I am married to the house carpenter
And a very nice young man."

4 "Oh! it's will you forsake your house carpenter
And go along with me?
I will take you on the banks of thc river,
On the banks of Sweet Willie."

5 She picked up her tender little one
And kissed it one, two, three.
"Stay at home, my tender little one,
And keep poor papa's company."

6 They had n't been a-sailing on the sea two weeks,
I'm sure it was not three,
Before she began for to weep,
And she wept most bitterly.

7 "What are you weeping for, my miss?
Are you weeping for my gold?
Or are you weeping for your house carpenter
Whose face you'll see no more?"

8 "No, I'm neither weeping for my house carpenter,
No, I'm neither weeping for your gold;
But I am weeping for my tender little babe
Whose face I'll see no more."

9 Oh! they had n't been a-sailing on the sea three weeks,
I'm sure it was not four,
Before the vessel it sprang for to leak
And sank for to rise no more.

10 "If I had as many dollars as the stars in the sky
And half as many more,
I wish that a cursed [*sic*] may fall upon my head
From fooling a young girl so."

11 "When I was a-lying across my bed
And his hand across my breast,
He made me believe by the faults of his tongue
That the sun rose in the west."

V

"The House Carpenter." Collected by Miss Juliet Fauntleroy. Sung by Mr. Alonzo Hogan and Miss Callie Hogan, of Lynch Station, Va. Campbell County. February, 1914. With music. The first stanza and half the second are supplied from the opening of "The False Young Man." Compare Virginia T, preceding.

1 "Come in, come in, my own true love,
Come in, come in," said she.
"I have n't spoken a word to my own true love
In five or seven years."

2 "I can't come in, I can't stay here,
For I have not a moment of time;
For I heard you were married to a house carpenter,
And your heart is no more mine.

3 "If you will leave your house carpenter,
And go along with me,
I'll carry you where the grass grows green,
On the banks of sweet Willee."

4 She picked her babe up in her arms,
And kissed it one, two, three,
Saying, "Stay at home, my sweet little babe,
And keep your father company."

W

"The House Carpenter." Collected by Miss Juliet Fauntleroy. Sung by Mr. Ed. Stinnet, of Lynch Station, Va. Campbell County. April 18, 1914. The first and fifth stanzas are supplied from "The False Young Man."

1 As I marched out one merry, merry morn,
To hear a bird sing sweet,
There I spied a pretty fair miss,
And I choosed her to be my bride.

2 "I could have married a king's daughter dear,
But if she would have married me;
But I refused that crown of gold,
And 't was all for the sake of thee."

3 "If you could have married a king's daughter dear,
I am sure you were to blame;
For I have married a house carpenter,
And I think he's a fine young man."

4 "If you will leave your house carpenter
And go along with me,
I will take you where the grass is ever green
On the bank of sweet Italy.

5 "I won't come in, nor I won't sit down,
I have but a moment of time;
I heard you had married to the house carpenter
And your heart be no more mine."

6 "If I will leave my house carpenter,
And go along with thee,
What have you to support me upon
And to keep me from poverty?"

7 She went upstairs and dressed in silk,
As fine as silk could be.
. . . .
. . . .

8 She picked up her little babe
And the kisses she gave her were three,
Saying, "You stay here, my poor little babe,
And keep your papa's company."

9 She was n't on the ship but about two weeks,
I'm sure it was not three,
Before the lady began to weep,
And she wept most bitterly.

10 Then she was n't on the ship but about three weeks,
I'm sure it was not four,
Before the ship began to sink,
And it sunk for to rise no more.

X

"The House Carpenter." Collected by Dr. Launcelot M. Harris. Sung by Mrs. Marshall, near Charlottesville, Va. Albemarle County. September 11, 1923. With music. Again the ending belongs to "The False Young Man."

1 "Well met, well met, my own true love;
Well met, well met," said he.
"I have lately returned from the salt water sea,
And it's all for the love of thee.

2 "I could have married a king's daughter dear,
And she would have married me;
But all for crowns of gold I refused,
And it's all for the love of thee."

3 "If you could have married a king's daughter dear,
I am sure I am not to blame;
For I am married to a house carpenter,[1]
And a nice young man is he."

4 "Won't you forsaken your house carpenter,
And go along with me?
I will take you to the banks of the river,
And to the banks of sweet Willie."

5 O, she picked it up, her little babe,
And kissed it one, two, three,
Saying, "Stay at home, my tender little babe,
And keep poor papa company."

6 O, she had not been sailing but two weeks,
I am sure it was not three,
Before she began for to weep,
And wept most bitterly.

7 "What are you weeping for, my miss?
Are you weeping for my gold?
Or are you weeping for your house carpenter?
His face you will see no more."

8 "I am neither weeping for my house carpenter,
I am neither weeping for your gold.
I am weeping for my tender little babe;
Its face I will see no more."

9 O, she had not been sailing but three weeks,
I am sure it was not four,
Before the vessel sprung for to leak,
For to sink to rise no more.

Mrs. M. has "forgotten the last verse," but says the song ends thus:

10 " . . . .
. . . .
He made me believe by the false of his tongue
That the sun rose in the west."

[1] In singing, the word is pronounced *car-ping-ter*, wtih the accent equally distributed over all three syllables.

Y

"The House Carpenter." Collected by Miss Juliet Fauntleroy. Sung by Mrs. John Maxie (*née* Lily Stone), of Altavista, Va. Campbell County. February 28, 1914. The three final stanzas, 12, 13, and 14, are supplied from such songs as "The Wagoner's Lad," "The Rejected Lover," "The False Young Man," etc.

1 "I've come, I've come, my own true love,
I've come, I've come," said he,
"Across salt rivers and salty seas,
And it was all for the sake of thee.

2 "It was not for the gold you possess,
Neither for your store;
I could have married the King's daughter fair,
I am sure she would have married me."

3 "Well, if you could have married the King's daughter fair,
I'm sure you were to blame;
For I have married a house carpenter
And I think him a fine young man."

4 "Oh, kind miss, will you forsake your house carpenter,
And go along with me?"
"Pray, what have you to maintain me upon,
To keep me from slavery?"

5 "Oh, kind miss, I have money in the thousands,
You shall have at your command,
If you will leave your house carpenter
And go along with me."

6 She taken her poor little babe,
The kisses she gave it were one, two, three.
"Stay here," she said, "my dear little babe,
And keep your papa company, till I return again."

7 This kind miss dressed first in crimson and red,
And then she dressed in green,
And when she walked out on the street,
She shined as any queen.

8 The ships had not been on water two weeks,
If two, I'm sure it was not three,
Before she began to weep,
And she wept most bitterly.

9 "Oh, kind miss, what are you weeping for?
Are you weeping for your store?
Or are you weeping for your house carpenter
You left so far away?"

10 "I am not weeping for my store,
Nor I am not weeping for my house carpenter
I have left so far away.
I am weeping for my poor little babe
I never shall see no more."

11 The ships had not been sailing on the waters three weeks,
If three, I'm sure it was not four,
Before the ship began to sink
And it sank to rise no more.

12 Oh, I have seen green grass all trodden under foot
Rise up and grow again.
Oh, love it is a killing thing,
For I am sure I have felt the pain.

13 It's first to love, and then to hate,
And then to love again.
Oh, love it is a killing thing,
Have you ever felt the pain?

14 Oh, I wish I had never been born,
Or had died when I was young;
I would never have been here to shed a tear,
Nor to listen to your lying tongue.

Z

"The House Carpenter." Collected by Miss Juliet Fauntleroy. Sung by Miss Daisy Quarles, of White Rock, Va. Bedford County. October 17, 1915. Again the final stanzas, 11 and 12, belong to other songs. Compare Virginia Y, preceding, stanzas 12 and 13, and see its head-note.

1 "We have, we have, my old true love,
I am glad that I have met with thee;
For I am just from the salt water sea,
And it is all for the sake of thee.

2 "I could have married a king's daughter fair,
I am sure she would have married me;
It was not for the gold that she possessed,
It was all for the sake of thee."

3 "If you could have married a king's daughter fair,
I'm sure you were to blame;
For I have married a house carpenter,
And I think he is a fine young man."

4 "Oh! won't you forsake your house carpenter
And go a long with me?
I will carry you where the grass grows green
On the edge of sweet Willie."

5 She dressed herself all over in red,
And then she dressed in green,
And as she marched on down the street
She shined as any queen.

6 This lady had not been on the sea two weeks,
I am sure it was not three,
Before she began to weep,
And she wept most bitterly.

7 "Are you weeping for my gold?" said he,
"Are you weeping for my store?
Are you weeping for the house carpenter
Which you never shall see more?"

8 "I neither am weeping for your gold," said she,
"Neither for your store;
I am weeping for the house carpenter
Which I never shall see more."

9 This lady had n't been on sea three weeks,
I am sure it was not four,
Before the ship it sprang a leak,
And it sank to rise no more.

10 She said, "Cursed be all sailor men!"
She cursed a sailor's life,
Which had robbed her of her rest
And deprived her of her life.

11 I've seen green leaves, all trodden under foot,
To rise up and grow again;
True love is a killing thing;
Did you ever feel the pain?

12 'T is first to love and then to hate
And then to love again;
True love it is a killing thing;
Did you ever feel the pain?

AA

"James Harris" or "The House Carpenter's Wife." Collected by Miss Nancy E. Pearson, of Christiansburg, Va. Montgomery County. November 10, 1917. With stanza 11, which is the intruder here, compare Virginia Y 14, and see its head-note.

1 "Well met, well met, my true love,
Well met, well met, I say.
For I've just returned from the salt lake sea,
And it was all for the sake of thee.

2 "I could have married a king's daughter,
I'm sure she'd married me,
But I refused her crown of gold
All for the sake of thee."

3 "If you could have married a king's daughter,
I'm sure you were to blame;
For I have married a house carpenter,
And I think he's a nice young man."

4 "If you leave your house carpenter
And go along with me,
I'll take you where the grass grows green
On the banks of the deep blue sea."

5 "If I was to leave my house carpenter
And go along with thee,
What would you have to support me on
On the banks of the deep blue sea?"

6 "I have a hundred ships sailing on the sea,
All sailing for dry land,
And a hundred and ten jolly sea men
Shall be at your command."

7 She called her little babe to her house
And kisses gave it three,
Saying, "You stay here with your papa
And keep him company."

8 She had not been on board two weeks,
I'm sure it was not three,
Till this young lady began to weep,
And she wept mighty bitterly.

9 "Are you weeping for my riches,
Or are you weeping for stores?
Are you weeping your house carpenter
Which you never shall see any more?"

10 "I'm not weeping for your riches,
Or neither for your stores;
For I'm weeping for my sweet little babe
Which I never shall see any more.

11 "I wish to God I'd never been born,
Else died when I was young;
My cheeks would never have been bathed with tears
By no man's lying tongue."

12 She had not been on board three weeks,
I'm sure it was not four,
Till this old ship she burst a leak
And sunk to rise no more.

APPENDICES

A

No title given. Reported by Professor James M. Grainger. Collected by Miss Ira McAlpin. Sung by Mrs. Charles McAlpin, of Lexington, Va. Rockbridge County. March 14, 1914. In the confusion of songs the story has been completely lost. Stanzas 2 and 3 belong to "The House Carpenter"; the chorus and stanzas 5 and 6 belong to "The Lass of Roch Royal"; stanzas 1, 4, and 7 belong almost indiscriminately to the cycle of songs so often blended with this ballad, such as "The True Lover's Farewell," "The False Young Man," "The Rejected Lover," and others. See the head-note.

1 As I was walking out early one morn,
Thinking of sweet wine,
I overtook that sweet little girl
That broke this heart of mine.

Chorus

Saddle me the milk-white horse,
Saddle me the brown,
Saddle me the swiftest horse
That ever laid foot on ground.

2 "See those fairy banks of heaven
White as driven snow?
They are the fairy banks of heaven
Where you and I can't go.

3 "See those cloudy banks of heaven
Dark as driven woe?
They are the cloudy banks of torment
Where you and I shall go."

4 I'm going away but not to stay,
If I go ten thousand miles.

5 "Who will shoe your pretty white foot?
Who will glove your hand?
Who will kiss your ruby lips
When I come from foreign land?

6 "Your father will shoe your pretty white foot;
Your mother will glove your hand;
And I will kiss your sweet ruby lips
When I come from foreign land."

7 Wish I were a little babe
Sitting on my father's knee,
Or I were dead and in my grave
With green grass growing over me.

B

"A-Roving." Collected by Miss Alfreda M. Peel. Sung by Mrs. Shields, of Gralman, Va. Roanoke County. December 3, 1916. Again a mere jargon of many songs, much like Appendix A. Stanzas 3, 4, and 5 belong to "The House Carpenter"; the chorus, to "The Lass of Roch Royal"; stanzas 1, 2, 6, and 7 represent practically all the songs hitherto found blended with this ballad, plus "Cold Winter's Night" and others.

1 "A-roving a-roving one cold winter night,
A-drinking off good wine,
When I over looked that pretty little girl
That broke that heart of mine.

2 "I am going away ten thousand miles,
Ten thousand miles or more,
And I am coming back again
If it be ten thousand more."

Chorus

"Oh, who will shoe your pretty little foot,
And who will love your hand?
And I will shoe your foot, my dear,
When I come from a foreign land."

3 She picked up her sweet little babe,
And kisses gave it three,
Saying, "Lie there, lie there, my sweet little babe,
Lie there in the room with me."

4 She had not been on the sea two weeks,
I'm sure it was not three,
Till this fair one began to weep,
And she wept most bitterly.

5 "Are you weeping for my gold?" said he,
"Are you weeping for my store?"
"I'm not weeping for your gold," said she,
"Nor weeping for your store.
But I am weeping for my sweet little babe
Whose face I'll see no more."

6 He threw his left foot in the stirrup,
The bridle in his hand,
He rode and he rode with very much speed,
Till his nose began to bleed.

7 "I wish to the Lord I'd never been born
Or died when I was young,
As here in this lone wilderness
Lamenting for one who's gone."

41

THE HEIR OF LINNE

(CHILD, No. 267)

ONLY one other text of this ballad has been found in America. See *Journal*, XXVIII, 156 (Perrow, North Carolina). The Virginia text was first announced in *Bulletin*, No. 6, p. 7. No American melody has been noted.

The Virginia text evidently belongs to the version published by Percy in his *Reliques*, 1765, II, 309, 1794, II, 128. This version is practically Child A "revised and completed by the insertion of supplemental stanzas suggested by a modern ballad on a similar subject." Except for the introduction of the lonesome lodge, the rope, and the hundred marks instead of twenty pounds, the Virginia text might pass as a much compressed variant of Child A. As this compression and exclusion of stanzas somewhat obscures the narrative, Child's summary of the story of his A should prove helpful:

"The heir of Linne, a Scots lord, took to cards, dice, and wine, sold his lands to John o the Scales, and went on in dissolute ways for three fourths of a year longer; then he was forced to go to Edinburgh and beg his bread. Some gave him, some refused him, some bade him go to the devil. Brooding over his destitution, he remembered that his father had left him a paper which he was not to look into till he should be in extreme need. This paper told of a castle wall in which stood three chests of money. Filling three bags of gold, he went to John o Scales's house. John's wife wished herself a curse if she trusted him a penny. One good fellow in the company offered to lend him forty pence, and forty more, if wanted. John o Scales tendered him his lands back for twenty pounds less than they had been sold for. The heir of Linne called the lords present to witness, threw John a penny to bind the bargain, and counted out the money from his bags. Then he gave the good fellow forty pounds, and made him keeper of his forest, and beshrewed himself if ever he put his lands on jeopardy again." Of Percy's alterations suggested by "The Drunkard's Legacy," the chief ones visible in the Virginia text are the three mentioned above. The Virginia text is just half the length of Child A and less than a third as long as the Percy text.

"Heir of Linne." Collected by Miss Alfreda M. Peel. Recited by Mrs. Neighbors (aged 90), of Salem, Va. Roanoke County. May 27, 1917.

1 "Welcome, welcome, Lord of Linne,
Let naught disturb your merry cheer;
If you will sell your lands so broad,
Good store of gold I'll give thee here."

2 "Swear me now upon the rood,
That lonesome lodge thou 'lt never spend;
For when all the world doth frown on thee,
Thou there shall find a faithful friend."

3 "Now well-a-day," said the heir of Linne,
"Now well-a-day, and woe is me;
For when I had my lands so broad,
On me they lived full merrily."

4 He looked up and he looked down,
In hope some comfort for to win,
But bare and lonely were the walls.
"Here's sorry cheer," said the heir of Linne.

5 Two were full of beaten gold,
The third was full of white money;
And over them in broad letters
These letters were written plain to see.

6 "Once more, my son, I set thee clear
Amend thy life and folly past;
. . . .
That rope must be thy end at last."

7 Thus bespake a good fellow,
Which sat at John o' Scales his board,
Said, "Turn again, thou heir of Linne,
Some time thou was a real good lord.

8 "Some time a good fellow thou hast been
And spared not your gold and fee;
There for I'll lend thee forty pence,
Another forty if need be.

9 "And ever I pray thee, John o' Scales,
To let him sit in company;
For well I wot thou had'st his land,
And a good bargain was to thee."

10 Then spake him John o' Scales,
All would he answer him again,
"Now Christ's curse on my head," said he,
"But I did lose by that bargain.

11 "And here I offer the heir of Linne,
Before these lords so fair and free,
Thou shalt have it back again better and cheap,
By hundred marks than I had of thee."

12 "I'll draw you to record, lord," said he.
With that he cast him a god's-penny,
"Now, by my fay," said the heir of Linne,
"And here, good John, is thy money."

13 He pulled forth three bags of gold,
And laid them down upon the board.
All woe-begone was John o' Scales
So he could say never a word.

14 He told him forth the good red gold,
He told it forth with rattle and din.
"The gold is thine, the land is mine,
And now I again am Lord of Linne."

15 "Now well-a-day," said Joan of Scales,
"Now well-a-day, and woe's my life;
Yesterday I was Lady of Linne,
Now I'm but John o' Scales his wife."

16 "Now fare thee well," said the heir of Linne,
"Farewell now, John o' Scales," said he,
"Christ's curse light on me, if ever again
I bring my lands in jeopardy."

42

THE SUFFOLK MIRACLE

(Child, No. 272)

Two fairly complete texts and one fragment, with two melodies, have been found in Virginia, all contributed by Mr. Cecil J. Sharp, and as they were found on Mr. Sharp's last collecting trip in the South, not elsewhere published by him. Campbell and Sharp (No. 31) print three texts of the ballad, two from North Carolina, one from Tennessee; Cox (No. 27) prints one text from West Virginia; and Brown (p. 9) reports one from North Carolina. These five variants plus the Virginia three constitute the American survivals of this ballad.

The Virginia texts, like all the American representatives of this ballad, have confused certain stanzas and lost others, but the main outlines of the story are preserved as in the Child version. The story is thus epitomized by Child: "A young man loved a farmer's daughter, and his love was returned. The girl's father sent her to his brother's, forty miles off, to stay till she should change her mind. The man died. A month after, he appeared at the uncle's at midnight, and, as he came on her father's horse and brought with him her mother's travelling gear, he was allowed to take the girl away with him. As they rode, he complained of headache, and the girl bound her handkerchief about his head; he was cold as clay. In two hours they were at her father's door. The man went to put up the horse, as he said, but no more was seen of him. The girl knocked, and her father came down, much astonished to see her, and still more astonished when she asked if her lover, known by her father to be dead, had not been sent to bring her. The father went to the stable, where the girl said the man would be; there was nobody there, but the horse was found to be 'all in a sweat.' After conferences, the grave was opened, and the kerchief was found about the head of the mouldering body. This was told to the girl, and she died shortly after." The Virginia texts omit the final incident of the death of the girl, nor are they particularly close to the Child version in language. The Virginia variants serve to corroborate Professor Child's statement that this ballad could hardly be admitted to the select company of popular ballads on its own merits, but only because "in a blurred, enfeebled, and disfigured shape, it is the representative in England of one of the most remarkable tales and one of the most impressive and beautiful ballads of the European continent." And he proceeds to trace its affiliations in other literatures.

A

"The Suffolk Miracle." Collected by Mr. Cecil J. Sharp and Miss Karpeles. Sung by Mr. Dol Small, at Nellysford, Va. Nelson County. May 22, 1918.

1 There was an old and wealthy man,
He had a daughter great and grand;
She were neat, handsome and tall,
She had a handsome face withal.

2 A many a squire came this way,
This handsome lady for to see;
But at length there was a widow's son,
'T was found he were her chosen one.

3 It's when her old folks came this to know,
They sent him two thousand miles from home,
Which broke this young man's tender heart,
To think that he and his love must part.

4 It were on a cold and stormy night,
He started for his heart's delight.
He rode till he came to the place he knew.
Says he: "My love, I've come for you.

5 "It's your father's request, your mother's heed,
I've come for you all in great speed,
And in two weeks or a little more,
I'll set you safe at your father's door."

6 They rode till they came to the old man's gate.
He did complain his head did ache.
With a handkerchief that he had out,
With it she tied his head about.

7 They rode till they came to the old man's stile.
Says he: "My love, let's tarry awhile.
Alight, alight, alight," says he,
"And I will put your steeds away."

8 She knocked upon her father's door.
The sight of her love she saw no more.
"It's welcome home, my child," says he.
"What trusty friend hath come with thee?"

9 "It's the one I love, I love so well,
I love him better than tongue can tell."
Which made the hair stand on the old man's head,
To think that he'd been twelve months dead.

10 Then princes grand and judges too
Were sent for to witness this great one do (wonder?):
It's although he had been twelve months dead,
The handkerchief were around his head.

11 Now this is a warning to young and old
Who love your children better than gold.
For if you love them, give them their way,
For fear that love will lead astray.

B

"The Suffolk Miracle." Collected by Mr. Cecil J. Sharp and Miss Karpeles. Sung by Mrs. Frances Richards, at Callaway, Va. Franklin County. August 16, 1918. With music.

1 Twelve months he rose, put on his clothes,
Then off to her he then did go.

2 "Here's your mother's cloak and your father's steed,
That's sent for you within great speed."

3 He mounted on and she got behind him,
And they rode swiftly as the wind.

4 Before she got to her father's gate,
He did complain his head did ache.

5 She taken her own handkerchief,
And around his head she bound it around.

6 He set her at her father's door.
The sight of him she saw no more.

7 "Come in, come in, dear daughter, dear;
You are welcome, dear child, to me."

8 Saying: "Do you send the any more (*sic*)
Whom I once loved till I could love no more?"

9 It made the hair rise on this old man's head
In knowing he had been twelve months dead.

10 This old man rose, put on his clothes,
Saying: "This young man's grave is to be undone."

11 And when they undone this young man's grave,
The handkerchief bound round his head.

12 Saying: "If love can bring the dead decay,
I say, pray give to them their way."

13 And ain't this warning to both young and old
To love their children better than gold?

C

"The Suffolk Miracle." Collected by Mr. Cecil J. Sharp. Sung by Mrs. Laura Beckett, at St. Peter's Settlement, Callaway, Va. Franklin County. August 16, 1918. With music.

1 "O father, father, don't you know?
The one I loved I will endure."

43

OUR GOODMAN

(CHILD, No. 274)

FIVE texts and five tunes are the harvest of this ballad in Virginia, two of the texts being without tunes, and two of the tunes without words. Virginia A is Child A, Virginia B Child B, both with variations. Virginia C, D, and E are closer to Child A than to B, but show numerous divergences. Virginia B is the rarest version here given, as most of the texts so far recovered in America have belonged to Child A. As an appendix is printed "A Jacobite Song," which though it comes from a Virginia collector is of West Virginia, Canadian, and British navy ancestry. It seems to correspond to the piece printed in Smith's *Scotish Minstrel*, where the goodwife is found to be concealing her cousin McIntosh, a Tory. None of the more or less ribald stanzas sometimes added to or superimposed upon this ballad have found access to the Virginia files; hence the problem of their publication does not arise. The Virginia titles are "Our Goodman," "Hobble and Bobble," "Home Comes the Good Old Man," "Down Came the Old Man," "The Old Man," and "Cairo Gal," which the singer also called, "A Blackguard Song."

For American texts, see Barry, No. 17; Brown, p. 9 (North Carolina); *Bulletin*, Nos. 2–5; Campbell and Sharp, No. 32 (North Carolina); Cox, No. 28; Finger, p. 161; Hudson, No. 20 (Mississippi); Jones, p. 301 (fragment); *Journal*, XVIII, 295 (Barry, Massachusetts); XXX, 199 (Parsons, North Carolina); Mackenzie, *Ballads*, No. 14; C. A. Smith, p. 17 (Virginia, fragment and two melodies, British melody); Reed Smith, *Ballads*, No. 14. For additional references, see *Journal*, XXIX, 166; XXX, 328; XXXV, 348.

A

"Our Goodman." Collected by Miss Martha M. Davis. Sung by a mountain woman of Elkton, Va. Rockingham County. January 3, 1914.

1 Down came the old man
Hummin' like a bee,
Found a horse a-standin'
Where his own ought to be.

2 He turned to his wife
And he said unto she,
"What's this horse a-doin' here
Without leave o' me?"

3 "You old fool, you blind fool,
You fool, you cannot see;
It's nothing but a milk cow
My mother sent to me."

4 "I've traveled many miles
And many miles before;
A saddle on a milk cow
I never saw before."

5 Down came the old man
Hummin' like a bee,
Found a man a-standin'
Where himself ought to be.

6 He turned to his wife
And he said unto she,
"What's this man a-doin' here
Without leave o' me?"

7 "You old fool, you blind fool,
You fool, you cannot see;
It's nothing but a milkmaid
My mother sent to me."

8 "I've traveled many miles
And many miles before;
Breeches on a milkmaid
I never saw before."

9 Down came the old man
Hummin' like a bee,
Found a hat a-hangin'
Where his own ought to be.

10 He turned to his wife
And he said unto she,
"What's this hat a-doin' here
Without leave o' me?"

11 "You old fool, you blind fool,
You fool, you cannot see;
It's nothing but a milk churn
My mother sent to me."

12 "I've traveled many miles
And many miles before;
But fur on a milk churn
I never saw before."

13 Down came the old man
Hummin' like a bee,
And he found a sword
Where his own ought to be.

14 He turned to his wife
And he said unto she,
"What's this sword a-doin' here
Without leave o' me?"

15 "You old fool, you blind fool,
You fool, you cannot see;
It's nothin' but a churn dasher
My mother sent to me."

16 "I've traveled many miles
And many miles before;
Edge on a milk dasher
I never saw before."

B

"Hobble and Bobble." Sent in by Miss Juliet Fauntleroy. Collected by Mrs. H. W. Adams. Sung by an old Colored man, Henry Payne, near Altavista, Va. Campbell County. May 11, 1914. With music (sent June 6, 1914).

1 I walked into my stable,
And the sight that I did see,
It was some gentlemen's horses,
One, or two, or three.

2 I called to my kind wife,
So kindly she answered me.[1]
"What are those horses doing there
Without a lief[2] from me?"

3 "Whole couple, blind couple,[3]
Fool, can't you see?
It's nothing but some old milk cows
My mother sent here to me."

4 "Hobble and bobble,
Very well done,
Saddle and bridle on an old milk cow
Is a thing I never did see."

[1] Variant two lines: "I hailed to my kind wife,
So kind she answered me."

[2] Almost certainly for *leave*, but the original word is retained.

[3] For "Old cuckold, blind cuckold." The word *cuckold* evidently meant nothing to the singer. Cf. Child B.

5 I walked into my yard,
And the sight that I did see,
It was some gentlemen's hound dogs there,
One, or two, or three.

6 I called to my kind wife,
So kindly she answered me.
"What are those dogs doing there
Without a lief from me?"

7 "Whole couple, blind couple,
Fool, can't you see?
It's nothing but the old cow's calves
My mother sent here to me."

8 "Hobble and bobble,
And very well done,
The born cows' calves and the hound dogs' ears
Are things I never did see."

9 I walked into my porch,
The sight that I did see,
It was some gentlemen's hats in there,
One, or two, or three.

10 I called to my kind wife,
So kindly she answered me.
"What are those hats doing there
Without a lief from me?"

11 "Whole couple, blind couple,
Fool, can't you see?
It's nothing but some old wash pans
My mother sent here to me."

12 "Hobble and bobble,
Very well done,
A hat band on an old wash pan
Is a thing I never did see."

13 I walked into my chamber,
The sight that I did see,
It was some gentlemen's big coats there,
One, or two, or three.

14 I called to my kind wife,
So kindly she answered me.
"What are those big coats doing there
Without a lief from me?"

15 "Whole couple, blind couple,
Fool, can't you see?
It's nothing but some blankets,
My mother sent here to me."

16 "Hobble and bobble,
Very well done,
Sleeves and pockets on a blanket
Is a thing I never did see."

17 I walked into my dining room,
The sight that I did see,
It was some gentlemen's boots in there,
One, or two, or three.

18 I called to my kind wife,
So kindly she answered me.
"What are those boots doing there,
Without a lief from me?"

19 "Whole couple, blind couple,
Fool, can't you see?
It's nothing but some coffee pots
My mother sent here to me."

20 "Hobble and bobble,
Very well done,
Boot straps on a coffee pot
Is a thing I never did see."

21 I walked up to my table,
The sight that I did see,
It was some gentlemen sitting there,
One, or two, or three.

22 I called to my kind wife,
So kindly she answered me.
"What are those gentlemen doing there
Without a lief from me?"

23 "Whole couple, blind couple,
Fool, can't you see?
It's nothing but some cabbage heads
My mother sent here to me."

24 "Hobble and bobble,
Very well done,
But hair on a cabbage head
Is a thing I never did see."

C

"The Old Man." Collected by Miss Juliet Fauntleroy. Sung by Mrs. Maxie (*née* Holland), of Altavista, Va. Franklin County. April 7, 1914. With music.

1 "Lordy, Lordy, my dear wife,
Pray tell me what I see;
Whose horse is that in yonders stall
Where my horse ought to be,
Where my horse ought to be, my love,
Where my horse ought to be?"

2 "You silly fool, you blind fool,
You fool, you cannot see;
It's nothing but a milk cow
My mother gave to me," etc.

3 "I've traveled and I've traveled,
Ten thousand miles or more,
And a bridle upon a milk cow
I never saw before," etc.

4 "Lordy, Lordy, my dear wife,
Pray tell me what I see;
Whose coat is that in yonders hall
Where my coat ought to be?"

5 "You silly fool, you blind fool,
You fool, you cannot see;
It's nothing but a blanket
My mother gave to me."

6 "I've traveled and I've traveled,
Ten thousand miles or more,
But sleeves in a blanket
I never saw before."

7 "Lordy, Lordy, my dear wife,
Pray tell me what I see;
Whose head is that in the bed with you
Where my head ought to be?"

8 "You silly fool, you blind fool,
You fool, you cannot see;
It's nothing but a cabbage head
My mother gave to me."

9 "I've traveled and I've traveled,
Ten thousand miles or more,
But hair upon a cabbage head
I never saw before."

D

"Home Comes the Good Old Man." Collected by Miss Juliet Fauntleroy. Sung by Mrs. James Dearing, of Lynchburg, Va. Campbell County. May 10, 1914. With music.

1 Home comes the good old man,
Home comes he,
He finds a horse a-standing
Where his own horse ought to be.

2 "My own wife, my dear wife,
What can the matter be?
I find a horse a-standing
Where my own horse ought to be."

3 "You old fool, you blind fool,
Can't you plainly see
It's nothing but a milk cow
My mother gave to me?"

4 "I've traveled many thousand miles,
I'll travel many more,
But I never saw a milk cow
With a saddle on before."

5 "My own wife, my dear wife,
What can the matter be?
I find a hat a-hanging
Where my own hat ought to be."

6 "You old fool, you blind fool,
Can't you plainly see
It's nothing but a milk pail
My mother gave to me?"

7 "I've traveled many thousand miles,
I'll travel many more,
But I never saw a milk pail
With a handle (?) on before."

8 "My own wife, my dear wife,
What can the matter be?
I find a coat a-hanging
Where my own coat ought to be."

E

"Cairo Gal." Collected by Miss Juliet Fauntleroy. Sung by Mrs. James Sprouse, at Lawyers, Va. Campbell County. September 4, 1915. "Cairo Gal" is "'A Blackguard Song,' Mrs. Sprouse says" (Miss Fauntleroy).

1 "Wife, Oh wife,
How is this to be?
Another man's horse
Where mine ought to be."

2 "You old fool, Oh blind fool,
Blind and cannot see,
'T aint nothing but a milk cow
My mammy sent to me."

3 "I've been all round this wide, wide world,
A thousand miles or more,
I never seed a milk cow
With a saddle on before."

4 "Wife, Oh wife,
How is this to be?
Another man's boots
Where mine ought to be."

5 "You old fool, Oh blind fool,
Blind and can not see,
'T aint nothing but a churn
My mammy sent to me."

6 "I've been all round this wide, wide world,
A thousand miles or more,
But I never seed a churn
With heels on before."

F

"Home Comes the Good Old Man." Collected by Miss Juliet Fauntleroy. Sung by Mrs. F. P. Christian. Campbell County. July 26, 1914. Music only.

G

"Down Came the Old Man." Collected by Mrs. George D. McLaughlin, of Benicia, California. Sung by Mr. George D. McLaughlin, of Virginia. Rockbridge County. May 15, 1916. Music only.

APPENDIX

"A Jacobite Song." Collected by Miss Martha M. Davis, Contributed by Miss Winifred Patterson, of Garoway, West Virginia. Rockingham County. April 6, 1914. Miss Davis writes: "Her great grandfather was an officer in the British navy and learned this from the sailors. Miss Patterson was born in Canada." The Scottish dialect spelling suggests a printed source, but none is mentioned.

1 Hame cam oor gudeman at e'en,
an hame cam he,
And there he saw a saddled horse
where na horse shud be.
"And how is this and wha is this
and how cam this ta be?
How cam this horse here
wi oot the leave o' me?"

2 "A horse?" quoth she.
"Aye! a horse!" quoth he.
"A ye old blind dottard carl (*or* fool),
and blinder might ye be,
It's nothing but a milch coo
my mither sent to me."

3 "A milch coo?" quoth he.
"Aye! a milch coo!" quoth she.
"Ah, far hae I ridden and muckle
hae I seen
But a saddle on a milch coo saw
I never ane."

4 Hame cam oor gudeman at e'en,
an hame cam he,
And there he saw a pair of boots
where na boots shud be.
"And how is this and wha is this
and how cam this ta be?
And how cam tha boots here
wi oot the leave o' me?"

5 "Boots?" quoth she.
"Aye! boots!" quoth he.
"A ye old blind dottard carl,
and blinder might ye be,
It's but a pair of milk stoops
my mither sent to me."

6 "Milk stoops?" quoth he.
"Aye, milk stoops!" quoth she.
"Ah, far hae I ridden, and muckle
hae I seen,
But siller spurs on milk stoops saw
I never ane."

7 Hame cam oor gudeman at e'en,
and hame cam he,
And there he saw a siller sword
where na sword shud be.
"What's this now, gude wife, and
what's this I see?
And how cam tha sword here
wi oot the leave o' me?"

8 "A sword?" quoth she.
"Aye, a sword!" quoth he.
"A ye auld blind dottard carl,
and blinder might ye be,
It is but a porridge stick
my mither sent to me."

9 "A porridge stick?" quoth he.
"Aye! a porridge stick!" quoth she.
"Weel far hae I ridden and muckle
hae I seen,
But tassels upon porritch sticks saw
I never ane."

Stanzas about the hat come here.

10 Hame cam oor gudeman at e'en,
and hame cam he,
And there he saw a sturdy man
where na man shud be.
"And how's this now, gude wife,
and how cam this ta be?
And how cam this man here
wi oot the leave o' me!"

11 "Oh! woe's me! an woe's me!
It's but ma cousin Mackintosh
from the North Countree."
"We'd be all hanged and quartered, Kate,
wi oot the leave o' me."

44

GET UP AND BAR THE DOOR

(Child, No. 275)

Only six lines of this ballad, and they somewhat confused, have been found in Virginia, though the excellent West Virginia text, the only other trace of the ballad in American tradition, hails penultimately from Loudoun County, Virginia. The Virginia fragment belongs to the Child A version. The story of this version as summarized by Child, is this: "A housewife is boiling puddings anight; a cold wind blows in, and her husband bids her bar the door; she has her hands in her work and will not. They come to an agreement that whoever speaks first shall bar the door. Two belated travellers are guided to the house by the light which streams through the opening. They come in, and, getting no reply to their questions or response to their greetings, fall to eating and drinking what they find; the goodwife thinks much, but says naught. One of the strangers proposes to the other to take off the man's beard, and he himself will kiss the goodwife. Hot water is wanting (for scalding), suggests the second; but the boiling pudding-bree will serve, answers the first. The goodman calls out, Will ye kiss my wife and scald me? and having spoken the first word has to bar the door."

The first line of the Virginia fragment seems to have been influenced by the preceding ballad of "Our Goodman"; line 2 is Child A 10, line 2; line 3 is Child A 10, line 1; line 4 is Child A 11, line 2; lines 5 and 6 are Child A 10, lines 3 and 4. The Cox text agrees with Child B.

The fragment is Virginian by residence rather than by ancestry. The Mr. Robert Fleming who recited it to Mr. Stone learned the ballad in Scotland years ago, but as he had not repeated it for over fifty years, he could recall no more of it. This Scottish ancestry accounts for the dialect spelling.

The fragment was first announced in *Bulletin*, No. 9, p. 7. Add Cox, No. 185 (Combs, p. 147). No other American variant has been printed; but Jones has found the song in Michigan, and it sometimes occurs in American song-books. A burlesque version ("Get up and Shut the Door") may be found in *Delehanty and Hengler's Song and Dance Book* (copyright 1874), p. 169.

"Get up and Bar the Door." Collected by Mr. John Stone. Recited by Mr. Robert Fleming, of Norton, Va. Wise County. November 8, 1921.

1 Our guidman came hame at e'en,
   And an angry man was he.
. . . .
   . . . .

2 Up starts our guidman
And give three skips on the floor:
"Will ye kiss my wife before my face
And scuid me with puddin bra?" [1]

[1] The Child line is, "And scad me wi pudding-bree." The Virginia line might mean either "scald me with pudding broth" or "scald me with fine pudding." The former is probably the meaning. Either Mr. Fleming's Scottish accent has suffered from his American residence, or Mr. Stone's Scottish recording is uncertain.

45

THE WIFE WRAPT IN WETHER'S SKIN

(Child, No. 277)

A dozen texts and two melodies of this ballad have been recovered in Virginia, most of them under the usual American title of "Dandoo," the rest under the Child title, except for one called "Dindo-Dan." As the texts are all short and as they show considerable minor variation, especially in the character and position of the burden, all twelve items, varying in length from three to nine stanzas, are given here. All these variants would seem to belong to a single version, one which does not appear among the regular Child versions, though a somewhat similar text is printed in Child's final Additions and Corrections, V, 304. They belong rather to the usual American "Dandoo" version, variants of which have been printed by Belden, Campbell and Sharp, Cox, Pound, and others (see below). The Virginia texts follow the B rather than the A version of Miss Pound's *American Ballads and Songs*, No. 6.

The story told often in fragmentary form by the following texts is the usual one of an unruly wife reformed by a beating, responsibility for which the husband escapes by the technicality of wrapping his wife in a wether's skin and beating the skin. Child has pointed out that the story of the ballad is probably traditionally derived from the old tale of "The Wife Lapped in Morrel's Skin," Morrel being the husband's old horse flayed to assist at the wife-taming.

For American texts, see Belden, No. 12 (fragment); Brown, p. 9 (North Carolina); *Bulletin*, Nos. 4, 5, 7–10; Campbell and Sharp, No. 33 (Virginia, Kentucky; cf. Sharp, *Songs*, I, No. 6); Child V, 304 (Massachusetts from *The Journal of American Folk-Lore* VII, 253); Cox, No. 29; Hudson, No. 21 (and *Journal*, XXXIX, 109; Mississippi); *Journal*, VII, 253 (Newell, Massachusetts); XIX, 298 (Belden, Missouri); XXX, 328 (Kittredge, Missouri, fragment); Pound, *Ballads*, No. 6; Shearin and Combs, p. 8 (fragment). For additional references, see Cox, p. 159; *Journal*, XXX, 328.

A

"The Wife Wrapped in Wether's Skin." Collected by Mr. John Stone. Sung by Mr. George Hart, of Konnarock, Va. Washington County. November 8, 1921.

1 There was an old man and he lived in the west,
Clang-clish-a-ma-clingo,
He had him a wife that was none of the best,
Lam-berrum-king-derrum-mingo.

2 This old man went out to plow,
Clang-clish-a-ma-clingo,
With one eye open, t'other one shut,
Lam-berrum-king-derrum-mingo.

3 This old man came in from the plow,
Clang-clish-a-ma-clingo,
He says to his wife: "Is dinner ready now?"
Lam-berrum-king-derrum-mingo.

4 "There is a piece of bread all on the shelf;
If you want any better, you can get it yourself."

5 This old man went out to his sheep fold
And he killed him a wether both fat and old.

6 He hung it up upon a pin
And at two jerks he jerked off the skin.

7 He tacked the hide to his wife's back
And with two sticks he made it crack.

8 "I'll tell my daddy, and that you'll see,
How you have lambasted me."

9 "You can tell your daddy and all of your kin
How I dressed my wether's skin."

B

"Dindo-Dan." Contributed by Mrs. A. D. Stone, of Lexington, Va. First learned in Louisiana. Rockbridge County. October 26, 1915.

1 There was an old man lived in the west,
Dindo-Dan,
Who married the wife he loved the best,
Clara ma clish shango clingo,
There was an old man lived in the west
Who married the wife he loved the best.
With a larro, cle marro, clearreo don clingo.

2 This good old man came home from plow,
Says, "Wife, is my supper ready now?"

3 "I am not your dog, I am not your slave."
This was the answer his wife gave.

4 This good old man to his sheepfold went
And took a skin on two sticks bent.

5 He put the skin on his wife's back,
And with two sticks he did whick whack (*clapping the hands*).

6 "I will tell my father and brothers three (*sobbing*)
That with two sticks you did beat me."

7 "You may tell your father and all your kin
That I did beat my mutton skin."

C

"The Wife Wrapt in Wether's Skin." Collected by Mr. Cecil J. Sharp and Miss Karpeles. Sung by Mrs. Puss Smith at Charlottesville, Va. Albemarle County. September 25, 1916. Cf. Campbell and Sharp, No. 33, A. The first stanza there printed is taken from this (Mrs. Smith's) variant. The rest comes from Mr. Chisholm (Virginia D). The two are very close together, however.

1 There was an old man he had a wife,
Dandoo, dandoo,
There was an old man he had a wife,
Cling a ma clang a ma clearo,
There was an old man he had a wife,
And she plagued him of his life.
To my kum lam slam dam,
Clearey O Jimmy go.

2 When this old man came in from his plough,
Says: "Old woman, is my supper ready now?"

3 She says, "There's a piece of meat and bread upon the shelf.
If that don't do, go and cook it yourself."

4 This old man went out to his sheep-pen,
And soon had off an old wether's skin.

5 He placed it on his old wife's back,
And with two sticks went whickety whack.

6 "I'll tell your daddy and mammy and all your kin
How I tanned my wether's skin."

D

"The Wife Wrapt in Wether's Skin." Collected by Mr. Cecil J. Sharp and Miss Karpeles. Sung by Mr. N. B. Chisholm, at Woodridge, Va. Albemarle County. September 21, 1916. With music. Cf. Campbell and Sharp, No. 33, A. The first stanza of the song there printed was obtained not from Mr. N. B. Chisholm but from Mrs. Puss Smith, at Charlottesville, Va. (see Virginia C). In other words, Mr. Sharp has combined the texts of two singers in his printed version.

1 When this old man came in from his plough,
Dandoo, dandoo,
When this old man came in from his plough,
Cling a ma clang a ma clearo,
When this old man came in from plough,
Says: "Have you got my breakfast now?"
To my kum lam, slam, dam,
Clearey O Jimmy go.

2 She says: "There's a piece of bread upon the shelf,
If that don't do go bake it yourself."

3 This old man went out to his sheep-pen,
And soon had off an old wether's skin.

4 He placed it on his old wife's back,
And with two sticks went wickety-wack.

5 "I'll tell your daddy and mammy and all your kin
How you tanned your wether's skin."

E

"Dandoo." Collected by Mr. John Stone. Sung by Mrs. Martha C. Throckmorton, of Bluemont, Va. Loudoun County. September 23, 1922.

1 There was an old man lived in the west,
Dandoo, dandoo,
There was an old man lived in the west,
Clish-clash-a-ma-clingo,
There was an old man lived in the west,
He married a wife that was none of the best.
Lie-claro-cling-the-baro-cling-clash-and-ma-clingo.

2 The old man he went out to plow
And he said, "Is my breakfast ready now?"

3 "There's a piece of cold bread upon the shelf,
And if that's not enough, you can bake it yourself."

4 The old man went out into the fold,
He caught a wether that was tough and old.

5 He laid the skin upon her back
And with a stick he made it whack.

6 "Go tell your mother and all your kin
I tanned your back with a wether's skin."

F

"The Wife Wrapt in Wether's Skin." Collected by Mr. John Stone. Recited by Mr. J. K. Mathews, of Bentonville, Va. Warren County. September 23, 1922.

1 There was an old man lived in the west,
Dandoo,
There was an old man lived in the west,
Dandoo,
There was an old man lived in the west,
He married a wife that was none of the best.
Come-clish-e-ma-clash-i-ma-clingo.

IN THE BALLAD COUNTRY OF VIRGINIA

2 This little old man went out to plow;
He came in and says, "Is my dinner ready now?"

3 "There's a piece of cold cheese on the shelf;
If you want any more, you can get it yourself."

4 He wrapped a sheepskin around her back;
He got him some switches and made them go whickety-whack.

5 "I'll tell my brothers and sisters three
How you have been treating me."

6 "You can tell your brothers and all your kin
How I beat my old sheepskin."

G

"Dandoo." Contributed by Miss Ellen Dana Conway (teacher of history in the High School), of Pocahontas, Va. Spottsylvania County. October 28, 1915.

Miss Conway's accompanying letter is a good illustration of the spirit in which ballads were sent in, especially by the teachers of the state: "While reading the current issue of the Journal of Education this evening, I saw your plea for information concerning certain ballads. Among them I noticed one entitled 'The Wife Wrapped in Wether's Skin' and I saw that it was also called 'Dandee' [misprint for 'Dandoo']. There is an absurd old song called 'Dandoo' which as a child I often heard sung in my native county of Spottsylvania, that may perhaps be a much mangled version of the ballad you mention. There is a very slight vague suggestion of likeness in the names and in the story related in each. This resemblance is, however, so problematical as to recall the case of the student who said he was sure the name Middletown was derived from Moses, and when asked how he derived it, said he did so by 'eliminating oses and adding iddletown.' The cases are quite similar.

"I never saw the song in print, of course, and remember only a fragment of it, together with the fact that it had a very monotonous air and was warranted to put the crossest baby to sleep in ten minutes — a measure of self-defence on the child's part, no doubt.

"Under the circumstances, I wouldn't have risked wasting your time in sending the thing, except for your statement that 'any fragment of one of these ballads will be a veritable treasure trove to the Virginia Folk-Lore Society.' Far be it from a mere history teacher like me to lose any chance of presenting these good folks with a treasure trove! I am therefore sending you on a separate sheet what will no doubt prove to be a perfectly useless version of a singularly idiotic old song. If so, pray excuse me, for as my laundress says, 'I means well.'"

1 There was an old man who lived in the west,
He had a wife, she was none of the best.
Dandoo! Dandoo!

2 When this old man came in from the plow,
"Pray, wife, is supper ready now?"
Dandoo! Dandoo!

3 "There's a piece of bread upon the shelf;
If you want any more you may cook it yourself."
Dandoo! Dandoo!

4 He laid a switch on his wife's back,
And make it go ty-whick-e-ty-whack.
Dandoo! Dandoo!

5 "I'll tell mother and father and brothers three
What a terrible whipping you gave me."
Dandoo! Dandoo!

H

"The Wife Wrapped in Wether's Skin." Collected by Mr. John Stone. Sung by Mrs. Oscar Plummer, of Park, Va. Grayson County. November 8, 1921.

1 The old man come in from the plow:
"Wife, I'm ready for my breakfast now."

Tu-ma-ri-do-link-a-dink-tum,
Tu-ma-ri-do-link-a-dink-dum-dandy.

2 "Piece of cornbread on the shelf;
If you get any more, you'll cook it yourself."

3 Two fat muttons in one pen,
And the hide he jerked off of one of them.

4 He stretched that hide across her back,
And a great big stick for to make it crack.

5 "Go send for your daddy and all of your kin;
I'll show him how to tan my mutton skin."

I

"Dandoo." Contributed by Miss G. B. Grinnan, of University, Va. Gloucester County. August 12, 1916.

1 There was an old man lived in the west,
Dandoo, dandoo,
There was an old man lived in the west,
Clishime, clasheme, clingo,
There was an old man lived in the west,
He had a wife, she was none of the best.
Curiorum, dingdorum, clingo.

2 He asked his wife for something to eat,
A piece of bread or a piece of meat.
"There's a piece of bread upon the shelf,"
Dandoo, dandoo,
"There's a piece of bread upon the shelf;
If you want any more you must get it yourself."
Curiorum, dingdorum, clingo.

3 He killed a mutton very fat,
Dandoo, dandoo,
And swore she should have none of that,
Clishime, clasheme, clingo.
He tied the skin upon her back,
Dandoo, dandoo,
Then two sticks went whichity-whack.
Curiorum, dingdorum, clingo.

J

"Wife Wrapped in Wether's Skin" or "Dandoo." Collected by Mr. John Stone. Sung by Mr. and Mrs. J. A. Mitchell, of Brightwood, Va. Madison County. August 2, 1920. With music.

1 A little old man lived in the West,
Dandoo,
A little old man lived in the West,
Meclimeclash-to-meclingo,
A little old man lived in the West,
He married a girl and none of the best.
Lam-squire-beri-mire-mecory-mecory-
mingto-meclimeclash-to-meclingo.

2 Little old man went out to the field to plow,
Dandoo,
Little old man went out to the field to plow,
Meclimeclash-to-meclingo,
Little old man went out to the field to plow,
And he came to the house: "Is my breakfast ready now?"
Lam-squire-beri-mire-mecory-mecory-
mingto-meclimeclash-to-meclingo.

3 "There's a little piece of bread and meat on the shelf,"
Dandoo,
"There's a little piece of bread and meat on the shelf,"
Meclimeclash-to-meclingo.
"There's a little piece of bread and meat on the shelf;
If you want any more just get it yourself."
Lam-squire-beri-mire-mecory-mecory-
mingto-meclimeclash-to-meclingo.

K

"Dandoo." Collected by Mr. John Stone. Sung by Bob Lawson (Colored). Albemarle County. November 3, 1920. Bob "learned it, when a boy, from an old white man" (Mr. Stone).

1 Dandoo, dandoo. Clish, miclosh, miclingo.
Old man went out to plow,
Came back, says, "Is my breakfast ready now?"

2 Dandoo, dandoo. Clish, miclosh, miclingo.
"There's a little piece of bread and meat on the shelf.
Want any more, go bake it yourself."

3 Dandoo, dandoo. Clish, miclosh, miclingo.
Old man went out and got a bundle of switches,
Came back and went whickety whack on the old woman's back.

L

"Wife Wrapt in a Wether's Skin." Collected by Miss Alfreda M. Peel. Sung by Miss Joe Neighbors, of Salem, Va., Roanoke County, August 10, 1919.

1 He beat her hard upon her back,
With two sticks played whickety-whack.

2 "I tell my father and my brothers two
Of this wicked thing you do."

3 "Tell your father and all your kin;
I've only whipped my old wether's skin."

46

THE FARMER'S CURST WIFE

(Child, No. 278)

The ballad is represented by fifteen texts and six tunes in the Virginia archives. Of these, thirteen texts and all six tunes are here printed. Most of the Virginia texts show a likeness to the Child A version, but some exhibit features found only in Child B. It is clear that both versions are represented, with many interesting variations, not least in the philosophical stanza or stanzas at the end. The tripping tunes, some of them with a whistled burden, fit perfectly the comic story of the ballad, which is thus summarized by Child: "The devil comes for a farmer's wife and is made welcome to her by the husband. The woman proves to be no more controllable in hell than she had been at home; she kicks the imps about, and even brains a set of them with her pattens or a maul. For safety's sake, the devil is constrained to take her back to her husband." The moral of the tale is often pointed. "The Old Man under the Hill" seems to be the only unusual Virginia title; it is not, of course, the usual song of that name, though the title of that song may have been appropriated.

The material here given more than doubles the American store of this ballad. Other American references are Barry, No. 28; Belden, No. 13 (fragment); *Bulletin*, Nos.4–6, 8–10; Campbell and Sharp, No. 34 (North Carolina, Virginia); Cox, No. 30; *Journal*, xix, 298 (Belden, Missouri); xxiv, 348 (Barry, Massachusetts, fragment, Maine); xxvii, 68 (Barry, Massachusetts); xxx, 329 (Kittredge, Missouri, fragments); Mackenzie, *Ballads*, No. 15; Sharp, *Songs*, ii, No. 3 (Kentucky). For additional references, see Cox, p. 164; *Journal*, xxx, 329.

A

"The Farmer's Curst Wife." Collected by Mr. John Stone. Sung by Mr. C. A. Sours, of Bentonville, Va. Warren County. September 23, 1922.

1 There was an old man, he had a farm,
  Sing fol-e-rol-dolli-sing-fol-e-rol-da,
  Sing fol-e-rol-dolli-sing-fol-e-rol-da.
He had no oxen to carry it on,
  Sing fol-e-rol-dolli-sing-fol-e-rol-da,
  Sing fol-e-rol-dolli-sing-fol-e-rol-da.

2 He hooked up his pig and began to plow;
He seen the old devil coming over the brow.

3 "And now, old devil, I'll have you undone;
For I believe you're after my oldest son."

4 "It's not your oldest son I crave,
But it's your scolding wife I am determined."

5 "O take her on with all your heart!
Be sure that you and her don't part."

6 He picked her up all on his back,
And away to hell clickety-clack.

7 He took her to the devil's door;
He threw her sprawling in the floor.

8 One little devil came running with a chain;
She up with her foot and kicked out his brains.

9 One little devil called her a liar;
She up with her foot, kicked nine in the fire.

10 One little devil peeped over the wall,
Cried, "Take her away, daddy, she'll murder us all."

11 He picked her up all on his back,
And away he went a-lugging her back.

12 Seven years going, seven years coming,
She called for the pie she left in the oven.

13 That's where the women got the advantage of the men:
They can go to hell and get back again.

B

"The Farmer's Curst Wife." Collected by Miss Juliet Fauntleroy. Sung by Mr. Beaver Arthur, near Lynch Station, Va. Pittsylvania County. November 26, 1915. Miss Fauntleroy writes: "Mr. Arthur said he learned this ballad in 1876 from Mack Witt, the son of a blacksmith in Pittsylvania County, Va." She adds: "Mrs. Creasy also sang for me 'The Farmer's Curst Wife.' Her version was just like Mr. Beaver Arthur's except for the last verse, which resembles one in Mrs. Sprouse's version. Here it is: —

All young men take warning and heed,
For an old wife is the very last thing you need."

1 There was an old farmer in London did dwell,
Oh me, sing tu le la lu,
He had an old wife, not wishing her well,
Tu le la, lu le la, lu.

2 The devil he came to his plow one day,
Saying, "One of your family I'll carry away."

3 "Well, you can have my oldest son,
If that don't do, take two for one."

4 "Well, 't aint your oldest son I crave,
It's your old wife I'll carry away."

5 "Well, take her, dear devil, with all my heart,
Hoping to God you'll never more part."

6 He gathered ("gethered") her up into his old sack,
'T was first ("fust") on his shoulder and then on his back.

7 When he got to the iron gate,
She fell out the old sack and skun her old face.

8 There ("Thar") came three devils with balls and chains,
She hauled off her fetters ("flatters") and slapt out their brains.

9 A court together the devil did call:
"If ("Ef") she stays here much longer she'll conquer us all."

10 He gathered ("gethered") her up into his old sack,
And like an old fool he went waggin' her back.

11 While traveling along through showers of rain,
Says ("Sez") he, "Here's your old wife I've brought back again."

12 "Well," says the old farmer, "I was born for a cuss;
I sent my wife to the devil, and he brought her back wuss."

C

"The Farmer's Curst Wife." Collected by Mr. John Stone. Sung by Mr. Charles Vest. Louisa County. September 13, 1917. With music. Mr. Vest "is an old Mosby man and heard this ballad while in the army. I heard him sing it fifteen years ago and have never forgotten the song itself though I could think of neither the tune nor the words. Last week I went over to Louisa and got him to sing it for me. He had forgotten it, but recalled it" (Mr. Stone).

1 There was an old farmer and he had a little farm. (*Whistle*)
He had no horses to carry it on.
Sing fol-de-rol-dol-de-rol-di-do.

2 He hitched his oxen (up) to the plow; (*Whistle*)
Mr. Devil come along a-crossing his brow.
Sing fol-de-rol-dol-de-rol-di-do.

3 "Now, Mr. Devil, what is it you crave?" (*Whistle*)
"Your derned old scolding wife I'll have."
Sing fol-de-rol-dol-de-rol-di-do.

4 "Now, Mr. Devil, I'll tell you apart, (*Whistle*)
You can take her will all my heart."
Sing fol-de-rol-dol-de-rol-di-do.

5 He threw her over across his back (*Whistle*)
And off he went a-clickety-clack.
Sing fol-de-rol-dol-de-rol-di-do.

6 When he got her to his door, (*Whistle*)
He threw her sprawling on the floor.
Sing fol-de-rol-dol-de-rol-di-do.

7 One little devil came dragging a chain. (*Whistle*)
She up with her foot and kicked out his brains.
Sing fol-de-rol-dol-de-rol-di-do.

8 One little devil says, "Take her up higher." (*Whistle*)
She up with her foot and kicked him in the fire.
Sing fol-de-rol-dol-de-rol-di-do.

9 One little devil peeped over the wall: (*Whistle*)
"Take her back, pap, she'll kill us all."
Sing fol-de-rol-dol-de-rol-di-do.

10 So the devil he bundled her up in a sack, (*Whistle*)
And like an old fool came lugging her back.
Sing fol-de-rol-dol-de-rol-di-do.

11 Now what will become of the women? (*Whistle*)
Won't have them in hell and they can't get to heaven.
Sing fol-de-rol-dol-de-rol-di-do.

D

"The Farmer's Curst Wife." Collected by Professor D. R. Carpenter and Mr. John Stone. Sung by Mrs. J. A. Mitchell and others, near Brightwood, Va. Madison County. August 2, 1920. Mr. Stone writes: "Her daughters, Miss Mary Mitchell and Mrs. Holland Hoffman, also sang the ballad. Prof. D. R. Carpenter, of Salem College, who lives near Brightwood, Va., spent the whole of that day driving me about in his car to meet prospective ballad singers. We spent a large part of the day at Mr. Mitchell's. Mr. Mitchell, Mrs. Mitchell, and their two grown daughters, all sang for us. From them we got two complete ballads, three fragments, and four tunes."

1 Once there was a man, he bought him a farm, (*Whistle*)
He had no oxen to carry it on. (*Whistle*)

2 He hitched up his pig and began to plow,
Old Mr. Devil passed over the brow.

3 "Old Mr. Devil, I'll have you undone,
For you are after my oldest son."

4 "It's not your oldest son I crave;
It's your damned old scolding wife I'll have."

5 He took her up all on his back
. . . .

6 When he got to the devil's great door,
He throwed her sprawling into the floor.

7 One little devil came bringing a chain;
She up with her foot and kicked out his brains.

8 One little devil says, "Take her up higher."
She up with her foot and kicked him in the fire.

9 One little devil peeped over the wall;
"Carry her back, daddy, she'll murder us all."

10 He took her up all on his back,
And like a damned fool came lugging her back.

11 Gentlemen, a woman can do more than a man:
Into hell and safe back to land.

E

"The Farmer's Curst Wife." Collected by Mr. Cecil J. Sharp and Miss Karpeles. Sung by Mr. N. B. Chisholm, at Woodridge, Va. Albemarle County. September 21, 1916. With music. Printed by Campbell and Sharp, p. 140.

1 There was an old man lived under the hill,
Sing tiro rattle-ing day,
If he ain't moved away he's living there still,
Sing tiro rattle-ing day.

2 This old man went out to his plough
To see the old devil fly over his mow.

3 The old man cries out: "I am undone,
For the devil has come for my oldest son."

4 "It's not your oldest son I want,
But your damned old scolding wife I'll have."

5 He took the old woman upon his back,
And off he went with her packed in a sack.

6 He packed her back in one corner of hell,
Saying: "I hope the old devil will use you well."

7 Twelve little devils came walking by,
Then she up with her foot and kicked eleven in the fire.

8 The odd little devil peeped over the wall,
Saying: "Take her back, daddy, or she will kill us all."

9 She was six months going and eight coming back,
And she called for the mush she left in the pot.

10 The old man lay sick in the bed.
With an old pewter pipe she battered his head.

11 The old man cries out: "I am to be cursed;
She has been to hell and come back worse."

F

"The Farmer's Curst Wife." Collected by Mr. John Stone. Sung by Mr. T. C. Commins, of Rumford, Va. King William County. September 13, 1917. With music.

1 There was an old farmer who in Gloucester did dwell, (*Whistle*)
He had an old wife whom he wished was in hell.
Sing Tol-le-rol-dol,
Sing Tol-le-rol-diddle-dee-dee.

2 The devil he made his appearance one day, (*Whistle*)
And said, "One of your family I must take away."
Sing Tol-le-rol-dol,
Sing Tol-le-rol-diddle-dee-dee.

3 "Then you may take my oldest son, (*Whistle*)
If he won't do, take two for one."
Sing Tol-le-rol-dol,
Sing Tol-le-rol-diddle-dee-dee.

4 "Your oldest son I do not crave, (*Whistle*)
But your old wife I must have."
Sing Tol-le-rol-dol,
Sing Tol-le-rol-diddle-dee-dee.

5 He packed her up in a sack, (*Whistle*)
And slung the sack across his back.
Sing Tol-le-rol-dol,
Sing Tol-le-rol-diddle-dee-dee.

6 When he arrived at hell's gate, (*Whistle*)
He chucked her in and she fell on her pate.
Sing Tol-le-rol-dol,
Sing Tol-le-rol-diddle-dee-dee.

7 She spied two little devils fettered with chains, (*Whistle*)
She took up their fetters and knocked out their brains.
Sing Tol-le-rol-dol,
Sing Tol-le-rol-diddle-dee-dee.

8 Three little devils sitting on the wall, (*Whistle*)
Cried, "Father, take her back or she'll murder us all."
Sing Tol-le-rol-dol,
Sing Tol-le-rol-diddle-dee-dee.

9 So he rammed her back into the sack, (*Whistle*)
And like an old fool came trudging her back.
Sing Tol-le-rol-dol,
Sing Tol-le-rol-diddle-dee-dee.

10 This proves that the women are worse than the men, (*Whistle*)
For when sent to hell they come back again.
Sing Tol-le-rol-dol,
Sing Tol-le-rol-diddle-dee-dee.

G

"The Farmer's Curst Wife." Collected by Mr. John Stone. Sung by Miss Bertha Mayo, of Wilmington, Va. Fluvanna County. November 3, 1920. "She learned it from her father" (Mr. Stone).

1 There was an old man in Yorkshire dell,
He had three sons and he wished them not well.
Sing Ta-la-la-la.

2 The devil appeared to him one day:
"There is one of your family I must take away."
Sing Ta-la-la-la.

3 "You can take my oldest son;
If he won't do, take two for one."

4 "It's not your oldest son I crave;
It's your wife I must have."

5 "You can take her with all my heart;
I think you and her will never part."

6 The old devil he packed her in a sack,
Soon found himself at the old home gate;
He dumped the old critter off on her feet.

7 Three devils they met with a ball and chain;
She up with a club and beat out their brains.

8 "Now a jury we must call;
If we don't return her, she'll murder us all."

9 The old devil then he packed her up in a sack,
First on shoulder, then on back,
Just like an old fool come wagging her back.

10 This shows that the women are worse than the men:
Been to the devil and brought her back again.

H

"The Farmer's Curst Wife." Collected by Miss Juliet Fauntleroy. Sung by Mrs. James Sprouse, of Lawyers, Va. Learned from her cousin, Fletcher Gill. Campbell County. September 4, 1915. With music.

1 Up came the devil to the farmer one day,
Oh me, sing tu le la, lu,
Said, "One of your family I mean to take away,"
Sing tu le la, lu le la, lu.

2 "Well, you may have my oldest son,"
Oh me, sing tu le la, lu,
"If that won't do, take two to one,"
Sing tu le la, lu le la, lu.

3 "It is n't your oldest son I want,"
Oh me, sing tu le la, lu,
"It's your old wife I'm going to take away,"
Sing tu le la, lu le la, lu.

4 So up came the devil with his ball and his chain,
Oh me, sing tu le la, lu,
She up with a shoe and she smacked out his brain,
Sing tu le la, lu le la, lu.

5 Up popped seven little devils with their heads over the wall,
Oh me, sing tu le la, lu,
"Take her on back, don't she'll conquer us all,"
Sing tu le la, lu le la, lu.

6 So he gathered her up in his old sack,
Oh me, sing tu le la, lu,
Away he went, a-wagging her back,
Sing tu le la, lu le la, lu.

7 Young men, young men, take warning from this,
Oh me, sing tu le la, lu,
Let get you a wife be the last thing you do,
Sing tu le la, lu le la, lu.

8 Let get you a wife be the last thing you do,
Oh me, sing tu le la, lu,
For if you give them to the devil, he'll bring them back again,
Sing tu le la, lu le la, lu.

I

"The Farmer's Curst Wife." Collected by Mr. John Stone. Sung by Mr. C. F. Carpenter and brother, of Bolar, Va. Highland County. November 3, 1920. With music. Mr. Stone writes: "In this song I have pieced together two fragments given to me by Mr. C. F. Carpenter and his brother, both from Bolar, Highland County, Va. Both fragments had practically the same tune."

1 There was an old man when he was first born,
Old Marindy Marowly,
He had no horses to plow up his corn,
With his left leg, right leg, over leg, under leg,
Old Marindy Marowly.

2 He called up his pigs and he yoked up his sows
And plowed up his corn the devil knows how.

3 The old woman came home in a powerful fright;
Says she, "I saw the devil this night."

4 He packed her up upon his back
Just like a brave pedlar carrying his pack.

5 He carried her up just to the door,
Give her a kick, saying, "Go in at that door."

6 He (She?) saw little Rufus all bowing in chains
And he(?) up with his foot and kicked out his brains.

7 The children raised a powerful squall;
Said, "Take her away, he'll (?) kill us all."

J

"The Old Man under the Hill." Reported by Miss Martha M. Davis. Contributed by Mrs. J. C. Byrd, of Harrisonburg, Va., Rockingham County. April 1, 1915. Mrs. Byrd "learned it from a young girl, she thinks, in Page County, about thirty years ago" (Miss Davis).

1 There was an old man lived under the hill,
Tra-la-la-le-la-le,
And if he's not dead, he's living there still,
Tra-la-la-le-la-le.

2 His wife she would not say her prayers,
So he picked her up and threw her down stairs.

3 The devil came in while saying his prayers;
He said, "Come along and go with me."

4 He took her up on his old back,
Just like a pedlar shouldering his pack.

5 He took her up to his old gate,
And said, "Get you in there, you old bald pate."

6 And when they found what he had there,
They said, "Take her out, dad, she'll kill us all here."

7 This shows that women are worse than men,
For they go to hell and are kicked out again.

K

"The Farmer's Curst Wife." Collected by Mr. John Stone. Recited by Mrs. Caroline Littlepage Cook Moseley, of Drewry's Bluff, Va. Chesterfield County. June 29, 1921. "She heard her mother sing it years ago" (Mr. Stone).

1 There was an old farmer in Yorkshire did dwell,
Ha, ha, ha, ha.
He had a sweet wife and he wished her in hell,
Sing fol-de-rol-fol-de-rol-fol-de-rol-de-re.

2 One day the devil appeared at his plow:
"You have a sweet wife and you wished her in hell."

3 "Take my oldest son;
If that won't do, take two for one."

4 "It's not your oldest son I crave;
It's your sweet wife and she I must have."

5 So the devil he put her in a sack
And flung her across his back.

6 When she saw young devils in chains,
She picked up her fetters and knocked out their brains.

7 It shows that women are worse than the men.
When they are sent there, they are sent back again.

L

"The Farmer's Curst Wife." Collected by Mr. John Stone. Sung by Mrs. Weathers, of Rumford, Va. King William County. September 13, 1917. With music. "Mrs. Weathers heard Mr. Caperton Braxton sing this ballad when they were school children" (Mr. Stone).

1 There was an old farmer in Yorkshire dell, (*Whistle*)
He had an old wife and he wished her in — well . . . .

Sing fol-de-rol-rol,
Sing fol-de-rol-rol,
Sing fol-de-rol-rol-rol-ray.

2 So when he arrived at old hell's gate,
He pitched the old woman upon her pate.

3 She saw two devils bound in chains,
She took up their fetters and beat out their brains.

4 Two little imps climbed upon the wall,
Crying, "Take her away or she'll kill us all."

5 So the devil he bundled her up in a sack,
And like an old fool came lugging her back.

6 This proves that women are worse than men,
She was carried to hell and brought back again.

M

"The Farmer's Curst Wife." Collected by Mr. John Stone. Sung by Miss Emma Carpenter. Madison County. November 3, 1920. With music.

1 There was an old farmer and he had a little farm,
Lily-fa-le-lily-fa-la.
He had no horses to plow up his ground,
Lily-fa-lily-fa-la-re-do.

2 He hitched up his hogs and set them to plow,
And how he did plow the devil knows how.

3 The devil he took her up on his back
And away he went a-whickety-whack.

4 The little devils run all over the wall,
Say, "Carry her back, daddy, she'll conquer us all."

47

THE SWEET TRINITY (THE GOLDEN VANITY)

(Child, No. 286)

One complete text, A, and five more or less fragmentary ones, with one tune, have been found in Virginia. The titles are "The Lowlands Low," "The Green Willow Tree," "The Golden Vanity," "The Turkey-rogherlee and the Yellow Golden Tree," and "Sailing in the Lowlands Low." All the Virginia items are printed here. They are all closely related to the Child C version, as shown especially by the final death of the cabin-boy, either from exhaustion in the sea, as in A, or on deck, as in B. But there are verbal suggestions of other versions; for instance, stanza 1 of the Virginia E fragment suggests Child B 9. Several Virginia texts of a later "Lowlands Low" song, also known in Virginia as "Young Edmund," which belong to the English song of "Young Edwin in the Lowlands Low" have of course been excluded as out of place here. The story of the ballad is given with fair completeness in Virginia A.

For Americans texts, see Barry, No. 1; Belden, No. 78; Brown, p. 9 (North Carolina); *Bulletin*, Nos. 3, 4, 8–10; Campbell and Sharp, No. 35 (North Carolina); Colcord, p. 79; Cox, No. 32; Hudson, No. 22 (Mississippi); *Journal*, xviii, 125 (Barry, Vermont, two texts with two melodies); xxiii, 429 (Belden, Missouri); xxx, 331 (Kittredge, Missouri); McGill, p. 97; Pound, *Ballads*, No. 10; Shearin, p. 4; Shearin and Combs, p. 9 (fragment); Shoemaker, p. 126; Wyman and Brockway, p. 72. For additional references, see Cox, p. 169; *Journal*, xxx, 330.

A

"The Green Willow Tree." Collected by Miss Eunice Harris, of the Farmville Ballad Club. From Mrs. J. S. Harris, of Prospect, Va. Sung by Mrs. Goodwin. Prince Edward County. March 23, 1914. Printed in *The Focus* for April, 1914, p. 158.

1 There was a ship that sailed from South America
Known by the name of *The Green Willow Tree*,
As she sailed in the lowlands, lowlands, lowey,
As she sailed in the lowlands low.

2 Short time had she been sailing, dauntless and free,
When there hove in sight a Turkish robery,
As she sailed in the lowlands, lowlands, lowey,
As she sailed in the lowlands low.

3 Up steps the captain, saying, "What shall we do?
Yonder is a Turkish robery;
She will sink us in the lowlands, lowlands, lowey,
Sink us in the lowlands low."

4 Forward there came out the captain's boy,
Saying, "What will you give to me
If I sink them in the lowlands, lowey,
Sink them in the lowlands low?"

5 "I will give you gold and then set you free,
Besides my youngest daughter your wedded wife to be,
If you will sink them in the lowlands, lowey,
Sink them in the lowlands low."

6 At once he took the task and away swam he,
And soon reached the Turkish robery,
Where they had anchored in the lowlands, lowey,
Anchored in the lowlands low.

7 He had a little instrument just fitted for use,
With which he cut some gashes and let in a sluice,
As they lay at anchor in the lowlands, lowey,
At anchor in the lowlands low.

8 Some with their hats and some with their caps
All tried their best to stop the water gaps,
As they were sinking in the lowlands, lowey,
Sinking in the lowlands low.

9 His task being accomplished, back swam he,
And soon regained *The Green Willow Tree*,
Where she was sailing in the lowlands, lowey,
Sailing in the lowlands low.

10 He hailed the Captain, "Will you keep your word?
Will you lay to and take me on board?
Or will you sink me in the lowlands, lowey,
Sink me in the lowlands low?"

11 "No, I will not be as good as my word,
I will not lay to and take you on board,
But I will sink you in the lowlands, lowey,
Sink you in the lowlands low."

12 "If it were not for the guards you have on board,
I'd leave you just the same, I would upon my word,
I would sink you in the lowlands, lowey,
Sink you in the lowlands low."

13 His appeals were useless and away swam he,
Bidding adieu to *The Green Willow Tree*,
As he was sinking in the lowlands, lowey,
Sinking in the lowlands low.

B

"The Golden Vanity," Collected by Mr. John Stone. Sung by Mr. J. A. Wyatt. King William County. September 11, 1922.

1 There was a ship and she sailed across the sea,
And they called her *The Golden Banneree.*
First on deck there was a cabin boy:
"Captain, what'll you give me for the ship if I'll destroy,
If I sink her in the lowland sea?"

2 "I'll give you gold and silver," the captain he replied,
"And all the more I'll give you my daughter for your bride,
If you'll sink her in the lowland sea."

3 The boy grabbed the anchor and overboard he went;
The boy began to bow [1] and the ship began to sink,
And he sank her in the lowland sea.

4 The boy swam around to the other side:
"O captain, pull me in, for I'm drowning in the tide."
"I won't pull you in," the captain he replied,
"I'll never do, indeed, for my daughter to be your bride."

5 "I'll cut you and I'll shoot you and I'll drown you in the tide,
And I'll bury you in the lowland sea."

6 The boy swam around to the other side:
"Mate, pull me in, for I'm drowning in the tide."
The mate pulled him in, and on deck he died.

7 They wrapped and they wound him so very neat and wide
And they buried him in the lowland sea.[2]

C

"The Lowlands Low." Collected by Mr. John Stone. Sung by Mrs. Oscar Plummer, of Park, Va. Grayson County. November 8, 1921.

1 "O captain, O captain, and what'll you give me
If I will destroy the Boat-O-Robberee?"
"I'll give you gold and I'll give you fee
And my oldest daughter, and married you shall be,
If you'll sink her in the lonesomes lowlands low,
If you'll sink her in the lonesomes lowlands low."

[1] Evidently for *bore*, which the singer pronounced *bo'*.

[2] The stanza divisions are here given as indicated and numbered in the original manuscript, though they are open to some question.

2 He swam on his belly and he swam on his back
Until he came to the Boat-O-Robber's deck.
Him a-having the instruments suitable for the use,
Cut a hole in the bottom and let in the juice,
And he sunk her in the lonesomes lowlands low,
And he sunk her in the lonesomes lowlands low.

3 He swam upon his belly and he swam upon his back
Until he came to his own boater's deck.
"Captain, O captain, be as good as your word,
Captain, O captain, be as good as your word,
For I've sunk her in the lonesomes lowlands low,
For I've sunk her in the lonesomes lowlands low."

4 "I'll neither give you gold nor neither give you fee,
Nor my oldest daughter, nor married you shan't be,
If you've sunk her in the lonesomes lowlands low,
If you've sunk her in the lonesomes lowlands low."

5 "If it was n't for the honor that I have for your men,
I'd just serve you as I've just served them;
I'd sink you in the lonesomes lowlands low,
I'd sink you in the lonesomes lowlands low."

D

"The Turkey-rogher lee and the Yellow Golden Tree" or "Lowlands Low." Collected by Professor Carpenter and Mr. John Stone. Sung by Mrs. J. A. Mitchell. Madison County. November 3, 1920. With music. "Mrs. Mitchell's daughters, Miss Mary Mitchell and Mrs. Holland Hoffman, also joined in the singing of this ballad. Mrs. Mitchell got it about fifty years ago from Mrs. Sally Yowell, who, I think, was Mrs. Mitchell's grandmother" (Mr. Stone).

1 "I'll give you gold and I'll give you fee,
    Sing o'er the lowlands O,
I'll give you gold and I'll give you fee,
And my oldest daughter your wedded wife shall be,
If you'll sink her in the lowlands, so lowly and so low,
If you sink her in the lowlands, O so low."

2 "I won't give you gold and I won't give you fee,
    Sing o'er the lowlands O,
I won't give you gold and I won't give you fee,
And my oldest daughter your wedded wife shan't be,
O you've sunk her in the lowlands, so lowly and so low,
O you've sunk her in the lowlands, O so low."

3 "If it was n't for the ship and it was n't for the men,
Sing o'er the lowlands O,
If it was n't for the ship and it was n't for the men,
I'd serve you as I've just served them,
I'd sink her in the lowlands, so lowly and so low,
I'd sink her in the lowlands, O so low."

E

"Lowlands Low." Collected by Miss Corita G. Seoane. Sung by Miss Webster, of Merrifield, Va. Fairfax County. February 11, 1914.

1 Some with their hats, and some with their caps,
Are trying for to stop those water-erie gaps,
As they're sailing in the lowlands, lonesome low,
As they're sailing in the lowlands low.

2 Then he turned on his back, and down sank he,
And he bade farewell to the low country,
As they're sailing in the lowlands, lonesome low,
As they're sailing in the lowlands low.

F

"Sailing in the Lowlands Low." Collected by Mr. John Stone. Sung by Mrs. J. B. Clark, of Waverly, Va. Sussex County. July 13, 1921. Mrs. Clark, writes Mr. Stone, "heard it sixty years ago in Prince William County, Va."

1 "O captain, captain, what will you give me
To sink this roguish rascal in the sea, sea, sea?"
"I'll give unto thee gold and silver free,
And my oldest daughter shall be married unto thee, thee, thee,
While I'm sailing on the lonesome sea, sea, sea,
While I'm sailing on the lonesome sea."

48

THE MERMAID

(CHILD, No. 289)

THIRTEEN texts, whole or fragmentary, and two tunes are the contribution of this ballad to the Virginia archives, under the titles "The Stormy Winds Do Blow," "The Stormy Winds How They Blow," "The Stormy Winds," and "The Wreck," as well as "The Mermaid." Only one repetitive fragment is here excluded. The twelve remaining variants are quite similar, and in the main follow the Child sequence B–C–D. But the speech of the cook which appears in Virginia A, D, K, L, is more like Child E and F. Virginia A shows the impress of another section of the country (see the footnote). Virginia B and C come from the same singer but show certain variations; they are placed in juxtaposition for comparison. An interesting feature of the fuller variants is the use made of the "stormy winds" stanza; usually it is the chorus, sometimes the first stanza and chorus, sometimes first and last stanza, sometimes (once) it is omitted.

The ship sets sail, as in Child B, C, D, on Friday, a day of ill omen. The appearance of a mermaid is a signal of despair to seamen in this ballad as in certain versions of "Sir Patrick Spens" (Child, No. 59, J, L, P, Q). As Child there (II, 19) remarks, "If nothing worse, mermaids at least bode rough weather, and sailors do not like them. . . . They have a reputation for treachery: there is in a Danish ballad . . . one who has betrayed seven ships."

The popularity of this ballad in college and other songbooks has often been pointed out (see Cox and Mackenzie, head-notes). For other traditional American texts, see Barry, No. 7; *Bulletin*, Nos. 2–5, 8–10; Cox, No. 33; Heart Songs, p. 360; Hudson, No. 23 (Mississippi); *Journal*, XVIII, 136 (Barry, Vermont, text and melody); XXII, 78 (Barry, Vermont, melody only); XXV, 176 (Belden, Missouri); XXVI, 175 (Kittredge, Massachusetts); McGill, p. 46; Mackenzie, *Ballads*, No. 16; Pound, *Syllabus*, p. 10 (fragment); Pound, *Ballads*, No. 11; Spaeth, *Read 'em and Weep*, 1927, p. 81. For additional references, see Cox, p. 172; *Journal*, XXX, 333.

A

"The Mermaid." Contributed by Miss Maria P. Duval, of Staunton, Va. Sung by her mother. Augusta County. March 10, 1914. The mention of Salem and Boston shows that this ballad has been subject to New England influence. Perhaps it is natural that so nautical a story should bear the impress of a more maritime section of the country, but a longer residence in Virginia would doubtless have substituted Norfolk, Portsmouth, or Newport News for the New England places.

1 'T was Friday morn when we set sail,
And we were not far from the land,
When the captain spied a lovely mermaid
With a comb and a glass in her hand.

Chorus

Oh! the ocean waves may roll,
And the stormy winds may blow,
While we poor sailors go skipping to the tops,
And the land-lubbers lie down below, below, below,
While the land-lubbers lie down below.

2 Then out spake the captain of our gallant ship,
And a well-spoken man was he:
"I have married me a wife in Salem town,
And tonight she a widder will be!"

3 Then out spake the cook of our gallant ship,
And a fat old cookie was he:
"I care much more for my pottles and my kets[1]
Than I do for the depths of the sea."

4 Then out spake the boy of our gallant ship,
And a well-spoken laddie was he:
"I've a father and a mother in Boston city,
But tonight they childless will be.

5 "Oh! the moon shines bright, and the stars give light;
Oh! my mammy'll be looking for me;
She may look, she may weep, she may look to the deep,
She may look to the bottom of the sea."

6 Then three times around went our gallant ship,
And three times around went she;
Then three times around went our gallant ship,
And she sank to the depths of the sea.

B

"The Stormy Winds." Reported by Mrs. J. M. Grainger, of the Farmville Ballad Club. Contributed by Mr. Inslee Deaderick, of Knoxville, Tennessee. Prince Edward County. March, 1914. With music. Printed, with music, in *The Focus* for March, 1914, pp. 98–99.

1 'T was Friday morn when we sot sail,
And we were not far from land,
When we all espied a fair mermaid
With a comb and a glass in her hand, in her hand,
With a comb and a glass in her hand.

[1] A rare ballad indulgence in *Spoonerism*.

Chorus

The stormy winds do blow, blow, blow,
    And the raging seas, how they flow,
While we poor sailors are climbing to the top,
    The landsmen are lying down below, down below,
    The landsmen are lying down below.

2 Then up spake the captain of our gallant ship,
    And a well-spoken man was he,
"I've a wife and a child in my own native land,
    Who this night shall be weeping for me, oh, for me,
    Who this night shall be weeping for me."

3 Then up spake the boy of our gallant ship,
    And a well-spoken boy was he,
"I've a father and a mother in my own native land,
    Who this night childless shall be, oh, shall be,
    Who this night childless shall be."

4 Then three times around turned our gallant ship,
    And three times around turned she,
And as she turned the third time around,
    She sank to the bottom of the sea, of the sea,
    She sank to the bottom of the sea.

C

"The Stormy Winds Do Blow." Reported by Mrs. J. M. Grainger, of the Farmville Ballad Club. Sung by her father, Mr. Inslee Deaderick, of Knoxville, Tennessee. Prince Edward County. January 17, 1914. Printed in *The Focus* for January, 1914, p. 447.

1 'T was Friday morn we all set sail,
    And we were not far from land,
When all at once we espied a mermaid
    With a comb and a glass in her hand,
        In her hand,
    With a comb and a glass in her hand.

Chorus

The stormy winds do blow, blow, blow,
    And the raging sea how they flow;
While we poor sailors are climbing to the top,
    And the landsmen lying down below,
        Down below,
    And the landsmen lying down below.

2 Then up spoke the captain of that gallant ship,
And a right gallant captain was he:
"I've a father and mother in me own native land,
Who'll be watching and waiting for me,
For me,
Who'll be watching and waiting for me."

3 Then up spoke the bo'sun of that gallant ship,
And a right gallant bo'sun was he:
"I've a wife and a child in me own native land,
Who'll be watching and waiting for me,
For me,
Who'll be watching and waiting for me."

4 Then three times around went our gallant ship,
And three times around went she;
And the last time around she . . . .
And sank to the bottom of the sea,
Of the sea,
And sank to the bottom of the sea.

D

"The Mermaid." Collected by Mr. John Stone. Sung by Mrs. Geo. W. Johnson, of Tunstall, Va. New Kent County. September 11, 1922.

1 'T was Friday morn when we set sail,
And we were not far from the land,
When the captain spied a mermaid fair
With a comb and a glass in her hand.

Chorus

Oh, the ocean waves they roll,
And the stormy winds they blow,
While we poor sailors go toiling to the top
And the land-lubbers lie down below, down below,
And the land-lubbers lie down below.

2 Then up steps the captain of our gallant little ship,
And a well-spoken man was he:
"I've married a wife in Salem town
Who this night a widow will be."

3 Then up spoke the cook of our gallant little ship,
And a well-spoken man was he:
"I care much more for my kettles and my pots
Than I do for the depths of the sea."

4 And three times around went our gallant little ship,
And three times around went she;
And as she was going the last time around,
She went to the bottom of the sea.

E

"The Mermaid." Collected by Mrs. James A. Otey, of Blacksburg, Va. Sung by Mr. Robert M. Patterson, of Walnut Spring, Va. Montgomery County. February 21, 1916.

1 'T was Friday night when we set sail,
And we were not very far from land,
When the captain spied a pretty mermaid
With a comb and brush in her hand.

Chorus

The stormy winds may blow, blow, blow,
And the raging seas how they go,
While we poor sailors are running up aloft
And the land-lubbers lying down below.

2 Up spoke the captain of our gallant ship,
And a brave looking man was he:
"I've a wife and five children in my far native land
Whom I fear that I never more will see."

3 Up spoke the little cabin boy,
And a smart little lad was he:
"I've a poor old mother in my far native land
Whom I fear that I never more will see."

Up spoke in turn any officer of the crew, as the singer can think them up.

4 Three times around spun our gallant ship,
And three times around spun she;
And as she was spinning the third time around,
She sank to the bottom of the sea.

F

"The Mermaid." Collected by Miss Martha M. Davis. Sung by Miss Fannie Speck, of Harrisonburg, Va. Rockingham County. March 15, 1913. With music. "Miss Speck is of old Virginia stock, Rockingham County, a teacher in the Harrisonburg Graded School. 'The Mermaid' was sung by her mother to the children around the fireside. The fourth stanza was added by a sister of Miss Speck" (Miss Davis).

1 Last Friday morn when we set sail,
We had n't sailed far from land,
Till we spied, till we spied a pretty fair maid
With a comb and a glass in her hand, her hand, her hand,
With a comb and a glass in her hand.

2 Up stepped one of our gallant men,
And a well-spoken man was he:
He cried, "I've a wife in London's famous town,
And a widow this night she shall be, shall be, shall be,
And a widow this night she shall be."

3 'T is three times round goes our gallant ship,
And three times around go we,
Till we sink, till we sink to the bottom of the sea,
Till we sink to the bottom of the sea, the sea, the sea,
Till we sink to the bottom of the sea.

4 The moon shines bright, the stars give light,
And my mother is looking for me;
She may look, she may look with a watery eye,
She may look to the bottom of the sea, the sea, the sea,
She may look to the bottom of the sea.

G

"The Stormy Winds How They Blow." Collected by Col. E. Berkeley, of Haymarket, Va. Contributed by Miss Alice Maude Ewell. Prince William County. February 2, 1914.

1 The stormy winds how they blow, blow, blow,
The raging seas how they flow,
While we poor sailors are toiling in the tops,
The landsmen are lying down below, down below,
The landsmen are lying down below.

2 Then up stepped the captain of our gallant crew,
And a very gallant man was he:
"I have a wife and children in my own native land
Who this night are looking out for me, for me,
Who this night are looking out for me."

3 Then up stepped the mate of our gallant crew,
And a very gallant man was he:
"I've a father and mother in my own native home
Who this night are looking out for me, for me,
Who this night are looking out for me."

4 Three times around went our gallant ship,
Three times around went she,
And as she was turning the third time around,
She settled to the bottom of the sea, of the sea,
She settled to the bottom of the sea.

5 The stormy winds how they blow, blow, blow,
The raging seas how they flow,
While we poor sailors are toiling in the tops,
With the landsmen they all settled down below, down below,
With the landsmen they all settled down below.

H

"The Stormy Winds How They Blow." Collected by Miss Ellen B. Bouldin, of Houston, Va. Sung by her brother. Halifax County. February 12, 1914.

1 O the stormy winds how they blow, blow, blow,
And the raging billows how they roar,
While we poor sailors toiling at the masts,
And the landsmen lying down below, down below,
And the landsmen lying down below.

2 Up stepped a youth, a gallant youth was he,
Of our most gallant crew;
Says he, "I've a mother *on a distant shore* [1]
Who this night is looking out for me, for me,
Who this night is looking out for me."

Chorus: The first stanza is used as chorus after the second and after all later stanzas.

3 Up stepped the captain, a gallant man was he,
Of our most gallant crew;
Says he, "I've a wife and three little ones
Who this night are looking out for me, for me,
Who this night are looking out for me."

4 Three times around went our gallant ship,
Three times around went she;
The fourth time she turned *she trembled in the blast* [1]
And sank to the bottom of the sea, of the sea,
And sank to the bottom of the sea.

[1] "I am not sure about the underlined words" (Miss Bouldin).

I

"The Wreck." Collected by Miss Juliet Fauntleroy. Sung by Miss Ethel Hancock, at Altavista, Va. Franklin County. September 10, 1915.

1 The stormy winds did blow, blow, blow,
While the lamp was burning dimly down below.

2 Three times around sailed our gallant ship,
Three times around sailed she;
And as she was sailing the third time around,
She sank to the bottom of the sea,
She sank to the bottom of the sea.

J

"The Mermaid." Collected by Mr. John Stone. Recited by Mrs. D. W. Owen, of Denniston, Va. Halifax County. July 31, 1922.

The stormy wind doth blow,
And the raging sea overflow,
And we poor sailors cling to the mast
While the land loafers lie down below, down below,
While the land loafers lie down below.

K

"The Mermaid." Collected by Mr. John Stone. Sung by Mrs. H. F. Fauntleroy, of Tunstall, Va. New Kent County. September 11, 1922.

Then up steps the cook of our gallant little ship,
And a well-spoken man was he:
"I care not a damn for my kettles and my pots,
For they'll soon be at the bottom of the sea."

L

"The Mermaid." Collected by Mr. John Stone. Recited by Mrs. H. T. Stevens, of Igo, Va. King George County. September 11, 1922.

"I care more tonight for my kettles and my pots,
Than I do for my lovers all three."

49

JOHN OF HAZELGREEN

(CHILD, No. 293)

THE ten texts and three melodies here given seem to be the only traditional copies of this ballad to be printed from America. One repetitive text has been excluded. The Virginia variants A to I evidently belong to a single version which is not particularly close to any Child version. Virginia J, on the other hand, is fairly close to Child E and to the "Jock of Hazeldean" which Scott built upon the traditional Child E. The first stanza of all three is practically identical, but the beginning of the second Virginia stanza is more like the beginning of Scott's third stanza than like the traditional second stanza. But the traditional name "Hazelgreen" is retained for the hero, and as the contributor assures us that the version was "known and sung in Louisa Co., Va., in the '50's," the song was surely, in spite of its semi-Scottish language, traditional in Virginia.

The story of the ballad is more fully told by the A to I variants, but even there it is a bit fragmentary. A walker discovers a fair maid in distress, and offers her his eldest son in marriage. She scorns his offer, saying that she loves John of Hazelgreen, whom she describes in glowing terms. She rides to the town, where she is met by her lover with kisses and promises of fidelity. How much of the story has been dropped out in the Virginia versions will be shown by a comparison of this with the Child summary: "A gentleman overhears a damsel making a moan for Sir John of Hazelgreen. After some compliment on his part, and some slight information on hers, he tells her that Hazelgreen is married; then there is nothing for her to do, she says, but to hold her peace and die for him. The gentleman proposes that she shall let Hazelgreen go, marry his eldest son, and be made a gay lady; she is too mean a maid for that, and, anyway, had rather die for the object of her affection. Still she allows the gentleman to take her up behind him on his horse, and to buy clothes for her at Biggar, though all the time dropping tears for Hazelgreen. After the shopping they mount again, and at last they come to the gentleman's place, when the son runs out to welcome his father. The son is young Hazelgreen, who takes the maid in his arms and kisses off the still-falling tears. The father declares that the two shall be married the next day, and the young man shall have the family lands." In comparison with this rather involved narrative, the Virginia ballad is simply a maid's lamentation ended by a lovers' union.

These Virginia variants are reported in *Bulletin*, Nos. 3–7, 10, No other American texts have been printed.

A

"John o' the Hazelgreen." Collected by Miss Martha M. Davis. Sung by a mountain woman. Rockingham County. November 16, 1915. With music.

1 As I walked out one May morning
Down by the greenwood side,
There I spied a pretty fair maid,
And all alone she cried.

2 "If you go home, it's home with me,
It's home with me to stay,
You may have my oldest son
A husband for to be."

3 "I neither want your oldest son,
He's neither lord nor king;
For I intend to be the bride of none
But John o' the Hazelgreen.

4 "His arms are long, his shoulders broad,
He's the flower of all his kin:
His hair hangs down like links of gold,
John o' the Hazelgreen."

5 As she rode down the lengthy road
And drew near to the town,
Out stepped John o' the Hazelgreen
And holp his lady down.

6 Three times he kissed her ruby lips,
Three times he kissed her chin;
He took her by her lily-white hand
And led his lady in.

7 "If ever you have forsaken me,
I hope sweet heaven will forsake you,
And send you down to the torment place,
And there forever be."

8 "If ever I have forsaken you,
The rocks must melt in the sun,
The fire shall freeze to ice,
And the raging sea shall burn."

B

"Jack o' Hazelgreen." Collected by Martha M. Davis. Sung by a mountain woman in Elkton, Va. Rockingham County. January 3, 1914.

1 As I spied a pretty fair maid
And all alone she cried
. . . .
. . . .

2 "If you go home, it's home with me,
It's home with me to stay,
And you may have my eldest son
A husband for to be."

3 "I neither want your oldest son,
He's neither lord nor king;
I intend to be the bride of none
But Jack o' Hazelgreen."

4 As she rode down the lengthy road
She drew near to the town;
Out stepped John o' the Hazelgreen
And holp his lady down.

5 "If you forsaken me, my dear,
I hope sweet heaven will forsake you,
And send you down to the torment place,
And there forever be."

6 "If I forsaken you, my dear,
I hope sweet heaven will forsake me,
And send me down to the torment place,
And there forever be."

C

"John o' the Hazelgreen." Collected by Miss Martha M. Davis, of Harrisonburg, Va. Rockingham County. March 7, 1914.

1 As she rode down the lengthy road
And drew near to the town,
Up stepped John o' the Hazelgreen
And holped his lady down.

2 His arms were long, his shoulders broad,
He's the flower of all his kin;
His hair hangs down like links of gold,
John o' the Hazelgreen.

3 It is forty times he kissed her cheeks,
And forty times her chin,
And forty times her ruby lips,
John o' the Hazelgreen.

4 "If ever I have forsaken you,
The rocks must melt in the sun,
The fire must freeze to ice,
And the raging sea shall burn.

5 "If ever I have forsaken you,
I hope heaven will forsake me,
And send me down to the torment place,
And there forever be."

D

"John of Hazelgreen." Collected by Mr. John Stone. Sung by Mr. Thomas H. Bailey, of Shenandoah, Va. Page County. November 10, 1919. With music. "Mr. Bailey heard Mrs. Martha Lee Graves, of Page County, sing it years ago. The tune is practically the same as the tune of 'Say Au Revoir but not Good-bye.' I wonder which borrowed from the other? To get this song I walked about thirty-three miles, rode about seventeen miles on the train, and slept less than two hours, part of that being under a tree in the woods, and part in a railway station. I crossed the Blue Ridge mountains twice and made the round trip in about twenty-eight hours" (Mr. Stone).

1 As I walked out one fair May morning
Down by the Haywood side,
There I saw a pretty fair miss,
And all alone she cried.

2 "You are welcome home with me.
And you can have my oldest son,
A loving husband for to be."

3 "I neither want your oldest son
Nor a lord nor a king;
I never can be the bride of none
But John over the Hazelgreen.

4 "His arms is long, his shoulders is broad,
He is the flower of all his king,
His hair hangs down like links of gold,
John over the Hazelgreen."

5 As we rode 'long the lonesome road,
The road drew near the town;
Up steps John of the Hazelgreen
And helps his lady down.

6 Forty times he kissed her cheeks,
And forty times her chin,
And forty times her rosy lips,
And led his lady in.

7 "If ever I forsaken you,
I hope heaven will forsaken me,
And send me down to the torment place,
There forever to be."

E

"John of Hazelgreen." Collected by Mr. John Stone. Sung by Miss Ruby Herndon, of Mt. Fair, Va. Albemarle County. November 3, 1920. With music. "This song was given to me by Miss Ruby Herndon, one of my pupils. She got it from her mother, who heard it years ago. They sang it for me together" (Mr. Stone).

1 As I was walking out one wondering morn
  Down by the greenwood side,
It there I spied a handsome lady.
  "I'm all alone," she cried.

2 "You are welcome home, you are welcome home,
  You are welcome home with me;
For you may have my oldest son
  A husband for to be."

3 "I do not want your oldest son,
  He's neither a lord nor a king;
I never intend to be the bride of but one:
  That's John over the Hazelgreen.

4 "His shoulders are broad, his arms are long,
  He's the fairest of all the king;
His hair swings down like the links of gold,
  John over the Hazelgreen."

5 Thirty times he kissed her cheeks,
  Forty times her chin,
And fifty times her ruby little lips,
  And let his lady in.

6 He stepped into his carriage gay
  And rode off to the town;
John jumped over the Hazelgreen
  And helped his lady down.

F

"John of Hazelgreen." Collected by Mr. John Stone. Sung by Mr. Podger Garrison, of Blackwell's Hollow, Va. Albemarle County. November 10, 1919. "'Podg' not only sings ballads but he also makes them. He sang two of his own compositions for me. One was about a coon hunt and the other about a mock fight in the snow" (Mr. Stone).

1 I walked out one pretty fair morn
  Down by the greenwood side,
And there I spied a pretty fair miss,
  And all alone she cried.

2 "You'd as well come home, my pretty fair miss,
You'd as well go home," said he.
"For you may have my oldest son
A husband for to be."

3 "I don't want your oldest son,
For he is neither a lord nor a king,
For I never intend to be the bride of none
Save John of the Hazelgreen."

4 As I was riding along the road,
The road drew near thc town;
Up stepped John of the Hazelgreen
And he hoped his lady down.

5 Forty times he kissed her cheeks,
And forty times her chin,
And forty times her ruby lips,
And led his lady in.

6 "If ever I forsaken of you,
Pray seven forsaken of me,
And send me down into the torment place
Forever and eternity."

G

"John of the Hazel Green." Collected by Miss Roxie Martin and Mr. Judson McManaway. Told by a very old white woman. Albemarle County. June 1, 1917.

1 As I walked out one early May morning
Down by the greenwood side,
There I spied a pretty fair maiden,
All alone she cried.

2 "You're welcome home, you're welcome home,
You're welcome home with me;
For you shall have my oldest son,
Your husband for to be."

3 "I don't want your oldest son,
He's neither lord nor king;
I'll be the bride of none
But John o' the Hazel Green."

4 His arms are long, his shoulders broad,
He's lord of all, he's king;
His hair hangs down like links of gold,
He's John o' the Hazel Green.

5 As she was riding down that lengthy road,
That road that leads to town,
Up steps John of the Hazel Green
And helps the lady down.

6 "If ever I've forsaken you,
Heaven may me forsake,
And send me down to torment,
And there I'll ever be."

H

"John of Hazelgreen." Collected by Mr. John Stone. Sung by Mr. Raz Shifflet, of Brown's Cove, Va. Albemarle County. November 1, 1922.

1 "Will you go home with me tonight?
You may have my oldest son."
"But I neither want you nor your oldest son,
John over the Haz of Green.

2 "Your arms is long and shoulders is broad,
And you are the flower of all the kin;
But I never intend to be the bride of none,
John over the Haz of Green."

3 He rode along that lengthum road,
And the road went near through town,
And up steps John, being a bold young man,
And he hope his lady down.

I

"John o' the Hazelgreen." Collected by Miss Martha M. Davis. Sung by Mrs. Davis, of Elkton, Va. Rockingham County. December 27, 1917. "Evidently second stanza of version already reported. Given by one Mrs. Davis, an old woman on Blue Ridge — the foot-hills — near Elkton, Va., in the summer of 1916. This was the only stanza she could recall" (Miss Davis).

As I drew nearer and nearer to her
To hear what she did mean,
All her lamentation was,
"John o' the Hazelgreen."

J

"Jock o' Hazelgreen." Collected by Mrs. J. B. Ferneyhough, of Richmond, Va. Contributed by Mrs. Olivia D. Waller. Louisa County. November 23, 1915. Mrs. Ferneyhough says that this version was "known and sung in Louisa County, Va., in the '50's."

1 "Why weep ye by the tide, Ladye,
Why weep ye by the tide?
I 'll wed thee to my youngest son,
And ye shall be his bride;
And ye shall be his bride, Ladye,
The fairest to be seen."
But a' she loot the tears come down
For Jock o' Hazelgreen.

2 "A chain of gold ye shall not lack,
Nor braid to bind your hair,
Nor trusty steed nor silken plaid,
And all that ladies wear.
And ye the fairest of them all
Shall ride a fairie queen."
But a' she loot the tears come down
For Jock o' Hazelgreen.

50

THE BROWN GIRL

(Child, No. 295)

The Virginia contribution of eleven texts and three melodies more than doubles the gleanings of this ballad in America. For other American items, see Barry, No. 19 (and melody from Vermont in *Journal*, xviii, 295); and Campbell and Sharp, No. 36 (six texts and five tunes from North Carolina and Virginia). The Virginia items are reported in *Bulletin*, Nos. 5, 7, 8, 9, 11. One fragment of this ballad combined with "The Death of Queen Jane" (Child, No. 170) was not reported in the *Bulletin* but appears as Virginia, No. 35, which see.

The Virginia variants A to J seem to belong to a single version of the ballad, one that has little in common with either of the Child versions, though its phraseology is occasionally reminiscent of Child B, not of A. The Campbell and Sharp texts A to F represent the same version, which we may therefore call the usual American version. In it the girl is no longer brown, and the lovers have exchanged positions; the man is now the proud one who, once scorned, will not forgive and thus save the life of the sick girl, upon whose grave he will rather dance. These essential changes and others must be made in Child's summary, which runs thus: "A young man who has been attached to a girl sends her word by letter that he cannot fancy her because she is so brown (he has left her for another maid in B). She sends a disdainful reply. He writes again that he is dangerously ill (he is love-sick in B), and begs her to come to him quickly and give him back his faith. She takes her time in going, and when she comes to the sick man's bedside, cannot stand for laughing. She has, however, brought a white band with her, which she strokes on his breast, in sign that she gives him back the faith which he had given her. But as to forgiving and forgetting, that she will never do; she will dance upon his grave." The Virginia version of the unrelenting male lover over-cruel to the dying Sally because she has rejected him is certainly less moving and less grateful than the picture of the proud brown girl who refuses the death-bed advances of her once scornful lover. The name Sally or Sarah gives place once to Marthy, in Virginia F. The style of the Virginia ballad shows unmistakably the influence of the broadside press.

Indeed, it is with some hesitation that these texts have been definitely assigned to "The Brown Girl." But if they are not strictly a version of that ballad, they may well be, and almost certainly are, founded on "The Brown Girl" or perverted from it. Hence, and also following the authority of Campbell and Sharp, they are printed here as variants of the ballad rather than as appendices to it.

A

"The Brown Girl." Collected by Mr. John Stone. Sung by Mr. George Hart, of Konnarock, Va. Washington County. November 8, 1921. "Mr. Hart learned it from his sister years ago. . . He sang seventeen ballads for me. We sat under a tree in the mountains for nearly six hours without getting out of our seats, while he sang and recited ballads and I copied them" (Mr. Stone).

1 There was a rich lady, from London she came,
She called herself Sally, pretty Sally, by name.
Her riches was more than the king doth possess,
Yet her beauty was more than her wealth at the best.

2 There was a young gentleman, a rich merchant's son,
And the least of his income was five hundred pound;
He was tangled in love and he knew not for why,
'T was on this fair damsel could scarce cast an eye.

3 "I don't scorn for to hate you or any other man,
But as for to love you, it's more than I can.
So drop your intentions and end your discourse,
For I never will marry you, at least ways I'm forced."

4 Six months had rolled around, full six months had passed,
Till this fair young damsel proved sick at the last.
She was tangled in love and she knew not for why,
She sends for this young man she once did deny.

5 "Am I the doctor you sent for so sly
Or am I the young man you once did deny?"
"O you are the doctor can kill or can cure,
And without your assistance, I'm ruined, I'm sure."

6 "O Sally, O Sally, pretty Sally," says he,
"O don't you remember when you slighted me?
You laughed at my courtship, you have slighted me with scorn,
And now I'll reward you for things past and gone."

7 "For things past and gone, love, forget and forgive,
And grant me some longer in this world to live."
"I never will forgive you, enduring of my breath,
But I'll dance on your grave when you are laid in the earth."

8 So off her finger she pulled a gold ring,
Saying, "Take this and wear it while dancing on me."
"Your ring I'll deny, and your body I'll disdain.
So now I will leave you in sorrow and pain."

B

"The Brown Girl." Collected by Mr. John Stone. Sung by Mrs. J. C. Eakle, near Bolar, Va. Bath County. November 3, 1920.

1 There was a rich Irish lady, from Ireland she came,
There was a rich Irish lady, and Sarah by name.

2 Her riches were more than the king could possess,
But her behavior and beauty were more than all thus.

3 That lengthy [1] young squire a-courting her came,
That lengthy young squire came her for to see.

4 She spitefully used him and denied him with scorn,
And the less he'll revoir (?) [2] her for what she has done.

5 Six months had not ended nor scarcely had passed,
Till this rich Irish damsel fell sick at the last.

6 Being tangled in love, she knew not for why,
She sent for that young man whom she once did deny.

7 "Am I the doctor that you sent for me?
Or am I the young man whom you wanted for to see?"

8 "You are the doctor that can kill or can cure,
And without your assistance, I'm dying, I'm sure."

9 "O Sarah, O Sarah, O Sarah," said he,
"Don't you remember how you once did slight me?"

10 "Forget and forgive for what's past and gone,
And 'low your darling Sarah some longer to live."

11 "I'll never forget you, I'll never forgive you, nor that ain't half all;
For I'll dance on your grave, girl, after you're laid in the dust."

12 Off of her fingers she pulled diamond rings three,
Saying, "Take and wear those while you 're dancing o'er me.

13 "Let no more of your flying colors be seen
While you 're dancing over Sarah, o'er Sarah, the queen."

14 Sarah is dead now, that you all may suppose,
And she has left some of those ladies all of her fine clothes.

15 And she has took up her lodging in the banks of cold clay,
And the last of her red rosy cheeks lies moldering away.

[1] For *at length a*, probably.

[2] For *revile*, probably.

C

"The Brown Girl." Collected by Mr. John Stone. Recited by Mrs. Jennie Allison, of Saltville, Va. Smyth County. November 8, 1921. "She learned it from her mother, who learned it from the soldiers in the War between the States. When in winter quarters, the soldiers would meet at parties from house to house and often sing all night. In that way, many songs were spread" (Mr. Stone).

1 A rich Irish lady from London she came,
They called her Pretty Sally, Pretty Sally, by name.
Her riches so noble, her beauty so fair,
And on a young squire she scarcely cast an eye.

2 About six months afterwards, it was a sad surprise,
This young girl was seen with tears in her eyes.
She was wounded and wounded she knew not for why,
She sent for the squire to come see her die.

3 "O Sally, O Sally, O Sally," said he,
"Don't you remember when you slighted me?
You laughed at my courtship and treated me with scorn,
And now I'll reward you for time past and gone."

4 "For time past and gone, O forget and forgive,
And spare me some longer in this vain world to live."
"No, that I won't do, Sally, as long as I have breath,
But I'll dance on your grave when you are laid in cold death."

5 Off of her fingers she pulled diamond rings three,
Saying, "Take these and wear them while dancing o'er me."
"No, that I won't do, Sally, but as long as I have breath
I'll dance on your grave when you are laid in cold earth."

D

"The Brown Girl." Collected by Miss Alfreda M. Peel. Sung by Miss Isobel Nicewander, of Bland, Va. Bland County. September 3, 1923. The sense of this variant is badly confused.

1 "Oh Sarah, Oh Sarah," said he,
"Do n't you remember when you first courted me?

2 "Oh, I asked you in kindness, you answered me in scorn,
And now you'll remember the days passed and gone."

3 He lay wounded in love, and they knew not for why;
She sent for this young maid she once did deny.

4 "Am I your doctor, am I your cure?
Am I your doctor you sent for me here?"

5 "Yes, you are my doctor, you are my cure,
And without your assistance I'm ruined, I'm sure.

6 "And the time passed and gone, dear, I hope you'll forgive,
And grant some longer time for to live."

7 "I never will forgive you, as long as I live,
I'll dance on your grave when you're laid in the ground."

8 And off of her fingers her rings, her rings she pulled three,
"Take them and wear them while I'm dancing on thee."

9 "I'd freely forgive him, but he won't forgive me;
My fall is ten thousand times under the sea."

E

"The Brown Girl." Collected by Mr. John Stone. Sung by Miss I. C. Young, of South Norfolk, Va. Norfolk County. November 10, 1919.

1 There was a young lady from Old England came,
Sweet Sally of Salsworth, they called her by name.

Several stanzas are missing here.

2 "Am I the doctor that you send for me here,
Or am I the young man that you love so dear?"

3 "You are the doctor that can kill or can cure,
And without your relief, love, I am ruined, I'm sure."

4 "When I first courted you, you denied me with scorn,
And now I'll repay you for all's past and gone."

5 "For all's past and gone, love, forget and forgive,
And grant me, I pray you, some longer to live."

6 "No, I won't, Sally, sweet Sally," said he,
"But I'll dance on your grave when you're cold in the clay."

7 Then off of her fingers she pulled diamond rings three,
Saying, "Wear them for my sake when dancing o'er me."

F

"The Brown Girl." Collected by Mr. John Stone. Sung by Mr. Charles H. Lowry, near South Boston, Va. Halifax County. June 29, 1921.

1 "O Marthy, O Marthy, O Marthy," says he,
"I'm feared that your beauty might ruin me.
Without your hatrance turns to love and love no other one,
I'm sure that your beauty might ruin me.

2 "You laughed at my courtship,
You treated me with scorn,
But now I 'll reward you
For the time that's past and gone.

3 "The time that's past and gone, love,
The time you turned me away."
"Dear lord, remember me
When you're dancing on my grave."

G

"The Brown Girl." Collected by Mr. Cecil J. Sharp and Miss Karpeles. Sung by Mr. N. B. Chisholm, at Woodridge, Va. Albemarle County. September 23, 1916. With music. See Campbell and Sharp, p. 147, where the first stanza and the melody of this variant are printed.

1 "Are you the doctor they sent for me here,
Or are you the young girl that I loved so dear,
Or are you the doctor can kill or can cure?
Without your assistance I'm ruined, I'm sure."

2 "And stand by your bed till you breathe the last breath,
And I'll dance on your grave when you're cold in the earth."

3 She pulled from her fingers gold diamond rings three,
Saying: "Take them and wear them when you're dancing on me.
I'll freely forgive you, although you won't me.
Farewell to this vain world, it's all vanity."

H

"The Brown Girl." Collected by Mr. John Stone. Sung by Miss Emma Carpenter, of Brightwood, Va. Madison County. November 3, 1920.

1 A rich Irish lady from London she came,
A beautiful fair damsel called Sally by name.

2 "Am I the doctor you sent for me here,
Or am I the doctor that can kill or can cure?"

3 "You are the doctor that can kill or can cure;
Without your assistance I am ruined, I'm sure."

I

"The Brown Girl." Collected by Mr. John Stone. Sung by Mrs. Rosson, of Alexandria, Va. Rockingham County. November 10, 1919. With music.

1 A fair Irish lady from Ireland came,
Fair Sally, fair Sally, fair Sally by name.

2 This lady took sick and likened to die,
And sent for this young man who had scarce cast an eye.

J

"The Brown Girl." Collected by Mr. John Stone. Sung by Mrs. W. K. Rogers, near Bolar, Va. Bath County. November 3, 1920. With music. "She heard her sister sing it" (Mr. Stone).

1 There was a lady from Ireland she came
She called herself Sally, pretty Sally, by name.

2 Her riches were more than her king could possess,
And her beauty was more than her wealth at the best.

51

TROOPER AND MAID

(Child, No. 299)

The ballad has yielded two texts and one melody in Virginia. They were first reported in *Bulletin*, Nos. 4, 7, 8. Other American texts are Campbell and Sharp, No. 37 (North Carolina, Tennessee); and Shearin and Combs, p. 9. Brown (p. 9) reports the song from North Carolina. The Virginia texts are not particularly close to any Child version, but are perhaps nearest to Child B. They are compressed but very good versions, containing most of the Child story, as follows: "A trooper comes to the house of his mistress in the evening and is kindly received. They pass the night together and are awakened by the trumpet. He must leave her; she follows him some way, he begging her to turn back. She asks him repeatedly when they are to meet again and marry. He answers, when cockle shells grow siller bells, when fishes fly and seas gang dry, etc." Such questions and answers are common in the ballads, especially as an ending; compare "Edward" and "The Twa Brothers." In Virginia A, the lovers are awakened not by a trumpet but by the war drum, and the trooper's reply as to when they will get married is "when gray goose quills turn to silver pins," a variant not found in Child. In neither Virginia text does the girl follow the trooper or he beg her to return.

A

"The Trooper and Maid." Collected by Miss Martha M. Davis. Sung by Mrs. Sarah Finchum, of Elkton, Va. Rockingham County. November 16, 1915. With music.

1 There was a man a-coming from the south,
It being dark and gloomy.
She knew the soldier by his horse
Because she loved him dearly.
Dearly, O dearly,
She knew the soldier by his horse,
Because she loved him dearly.

2 She caught him by the bridle rein,
She led him to the stable:
"Here's oats and corn for the soldier's horse,
Come feed him at your leisure."

3 She took him by his lily-white hand,
She led him to the table:
"Here's cakes and beer for you, my dear,
Come eat and drink with pleasure."

4 She tripped up stairs to make his bed,
She made it soft and easy;
Then she came tripping down the steps,
Saying, "At last, my dear, it's ready."

5 He pulled off his lily-white robe,
He laid it on the table,
A sword and pistol by its side,
Saying, "At last, my dear, I'm able."

6 He had been in bed not more than two hours,
When he heard the war drum beating,
He 'rose, he 'rose and put on his clothes,
Saying, "Alas, my dear, I leave you."

7 "O when are you a-coming back?
And when will we get married?"
"When gray goose quills turn to silver pins,
O then, my dear, we'll marry."

B

"The Trooper and the Maid." Collected by Mr. John Stone. Sung by Mr. George Hart, of Konnarock, Va. Washington County. November 8, 1921.

1 The soldier rode from east to west,
And he rode both late and early.
The lady knew him by his vest
Because she loved him dearly. } *Repeat*

2 She took his horse by the bridle reins,
And she led him to the stable:
"Here's oats and corn for the soldier's horse,
Come feed him, we are able." } *Repeat*

3 She took him by the little white hand,
And she led him to the table:
"Here's cakes and wine for you, young man,
Come eat and drink, we are able,
Come eat and drink, we are able,
Come eat and drink, we are able,
Here's cakes and wine for you, young man,
Come eat and drink, we are able."

4 She pulled off her costly robe
And folded it onto the table,
And he pulled off his bugle coat
And jumped in the bed with the lady. } *Repeat*

5 They had n't lay but about three hours
Till they heard some trumpet blowing:
"The time has come that I must go."
"Although, my love, I'm ruined. } *Repeat*

6 "O when will you return again?
Or when will we get married?"
"When silver bells turns to conch shells,
O then, my love, we'll marry." } *Repeat*

II. BALLAD MUSIC

NOTE

For a general introduction to these melodies, see the section on "The Music and Its Treatment," Introduction, pp. 16–20.

In several places in the songs that follow, it will be found that two syllables will have to be sung to one note; for example, "followed" in No. 3 (B), "followed" and "away" in No. 3 (D), "yellow" and "any" in No. 3 (P), "daughters" and "seventh" in No. 3 (Q), "William" in No. 4 (B), "Johnny" and "Mother" in No. 6 (B), and so on. Though it would have been a simple matter to double each of these notes (halving the time, of course), it has been thought wiser to leave the music as found, for any or all of the following reasons: to emphasize the fact that the fitting of the words to the tune is not final or authoritative; to avoid doing even this minor violence to the notation as it was sent in; to leave the music in a form which more nearly satisfies subsequent stanzas; to provide for the possibility, sometimes the strong probability, that the dissyllable was squeezed into a monosyllable, or one syllable somehow dropped out in the singer's pronunciation or left unvoiced between the notes. The single note often represents the original singing more accurately than would the technically stricter but more staccato doubled note. Various musical authorities have given their assurance that this departure from strict syllabic notation is not a musical barbarity, especially in the treatment of folk music. The arrangement of the words under the music is such that the singer can scarcely go wrong.

No. 1 THE DEVIL'S NINE QUESTIONS

Sent in by Miss Alfreda M. Peel; noted by Miss Evelyn Rex; sung by Mrs. Rill Martin, of Giles County, Virginia; September 11, 1922.

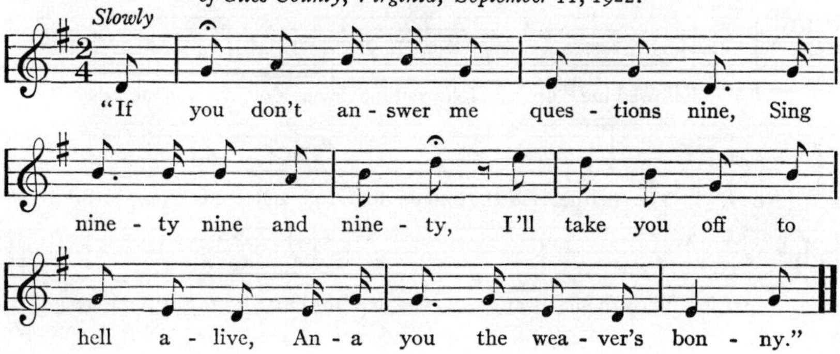

No. 2 THE FALSE KNIGHT ON THE ROAD

Collected by Miss Martha M. Davis; sung by Mrs. Sarah Finchum, of Elkton, Virginia; Rockingham County; November 23, 1918.

No. 3 (*B*) PRETTY POLLY

Collected by Mr. John Stone; sung by Hill Jackson (Colored), of Brown's Cove, Virginia; Albemarle County; November 3, 1920 (words sent previously).

No. 3 (*D*) THE NINE KING'S DAUGHTERS

Collected by Miss Juliet Fauntleroy; sung by Mr. Ed. Stinnet and by Mrs. Wildman, of Lynch Station, Virginia; Campbell County; June 4, 1914.

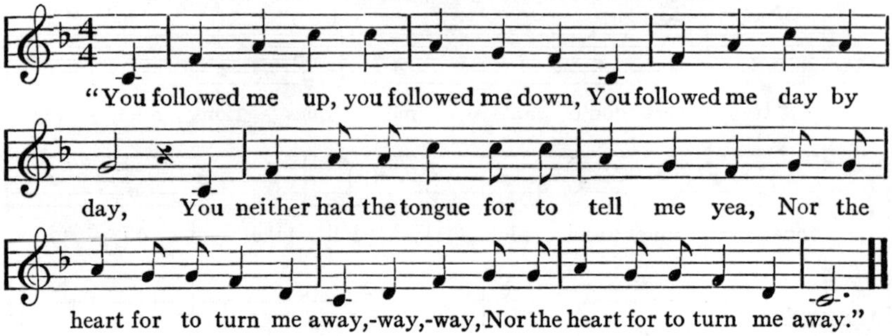

No. 3 (*F*) THE SEVEN KING'S DAUGHTERS

Collected by Miss Alfreda M. Peel; sung by Miss Odell Roop, of Vinton, Virginia; Roanoke County; September 11, 1922.

No. 3 (*P*) PRETTY POLLY

Collected by Miss Olive Flora Bryson, of East Radford, Virginia; sung by an old lady in Lee County; November 3, 1920.

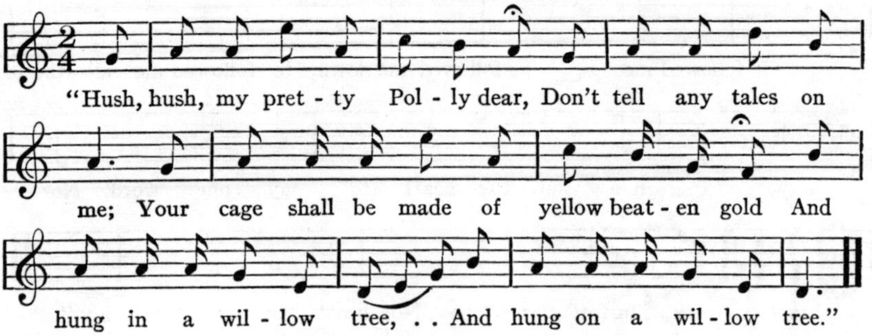

No. 3 (*Q*) THE SEVEN KING'S DAUGHTERS

Collected by Miss Juliet Fauntleroy; sung by Mrs. Dan Maxie (née Holland), of Altavista, Virginia; Franklin County; March 23, 1914.

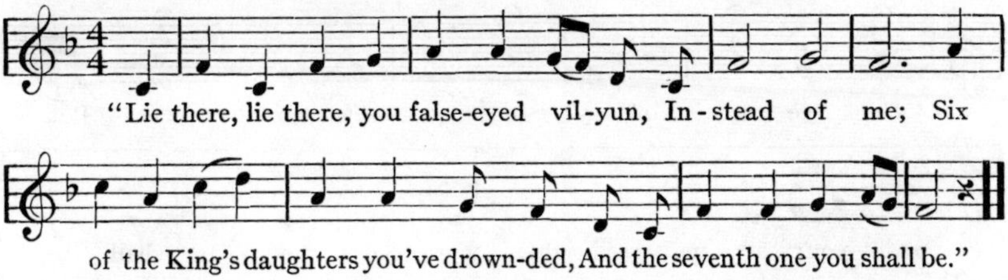

No. 3 (*R*) THE FALSE HEARTED KNIGHT

Collected by Miss Alfreda M. Peel; sung by Mrs. Harrington, of Roanoke, Virginia; Roanoke County; December 2, 1919.

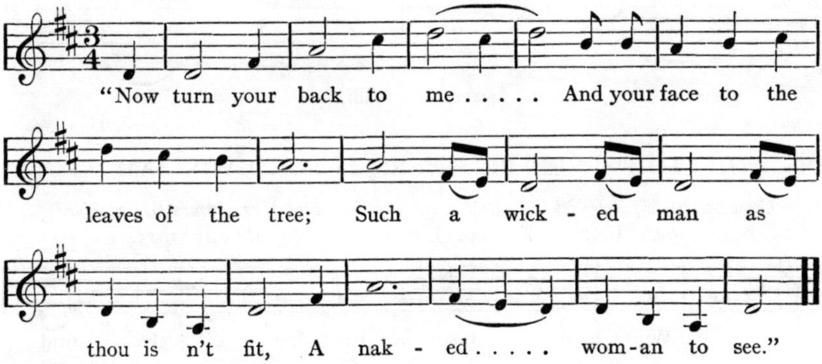

No. 3 (*S*) LADY ISABEL AND THE ELF KNIGHT

Collected by Miss Alfreda M. Peel; noted by Miss Evelyn Rex; sung by Miss Lucile Noel, of Vinton, Virginia; Roanoke County; November 30, 1923.

No. 4 (*B*) THE SEVEN BROTHERS, OR THE SEVEN SLEEPERS

Collected by Miss Martha M. Davis; sung by Mrs. Rosie Morris, of Elkton, Virginia; Rockingham County; August 30, 1922.

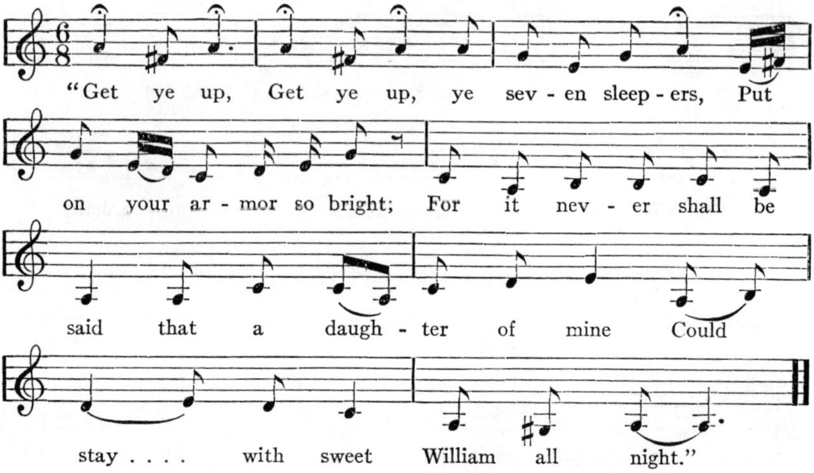

No. 4 (*D*) THE SEVEN BROTHERS, OR LORD WILLIAM

Collected by Miss Juliet Fauntleroy; sung by Mr. and Mrs. James B. Crawford, near Altavista, Virginia; Campbell County; May 27, 1915.

No. 5 (*A*) THE OLD LORD OF THE NORTH COUNTRY, OR THE THREE SISTERS

Collected by Mr. John Stone; sung by Mr. A. S. Furcron; Fauquier County; November 10, 1919.

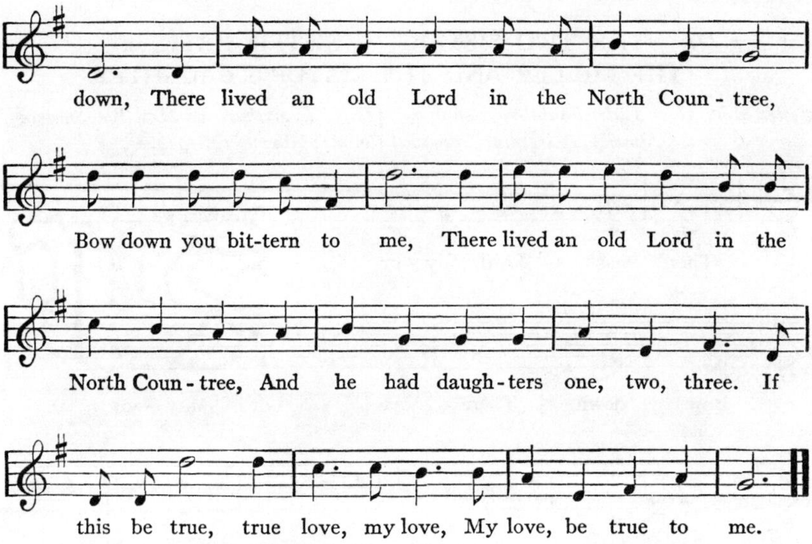

No. 5 (*B*) THE OLD WOMAN OF THE NORTH COUNTRIE

Collected by Mr. B. C. Moomaw, Jr., of Barber, Virginia; sung by Mr. Sam Pritt; Alleghany County; November 28, 1924.

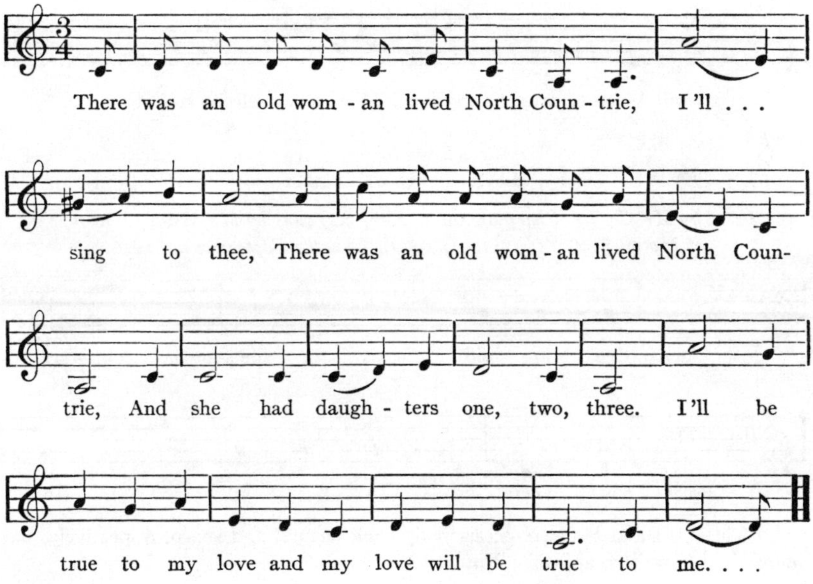

No. 5 (*D*) THE TWO SISTERS, OR SISTER KATE, OR THE MILLER AND THE MAYOR'S DAUGHTER

Collected by Miss Juliet Fauntleroy; sung by Mrs. L. L. Arthur and Mrs. Bob Stone, of Altavista, Virginia; Campbell County; March 14, 1914.

No. 5 (*F*) THE TWO SISTERS

Collected by Mr. Cecil J. Sharp and Miss Karpeles; sung by Mr. Wesley Batten (53), of Mount Fair, Virginia; Albemarle County; September 22, 1916.

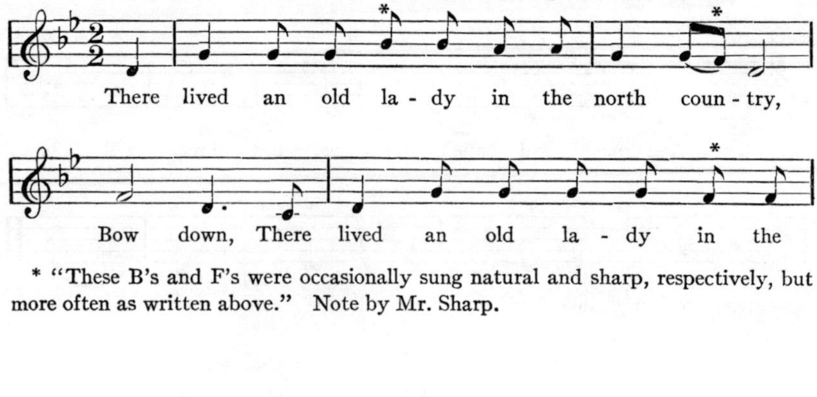

* "These B's and F's were occasionally sung natural and sharp, respectively, but more often as written above." Note by Mr. Sharp.

* "These B's and F's were occasionally sung natural and sharp, respectively, but more often as written above." Note by Mr. Sharp.

No. 5 (*G*) THE TWO SISTERS

Collected by Mr. Cecil J. Sharp and Miss Karpeles; sung by Miss Louisa Chisholm, at Woodridge, Virginia; Albemarle County; September 23, 1916.

No. 5 (*J*) THE TWO SISTERS

Collected by Mr. Cecil J. Sharp and Miss Karpeles; sung by Mr. Nuel Walton, at Mount Fair, Brown's Cove, Virginia; Albemarle County; September 26, 1916.

No. 6 (*A*) JOHN WILLOW, MY SON

Collected by Miss Juliet Fauntleroy; sung by Mrs. James B. Crawford, of Altavista, Virginia; Campbell County; September 9, 1915.

No. 6 (*B*) **JOHNNY RILLUS**

Collected by Mr. John Stone; sung by Mrs. Emily Via, of Stage Junction, Virginia; Fluvanna County; November 3, 1920.

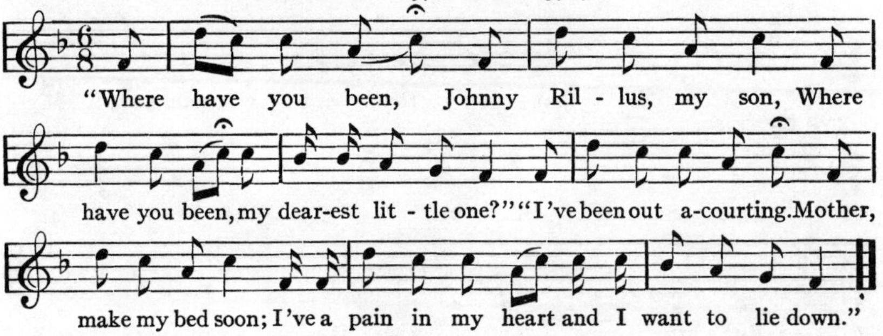

No. 6 (*F*) **JOHNNY RILLA**

Collected by Mr. John Stone; sung by Mrs. Ella Wood, of Doylesville, Virginia; Albemarle County; November 10, 1919.

No. 6 (*N*) **LORD RANDAL**

Contributed by Miss Alfreda M. Peel, of Salem, Virginia; noted by Miss Wingfield; Bland County; November 30, 1923.

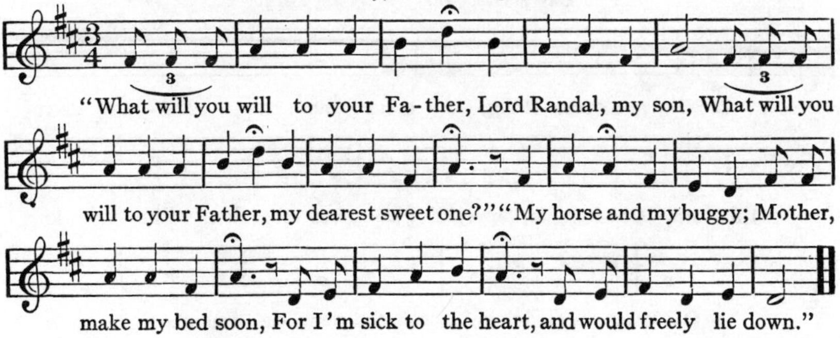

No. 7 (*C*) WHAT IS THAT ON THE END OF YOUR SWORD?

Collected by Miss Martha M. Davis; sung by Mrs. Archibald Cummins, of Berryville, Virginia; Clark County; April 23, 1913.

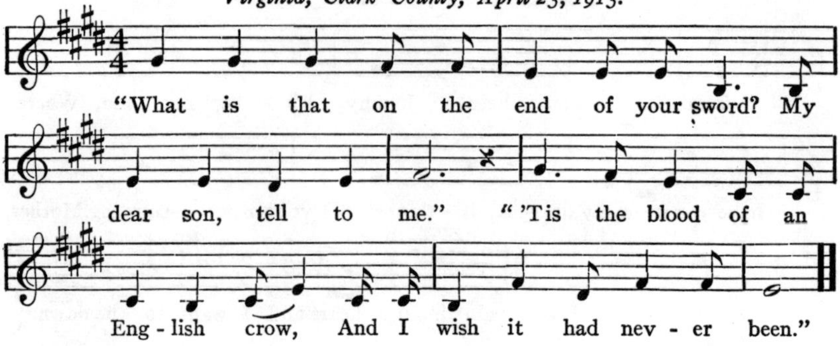

No. 7 (*D*) EDWARD

Collected by Mr. John Stone; sung by Mrs. Travers D. Moncure, of Aylett, Virginia; King William County; September 13, 1917.

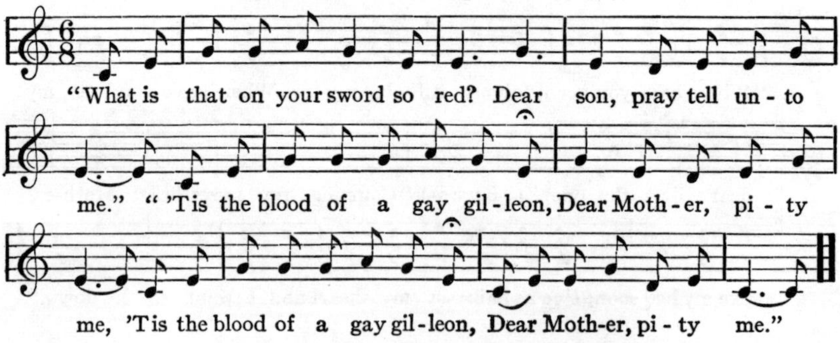

No. 8 (*A*) BANGUM AND THE BOAR

Collected by Miss Juliet Fauntleroy; sung by Mr. H. W. Adams, near Altavista, Virginia; Campbell County; May 24, 1914.

No. 8 (*B*) OLD BANG 'EM

Reported by Prof. James M. Grainger; contributed by Miss Evelyn Purcell, of the Farmville Ballad Club; Albemarle County; November 20, 1913.

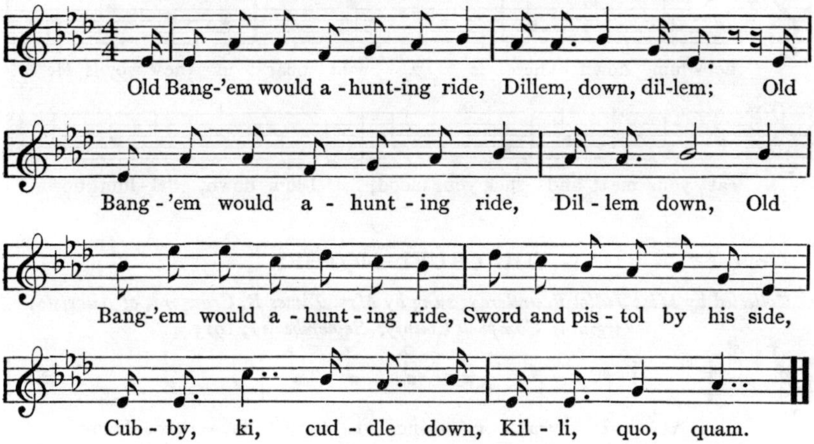

No. 8 (*F*) OLE BANGUM

Collected by Miss Dorothy Scarborough; sung by Mrs. Landon Randolph Dashiell; music noted by Mr. Shepard Webb, of Richmond, Virginia; Fauquier County; April 11, 1921.

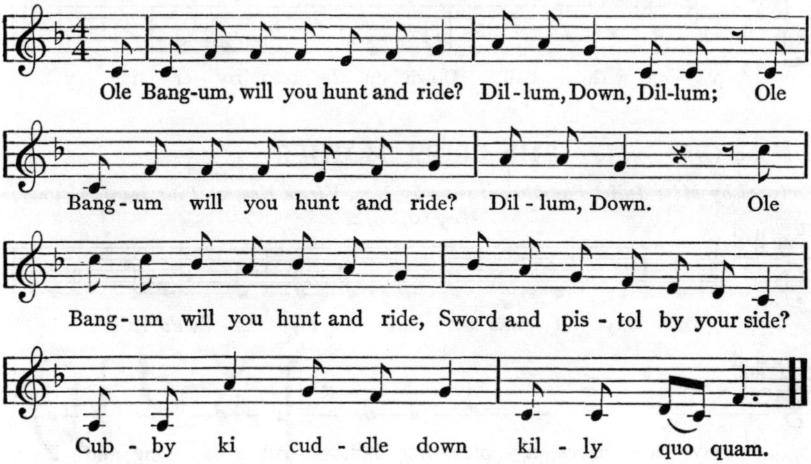

No. 8 (*G*) **SIR LIONEL**

Collected by Mr. Cecil J. Sharp and Miss Karpeles; sung by Mrs. Betty Smith and Mr. N. B. Chisholm, at Woodridge, Virginia; Albemarle County; September 28, 1916.

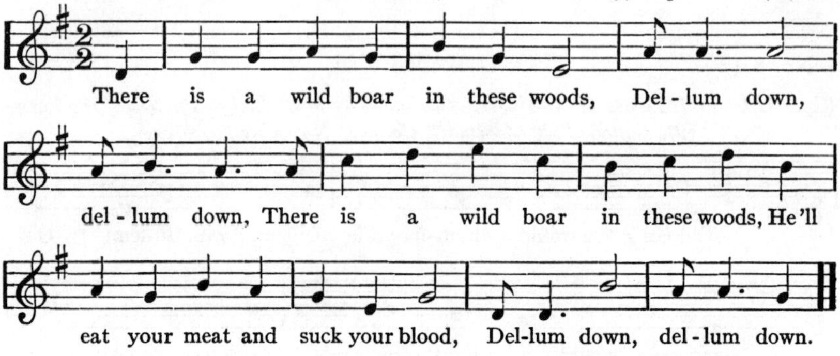

No. 9 (*A*) **THE CRUEL MOTHER**

Collected by Miss Juliet Fauntleroy; sung by Mrs. James B. Crawford, of Altavista, Virginia; Campbell County; September 11, 1915.

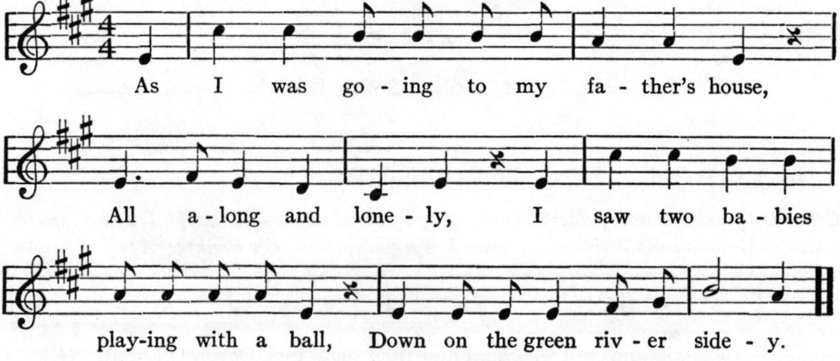

No. 9 (*B*) **THE CRUEL MOTHER**

Collected by Miss Juliet Fauntleroy; sung by Mrs. Virgie Keesee; Pittsylvania County; May 26, 1915.

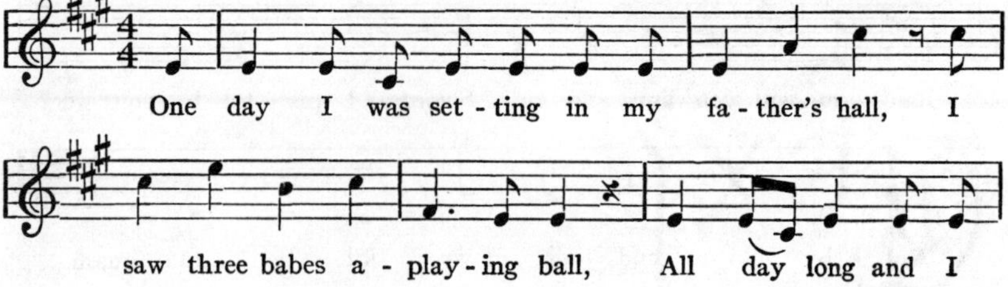

No. 9 (*C*) THE CRUEL MOTHER

Collected by Miss Martha M. Davis, of Harrisonburg, Virginia; sung by a mountain woman; Rockingham County; May 9, 1916.

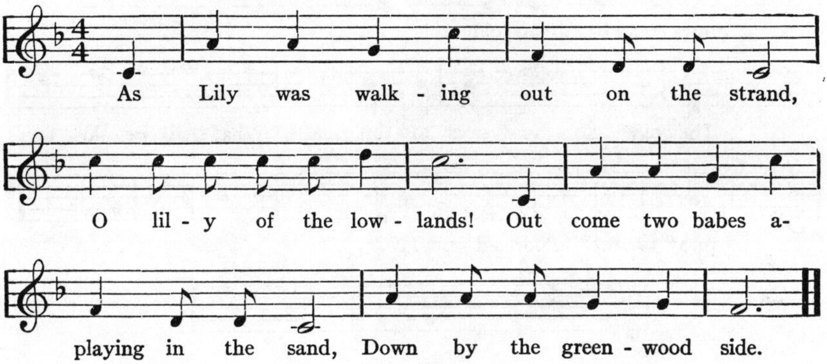

No. 9 (*E*) THE CRUEL MOTHER

Collected by Mr. Cecil J. Sharp and Miss Karpeles; sung by Mr. N. B. Chisholm, at Woodridge, Virginia; Albemarle County; September 28, 1916.

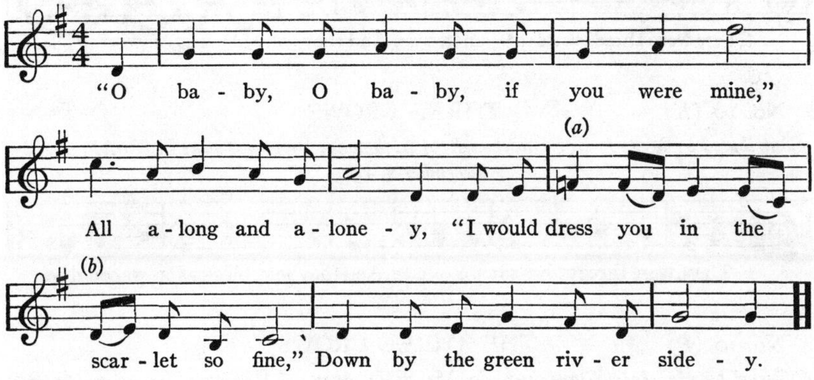

No. 10 (*I*) THE THREE RAVENS

Collected by Mr. Cecil J. Sharp; sung by Mr. Ben Burgess (76) at Charlottesville, Virginia; Albemarle County; September 28, 1916.

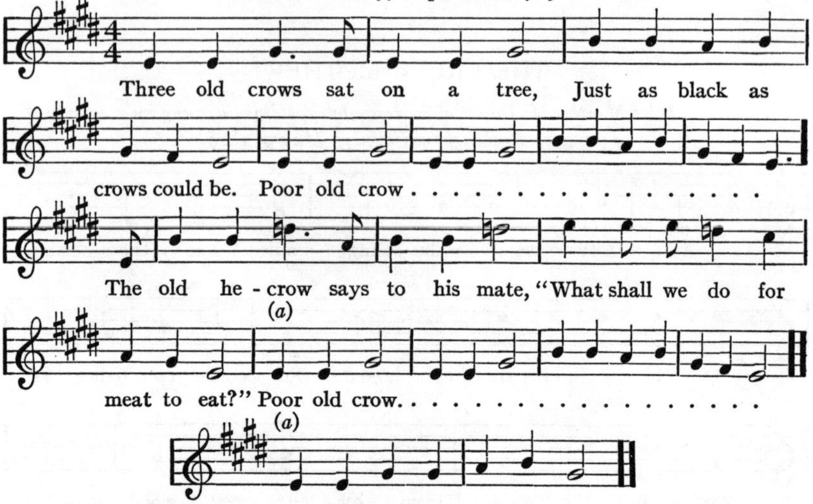

No. 10 (*J*) THE THREE CROWS

Collected by Mrs. J. B. Ferneyhough, of Richmond, Virginia; sung by Miss Elizabeth Grubb; Norfolk County; October 15, 1919.

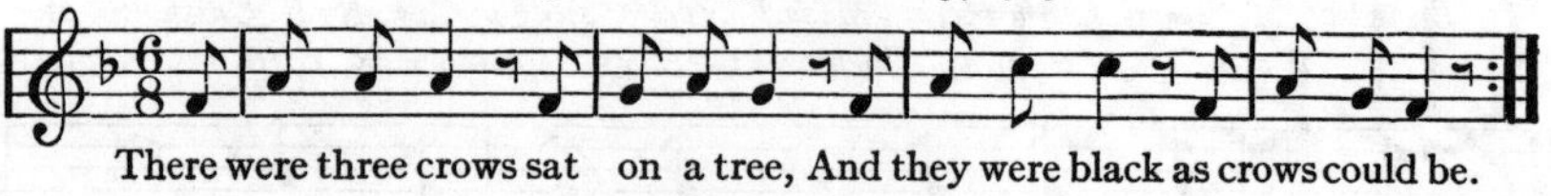

No. 10 (*K*) THREE CROWS

Contributed by Mrs. J. B. Ferneyhough, of Richmond, Virginia; sung in Norfolk County; December 2, 1919.

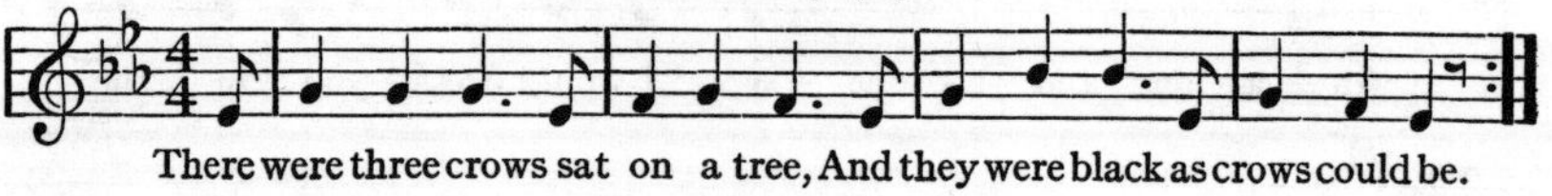

No. 10 (*P*) THE THREE CROWS

Collected by Mr. John Stone; sung by Mr. J. D. Fray, of Madison, Virginia; Madison County; November 3, 1920.

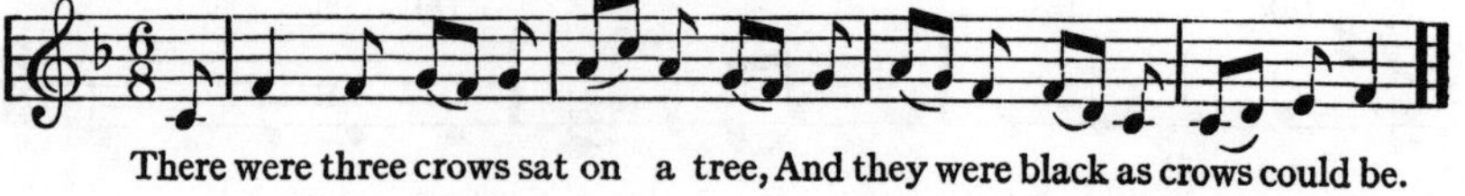

No. 11 (*A*) THE TWO BROTHERS

Collected by Mr. John Stone; sung by Miss Etta Shifflett, of Blackwell's Hollow, Virginia; Albemarle County; November 10, 1919.

No. 11 (*D*) THE TWO BROTHERS

Collected by Mr. Cecil J. Sharp and Miss Karpeles; sung by Mr. Nuel Walton, at Mount Fair, Brown's Cove, Virginia; Albemarle County; September 28, 1916.

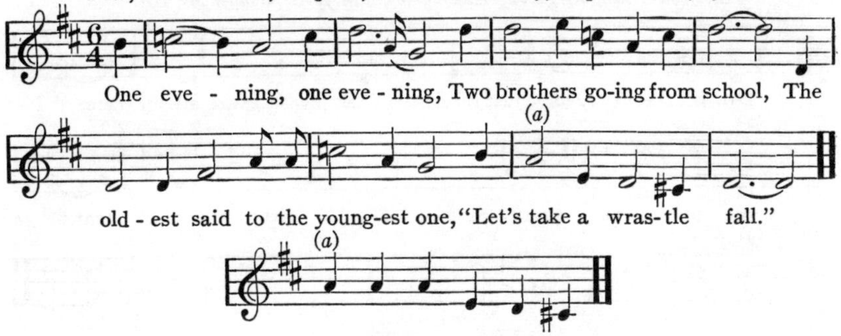

No. 11 (*E*) THE TWO BROTHERS

Collected by Miss Juliet Fauntleroy; sung by Mr. Dan Maxie, at Altavista, Virginia; Franklin County; May 9, 1914.

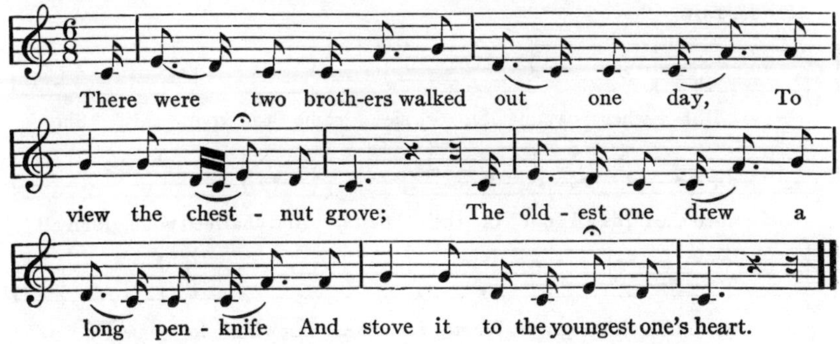

No. 11 (*F*) THE TWO BROTHERS

Collected by Miss Martha M. Davis; sung by Mrs. Rosie Morris, of Elkton, Virginia; Rockingham County; August 30, 1922.

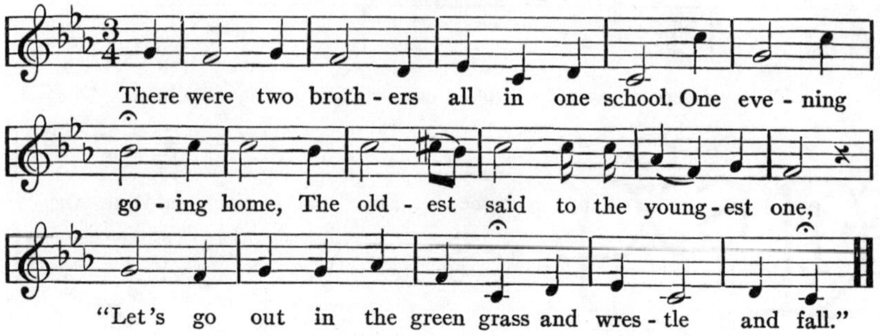

No. 11 (*H*) THE TWO BROTHERS

Collected by Mr. Cecil J. Sharp and Miss Karpeles; sung by Mrs. Rosie Smith (33), at Charlottesville, Virginia; Albemarle County; September 20, 1916.

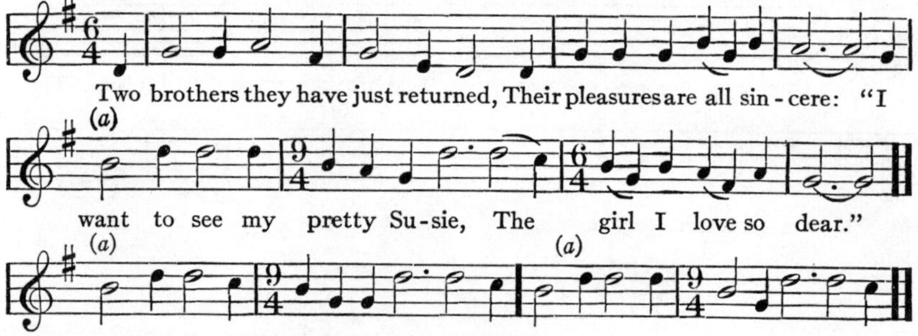

No. 11 (*I*) THE TWO BROTHERS

Collected by Mr. Cecil J. Sharp and Miss Karpeles; sung by Mr. Ozro Keeton (25) and his mother, at Mount Fair, Brown's Cove, Virginia; Albemarle County; September 28, 1916.

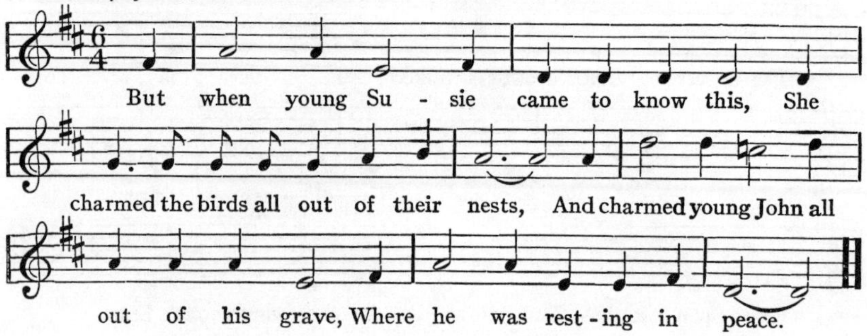

No. 12 (*D*) LORD BATEMAN AND THE TURKISH LADY, OR THE TURKISH LADY

Collected by Mr. B. C. Moomaw, Jr.; sung by Mr. Sam Pritt, of Barber, Virginia; Alleghany County; November 28, 1924.

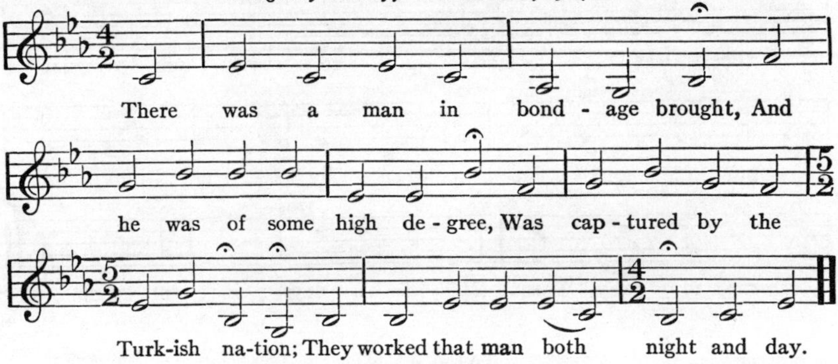

No. 12 (*I*) THE TURKISH LADY

Collected by Miss Martha M. Davis; sung by Mrs. M. Leake, of Harrisonburg, Virginia; Rockingham County; November 21, 1918.

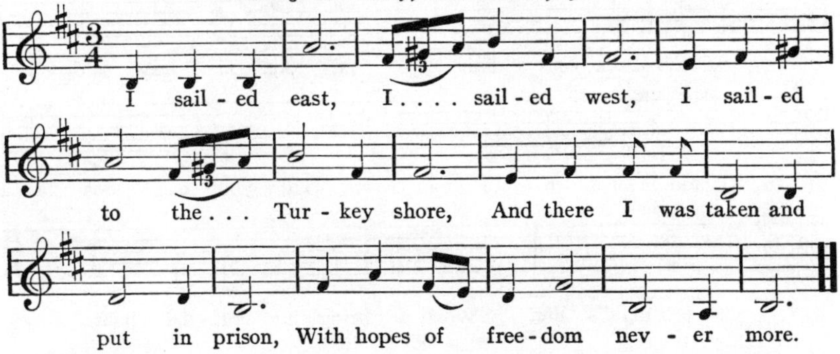

No. 13 (*B*) THE CHERRY TREE CAROL

Collected by Mr. John Stone; sung by a Negro woman in Culpeper County, Virginia; November 15, 1916.

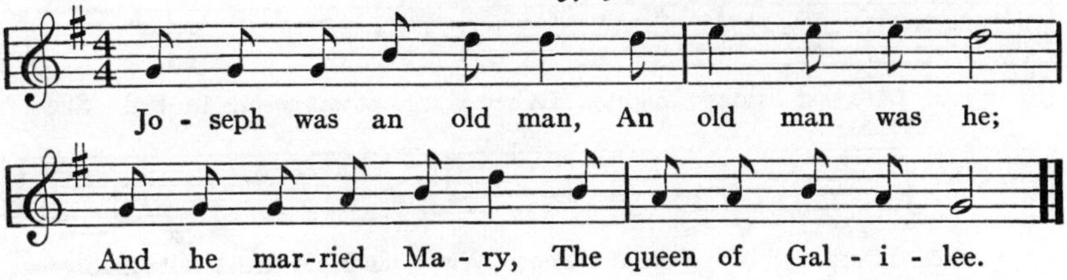

No. 14 LAZARUS AND DIVES, or THE RICH MAN DIVES

Collected by Mr. B. C. Moomaw, Jr.; sung by Mr. Sam Pritt, of Barber, Virginia; Alleghany County; November 28, 1924.

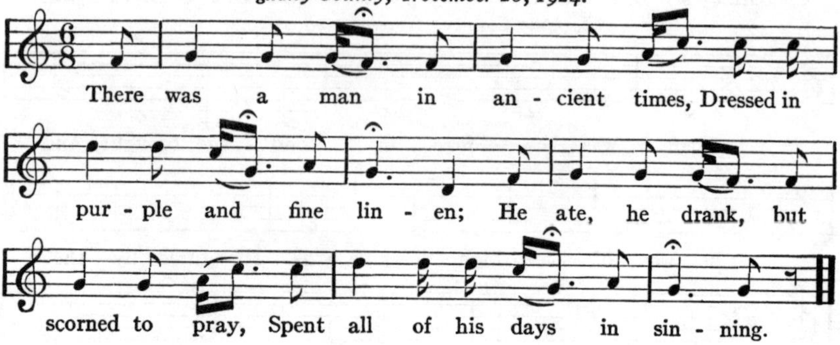

No. 15 FAIR ANNIE

Collected by Mr. John Stone; music written by Mrs. Mary Greiner and Miss Ella Mock; sung by Mrs. Martha Elizabeth Lethcoe, of Damascus, Virginia; Washington County; November 8, 1921.

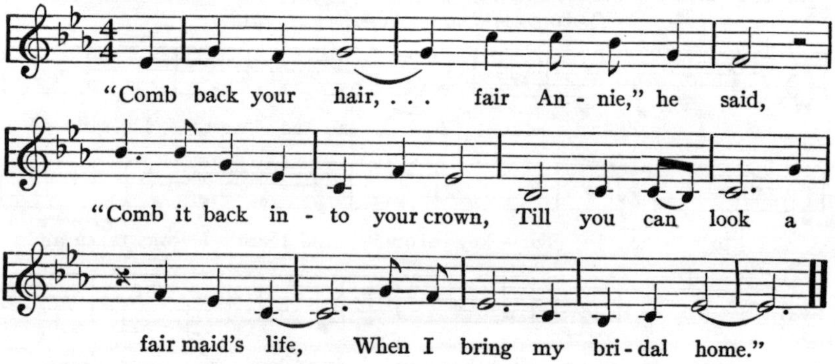

No. 17 (B) SIR HENRY AND LADY MARGARET

Collected by Miss Alfreda M. Peel; sung by Mrs. Witt, of Salem, Virginia; Roanoke County; February 9, 1919, or November 30, 1923.

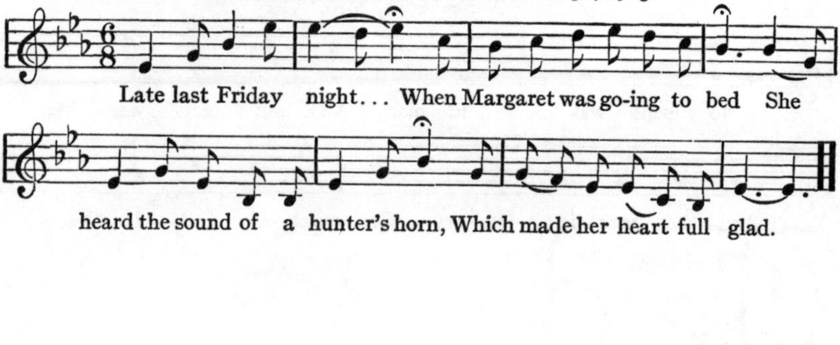

No. 17 (*D*) **YOUNG HUNTING**

Collected by Mr. Cecil J. Sharp and Miss Karpeles; sung by Mrs. Orilla Keeton, at Mount Fair, Virginia; Albemarle County; September 26, 1916.

NOTE: Subsequent stanzas are sung without the notes marked *, and with the following change for the section marked *a* . . . . *a*:

No. 17 (*E*) **LORD HENRY**

Collected by Miss Alfreda M. Peel, of Salem, Virginia; Giles County; April 23, 1922.

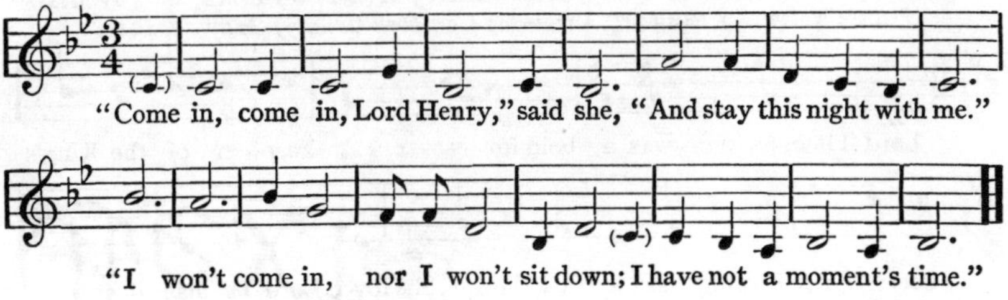

No. 17 (*F*) YOUNG HUNTING

Collected by Mr. John Stone; sung by Mrs. Brice Walton, at Mount Fair, Virginia; Albemarle County; November 10, 1919.

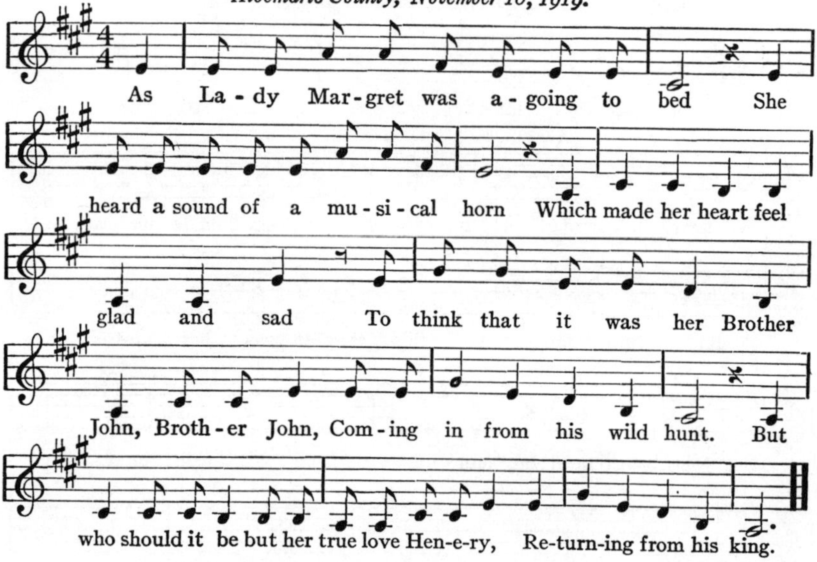

No. 18 (*A*) LORD THOMAS AND FAIR ELENOR

Collected by Messrs. Carpenter and Stone; sung by Mrs. J. A. Mitchell, Miss Mary Mitchell, and Mrs. H. Hoffman; Madison County; November 3, 1920.

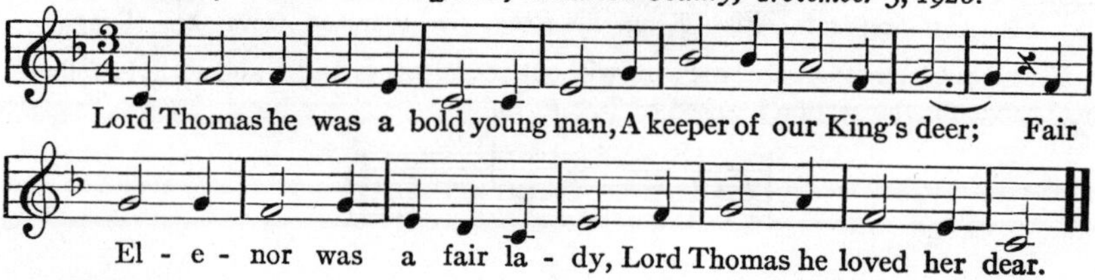

No. 18 (*B*) LORD THOMAS AND FAIR ELEANOR

Reported by Miss Juliet Fauntleroy; contributed by Miss Mary Finch; sung by Miss Jennie Nelson, of Rustburg, Virginia; Campbell County; May 24, 1919.

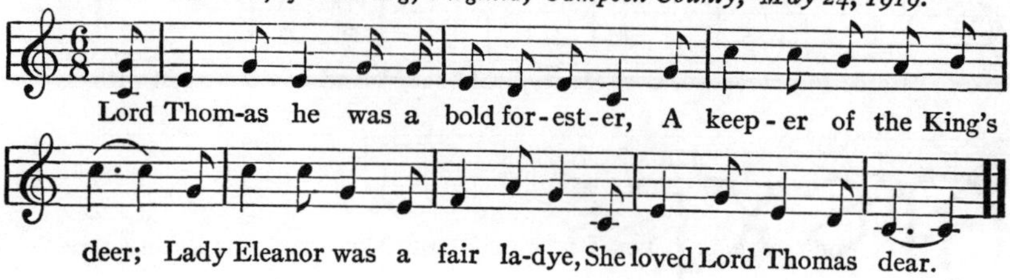

No. 18 (*D*), I FAIR ELLEN

Sent by Miss Alfreda M. Peel; noted by Miss Mildred McLaughlin; sung by Sis Sears, of Salem, Virginia; Roanoke County; November 5, 1916.

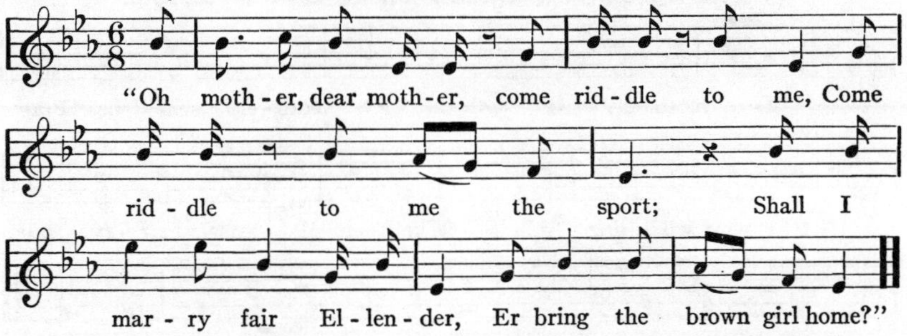

No. 18 (*D*), II LORD THOMAS AND THE BROWN GIRL

Collected by Miss Alfreda M. Peel; sung by Sis Sears, of Salem, Virginia; Roanoke County; November 30, 1923.

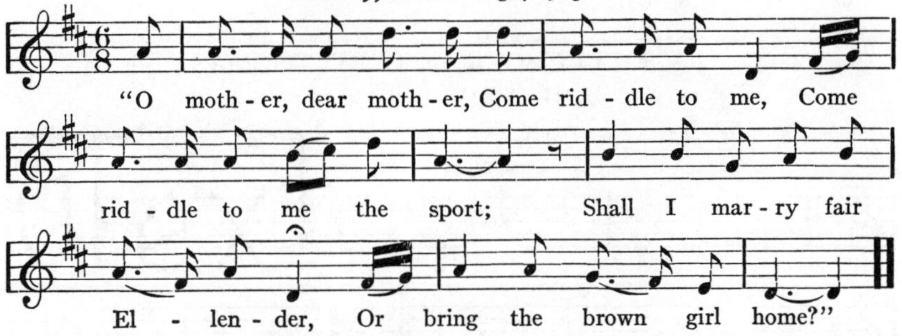

No. 18 (*L*) THE BROWN GIRL, OR LORD THOMAS AND FAIR ELLENDER

Collected by Miss Juliet Fauntleroy; sung by Mrs. Dan Maxie, née Holland, of Altavista, Virginia; Franklin County; March 9, 1914.

No. 18 (*R*) LORD THOMAS AND FAIR ELINOR

Collected by Mr. Cecil J. Sharp and Miss Karpeles; sung by Mrs. Kate Campbell, at Woodridge, Virginia; Albemarle County; September 28, 1916.

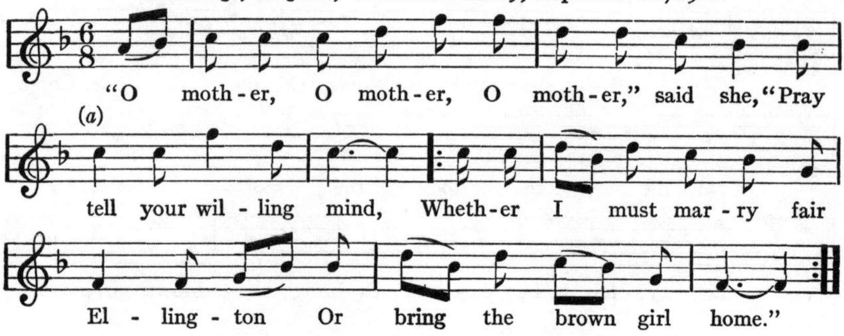

No. 18 (*S*) FAIR ELLENDER, OR LORD THOMAS AND FAIR ELLINOR

Collected by Miss Martha M. Davis, of Harrisonburg, Virginia; Rockingham County; May 9, 1916.

No. 19 (*E*) SWEET WILLIAM AND LADY MARGARET

Collected by Mr. John Stone; sung by Mr. T. C. Clark, of Whitehall, Virginia; Albemarle County; November 3, 1920.

No. 19 (*F*) LADY MARGET

Collected by Miss Martha M. Davis; sung by Mrs. William Keister; Rockingham County; July 31, 1913.

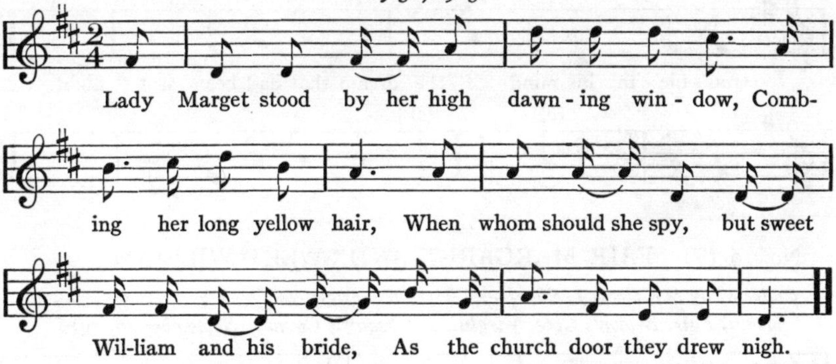

No. 19 (*G*) FAIR MARGARET AND SWEET WILLIAM

Collected by Miss Nancy Pearson; sung by Mr. Armistead, of Cobbs Creek, Virginia; Mathews County; March 20, 1916.

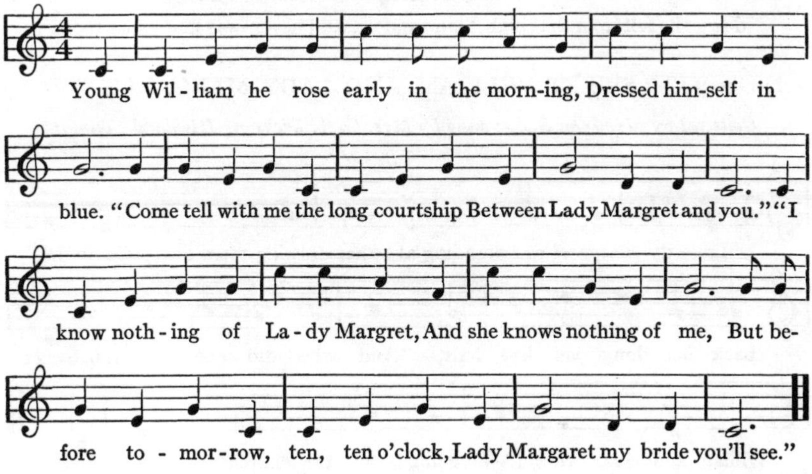

No. 19 (*I*) FAIR MARGARET AND SWEET WILLIAM

Collected by Mr. Cecil J. Sharp and Miss Karpeles; sung by Mr. N. B. Chisholm, at Woodridge, Virginia; Albemarle County; September 23, 1916.

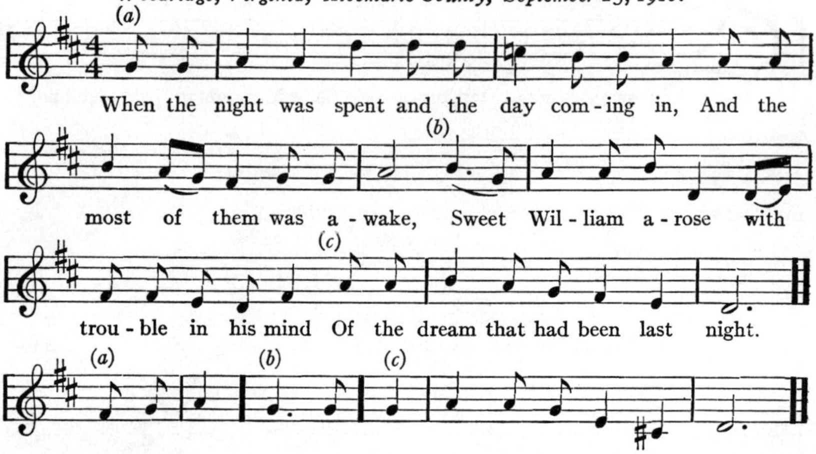

No. 19 (*J*) FAIR MARGARET AND SWEET WILLIAM

Collected by Mr. Cecil J. Sharp and Miss Karpeles; sung by Mrs. Orilla Keeton at Mount Fair, Brown's Cove, Virginia; Albemarle County; September 26, 1916.

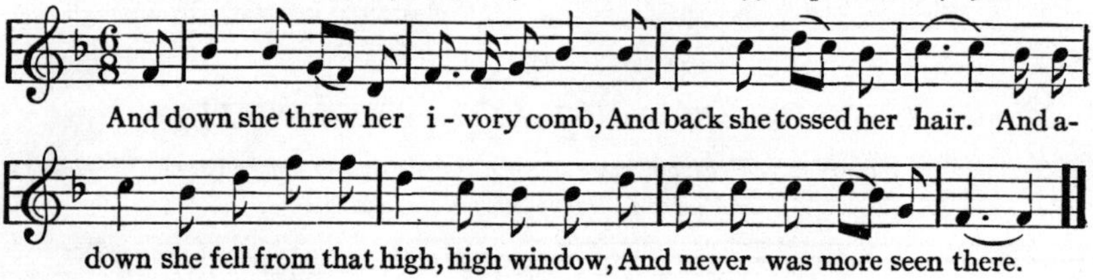

No. 19 (*K*) SWEET WILLIAM AND LADY MARGARET

Collected by Mr. John Stone; sung by Mrs. C. A. Dickson; Highland County; November 3, 1920.

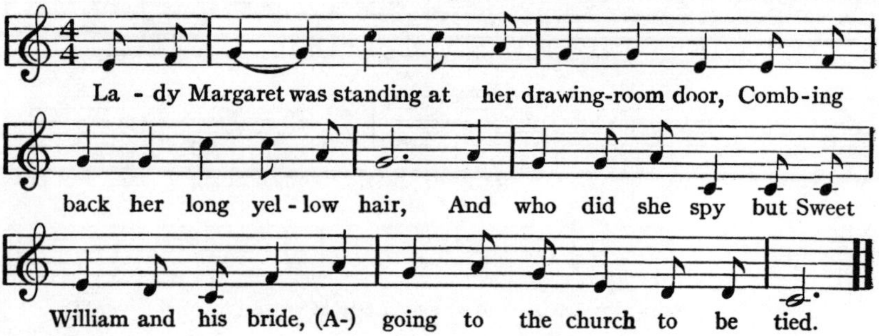

No. 19 (*M*) LADY MARGARET

Collected by Miss Juliet Fauntleroy; sung by Mr. Alonzo Hogan and Miss Callie Hogan, Lynch Station, Virginia; Campbell County; February, 1914.

No. 19 (*P*) LADY MARGARET AND SWEET WILLIAM

Collected by Mr. John Stone; sung by Mr. Raz Shifflett, of Blackwell's Hollow, Virginia; Albemarle County; November 2, 1920.

No. 20 (*B*) LORD LOVEL

Collected by Miss Alfreda M. Peel; sung by Mrs. John Roberts, of Roanoke, Virginia; Roanoke County; October 19, 1919.

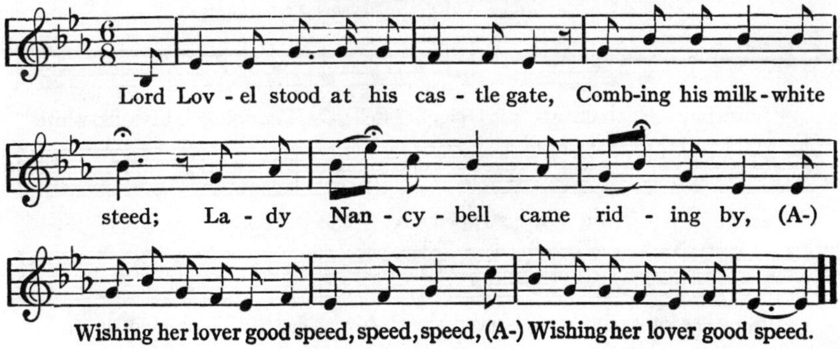

No. 20 (*E*) **LORD LOVEL**

Collected by Miss Juliet Fauntleroy; sung by Mrs. Frank P. Christian, of Lynchburg, Virginia; Campbell County; May 24, 1914.

No. 20 (*L*) **LORD LOVEL**

Collected by Mr. John Stone; sung by Mr. Thomas H. Bailey; Page County; November 10, 1919.

No. 20 (*O*) **LORD LOVEL**

Collected by Mr. John Stone; sung by Mrs. Mary E. Bell, of Shirley, Virginia; Charles City County; September 13, 1917.

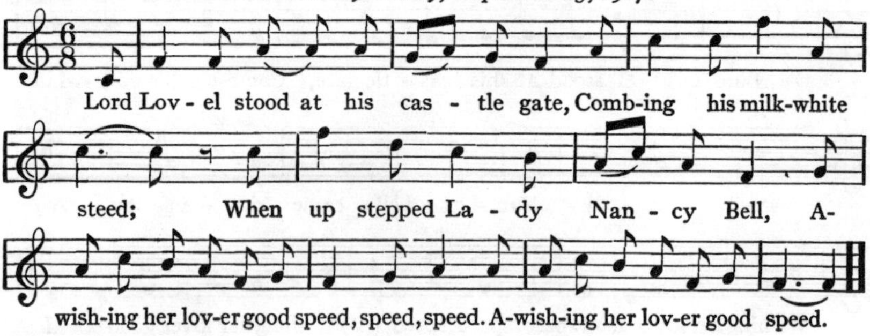

No. 21 (*A*) LASS OF ROCH ROYAL

Collected by Mr. John Stone; sung by Mrs. Terry; King William County; November 15, 1916.

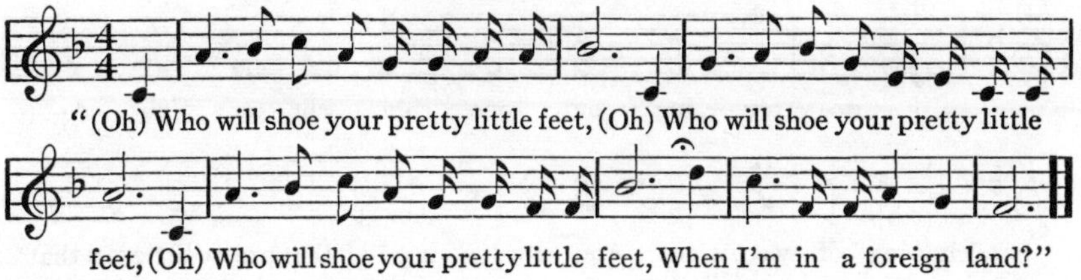

No. 21 (*U*) LOVE GREGORY

Collected by Mr. John Stone; sung by Mrs. C. A. Dickson; Highland County; November 3, 1920.

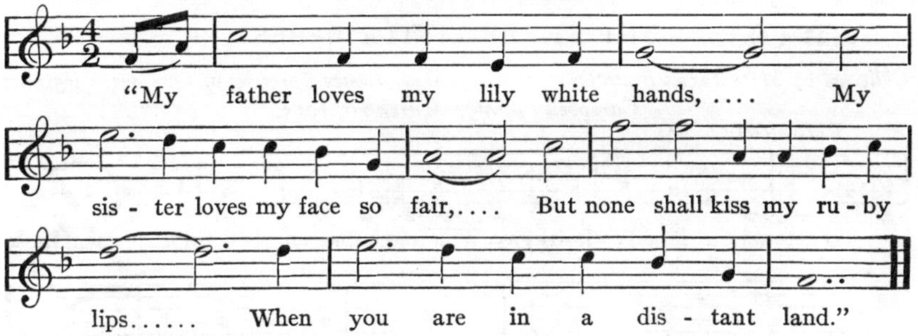

No. 21 (Appendix, *A*) LASS OF ROCH ROYAL

Collected by Mr. John Stone; sung by Mrs. Nathaniel Stone, of Culpeper, Virginia; Culpeper County; November 15, 1916.

No. 21 (Appendix, *G*) COLD WINTER'S NIGHT

Collected by Miss Juliet Fauntleroy; sung by Mrs. Maxie, Altavista, Virginia; Franklin County; April 7, 1914.

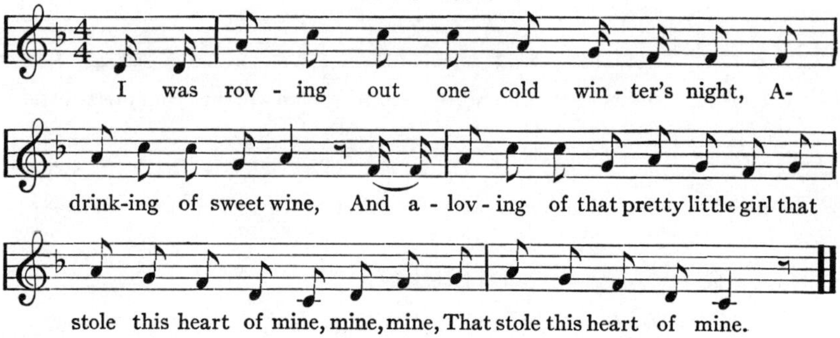

No. 22 (*J*) THE THREE LITTLE BABES

Collected by Miss Juliet Fauntleroy; sung by Mrs. James Sprouse, of Lawyers, Virginia; Campbell County; March 20, 1915.

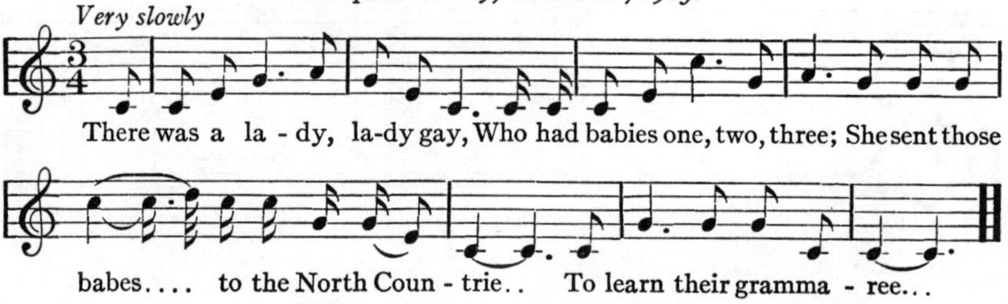

No. 22 (*L*) LADY GAY

Collected by Miss Martha M. Davis, of Harrisonburg, Virginia; Rockingham County; March 2, 1916.

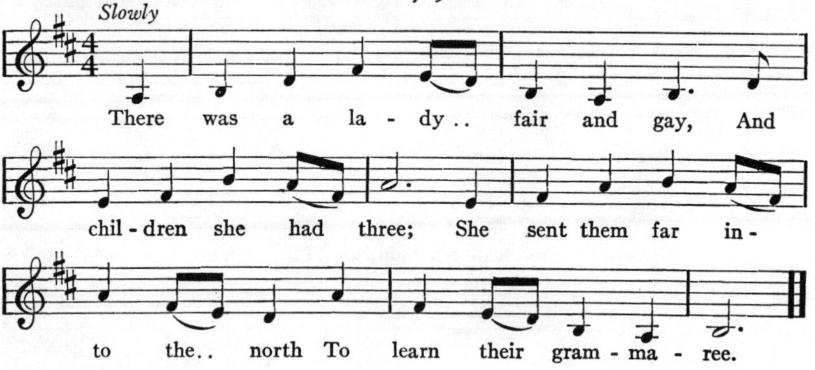

No. 23 (*F*) LORD DANIEL'S WIFE

Collected by Miss Alfreda Peel; music written by Miss Daisy Wingfield, of Roanoke County; sung by Mrs. Nancy Kitts and Miss Rosa Tickle, of Bland, Virginia; Bland County; November 30, 1923.

No. 24 (*G*) BARBARA ALLEN

Collected by Miss Juliet Fauntleroy; sung by Mrs. Seely Ann Kegly, of Altavista, Virginia; Grayson County; September 21, 1915.

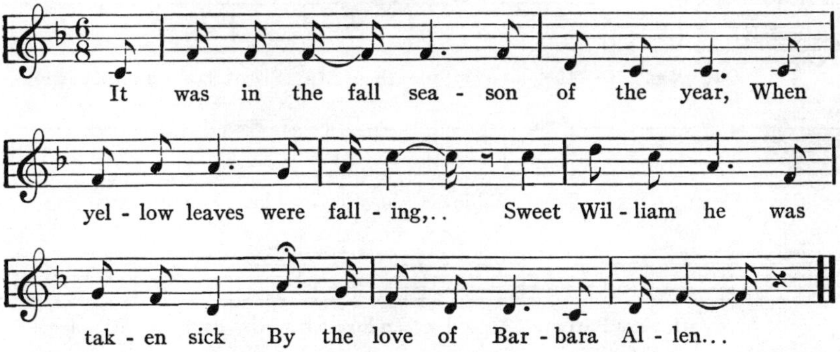

No. 24 (*H*) BARBARA ALLEN

Collected by Miss Juliet Fauntleroy; sung by Mrs. John Maxie, née Lily Stone, near Altavista, Virginia; Campbell County; June 29, 1914.

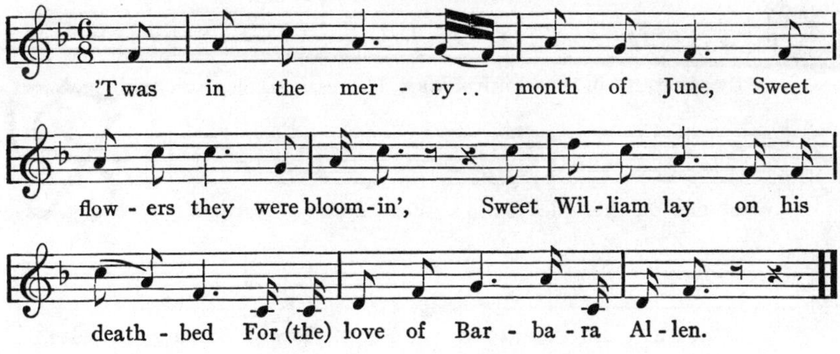

No. 24 (*I*) BARBARA ALLEN

Collected by Miss Alfreda M. Peel; sung by Texas Gladden, near Salem, Virginia; Roanoke County; May 27, 1917.

No. 24 (*U*) BARBARA ALLEN

Collected by Miss Juliet Fauntleroy; sung by Mr. Hall, near Altavista, Virginia; Campbell County; May 28, 1914.

No. 24 (*Y*) BARBARA ALLEN

Collected by Mr. John Stone; sung by Mr. Ed. Davis, of Shipman, Virginia; Nelson County; November 15, 1915.

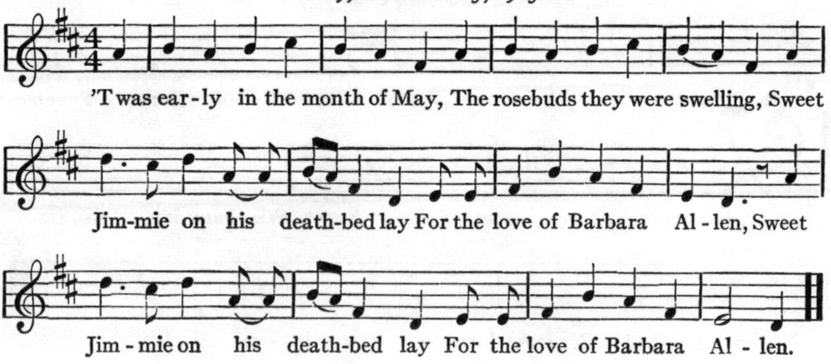

No. 24 (*AA*) BARBARA ALLEN

Collected by Miss Juliet Fauntleroy; sung by Mrs. H. W. Adams, near Altavista, Virginia; Campbell County; June 21, 1914.

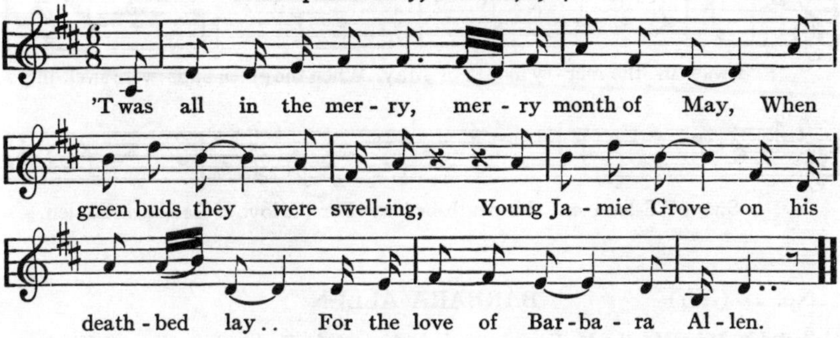

No. 24 (*DD*) BARBARA ALLEN

Collected by Mr. John Stone; sung by Mrs. C. A. Dickson, of Trimble, Virginia; Highland County; November 3, 1920.

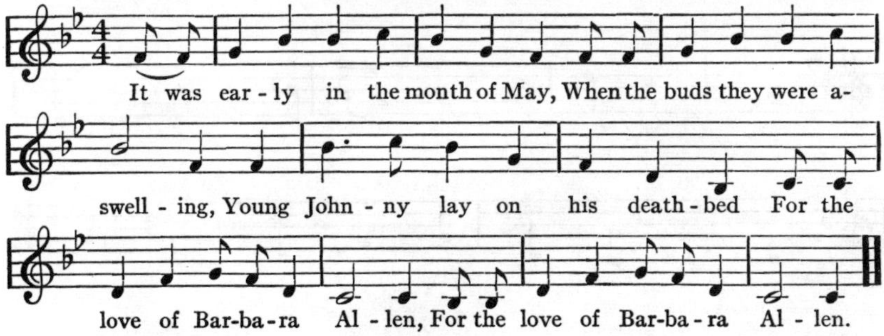

No. 24 (*FF*) BARBARA ALLEN

Collected by Miss Alfreda M. Peel; music by Miss Evelyn Rex, Richmond, Virginia; sung by Sis Sears, of Salem, Virginia; Roanoke County; November 30, 1923.

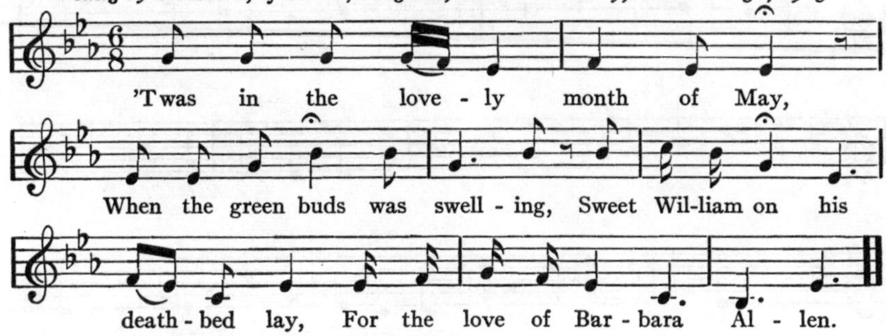

No. 24 (*GG*) BARBARA ALLEN

Collected by Mr. John Stone; heard in many places in Virginia; September 15, 1915.

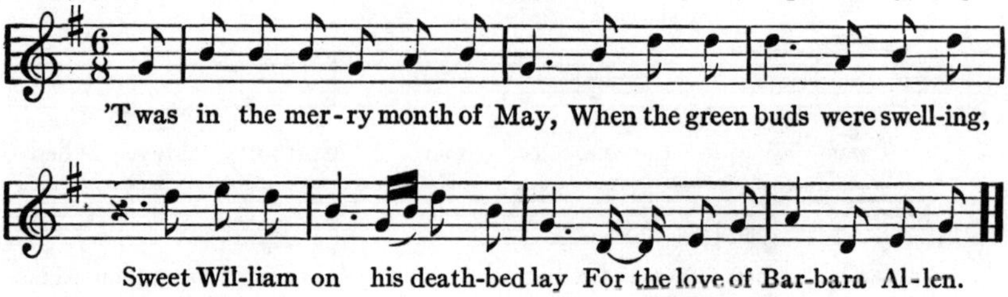

No. 24 (*HH*) BARBARA ALLEN

Collected by Miss Martha M. Davis; sung by old people in Rockingham County; Virginia; December 14, 1914.

No. 24 (*II*) BARBARA ALLEN

Collected by Miss Martha M. Davis; sung by Mrs. N. W. Hough, of Lynchburg, Virginia; Campbell County; December 12, 1914.

No. 24 (*JJ*) **BARBARA ALLEN**

Collected by Mr. Cecil J. Sharp; sung by Mr. N. B Chisholm, of Woodridge, Virginia; Albemarle County; September 28, 1916.

No. 25 (*B*) **JOHNNY COLLINS**

Collected by Mr. John Stone; sung by Mrs. Julie Simmons; Highland County; November 3, 1920.

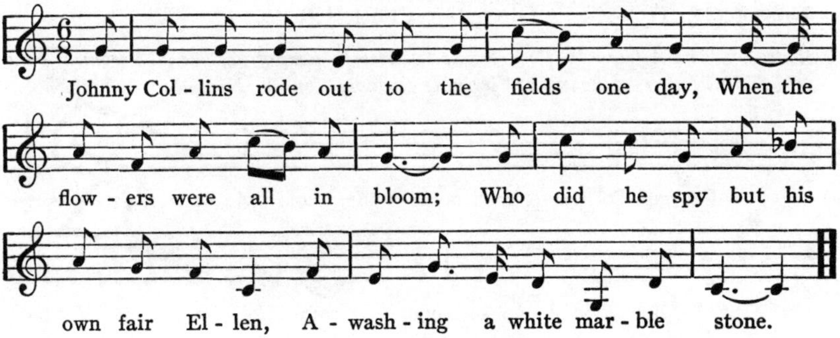

No. 25 (*C*) **GEORGE COLLINS**

Collected by Miss Juliet Fauntleroy; sung by Mrs. Lit Arthur, née Taylor, of Altavista, Virginia; Campbell County; March 14, 1914.

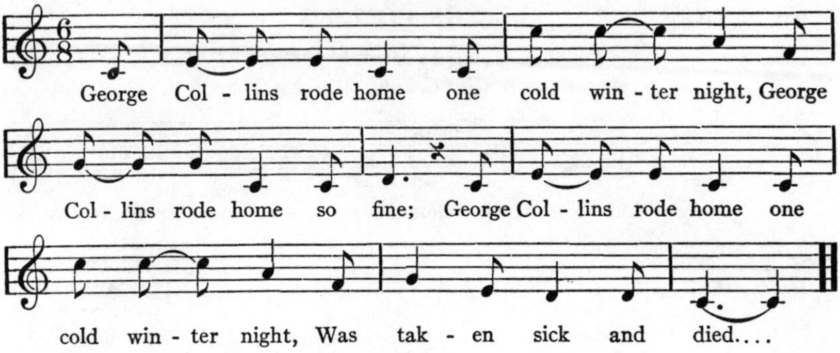

No. 25 (*D*), I GEORGE COLLINS

Collected by Miss Alfreda M. Peel; sung by Mrs. Lester, of Roanoke, Virginia; Roanoke County; May 27, 1917.

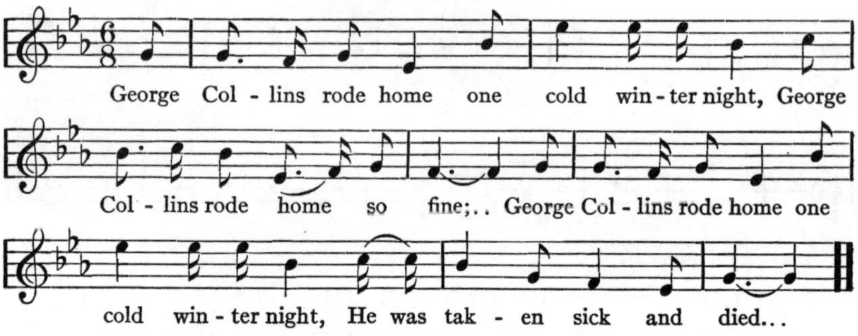

No. 25 (*D*), II GEORGE COLLINS

Collected by Miss Alfreda M. Peel; music by Miss E. Rex, of Richmond, Virginia; sung by Mrs. Lester, of Roanoke, Virginia; Roanoke County; November 30, 1923.

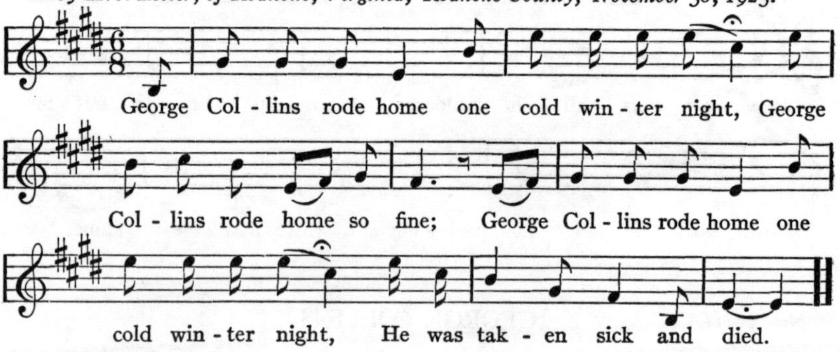

No. 25 (*E*) GEORGE COLLINS

Collected by Miss Juliet Fauntleroy; sung by Mrs. Dan Maxie, née Holland, of Altavista, Virginia; Franklin County; March 2, 1914.

No. 26 (*B*) LAMPKIN

Reported by Miss Martha M. Davis; contributed by Mrs. Thomas Ware; sung by an old Colored servant, Fanny Fletcher; Clarke County; September 5, 1914.

As contributed:

As possibly sung:

No. 27 (*B*) MAID FREED FROM THE GALLOWS

Collected by Mr. Cecil J. Sharp and Miss Karpeles; sung by Mrs. Orilla Keeton, at Mount Fair, Brown's Cove, Virginia; Albemarle County; September 26, 1916.

No. 27 (*E*) THE HANGERMAN'S TREE, or FREED FROM THE GALLOWS

Collected by Miss Juliet Fauntleroy; sung by Mrs. Maxie, née Holland, of Altavista, Virginia; Franklin County; March 23, 1914.

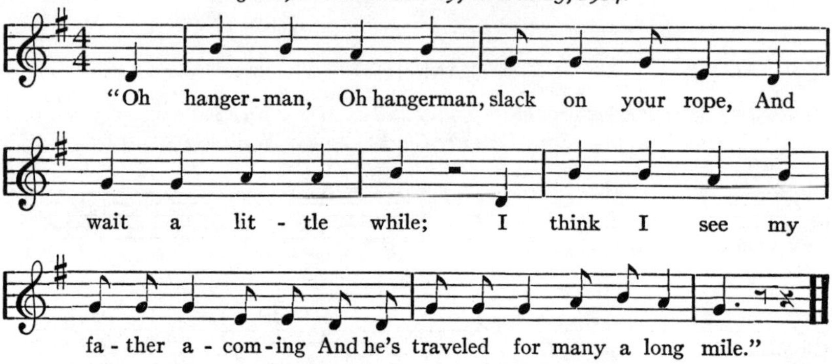

No. 27 (*F*) MAID FREED FROM THE GALLOWS

Collected by Mr. Cecil J. Sharp and Miss Karpeles; sung by Mr. N. B. Chisholm, at Woodridge, Virginia; Albemarle County; September 27, 1916.

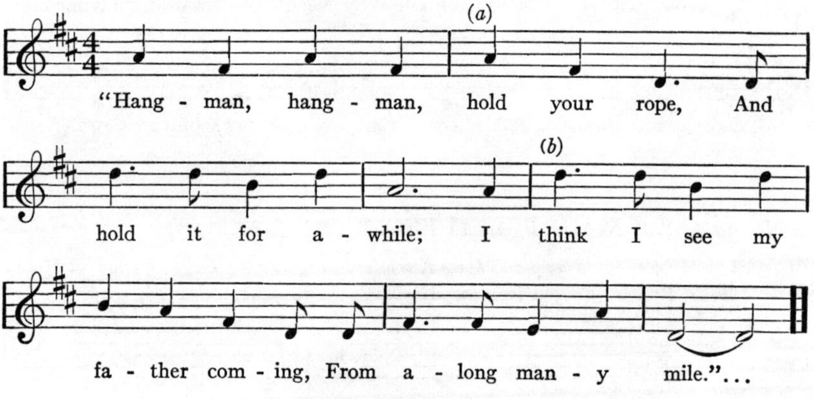

(*b*) *Mrs. Betty Smith's version.*

No. 27 (*M*) THE MAID SAVED

Collected by Mr. John Stone; sung by Mr. Ed. Davis, of Shipman, Virginia; Nelson County; September 15, 1915.

No. 27 (*N*) HANGSMAN

Collected by Mr. John Stone; sung by Mr. J. D. Carpenter; Madison County; November 3, 1920.

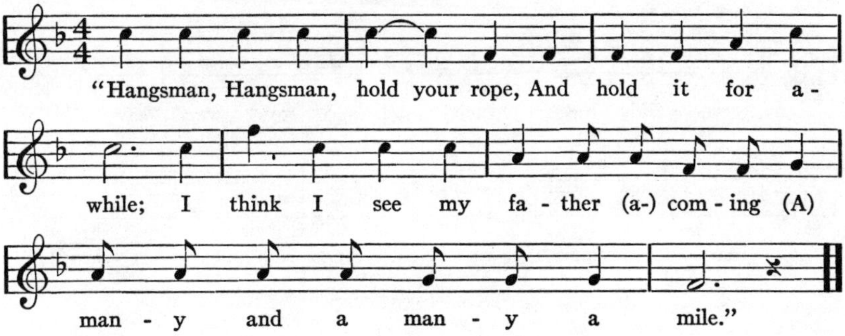

No. 28 (*B*) THE BAILIFF'S DAUGHTER OF ISLINGTON

Contributed by Professor Willoughby Reade, of the Episcopal High School, Alexandria, Virginia; from a childhood recollection; Alexandria County; November 16, 1928.

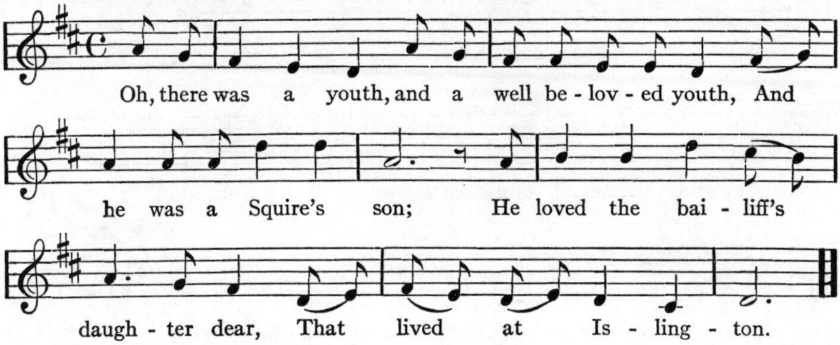

No. 30 THE DEATH OF ROBIN HOOD

Collected by Miss Martha M. Davis; dictated by her grandmother, in 1882; Rockingham County; April 8, 1913.

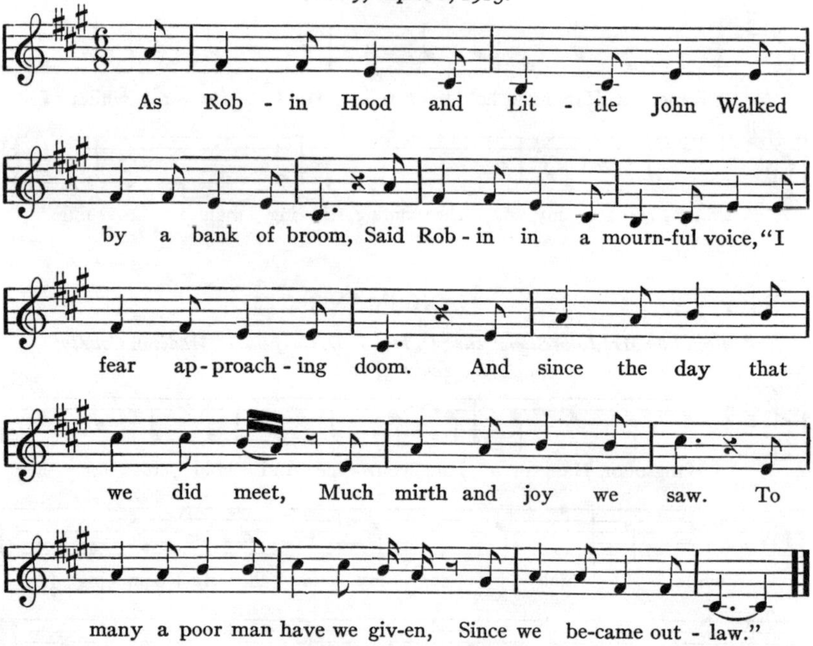

No. 31 ROBIN HOOD AND ARTHUR O'BLAND

Collected by Miss Martha M. Davis; dictated by her grandmother, in 1882; Rockingham County; April 8, 1913.

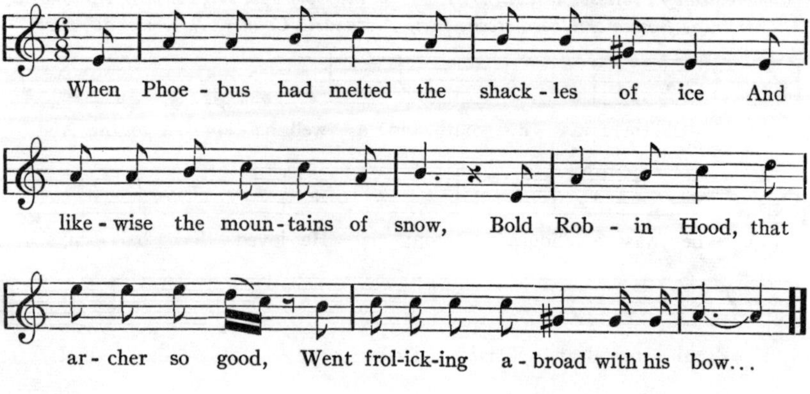

No. 32 THE RESCUE OF WILL STUTLY

Collected by Miss Martha M. Davis; dictated by her grandmother, in 1882; Rockingham County; April 8, 1913.

No. 33 (*A*) THE JEW'S DAUGHTER

Collected by Miss Martha M. Davis, of Harrisonburg, Virginia; Rockingham County; April 26, 1913.

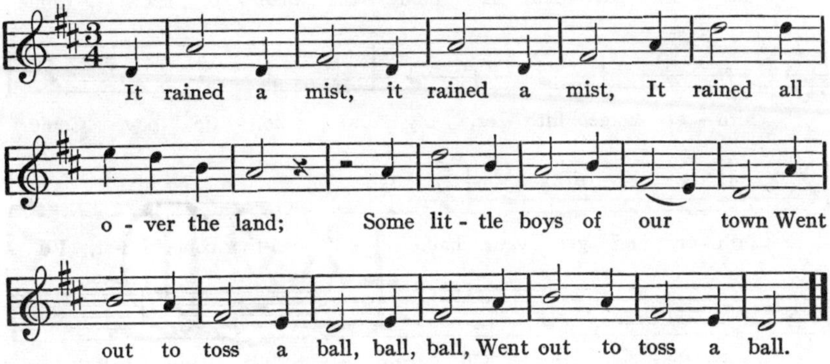

No. 33 (*C*) IT RAINED A MIST

Collected by Miss Alfreda M. Peel; sung by Miss Marie Hatfield, of Vinton, Virginia; Roanoke County; April 24, 1923.

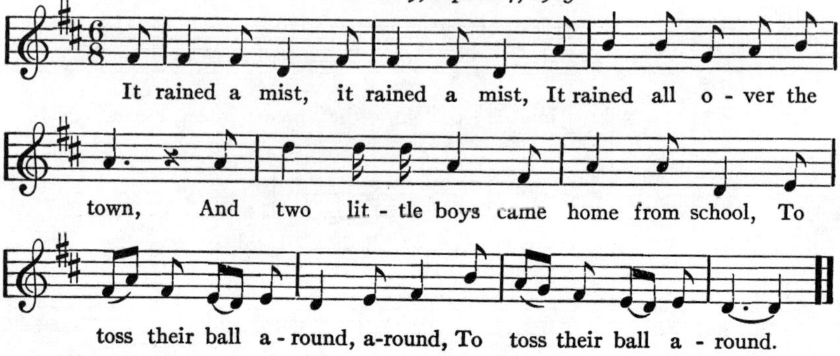

No. 33 (*E*) A LITTLE BOY THREW HIS BALL SO HIGH

Contributed by Mrs. Landon Dashiell, of Richmond, Virginia; sung by herself; Fauquier County; April 11, 1921.

No. 33 (*F*) IT RAINED A MIST

Collected by Miss Juliet Fauntleroy; sung by Mr. Jesse Burgess, of Altavista, Virginia; Campbell County; April 30, 1915.

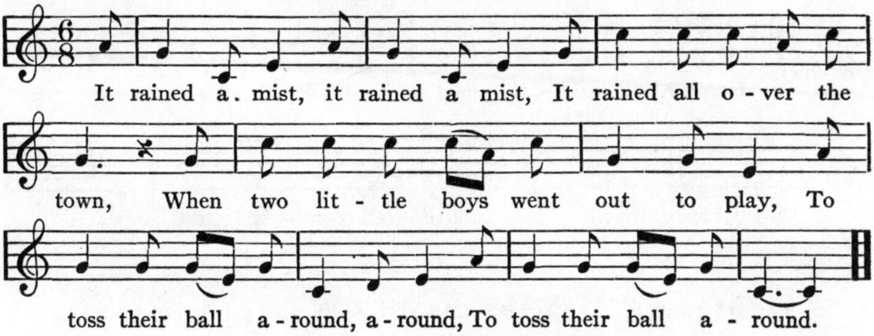

No. 33 (*I*) SIR HUGH, OR LITTLE HARRY HUGHES

Collected by Miss Juliet Fauntleroy; sung by Miss Charlotte Rodé, near Rustburg, Virginia; Campbell County; March 1, 1914.

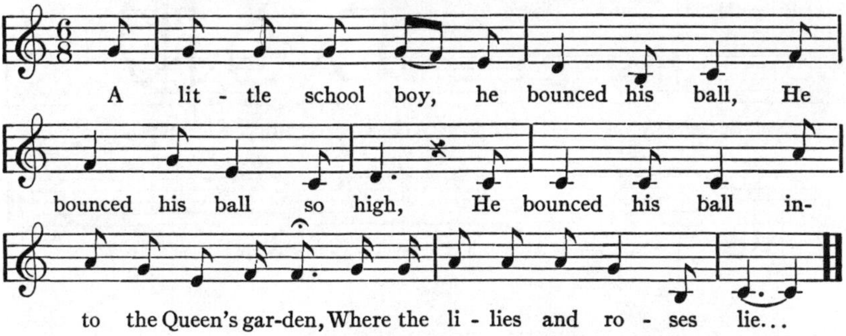

No. 33 (*K*) THE JEW'S DAUGHTER

Collected by Mr. John Stone; sung by Mr. Ed. Davis and Mrs. Marion Browning, of Shipman, Virginia; Nelson County; November 15, 1916.

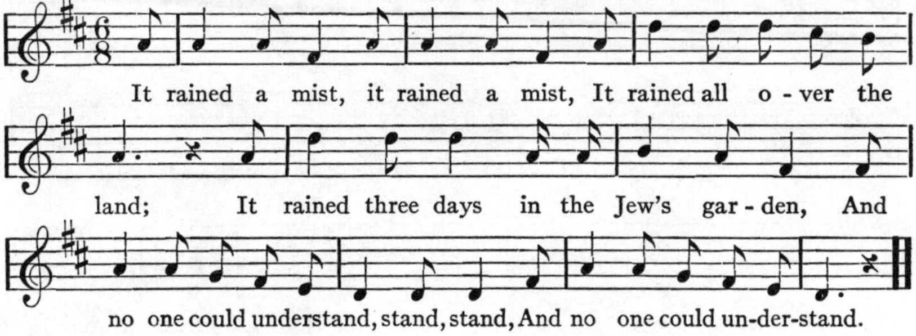

No. 33 (*L*) SIR HUGH

Contributed by Mr. and Mrs. George D. McLaughlin, of Benicia, California; learned in Rockbridge County, Virginia; May 15, 1916.

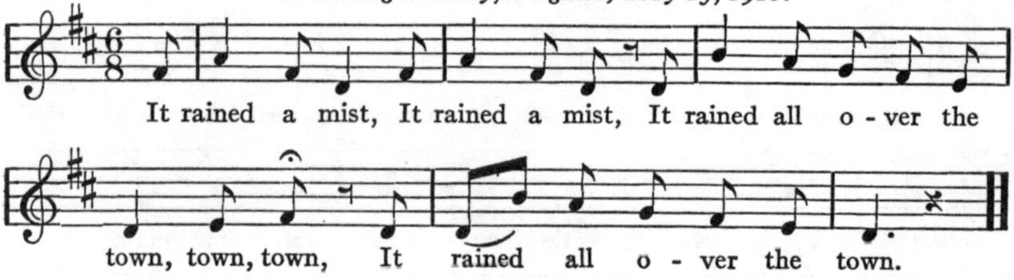

No. 36 (*A*) and (*B*) MARY HAMILTON

Collected by Miss Alfreda M. Peel; music by Miss Evelyn Rex; sung by Mrs. Libert Chandler, of Salem, Virginia; Roanoke County; November 30, 1923.

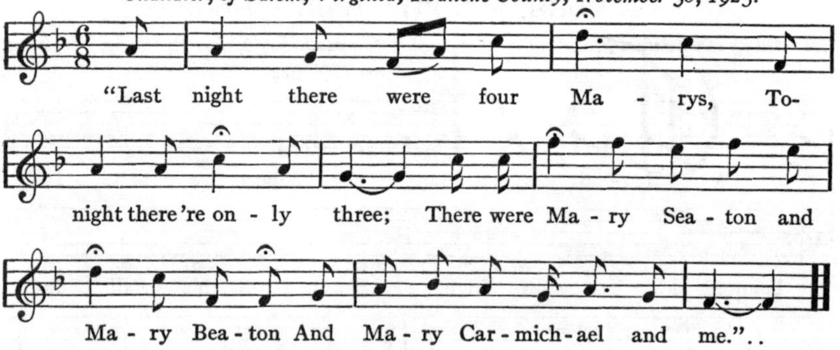

No.37 (*A*) THE GYPSY LADDIE

Collected by Miss Alfreda M. Peel; music by Miss Wingfield; sung by Miss Myrtle Harman, of Bland, Virginia; Bland County; August 28, 1923.

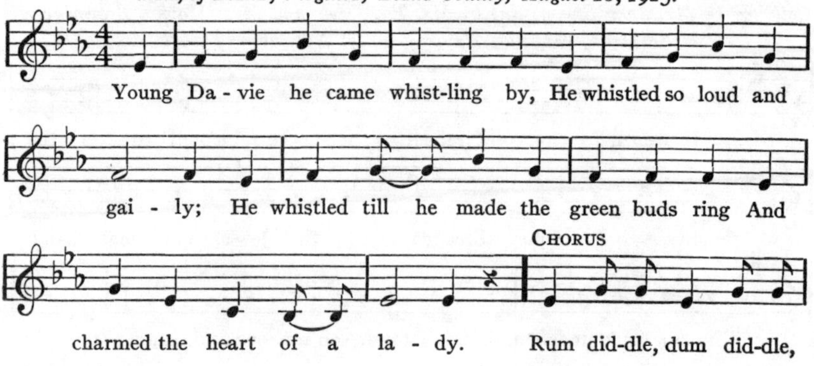

No. 37 (*D*) THE GYPSY LADDIE

Collected by Mr. John Stone; sung by Misses Fannie and Hattie Via, of Stage Junction, Virginia; Fluvanna County; November 3, 1920.

No. 37 (*H*) GYPSY LADDIE

Collected by Mr. Cecil J. Sharp and Miss Karpeles; sung by Mr. N. B. Chisholm, at Woodridge, Virginia; Albemarle County; September 27, 1916.

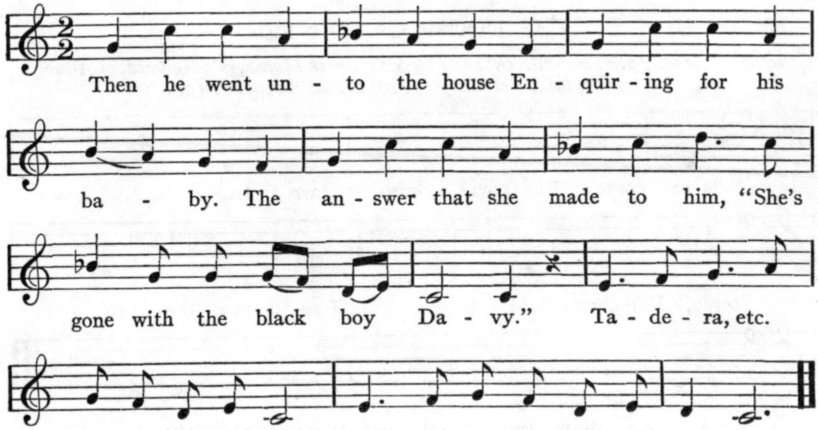

No. 39 (*B*) GEORGIE

Collected by Mr. Cecil J. Sharp; sung by Mrs. Laura Donald, at Dewey, Virginia; Bedford County; June 6, 1918.

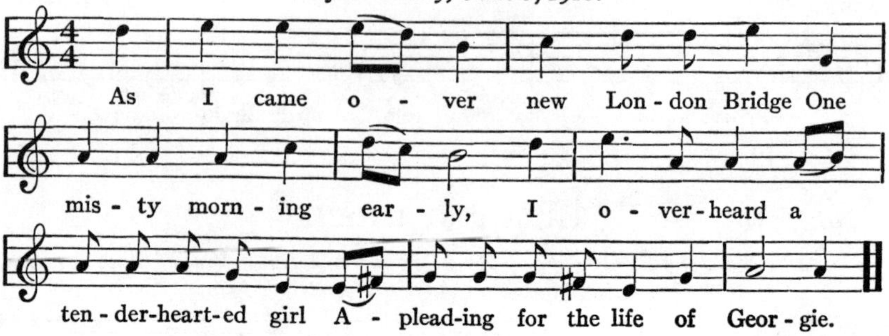

No. 40 (*C*) THE HOUSE CARPENTER

Collected by Miss Alfreda M. Peel; noted by Miss Evelyn Rex, of Richmond, Virginia; sung by Miss Rushia Richardson, of Vinton, Virginia; and by Sis Sears, of Salem, Virginia; Roanoke County; September 11, 1922.

No. 40 (*D*) THE HOUSE CARPENTER

Collected by Miss Juliet Fauntleroy; sung by Mrs. Jesse Maxie, née Holland, of Altavista, Virginia; February 19, 1914, and August 1, 1914.

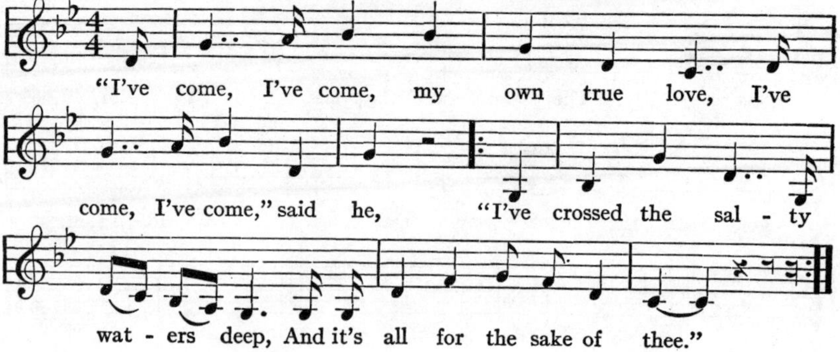

No. 40 (*G*) THE HOUSE CARPENTER

Collected by Miss Martha M. Davis; sung by an old nurse in Fairfax County, Virginia; August 14, 1914.

No. 40 (*H*) THE HOUSE CARPENTER

Collected by Mr. John Stone; sung by Mrs. J. A. Mitchell and Miss Mary Mitchell and Mrs. Holland Hoffman, of Criglersville, Virginia; Madison County; November 3, 1920.

No. 40 (*Q*) THE HOUSE CARPENTER

Collected by Mr. John Stone; sung by Mr. C. F. Carpenter, of Bolar, Virginia; Highland County; November 3, 1920.

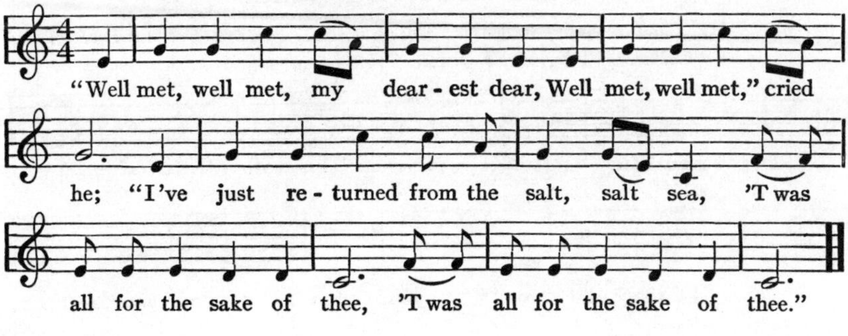

No. 40 (*V*) THE HOUSE CARPENTER

Collected by Miss Juliet Fauntleroy; sung by Mr. Alonzo Hogan and Miss Callie Hogan, of Lynch Station, Virginia; Campbell County; February, 1914.

No. 40 (*X*) THE HOUSE CARPENTER

Collected by Dr. Launcelot M. Harris; sung by Mrs. Marshall, near Charlottesville, Virginia; Albemarle County; September 11, 1923.

No. 42 (*B*) THE SUFFOLK MIRACLE

Collected by Mr. Cecil J. Sharp and Miss Karpeles; sung by Mrs. Frances Richards, at Callaway, Virginia; Franklin County; August 16, 1918.

steed, That has sent for you with - in great speed."

(a)

No. 42 (*C*) THE SUFFOLK MIRACLE

Collected by Mr. Cecil J. Sharp; sung by Mrs. Laura Beckett, at St. Peter's Settlement, Callaway, Virginia; Franklin County; August 16, 1918.

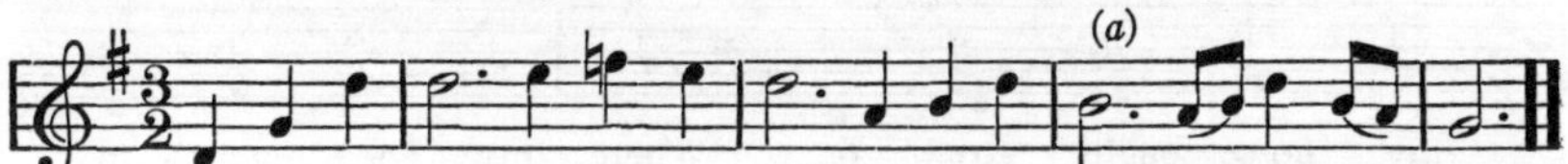

"O fa-ther, fa-ther, don't you know? The one I loved I will en - dure."

(a)

No. 43 (*B*) HOBBLE AND BOBBLE

Collected by Miss Fauntleroy and Mrs. Adams; sung by Henry Payne (Colored), near Altavista, Virginia; Campbell County; June 6, 1914.

I walked in - to my sta - ble And the sight that I did see, It

was some gentlemen's hors - es, One or two or three.

This tune played for three stanzas and followed by:

Hob - ble and bob - ble and ve - ry well

done, but a.......... thing I nev - er did see....

No. 43 (*C*) THE OLD MAN

Collected by Miss Juliet Fauntleroy; sung by Mrs. Maxie, née Holland, of Altavista, Virginia; Franklin County; April 7, 1914.

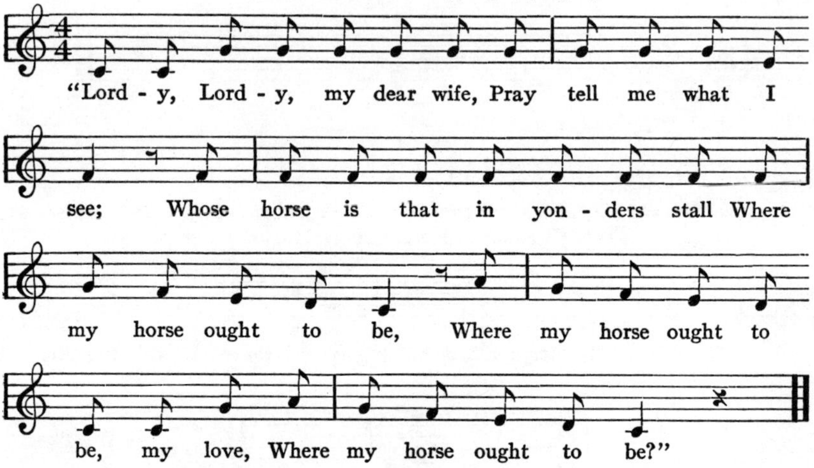

No. 43 (*D*) HOME COMES THE GOOD OLD MAN

Collected and noted by Miss Juliet Fauntleroy; sung by Mrs. James Dearing, of Lynchburg, Virginia; Campbell County; May 10, 1914.

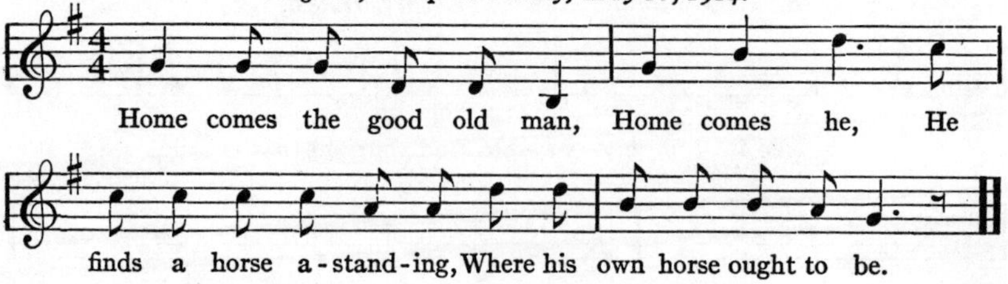

No. 43 (*F*) HOME COMES THE GOOD OLD MAN

Collected by Miss Juliet Fauntleroy; sung by Mrs. F. P. Christian, of Campbell County, Virginia; July 26, 1914.

No. 43 (*G*) DOWN CAME THE OLD MAN

Collected and noted by Mrs. George D. McLaughlin, of Benicia, California; sung by Mr. George D. McLaughlin, of Virginia; Rockbridge County; May 15, 1916.

No. 45 (*D*) THE WIFE WRAPT IN WETHER'S SKIN

Collected by Mr. Cecil J. Sharp and Miss Karpeles; sung by Mr. N. B. Chisholm, at Woodridge, Virginia; Albemarle County; September 21, 1916.

No. 45 (*J*) WIFE WRAPPED IN WETHER'S SKIN OR DANDOO

Collected by Mr. John Stone; sung by Mr. and Mrs. J. A. Mitchell, of Brightwood, Virginia; Madison County; August 2, 1920.

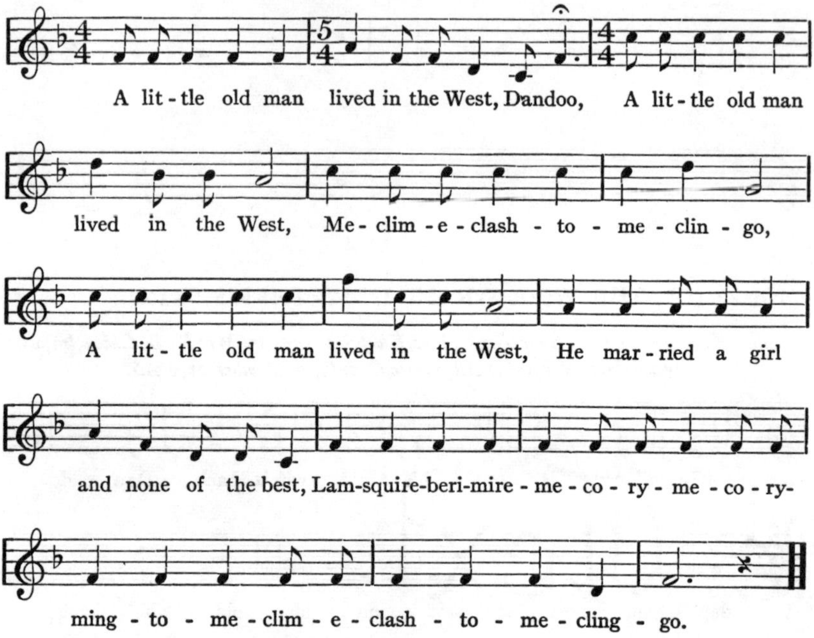

No. 46 (*C*) THE FARMER'S CURST WIFE

Collected by Mr. John Stone; sung by Mr. Charles Vest, of Louisa County, Virginia; September 13, 1917.

No. 46 (*E*) THE FARMER'S CURST WIFE

Collected by Mr. Cecil J. Sharp and Miss Karpeles; sung by Mr. N. B. Chisholm, at Woodridge, Virginia; Albemarle County; September 21, 1916.

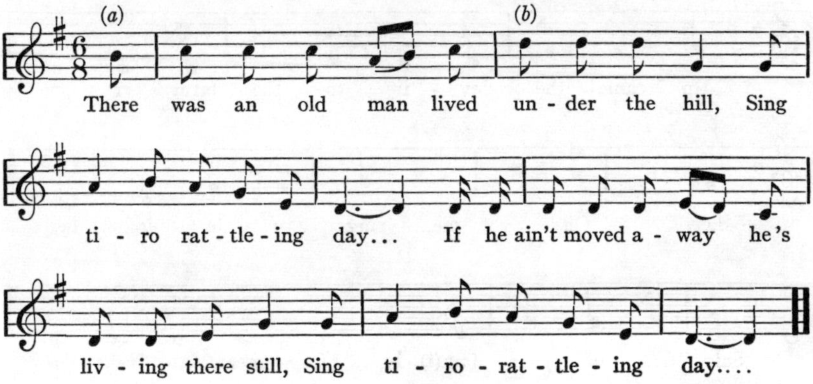

No. 46 (*F*) THE FARMER'S CURST WIFE

Collected by Mr. John Stone; sung by Mr. T. C. Cummins, of Rumford, Virginia; King William County; September 13, 1917.

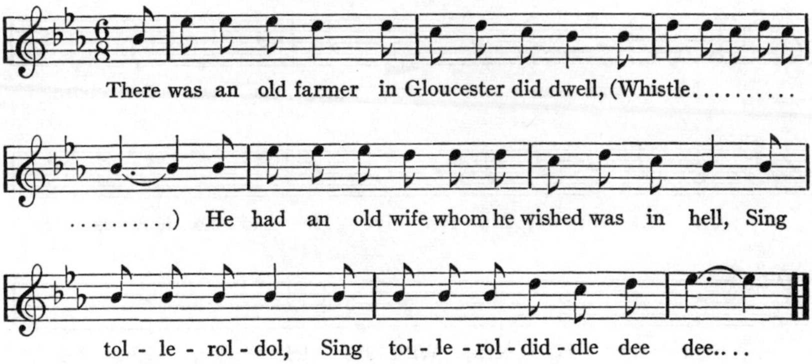

No. 46 (*H*) THE FARMER'S CURST WIFE

Collected by Miss Juliet Fauntleroy; sung by Mrs. James Sprouse, of Lawyers, Virginia; Campbell County; September 4, 1915.

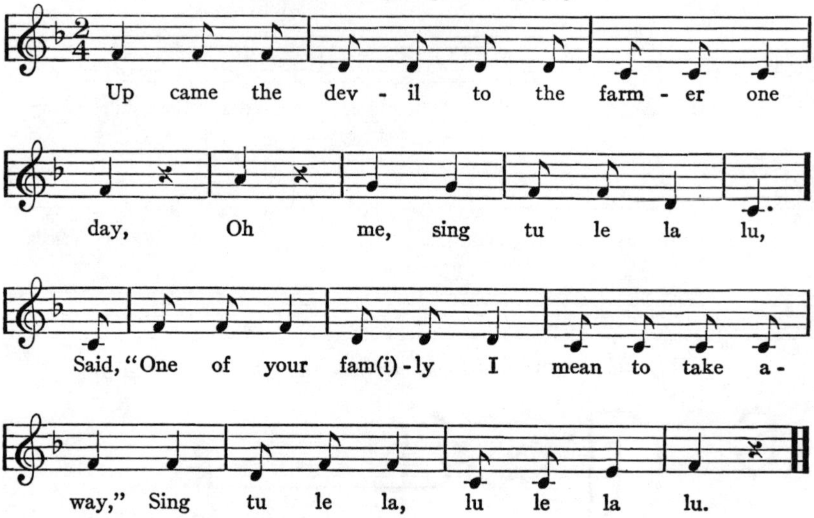

NOTE: Second couplet is sometimes sung thus:

No. 46 (*I*) THE FARMER'S CURST WIFE

Collected by John Stone; sung by Mr. C. F. Carpenter and brother, of Bolar, Virginia; Highland County; November 3, 1920.

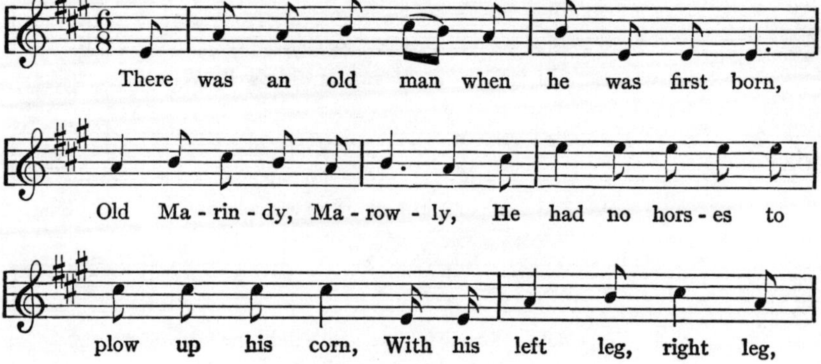

No. 46 (*L*) THE FARMER'S CURST WIFE

Collected by Mr. John Stone; sung by Mrs. Weathers, of Rumford, Virginia; King William County; September 13, 1917.

No. 46 (*M*) THE FARMER'S CURST WIFE

Collected by Mr. John Stone; sung by Miss Emma Carpenter, of Madison County, Virginia; November 3, 1920.

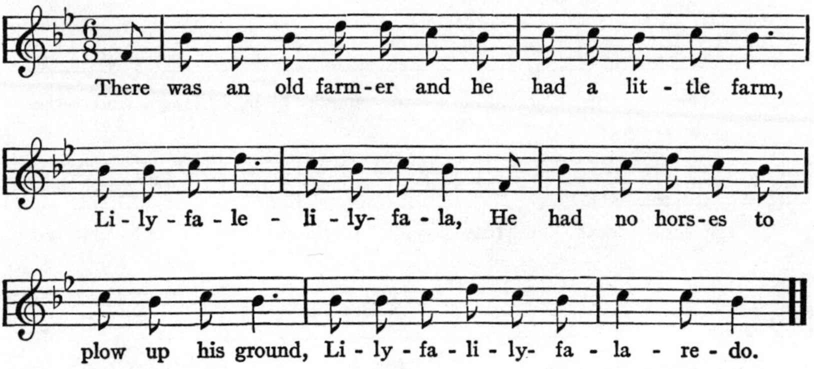

No. 47 (*D*) THE TURKEY–ROGHERLEE AND THE YELLOW GOLDEN TREE, or LOWLANDS LOW

Collected by Professor Carpenter and Mr. John Stone; sung by Mrs. J. A. Mitchell, Miss Mary Mitchell, and Mrs. Holland Hoffman; Madison County; November 3, 1920.

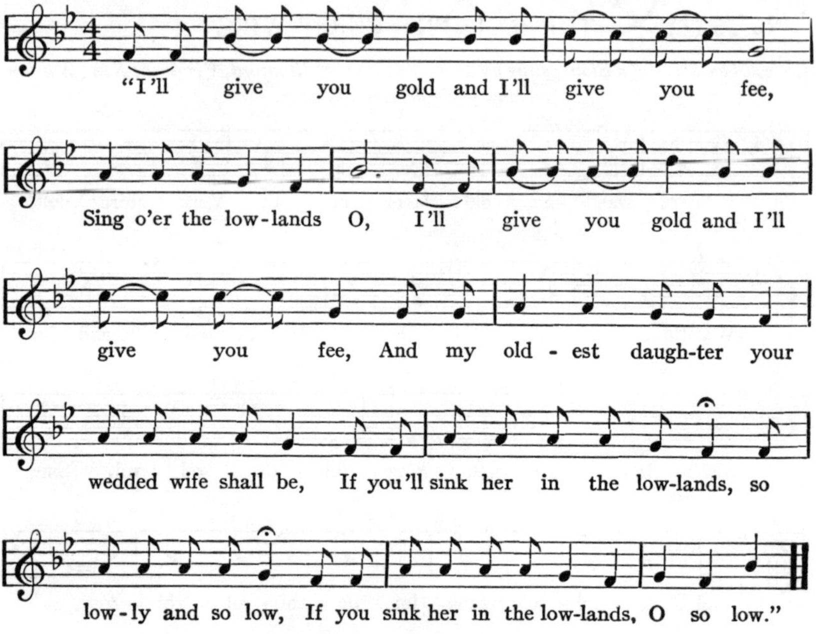

No. 48 (*B*) THE STORMY WINDS

Reported by Mrs. J. M. Grainger of the Farmville Ballad Club; contributed by Mr. Inslee Deaderick, of Knoxville, Tennessee; Prince Edward County; March, 1914.

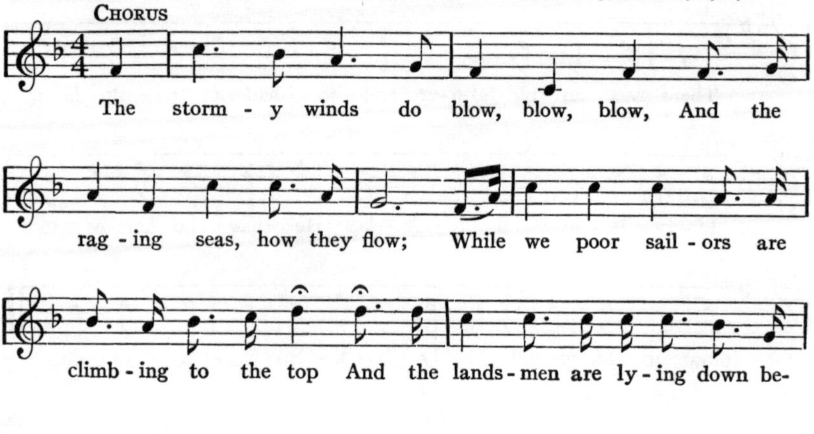

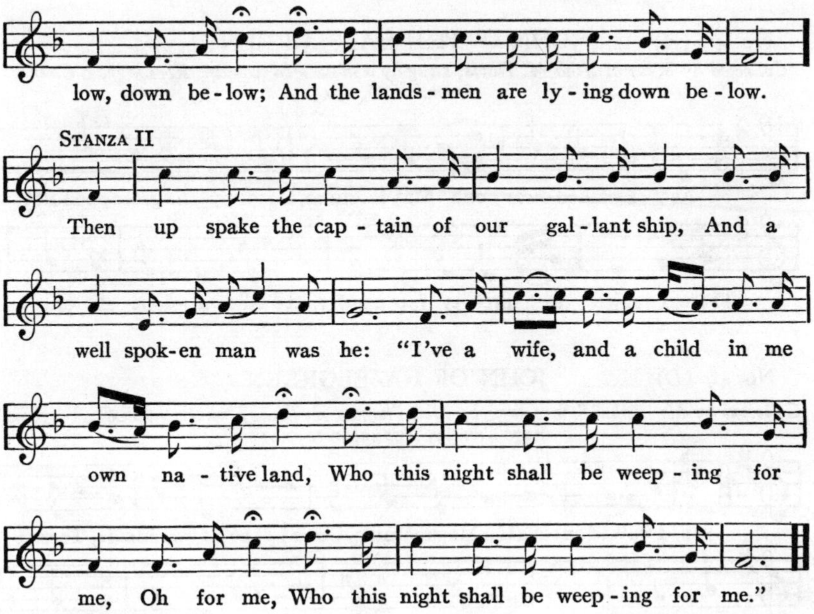

NOTE: The first stanza is sung to the tune of the chorus, all subsequent stanzas to the music of Stanza II, above.

No. 48 (*F*) THE MERMAID

Collected by Miss Martha M. Davis; sung by Miss Fannie Speck, of Harrisonburg, Virginia; Rockingham County; March 15, 1913.

No. 49 (*A*) JOHN O' THE HAZELGREEN

Collected by Miss Martha M. Davis; sung by a mountain woman; Rockingham County; November 16, 1915.

No. 49 (*D*) JOHN OF HAZELGREEN

Collected by Mr. John Stone; sung by Mr. Thomas H. Bailey, of Shenandoah, Virginia; Page County; November 10, 1919.

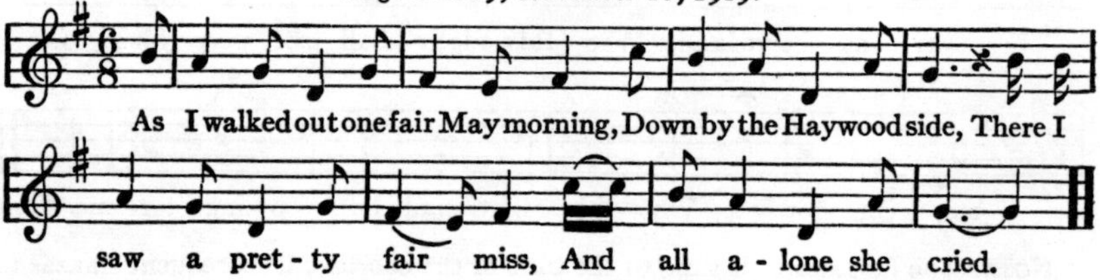

No. 49 (*E*) JOHN OF HAZELGREEN

Collected by Mr. John Stone; sung by Miss Ruby Herndon, of Mount Fair, Virginia; Albemarle County; November 3, 1920.

No. 50 (*G*) THE BROWN GIRL

Collected by Mr. Cecil J. Sharp and Miss Karpeles; sung by Mr. N. B. Chisholm, at Woodridge, Virginia; Albemarle County; September 23, 1916.

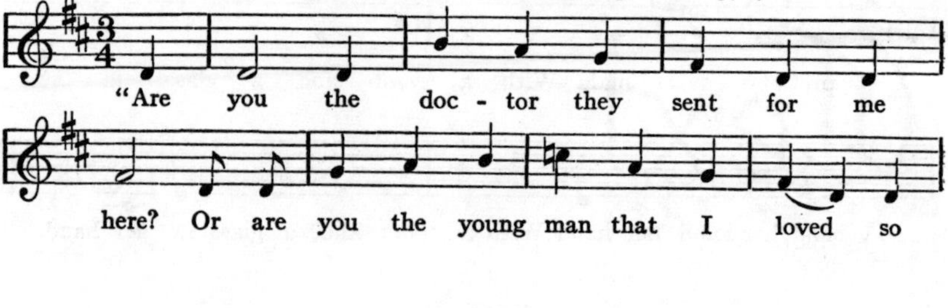

No. 50 (*I*) THE BROWN GIRL

Collected by Mr. John Stone; sung by Mrs. Rosson, of Alexandria, Virginia; Rockingham County; November 10, 1919.

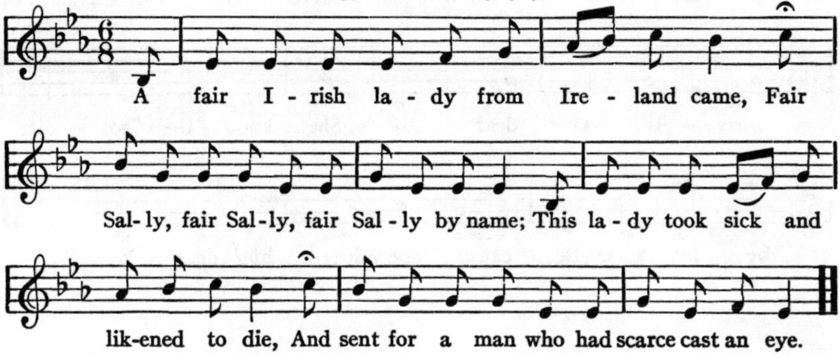

No. 50 (*J*) THE BROWN GIRL

Collected by Mr. John Stone; sung by Mrs. W. K. Rogers, near Bolar, Virginia; Bath County; November 3, 1920.

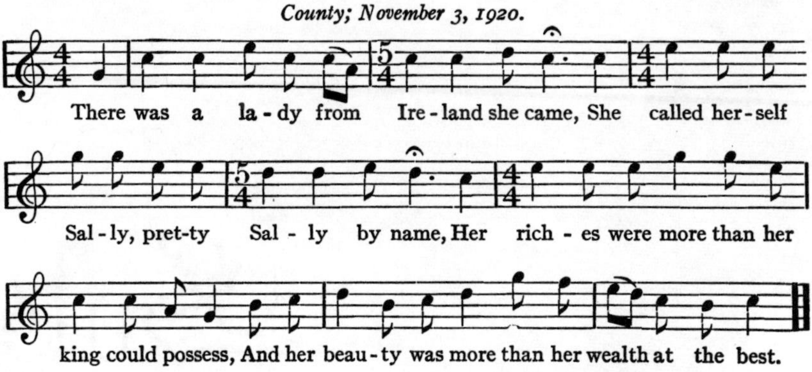

No. 51 (*A*) THE TROOPER AND MAID

Collected by Miss Martha M. Davis; sung by Mrs. Sarah Finchum, of Elkton, Virginia; Rockingham County; November 16, 1915.

APPENDICES

APPENDIX A

A List of Additional Ballad Material Collected by the Virginia Folk-Lore Society but not Included in this Volume

For the following twenty-eight ballads, all the material collected has been presented in full in the body of this book: Nos. 1, 2, 8, 9, 11, 13, 14, 15, 16, 26, 28, 29, 30, 31, 32, 34, 35, 36, 37, 38, 39, 41, 42, 43, 44, 45, 47, 51. The excluded items of the remaining twenty-three ballads are here listed chronologically under each ballad head in the order of their receipt by the archivist, with the data of collection for each item, and the number of stanzas.

3

Lady Isabel and the Elf-Knight

(Child, No. 4)

1. *The Pretty Gold Leaf.* Collected by Miss May Blankenship, of Naruna, Va. Campbell Co. April, 1914. Eight stanzas. No music.
2. *Bonnie Brown.* Sent by Mrs. Olin Fisk Wiley, of Richmond, Va. Wise Co. Oct. 30, 1915. Seven stanzas. No music.
3. *Pretty Polly.* Sent in by Mr. John Stone. Collected by Miss Lucy Menefee, of Lynchburg, Va. Heard in Appomattox Co. Nov. 8, 1919. Two stanzas. No music.
4. *Pretty Polly.* Sent in by Miss Gladys A. Whitmore. Sung by Mrs. H. S. Duffey, of Winchester, Va. Frederick Co. May 29, 1920. Four stanzas. No music.
5. *The Seventh King's Daughter.* Collected by Miss Alfreda M. Peel, of Salem, Va. Sung by Mrs. Fore, of Roanoke, Va. Roanoke Co. Aug. 28, 1920. Five stanzas. No music.
6. *Lady Isabel and the Elf-Knight, or Pretty Polly.* Collected by Mr. John Stone. Sung by Mrs. Mollie Binns, of Claremont, Va. Surry Co. July 13, 1921. Three stanzas. No music.
7. *Lady Isabel and the Elf-Knight.* Collected by Mr. John Stone. Sung by Mr. J. W. Wyatt, of Dante, Va. Russell Co. Nov. 8, 1921. Two stanzas. No music.
8. *Lady Isabel and the Elf-Knight.* Collected by Mr. John Stone. Recited by Mrs. S. V. Helton, of Saltville, Va. Smyth Co. Nov. 8, 1921. Five stanzas. No music.
9. *Lady Isabel and the Elf-Knight.* Collected by Mr. John Stone. Recited by Mr. J. A. Wyatt. King and Queen Co., Va. Sept. 11, 1922. Six stanzas. No music.

4

Earl Brand

(Child, No. 7)

1. *Seven King's Sons.* Collected by Miss Roxie Martin and Mr. J. M. McManaway. Albemarle Co., Va. June 1, 1917. Eight stanzas. No music.

5

The Twa Sisters

(Child, No. 10)

1. *I'll Be True to My Love.* Collected by Mrs. C. L. Scott. Amherst Co., Va. Nov. 30, 1915. Eight stanzas. No music.
2. *The Two Sisters.* Collected by Mr. John Stone. Sung by Miss Emma Carpenter. Madison Co., Va. Nov. 3, 1920. One stanza. No music.

6

Lord Randal

(Child, No. 12)

1. *Lord Randal, or Johnnie Riller.* Collected by Miss Martha M. Davis, from the singing of a mountain woman. Rockingham Co., Va. Jan. 20, 1914. Five stanzas. No music.
2. *Johnnie Rolus.* Collected by Miss Florida Ashby. Recited by her mother. Fluvanna Co., Va. Aug. 29, 1916. Two stanzas. No music.

7

Edward

(Child, No. 13)

1. (No title.) Contributed by Dr. Hugh Mercer Blain, of Baton Rouge, La., as sung by his grandmother, Mrs. Susan Isham Blain, of Va. Feb. 24, 1914. Six stanzas. No music.

10

The Three Ravens

(Child, No. 26)

1. *The Three Ravens.* Contributed by Miss E. W. Holland, of Berryville, Va. Sung by Mrs. J. T. Kane. Clark Co., Va. Oct. 20, 1915. One stanza. No music.
2. *The Three Crows.* Contributed by Miss Helen Boulden Towles. Transmitted by Mr. E. F. Shewmake, Jr. Lancaster Co., Va. June, 1916. Three stanzas. No music.
3. *The Two Crows.* Contributed by Miss Margaret Martin. Washington Co., Va. Sept. 29, 1916. Two stanzas. No music.

4. *The Three Crows*. Collected by Mr. John Stone. Given by Mr. C. A. Dickson, of Trimble, Va. Highland Co. Nov. 3, 1920. Three stanzas. No music.
5. *The Three Ravens*. Collected by Mr. John Stone. Recited by Mr. John Doughty, of Cape Charles, Va. Northampton Co. July 13, 1921. Three stanzas. No music.
6. *The Three Ravens*. Collected by Mr. John Stone. Sung by Mrs. J. Waverly Thomas, of Smithfield, Va. Isle of Wight Co. July 13, 1921. Four stanzas. No music.
7 *The Three Crows*. Collected by Mr. John Stone. Sung by Miss Kate Wheeler and Mrs. Jennie Davis, of Abingdon, Va. Washington Co. Nov. 8, 1921. Two stanzas. No music.
8. *The Three Ravens*. Collected by Mr. John Stone. Recited by a lady in Essex Co., Va. Sept. 11, 1922. Three stanzas. No music.
9. *The Three Ravens*. Collected by Mr. John Stone, Recited by Mrs. H. T. Fountleroy, of Tunstall, Va. New Kent Co. Sept. 11, 1922. One stanza. No music.
10. *The Three Ravens*. Collected by Mr. John Stone. Sung by Mr. S. F. Barnes, of Nokomis, Va. Northumberland Co. Sept. 11, 1922. One stanza. No music.

12
Young Beichan
(Child, No. 53)

1. *Young Beichan*. Collected by Miss Martha M. Davis. Sung by "Granny L." Rappahannock Co., Va. March 2, 1916. Five stanzas. No music.
2. *There Was a Man in England Born*. Collected by Mrs. Olin F. Wiley. Contributed by Miss Belle Hamilton. Wise Co., Va. Dec. 1, 1916. Nine stanzas. No music.
3. *Lord Bateman*. Collected by Miss Roxie Martin and Mr. J. M. McManaway. Sung by a "religious" Negro woman. Albemarle Co., Va. June 1, 1917. Thirteen stanzas. No music.

17
Young Hunting
(Child, No. 68)

1. *Proud Lady Margaret*. Collected by Miss Roxie Martin. Albemarle Co., Va. Aug. 4, 1916. Thirteen stanzas. No music.

18
Lord Thomas and Fair Annet
(Child, No. 73)

1. *The Brown Girl*. Collected by Miss Juliet Fauntleroy. Sung by Mr. Walker, near Altavista, Va. Campbell Co. March 28, 1914. One stanza. No music.
2. *The Brown Girl*. Collected by Miss Juliet Fauntleroy. Sung by Mrs. Fanny Stone, near Altavista, Va. Campbell Co. March 28, 1914. Three stanzas. No music.

3. *Lord Thomas and Fair Eleanor.* Reported by Prof. James M. Grainger. Collected by Miss May Blankenship, of Naruna, Va. Campbell Co. April, 1914. Two stanzas. No music.
4. *Lord Thomas.* Collected by Dr. C. Alphonso Smith. Sung by Mr. J. C. Mays, of Craigsville, Va. Amherst (via Augusta) Co. Dec. 17, 1914. Eight stanzas. No music.
5. *Lord Thomas.* Collected by Miss Roxie Martin. Albemarle Co., Va. Aug. 4, 1916. Eleven stanzas. No music.
6. *Fair Ellendar and the Brown Girl.* Contributed by Miss Nancy Pearson. Found in Christiansburg, Va. Montgomery Co. Jan. 31, 1917. Fifteen stanzas. No music.
7. *Lord Thomas.* Collected by Miss Roxie Martin and Mr. J. M. McManaway. Sung by "Aunt Het" (Colored), at Brown's Cove, Va. Albemarle Co. June 1, 1917. Twelve stanzas. No music.
8. *Lord Thomas.* Collected by Miss Roxie Martin and Mr. J. M. McManaway. Sung by an old Colored woman at Brown's Cove, Va. Albemarle Co. June 1, 1917. Ten stanzas. No music.
9. *The Brown Girl, or Lord Thomas and Lady Eleanor.* Contributed by Mrs. N. E. Clement. Sung by an old lady, of Chatham, Va. Pittsylvania Co. July 25, 1917. Ten stanzas. No music.
10. *Lord Thomas and Fair Ellender.* Collected by Mr. John Stone. Sung by Mrs. Leona Dever, of Mustoe, Va. Highland Co. Nov. 3, 1920. Nine stanzas. No music.
11. *Lord Thomas and Fair Elinor.* Collected by Mr. John Stone. Sung by Mr. Charles H. Lowry, near South Hoston, Va. Halifax Co. June 29, 1921. Nine stanzas. No music.
12. *Lord Thomas and Fair Elinor.* Collected by Mr. John Stone. Recited by Mr. H. G. Cole, of Jetersville, Va. Amelia Co. June 29, 1921. Fourteen stanzas No music.
13. *Lord Thomas and Fair Elinor.* Collected by Mr. John Stone. Recited by Mrs. L. M. Henning, of Jefferson, Va. Powhatan Co. June 29, 1921. Eight stanzas. No music.
14. *Fair Ellender and the Brown Girl.* Collected by Mr. John Stone. Sung by Mr. J. W. Fields, of Coeburn, Va. Wise Co. Nov. 8, 1921. Two stanzas. No music.
15. *Fair Ellen and the Brown Girl.* Collected by Mr. John Stone. Recited by Mrs. Rhoda O'Bryhin, of Falmouth, Va. Stafford Co. Sept. 11, 1922. Seven stanzas. No. music.
16. *Fair Elinor and the Brown Girl.* Collected by Mr. John Stone. Recited by Mrs. Mary Jett Armstrong, of Falmouth, Va. Stafford Co. Sept. 11, 1922. Ten stanzas. No music.
17. *Fair Ellender and the Brown Girl.* Collected by Mr. John Stone. Sung by Rev. Wallace Wood, of Heathsville, Va. Northumberland Co. Sept. 11, 1922. One stanza. No music.

19

Fair Margaret and Sweet William

(Child, No. 74)

1. (No title given.) Collected by Mr. G. L. Harwell. Sung by an old lady at Mission Home. Greene Co., Va. June 16, 1915. Six stanzas. No music.

2. (No title given.) Collected by Miss Mattie W. Mills. Sung by her father, at Hylas, Va. Hanover Co. Aug. 20, 1915. Five stanzas. No music.
3. *Sweet Williams and Lady Marget.* Collected by Miss Roxie Martin. Contributed by Miss Hazel L. Garrison, of Brown's Cove, Va. Albemarle Co. Aug. 4, 1916. Seventeen stanzas. No music.
4. *Sweet William.* Contributed by Mrs. Olin F. Wiley. Wise Co., Va. Dec. 1, 1916. Fifteen stanzas. No music.
5. *Sweet William.* Contributed by Mrs. N. E. Clement. Sung by an old woman of Chatham, Va. Pittsylvania Co. July 25, 1917. Fourteen stanzas. No music.
6. *Lady Margaret and Sweet William.* Collected by Mr. John Stone. Sung by Miss Emma Carpenter, of Brightwood, Va. Madison Co. Aug. 2, 1920. Two stanzas. No music.
7. *Sweet William and Lady Margaret.* Collected by Mr. John Stone. Sung by Mrs. J. C. Eakle. Bath Co., Va. Nov. 3, 1920. Eleven stanzas. No music.
8. *Sweet William and Lady Margaret.* Collected by Mr. John Stone. Sung by Mrs. Leona Dever, of Mustoe, Va. Highland Co. Nov. 3, 1920. Thirteen stanzas. No music.
9. *Lady Margaret.* Collected by Mr. John Stone. Sung by Miss Lottie Shaffir, of Mustoe, Va. Highland Co. Nov. 3, 1920. Five stanzas. No music.
10. *Lady Margaret.* Contributed by Miss Lottie Shaffir, of Mustoe, Va. Sung by herself. Highland Co. Nov. 3, 1920. Seven stanzas. No music.
11. *Fair Margaret and Sweet William.* Collected by Mr. John Stone. Sung by Mr. George Hart, of Konnarock, Va. Washington Co. Nov. 8, 1921. Five stanzas. No music.
12. *Fair Margaret and Sweet William.* Collected by Mr. John Stone. Sung by Mrs. S. C. Nash, of Onville, Va. Stafford Co. Sept. 11, 1922. Five stanzas. No music.
13. (No title given.) Collected by Miss Alfreda M. Peel. Sung by Miss Isabel Nicewander. Bland Co., Va. Aug. 26, 1923. Two stanzas. No music.

20

Lord Lovel

(Child, No. 75)

1. *Lord Lovel.* Collected by Mrs. W. H. Taliaferro, of Charlottesville, Va. Albemarle Co. 1913. Eight stanzas. No music.
2. *Lord Lovel.* Reported by Prof. James M. Grainger. Contributed by Miss Evelyn Purcell, of the Farmville Ballad Club. Albemarle Co., Va. Dec. 21, 1913. Seven stanzas. No music.
3. *Lord Lovel.* Collected by Miss Corita G. Seoane. Sung by Mr. Albert Thompson, of Fairfax, Va. Fairfax Co. Jan. 10, 1914. Nine stanzas. No music.
4. *Lord Lovel.* Reported by Miss Edith B. Payne. Contributed by Miss Grace Ward. Recited by her grandmother, Mrs. L. G. Davis. Princess Anne Co., Va. Jan. 20, 1914. Eight stanzas. No music.
5. *Lord Lovel.* Reported by Miss Nancy Johnston. Contributed by Mrs. C. V. Cavitt, of Martinsville, Va. Botetourt Co. Jan. 25, 1914. Nine stanzas. No music.

6. *Lord Lovel and Lady Nancy Belle.* Reported by Miss Cornelia S. Adair, of Richmond, Va. Contributed by Mrs. Jacquelin Taylor. Sung by Miss Figgat, of Fincastle, Va. Botetourt Co. Nov. 1, 1914. Five stanzas. No music.
7. *Lord Lovel.* Collected by Mr. John Stone. Sung by Mrs. Mary J. Moore (84), of Charlottesville, Va. Albemarle Co. Nov. 15, 1915. Eight stanzas. No music.
8. *Lord Lovel.* Collected by Mr. Fred P. Myers. Sung by Mr. Thomas H. Bailey and Miss Lee Koonz, of Marksville, Va. Page Co. Nov. 26, 1915. Seven stanzas. No music.
9. *Lord Lovel.* Collected by Miss Roxie Martin. Albemarle Co., Va. Aug. 4, 1916. Eleven stanzas. No music.
10. *Lord Lovel.* Collected by Mr. John Stone. Sung by Mr. A. S. Furcron, of The Plains, Va. Fauquier Co. Nov. 10, 1919. Seven stanzas. No music.
11. *Lord Lovel.* Collected by Mr. John Stone. Sung by Mrs. C. A. Dickson. Highland Co., Va. Nov. 3, 1920. Three stanzas. No music.
12. *Lord Lovel.* Collected by Mr. John Stone. Sung by Mr. D. M. Pattie, of Madison, Va. Madison Co. Nov. 3, 1920. Two stanzas. No music.
13. *Lord Lovel.* Collected by Mr. John Stone. Recited by Miss Sallie E. Steed, of Lawrenceville, Va. Brunswick Co. June 29, 1921. One stanza. No music.
14. *Lord Lovel.* Collected by Mr. John Stone. Recited by Mrs. F. L. Maupin, of Williamsburg, Va. James City Co. July 13, 1921. One stanza. No music.
15. *Lord Lovel.* Collected by Mr. John Stone. Sung by Mrs. Charles Kellogg, of Cape Charles, Va. Northampton Co. July 13, 1921. One stanza. No music.
16. *Lord Lovel.* Collected by Mr. John Stone. Recited by Mrs. J. B. Clark, of Waverly, Va. Sussex Co. July 13, 1921. Two stanzas. No music.
17. *Lord Lovel.* Collected by Mr. John Stone. Sung by Mrs. Lucy Vaughan Cunningham, of Glade Spring, Va. Washington Co. Nov. 8, 1921. Seven stanzas. No music.
18. *Lord Lovel.* Collected by Mr. John Stone. Sung by Mrs. Clarence Williams, of Pinola, Va. Caroline Co. Sept. 11, 1922. Eight stanzas. No music.
19. *Lord Lovel.* Collected by Mr. John Stone. Sung by Mrs. Henry Latané Jones, of Walkerton, Va. King and Queen Co. Sept. 11, 1922. Nine stanzas. No music.
20. *Lord Lovel.* Collected by Mr. John Stone. Recited by Mrs. Mary Jett Armstrong, of Falmouth, Va. Stafford Co. Sept. 11, 1922. Eight stanzas. No music.
21. *Lord Lovel.* Collected by Mr. John Stone. Recited by Mrs. Martha C. Throckmorton, of Bluemont, Va. Loudoun Co. Sept. 23, 1922. Three stanzas. No music.

21

The Lass of Roch Royal

(Child, No. 76)

Note — No complete text of this ballad has been recovered in Virginia. Indeed, only two stanzas definitely belonging to the ballad have been found — the "shoe my foot" stanzas. Therefore, when more than two stanzas are indicated in this list it must be understood that the additional stanzas are either repetitive prolongations of the original two, or material introduced from other songs. See the head-note to the ballad, Virginia, No. 21.

1. *The Lass of Roch Royal.* Collected by Miss Martha M. Davis. Sung by a mountain woman of Elkton, Va. Rockingham Co. Jan. 20, 1914. Four stanzas. No music.
2. (No title given.) Reported by Prof. James M. Grainger. Collected by Miss Ira McAlpin. Sung by Mrs. Charles McAlpin, of Lexington, Va. Rockbridge Co. March 14, 1914. Seven stanzas. No music.
3. (No title given.) Collected by Miss Juliet Fauntleroy. Sung by Mrs. Bob Stone, *née* Taylor. Campbell Co., Va. March 14, 1914. Three stanzas. No music.
4. *Lass of Roch Royal.* Reported by Mrs. W. H. Taliaferro. Contributed by Miss Bettie Riddick, of Suffolk, Va. Nansemond Co. Feb. 5, 1915. One stanza. No music.
5. *The Lass of Roch Royal.* Collected by Miss Nancy Pearson, of Cobbs Creek, Va. Mathews Co. March 20, 1916. Four stanzas. No music.
6. *The Lass of Roch Royal.* Collected by Miss Nancy Pearson, of Cobbs Creek, Va. Mathews Co. March 20, 1916. Three stanzas. No music.
7. (No title given.) Contributed by Mr. Sterling Boisseau. Heard forty years ago in Dinwiddie Co., Va. July 18, 1916. One stanza. No music.
8. *A-Roving.* Collected by Miss Alfreda M. Peel. Sung by Mrs. Shields, of Graham, Va. Roanoke Co. Dec. 3, 1916. One stanza. No music.
9. *Oh, Who's Going to Shoe My Pretty Little Foot?* Collected by Miss Florence Adams, of Danville, Va. Franklin Co. Dec. 6, 1916. Three stanzas. No music.
10. (No title given.) Collected by Miss Gladys A. Whitmore. Sung by Mrs. H. S. Duffey, of Wincester, Va. Frederick Co. May 29, 1920. Two stanzas. No music.
11. *Lass of Rock Royal.* Collected by Miss Alfreda M. Peel. Sung by Mrs. Crop, of Salem, Va. Roanoke Co. June, 1921. Seven stanzas. No music.
12. *Love Gregor.* Collected by Mr. John Stone. Recited by Mrs. G. P. Coleman, of Williamsburg, Va. James City Co. July 13, 1921. Three stanzas. No music.
13. *Love Gregor.* Collected by Mr. John Stone. Sung by Misses Orelia and Annie D. Williams, of Cape Charles, Va. Northampton Co. July 13, 1921. Two stanzas. No music.
14. *Love Gregor.* Collected by Mr. John Stone. Sung by Miss Annie D. Williams, of Cape Charles, Va. Northampton Co. Nov. 8, 1921. Two stanzas. No music.

15. *Love Gregor.* Collected by Mr. John Stone. Sung by Mr. George Hart, of Konnarock, Va. Washington Co. Nov. 8, 1921. Three stanzas. No music.
16. *Love Gregor.* Collected by Mr. John Stone. Sung by Mrs. Rosa Opt Wilburn, of Pennington, Va. Lee Co. Nov. 8, 1921. Two stanzas. No music.
17. *Love Gregor.* Collected by Mr. John Stone. Recited by Mr. Wiley Compton, Dickenson Co., Va. Nov. 8, 1921. Two stanzas. No music.
18. *Love Gregor.* Collected by Mr. John Stone. Recited by Mrs. J. E. Kane, of Gate City, Va. Scott Co. Nov. 8, 1921. One stanza. No music.
19. *Love Gregor.* Collected by Mr. John Stone. Recited by Mrs. H. T. Stevens, of Igo, Va. King George Co. Sept. 11, 1922. Two stanzas. No music.
20. *Love Gregor.* Collected by Mr. John Stone. Recited by Mrs. George W. Johnson, of Tunstall, Va. New Kent Co. Sept. 11, 1922. One stanza. No music.
21. *Love Gregor.* Collected by Mr. John Stone. Recited by Mrs. W. A. Street and Miss Rosa Street, of Urbana, Va. Middlesex Co. Sept. 11, 1922. One stanza. No music.
22. *Love Gregor.* Collected by Mr. John Stone. Sung by Mrs. Frank Kennerly, of White Post, Va. Clark Co. Sept. 23, 1922. No music.

22

The Wife of Usher's Well

(Child, No. 79)

1. *The Lady Gay.* Collected by Mr. John Stone. Sung by Mr. A. L. Compton, of Gate City, Va. Scott Co. Nov. 8, 1921. Eight stanzas. No music.

23

Little Musgrave and Lady Barnard

(Child, No. 81)

1. *Lord Arnold's Wife.* Collected by Mr. John Adams. Sung by Charles Henry Payne (Colored), near Altavista, Va. Campbell Co. May 11, 1915. Eleven stanzas. No music.

24

Bonny Barbara Allan

(Child, No. 84)

1. *Barbara Allen.* Contributed by Mrs. T. W. Dexter, of Charlottesville, Va. Albemarle Co. May 31, 1913. One stanza. No music.
2. *Barbara Allen.* Collected by Miss Martha M. Davis. Sung by Mrs. Adams Gowl. Rockingham Co., Va. August 6, 1913. Ten stanzas. No music.
3. *Barbara Allen.* Sung by Louise Gray (Colored), of Charlottesville, Va. Albemarle Co. Dec. 15, 1913. Nine stanzas. No music.

4. *Barbara Allen*. Collected by S. Bruce Jones, of Baywood, Va. Grayson Co. Jan. 6, 1914. Eleven stanzas. No music.

5. *Barbara Allen*. Sent in by Miss Nancy Johnston. Contributed by Miss Annie Draper, of Martinsville, Va. Sung by her mother. Henry Co. Jan. 25, 1914. Five stanzas. No music.

6. *Barbara Allen*. Collected by Miss Ruth Gleaves. Recited by Isaac Carroll, a Negro ex-slave about 90 years old. Wythe Co., Va. Jan., 1914. Eight stanzas. No music.

7. *Barbara Allen*. Collected by Miss Lily C. Maxey. Sung by her father. Buckingham Co., Va. Jan., 1914. Nine stanzas. No music.

8. *Barbara Allen*. Collected by Miss Juliet Fauntleroy. Sung by Miss Callie Hogan and Mr. Alonzo Hogan, of Altavista, Va. Campbell Co. March 9, 1914. Nine stanzas. No music.

9. *Barbary Ellen*. Collected by Miss Juliet Fauntleroy. Sung by Mrs. Maxie, *nêe* Holland, of Altavista, Va. Franklin Co. March 28, 1914. Twelve stanzas. No music.

10. *Barbara Allen*. Contributed by Miss Nancy Johnston, of Martinsville, Va. Henry Co. April 15, 1914. Eight stanzas. No music.

11. *Barbara Allen*. Collected by Miss Juliet Fauntleroy and Mr. John L. Douglas, Jr. Sung by Pamela Payne (Colored), near Gladys, Va. Campbell Co. July 7, 1914. Five stanzas. No music.

12. *Barbara Ellen*. Contributed by Miss Alma Wilkinson, of Hillsville, Va. Carroll Co. July 26, 1915. Thirteen stanzas. No music.

13. *Barbara Allen*. Collected by Mr. John Stone. Sung by Mrs. Dora Maddox. Culpeper Co., Va. Nov. 15, 1915. Nine stanzas. No music.

14. *Barbara Ellen*. Collected by Miss Lauretta M. Yost. Sung by Miss Maude Boyd, of Endicott, Va. Floyd Co. March 11, 1916. Twelve stanzas. No music.

15. *Barbara Allen*. Collected by Miss Alfreda M. Peel. Sung by the mountaineers of Roanoke Co., Va. Nov. 5, 1916. Twelve stanzas. No music.

16. *Barbara Allen*. Collected by Miss Roxie Martin and Mr. J. M. McManaway. Sung by an old white woman in Albemarle Co., Va. June 1, 1917. Eleven stanzas. No music.

17. *Barbara Allen's Cruelty*. Collected by Mr. John Stone. Sung by Miss Sallie Faulkner, of Houston, Va. Halifax Co. Sept. 13, 1917. Eleven stanzas. No music.

18. *Barbara Allen*. Collected by Miss Gladys A. Whitmore. Sung by Mrs. H. S. Duffey, of Winchester, Va. Frederick Co. May 29, 1920. Eleven stanzas. No music.

19. *Barbara Allen*. Collected by Mr. John Stone. Sung by Mrs. J. C. Eakle. Bath Co., Va. Nov. 3, 1920. Six stanzas. No music.

20. *Barbara Allen*. Collected by Mr. John Stone. Sung by Mr. David P. Corbett. Highland Co., Va. Nov. 3, 1920. Three stanzas. No music.

21. *Barbe Allen*. Reported by Mr. John Stone. Contributed by Miss Elsie Bradds, of Covington, Va. Alleghany and Rockbridge Cos. Nov. 3, 1920. Ten stanzas. No music.

22. *Barbara Allen*. Collected by Mr. John Stone. Sung by Mr. T. N. Williams, of Emporia, Va. Greensville Co. June 29, 1921. Ten stanzas. No music.

23. *Barbara Allen.* Collected by Mr. John Stone. Sung by Mrs. A. E. St. John and Mrs. L. A. St. John, of Traffic, Va. Lunenburg Co. June 29, 1921. Eleven stanzas. No music.
24. *Barbara Allen.* Collected by Mr. John Stone. Recited by Mrs. C. S. Lowry, near South Boston, Va. Halifax Co. June 29, 1921. Five stanzas. No music.
25. *Barbara Allen.* Collected by Mr. John Stone. Recited by Mrs. Carrie Bryant, of South Emporia, Va. Greensville Co. June 29, 1921. One stanza. No music.
26. *Barbara Allen.* Collected by Mr. John Stone. Recited by Mr. Wallace, of Wattsboro, Va. Lunenburg Co. June 29, 1921. One stanza. No music.
27. *Barbara Allen.* Collected by Mr. John Stone. Sung by Mr. L. W. Williams, of Emporia, Va. Greensville Co. June 29, 1921. One stanza. No music.
28. *Barbara Allen.* Collected by Mr. John Stone. Recited by Mr. J. A. Cooper, of Williamsburg, Va. James City Co. July 13, 1921. One stanza. No music.
29. *Barbara Allen.* Collected by Mr. John Stone. Recited by Mr. and Mrs. B. F. Pollard, of Claremont, Va. Surry Co. July 13, 1921. Two stanzas. No music.
30. *Barbara Allen.* Collected by Mr. John Stone. Recited by Mr. A. J. Bury, of Chester, Va. Chesterfield Co. July 13, 1921. One stanza. No music.
31. *Barbara Allen.* Collected by Mr. John Stone. Sung by Mrs. Mollie Binns, of Claremont, Va. Surry Co. July 13, 1921. Eleven stanzas. No music.
32. *Barbara Allen.* Collected by Mr. John Stone. Recited by Mr. Wise Worrel, of Radford, Va. Montgomery Co. Nov. 8, 1921. Two stanzas. No music.
33. *Barbara Allen.* Collected by Mr. John Stone. Sung by Mr. J. W. Wyatt, of Dante, Va. Russell Co. Nov. 8, 1921. Two stanzas. No music.
34. *Barbara Allan.* Collected by Mr. John Stone. Sung by Prof. R. M. Addington, of Gate City, Va. Scott Co. Nov. 8, 1921. One stanza. No music.
35. *Barbara Allan.* Collected by Mr. John Stone. Recited by Mr. Felix Stapleton, of Gate City, Va. Scott Co. Nov. 8, 1921. Eight stanzas. No music.
36. *Barbara Allan.* Collected by Mr. John Stone. Sung by Mr. J. W. Fields, of Coeburn, Va. Wise Co. Nov. 8, 1921. Five stanzas. No music.
37. *Barbara Allan.* Collected by Mr. John Stone. Sung by Mr. Jeff Doss, of Damascus, Va. Washington Co. Nov. 8, 1921. Three stanzas. No music.
38. *Barbara Allen.* Collected by Mr. John Stone. Recited by Mr. H. B. Ellison, of Saltville, Va. Smyth Co. Nov. 8, 1921. One stanza. No music.
39. *Barbara Allan.* Collected by Mr. John Stone. Sung by Mrs. Thomas Phipps, of Saltville, Va. Smyth Co. Nov. 8, 1921. Ten stanzas. No music.
40. *Barbara Allan.* Collected by Mr. John Stone. Sung by Mr. J. A. Wyatt, King and Queen Co., Va. Sept. 11, 1922. Ten stanzas. No music.

41. *Barbara Ellen*. Collected by Mr. John Stone. Recited by Mrs. Mary Jett Armstrong, of Falmouth, Va. Stafford Co. Sept. 11, 1922. Five stanzas. No music.
42. *Barbara Allan*. Collected by Mr. John Stone. Sung by Mrs. S. C. Nash, of Onville, Va. Stafford Co. Sept. 11, 1922. Four stanzas. No music.
43. *Barbara Allen*. Collected by Mr. John Stone. Recited by Mrs. H. T. Stevens, of Igo, Va. King George Co. Sept. 11, 1922. One stanza. No music.
44. *Barbara Allan*. Collected by Mr. John Stone. Recited by Mrs. George Adkins, of Comorn, Va. King George Co. Sept. 11, 1922. One stanza. No music.
45. *Barbara Allan*. Collected by Mr. John Stone. Sung by Mr. J. H. Balderson, of Walnut Point, Va. Northumberland Co. Sept. 11, 1922. One stanza. No music.
46. *Barbara Allan*. Collected by Mr. John Stone. Sung by Mrs. Pearl Townsend Brown, of Urbana, Va. Middlesex Co. Sept. 11, 1922. Three stanzas. No music.
47. *Barbara Allan*. Collected by Mr. John Stone. Sung by Mrs. I. B. Hall, of Warsaw, Va. Richmond Co. Sept. 11, 1922. Four stanzas. No music.
48. *Barbara Allan*. Collected by Mr. John Stone. Recited by Mr. J. K. Mathews, of Bentonville, Va. Warren Co. Sept. 23, 1922. One stanza. No music.
49. *Barbara Allen*. Collected by Mr. John Stone. Recited by Mr. T. Hughes, of White Post, Va. Clark Co. Sept. 23, 1922. One stanza. No music.

50–56. *Barbara Allen*. (Seven fragments of a single line each are not listed.)

25

Lady Alice or Giles Collin

(Child, No. 85)

1. *George Collins*. Reported by Prof. J. M. Grainger. Contributed by Miss Elizabeth Painter, of the Farmville Ballad Club. Pulaski Co., Va. Feb., 1914. Six stanzas. No music.
2. *George Collie*. Reported by Prof. J. M. Grainger. Contributed by Miss Dixie McCabe, of the Farmville Ballad Club. Patrick Co., Va. Feb., 1914. Six stanzas. No music.
3. *George Collins*. Reported by Miss Alma Wilkinson. Contributed by Miss Sudie Fulcher. Sung by school children in Carroll Co., Va. July 26, 1915. Seven stanzas. No music.
4. *George Collins*. Reported by Miss Alma Wilkinson. Contributed by Miss Sudie Fulcher. Sung by school children in Carroll Co., Va. July 26, 1915. Five stanzas. No music.
5. *George Collins*. Collected by Miss Carrie Oglesby, of Pocahontas, Va. Tazewell Co. Nov. 29, 1915. Four stanzas. No music.
6. *George Collins*. Collected by Mr. John Stone. Sung by Mrs. M. C. Hurt, of Wytheville, Va. Wythe Co. Nov. 8, 1921. Five stanzas. No music.
7. *George Collins*. Collected by Mr. John Stone. Sung by Mrs. Oscar Plummer and her daughter, Miss Foxie Plummer, of Park, Va. Grayson Co. Nov. 8, 1921. Four stanzas. No music.

8. *George Collin, Giles Collins, Lady Alice.* Collected by Miss Martha M. Davis. Sung by Mrs. Rosie Morris, of Elkton, Va. Rockingham Co. Nov. 8, 1921. Three stanzas. No music.
9. *Lady Alice.* Collected by Mr. John Stone. Recited by Mrs. H. T. Stevens, of Igo, Va. King George Co. Sept. 11, 1922. One stanza. No music.
10. *John Collins.* Collected by Miss Mary Plummer McIlwaine, of Petersburg, Va. Sung by Miss Lottie Shaffir. Highland Co. August, 1924.

27

The Maid Freed from the Gallows
(Child, No. 95)

1. (No title given.) Contributed by Miss Katherine Middleton, of Rich Creek, Va. Sung by her mother in Rockbridge Co. July, 1914. Fifteen stanzas. No music.
2. *Hangman.* Collected by Miss Roxie Martin and Mr. J. M. McManaway. Sung by a woman from Blackwell's Hollow, Va. Albemarle Co. Aug. 4, 1916. Fifteen stanzas. No music.
3. *The Hangman.* Collected by Mr. John Stone. Sung by Miss Bertha Mayo, of Wilmington, Va. Fluvanna Co. Nov. 3, 1920. Fifteen stanzas. No music.
4. *The Hangman.* Collected by Mr. John Stone. Sung by Mr. H. A. Campbell, of Denbeigh, Va. Warwick Co. July 13, 1921. One stanza. No music.
5. *The Hangman.* Collected by Mr. John Stone. Sung by Mrs. Mollie Binns, of Claremont, Va. Surry Co. July 13, 1921. Fifteen stanzas. No music.
6. *The Maid Freed from the Gallows.* Collected by Mr. John Stone. Recited by Mrs. George Adkins, of Comorn, Va. King George Co. Sept. 11, 1922. Fifteen stanzas. No music.
7. *The Hangman.* Collected by Mr. John Stone. Recited by Dr. Darracott, of Tunstall, Va. New Kent Co. Sept. 11, 1922. One stanza. No music.
8. *Hangman.* Collected by Mr. John Stone. Recited by Mrs. Raymond Haynie, of Warsaw, Va. Richmond Co. Sept. 11, 1922. One stanza. No music.
9. *The Maid Freed from the Gallows.* Collected by Mr. John Stone. Sung by Mr. J. K. Mathews, of Bentonville, Va. Warren Co. Sept. 23, 1922. Fifteen stanzas. No music.

33

Sir Hugh or The Jew's Daughter
(Child, No. 155)

1. *The Jew's Daughter.* Contributed by Miss Martha M. Davis. Sung by Mrs. Lewis Payne. Rockingham Co., Va. March 26, 1913. Six stanzas. No music.
2. *The Jew's Daughter.* Collected by Miss Martha M. Davis. Sung by Mrs. Adam Gowl. Rockingham Co., Va. May 26, 1913. Ten stanzas. No music.
3. *The Jew's Daughter.* Collected by Mr. John Stone. Nelson Co., Va. Nov. 15, 1915. Three stanzas. No music.

40

James Harris (The Dæmon Lover)

(Child, No. 243)

1. *The House Carpenter.* Collected by Miss Corita G. Seoane, of Merrifield, Va. Fairfax Co. Dec. 28, 1913. Six stanzas. No music.
2. *The House Carpenter.* Collected by Miss Martha M. Davis. Sung by a mountain woman at Elkton, Va. Rockingham Co. Jan. 2, 1914. Nine stanzas. No music.
3. *The House Carpenter.* Collected by Miss Corita G. Seoane. Sung by Mr. Alexander Coulter, of Dranesville, Va. Fairfax Co. Jan. 19, 1914. Eleven stanzas. No music.
4. *The House Carpenter.* Reported by Mr. W. E. Gilbert. Contributed by Mr. Wise Worrell, of Radford, Va. Carroll Co. Jan. 21, 1914. Three stanzas. No music.
5. *The House Carpenter.* Collected by Miss Corita G. Seoane, of Merrifield, Va. Fairfax Co. Feb. 11, 1914. Ten stanzas. No music.
6. *The House Carpenter.* Collected by Miss Juliet Fauntleroy. Sung by Mrs. Dan Maxie, *née* Holland, of Altavista, Va. Franklin Co. Feb. 19, 1914. Twelve stanzas. No music.
7. *The House Carpenter.* Collected by Miss May Blankenship, of the Farmville Ballad Club. Sung near Naruna, Va. Campbell Co. April, 1914. Four stanzas. No music.
8. *The House Carpenter.* Collected by Miss Juliet Fauntleroy. Sung by Mrs. Quarles, of Castle Craig, Va. Campbell Co. June 19, 1914. Five stanzas. No music.
9. *The House Carpenter.* Collected by Miss Juliet Fauntleroy. Sung by Mrs. Essie Wallace Yowell, of Altavista, Va. Campbell Co. July 11, 1914. Eleven stanzas. No music.
10. *The House Carpenter.* Collected by Dr. C. Alphonso Smith. Sung by Mr. J. C. Mays, of Craigsville, Va. Amherst Co. Dec. 17, 1914. Four stanzas. No music.
11. *The House Carpenter.* Collected by Miss Juliet Fauntleroy. Sung by Mrs. Virgie Kezee, of Castle Craig, Va. Campbell Co. June 14, 1915. Seven stanzas. No music.
12. *The House Carpenter.* Collected by Miss Juliet Fauntleroy. Sung by Mrs. Hall, of Altavista, Va. Campbell Co. October 9, 1915. Twelve stanzas. No music.
13. *The House Carpenter.* Reported by Mr. Elgie G. Purvis. Contributed by Miss Kathleen Purvis, of Shipman, Va. Nelson Co. Nov. 5, 1915. Eleven stanzas. No music.
14. *The House Carpenter.* Collected by Miss Carrie Oglesby, of Pocahontas, Va. Tazewell Co. Nov. 29, 1915. Six stanzas. No music.
15. *The House Carpenter.* Collected by Miss Lauretta M. Yost. Sung by Miss Maude Boyd, of Floyd Co., Va. March 11, 1916. Twelve stanzas. No music.

16. *The House Carpenter.* Collected by Miss Roxie Martin. Sung near Brown's Cove, Va. Albemarle Co. Aug. 4. 1916. Thirteen stanzas. No music.
17. *The House Carpenter.* Collected by Miss Alfreda M. Peel. Sung by Mrs. B. P. Shelor, of Salem, Va. Roanoke Co. Dec. 17, 1916. Five stanzas. No music.
18. *The House Carpenter.* Collected by Miss Roxie Martin and Mr. J. M. McManaway. Found near Brown's Cove, Va. Albemarle Co. June 1, 1917. Twelve stanzas. No music.
19. *The House Carpenter.* Collected by Mr. John Stone. Sung by Miss Emma Carpenter, of Brightwood, Va. Madison Co. Nov. 3, 1920. Three stanzas. No music.
20. *The Daemon Lover.* Collected by Mr. John Stone. Recited by Mrs. Edith Gregory, of City Point, Va. Prince George Co. June 29, 1921. Three stanzas. No music.
21. *The House Carpenter.* Collected by Mr. John Stone. Sung by Mrs. M. C. Hurt, of Wytheville, Va. Wythe Co. Nov. 8, 1921. Twelve stanzas. No music.
22. *The House Carpenter.* Collected by Mr. John Stone. Sung by Mr. R. R. Rutter, of Damascus, Va. Washington Co. Nov. 8, 1921. Twelve stanzas. No music.
23. *The Daemon Lover.* Collected by Mr. John Stone. Sung by Mr. J. A. Wyatt. King William Co., Va. Sept. 11, 1922. Eleven stanzas. No music.

46

The Farmer's Curst Wife

(Child, No. 278)

1. *The Farmer's Curst Wife.* Collected by Miss Juliet Fauntleroy. Sung by Miss Jennie Nelson, of Rustburg, Va. Campbell Co. Oct. 20, 1915. One stanza. No music.
2. *The Farmer's Curst Wife.* Collected by Miss Juliet Fauntleroy. Sung by Mrs. Creasy, of Lynch Station, Va. Campbell Co. Sept. 15, 1916. Twelve stanzas. No music.

48

The Mermaid

(Child, No. 289)

1. *The Mermaid.* Collected by Mr. John Stone. Dictated by Supt. French, of Dickenson Co., Va. Nov. 8, 1921. Two stanzas. No music.

49

John of Hazelgreen

(Child, No. 293)

1. *John of the Hazel Green*. Collected by Miss Roxie Martin and Mr. Judson McManaway. Albemarle Co., Va. Aug. 4, 1916. Four stanzas. No music.

50

The Brown Girl

(Child, No. 295)

1. [(Combined with *The Death of Queen Jane*). Collected by Mr. Cecil J. Sharp and Miss Karpeles. From Virginia (county unnamed). Sept. 1, 1918. Eight (= five) stanzas. No music.]

APPENDIX B

List of Members of the Virginia Folk-Lore Society, 1913–1924

(All addresses are in Virginia unless otherwise noted.)

Adair, Miss Cornelia, Richmond.
Alderman, Dr. Edwin A., University.
Andrews, Miss Lulu O., New York, N. Y.

Bailey, Miss Callie, Jetersville.
Bain, Professor George M., Norfolk.
Barrett, Miss Susie, Newsomes.
Barry, Phillips, Esq., Ashburnham, Mass.
Bartlett, Mr. William I., Whitmell.
Baugh, Miss Ada, Broadway.
Beard, J. O., Middletown.
Beatty, John O., University.
Berkeley, Miss S. Campbell, Richmond
Beverley, Mrs. F. C., Whitmell.
Billingsley, Miss Elizabeth, Lignum.
Bingham, Miss Maude, Clifton Forge.
Blair, Miss Louisa C., Richmond.
Blakey, Mrs. W. W., Rappahannock.
Boatwright, President F. W., Richmond.
Bosher, Mrs. Kate Langley, Richmond.
Bouldin, Miss Ellen B., Houston.
Bourland, Dr. A. P., Washington, D.C.
Brown, J. Thompson, Charlottesville.
Brown, Miss Maria J., Shipman.
Bryan, Mrs. George, Richmond.
Bryan, John Stewart, Richmond.
Bryson, Miss Flora, East Radford.
Burke, Miss Eva C., Hampton.
Burruss, Dr. Julian A., Blacksburg.
Byrne, Miss Margaret, Luray.

Cameron, Miss Mary G., Goshen.
Campbell, Miss Marie, Barber.
Campbell, Miss Sarah, Bell Haven.
Carr, Miss Nellie E., Hampton.
Cason, Miss Mary D., Richmond.
Chandler, Dr. J. A. C., Williamsburg.
Chesterman, Evan R., Richmond.
Churchman, C. J., University.
Cocke, Mrs. Preston, Richmond.
Coleman, Miss Helen E., Midlothian.
Cook, Miss Sue B., Richmond.
Corling, Miss A. B., Richmond.
Costello, M. B., Leesburg.
Cottrell, S. C., Goochland.
Cottrell, Miss Virginia Lee, Richmond.
Cowden, Miss Ludie E., Apple Grove.
Cox, Miss Theodora C., Millwood.
Cox, Mrs. William Ruffin, Richmond.
Crump, Mrs. James, Richmond.
Currell, Professor W. S., Lexington.
Curry, Mrs. L. R., Ginter Park.
Curtiss, Miss Essie, Richmond.
Czarnomska, Miss Marie E. J., Sweet Briar.

Daniel, Mrs. J. R. V., Richmond.
Darden, Mrs. Paul L., Portsmouth.
Dashiell, Mrs. Parker, Richmond.
Davis, Professor Arthur Kyle, Jr., University.
Davis, Miss Lucy, Lynchburg.
Davis, Miss Martha M., Harrisonburg.
Davis, Miss Nannie C., Lynchburg.
De Jarnette, Mrs. A. H., Richmond.
Dibert, John, University.
Dingus, Dr. L. R., Richmond.
Dixon, F. M., University.
Doty, William Kavanaugh, Tappahannock.
Doughty, Miss Sarah, Cape Charles.
Dunn, Mrs. R. Powell, Richmond.
DuPuy, Miss Mary, Worsham.
Duval, Miss Elizabeth M., Hampton.

Early, Miss Ruth H., Lynchburg.
Edwards, Miss Mae W., Newport News.
Eggleston, President J. D., Hampden-Sidney.
Ellett, Miss Virginia Randolph, Richmond.
Elliott, J. W., Richmond.

Farragut, Loyall, New York, N. Y.
Faulkner, Professor W. H., University.
Fauntleroy, Miss Juliet, Altavista.
Ferneyhough, Mrs. J. Bowie, Richmond.
FitzHugh, Professor Thomas, University.
Flanagan, Miss Maizie, Fredericksburg.
Flory, Miss Katherine, Bridgewater.
Foster, James W., The Plains.

Gammon, Miss Mary Somerville, Fredericksburg.
Garnett, R. S., Lexington.
Gay, Miss E. Hazel, Richmond.
Gilbert, W. E., University.
Gilly, Miss Glossie, Big Stone Gap.
Gordon, Armistead C., Staunton.
Grainger, Professor James M., Farmville.
Green, Miss Lucy L., Alton.
Groh, Miss Katherine, Herndon.
Guerrant, Miss Sally A., Petersburg.

Haden, Mrs. H. E., Richmond.
Hamner, Miss Sallie, Richmond.
Handy, Professor H. B., Richmond.
Hardy, Miss E. V., Appomattox.
Harlowe, Miss Louise, Mineral.
Harouff, Miss M. Virginia, Burnsville.
Harris, Mrs. John T., Harrisonburg.
Harris, Miss M. P., Richmond.
Harris, Professor W. A., Richmond.
Harrison, E. Caskie, Charleston, W. Va.
Harrison, Fairfax, Washington, D. C.
Harrison, Henry Sydnor, Charleston, W. Va.
Harrison, J. Letcher, University.
Hart, Hon. Harris, Richmond.
Harvard College Library, Cambridge, Mass.
Hazen, Miss M. Edith, Bon Air.
Henderson, Miss Lucy, Richmond.
Henneman, Mrs. John Bell, Washington, D. C.
Hudnall, Professor R. H., Blacksburg.
Hunley, Professor W. M., University.
Hurdle, Miss Selina H., Amelia.
Hurst, James, Norfolk.
Hurt, Mrs. A. J., Chester.

Irwin, Miss Annie, Centralia.

Jarman, President J. L., Farmville.
Jones, Miss Lou Belle, Richmond.
Jones, Rev. Plummer F., Arvonia.
Jones, Professor W. G., Richmond.
Jones, Mrs. William G., Richmond.

Kent, Professor Charles W., University.
Kittredge, Professor George L., Cambridge, Mass.

Laughton, Miss Florence, Richmond.
Lecky, Mrs. Robert, Richmond.
Lefroy, Mrs. J. A., Richmond.
Lewark, Mrs. A. T., Claremont.
Lindsay, J. H., Charlottesville.
Lineweaver, W. S., Bridgewater.
Low, Mrs. Winifred Hopkins, Sandy Hook.
Louderback, Miss Fannie, Shenandoah
Lunger, Rev. Henry J., Charlottesville.
Lyons, Mrs. James, Ginter Park.

Maphis, Professor Charles G., University.
Martin, Miss Carry, Roanoke.
Martin, Professor M. A., Richmond.
McBryde, Professor John M., Jr., Sewanee, Tenn.
McConnell, Dr. John P., East Radford.
McCoy, Mrs. Victoria, Newsomes.
McCoy, Dr. W. K., Gum Spring.
McCullock, Miss Annie M., Apple Grove.
McIlwaine, Dr. H. R., Richmond.

McVeigh, Mrs. Llewellyn, Richmond.
McWhorter, Dr. A. W., Hampden-Sidney.
Mells, Mrs. Hinton Aubrey, Centralia.
Metcalf, Dr. J. C., University.
Metcalf, Mrs. J. C., University.
Michie, G. R. B., Charlottesville.
Montgomery, Col. B. F., New York, N. Y.
Montgomery, Professor W. A., Williamsburg.
Moomaw, B. C., Jr., Barber.
Moowmaw, Miss Margaret, Barber.
Moore, Dr. W. W., Richmond.
Morrow, Loyal C., University.
Moyston, Roy C., University.
Munce, Mrs. John S., Richmond.
Myers, Fred P., Washington, D. C.
Myers, Supt. John C., Harrisonburg.
Myers, Miss Nannie P., Petersburg.

Nelson, Mrs. William Hugh, Richmond.
Newman, Professor Carol M., Blacksburg.

O'Connell, Rt. Rev. Dennis J., Richmond.
Oglesby, Mrs. Carrie, Holdcroft.

Paxton, Mrs. Robert, Richmond.
Pearson, Miss Nancy, Cobb's Creek.
Peel, Miss Alfreda M., Salem.
Peterson, Isaac, Chicago, Ill.
Phamp, Miss S. L., Norfolk.
Phipps, W. M., University.
Pollard, Frank K., Sheppards.
Powell, Miss Louise, Midlothian.
Purcell, Miss Jo, South Boston.

Read, Miss Caroline M., Evington.
Reade, Professor Willoughby, Alexandria.
Rennie, Mrs. Channing Bruce, Richmond.
Rex, Miss Evelyn J., Richmond.
Roadcap, Miss Susan A., Goshen.
Robert, Mrs. R. R., Richmond.
Robinson, Dr. Morgan P., Richmond.
Rodeffer, Professor J. D., Salem.
Rodes, Miss Frances, Lynchburg.
Rolston, Henry F., Mt. Clinton.
Rowe, Miss Blanche V., Tazewell.
Royall, Miss Emily C., Richmond.
Russell, President E. H., Fredericksburg.
Rutherfoord, Miss Jane, Richmond.
Ryland, Dr. Garnett, Richmond.
Ryland, Miss Marion, Richmond.

St. Clair, Mrs. D. F., Glen Allen.
Sanger, Mrs. W. T., Richmond.
Saunders, Hon. John R., Richmond.
Sayre, Miss Margaret, Hampton.
Shannon, Professor Edgar F., Lexington.
Shepherd, David A., Sewanee, Tenn.
Showalter, Miss Lois, Cape Charles.
Singleton, Ogle R., Washington, D. C.
Singleton, William H., Washington, D. C.
Sinton, Miss Jane, Richmond.
Smith, Professor C. Alphonso, University.
Smith, President Henry Louis, Lexington.
Smith, Mrs. Isola, Richmond.
Smith, Mrs. J. Henry, Greensboro, N. C.
Smith, Miss Susie A., Middletown.
Smyth, Miss Amey Allen, Blacksburg.
Somers, Wilson E., Bloxom.
Southall, Mrs. John W., Richmond.
Spitzer, Miss Viola, Holdcroft.
Spofford, Mrs. Lydia R., Alexandria.
Stanard, Mrs. Mary Newton, Richmond.
Stearnes, Hon. R. C., Richmond.
Steger, S. H., University.
Steptoe, Miss Grace, Richmond.
Stockley, Mrs. J. W., Keller.
Stone, Professor John, Mt. Fair.
Strickler, H. M., Harrisonburg.
Strudwick, E., Jr., University.
Stuart, H. C., University.
Sumeford, Mrs. H. L., Drewry's Bluff.
Swem, E. G., Richmond.
Sydnor, Miss Eleanor, Ashland.
Sydnor, Miss M. Virginia, Greenville, S. C.

Tabb, B. West, Richmond.
Taliaferro, Mrs. W. H., Portsmouth.
Taylor, Miss Bessie P., Williamsburg.
Taylor, Miss Cornelia S., Richmond.
Thom, W. T., Washington, D. C.
Thurman, Dr. Francis Lee, Keswick.
Tidwell, Mrs. Edith C., Richmond.
Trinkle, Governor E. Lee, Richmond.
Trussell, Miss Lizzie, Timberville.
Tyler, Dr. Lyon G., Holdcroft.
Tyler, Supt. P. M., Chester.

Van Landingham, Professor H. A., Richmond.

Wallerstein, Miss Catherine, Richmond.
Wallerstein, Mrs. Joseph, Richmond.
Ward, C. E., Gala.
Warriner, Mrs. J. E., Richmond.
Warwick, L. H., University.
Webster, Rear-Admiral Harrie, Richmond.
Weeks, Professor Raymond, New York, N. Y.
Wicker, Miss Katherine, Hampton.
Wiley, Mrs. Olin F., Richmond.
Williams, Miss Evelyn Cary, Lynchburg.
Williams, H. E., Honaker.
Williams, J. E., Blacksburg.
Williamson, Miss Mary, Hollins.
Willingham, Miss Carrie, Richmond.
Willingham, Miss Elizabeth, Richmond.
Wilson, Dr. B. F., Harrisonburg.
Winston, Miss Annie, Richmond.
Winston, Miss Kate, Richmond.
Wise, Professor Henry A., Columbia, S. C.
Woolfork, Pichegru, University.
Wyman, Miss Loraine, New York, N.Y.

APPENDIX C

Distribution of the Virginia Ballads by Counties

County	Ballads
Accomac	3
Albemarle	66
Alleghany	7
Amelia	3
Amherst	3
Appomattox	1
Arlington (Alexandria)	2
Augusta	6
Bath	4
Bedford	2
Bland	8
Botetourt	2
Brunswick	1
Buchanan	1
Buckingham	1
Campbell	60
Caroline	1
Carroll	4
Charles City	2
Charlotte	1
Chesterfield	2
Clarke	5
Craig	1
Culpeper	4
Cumberland	1
Dickenson	2
Dinwiddie	1
Elizabeth City	1
Essex	2
Fairfax	14
Fauquier	4
Floyd	3
Fluvanna	8
Franklin	15
Frederick	4
Giles	5
Gloucester	3
Goochland	1
Grayson	10
Greene	4
Greensville	3
Halifax	7
Hanover	1
Henrico	5
Henry	3
Highland	18
Isle of Wight	1
James City	5
King and Queen	4
King George	7
King William	8
Lancaster	1
Lee	2
Loudoun	5
Louisa	3
Lunenburg	2
Madison	13
Mathews	4
Mecklenburg	2
Middlesex	4
Montgomery	8
Nansemond	1
Nelson	10
New Kent	6
Norfolk	3
Northampton	7
Northumberland	5
Nottoway	1
Orange	1
Page	3
Patrick	4
Pittsylvania	8
Powhatan	1
Prince Edward	5
Prince George	1
Prince William	2
Princess Anne	3
Pulaski	6
Rappahannock	1
Richmond	2
Roanoke	27
Rockbridge	7
Rockingham	48
Russell	4
Scott	4
Shenandoah	1
Smyth	12
Southampton	1
Spottsylvania	3
Stafford	11
Surry	6
Sussex	3
Tazewell	2
Warren	5
Warwick	1
Washington	29
Westmoreland	2
Wise	15
Wythe	9
York	1
County not designated	7

APPENDIX D

Table of Totals for Each Ballad

Virginia No.	Child No.	Title	Total Items Available	Total Items Used in This Book [1]	Total Musical Variants—All Used
1	1	Riddles Wisely Expounded........	1	1	1
2	3	The Fause Knight Upon the Road .	1	1	1
3	4	Lady Isabel and The Elf-Knight...	28	19	7
4	7	Earl Brand..................	6	4–5	2
5	10	The Twa Sisters...............	13	11	6
6	12	Lord Randal..................	18	14–16	4
7	13	Edward......................	6	5	2
8	18	Sir Lionel....................	7	7	4
9	20	The Cruel Mother..............	5	5	4
10	26	The Three Ravens (The Twa Corbies).................	29	17–19	4
11	49	The Twa Brothers..............	11	11	6
12	53	Young Beichan................	12	9	2
13	54	The Cherry-Tree Carol..........	3	3	1
14	56	Dives and Lazarus.............	1	1	1
15	62	Fair Annie....................	1	1	1
16	65	Lady Maisry..................	2	2	0
17	68	Young Hunting................	7	6	4
18	73	Lord Thomas and Fair Annet	36	19	7
19	74	Fair Margaret and Sweet William..	29	16	8
20	75	Lord Lovel....................	37	15–16	4
21	76	The Lass of Roch Royal..........	52	21–30	4
22	79	The Wife of Usher's Well.........	13	12	2
23	81	Little Musgrave and Lady Barnard	7	6	1
24	84	Bonny Barbara Allen............	92	36	12
25	85	Lady Alice....................	18	7–8	5
26	93	Lamkin......................	4	4	1
27	95	The Maid Freed from the Gallows .	34	22–25	5
28	105	The Bailiff's Daughter of Islington..	2	2	1
29	114	Johnie Cock..................	1	1	0
30	120	Robin Hood's Death............	1	1	1
31	126	Robin Hood and the Tanner	1	1	1

[1] The alternative figures in this column indicate the totals without and with appendices, respectively, where appendices appear.

TABLE OF TOTALS FOR EACH BALLAD (*continued*)

Virginia No.	Child No.	Title	Total Items Available	Total Items Used in This Book	Total Musical Variants — All Used
32	141	Robin Hood Rescuing Will Stutly	1	1	1
33	155	Sir Hugh, or, The Jew's Daughter	16	13	7
34	162	The Hunting of the Cheviot	1	1	0
35	170	The Death of Queen Jane	1	1	0
36	173	Mary Hamilton	2	2	1
37	200	The Gypsy Laddie	8	8	3
38	201	Bessy Bell and Mary Gray	4	4	0
39	209	Geordie	4	4	1
40	243	James Harris (The Dæmon Lover)	52	29	7
41	267	The Heir of Linne	1	1	0
42	272	The Suffolk Miracle	3	3	2
43	274	Our Goodman	8	7–8	5
44	275	Get Up and Bar the Door	1	1	0
45	277	The Wife Wrapt in Wether's Skin	12	12	2
46	278	The Farmer's Curst Wife	15	13	7
47	286	The Sweet Trinity (The Golden Vanity)	6	6	1
48	289	The Mermaid	13	12	2
49	293	John of Hazelgreen	11	10	3
50	295	The Brown Girl	11	10	3
51	299	Trooper and Maid	2	2	1
TOTALS			650	420–440	148

INDEX OF TITLES

INDEX OF TITLES

(The titles here listed are those used by Child, plus the more usual or distinctive Virginia titles.)